Social Security Programs and Retirement around the World

**A National Bureau
of Economic Research
Conference Report**

Social Security Programs and Retirement around the World
Fiscal Implications of Reform

Edited by **Jonathan Gruber and David A. Wise**

The University of Chicago Press

Chicago and London

JONATHAN GRUBER is professor of economics at the Massachusetts Institute of Technology, and director of the Program on Children at the NBER, where he is a research associate. DAVID A. WISE is the John F. Stambaugh Professor of Political Economy at the John F. Kennedy School of Government, Harvard University, and director of the Programs on Aging and Health Care at the National Bureau of Economic Research.

The University of Chicago Press, Chicago 60637
The University of Chicago Press, Ltd., London
© 2007 by the National Bureau of Economic Research
All rights reserved. Published 2007
Printed in the United States of America

16 15 14 13 12 11 10 09 08 07   1 2 3 4 5
ISBN-10: 0-226-31017-5 (cloth)
ISBN-13: 978-0-226-31017-6 (cloth)

Library of Congress Cataloging-in-Publication Data

Social security programs and retirement around the world : fiscal
    implications of reform / edited by Jonathan Gruber and David A.
    Wise.
        p. cm. — (A National Bureau of Economic Research conference
        report)
        "This volume presents the third phase of the project"—P.
        An analysis and country-by-country comparison of the effects of
    social security incentives on retirement behavior in Belgium, Canada,
    Denmark, France, Germany, Italy, Japan, The Netherlands, Spain,
    Sweden, the UK, and the United States.
        ISBN-13: 978-0-226-31017-6 (cloth : alk. paper)
        ISBN-10: 0-226-31017-5 (cloth : alk. paper)
        1. Social security—Finance. 2. Retirement—Economic aspects.
    3. Retirement income. 4. Older people—Employment. I. Gruber,
    Jonathan. II. Wise, David A. III. National Bureau of Economic
    Research. IV. Series.
    HD7091.S6244 2007
    368.4'3—dc22

                                                          2006051468

Relation of the Directors to the
Work and Publications of the
National Bureau of Economic Research

1. The object of the NBER is to ascertain and present to the economics profession, and to the public more generally, important economic facts and their interpretation in a scientific manner without policy recommendations. The Board of Directors is charged with the responsibility of ensuring that the work of the NBER is carried on in strict conformity with this object.

2. The President shall establish an internal review process to ensure that book manuscripts proposed for publication DO NOT contain policy recommendations. This shall apply both to the proceedings of conferences and to manuscripts by a single author or by one or more co-authors but shall not apply to authors of comments at NBER conferences who are not NBER affiliates.

3. No book manuscript reporting research shall be published by the NBER until the President has sent to each member of the Board a notice that a manuscript is recommended for publication and that in the President's opinion it is suitable for publication in accordance with the above principles of the NBER. Such notification will include a table of contents and an abstract or summary of the manuscript's content, a list of contributors if applicable, and a response form for use by Directors who desire a copy of the manuscript for review. Each manuscript shall contain a summary drawing attention to the nature and treatment of the problem studied and the main conclusions reached.

4. No volume shall be published until forty-five days have elapsed from the above notification of intention to publish it. During this period a copy shall be sent to any Director requesting it, and if any Director objects to publication on the grounds that the manuscript contains policy recommendations, the objection will be presented to the author(s) or editor(s). In case of dispute, all members of the Board shall be notified, and the President shall appoint an ad hoc committee of the Board to decide the matter; thirty days additional shall be granted for this purpose.

5. The President shall present annually to the Board a report describing the internal manuscript review process, any objections made by Directors before publication or by anyone after publication, any disputes about such matters, and how they were handled.

6. Publications of the NBER issued for informational purposes concerning the work of the Bureau, or issued to inform the public of the activities at the Bureau, including but not limited to the NBER Digest and Reporter, shall be consistent with the object stated in paragraph 1. They shall contain a specific disclaimer noting that they have not passed through the review procedures required in this resolution. The Executive Committee of the Board is charged with the review of all such publications from time to time.

7. NBER working papers and manuscripts distributed on the Bureau's web site are not deemed to be publications for the purpose of this resolution, but they shall be consistent with the object stated in paragraph 1. Working papers shall contain a specific disclaimer noting that they have not passed through the review procedures required in this resolution. The NBER's web site shall contain a similar disclaimer. The President shall establish an internal review process to ensure that the working papers and the web site do not contain policy recommendations, and shall report annually to the Board on this process and any concerns raised in connection with it.

8. Unless otherwise determined by the Board or exempted by the terms of paragraphs 6 and 7, a copy of this resolution shall be printed in each NBER publication as described in paragraph 2 above.

Contents

Acknowledgments

This is the third volume presenting results of an ongoing project on social security and labor supply organized through the Program on the Economics of Aging at the National Bureau of Economic Research.

Funding for the project was provided by the National Institute on Aging grant numbers P01-AG05842 and P30-AG12810 to the National Bureau of Economic Research. Funding for individual papers is noted in specific chapter acknowledgments.

Any opinions expressed in this volume are those of the respective authors and do not necessarily reflect the views of the National Bureau of Economic Research or the sponsoring organization.

Introduction

Jonathan Gruber and David A. Wise

Under pay-as-you-go social security systems, most developed countries have made promises they can't keep. The systems in their current forms are not financially sustainable. What caused this problem? It has been common to assume that the problem was caused by aging populations. The percentage of older persons has increased very rapidly relative to the number of younger persons and this trend will continue (see figure I.1).[1] Thus, the proportion of retirees has increased relative to the number of employed persons who must pay for the benefits of those who are retired. In addition, persons are living longer, so that those who reach retirement age are receiving benefits longer than they used to. The combined effect of aging populations and increasing longevity has been compounded by another trend: older persons are leaving the labor force at younger and younger ages, further increasing the ratio of retirees to employed persons (see figure I.2). What has not been widely appreciated is that the provisions of social security programs themselves often provide strong incentives to leave the labor force. By penalizing work, social security systems magnify the increased financial burden caused by aging populations and thus contribute to their own insolvency.

Several years ago we began an international project to study the relationship between social security program provisions and retirement. This volume presents the results of the third phase of the project. The first phase

Jonathan Gruber is a professor of economics at the Massachusetts Institute of Technology, and a research associate of the National Bureau of Economic Research. David A. Wise is the John F. Stambaugh Professor of Political Economy at the John F. Kennedy School of Government, Harvard University, and director of the program on aging at the National Bureau of Economic Research.

1. In this figure, "Now" varies from country to country but is generally the early 1990s.

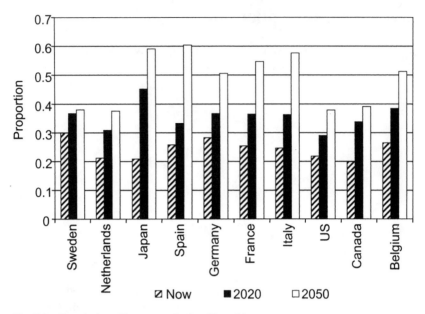

Fig. I.1   Population 65+ to population 20 to 64

described the retirement incentives inherent in plan provisions and documented the strong relationship across countries between social security incentives to retire and the proportion of older persons out of the labor force (Gruber and Wise 1999b). The second phase illustrated the large effects that changing plan provisions would have on the labor force participation of older workers. This third phase shows the consequent fiscal implications that extending labor force participation would have on net program costs—reduced government social security benefit payments less increased government tax revenues.

The findings are conveyed by simulating the implications of illustrative reforms. One reform increases benefit eligibility ages by three years. Another actuarially reduces benefits received before the normal retirement age. A common reform prescribes the same provisions in each country. The financial implications of the illustrative reforms are very large in many instances, often as much as 20 to 40 percent of current program costs. The savings amount to as much as 1 percent or more of country GDP.

The results of the ongoing project are the product of analyses conducted for each country by analysts in that country. Researchers who have participated in the project are listed here (the authors of the country papers in this volume are listed first; others who participated in one of the first two phases are listed second and are shown in italics).

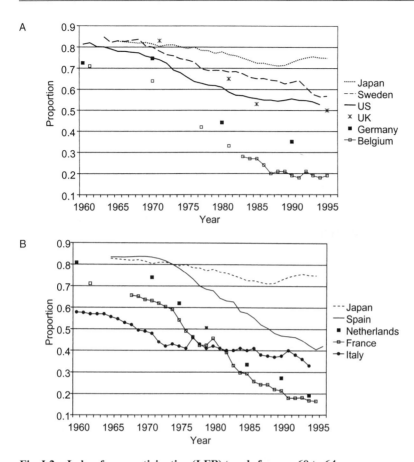

Fig. I.2   Labor force participation (LFP) trends for men 60 to 64

Belgium	Raphaël Desmet, Alain Jousten, Sergio Perelman, Pierre Pestieau, *Arnaud Dellis,* and *Jean-Philippe Stijns*
Canada	Michael Baker, Jonathan Gruber, and Kevin Milligan
Denmark	Paul Bingley, Nabanita Datta Gupta, and Peder J. Pedersen
France	Emmanuelle Walraet, Ronan Mahieu, and *Didier Blanchet*
Germany	Axel Börsch-Supan, Simone Kohnz, *Giovanni Mastrobuoni,* and *Reinhold Schnabel*
Italy	Agar Brugiavini and Franco Peracchi
Japan	Akiko Sato Oishi, Takashi Oshio, and *Naohiro Yashiro*
The Netherlands	Arie Kapteyn and Klaas de Vos

Spain	Michele Boldrin, Sergi Jiménez-Martín, and *Franco Peracchi*
Sweden	Mårten Palme and Ingemar Svensson
United Kingdom	Richard Blundell, Carl Emmerson, *Paul Johnson, Costas Meghir,* and *Sarah Smith*
United States	Courtney Coile, Jonathan Gruber, and *Peter Diamond*

An important goal of the project has been to present results that were as comparable as possible across projects. Thus the papers for each phase were prepared according to a detailed template that we prepared in consultation with country participants. In many cases the country papers contain analyses in addition to those prescribed in the template, usually pertaining to reforms or reform proposals in individual countries.

Before discussing in more detail the results of this phase of the project, we summarize the results of the previous two phases. We give particular attention to the second phase, which provides the empirical base for the analysis in this volume.

Phase I

The goal of the first stage of this project was to describe the incentives inherent in the social security provisions and to relate their incentives to the labor-force participation of older workers across nations. The core of each Phase I paper is a detailed analysis of the retirement incentives inherent in the provisions of that country's retirement income system, based on a template that described—in detail—how the incentives were to be calculated. By making the same analytic calculations and by presenting the same simulations in each of the countries, the individual studies could provide a means of comparing the retirement incentives among the countries. Each of the country papers presents completely parallel labor-force (and other) data for men and women. To simplify the exposition here, only data for men are discussed, but the effect of the social security incentives to leave the labor force, as later discussed, appear to be at least as important for women as for men.

Unused Labor-Force Capacity

The proportion of men out of the labor force between ages 55 and 65 in 11 countries is shown in figure I.3. The term *unused labor-force capacity* is used to emphasize that incentives to induce older persons to leave the labor force reduce national economic production, recognizing of course that not all persons in these age ranges want to work or are able to work. For the 55 to 65 age group the percentage ranges from close to 0.7 in Belgium to about 0.2 in Japan. Subsequent results show the relationship between social security plan provisions to leave the labor force and this measure of

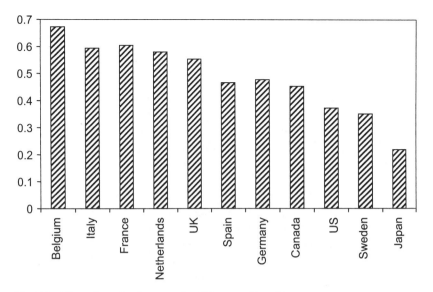

Fig. I.3   Unused productive capacity: Men age 55 to 65

unused labor-force capacity. We first describe the measurement of incentives to retire.

Measuring Incentives to Retire

Three key features of social security systems have an important effect on labor-force participation incentives. The first is the age at which benefits are first available. This is called the *early retirement age* (ERA), or the age of first eligibility. Across the countries participating in this study, the first eligibility age ranges from about 53 for some employee groups in Italy to 62 in the United States. In none of the countries in this project does a significant portion of persons retire before the first eligibility age. The normal retirement age (NRA)—for example, 65 in the United States—is also important, but typically much less important than the early retirement age. In most countries, few people currently work until the normal retirement age.

The second important feature of plan provisions, which is strongly related to the extent to which people continue to work after the early retirement age—and which we emphasized in this phase of the analysis—is the pattern of benefit accrual after the age of first eligibility. The idea can be explained this way: consider two components of total compensation for working an additional year. One component is current wage earnings. The other component is the increase in future, promised social security benefits. Consider a person who has attained the social security early retirement age (when benefits are first available) and suppose that person is considering whether to work for an additional year. It is natural to suppose that if benefit receipt is delayed by a year, then benefits—when they are received—might be increased, to offset the receipt of benefits for one less year. But in most countries this is not the case. Once benefits are available, a person who continues to work for an additional year will receive less in social security benefits over his or her lifetime than if he or she quit work and started to receive benefits at the first opportunity. That is, the present value of expected social security benefits declines. In many countries, this loss of social security benefits can offset a large fraction of the wage earnings a person would receive from continued work. Thus there is an implicit tax on work, and total compensation can be much less than net wage earnings.

A bit more formally, consider the difference between the expected discounted value of social security benefits (social security wealth) if retirement is age $a + 1$ and the present value if retirement is at age $a - SSW(a + 1) - SSW(a)$. This difference is called the *accrual of benefits* between age a and age $a + 1$. It is this value that is often negative. If the accrual is positive, it adds to total compensation from working the additional year; if the accrual is negative, it reduces total compensation. The ratio of the accrual to net wage earnings is an implicit tax on earnings if the accrual is negative and an implicit subsidy to earnings if the accrual is positive. Thus a negative accrual discourages continuation in the labor force and a positive accrual encourages continued labor force participation. This accrual rate, and the associated tax rate, is one of the key calculations that was made in the same way for each of the countries. As it turns out, the pension accrual is typically negative at older ages: continuation in the labor force means a loss in the present discounted value of pension benefits, which imposes an implicit tax on work and provides an incentive to leave the labor force. In many countries, the implicit tax on work is 80 percent or more the first year after benefit eligibility.

This feature of plan provisions is related to a technical term called *actuarial adjustment*. In the United States, for example, if benefits are taken at 64 instead of 65, they are reduced just enough to offset the receipt of benefits for one additional year. If they are taken at 63 instead of 65 they are reduced just enough to offset the receipt of benefits of two additional years, and so forth.[2] Under some plan provisions, there is no actuarial adjustment. The importance of this feature is stressed in the following discussion.

A third, important feature of social security systems is that in many European countries disability insurance and special unemployment programs essentially provide early-retirement benefits before the official social

---

2. Under current law, benefits in the United States are actuarially fair between 62 and 65, but are increased less than actuarially if the receipt of benefits is delayed beyond age 65, thus providing an incentive to leave the labor force at 65. Benefits will eventually become actuarially fair after age 65 as well.

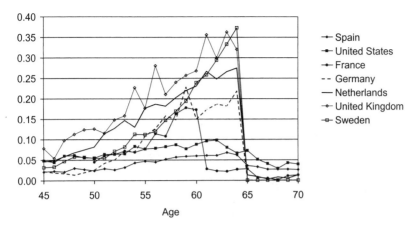

Fig. I.4   **Proportion of men collecting disability benefits, by age**

security early retirement age. Figure I.4 shows the proportion of men collecting disability benefits by age in seven of the countries.[3] At age 45, the proportion of men collecting disability benefits is rather close in all of the countries; the range is from 2 to 5 percent in all of the countries except the Netherlands, where the rate is 8 percent. At age 64, however, the range is from about 7 percent in Spain and the United States to over 37 percent in Sweden.[4] In each of the countries with very high proportions, the rate essentially falls to zero at the normal retirement age, which is 65 in Sweden, the United Kingdom, The Netherlands, and Germany, and 60 in France. At the normal retirement age, benefits are obtained from country social security programs rather than disability programs. It is evident that the receipt of benefits from a disability program does not always indicate that a person is physically disabled.

Figure I.5 shows the pathways to retirement in Germany from 1960 to 1995. It is clear that the proportion of persons retiring at the normal retirement age (65) declined substantially over this period, while the proportion retiring under disability and unemployment programs and under the social security early-retirement program (age 63) increased correspondingly. In Germany, many employees retire as early as age 57, under a disability program. In 1995, 65 percent of men retired under a disability or special unemployment program. Where these programs are important they are incorporated into the social security incentive calculations. Appendix table IA.1 provides a brief summary of the programs accounted for in each country. In addition, Appendix table IA.2 provides a selected summary of

3. To reduce the complexity of the figure, data are shown only for selected countries.
4. The data for Italy are similar to the data for Spain. The rates for Belgium and Canada are similar, and follow a path approximately midway between the path for the United States and the path for Germany.

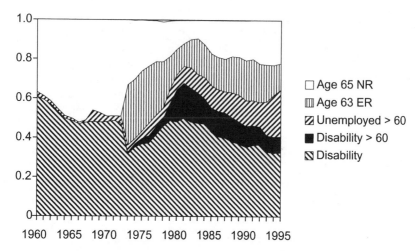

Fig. I.5   Germany: Pathways to retirement for men, 1960 to 1995

the data files used in each country. For more detail, the country papers must be consulted.

Retirement Incentives and Labor Force Participation

To summarize the social security incentive to retire in each country we proposed a simple measure. At each age, beginning with the early retirement age, the implicit tax on work was calculated in each country. These implicit tax rates on work were then summed, beginning with the early retirement age and running through age 69. This measure we called the *tax force* to retire. The sum is shown for each of the countries in figure I.6. This tax force to retire ranges from over 9 in Italy to about 1.5 in the United States.

The Tax Force to Retire and Unused Labor-Force Capacity

The key finding from Phase I of the project is shown in figures I.7 and I.8. Figure I.7 shows the relationship between the tax force to retire and unused labor force capacity—the proportion of men between ages 55 and 65 that is out of the labor force. It is clear that there is a very strong correspondence between the two. Figure I.8 shows the same data for all of the countries except Japan, and rescales the tax force measure to achieve a linear relationship between the tax force to retire and unused labor force capacity. The relationship between the two is perhaps even more evident. The proportion of variation in unused labor force capacity that is explained by the tax force to retire is 86 percent (as indicated by the R-squared value).

The results of the first phase were reported in Gruber and Wise (1999b). The introduction (Gruber and Wise 1999a, 34–35) concluded this way:

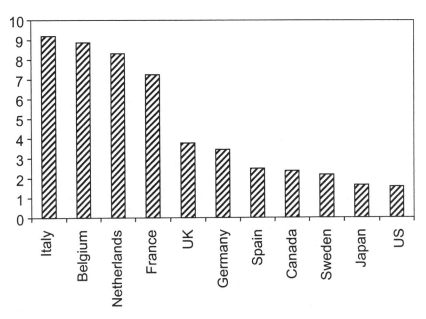

Fig. I.6   Sum of tax rates on work from early retirement age to 69

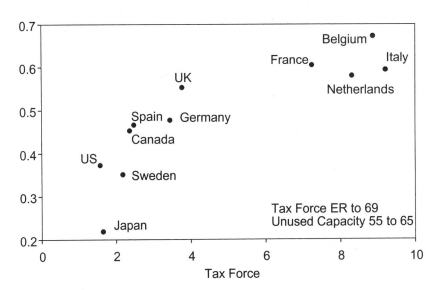

Fig. I.7   Unused capacity versus tax force to retire

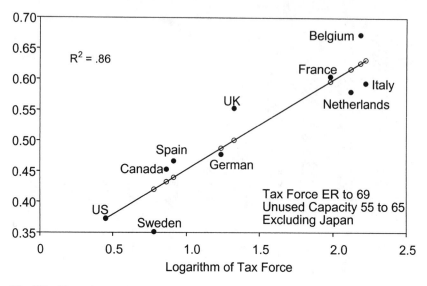

Fig. I.8   Unused capacity versus tax force to retire

The populations in all industrialized countries are aging rapidly and individual life expectancies are increasing. Yet older workers are leaving the labor force at younger and younger ages. In several countries in our study, participation rates for men 60 to 64 have fallen from over 70 percent in the early 1960s to less than 20 percent now. This decline in labor force participation magnifies population trends, further increasing the number of retirees relative to the number of persons who are working. Together these trends have put enormous pressure on the financial solvency of social security systems around the world. Ironically, we argue, the provisions of the social security systems themselves typically contribute to the labor force withdrawal.

It is clear that there is a strong correspondence between the age at which benefits are available and departure from the labor force. Social security programs often provide generous retirement benefits at young ages. In addition, the provisions of these programs often imply large financial penalties on labor earnings beyond the social security early retirement age. Furthermore, in many countries disability and unemployment programs effectively provide early retirement benefits before the official social security early retirement age. We conclude that social security program provisions have indeed contributed to the decline in the labor force participation of older persons, substantially reducing the potential productive capacity of the labor force. It seems evident that if the trend to early retirement is to be reversed, as will almost surely be dictated by demographic trends, changing the provisions of social security programs that induce early retirement will play a key role.

Phase II

The first stage of the project established two key results: (1) that the social security systems in many countries provide enormous incentives to leave the labor force at older ages; and (2) that there is a strong correspondence between social security incentives to retire and the withdrawal of older workers from the labor force. The relationships in the first volume, however, did not provide a means of estimating the magnitude of the effect on labor force participation of changes in plan provisions.

The goal of the second phase of the project was to estimate how much the retirement age would change if social security provisions were changed. This analysis was based on within-country analysis of the determinants of retirement, considering the relationship between retirement and the incentives faced by individual employees. That is, rather than considering systemwide incentives for representative persons (such as those with median earning histories), and comparing these incentives to aggregate labor force participation across countries, we turned to microeconometric analyses within countries. The results of these analyses are based on differences in individual circumstances within a given country. Persons in a given country who are similar in many respects face quite different retirement incentives. It is these differences in retirement incentives—among otherwise similar persons—and the corresponding differences in individual retirement decisions that are used to determine the effect of the incentives on retirement.

In Phase II, the investigators in each country put together large microdata files that combined information on individual retirement decisions with retirement incentives (together with other individual data). Individual measures of social security retirement incentives—which vary substantially within a country—were calculated based on the methods developed for the first phase of the project. A key incentive measure was the *option value* of delayed retirement. This forward-looking measure is based on the potential gain (or loss) in wage earnings plus social security wealth if receipt of benefits is delayed. The financial value of retiring at the current age is compared with the age at which the financial value is the greatest, which could be the current age or could be many years in the future. That is, this constructed economic variable describes the financial gain or loss from continuing to work. Estimation using this measure goes back to the procedure Stock and Wise (1990a, 1990b) used to analyze the effect on retirement of employer-provided defined-benefit pension plans in the United States. Estimates were also obtained based on the related peak value measure proposed by Coile and Gruber (2001), which is based on the potential gain (or loss) in social security wealth only if receipt of benefits is delayed. Although the focus of the analysis is on forward-looking measures of the incentive to retirement—or for continued work—a natural starting point is a measure that looks ahead only one year, the single-year accrual measure. This measure captures the effect of another year of work on future benefits. Thus, as a base for comparison, the country analyses present the single-year accrual incentive measure as well.

As in the first phase, the analysis in each country followed a detailed template, so that results could be compared across countries. The micro-analysis in each country is based on a sample of individuals. In some cases, the data come largely from administrative records, while in other cases, the data were obtained from special surveys. The coverage is not precisely the same in each country. Nonetheless, it was possible to estimate the same models in each country, even though the population covered by the country data sets differed in some respects.

The key advantage of the microestimation is that in each country the effects of changes in plan provisions could be predicted. A second key feature of the microanalyses is that they allow consideration of several features of social security systems—as well as individual attributes—that may simultaneously affect retirement decisions. In particular, the microestimation results make it possible to jointly estimate the effect on retirement of the age at which benefits are first available and the incentive to retire once benefits are available. Both of these features were shown in the first stage of the project to be important determinants of the age of retirement.

The analysis in Phase II, however, posed several estimation challenges. Perhaps the most difficult was to identify the effect on retirement of the first eligibility age—in particular, to distinguish the effect of the eligibility age from the effect of the incentive measure, given eligibility. This was an important consideration, because a key empirical regularity across all countries was that retirement before the first eligibility age is rare and there is typically a jump in retirement at successive eligibility ages, in particular the age of first eligibility. This empirical regularity is discussed in some detail in the introduction to the Phase II volume (Gruber and Wise 2004a). To address this and other identification issues, each country estimated two different specifications of the base retirement model with respect to age: a model including a linear age trend and a model including age-specific dummy variables.

Parameter Estimates

The results in the second volume produced a striking finding: in virtually every country, in virtually every specification, the retirement incentives inherent in most social security programs are strongly related to departure from the labor force. In ten of the twelve countries we studied, the incentive measure effects were uniformly negatively related to retirement (a higher option value or peak value of continued work led to less retirement) and significantly different from zero. The results were robust to the use of both linear age and age-dummy variables. In two of the countries, Italy and Spain, the peak value and option value effects were typically not significant and sometimes of the wrong sign.[5] In these two countries, the single-year accrual effect is negative and significantly related to retirement in four of the six cases.

Thus, overall, we found the results from these twelve separate analyses to be strikingly consistent. The incentives inherent in retirement income programs are clear determinants of individual retirement behavior. The estimates themselves strongly suggest a causal interpretation of the cross-country results presented in our first volume. The results point to an important relationship between incentive effects and labor-force participation, independent of cultural difference among countries. The magnitudes of the implied effects are also very comparable across countries, as shown by the simulations discussed in the following.

Simulations

To demonstrate the effect of plan provisions on retirement, the estimates for each country were used to simulate the effect of three illustrative changes in plan provisions. Two illustrative plan changes were simulated in Phase II of the project, and a third was added in Phase III. All three are described here:

(1) The Three-Year Reform in eligibility ages. This illustrative simulation increases all eligibility ages by three years, including the early retirement age, the normal retirement age, and the ages of receipt of disability benefits—in countries in which disability, unemployment, or other retirement pathways are important, the eligibility age for *each* of the programs is delayed by three years.

(2) The Actuarial Reform. This reform reduces benefits actuarially if taken before the normal retirement age and increases benefits actuarially if taken after the normal retirement age.

(3) The Common Reform. This illustrative simulation is intended to predict the effect of the same reform (the common reform) in each country. Under the Common Reform, the early retirement age is set at age 60 and the normal retirement age at 65. Benefits taken before age 65 are reduced actuarially by 6 percent for each year before age 65. Benefits taken after age 65 are increased by 6 percent for each year the receipt of benefits is delayed. In addition, the replacement rate at age 65 is set at 60 percent of (projected) age 60 earnings.

5. In the United Kingdom, the option value incentive measures are significant when a bootstrap method that accounts for repeated observations for the same person is used to calculate standard errors. Also, in the United Kingdom, both the peak value and the option value incentive measures are very significant—under conventional standard error estimates—when cohort indicator, instead of age indictor, variables are used.

It is clear that an increase in eligibility ages will typically increase labor-force participation in each country. The implications of the Actuarial and Common reforms are less obvious, so we illustrate their likely effects across different countries, using the examples of Germany and the United States.

In Germany there was no actuarial adjustment before the 1992 reform legislation, and until recently most employees still retired under provisions that did not include actuarial adjustment. The magnitude of the combined effect of early retirement under the disability program in Germany and no actuarial adjustment is illustrated conceptually in figure I.9. The official social security normal retirement age in Germany is 65. Suppose that at that age, benefits would be 100 units per year. Many employees can receive benefits at age 57 through the disability program. The disability benefits at 57 are essentially the same as normal retirement benefits at age 65. That is, a person eligible for disability benefits at age 57 who did not take the benefits at that age would forego 100 units per year. This results in a baseline profile of benefits that starts at age 57 and remains flat at 100 units per year.

On the other hand, suppose benefits were reduced actuarially if taken before age 65 and increased actuarially if taken after age 65. Then benefits taken at 57 would be about 60 instead of 100. Benefits if taken at 70 would be about 140 instead of 100. There would be no incentive to take benefits early. Indeed, there would be no social security incentive to take benefits at any specific age, once benefits were available.

Figure I.10 shows a comparable figure for the United States. In both countries, the normal retirement age is 65. Benefits in the United States are first available at 62, however, compared to the common receipt of benefits from a

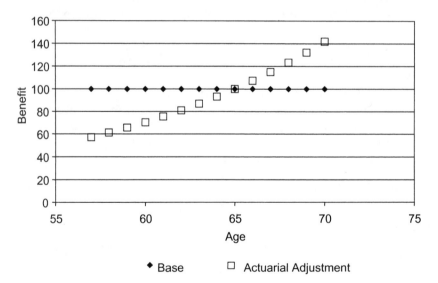

Fig. I.9   Germany: Base versus Actuarial Reform

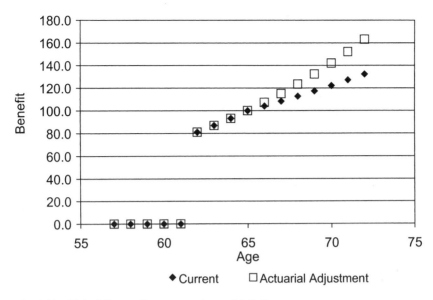

Fig. I.10   United States: Base versus Actuarial Reform

disability program at age 57 in Germany. In addition, benefits taken before age 65 in the United States are reduced actuarially. Benefits at 62 are 80 percent of benefits at 65. The increase in benefits after age 65 is less than actuarially fair, however.[6] Thus a reform to adjust benefits actuarially in the United States would have no effect before age 65, and only a small effect thereafter. It should be clear from figures I.9 and I.10 that increasing the first eligibility age—without any actuarial adjustment—would increase labor force participation in both countries, although the size of the effect is likely to be greater in Germany than in the United States because benefits at the first eligibility age are much larger in Germany than in the United States. Under this illustrative reform, in Germany benefits would be zero at age 57, 58, and 59. Benefits would first be available at age 60. In the United States, this illustrative reform would increase the age of first eligibility from 62 to 65.

Continuing to use a conceptual representation of social security provisions in Germany as an example, figure I.11 shows the effect of the Common Reform in Germany, and, for comparison, shows the Actuarial Reform as well. The Common Reform incorporates actuarial reduction in benefits before and actuarial increase in benefits after the normal retirement age, as described in figure I.9. In addition, the Common Reform in Germany implies a substantial reduction in benefits at the age 65 normal retirement age. And, the Common Reform in Germany would increase the

6. Under current legislation, the increase will be gradually increased to be actuarially fair by 2008.

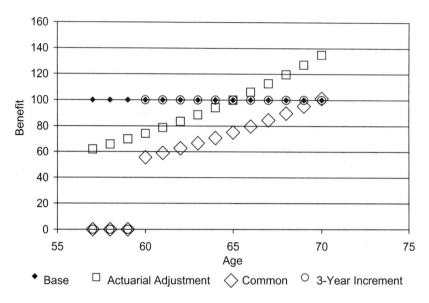

Fig. I.11   Germany: Base, Three-Year Reform, Actuarial Reform, Common Reform

age of first eligibility by three years (and thus incorporate the three-year in-crement in eligibility). In short, the receipt of benefits is delayed from 57 to 60, benefits at the normal retirement age are reduced from 100 to 75, and normal retirement age benefits are adjusted actuarially if taken before or after the normal retirement age.

The diagram suggests that the combined effect of these changes is likely to be large in Germany. Benefits before age 57 are no longer available. When they are available at age 60, there is no financial incentive to take benefits then as opposed to some later age, and when the normal retirement age is reached there is no financial incentive to take benefits at that age as opposed to some later age. (The following results show that the actuarial reduction accounts for a large fraction of the labor force participation effect of the Common Reform in Germany.)

Figure I.12 is a conceptual representation of the Common Reform in the United States. The Common Reform provides benefits two years earlier than the current early retirement age of 62. In addition, the Common Reform rep-resents an approximately 33 percent increase in benefits at the normal re-tirement age. These two features of the Common Reform should be expected to reduce the labor force participation of older workers in the United States. (In addition, the Common Reform provides for an actuarially fair increase in benefits after age 65, which would provide some incentive to remain in the labor force for persons who were still employed at ages older than 65.)

The cases of Germany and the United States are representative of the other nations in our sample. Most European nations have a system similar

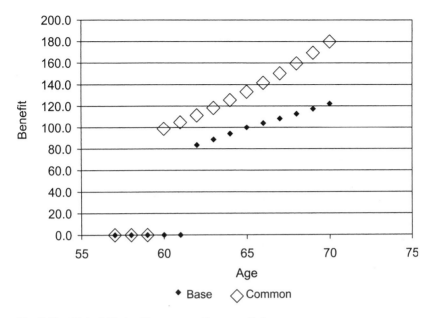

Fig. I.12   United States: Base versus Common Reform

to Germany's, so that we would expect very large increases for them in labor force participation from all of the reforms. Canada is more similar to
the United States, so that raising eligibility ages will raise labor force participation, the Common Reform will lower participation, and the Actuarial Reform will have little effect.

In general, specific features of the current plan in each country suggest
how the Common Reform should change labor force participation in that
country. Thus, in part, the Common Reform is used to confirm that the
simulation results, when compared across countries, conform to expectations based on current plan provisions.

Results

As emphasized previously, we made calculations based on two principle
estimation specifications—option value (OV) and peak value (PV)—and
three simulation methods. The three simulation methods are:

- S1: Use the retirement model with linear age.
- S2: Use the retirement model with age dummies, and assume that the
  age dummies' effects purely represent a taste for leisure and do not
  change when the system is reformed.
- S3: Use the retirement model with age dummies, and assume that the
  deviation of age dummies from a linear age trend purely represents
  effects of the retirement system.

Arguments can be made for all three approaches. The advantage of the first approach is that it allows us to remain neutral regarding the meaning of age-specific retirement patterns, but at the risk of misspecifying the regression model. But once age dummies are included, we do not know exactly whether they should be interpreted as variations in taste for leisure by age or as program effects. Thus, in this section, we will rely on the results from simulation approach S1, as a middle ground; the actual chapters in the second and third volumes show the results from all simulation methods.

Three-Year Reform in Eligibility Ages and Labor Force Participation

The basic findings can be shown in two figures. Figure I.13 shows the effect of the Three-Year Reform in eligibility ages, based on the method that we believe is most likely to reflect the long-run effect of such a reform. To help standardize for the wide variation across countries in the age at which retirement begins, each bar shows the reduction in the fraction of the population out of the labor force four years after the age at which a quarter of the population has retired (which is an effective retirement age). There are two notable features of this figure. The first is that the average reduction in the out-of-labor force (OLF) proportion is very large—47 percent. The second is the similarity across countries. The reduction is between 34 and 55 percent in nine of the twelve countries. In Germany and Sweden, the reductions are 77 and 68 percent, respectively. (The average reduction is 28 percent, using the simulation method that we believe is likely, on average, to substantially underestimate the response to the Three-Year Reform.)

The Common Reform and Labor Force Participation

Figure I.14 shows the effect on the OLF proportion of the Common Reform. In this figure, it is clear that the greatest reductions in the OLF proportion under the Common Reform are realized in the countries with the youngest effective retirement ages. For the six countries with substantial retirement before age 60, the average *reduction* in the OLF proportion is 44 percent. For the six countries in which most retirement is after age 60, there is a 4 percent average *increase* in the OLF proportion.

The systematic pattern of these results shows a strong congruence with intuition. For the six countries with the youngest effective retirement ages, the Common Reform represents a substantial *increase* in the youngest eligibility age, and the actuarial reduction in most of these countries means that benefits at this age are much lower than under the base country plans. Thus, for these countries, the OLF proportion should decline under the reform, and that is the case for every country but Canada. But for the six countries with older retirement ages, the Common Reform may reduce the earliest eligibility age—as in the United States—and may provide a greater incentive to leave the labor force. In addition, the 60 percent replacement rate at the normal retirement age represents an increase for some countries,

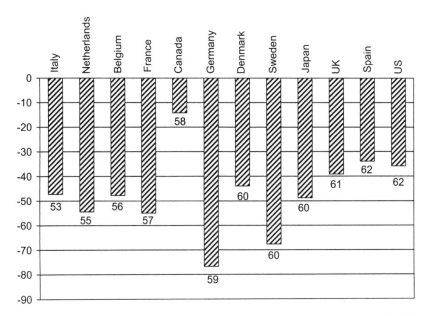

Fig. I.13   OLF change 25 percent age + 4 years, base versus 3-year delay: OV-S3

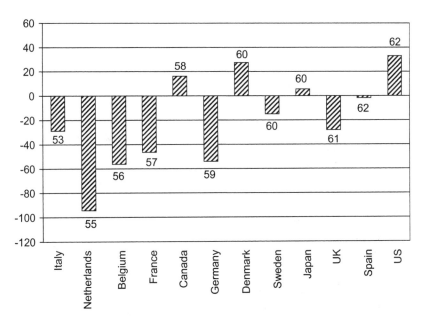

Fig. I.14   OLF change 25 percent age + 4 years, base versus Common
Reform: OV-S3

such as the United States, but a reduction in the replacement rate for other countries. Consequently, in three of these six countries, there is an increase in the OLF proportion under the Common Reform simulation, and on average there is an increase in the OLF proportion. (The seemingly anomalous result for Canada is explained by the fact that Canada is the only country in which the 25 percent age is below the nominal social security entitlement age; the 25 percent age is 58, while the social security entitlement age is 60. In addition, Canada has relatively low benefits at the early retirement age (60). Thus, the Common Reform significantly increases benefit levels, providing an additional inducement to retirement.)

A key reason for simulating the Common Reform was to determine whether the results would correspond with intuition based on current plan provisions. That the correspondence is close, we believe, helps to add credence to the estimation and simulation methods and to the overall results.

We concluded the introduction to this phase of the project (Gruber and Wise 2004a, 35–36) with these comments:

> The results of the country analyses reported in this volume confirm the strong causal effect of social security program retirement incentives on labor force participation. But perhaps more important, the results in this volume show the large magnitude of these effects. Across 12 countries with very different social security programs and labor market institutions, the results consistently show that program incentives accord strongly with retirement decisions. The magnitude of the estimated effects varies from country to country, but in all countries the effects are large.
>
> In short: the results in this volume provide an important complement to the first volume. The results leave no doubt that social security incentives have a strong effect on retirement decisions. And the estimates show that the effect is similar in countries with very different cultural histories, labor market institutions, and other social characteristics. While countries may differ in many respects, the employees in all countries react similarly to social security retirement incentives. The simulated effects of illustrative reforms reported in the country papers make clear that changes in the provisions of social security programs would have very large effects on the labor force participation of older employees.

Phase III

Using the estimates from Phase II, Phase III of the project describes the fiscal implications of changes in program provisions. What would be the financial implications of changing the provisions of social security systems? Again, the results are demonstrated by simulating the fiscal effects of illustrative reforms. In this phase, all three illustrative reforms described earlier are simulated. In addition to the Three-Year Reform and the Common Reform, we also simulate separately an Actuarial Reform. As noted, in the United States and in Canada, for example, benefits taken before the early retirement age are reduced actuarially (so that, on average, benefits received over a lifetime do not depend on the age at which receipt of benefits begins), so that this simulation closely parallels existing law. In many European countries, however, there is little or no actuarial reduction if benefits are taken early. This provides a very large incentive to leave the labor force early, so that in many countries, moving to an actuarially fair system can have very large fiscal implications.

The goal of the analysis in this phase is not to calculate the long-run balance sheets of a social security system, as is undertaken, for example, by the United States Social Security Administration (SSA). Rather, the approach taken here is to illustrate the fiscal implications by calculating the implications of reform for a specific cohort or for a group of cohorts. For example, in the United States, the estimates show the fiscal implications of changes in social security provisions for the cohort born between 1931 and 1941 (reaching age 65 between 1996 and 2006). The calculations in Phase III, like those in Phases I and II, are made according to a detailed template so that the results can be compared across countries.

In each country, the simulations proceed in several steps:

1. Using the retirement models estimated in Phase II of the project, predict the distribution of retirement ages under current law (the base case).

2. For this distribution of retirement ages, compute the fiscal position of the cohort—total expected benefits paid to the cohort and total expected taxes (both social security and other taxes) paid by the cohort.

3. Use the retirement models to predict the distribution of retirement ages under a reform.

4. For the new distribution of retirement ages, compute the fiscal position of the cohort.

5. Calculate the difference between fiscal positions under the base and the reform systems to obtain the fiscal implication of reform.

6. Divide the fiscal implication into two components: The *mechanical* effect is the effect of the reform assuming no behavioral response (change in retirement ages) to the reform. The *behavioral* effect is the additional incremental effect due to retirement response to the reform.

To illustrate the method used in each of the country papers, we describe key calculations for two countries—the effects of the reforms in Canada, focusing on the Three-Year Reform, and effects of the Actuarial Reform in Germany. These examples also help to highlight how the details of the current plan provisions, including the treatment of different components of the current system, influence the effect on the illustrative reform. We then show comparative results across countries.

Canada—Three-Year Reform

We illustrate the results presented in each paper using results for Canada as an example. (Values are shown in Euros, converted from Canadian dollars at the December 31, 2001, exchange rate—C$1.4185 = €1.00). The Canadian retirement system has three central components:

1. The Old Age Security (OAS) pension is a lump sum that is paid to all citizens 65 and older. (It was $442.66 in March 2002 [€312.06] at the December 31, 2001 exchange rate.) The OAS is indexed to the CPI and is fully taxable. (It also includes a "claw-back" provision for very high-income recipients.)

2. The Guaranteed Income Supplement (GIS) is an income-tested supplement for low-income OAS beneficiaries. (In January to March 2002 it was $526.08 for married couples and $342.67 for single persons [€370.85 and €241.57], respectively.) The GIS is indexed to the CPI and is not subject to income taxes. These benefits are not adjusted actuarially.

3. The largest component of the social security system (called the Income Security System in Canada) is the combination of the Canada Pension Plan (CPP) and the Quebec Pension Plan (QPP). The actuarial reduction applies only to the CPP/QPP component, for which the normal retirement age is 65 and the early retirement age is 60. The reduction rate is 0.5 percent per month (6 percent per year), so that those retiring at 60 receive 70 percent of the age-65 benefit. The CPP/QPP replaces at most 25 percent of preretirement income.

For this discussion, we focus on the Three-Year Reform but show key data for the other reforms as well. The main results are shown in two tables in each of the country papers. The example for Canada shows how these tables are organized and how to interpret the entries.

Table I.1 shows the total effect of each of the three reforms. As noted earlier, reforms were simulated for each country using six methods—three simulation approaches, each implemented based on the option value and the peak value incentive measures. Here we show the results for the option value model and for simulation method S1. Each of the country papers presents a table with six panels—one for each of the estimation-simulation methods—in which each panel looks like table I.1, shown here.

The first four columns show the present discounted value (PDV) of benefits and taxes under the base plan and under each of the three illustrative reforms. For example, the PDV of future benefits payments under the base plan is €111,084. Under the Three-Year Reform, the PDV is reduced to €91,491. Total taxes under the base plan are €134,034, and are composed of payroll taxes (15,182), income taxes (81,313), and consumption taxes (37,540).[7] Total taxes increase slightly, to €139,161 under the Three-Year Reform.

---

7. Consumption tax revenues are imputed based on the income associated with each policy. Payroll tax revenues include the share of general revenues that are associated with social security programs, as imputed in each country.

Table I.1   **Canada illustration: Total fiscal effect of reform—OV-S1**

| Cost or revenue item | Present discounted value | | | | Total change relative to base (%) | | |
	Base	Three-Year Reform	Actuarial Reform	Common Reform	Three-Year Reform	Actuarial Reform	Common Reform
Benefits	111,084	91,491	111,084	187,796	–17.60	0.00	69.10
Taxes							
Payroll	15,182	16,821	15,182	12,537	10.80	0.00	–17.40
Income	81,313	85,075	81,313	93,608	4.60	0.00	15.10
Consumption	37,540	37,265	37,540	41,314	–0.70	0.00	10.10
Total	134,034	139,161	134,034	147,459	3.80	0.00	10.00

Notes: The first four columns show the PDV of benefits and taxes under the base plan and under each of the three illustrative reforms. The last three columns show the change relative to the base, for benefits and for taxes.

The last three columns show the total change relative to the base. For example, the Three-Year Reform reduces benefits by 17.6 percent and increases tax receipts by 3.8 percent. The change in benefits minus the change in taxes (–19,593 – 5,127 = –€24,720) is 22.3 percent of the base benefit costs (€111,084) of the program. This percentage is explicitly shown in table I.2 and is the key result of the simulation.

The Actuarial Reform has no effect in Canada because, as previously mentioned, benefits are adjusted actuarially under the base (current) plan, so the Actuarial Reform is not a change. The Common Reform increases program costs substantially in Canada, primarily because benefits under the Common Reform are much larger than current benefits in Canada.

Table I.2 shows the total effect of the reform, shown in table 1, decomposed into mechanical and behavioral components. Again, each of the country papers presents a second key table with six panels, and each of the panels is organized like table I.2. The mechanical component is the effect of the reform, assuming no behavioral—labor force participation—response to the reform. The behavioral component is the additional incremental effect resulting from the labor force supply response to the reform. For example, the Three-Year Reform's mechanical effect reduces benefits by €19,452. The behavioral response—a substantial increase in the typical retirement age—in fact reduces benefits a bit more. (This apparent anomaly is the result of specific features of the Canadian social security system and is explained subsequently.) The mechanical effect reduces total taxes by €4,753 (and is also explained later). The behavioral effect—prolonging participation in the labor force—leads to an increase in taxes of €9,905. The total effect on taxes is an increase of €5,127. The net change in benefits minus tax revenues is –€24,720, which is equivalent to 22.3 percent of the base (current) cost of the program. This change as a percentage of base benefits is perhaps the single best summary of the effect of the illustrative

Table I.2 Canada illustration: Decomposition of total effect of reform, change in present discounted value—OV-S1

	Three-Year Reform			Actuarial Reform			Common Reform		
	Mechanical	Behavioral	Total	Mechanical	Behavioral	Total	Mechanical	Behavioral	Total
Benefits	-19,459	-134	-19,593	0	0	0	79,151	-2,438	76,713
Total taxes	-4,778	9,905	5,127	0	0	0	36,231	-22,806	13,425
Net change	-14,681	-10,039	-24,720	0	0	0	42,920	20,368	63,287
Change as % of base benefits	-13.20	-9.00	-22.3	0.00	0.00	0.00	38.60	18.30	57.00

Notes: The table shows the total effect of the reform (shown in table I.1) decomposed into mechanical and behavioral components. The first row shows the change in benefits. The second row shows the change in all taxes. The third row shows the net change (the change in benefits minus the change in taxes). The fourth row shows the net change as a percent of base benefits (shown in table I.1).

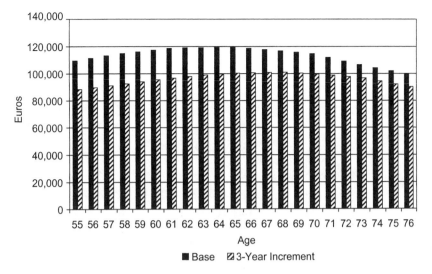

Fig. I.15   Canada: SSW by age of labor force exit

reform. Comparable percentages apply to each of the reforms in each of the countries and are used in the following discussion to provide cross-country comparisons.

A series of figures helps to explain the results in tables I.1 and I.2, focusing on the Three-Year Reform. Figure I.15 shows the present discounted value of social security wealth by age of retirement, under the base plan and under the Three-Year Reform. Benefits taken at any age are lower under the Three-Year Reform. There are two reasons for the pattern across ages. First, the age-65 normal retirement age under the base plan is increased to 68 under the Three-Year Reform. Thus, benefits taken at 55, for example, are lower under the Three-Year Reform because they are discounted actuarially from 68 to 55 instead of from 65 to 55. Second, while the CPP and QPP are actuarially adjusted, so that receiving them later does not affect their PDV, the GIS and OAS are not. So if the age of receipt of these programs is delayed, the PDV of benefits at all ages is lowered.

Figure I.16 shows the relationship between total taxes and retirement age. Taxes increase sharply with age, but *at any age* of exit from the labor force, taxes are less under the Three-Year Reform. This is because the OAS component of the social security benefit—which is taxable—is received for three fewer years under the Three-Year Reform. Thus, prolonging labor force participation yields increased tax revenues from taxes on the increased wage earnings. But this increase is partially offset by the reduction in future taxable social security benefits under the Three-Year Reform.

Figure I.17 shows the distribution of retirement ages under the base and under the Three-Year Reform. The upward shift in the distribution is clear.

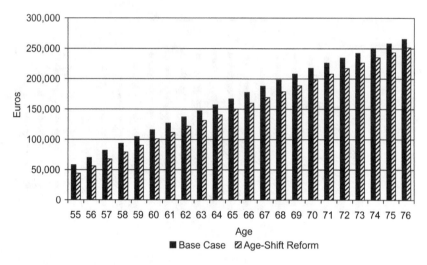

Fig. I.16   Canada: Total taxes by age of labor force exit

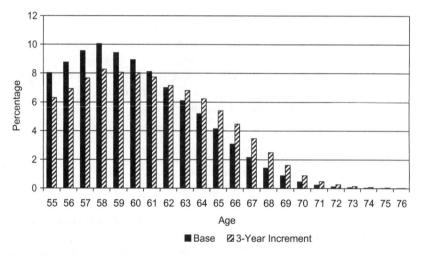

Fig. I.17   Canada: Distribution of labor force exit ages, OV-S1 model

The behavioral component of benefits and taxes reported in table I.2 is due to this upward shift in retirement ages.

Figure I.18 shows how the total effect reported in table I.2 arises, by considering the change in expected totals by age. The bars labeled *total benefits* show the change in expected benefits, by age. For example, the expected payment to persons at age 55 is lower because fewer persons retire at this age and because they receive lower payments, as shown in figure I.15. The expected payment of benefits to persons age 64 or older, however, is in-

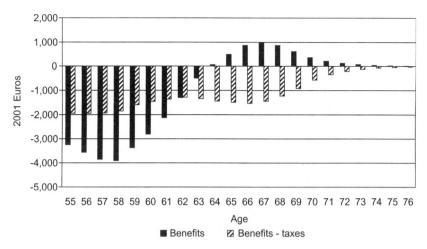

Fig. I.18   Canada: Total effect of Three-Year Reform by age of retirement, OV-S1 model

creased under the Three-Year Reform. Even though the benefit per person is lower under the Three-Year Reform, more people retire at these ages, leading to an increase in the expected payment to these older persons. Aggregated over all ages—weighted by the proportion of persons retiring at each age—the reduction is €19,593, shown under benefits total in table I.2.

The lighter bars show the change in the expected benefit payments by age, less the expected tax revenues of persons who retire at each age. Expected benefits minus tax revenues are lower at each age under the Three-Year Reform. The reduction in the expected value of benefits minus taxes is less than the reduction in benefits at younger ages because persons who retire at these ages pay lower taxes on future social security benefits than they used to, as explained with reference to figure I.15. Nonetheless, there is a net gain to the government budget. The important feature shown by this figure is that even at older ages—at which the expected benefits are increased under the Three-Year Reform, because more persons are retiring at these ages—the added taxes paid by these persons when they are working more than offset the greater expected benefits paid to persons at these ages. The net reduction in benefits minus taxes across all retirement ages is €24,720, as shown in table I.2.[8]

Finally, figure I.19 shows the fiscal effect of the Three-Year Reform as a percentage of GDP. This figure shows the estimated effect for each of the

8. The sum over the values in the figure is not exactly 24,720. Figure 18 shows the average benefits and taxes at each age (figure I.16) times the average retirement rates at each age (figure I.17). The 24,720 in table I.2 comes from taking each individual in the sample and multiplying benefits and taxes by probabilities of retirement, and then taking the average. The bars in figure I.18 sum to 24,193.

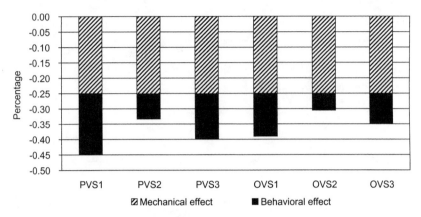

Fig. I.19   Canada: Fiscal implication of Three-Year Reform as percent of GDP, by estimation method

six methods used to obtain estimates. The reduction in government benefits payments minus revenues ranges from about .30 to .45 percent of GDP, depending on the estimation method.

Figures like those for Canada are shown in each of the country papers, but the figures that the country authors have selected to show vary from country to country. Tables showing results like those in tables I.1 and I.2, however, are shown for each country.

Germany—Actuarial Reform

Germany has a very generous social security system, with very strong incentives to retire early. In addition to the social security program per se, a large fraction of workers in Germany retire through disability and unemployment programs, as previously described. These programs essentially provide early-retirement benefits before the age-60 social security early retirement age. Indeed, these programs provide the principle path to retirement in Germany. And as described earlier, once benefits are available, there is no actuarial reduction in benefits taken before the age-65 normal retirement age (although recent reforms have introduced some actuarial reduction). For example, early retirement benefits taken at age 60, or benefits from the disability program taken at age 57, are the same as the age-65 normal retirement benefits. This provides an enormous incentive to take benefits when they are first available. If they are not taken, they are simply lost; there is no offsetting increase in benefits if they are received for fewer years.

Suppose that benefits in Germany were actuarially fair, so that benefits received prior to age 65 were reduced by 6 percent per year, and benefits received after 65 were increased 6 percent per year. What would be the fiscal implications of such a change? Table I.3 shows the effect of this change on the mean retirement age for the sample of workers used in the analysis. The mean retirement age for men under the current provisions is 61.91. The base simulation yields a mean retirement age very close to the sample mean. The actuarially fair reduction in benefits is estimated to increase the retirement age by about three years, for both men and women. Figure I.20 shows the change in the distribution of retirement ages for men; there is a clear shift to older ages throughout the distribution.

The fiscal implications of this change are shown in table I.4. As described previously, the total effect of the reform is decomposed into two parts—the mechanical effect that would exist if retirement ages did not change, and the behavioral effect that is due to change in retirement ages. Benefits received at any age less than 65 are reduced by the actuarial reduction. If there were no change in retirement ages, the average benefit per worker would be reduced by €37,056. But the behavioral response to the reform increases the average retirement age, as shown in table I.3 and figure I.20. This increases the average benefit by €19,632. The total (net) effect on benefits is a reduction of €17,423.

Table I.3   German illustration: Effect of actuarial reduction in benefits on
                   retirement age—OV model

Model	Men	Women
Sample frequencies	61.91	61.73
Base simulation	62.05	62.01
Actuarially fair simulation	65.18	64.57

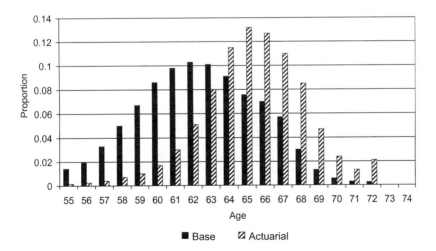

Fig. I.20   Germany: Distribution of retirement ages for base and Actuarial Reform, OV-S1 method

Table I.4   German Illustration: Fiscal implications of Actuarial Reform—Change in PDV, euros per worker (OV model, dummies shifted)

	Mechanical effect	Behavioral effect	Total effect
Benefits	−37,056	19,632	−17,423
Contribution	0	16,766	16,766
All taxes	−1,558	50,608	49,049
Net change	−35,497	−47,741	−83,238
% change	−18.27	−24.58	−42.85

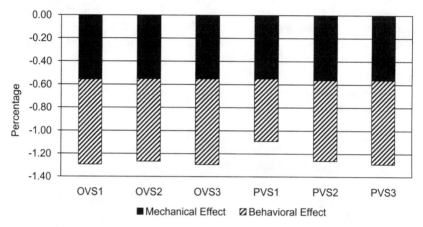

Fig. I.21   Germany: Fiscal implications of Actuarial Reform as percentage of 2001 GDP, by estimation method

In addition to the change in benefits, the reform has further fiscal implications. Contributions to the social security system are increased if employees continue to work. This behavioral effect is +€16,766.

In addition, if employees work longer, they pay more in other taxes. The total increase in taxes is €49,049 per worker (including taxes for health and other insurance programs, income taxes, and VAT tax). The net change in benefits *minus* the change in contributions and taxes is –€83,238. This net *reduction* in the total government benefit payments minus revenues is equivalent to 42.85 percent of base benefits under the current system. The fiscal effect of the reform as a percent of GDP is shown in figure I.21, which shows the estimated effect for each of six estimation and simulation methods. On balance, the reduction in benefits minus all taxes is about 1.2 percent of GDP.

Cross-Country Comparisons

Calculations like those illustrated for Canada and Germany were made by each of the country teams for each of the three illustrative reforms. As

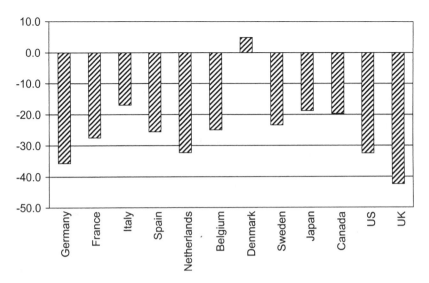

Fig. I.22   Total fiscal effect of Three-Year Reform, as percentage of base cost

the illustrations highlight, the effect of each of the reforms depends on the provisions of the current system in each country. An increase in eligibility ages is expected to reduce expenditures and increase tax revenues in all countries. But even in this case, the added tax revenue from increased labor-force participation can be at least partly offset by lower taxes resulting from lower future social security benefits, as in Canada. The Actuarial Reform, which has large effects in Germany, should have little effect in countries like the United States and Canada, where the system is already actuarially fair.

Results across all countries are shown in the next five figures. Like the results for the first two phases of the project, these results are taken from the individual country papers. For these comparisons, we use the estimates based on the option value specification and simulation method S3—sometimes referred to as OV-S3, or as option value-age dummies shifted. The figures show the total fiscal effect of the reforms. To reduce complexity, the figures do not divide the total effect into the mechanical and the behavioral components that can be seen in the country papers. The behavior effects of the Three-Year Reform in eligibility ages and of the Common Reform on labor force participation are shown in figures I.13 and I.14, respectively.

Figure I.22 shows the total fiscal effect of the Three-Year Reform in eligibility ages. For example, in Germany, the reduction in government benefit payments minus the increase in tax revenues—resulting from a three-year increment in all eligibility ages—would be equivalent to about 36 percent of the current cost of the program. Across all countries, the average decrease in government benefit payments minus tax revenues is equivalent to

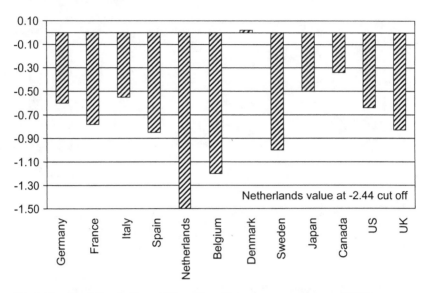

Fig. I.23   Total fiscal effect of Three-Year Reform, as percentage of GDP

27 percent of current program cost. The anomalous positive total fiscal effect in Denmark is due to the replacement of three years of Old Age Pension benefits with benefits from a more generous early retirement program.

Figure I.23 shows the decrease in government benefit payments minus tax revenues—resulting from the Three-Year Reform—as a percent of gross domestic product. The average decrease over all countries is equivalent to 0.97 percent of GDP and is greater than 0.50 percent or greater in all but two of the countries—again reported as a reduction in government benefit payments minus tax revenues.

Figure I.24 shows the fiscal effect of the Actuarial Reform as a percentage of base cost. As expected, there is large variation across countries. As noted earlier, in the United States and Canada, where adjustment is already close to actuarial, the effect is small. In Germany, where until recently there was no actuarial adjustment, the effect is very large, as explained in detail previously.

In France, the actuarial increase in benefits after the age-60 early retirement age would prolong participation in the labor force and would increase benefits for many retirees. The early retirement age in France is 60 and the normal retirement age depends on the number of validated participation quarters. (The normal retirement age is the minimum of 65 and is the age at which a person attains 150 validated quarters.) But under the current system there is no actuarial adjustment of benefits if they are taken after the age of first eligibility, and the reduction in benefits if they are taken before the normal retirement age is greater than actuarially fair. For per-

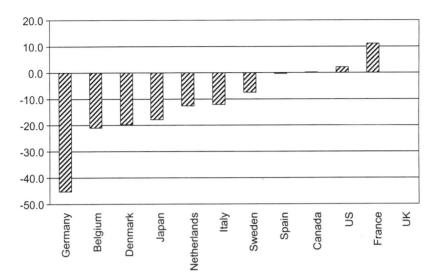

Fig. I.24   Total fiscal effect of Actuarial Reform, as percentage of base cost

sons with more than 150 validated quarters, the actuarial upward adjustment of benefits after age 60 would increase their pension benefits. The reduction in benefits if taken with less than 150 quarters is less under the Actuarial Reform. So both the behavioral and the mechanical effects of the Actuarial Reform increase the cost of benefits.

On average, across all countries the decrease in government expenditure minus revenue is equivalent to about 26 percent of the base cost—reported as a reduction in government benefit payments minus tax revenues. Because of particular features of the current system in the United Kingdom, the Actuarial Reform has not been simulated for that country.

Figure I.25 shows the fiscal effect of the Common Reform as a percentage of base cost. In accord with intuition, the total net government revenue as a percent of program base cost varies greatly. In the United States, for example, benefits under the Common Reform are more generous than current benefits and, are available at age 60 instead of the current age-62 early retirement age. Also, in the United Kingdom, the Common Reform benefits are much more generous than current benefits, and the age-60 early retirement age is younger than the current early retirement age for some participants.

Figure I.26 shows the fiscal effects of each of the reforms on the same figure, ordered by the effect of the Common Reform. This figure helps to emphasize the sometimes intricate relationship between current plan provisions and the effects of the illustrative reforms. In the United States and Canada, for example, the Three-Year Reform reduces (net) program costs. The Actuarial Reform has essentially no effect in Canada, where the

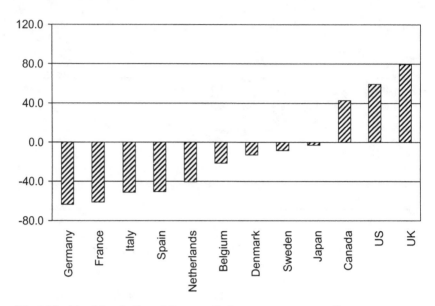

Fig. I.25   Total fiscal effect of Common Reform, as percentage of base cost

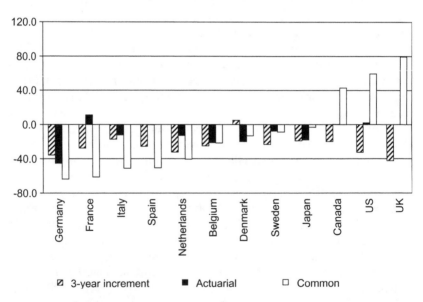

☒ 3-year increment   ■ Actuarial   ☐ Common

Fig. I.26   Total fiscal effect of Three-Year Reform, Actuarial, and Common Reforms, as percentage of base cost

system is already actuarial, and little effect in the United States, where the system is close to actuarial. But in both of these countries the Common Reform provides higher benefits than provided by their current system, and in the United States, benefits are available two years earlier than the current early retirement age. Thus, the Common Reform substantially increases program costs in these countries.

Another example: in France, the Three-Year Reform would reduce net program costs. The actuarial adjustment alone would increase benefit payments, as previously described. But the Common Reform provides much lower benefits than the current system in France. In addition, the Common Reform sets the normal retirement age at 65, and benefits are actuarially reduced between 65 and the age-60 early retirement age. Thus, on balance, the Common Reform implies a substantial reduction in net program cost in France.

Although not detailed in this introduction, the results for each of the countries are determined by the precise relationships between the current plan provisions and the illustrative reform.

Conclusions: Looking Back and Going Forward

Our introduction to Phase I of the project emphasized the striking relationship across countries between social security program incentives to retire and the proportion of older persons out of the labor force (figures I.7 and I.8). The weight of the evidence, we judged, was that the relationship was largely causal.

The results of the country analyses reported in Phase II of the project—based on within-country analysis of microdata—confirmed the strong causal effect of social security program retirement incentives on labor force participation and showed the large magnitude of these effects. The results left no doubt that social security incentives have a strong effect on retirement decisions. Across twelve countries, the results consistently showed that program incentives strongly accord with retirement decisions. The magnitude of the estimated effects varies from country to country, but in all countries the effects were found to be large. And the estimates show that the effect is similar in countries with very different cultural histories, labor market institutions, and other social characteristics. While countries may differ in many respects, employees in all countries react similarly to social security retirement incentives. The simulated effects of illustrative reforms reported in the country papers made clear that changes in the provisions of social security programs would have very large effects on the labor force participation of older employees.

In this phase of the project, we built on the estimates obtained in the second phase to analyze the fiscal implications of program provisions. In particular, we estimated the financial implications of three illustrative program reforms. The results make clear that reforms like those considered in this volume can have very large fiscal implications for the cost of social security benefits as well as for government revenues engendered by changes in the labor force participation of older workers.

On average, across the twelve countries, we judge that a three-year increase in program eligibility ages would reduce government benefits payments minus tax revenues by 27 percent of current program cost. The average reduction is approximately 0.72 percent of country GDP. While the estimates vary by method of estimation—as reported in each of the country papers—we believe that these averages reflect the most likely long-run effect of the illustrative reforms. Actuarial reform alone would have a very large effect in some countries—reducing net government cost by over 40 percent in five countries—depending on the extent of actuarial adjustment to benefits under the current program provisions.

In the second phase of the project, we used estimates of the labor force participation effects of the Common Reform to judge the plausibility of the estimates. In this third phase we estimated the fiscal implication of the Common Reform. Again, we find that the results accord strongly with intuition, based on the provisions of the current plans. In accord with intuition, the Common Reform yields both increases and reductions in government revenue equivalent to a large fraction of current program costs. We believe that this adds credence to the methods used for estimation of the fiscal effects of the illustrative reforms.

In short, the fiscal effects of reform can be very large. Some combination of increases in the early retirement age, actuarial adjustment of benefits, and change in the benefit level can change net government revenue substantially. In many countries, the illustrative reforms simulated by the participants in this project yield reductions in government benefit payments minus tax revenues equivalent to 20 to 50 percent of current program cost.

Finally, having emphasized the potential for changes in plan provisions to increase the labor force participation of older workers and to relieve the financial pressure on social security systems, we consider how such changes in social security systems may already be having an effect in some countries. Figure I.27, panels A and B, is the same as figure I.2, panels A and B, but it has been updated to include labor force participation rates of men from about 1995 to about 2003. In many of the countries there seems to be a clear reversal in the decline in labor force participation. In some countries the reversal can be traced to changes in social security provisions, while in others it seems to be associated with economy-wide trends in labor market conditions.

Consider Denmark first. Except for updating the series, the only other change is the addition of data for Denmark, which was added to the project after the first phase. In 1999, the Post Employment Wage (PEW) program was changed to provide incentives to stay in the labor force until age

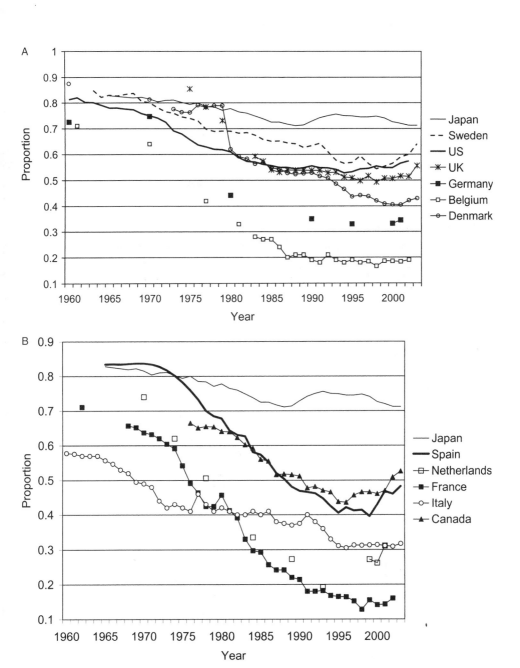

Fig. I.27   LFP trends for men 60 to 64, updated

62. (When the PEW program was introduced, in 1979, it induced an almost-immediate drop of 17 percentage points in the labor force participation rate of men 60 to 64.)

In Sweden, the explanation for the increase in the labor force participation of men 60 to 64 lies primarily in changes in the eligibility requirement for the disability program. The provision that unemployed workers older than age 60 were eligible for a disability pension was abolished in 1991, and the provision that these unemployed workers were eligible because of a combination of medical and labor market reasons was abolished in 1997. The most important change was likely the 1995 provision that enabled the social security administration to reconsider the right to a disability pension. Consistent with these changes, from 1993 to 2002 the percentage of men aged 60 to 64 with a disability pension was reduced from 30 to 23 percent. In addition, the Swedish economy has recovered from the 1990s recession that limited labor force demand.

In Germany, the reversal of the downward trend in the labor force participation of men 60 to 64 that began in 1997 coincides with the introduction of partial actuarial reduction in benefits taken before the early retirement age. In the United States, the downward trend was reversed about 1995. While the reason for the reversal is unclear, it seems likely that the decline in employer-provided defined-benefit pension plans—with strong incentives to retire early—and the rapid spread of personal retirement plans—with no retirement incentive effects—has been part of the explanation.

In the United Kingdom there has been a general increase in labor force participation rates at all ages, but there was no apparent change in social security plan provisions that might have led to an increase for men 60 to 64. In Canada there were no changes in social security provisions that could account for the increase in the labor force participation of men 60 to 64. There was, however, a general improvement in labor market conditions after the mid-90s, with a fall in the overall unemployment rate from 10.4 percent in 1995 to 7.6 percent in 2003. In Spain, the reforms during the 1997 to 2002 period did not substantially change the retirement incentives faced by older workers. There was, however, a large increase in the labor force—from about 12.5 million in 1995 to over 17 million in 2004—apparently due to an increase in the demand for labor. And during this period, labor force participation increased from 50.8 to 55.7 percent.

We do not yet have a succinct explanation for the increase in the labor-force participation in The Netherlands. Early retirement provisions in The Netherlands are the result of collective bargaining by sector, or even by firm, and hence it is hard to easily identify and summarize changes in plan provisions.

Thus far in the project, we have considered the early retirement incentives inherent in many social security programs, the reduction in the labor force participation of older workers induced by these penalties on work, and the consequent financial implications of the induced early retirement. Going forward, we will direct our attention to several new issues, including the relationship between social security system provisions and the well-being of the elderly and the young, the relationship between social security system provisions and the employment of the young, and how the relationship between health status and retirement varies with social security (including disability) program provisions.

References

Coile, Courtney C., and Jonathan Gruber. 2001. Social security incentives for retirement. In *Themes in the economics of aging,* ed. D. A. Wise, 311–41. Chicago: University of Chicago Press.

Gruber, Jonathan, and David A. Wise. 1999a. Introduction and summary. In *Social security programs and retirement around the world,* ed. J. Gruber and D. A. Wise, 73–100. Chicago: University of Chicago Press.

Gruber, Jonathan, and David A. Wise, eds. 1999b. *Social security and retirement around the world.* Chicago: University of Chicago Press.

Gruber, Jonathan, and David A. Wise. 2004a. Introduction and summary. In *Social security programs and retirement around the world: Micro-estimation,* ed. J. Gruber and D. A. Wise, 1–40. Chicago: University of Chicago Press.

Gruber, Jonathan, and David A. Wise, eds. 2004b. *Social security and retirement around the world: Micro-estimation.* Chicago: University of Chicago Press.

Stock, James H., and David A. Wise. 1990a. The pension inducement to retire: An option value analysis. In *Issues in the economics of aging,* ed. D. A. Wise, 205–24. Chicago: University of Chicago Press.

Stock, James H., and David A. Wise. 1990b. Pensions, the option value of work, and retirement. *Econometrica* 58 (5): 1151–80.

Appendix

Table IA.1   Programs considered in the analysis, by country

Country	Social security	Early retirement	Unemployment	Disability	Other
		Programs considered			
Belgium	Retirement Income System	For salaried workers and civil servants	Old age unemployment support	Not included	
Canada	Canada/Quebec Pension Plan, Guaranteed Income Supplement, Old Age Security	Included	Not included	Not included	
Denmark	Old-Age Pension (OAP)	Post-Employment Wage (PEW), Public Employee Pension (PEP)	Transitional Benefit Program	Disability pension	
France	Private sector and public sector	For the private sector	For the private sector	Not included	
Germany	Gesetzliche Rentenversicherung and Beamtenpensionen	Included	Included	Included	
Italy	Old age pension, disability and survivors	Included	Included	Included	
Japan	Employees' Pension Insurance (EPI), Zaishoku Pension Benefits (EPI benefits subject to earnings test)	Included	Included	Included	Wage subsidy to elderly workers
The Netherlands	Included	Included in occupational pension plans	Included	Included	
Spain	Included		Included	Included	
Sweden	Public and occupational pensions		Included	Included	Sickpay insurance
United Kingdom	Basic State Pension and State Earnings-Related Pension Scheme (SERPS)		Included	Invalidity benefit	Income support (Means-tested benefit)
United States	Included		Not included	Not included	

Table IA.2	Selected data sources, by country	
Country	Data sources	Year
Belgium	Fiscal Revenue Statistics (SFR)	1989–96
	Individual Pension Account (CIP)	
	Census	1991
Canada	Longitudinal Worker File (Statistics Canada)	
Denmark	Danish Integrated Database (IDA), 2% sample	1980–2001
France	Echantillon Interrégime de Retraités (EIR)	1997
	Annual declarations of social data (DADS)	
	Wage files for civil servants (State Service)	
	Unemployment files (UNEDIC)	
Germany	German Socio-Economic Panel (GSOEP)	
	Administrative data from German Association of Public Retirement	
	Insurance providers	
	Administrative data from German Department of Labor and Social Security (BMAS)	
Italy	Instituto Nazionale Pevidenza Sociale (INPS)-Workers archive	1973–97
Japan	Survey on Labor Market Participation of Older Persons	1996
The Netherlands	Netherlands Socioeconomic Panel (SEP)	1984–96
	CentER Savings Survey	1997
Spain	Administrative records from Spanish SSA (HLSS)	
	Encuesta de Población Activa (EPA)	
	Estadística de Convenios Colectivos	
	National accounts from Bank of Spain	
Sweden	Longitudinal Individual Data (LINDA)—based on Income and Wealth Register, Population Census, and National Social Insurance Board Registers	Panel data 1983–97
United Kingdom	UK Retirement Survey (RS)	Panel data
	Family Expenditure Survey (FES)	1988–89, 1994
United States	Health and Retirement Survey (HRS)	1951–91, 1992

1

Microsimulation of Social Security Reforms in Belgium

Raphael Desmet, Alain Jousten, Sergio Perelman, and Pierre Pestieau

1.1 Introduction

The various Belgian social security schemes are facing an uncertain future. The general trend toward demographic aging across all of the developed world and large parts of the developing world has not left Belgium unaffected. Demographic aging is the result of a combination of two trends. First, there has been a substantial decrease in fertility rates of women over the last few decades. Second, we have observed a strong increase in life expectancy across most categories in the population. Unfortunately, these trends have a strongly negative financial impact on a variety of social insurance and social protection programs, ranging from child support payments, the health care sector, to questions of retirement income and long-term care arrangements. While the problem can be approached in a myriad of ways, we approach it from the perspective of the social security system, thus largely leaving aside the question of health care and long-term care costs. While it is true that this focus inhibits a truly global view of the financial consequences of aging for government budgets, it is also true that introducing them would cause tremendous problems in terms of modeling

Raphael Desmet is researcher at the Federal Planning Bureau in Brussels, Belgium. Alain Jousten is professor of economics at Haute Ecole de Commerce (HEC)—University of Liège, research fellow at the Institute for the Study of Labor (IZA) and research associate at the Centre for Economic Policy Research (CEPR). Sergio Perelman is professor of labor economics at HEC—University of Liège and research director of Research Center on Public and Population Economics (CREPP). Pierre Pestieau is professor of economics at HEC—University of Liège and research fellow at Center of Operation Research, Econometrics and Mathematical Economics (CORE), Paris-Jourdan Sciences Economiques (PSE).

Financial support from the Fonds de la Recherche Fondamentale Collective (FRFC; 2.4544.01) is gratefully acknowledged. All remaining errors are entirely our own. Comments welcome at ajousten@ulg.ac.be.

the evolution of health care costs, as well as in terms of a loss of international comparability.

For the social security systems to survive this demographic process, higher contribution levels and/or lower benefits will have to be introduced, given the outright pay-as-you-go (PAYG) nature of these systems. Indeed, a straight increase in the public debt financing of the demographic transition is not truly an option in Belgium, as it would be totally incompatible with the Maastricht criterion of the European Economic Monetary Union (EMU) relating to the level of GDP.[1] But even beyond this purely institutional limit, a further increase in public debt levels is also financially unsustainable, as it would quickly cause a snowball effect like the one observed in Belgium in the 1980s.

Leaving aside these purely demographic considerations, other factors are challenging the way the Belgian social security institutions and systems are organized. First, there is the potential for increased labor mobility. At present, mobility between jobs in the public sector, the private sector, and in self-employment is rather limited, at least partly because of the way the three systems work. The needs of the labor market of the future, with its increased degree of flexibility, may thus induce large changes in the way the three corresponding social security systems work. International job mobility is also becoming more and more important, particularly for a small, open economy in the heart of Europe like Belgium. Jousten and Pestieau (2002) argue that both levels of intra- and intergenerational redistribution will be heavily affected by increased international labor mobility, even if the phenomenon is limited to some subgroups of the population.

The second and biggest nondemographic challenge is the widespread use of a variety of early retirement programs. In fact, Belgium excels in the use of these programs, as the world-leading low average retirement age of approximately 57 for men clearly illustrates.[2] Originally these systems were motivated by several objectives. Faced with an environment of industrial restructuring, early retirement seemed to be the royal route out of the problem for all partners involved. First, it allowed companies to lay off old workers and, if needed, hire cheaper young workers, while the government supported a large chunk of the costs.[3] Second, older workers were also encouraged by the trade unions to leave so as to free up space for younger ones. To the present day, many older workers believe that they make a decision that is beneficial to their younger counterparts. Third, successive governments since the 1970s were also political gainers, though financial

1. Belgian national debt currently hovers at a level of approximately 110 percent of GDP.

2. The average age of retirement of 57.6 for men was estimated by Blöndal and Scarpetta (1998) on the basis of Labor Force Surveys. In this study we estimated an average retirement age of 58.4 for men and 57.4 for women.

3. Belgium is a country where the age profile of wages is steeply increasing, with the length of the working career making older workers quite expensive.

losers, in this consensus toward early retirement, because it allowed the government to show a better performance in terms of unemployment (particularly youth unemployment) and guaranteed a social peace. Lately, however, these early retirement schemes have undergone some scrutiny. Not surprisingly, the beneficial labor market effects have been rather modest if not completely absent.[4] Recent discussions and decisions at the government level clearly move toward the direction of lifting the effective early retirement age, and hence also the sector-specific mandatory retirement ages. Financial costs of early retirement programs to the federal government have been huge, both on the income (contributions, taxes) and on the expenditure side (early retirement benefits).

The goal of this chapter is to simulate the impact of reforms of retirement income systems. The impact we are interested in resides on two levels. First, we consider the financial and behavioral impact on individuals and families. Second, we consider the financial impact on the federal government budget. We do not restrict our attention to the budgetary impact on the social security systems, but rather on all of the federal government's finances. Such reforms will have both an automatic effect on fiscal contributions, by changing contributions and benefits for a given work history (the *mechanical* effect), and an additional effect through labor supply responses to the reform (the *behavioral* effect). We will estimate the fiscal implications of both the mechanical and the behavioral effect, using our retirement probit models derived in Dellis et al. (2004) to predict labor supply responses. The result will be an estimate of the steady-state impact of the reforms on the financial balance sheet of retirement income systems.

The structure of the chapter is as follows. Section 1.2 describes the essential features of the various public retirement and early retirement systems in Belgium. In section 1.3 we explain the different components of our administrative dataset, as well as the key results of Dellis et al. (2004), which we heavily rely upon. The following section (1.4) describes the simulation methodology used. The approach can be qualified as being of a steady-state type. Our methodology implicitly assumes that there is a time-invariant social security program and time-invariant behavior, though this has obviously not been the case for the systems and the people analyzed in our sample, where both behaviors and system characteristics have evolved over time. Section 1.5 describes the simulation results obtained. Again, it is important to stress that these results have to be interpreted with due diligence because of the limitations inherent in our simulation approach. Though the results might be rather accurate for the cohort of 50-year-old workers, this might not be the case for the more general population at other ages or for other cohorts. Section 1.6 is devoted to the conclusions.

---

4. See Sneesens et al. (2003).

1.2   Social Security Schemes

The Belgian retirement income system relies on three very unequal pillars.[5] First, there are the dominant public social security programs, which represent the largest part of pension income for a wide majority in the population. A second pillar consists of company pension schemes, which play only a minor role as a source of income for the average Belgian worker. Essentially, they are currently confined to the higher-income individuals in the private sector and to the self-employed, a finding that is at least in part due to their tax treatment. A third type of retirement income comes from individual retirement savings. These take multiple forms: there are tax-favored individual pension savings accounts with a maximum annual contribution of €580 per person,[6] or under the form of more traditional savings vehicles, such as the tax-favored savings accounts, investments in trust funds, life insurance, and so on.

The first pillar, public retirement programs, essentially consists of four components. There are three large sectoral social security programs, one for the public sector, one for the private sector wage earners, and one for the self-employed. Some special categories of workers, such as coal mine workers and military personnel, have special retirement systems that we will not explicitly model in the present chapter. A fourth large category of public retirement income consists of the guaranteed minimum pension system, which operates on a means-tested basis.

1.2.1   Wage Earner's Scheme

The wage earner's scheme is by far the largest one, based on the number of people affiliated with the program. The program allows for retirement starting at age 60, with a normal retirement age (NRA) fixed at 65. The choice of retirement age does not induce any actuarial adjustment under current rules.

However, in the case of most workers, the choice of retirement age is not completely neutral with respect to the benefit amount, because a full earnings history consists of forty-five years of work for men, a condition that many people do not satisfy at the age of 60. For those having more than forty-five working years, a dropout-year provision operates, replacing low-income years by higher ones. The situation has so far been slightly different for women, who only needed forty years to complete a career. A transition (between 1997 and 2009) is under way to progressively increase the complete career requirement to forty-five years of work. Hence, for most women included in our dataset, a full career still consists of forty years of work.

5. The present section describes the system as in place in the late 1990s. It relies heavily on Dellis et al. (2004).

6. All financial data are presented in EUR of 31/12/2001. Administrative parameters cited in absolute EUR amounts are those applicable to the year 2001, unless specified otherwise.

Benefits are computed based on earnings during periods of affiliation. The benefit formula, which is subject to floors and ceilings, can be represented as follows:

$$\text{Benefits} = \frac{n}{N} \times \textit{average wage} \times k,$$

where n represents the number of years of affiliation with the wage earner's scheme, N the number of years required for a full career (in our case either forty or forty-five) and k is a replacement rate, which takes on the value of 0.6 or 0.75, depending on whether the social security recipient claims benefits as a single person or as a household. The variable *average wage* corresponds to indexed average wages over the period of affiliation, with indexation on the price index combined with additional discretionary adjustments for the evolution of growth. A peculiar feature of the Belgian wage earners' scheme is that periods of one's life spent on replacement income (unemployment benefits, disability benefits, workers compensation) fully count as years worked in the computation of the average wage, and hence of the social security benefit. For any such periods, fictive wages are inserted into the average wage computation. In line with the general philosophy of the Belgian social insurance system—that any such spell on a replacement income system is purely involuntary—imputed wages are set equal in real terms to those that the workers earned before entering these replacement income programs.

Wage earners' pensions are shielded against inflation through an automatic consumer price index (CPI) adjustment and are subject to an earnings test. Currently, the earnings limit is approximately €7,450 per year. For earnings above this limit, pension entitlement is suspended. Benefits are also paid to surviving spouses, or more generally, surviving dependents of deceased wage earners.

The wage earner system is essentially based on the PAYG principle, and financed through payroll taxes that are levied both on the employers and the employees, with a combined tax rate of 16.36 percent (no earnings limit). The system also receives annual subsidies and transfers from the Belgian federal budget that amount to approximately 10 percent of overall benefits for the period considered.

Next to the official wage earner scheme, several forms of early retirement programs have been developed: mandatory collective early retirement and individual early retirement. During the 1980s and the 1990s, an arsenal of mandatory early retirement schemes was put in place. All of these arrangements were and are based on collective agreements, which are negotiated with the active involvement of employees and employers, sometimes at the sector level, sometimes at the level of an individual company or production site. For some companies in a difficult economic position, mandatory retirement ages as low as 50 were introduced. Individual early retirement differentiates itself from its collective counterpart by the fact that it is based on an individual's decision to retire from work. During the years analyzed in our sample, the most prevalent way to do this is to pass through the unemployment system, in which the unemployed aged 50 or more are considered "aged unemployed" and are no longer subject to show up at the unemployment office on a regular basis.[7] Further, there is no control on availability to work, nor are there benefit cuts due to long-term unemployment.[8] Therefore, people unwilling to continue to work can ask their employer to lay them off. Similarly, employers can use the system to shed older, more expensive workers. The latter are often willing to do so because of a lack of experience rating in the unemployment insurance system. In the early years of the new millennium, a new technique has even reinforced the use of the unemployment insurance system as a retirement route. The technique, called *canadry dry* pensions, consists in a lump-sum transfer from the employer at the time the company lays off its worker. This lump sum is not formally a retirement pension, but clearly looks like one.

1.2.2   Public Sector Employees

Public sector pensions are paid out of the general federal budget and are officially considered as deferred income rather than old-age insurance. The only official insurance element is a coverage for survivor benefits, which is financed through a 7.5 percent payroll tax. No spousal benefits are available. Civil servants face compulsory retirement at the latest at age 65, for both men and women. However, for the private sector, there is a multitude of ways of retiring earlier than this normal age of 65.[9] There is disability protection, which is a much more plausible route to retirement than in the private-sector system, as the screening is considered to be much less severe. Most importantly however, it is possible to opt for an incomplete career and retire at 60. For some particular categories of workers, the normal retirement age is lower than 65, and early retirement provisions are sometimes extremely generous (military servicemen, teachers). Public sector pensions are based on the income earned by an individual during the last five years before retirement. Benefits are computed according to a rather complicated formula but can never exceed 75 percent of the average wages over the last five years. The benefit formula can be represented as follows:

7. Disability is not a major route toward early retirement, due to rather stringent qualifying conditions and rather advanced screening.
8. The system of the aged unemployed was reformed in July 2002. The rules were tightened for new entrants to the unemployment system, with grandfathering rules applicable to those already in the system. The minimum age for a full waiver of obligations under the unemployment insurance system was raised to 56. A new system of "mini-waiver" was introduced onto the periodic visits to unemployment insurance as of age 50, but the person still needs to be ready to accept a job.
9. Currently, less than 15 percent of civil servants retire at the age of 65.

benefit = average wage over last five years × min (*fract*; 0.75),

where *fract* is a fraction with a numerator consisting of the number of years the person worked in the public service, the denominator being a benefit accrual factor. This latter benefit accrual factor, also called *tantième,* depends on the rank the person occupies in the hierarchy. This denominator ranges from 30 to 60, taking the value of 30 for the highest-ranking civil servants (high court judges, university professors) and 60 for the lowest ranks. As in the private sector wage earners' scheme, the system is earnings tested. The system also applies floors and ceilings, which are, however, much more generous than for private sector retirement benefits. Most notably, higher-income individuals get a much better deal in the public sector than in the private sector. This finding is reinforced once we consider indexation rules, as public sector pensions are indexed on average wages (*péréquation*). Public servants therefore enjoy the benefits of productivity increases in the economy even beyond the moment when they actively contribute to them as workers.

1.2.3   Self-Employed

The self-employed retirement scheme is the latest one to have been introduced, as it has only existed since 1956. It is also the least generous of the three big social security systems, with retirement benefits close to the level of the guaranteed minimum income (see the following). The self-employed are not entitled to unemployment benefits, nor to early retirement benefits. Disability benefits exist, but both qualifying conditions and financial characteristics of the system make it a most unlikely exit route to retirement. For a very long time, old-age pensions have been independent of earnings levels. However, since 1984, the system is progressively being transformed to allow for a stronger link between contributions and benefits. Additional earnings past 1984 enter the pension computation formula at their correct value, instead of some fictive amount. Full benefits are available at age 65 for men with a complete earnings history of forty-five years. However, anticipated retirement is possible as early as age 60, with an actuarial reduction of 5 percent per year of anticipation. As for the wage earners' scheme, women are in a transitory phase, with the complete career requirement shifting from forty years of work to forty-five, and normal retirement age from 60 to 65.

The social security system of the self-employed is financed through two broad categories of income. First, there are direct social insurance contributions levied under the form of a tax of 16.7 percent on the first €46,035 of income, and 12.27 percent on the income in the bracket between €46,035 and €67,352. Income above the latter threshold is not subject to social insurance taxation. More than 75 percent of the contributions raised using this social insurance taxation are used for the pension system of the self-employed; the remainder serves to cover health care and other social insurance benefits for the self-employed. Second, the federal government pays a large subsidy to the system, which amounted to more than a third of benefits in the years 2003 and 2004.

1.2.4   Guaranteed Minimum Income

The guaranteed minimum income pensions are fully paid for by general government revenue, and are means tested. This type of pension is only available after the legal retirement age.

1.3   The Model

We opt for an approach of microsimulation relying on the data and estimates used in Dellis et al. (2004). The underlying data stem from five different sources, most of which are of administrative origin. The different data were merged using the national identification number, which is the Belgian equivalent to the U.S. Social Security number.

The first component of the data is the SFR (Fiscal Revenue Statistics) files, which are collected by the Finance Ministry and then processed by the INS (National Statistics Office). We use the SFR files for the years 1989 to 1996 to extract all the information relevant for the computation of individual tax liabilities. Variables available include wage income and income from other professional activities, household size and type, number of dependents in the household, age and income of spouse, social insurance transfers and private pension receipt, house ownership status (owner, renter), taxable real estate income, and contributions to second- and third-pillar pensions. The second component is the CIP (Individual Pension Account), which includes all career information relevant for the wage earner pension computation: gross wages, days of work, days on social insurance programs, and so forth. The third and fourth components are the equivalent datasets for the self-employed and civil servants, both of whose files are less detailed than the one for wage earners. Finally, information from the census (1991) is merged in to determine education levels, so as to be able to use survival tables that are education-level specific.

Dellis et al. (2004) used a multistep sample selection procedure to obtain a sample of households where at least one member of the household is in the 50 to 64 age bracket and has not yet retired. A total of 21,818 households was used to separately analyze retirement decisions of men and women. Using the data, the authors estimated the parameters of retirement probit models. Among the explanatory variables in the estimation, the authors paid particular attention to financial incentive measures. We use several different indicators to measure the impact of the social security systems' incentives. First is the concept of household social security wealth

(SSW), which is the present discounted value of all future benefit flows from a given social security system. Discounting is done allowing for both time preference and mortality adjustments. Further, SSW also has to allow for the possibility of people being subject to different retirement income systems. The authors apply the official rules that exist for cumulating benefits from the three main public systems. Hence, the total SSW is the weighted sum of the different pathways to retirement available to the individual or to the couple. The weights on the early-retirement routes and the unemployment/disability routes correspond to the sum of observed frequencies of these routes among all people of any given age up to age 65, when the public retirement system takes the residual weight. For wage earners, we group the unemployment insurance and disability insurance paths, as the two systems produce very similar benefit structures. Doing so, we give an upper bound on incentives for people to retire, as we render all disability voluntary. Given the lack of information for the public sector, we consider as early retirees all persons retiring before the age of 60.

The next two incentive indicators are forward-looking measures. *Peak value* (PV) represents the difference between SSW at its peak and SSW today. The other forward-looking measure is the concept of *option value* (OV), such as defined by Stock and Wise (1990), which is based on a utility maximization framework. The utility function V_t underlying the computation of the option value process can be summarized by the following mathematical expression:

$$V_t(r) = \sum_{s=t}^{r-1} \beta^{s-t} Y_s^\gamma + \sum_{s=r}^{S} \beta^{s-t} [k B_s(r)]^\gamma,$$

where the first expression on the right-hand side represents the utility derived from labor income Y, and the second expression represents utility derived from retirement income $B_s(r)$; β is the time-preference rate, which we assume to be approximately 0.97, which corresponds to a discount rate of 3 percent; γ corresponds to a parameter of concavity and is set to $\gamma = 0.75$. Finally, $k = 1.5$ expresses the relative weight of utility of retirement income as compared to wage income. It reflects the fact that the income without effort generates more utility than income with effort.

The concept of option value $G_t(r^*)$ is then defined as the difference in utility terms between retiring at the best point in the future (r^*) and now (t).

$$G_t(r^*) = V_t(r^*) - V_t(t)$$

The key estimates of the authors are summarized in tables 1.1 and 1.2.

1.4 Simulation Methodology

For our simulations purposes, we restrict our attention to a subsample of the previously discussed dataset. We use a cross-section of individuals

Table 1.1   **Retirement probits for men**

	Peak value				Option value			
	Age		Age dummies		Age		Age dummies	
	Coefficient	Standard error	Coefficient	Standard error	Coefficient	Standard error	Coefficient	Standard error
Intercept	-7.5957	0.2698	-2.4346	0.1690	-7.5110	0.3387	-2.2976	0.1709
Incentive measures								
SSW (in thousands)	-0.0008	0.0003	-0.0008	0.0003	-0.0001	0.0003	-0.0001	0.0003
Probability effect	(-0.0079)		(-0.0082)		(-0.0008)		(-0.0001)	
PV, OV (in thousands)	-0.0380	0.0016	-0.0364	0.0017	-0.0392	0.0054	-0.0327	0.0054
	(-0.3769)		(-0.3505)		(-0.4111)		(-0.3383)	
Demographic variables								
Age	0.1049	0.0039			0.1050	0.0053		
Married	0.1027	0.0499	0.1026	0.0505	0.0294	0.0488	0.0342	0.0495
Active spouse	-0.0501	0.0394	-0.0515	0.0399	-0.0857	0.0383	-0.0839	0.0388
Age difference	-0.0003	0.0039	-0.0001	0.0039	-0.0009	0.0038	-0.0015	0.0039
Dependent	-0.0999	0.0361	-0.0911	0.0364	-0.0729	0.0352	-0.0754	0.0355
Income earnings variables								
Life cycle earnings	0.0138	0.0066	0.0151	0.0068	0.0155	0.0066	0.0180	0.0068
Earnings (in thousands)	-0.0084	0.0012	-0.0084	0.0012	0.0014	0.0018	-0.0002	0.0018
Spouse earnings (in thousands)	0.0043	0.0024	0.0044	0.0024	0.0037	0.0024	0.0031	0.0024

Age and schemes dummies

Age51			0.0523	0.0827			0.0134	0.0808
Age52			0.2779	0.0779			0.2289	0.0763
Age53			0.3191	0.0788			0.2087	0.0773
Age54			0.4516	0.0773			0.2871	0.0760
Age55			0.6751	0.0720			0.5664	0.0718
Age56			0.6429	0.0740			0.5003	0.0745
Age57			0.8546	0.0723			0.7359	0.0738
Age58			1.0048	0.0734			0.8659	0.0760
Age59			0.7310	0.0833			0.4475	0.0869
Age60			1.4439	0.0745			1.4456	0.0816
Age61			1.4396	0.0806			1.4302	0.0876
Age62			0.9767	0.0958			0.9868	0.1028
Age63			1.0380	0.1023			1.0364	0.1097
Age64			0.9208	0.1129			0.9320	0.1198
Age65			1.9180	0.1083			1.9801	0.1191
Civil servant	0.6314	0.1258	0.6177	0.1277	0.3850	0.1254	0.3858	0.1281
Self-employed	-0.0328	0.1235	-0.0216	0.1254	-0.0408	0.1244	-0.0396	0.1271
Pseudo R^2		0.1901		0.2067		0.1512		0.1741

Source: Dellis et alii (2004).

Note: Financial values in US$ at the exchange rate of 0.942 EUR/US$ as of 31/12/1999.

Table 1.2   **Retirement probits for women**

	Peak value				Option value			
	Age		Age dummies		Age		Age dummies	
	Coefficient	Standard error	Coefficient	Standard error	Coefficient	Standard error	Coefficient	Standard error
Intercept	-6.2897	0.4100	-1.8504	0.2497	-4.7976	0.5161	-1.5951	0.2554
Incentive measures								
SSW (in thousands)	-0.0003	0.0003	-0.0001	0.0004	-0.0007	0.0004	-0.0004	0.0004
Probability effect	(-0.0042)		(-0.0001)		(-0.0089)		(-0.0048)	
PV, OV (in thousands)	-0.0307	0.0023	-0.0222	0.0024	-0.0793	0.0089	-0.0651	0.0091
Probability effect	(-0.3940)		(-0.2868)		(-1.0341)		(-0.8434)	
Demographic variables								
Age	0.0887	0.0060			0.0641	0.0080		
Married	0.2222	0.0708	0.2030	0.0725	0.2269	0.0709	0.2079	0.0729
Active spouse	-0.0367	0.0552	-0.0606	0.0566	-0.0784	0.0544	-0.0920	0.0560
Age difference	0.0206	0.0063	0.0145	0.0064	0.0288	0.0066	0.0226	0.0068
Dependent	-0.1539	0.0586	-0.1687	0.0590	-0.1346	0.0580	-0.1575	0.0587
Income earnings variables								
Life cycle earnings	0.0081	0.0104	0.0062	0.0106	0.0069	0.0106	0.0053	0.0107
Earnings (in thousands)	-0.0090	0.0027	-0.0084	0.0027	0.0125	0.0038	0.0102	0.0039
Spouse earnings (in thousands)	-0.0021	0.0020	-0.0017	0.0020	-0.0011	0.0020	-0.0010	0.0021

Age and schemes dummies

	(1)		(2)		(3)		(4)	
Age51			0.0094	0.0923			-0.0462	0.0922
Age52			0.2391	0.0877			0.1767	0.0876
Age53			0.3247	0.0897			0.2195	0.0899
Age54			0.2192	0.0951			0.0871	0.0955
Age55			0.4942	0.0888			0.3306	0.0906
Age56			0.3489	0.0942			0.1500	0.0973
Age57			0.5099	0.0951			0.2681	0.1001
Age58			0.3334	0.1060			0.0456	0.1128
Age59			0.2208	0.1161			-0.1246	0.1261
Age60			1.4579	0.0973			1.2533	0.1123
Age61			1.6646	0.1124			1.4447	0.1243
Age62			0.5275	0.1795			0.2841	0.1881
Age63			0.4805	0.1976			0.2177	0.2072
Age64			0.9965	0.1988			0.6746	0.2108
Age65			1.3057	0.2116			1.0055	0.2218
Civil servant	0.2851	0.1224	0.2128	0.1248	0.1541	0.1228	0.1287	0.1252
Self-employed	-0.2508	0.1292	-0.2766	0.1319	-0.2041	0.1300	-0.2281	0.1330
Pseudo R^2	0.1536		0.1918		0.1365		0.1860	

Source: Dellis et alii (2004).

Note: Financial values in US$ at the exchange rate of 0.942 EUR/US$ as of 31/12/1999.

instead of the entire age range (50 to 64). More specifically, we consider preretirement-age workers (male and female) aged 50 and then age them forward. We also include their spouses in our analysis. More specifically, we select all 50-year-old men and 50-year-old single females of the sample. Married 50-year-old females are excluded from the sample to avoid double counting, as our sample will account for the fiscal impact of all married females. This way, the cohort can be defined as a representative sample of Belgian 50-year-old workers and their spouses. To ensure a sufficient sample size, we use a synthetic age-50 cohort made up of individuals aged 50 in 1993, 1994, or 1995. This gives us a total sample size of 4,927 individuals, 2,515 men, 2,020 dependent women, and 392 working women.

We first estimate the probability that each worker will exit the labor force via death or retirement at each future age. Exit probabilities are computed using the estimates of tables 1.1 and 1.2 under the baseline setting with regard to all variables, including the SSW and peak and option value indicators. Spouses are supposed to retire at the early retirement age of the corresponding retirement scheme. In a second step, all these probabilities then serve as weights in the computation of the present discounted value (PDV) of the in- and outflows from the government budget. The financial flows considered are all flows from age 50 up until death.[10] This marks a difference with respect to Dellis et al. (2004), as we consider the full budgetary costs and benefits of the synthetic cohort as it ages. The total impact of individuals on the government's budget is measured as the difference between the outflows from the budget as measured by the flow of social security and other social insurance program benefits (unemployment and early retirement) and inflows as measured by payroll, income, and consumption taxes. Payroll taxes include health, retirement, unemployment, disability, professional sickness, and workers' compensation contributions.

Next to the previously mentioned payroll taxes, we include income taxes on labor and pension income as well as consumption taxes under the form of value added tax (VAT). We incorporate direct taxes in accordance with the Belgian Personal Income Tax Code IPP (Personal Income Tax), thus also including the favorable tax treatment of pension income. However, to render the computation feasible, we have fully individualized the tax accounts of husbands and wives, while the tax code only allows a partial splitting of incomes of spouses. Further, we decided to ignore some other tax code provisions. For example, we left aside the possibility of itemizing deductions in favor of the standard flat-rate deduction, and we ignored taxation of private annuity income. The likely impact of these simplifications is difficult to assign, as these omissions are to some degree offsetting. Regarding consumption taxes, we rely on consumption data by income quar-

10. To ensure international comparability across the different countries considered, we discount all financial variables back to the age of 55, using a 3 percent real discount rate.

tiles from the Household Budget Survey of the INS. Using the expenditure shares of different products in the typical household consumption basket by income quartile and weighting the corresponding VAT rates accordingly, the INS data imply an average VAT rate by income of 10.65 percent for the lowest income quartile, 10.60 for the second, 10.04 for the third and 9.14 for the top income quartile. We apply these average rates for all age groups in a uniform way.

The concept of PDV is the basis for comparison among different policy reform scenarios. We do so by reestimating the exit probabilities, benefits, contributions, and taxes under several reform proposals for both spouses so as to obtain new PDV estimates. We even break down the total effect of a reform on the PDV into its components: the mechanical budgetary effect (with unchanged retirement probabilities with respect to the prereform situation) and the fiscal implications of the behavioral effect. We use the terminology *fiscal implications of the behavioral effect* to measure the budgetary impact of the labor supply reactions (which is, properly speaking, the change in the behavior of the individual). Indeed, this distinction is rather important, as it is quite imaginable to have a strong labor supply reaction while at the same time having a very limited budgetary impact thereof due to a high degree of actuarial neutrality.

1.5   Simulation Results

We consider four different reforms. The first three share a common feature in that they are not intended as policy recommendations, but rather are to allow for international comparisons. The fourth simulation is an interesting country-specific reform of the retirement system, whose only aim is to illustrate the impact of a partial reform within the Belgian institutional setting. None of the four reforms, however, pursues an objective of budget neutrality with respect to the baseline, which corresponds to the current institutional setting and hence not necessarily to one that is viable in the long run. Nor do any of these reforms aim at establishing a balanced and viable budget in the long run.[11] The first two reforms have already been explored in Dellis et al. (2004) with respect to their impact on the SSW and accrual variables. However, the present exercise clearly distinguishes itself from the previous results as it incorporates a complete analysis of all budgetary implications of a retirement-system change.

The first reform is called the Three-Year Reform, and consists of a simple increase within three years of all key parameters in all retirement and early retirement systems in the country. Thus, the early and the normal entitlement ages are increased by three years, as is the length of a normal career—from forty-five to forty-eight years. All other system characteristics remain

11. Hopefully they are more viable than the status quo.

unchanged. Implicitly, this approach includes the rather implausible condition that unemployment benefits are totally absent from the landscape between the ages of 50 and 53.

The second reform, the so-called Common Reform, creates a system that is identical across all countries. The Common Reform has a benefit equal to 60 percent of average real lifetime earnings at normal retirement age, which is defined to be at age 65. Past wages are deflated using real-wage indexing. Average lifetime earnings are supposed to correspond to the highest forty years of indexed earnings during an individual's working life. In case a worker has less than forty years of earnings, zeros are averaged in, while a career longer than forty years has an impact on the real average lifetime wage through a dropout-year provision. Early retirement is available as of the age of 60 (ERA), with an actuarial adjustment of 6 percent per year of anticipation. Benefits thus defined are capped at the 90th percentile of the wage distribution for men. Benefits are subject to income taxation under the same rules as in the prereform world. Survivor benefits are paid out at a rate of 100 percent of workers benefits, but are reduced one for one for every euro of benefits the recipients receives on his or her own earnings history. No other benefits are available, which thus represents a rather dramatic change in benefit availability before the age of 60 in a country like Belgium.

The third reform is called the Actuarial Reform. The approach can be situated midway between the previous two reforms; hence its results will be presented in second place in the tables and figures that follow. The reform keeps the structure of the sectoral social security schemes unchanged with respect to the present, including eligibility ages, minimum contribution periods, as well as formulae for the computation of the basic benefits. However, the reform introduces an actuarial adjustment factor to vary the benefit flow as a function of the age of exit from the labor force, or expressed differently, the entry age into retirement. The linear adjustment factor is 6 percent per year of deviation from the normal retirement age, which is currently 65 under all three major Belgian sectoral pension schemes. Means-tested programs as well as survivor and spousal benefits are kept unchanged in their generosity with respect to the baseline situation, unless they are directly linked to the worker's own benefits. The age-dependent nature of workers' retirement benefits thus implies a relative increase in the attractiveness of means-tested programs for younger retirees.

The last reform considered is a Belgian Reform. We consider a reform where the government reforms the current wage earner scheme by no longer crediting years spent on all kinds of social insurance programs, such as unemployment insurance, disability insurance, and early retirement in the individual's pension record. All other system characteristics are supposed to remain unchanged, thus leaving the early retirement and unemployment paths into retirement intact. Thus, people will be confronted with incomplete careers at the end of their working life. There is thus a smaller buffering effect against income shocks on a lifetime basis. Another way of looking at the problem is to notice that the reform introduces a stronger link between contributions and benefits, and hence reinforces the pure insurance aspect of the system.

For evaluating the results of the first three simulations, we use simulation methods S1, S2, and S3 of Dellis et al. (2004). Method S1 relies on estimates using a linear age trend, which is unchanged by the reform. It adjusts the eligibility probabilities for unemployment or early retirement benefit receipt and applies the postreform incentive and PDV measures. Method S2 is based on the age-dummy model without a shift of the dummies. It is essentially the same as S1. However, the age-dummy effects are far from linear, and hence it is possible that these dummies better pick up the non-linearities in the various retirement and early retirement systems, or alternatively, that tastes for leisure are not a linear function of age. Method S3 is based on the age-dummy models and considers a shift of dummies to perform the simulations in a specific way for each one of the reforms. For the first reform, all age dummies are shifted upward by three years. This also applies to those dummies at ages lower than the earliest eligibility age, so that the entire retirement hazard shifts forward. For the Common Reform we proceed in a similar way, but the impact of age dummies is modified in a different way. On the one hand, given that in this policy simulation alternative retirement pathways are assumed out, we apply the age-51 dummy to all ages up to age 59, just prior to the early retirement age, both for men and women. On the other hand, we keep the effect of age-60 and age-65 dummies unchanged, assuming that the Common Reform will not affect individual behavior at these particular ages. Finally, using these two dummy values, we imputed the values of the intermediary dummies, from age 61 to age 64, assuming a smooth path trend. As for the Actuarial Reform and the Belgian Reform, methods S2 and S3 are equivalent, as there is no change in the key early and normal retirement ages from the base case to the reform situation.

An initial, noticeable finding is that the PDV of benefits minus taxes is negative in all cases considered in table 1.3; thus, the results tell us that our cohort is a net contributor (benefits minus taxes and contributions) to the public finances. At first sight, this result looks rather surprising, as it is contrary to intuition and contrary to the finding that we can observe when purely focusing on the social security system. However, several factors help explain it. First, it is important to note that direct taxation is extremely heavy in Belgium. Second, discounting plays an important role in the results. While taxes are essentially front loaded in the Belgian tax and social insurance system, benefits are rather back loaded from a life-cycle perspective. Third, and last, it is important to notice that we consider only a single outflow of the government budget, while we consider a large array of

Table 1.3   Total fiscal effect of reform (in euros per worker)

	Present discounted value					Total change relative to base (%)			
	Base	Three-Year Reform	Actuarial Reform	Common Reform	Belgian Reform	Three-Year Reform	Actuarial Reform	Common Reform	Belgian Reform
				Peak value—S1					
Benefits	146,581	131,131	120,265	114,111	141,371	−10.5	−18.0	−22.2	−3.6
Taxes									
Payroll	58,408	61,934	64,857	63,625	59,312	6.0	11.0	8.9	1.5
Income	80,843	84,908	85,741	76,989	81,004	5.0	6.1	−4.8	0.2
Consumption	19,313	18,744	18,346	18,280	19,056	−2.9	−5.0	−5.4	−1.3
Total	158,564	165,586	168,944	158,893	159,372	4.4	6.5	0.2	0.5
				Peak value—S2					
Benefits	147,557	129,241	120,458	114,115	142,326	−12.5	−18.4	−22.7	−3.6
Taxes									
Payroll	57,307	61,548	63,516	62,234	58,166	7.4	10.8	8.6	1.5
Income	79,472	84,478	83,977	75,300	79,542	6.3	5.7	−5.3	0.1
Consumption	19,339	18,759	18,304	18,250	19,088	−3.0	−5.4	−5.6	−1.3
Total	156,119	164,785	165,797	155,784	156,796	5.6	6.2	−0.2	0.4
				Peak value—S3					
Benefits	147,667	129,248	120,458	114,735	142,326	−12.5	−18.4	−22.3	−3.6
Taxes									
Payroll	57,307	66,872	63,516	65,697	58,166	16.7	10.8	14.6	1.5
Income	79,472	90,849	83,977	79,219	79,542	14.3	5.7	−0.3	0.1
Consumption	19,339	19,264	18,304	18,479	19,088	−0.4	−5.4	−4.5	−1.3
Total	156,119	176,985	165,797	163,394	156,796	13.4	6.2	4.7	0.4

					Option value—S1				
Benefits	145,711	128,967	115,129	140,496	112,722	-11.5	-21.0	-22.6	-3.6
Taxes									
Payroll	58,981	62,731	63,293	59,439	62,491	6.4	7.3	6.0	0.8
Income	82,021	85,663	81,469	81,702	76,800	4.4	-0.7	-6.4	-0.4
Consumption	20,333	19,605	19,034	20,014	19,039	-3.6	-6.4	-6.4	-1.6
Total	161,335	168,000	163,795	161,155	158,330	4.1	1.5	-1.9	-0.1
					Option value—S2				
Benefits	145,529	126,448	115,273	140,477	112,682	-13.1	-20.8	-22.6	-3.4
Taxes									
Payroll	59,882	63,806	63,223	60,228	62,574	6.6	5.6	4.5	0.6
Income	82,656	86,643	80,937	82,286	76,560	4.8	-2.1	-7.4	-0.4
Consumption	20,354	19,549	18,996	20,043	19,001	-4.0	-6.7	-6.6	-1.5
Total	162,891	169,998	163,156	162,557	158,136	4.4	0.2	-2.9	-0.2
					Option value—S3				
Benefits	145,529	127,191	115,273	140,577	113,163	-12.6	-20.8	-22.2	-3.4
Taxes									
Payroll	59,882	68,464	63,223	60,228	64,393	14.3	5.6	7.5	0.6
Income	82,656	92,441	80,937	82,286	77,924	11.8	-2.1	-5.7	-0.4
Consumption	20,354	20,050	18,996	20,043	19,312	-1.5	-6.7	-5.1	-1.5
Total	162,891	180,955	163,156	162,557	161,629	11.1	0.2	-0.8	-0.2

Notes: The first five columns show the PDV of benefits and taxes under the base plan and under each of the four illustrative reforms. The last four columns show the change relative to the base, for benefits and for taxes.

inflows. For example, we consider all tax revenues, even though only some of them help toward financing goods and services for the elderly, while some public subsidies to the old (e.g., more generous reimbursement of health expenditures, nursing home care, long-term care, public transportation) do not appear on the outflow side.

When measuring the impact of the various reforms on the different components reported in table 1.3 as a proportion of the baseline benefits, we find that the Common Reform is the most powerful one in terms of the change in the PDV of benefits, followed by the Actuarial Reform. This finding is not too surprising, given the fact that Belgians leave the workforce rather early in their life cycle, and hence are fully hit by the actuarial adjustments (Actuarial and Common reforms) and the reduced availability of benefits before the early retirement age of the social security system (Common Reform). The same lack of availability of benefits before the age of 60 is also the main cause of the drop in income tax receipt under the Common Reform, with a drop of 5 percent in all but the PV S3 simulation methodology. Overall, it is fair to say that the impact as measured using the PV and OV estimates is rather similar.

As for the Belgian Reform, it only displays a rather modest effect in terms of its impact on the value of the PDV of benefits, while its likely cost in terms of redistribution is rather heavy. Several reasons help explain this result. First of all, the reform only affects the wage earners' schemes, which casts the order of magnitude of the change in a different light. Further, the effect of the changes only affects one particular form of retirement income, and does not affect payments, either through the unemployment or the early retirement systems. Hence, the changes only affect people retiring early through the change of the benefits they receive starting at age 65, as the latter remains the age at which people are switched into the retirement system. Therefore, for a person aged 50, the effect of the changes only apply on income he or she starts receiving in fifteen years' time, and this with an annual 3 percent real discount factor. For a person aged 65, nothing much changes in terms of benefits received, unless (obviously) the person had experienced a longer spell on a social insurance program in the past. Finally, the reform is somewhat buffered by the availability of means-tested minimum benefits, which increasingly become interesting substitutes for people with incomplete earnings histories due to sickness, unemployment, disability, and so forth.

To illustrate the distinction between the behavioral and mechanical effects of a reform, let us focus on the net benefits an individual receives in a world of absolute certainty with respect to his or her life span. We denote them as b, and they depend on a policy parameter x and on the age of retirement z, itself a function of x. We thus have

$$b[x, z(x)].$$

A reform consists of a change from x to x'. The effect ($Diff$) of such a reform is:

$$Diff = b[x', z(x')] - b[x, z(x)]$$

We can decompose $Diff$ into two parts, $Diff^m$ and $Diff^b$, corresponding to the mechanical and behavioral effects, with

$$Diff^m = b[x', z(x)] - b[x, z(x)],$$
$$Diff^b = b[x', z(x')] - b(x', z(x)],$$

and $Diff^m + Diff^b = Diff$.

Table 1.4 displays a strong behavioral effect for all scenarios. This is particularly true when considering the first reform using simulation technique S3, where the net behavioral effect of benefits minus contributions as a proportion of base benefits is the most powerful (more than a quarter of base benefits). Table 1.4 shows that the behavioral response for both OV and PV estimations of the latter scenario imply a fiscal impact of the behavioral response that represents more than 50 percent of the total effect, essentially because of the outright shift by three years of all dummies. At first sight it might be curious to have a fiscal implication of the behavioral effect that is negative, that is, that the cohort's contribution to the government budget increases as a reaction to the change in its behavior. However, the finding is less surprising when we notice that another important variable has changed as a consequence of this change in behavior, notably the length of the working life. Hence, the loss of the cohort in terms of net benefits minus taxes has to be seen as a tradeoff for the gain in income due to a higher-than-average working life.

Another puzzling point from table 1.4 is the indetermination in the sign of the behavioral effect on the PDV of benefits. It is positive in most cases, except for the Belgian Reform, as well as for the Three-Year Reform using simulation methodology S2 in the Option Value model. Table 1.5 illustrates the decomposition by age of retirement of the fiscal implication of the behavioral effect on benefits for a median household facing the Actuarial Reform. It appears that the behavioral effect is negative until age 60 and then turns positive, the sign coming from the sign of the probability change. Even with negative probability changes being larger than positive ones in absolute value, as is the case in our example, we can observe that the total behavioral effect for this household is positive. The structure of the postreform PDV of benefits by age of exit from the labor force helps to explain this finding. As the Actuarial Reform is much less penalizing in the age range 61 to 70 than between the ages of 50 and 60, the PDV of benefits is steeply increasing as a function of age of the labor force exit, and hence leads to a positive behavioral effect when aggregating overall possible exit ages. The same reasoning can be applied to the Common Reform and to a

Table 1.4   Decomposition of the total effect of reforms, change in PDV

	Change in present discounted value											
	Three-Year Reform			Actuarial Reform			Common Reform			Belgian Reform		
	Mechanical	Behavioral	Total	Mechanical	Behavioral	Total	Mechanical	Behavioral	Total	Mechanical	Behavioral	Total
					Peak value—S1							
Benefits	-19,582	4,132	-15,450	-34,745	8,429	-26,316	-35,323	2,853	-32,470	-5,073	-137	-5,210
Total taxes	-3,592	10,614	7,022	-10,691	21,070	10,379	-12,849	13,177	329	-1,360	2,168	808
Net change	-15,990	-6,482	-22,472	-24,054	-12,642	-36,696	-22,474	-10,325	-32,799	-3,713	-2,305	-6,018
Change as % of base benefits	-10.9	-4.4	-15.3	-16.4	-8.6	-25.0	-15.3	-7.0	-22.4	-2.5	-1.6	-4.1
					Peak value—S2							
Benefits	-20,635	2,210	-18,425	-36,142	8,934	-27,208	-36,498	2,945	-33,552	-5,242	-99	-5,341
Total taxes	-3,787	12,453	8,666	-10,963	20,641	9,678	-13,028	12,692	-335	-1,416	2,092	677
Net change	-16,849	-10,243	-27,092	-25,179	-11,707	-36,886	-23,470	-9,747	-33,217	-3,826	-2,191	-6,018
Change as % of base benefits	-11.4	-6.9	-18.3	-17.1	-7.9	-25.0	-15.9	-6.6	-22.5	-2.6	-1.5	-4.1
					Peak value—S3							
Benefits	-20,635	2,217	-18,418	-36,142	8,934	-27,208	-36,498	3,566	-32,932	-5,242	-99	-5,341
Total taxes	-3,787	24,653	20,866	-10,963	20,641	9,678	-13,028	20,302	7,275	-1,416	2,092	677
Net change	-16,849	-22,436	-39,284	-25,179	-11,707	-36,886	-23,470	-16,737	-40,206	-3,826	-2,191	-6,018
Change as % of base benefits	-11.4	-15.2	-26.6	-17.1	-7.9	-25.0	-15.9	-11.3	-27.2	-2.6	-1.5	-4.1

					Option value—S1							
Benefits	−18,530	1,785	−16,745	−33,796	3,203	−30,583	−34,554	1,565	−32,990	−4,947	−268	−5,216
Total taxes	−3,657	10,323	6,666	−10,882	13,343	2,461	−13,047	10,042	−3,004	−1,389	1,210	−179
Net change	−14,873	−8,538	−23,410	−22,904	−10,140	−33,044	−21,508	−8,478	−29,986	−3,558	−1,478	−5,036
Change as % of base benefits	−10.2	−5.9	−16.1	−15.7	−7.0	−22.7	−14.8	−5.8	−20.6	−2.4	−1.0	−3.5
					Option value—S2							
Benefits	−18,931	−150	−19,081	−33,102	2,846	−30,256	−34,194	1,346	−32,848	−4,729	−223	−4,952
Total taxes	−3,743	10,849	7,107	−10,764	11,029	265	−13,036	8,280	−4,755	−1,307	973	−334
Net change	−15,188	−11,000	−26,188	−22,338	−8,183	−30,521	−21,158	−6,934	−28,092	−3,422	−1,195	−4,618
Change as % of base benefits	−10.4	−7.6	−18.0	−15.3	−5.6	−21.0	−14.5	−4.8	−19.3	−2.4	−0.8	−3.2
					Option value—S3							
Benefits	−18,931	593	−18,338	−33,102	2,846	−30,256	−34,194	1,827	−32,367	−4,729	−223	−4,952
Total taxes	−3,743	21,806	18,064	−10,764	11,029	265	−13,036	11,774	−1,262	−1,307	973	−334
Net change	−15,188	−21,213	−36,401	−22,338	−8,183	−30,521	−21,158	−9,947	−31,105	−3,422	−1,195	−4,618
Change as % of base benefits	−10.4	−14.6	−25.0	−15.3	−5.6	−21.0	−14.5	−6.8	−21.4	−2.4	−0.8	−3.2

Notes: The table shows the total effect of the reform (shown in table 1.3) decomposed into mechanical and behavioral components. The first row shows the change in benefits. The second row shows the change in all taxes. The third row shows the net change (the change in benefits minus the change in taxes). The fourth row shows the net change as a percent of base benefits (table 1.3).

Table 1.5   Decomposition of the behavioral effect on benefits for a median household (Actuarial Reform—option value—S2)

	Base case		Actuarial Reform			
Age	PDV of benefits (a)	Probability of exit (%) (b)	PDV of benefits (c)	Probability of exit (%) (d)	Probability change (d) – (b) = (e)	Behavioral effect (e) · (c)
50	329,538	0.82	224,385	0.44	−0.38	−855
51	337,893	0.99	227,271	0.53	−0.47	−1,057
52	347,071	2.02	229,978	1.09	−0.92	−2,122
53	354,961	2.19	233,078	1.17	−1.02	−2,379
54	362,829	2.97	236,653	1.59	−1.38	−3,263
55	369,887	5.84	240,407	3.32	−2.51	−6,043
56	376,577	5.21	243,768	3.01	−2.20	−5,366
57	383,305	8.28	246,404	4.98	−3.30	−8,131
58	388,166	9.85	253,870	6.62	−3.23	−8,198
59	393,696	4.41	266,432	3.14	−1.27	−3,392
60	398,815	19.11	279,171	18.42	−0.69	−1,922
61	389,943	11.52	296,357	14.09	2.57	7,604
62	389,340	4.41	319,259	5.86	1.45	4,619
63	386,618	3.77	340,224	5.56	1.79	6,084
64	383,631	2.58	360,614	4.15	1.58	5,684
65	381,773	6.73	381,773	12.05	5.33	20,332
66	356,814	2.71	356,814	4.86	2.15	7,667
67	333,433	1.09	333,433	1.96	0.86	2,883
68	311,112	0.44	311,112	0.79	0.35	1,081
69	289,168	0.18	289,168	0.32	0.14	404
70	268,414	0.12	268,414	0.21	0.09	254
Total						13,886

certain degree to the Belgian Reform. In this case, as the structure of the postreform PDV of benefits does not greatly change from the base case, the negative probability changes, which typically extends from 50 to 56, creating a larger behavioral effect than the positive one within the age range of 57 to 70. As to the Three-Year Reform, the probability changes are so erratic that no typical rules can be found.

Figure 1A.1, panels A–G, in the appendix illustrate the effects of the Three-Year Reform along several different margins. Figure 1A.1, panel A displays the PDV of benefits per worker at any given age of retirement, as well as the impact thereon by the reform. Figure 1A.1, panel B summarizes the total of taxes paid by age of labor force exit. This figure again illustrates the fact that the elderly are still important contributors to the federal budget. This is particularly true for those working relatively late in their life cycle, as the fiscal pressure on the productive-factor labor is relatively high compared to the pressure on pension benefits. Figure 1A.1, panels C and E display the simulated patterns of labor force exit over the age range 50 to

70, which follow a rather smooth pattern for the S1 simulation methodology and a more erratic one for simulation methodology S3. The role of the shift in the age dummies becomes evident in figure 1A.1, panel E. Figure 1A.1, panels D and F display the age-specific impact of the reform, with a rather modest net change (PDV of benefits minus taxes) at all ages, whereas the change of the PDV of benefits is of varying sign and characterized by larger swings in magnitude. Clearly, the tax system (payroll, income, and consumption) plays an important role in the determination of the sign and magnitude of the net contribution to the federal budget at all possible exit ages. Figure 1A.1, panel G illustrates the power of these fiscal implications as a proportion of GDP. The figure shows that the mechanical effects are approximately of the same size for all possible simulation methodologies, but that the difference between these reforms stems from the behavioral effect.

Figures 1A.2, panels A, B, and C, 1A.3, panels A, B, and C, and 1A.4, panels A, B, and C in the appendix illustrate the key results for the other three reforms in terms of the changes in the PDV of benefits and in the retirement probabilities at the different ages, as well as the fiscal implications as a proportion of GDP. The latter indicator allows for a comparison of the total budgetary effect of the various reforms in terms of a common measure. It appears that—budgetarily speaking—the Actuarial Reform is the most powerful reform in all cases, excluding those relying on the S3 methodology. Even if the Common Reform has the strongest impact on the level of benefits because of its inherent ineligibility to retirement benefits before age 60, it is the Actuarial Reform that creates the strongest incentives for individuals to work longer. Indeed, a comparison of figure 1A.3, panel C and figure 1A.2, panel C shows that the retirement rate is lower for the Actuarial Reform before age 60, and a bit higher after this age.

1.6 Distributional Analysis

Table 1.6 and table 1.7 display the distributional implications of the reforms when splitting the population into five income categories. A common feature of the first three reforms is that the three middle earnings quintiles, hence the middle classes, bear the brunt of the reform. This is particularly true for the Common Reform, where the impact on the two extreme income quintiles is much less pronounced. The results are less extreme for the case of the Three-Year Reform, where the changes of all income quintiles are relatively close to one another as expressed in these relative terms. The Actuarial Reform again is the middle ground. Only the lowest-income quintile loses less in relative terms under this reform proposal.

The Belgian Reform, on the other hand, has a very different redistributive pattern. While income quintiles 3 and 4 again face the largest proportional change, as displayed in tables 1.6 and 1.7, it is now the lowest-income

Table 1.6   Distributional analysis of the total effect of the reform (change in PDV OV-S1)

	Present discounted value					Total change relative to base			
	Base	Three-Year Reform	Actuarial Reform	Common Reform	Belgian Reform	Three-Year Reform	Actuarial Reform	Common Reform	Belgian Reform
				Quintile 1 (highest)					
Benefits	178,937	162,404	144,532	139,462	176,790	-16,532	-34,405	-39,475	-2,146
Total taxes	344,551	355,545	348,705	336,867	344,937	10,994	4,154	-7,684	386
Net change						-27,527	-38,559	-31,790	-2,532
Change as % of base benefits						-15.4	-21.5	-17.8	-1.4
				Quintile 2					
Benefits	168,756	148,930	129,998	123,519	163,889	-19,825	-38,757	-45,237	-4,866
Total taxes	179,867	187,627	182,373	174,499	179,591	7,759	2,506	-5,369	-276
Net change						-27,584	-41,263	-39,868	-4,590
Change as % of base benefits						-16.3	-24.5	-23.6	-2.7

			Quintile 3						
Benefits	146,169	128,311	111,982	111,320	138,546	-17,857	-34,187	-34,848	-7,622
Total taxes	129,816	136,579	133,288	129,335	129,193	6,763	3,472	-481	-623
Net change						-24,620	-37,659	-34,368	-7,000
Change as % of base benefits						-16.8	-25.8	-23.5	-4.8
			Quintile 4						
Benefits	128,841	112,534	100,241	100,403	121,227	-16,307	-28,600	-28,438	-7,614
Total taxes	95,886	101,052	98,347	96,358	95,420	5,166	2,461	472	-466
Net change						-21,473	-31,061	-28,910	-7,148
Change as % of base benefits						-16.7	-24.1	-22.4	-5.5
			Quintile 5 (lowest)						
Benefits	107,197	93,953	90,059	89,672	103,394	-13,243	-17,137	-17,525	-3,803
Total taxes	62,1412	65,154	62,181	60,100	62,525	2,743	-230	-2,312	113
Net change						-15,896	-16,907	-15,213	-3,916
Change as % of base benefits						-14.9	-15.8	-14.2	-3.7

Notes: The table shows the distributional impact of reform decomposed by income quintile using OV-S1 estimates. The first five columns show the PDV of benefits and taxes under the base plan and under each of the four illustrative reforms. The last four columns show the change relative to the base, for benefits and for taxes. For each quintile, the first row shows the change in benefits.

Table 1.7   Distributional analysis of the total effect of the reform (change in PDV OV-S3)

	Present discounted value					Total change relative to base			
	Base	Three-Year Reform	Actuarial Reform	Common Reform	Belgian Reform	Three-Year Reform	Actuarial Reform	Common Reform	Belgian Reform
Quintile 1 (highest)									
Benefits	178,632	160,507	145,089	141,042	176,857	−18,125	−33,543	−37,590	−1,775
Total taxes	347,617	378,058	348,367	336,839	347,803	30,442	750	−10,777	187
Net change						−48,567	−34,293	−26,813	−1,962
Change as % of base benefits						−27.2	−19.2	−15.0	−1.1
Quintile 2									
Benefits	168,531	147,322	130,005	124,102	164,006	−21,209	−38,527	−44,429	−4,525
Total taxes	181,871	202,958	181,412	178,730	181,441	21,087	−459	−3,141	−430
Net change						−42,296	−38,068	−41,288	−4,096
Change as % of base benefits						−25.1	−22.6	−24.5	−2.4

Quintile 3

Benefits	145,861	126,299	112,007	111,834	138,538	-19,563	-33,854	-34,028	-7,324
Total taxes	131,559	149,047	132,702	134,240	130,749	17,489	1,143	2,681	-810
Net change						-37,051	-34,997	-36,709	-6,514
Change as % of base benefits						-25.4	-24.0	-25.2	-4.5

Quintile 4

Benefits	128,618	110,460	100,250	100,573	121,214	-18,158	-28,368	-28,045	-7,405
Total taxes	96,845	110,481	97,713	100,710	96,233	13,635	868	3,864	-612
Net change						-31,793	-29,236	-31,910	-6,793
Change as % of base benefits						-24.7	-22.7	-24.8	-5.3

Quintile 5 (lowest)

Benefits	107,308	92,616	90,171	89,036	103,608	-14,692	-17,136	-18,272	-3,699
Total taxes	62,565	70,500	61,603	63,090	62,591	7,934	-962	524	26
Net change						-22,626	-16,174	-18,796	-3,725
Change as % of base benefits						-21.1	-15.1	-17.5	-3.5

Notes: The table shows the distributional impact of reform decomposed by income quintile using OV-S3 estimates. The first five columns show the PDV of benefits and taxes under the base plan and under each of the four illustrative reforms. The last four columns show the change relative to the base, for benefits and for taxes. For each quintile, the first row shows the change in benefits.

quintile that loses out more than the first- and second-income quintiles. The reasons for this finding are multiple. First, they are due to the way the reform only affects those that are on the wage earner scheme. Hence, it does not affect civil servants who have relatively high life cycle earnings, therefore making them relatively more numerous in the upper-income quintiles. Second, the reform only touches those with incomplete careers, and hence essentially touches two categories of people. First, it affects those with unstable and incomplete career patterns due to sickness, invalidity, unemployment, or accident. Second, it changes incentives for those choosing to retire early. Hence, the reform is less important for higher-income white collar workers, who face lower probabilities of layoff, accident, sickness, and invalidity.

To get a better grasp of the distributive implications of these alternative extensions, we have used two standard measures of inequality and poverty: the Gini coefficient and the poverty rate, measured as the fraction of households with lifetime income (starting at age 50) below 50 percent of the average lifetime income.

The results are given in table 1.8 for the baseline and the Three-Year Reform. Not surprisingly, the comparison between these two cases indicates that the reform generates more inequality and more poverty than what we observe in the baseline. The reason is simple: retiring later mostly benefits high-income households that are concentrated in the top income quintiles.

This comparison is, however, only of a very partial relevance. Compared to the baseline, the reform scenario generates additional revenue to the system. By reallocating this additional revenue among households we could easily get a more favorable outcome from the standpoint of both poverty and inequality reduction.

Table 1.8   **Gini indexes and poverty rates**

	Base	Three-Year	Benefits reduction
		Peak value—S1	
Gini index	0.2351	0.2461	0.2550
Poverty rate	2.89	3.82	7.02
		Peak value—S2	
Gini index	0.2327	0.2422	0.2526
Poverty rate	2.79	2.82	6.78
		Option value—S1	
Gini index	0.2360	0.2459	0.2568
Poverty rate	2.99	4.27	6.95
		Option value—S2	
Gini index	0.2363	0.2449	0.2569
Poverty rate	3.06	3.37	7.02

Table 1.9   **Comparison of two reforms with comparable budgetary impact (in € per worker)**

| | Change in present discounted value | | | | | |
| | Three-Year | | | Benefits reduction (–25%) | | |
	Mechanical	Behavioral	Total	Mechanical	Behavioral	Total
		Peak value—S1				
Benefits	–19,582	4,132	–15,450	–36,979	–693	–37,671
Total taxes	–3,592	10,614	7,022	–12,627	1,407	–11,221
Net change	–15,990	–6,482	–22,472	–24,351	–2,099	–26,451
Change as % of						
base benefits	–10.9	–4.4	–15.3	–16.6	–1.4	–18.1
		Peak value—S2				
Benefits	–20,635	2,210	–18,425	–37,233	–621	–37,854
Total taxes	–3,787	12,453	8,666	–12,604	1,287	–11,317
Net change	–16,849	–10,243	–27,092	–24,629	–1,909	–26,537
Change as % of						
base benefits	–11.4	–6.9	–18.4	–16.7	–1.3	–18.0
		Option value—S1				
Benefits	–18,530	1,785	–16,745	–36,753	–834	–37,588
Total taxes	–3,657	10,323	6,666	–12,924	2,624	–10,300
Net change	–14,873	–8,538	–23,410	–23,830	–3,458	–27,288
Change as % of						
base benefits	–10.2	–5.9	–16.1	–16.4	–2.4	–18.7
		Option value—S2				
Benefits	–18,931	–150	–19,081	–36,724	–731	–37,454
Total taxes	–3,743	10,849	7,107	–12,967	2,281	–10,686
Net change	–15,188	–11,000	–26,188	–23,756	–3,012	–26,768
Change as % of						
base benefits	–10.4	–7.6	–18.0	–16.3	–2.1	–18.4

However, such a statement is not very precise. To get a sharper comparison, we first observe in table 1.9 that the Three-Year Reform brings additional resources equivalent to about 18 percent of overall benefits.[12] These resources could, for example, be used for financing the costs of the ongoing demographic shift, as illustrated by a drastic increase in the dependency ratio. Suppose that instead of raising the effective age of retirement, as in the Three-Year Reform, we apply a simple linear reduction of benefits to obtain the very same budgetary savings. We can then oppose two comparable or budget-neutral scenarios. Our computations show that the linear benefit reduction needed to get an 18 percent resource saving has to be larger than 18 percent. Indeed, as individuals can have behavioral reactions and as income taxes are paid on benefits, we have to apply a higher

12. This amount is obtained with the S2 simulation method. For simplicity, we refer only to this simulation method in the rest of this comparison.

reduction on gross benefits to finally get an additional revenue of 18 percent. A gross benefit reduction of 25 percent seems to work. In other words, if instead of adopting the Three-Year Reform we cut all benefits by 25 percent, we would end up with an aggregate benefit reduction of 18 percent. This is presented on table 1.9 for different calculations of the reform.

We now study the comparative incidence of these two reforms. As table 1.8 shows, both the poverty rate and the Gini coefficient are higher with the second than with the first reform.[13]

A general conclusion arises from this exercise. The benefit reduction reform represents the policy that would be implemented if nothing is done to limit the problem of financing aging. The Three-Year Reform is such a policy, which decreases the implicit tax on continued work, incites agents to work longer, leads to more revenue, less spending, and hence ultimately to smaller budgetary problems. A third type of parametric reform is an increase in social security contributions. This solution has to be ruled out in the current context of strong fiscal competition. Hence, a reform that is quickly undertaken and that keeps workers in the labor force is better in terms of redistribution than an emergency reform that decreases benefits linearly (for some time).

1.7   Conclusions

The analysis just presented shows the large potential budgetary impact of various hypothetical reforms. These reforms, though clearly selected for comparative and illustrative purposes, indicate the importance of behavioral effects that citizens display when faced with a varying landscape in terms of their social insurance architecture. Different real-life reform alternatives are imaginable in the Belgian context. Any such real-life alternative will have to include—at least to some degree—some elements analyzed in our stylized scenarios; for example, changes in the key retirement ages, the use of actuarial adjustment factors, and a convergence between the three main retirement systems—while at the same time not forgetting the labor-demand side. The Common Reform admittedly looks somewhat unrealistic. In that sense, our Belgian Reform is a first step in the direction of getting these hypothetical simulations closer to the field. By eliminating one particular aspect of our largely Bismarckian system, namely an aspect that is not insurance based, we reestablish a clearer link between contributions and benefits. The results indicate that even such a partial reform might have important consequences, not only in levels but also on the distributional side. The results of the present distributional analysis also illustrate the need to refine the analysis in future research.

However, we would like to insist on the fact that the analysis relies heavily on some assumptions we made—most notably, the limitation to the

---

13. For more on this, see Cremer and Pestieau (2003).

cohort of 50-year-olds and the steady-state assumption, both of which clearly limit the generality with which one can apply these results to real-world proposals. Hence there is a clear need for further research, to get the reform proposals closer in line with politically feasible and economically viable alternatives over the long run, as well as to check the robustness of our simulation approach.

This chapter shows that the social security system at large (i.e., including unemployment and disability insurance as well as early retirement schemes) induces Belgian workers to retire earlier than they ought to. Most reforms contemplated imply that we bring this comprehensive social security package closer to actuarial fairness. We realize that this is questionable and ought to be viewed as a first step toward a more complete analysis of reforms. Assume, indeed, that a fraction of these early retirees who draw benefits from disability benefits are truly disabled, and a fraction of those drawing benefits from unemployment insurance are truly involuntarily unemployed. A *good* reform should attempt to identify these workers and let them benefit from social insurance. This may imply improving the audit and control procedures, particularly for unemployment. Then, for the remaining voluntary early retirees, we would apply our alternative actuarial reforms.

Appendix

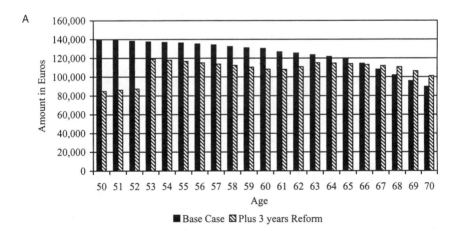

Fig. 1A.1   *A*, PDV of benefits by age of labor force exit (in EUR per worker); *B*, PDV of taxes by age of labor force exit (in EUR per worker); *C*, Distribution of age of labor force exit (option value–S1); *D*, Total effect by age of labor force exit (Three-Year Reform–option value–S1); *E*, Distribution of age of labor force exit (option value–S3); *F*, Total effect by age of labor force exit (Three-Year Reform–option value–S3); *G*, Fiscal implications of the Three-Year Reform as a percent of GDP

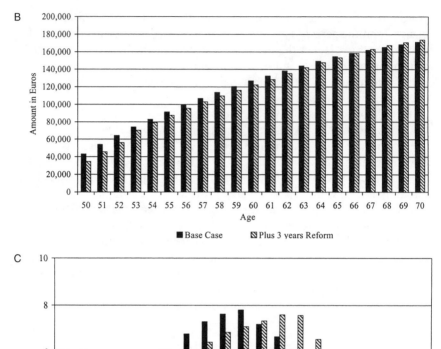

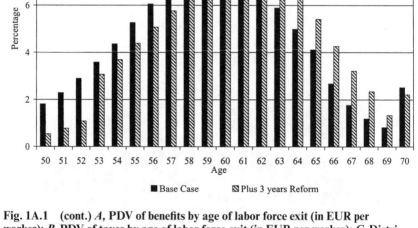

Fig. 1A.1 (cont.) *A*, PDV of benefits by age of labor force exit (in EUR per worker); *B*, PDV of taxes by age of labor force exit (in EUR per worker); *C*, Distribution of age of labor force exit (option value–S1); *D*, Total effect by age of labor force exit (Three-Year Reform–option value–S1); *E*, Distribution of age of labor force exit (option value–S3); *F*, Total effect by age of labor force exit (Three-Year Reform–option value–S3); *G*, Fiscal implications of the Three-Year Reform as a percent of GDP

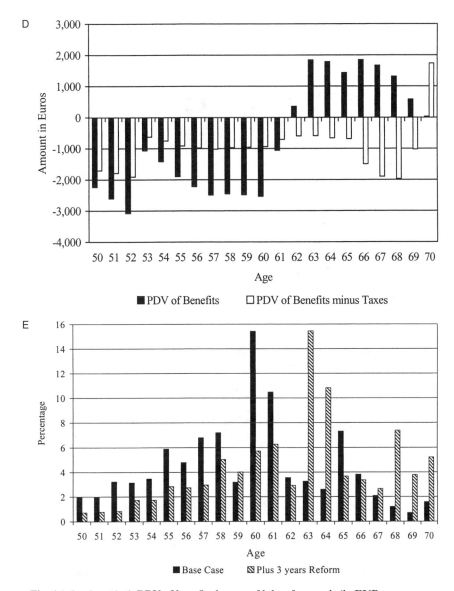

Fig. 1A.1 (cont.) *A*, PDV of benefits by age of labor force exit (in EUR per worker); *B*, PDV of taxes by age of labor force exit (in EUR per worker); *C*, Distribution of age of labor force exit (option value–S1); *D*, Total effect by age of labor force exit (Three-Year Reform–option value–S1); *E*, Distribution of age of labor force exit (option value–S3); *F*, Total effect by age of labor force exit (Three-Year Reform–option value–S3); *G*, Fiscal implications of the Three-Year Reform as a percent of GDP

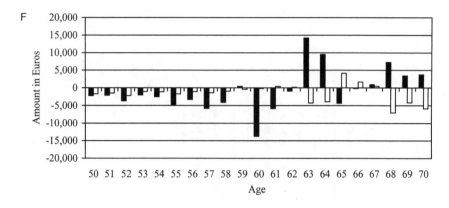

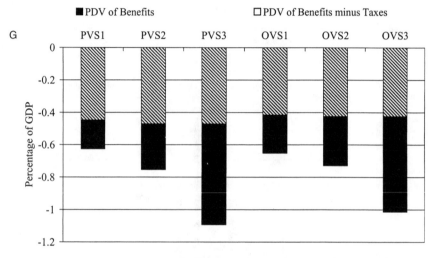

Fig. 1A.1   (cont.) *A,* PDV of benefits by age of labor force exit (in EUR per worker); *B,* PDV of taxes by age of labor force exit (in EUR per worker); *C,* Distribution of age of labor force exit (option value–S1); *D,* Total effect by age of labor force exit (Three-Year Reform–option value–S1); *E,* Distribution of age of labor force exit (option value–S3); *F,* Total effect by age of labor force exit (Three-Year Reform–option value–S3); *G,* Fiscal implications of the Three-Year Reform as a percent of GDP

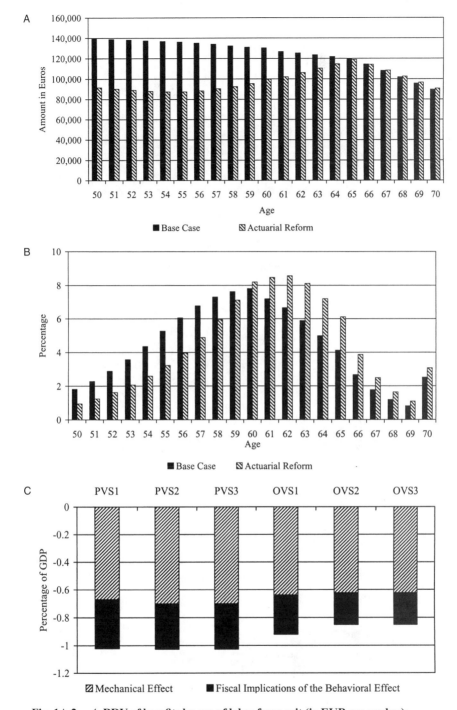

Fig. 1A.2 *A*, PDV of benefits by age of labor force exit (in EUR per worker); *B*, Distribution of age of labor force exit (option value–S1); *C*, Fiscal implications of the Actuarial Reform as a percent of GDP

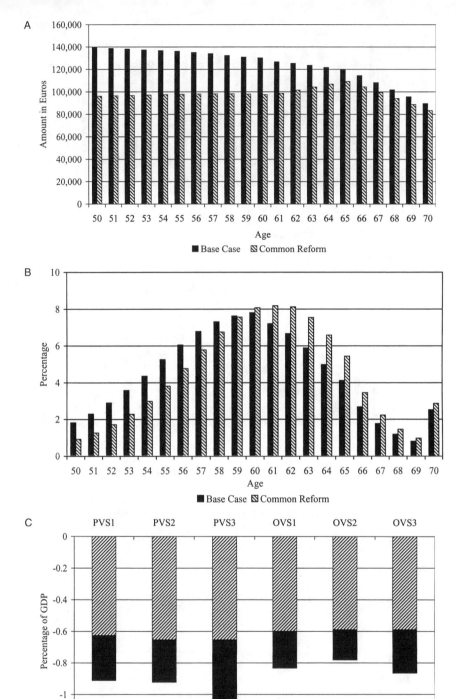

Fig. 1A.3   *A,* PDV of benefits by age of labor force exit (in EUR per worker);
B, Distribution of age of labor force exit (option value–S1); *C,* Fiscal implications
of the Common Reform as a percent of GDP

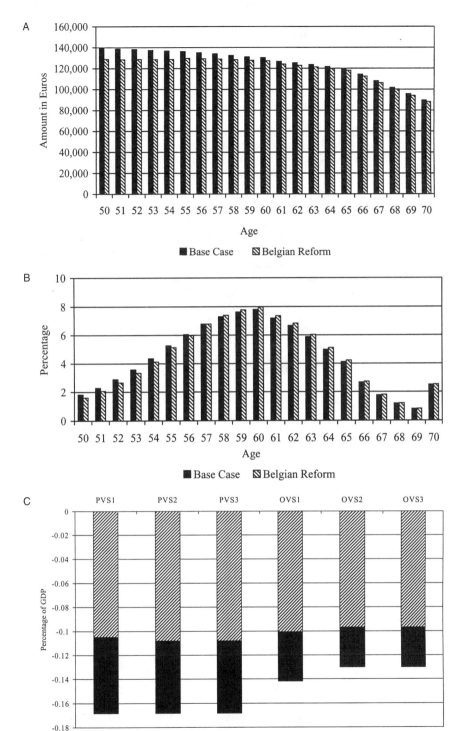

Fig. 1A.4 *A,* PDV of benefits by age of labor force exit (in EUR per worker); *B,* Distribution of age of labor force exit (option value–S1); *C,* Fiscal implications of the Belgian Reform as a percent of GDP

References

Blöndal, S., and S. Scarpetta. 1998. *Falling participation rates among older workers in the OECD countries.* Paris: Organization for Economic Cooperation and Development (OECD).

Cremer, H., and P. Pestieau. 2003. The double dividend of postponing retirement. *International Tax and Public Finance* 10 (4): 419–34.

Dellis, A., R. Desmet, A. Jousten, and S. Perelman. 2004. Micro-modeling of retirement in Belgium. In *Social security and retirement around the world,* ed. J. Gruber and D. Wise, 41–98. Chicago: University of Chicago Press.

Institut National de Statistique. 1995–1996. Enquête sur les budgets des ménages. Bruxelles: Institut National de Statistique.

Jousten, A., and P. Pestieau. 2002. Labor mobility, redistribution and pension reform in Europe. In *Social security pension reform in Europe,* ed. M. Feldstein and H. Siebert, 85–108. Chicago: University of Chicago Press.

Organization for Economic Cooperation and Development (OECD). 1994. *OECD Economic Survey: Belgium, Luxembourg.* Paris: OECD.

Pestieau, P., and J.-P. Stijns. 1999. Social security and retirement in Belgium. In *Social security and retirement around the world,* ed. J. Gruber and D. Wise, 37–71. Chicago: University of Chicago Press.

Sneesens, H., F. Shadman, and O. Pierrard. 2003. Effets des préretraites sur l'emploi. *Revue française d'économie* 1 (18): 133–55.

Stock, J., and D. Wise. 1990. Pensions, the option value of work, and retirement. *Econometrica* 58 (5): 1151–80.

Simulating the Response to Reform of Canada's Income Security Programs

Michael Baker, Jonathan Gruber, and Kevin Milligan

2.1 Introduction

Expenditures on public pensions in Canada are projected to be over C\$54 billion in 2002–2003. The extensive income security system in Canada, which consists of a demogrant, work-related pensions, and income-tested transfers, provides an important source of income for older Canadians. However, the system has experienced periodic crises when the streams of projected future expenditures and revenues fall out of alignment. The future may offer further turbulence. The elderly dependency ratio in Canada—the ratio of older persons to working-age persons—is projected to rise from 0.20 in 2000 to 0.40 in 2050 (Office of the Superintendent of Financial Institutions [1998]). As a result, this income security system may face pressure for reform in the years to come.

Any reforms that reduce program generosity will have two types of effects on public sector budgets. The first is a mechanical effect of the reduction. The magnitude of the government's benefit expenditures and tax receipts will change mechanically with any changes to the programs. The second effect is a dynamic effect, through changing retirement behavior. Our research has shown that the retirement decisions of older Canadians

Michael Baker is a professor of economics at the University of Toronto, and a faculty research fellow of the National Bureau of Economic Research. Jonathan Gruber is a professor of economics at the Massachusetts Institute of Technology, and a research associate of the National Bureau of Economic Research. Kevin Milligan is an assistant professor of economics at the University of British Columbia, and a faculty research fellow of the National Bureau of Economic Research.

This paper was prepared as part of the NBER Aging Program's International Social Security project. We thank participants at the International Social Security conference in Assmannshausen, Germany, in May 2002 for helpful comments.

are sensitive to the labor supply incentives in the income security system. This implies that reform to this system can have important indirect effects on fiscal balances through behavioral changes.

In this chapter we explore the fiscal implications of two alternative reforms, and describe how these implications depend on the types of behavioral responses estimated in our previous work. The first reform that we consider is a three-year increase in both the age at which individuals are eligible for early retirement benefits, and the normal retirement age for all retirement programs. The second is a move to a common income security system for all countries in this research project. The Common Reform replaces Canada's existing mix of demogrants and earnings-related benefits with one large earnings-related benefit, similar in structure to the existing Canada Pension Plan.

Our major findings are that both of these reforms would have enormous impacts on the fiscal position of the Canadian retirement income system. An increase of three years in the age of benefits eligibility would improve the government's fiscal position by about one-fourth of the base level of benefits, while the second reform raises net program expenditures by about 50 percent. For both reforms, we find very important behavioral as well as mechanical effects. The first reform significantly reduces the percentage of early retirement in Canada—between 21 and 49 percent of the reduction in program expenditures come from behavioral responses to this reform. The behavioral response manifests itself in the government budget through lower benefit payments paid to, and more taxes collected from, workers who retire later than under the base system. For the Common Reform, the fiscal implications of behavioral response are also large in magnitude but smaller relative to the mechanical effect of the increased benefits.

We also document important distributional implications of reform. A delay in retirement ages has somewhat larger negative effects for upper-income groups, as they see the largest effective reduction in their benefits. On the other hand, the Common Reform reduces effective benefits for the lowest-income groups, by removing the income-tested component of transfers, while at the same time dramatically increasing benefits for upper-income groups, whose benefits now reflect more fully their higher lifetime earnings.

In the balance of this chapter, we first describe, in detail, the components of Canada's retirement income system. This is followed by a recounting of the empirical results from our earlier work, upon which the simulations in this paper are based. We then lay out the simulation methodology employed. Finally, the results are presented, along with some concluding remarks.

2.2   Canada's Retirement Income System

The retirement income system in Canada has three pillars: (1) the Old Age Security Program, (2) the Canada and Quebec Pension Plans, and (3) private savings. The first pillar includes the Old Age Security pension (OAS), the Guaranteed Income Supplement (GIS), and the Allowance. The third pillar includes occupational pensions as well as other private savings, including those accumulated in Registered Retirement Savings Plans (RRSPs), which are a tax-subsidized savings vehicle. Our analysis focuses on reforms to the first two pillars of this system, which collectively are referred to as the Income Security (IS) system in Canada. We next provide a brief description of the components of all three pillars, however, to provide the proper context for our results.

2.2.1 The Old Age Security Program

The Old Age Security program is the oldest pillar of the current retirement system, dating back to 1952. All benefits paid out under the program are financed through general tax revenues rather than past or current contributions. Its principal component is the OAS pension, which is currently payable to anyone aged 65 or older who satisfies a residency requirement.[1] The pension is a demogrant, equal to $442.66 in March 2002. Individuals who do not meet the residence requirement may be entitled to a partial OAS benefit. Benefits are fully indexed to the Consumer Price Index (CPI) and are fully taxable under the Income Tax Act. There is also an additional "clawback" of benefits from high-income beneficiaries. Their benefits are reduced by 15 cents for every dollar of personal net income that exceeds $56,968.

A second component of the OAS program is the GIS. It is an income-tested supplement for OAS pension beneficiaries that has been in place since 1967. There are separate single and married benefits that in 2002 (January to March) were $526.08 and $342.67 (per person) monthly, respectively. The income test is applied annually, based on information from an individual's (and his or her partner's) income tax return. Income for the purpose of testing is the same as for income tax purposes, with the exclusion of OAS pension income. Unlike the OAS clawback, the income testing of GIS benefits is based on family income levels. Benefits are reduced at a rate of 50 cents for each dollar of family income, except for couples in which one member is age 65 or older and the other is younger than 60. For these couples, the reduction is 25 cents for each dollar of family income. The GIS is fully indexed to the CPI and is not subject to income taxes at either the federal or provincial level.

The final component of the OAS program is the Allowance, which until

---

1. Individuals must have been a Canadian citizen or legal resident of Canada at some point before application, and have resided in Canada for at least ten years (if currently in Canada) or twenty years (if currently outside Canada). The benefit is prorated for pensioners with less than forty years of Canadian residence, unless they are grandfathered under rules that apply to the persons who were over age 25 and had established attachment to Canada prior to July 1977.

recently was called the Spouse's Allowance.[2] This component was introduced in 1975. The Allowance is an income-tested benefit available to 60- to 64-year-old partners[3] of OAS pension recipients and to 60- to 64-year-old widows/widowers. For partners, the benefit is equal to the OAS pension plus the GIS at the married rate. An income test reduces the OAS pension portion of the Allowance by 75 cents for each dollar of family income until it is reduced to zero, and then the combined GIS benefits of both partners are reduced at 50 cents per dollar of family income. For a widowed partner, the benefit is equal to the OAS pension plus GIS at the widowed rate, and is taxed-back equivalently. The Allowance is also fully indexed to the CPI and again is not subject to income taxes at either the federal or provincial level.

2.2.2   The Canada/Quebec Pension Plan

The second pillar of the retirement system, and the largest component of the IS system, is the Canada Pension Plan (CPP) and Quebec Pension Plan (QPP). These programs, started in 1966, are administered separately by Quebec for the QPP and the federal government for the CPP.

In contrast to the OAS program, the CPP/QPP are contributory programs. They are financed by payroll taxes on both employers and employees, each at a rate of 4.7 percent (2002). The base for the payroll tax is earnings between the Year's Basic Exemption ($3,500) up to the Year's Maximum Pensionable Earnings (YMPE, $39,100 in 2002). The YMPE approximates average earnings and is indexed to its growth.

To be eligible for benefits, individuals must make contributions in at least one calendar year during the contributory period. The contributory period is defined as the period from attainment of age eighteen, or January 1, 1966, if later, and normally extended to age 70 or commencement of the retirement pension, whichever is earlier. Starting in 1984 for the QPP and 1987 for the CPP, benefits can be claimed as early as age 60. The normal retirement age is 65, and there is an actuarial reduction in benefits of 0.5 percent for each month the initial claim precedes this age, resulting in a maximum 30 percent reduction for claims on the 60th birthday. Symmetrically, benefits are increased by 0.5 for each month the initial claim succeeds age 65, to as late as age 70 (the maximum adjustment is therefore 30 percent). Finally, if an individual claims before age 65, their annual rate of earnings cannot exceed the maximum retirement pension payable at age 65 for the year in which the pension is claimed. This earnings test is only applied at the point of application, however. Subsequently, there is no check on the individual's earnings.[4]

2. Baker (2002) studies the retirement incentives in the Spouse's Allowance.

3. The Allowance is available to both spouses and common-law partners (same sex or opposite sex) of OAS pension beneficiaries.

4. There are no restrictions on returning to work after the benefit is being paid.

To calculate benefits, an individual's earnings history is first computed. The earnings history is based on earnings in the contributory period less any months (a) receiving a disability pension, (b) spent rearing small children,[5] (c) between age 65 and the commencement of the pension,[6] and (d) 15 percent of the remaining months. The last three of these exclusions cannot be used, however, to reduce the contributory period below 120 months after taking into account the offset for months of disability pension receipt. The ratio of each month of earnings in the contributory period to 1/12 of the YMPE for that period is then calculated, with the ratio capped at 1. Excess earnings in one month above 1/12 of the YMPE may be applied to months in the same calendar year in which earnings are below 1/12 of the YMPE.

Earnings over the earnings history period are then converted to current dollars in three steps. First, the average of the earnings ratios over the contributory period is calculated. Second, this average is multiplied by a pension adjustment factor. Until 1998, the pension adjustment factor was the average of the YMPE over the three years prior to (and including) the year of pension receipt. This average was raised to four years for benefits claimed in 1998 and five years for benefits beginning in 1999. Finally, the product of the earnings ratios and the pension adjustment factor is multiplied by 25 percent to arrive at the annual benefit. This benefit can be thought of as a pension that replaces 25 percent of earnings for someone who has average earnings over his or her lifetime. In 2002, the maximum possible monthly retirement benefit works out to $788.75.

While CPP/QPP retirement benefits are based solely on an individual's earnings history,[7] survivor pensions are either all or partly based on the earnings history of the deceased. Partners are eligible for survivor pensions if the deceased made contributions for the lesser of ten years or one third of the number of years in the contributory period. For survivors under age 65, benefits are equal to a flat-rate benefit plus 37.5 percent of the earnings-related pension of the deceased spouse. If the survivor is not disabled or has no dependent children the benefit is reduced by 1/120 for each month she or he is younger than age 45, such that no benefit is payable to individuals aged 35 or younger. Also, benefits to survivors who have dependent children and who are under age 35 only continue as long as the children are dependent.[8] For survivors aged 65 and above, the pension is equal to the

5. This is defined as months where there was a child less than seven years of age and the worker had zero or below average annual earnings.

6. Periods after age 65 to age 70 can be substituted for periods prior to age 65 if this will increase their future retirement pension.

7. Couples do have the option of sharing their benefits for income tax purposes, since taxation is at the individual level. Each spouse can claim up to half of the couple's total CPP/QPP pension credits. The exact calculation depends on the ratio of their cohabitation period to their joint contributory period.

8. Up to age 18, or age 25 if they are in school.

greater of (a) 37.5 percent of the deceased's retirement pension, plus 100 percent of the survivor's own retirement pension, or (b) 60 percent of the deceased's retirement pension, plus 60 percent of the survivor's own retirement pension. There is an upper cap on total payments equal to the maximum retirement pension payable in that year.[9] Under changes made effective in 1998, however, the rules for maximum payout are changed. The survivor simply receives the larger of her or his own retirement pension or her or his survivor pension plus 60 percent of the smaller. Finally, under the CPP, children of decreased contributors are also entitled to a (flat-rate) benefit if under 18 or a full-time student between 18 and 25 (the corresponding QPP benefit ends at age 18).[10]

A final dimension of the CPP/QPP is the disability benefit program. The basic benefit is made up of a flat-rate portion, paid to all disabled workers, and an earnings-related portion, which is 75 percent of the applicable CPP/QPP retirement pension, calculated with the contributory period ending at the date of disability. Fewer than 5 percent of Canadian men are on CPP/QPP disability (more information can be found in Gruber [2000]).

CPP/QPP benefits have been fully indexed to the CPI since 1973. Also, benefits are fully taxable by the federal and provincial governments.

2.2.3   Private Savings

The third pillar of the retirement income system is the proceeds of private savings. These can take a variety of forms, some of which are explicitly regulated by either federal or provincial governments. For many individuals, the most important form is private occupational pensions. In 1997, 41.2 percent of paid workers were covered by occupational pensions, with coverage slightly higher for males than for females (Statistics Canada 1999). Defined-benefit pensions are overwhelmingly the most common (86 percent of plan members in 1997) although the recent trend is toward more defined contribution plans.

The other main form of private savings having a public policy dimension is savings in Registered Retirement Savings Plans (RRSPs). Contributions are deducted from gross earnings in the calculation of taxable income. While in the RRSP, investment earnings on the contributions accumulate tax free. There is an annual limit on contributions that is lower for individuals who participate in an occupational pension plan. Unused contribution room can be carried forward indefinitely. Finally, there are rules cov-

---

9. If the surviving spouse is receiving his or her own CPP disability pension, the sum of the earnings-related portion of the two pensions cannot exceed the maximum retirement pension available in the year.

10. There is also a lump-sum death benefit, which is generally equal to one-half of the annual CPP/QPP pension amount up to a maximum ($3,500 in 1997). Under the 1997 legislation, this maximum is fixed at $2,500 for all years after 1997, and in the case of the QPP all death benefits are set at this level.

ering the start and minimum payout of these savings over the retirement years. More information on RRSPs can be found in Milligan (2002).

2.3 Base Empirical Model

The behavioral responses to the policy reforms considered in this chapter are predicted using an empirical model of retirement outlined and estimated in Baker, Gruber, and Milligan (2004). A full description and details of the estimation can be found in that paper. For the current purpose we provide a brief description of the data used to estimate the model as well as a discussion of the estimates on which our policy reform simulations are based.

The primary data source is the Longitudinal Worker File, developed by Statistics Canada.[11] This is a 10 percent random sample of Canadian workers for the period 1978–96. The data are the product of information from three sources: the T-4 file of Revenue Canada, the Record of Employment file of Human Resources Development Canada, and the Longitudinal Employment Analysis Program file of Statistics Canada.

T-4s are forms issued annually by employers for any employment earnings that exceed a certain annual threshold and/or trigger income tax, contributions to Canada's public pension plans, or Employment Insurance (EI) premiums.[12] Employers issue Record of Employment forms to employees in insurable employment whenever an earnings interruption occurs.[13] The Record of Employment file records interruptions resulting from events such as strikes, layoffs, quits, dismissals, retirement, and maternity or parental leave. Finally, the Longitudinal Employment Analysis Program data is a longitudinal data file on Canadian businesses at the company level. It is the source of information on the company size and industry of the jobs in which employees work.

The Longitudinal Worker File data provide information on the T-4 wages and salaries and three-digit industry for each job an individual holds in a given year, their age, and sex,[14] the province and size (employees) of the

11. The construction of the database is described in Picot and Lin (1997) and Statistics Canada (1998). Our description draws heavily on these sources.

12. The data include incorporated self-employed individuals who pay themselves a salary, but not other self-employed workers. The federal program that provides insurance against unemployment changed names from *Unemployment Insurance* to *Employment Insurance* in 1996. In this paper we use *Employment Insurance* throughout when referring to this program.

13. Over the sample period, insurable employment covers most employer-employee relationships. Exclusion includes self-employed workers, full-time students, employees who work less than fifteen hours per week and earn less than 20 percent of maximum weekly insurable earnings (20 percent × $750 = $150 in 1999). Individuals working in insurable employment pay Employment Insurance (EI) contributions on their earnings and are eligible for EI benefits subject to the other parameters of the EI program.

14. Information on the age and sex of individuals is taken from the T-1 tax returns, which individuals file each year. To obtain this information, therefore, it is necessary that he or she filed a tax return at least once in the sample period.

establishment for which they work,[15] and their job tenure, starting in 1978. Because T-4s are also issued for EI income, we also observe any insured unemployment/maternity/sickness spells. To extend the earnings histories we merged earnings information for 1975 through 1977 from the T-4 earnings files for these years. We then backcast earnings to 1971, using cohort-specific earnings growth rates calculated from the 1972, 1974, and 1976 Census Family files of the Survey of Consumer Finance,[16] applied to a three-year average of an individual's last valid T-4 earnings observations. Finally, histories back to 1966 (the initial year of the CPP/QPP) were constructed, using the earnings growth rates implied by the cross-section profile from the 1972 Survey of Consumer Finances, appropriately discounted for inflation and productivity gains using the Industrial Composite wage for the period 1966–70.[17]

The marital status and any spouses of individuals in our sample were identified using information from the T-1 family file maintained by Statistics Canada. T-4 earnings histories for the period 1966 to 1996 were then constructed for the spouses, using the procedures outlined previously.

The retirement model is estimated using the data on individuals' labor market decisions over the period 1985 to 1996. Separate samples of males and females aged 55 through 69 in 1985 were drawn, and then younger cohorts of individuals were added as they turn 55 in the years 1986–91.[18] Agricultural workers and individuals in other primary industries were excluded.[19] The sample was selected conditional on working, so the focus is on the incentives for retirement conditional on being in the labor force.

Work was defined as positive T-4 earnings in two consecutive years. Retirement was defined as the year preceding the first year of zero earnings after age 55. If an individual had positive earnings in one year and zero earnings in the following year, the year of positive earnings was considered the retirement year. Note that since T-4s are not issued to the unincorporated self-employed, this definition of retirement also captures any persons

15. The records of the Longitudinal Worker File data are at the person/year/job level. For some calculation it is necessary to aggregate the data to the person/year level. In years in which an individual has more than one job, there will be multiple measures of tenure, industry, firm size, and in some cases, province. In these cases the characteristics of the job with the highest earnings for the year are used.

16. We use samples of paid workers with positive earnings in the relevant birth cohorts.

17. The data on the Industrial Composite wage are from Statistics Canada (1983). The obvious limitation of this backcasting approach is that we will not predict absences from the labor market, which may be important at younger ages.

18. Individuals with missing age, sex, or province variables are excluded from the sample.

19. We make this exclusion because our definitions of retirement are based on earnings, and the earnings streams for these workers, given high rates of self-employment and special provisions in the Employment Insurance system for fishers and other seasonal workers, are difficult to interpret. For example, individuals in these industries are observed with years of very small earnings (in the hundreds of dollars) and no (or sporadic) evidence of EI benefits, who were too young to collect IS benefits. One possibility is that they are primarily unincorporated self-employed, and therefore the majority of their earnings are unobserved.

moving from paid employment into this sector.[20] Only the first observed retirement for each individual was considered. If a person reentered the labor market after a year of zero earnings, the later observations were not used. Finally, individuals were only followed until age 69.

An additional important piece of information for calculating retirement incentives is participation in an occupational pension plan. The Longitudinal Worker File data has no information on this participation. To provide some control for the effects of these pensions, we imputed a probability of participation in a private pension plan to each sample individual based on his or her three-digit industry. The probabilities were computed from the 1986 to 1990 Labour Market Activity Survey and the 1993 to 1996 Survey of Labour and Income Dynamics.

The retirement model estimated was

$$(1) \quad R_{it} = \delta_0 + \delta_1 ISW_{it} + \delta_2 ACC_{it} + \delta_3 AGE_{it} + \delta_4 EARN_{it} + \delta_5 APE_{it}$$
$$+ \delta_6 SPEARN_{it} + \delta_7 SPAPE + \delta_8 RPP_{it} + \delta_9 X_{it} + v_{it},$$

where R is a 0/1 indicator of retirement in the current year, ISW is the present discounted value of family IS wealth, ACC is a measure of the accrual in ISW with future additional years of work, AGE is alternatively a linear control for age or a full set of age dummies, $EARN$ and APE ($SPEARN$ and $SPAPE$) are cubics in an individual's (his or her spouse's) projected earnings[21] in year t and his or her Average Pensionable Earnings,[22] RPP is the probability of participation in a private pension plan, and X are controls for marital status, tenure, own and spouse's labor market experience, industry, establishment size, and province and year effects. Each individual contributes observations for each (consecutive) year that she or he has positive T-4 earnings after entering the sample up to the year of retirement or age 69, whichever comes first. The equation was estimated separately by sex as a probit.

For each year an individual is observed in the data, family ISW was constructed for the current year as well as for all potential future retirement years. As described in our previous paper, many of the provisions of the IS system are implemented in the calculation. Exclusions occurred where we did not observe the necessary information. These included any residency

---

20. While older individuals do work in unincorporated self-employment, the proportion doing so remains fairly constant over our sample period. For males, Canadian Census data (Individual Files for 1981, 1986, 1991, 1996) reveal that the proportion of the population of 60–64 year olds (65+ year olds) working in this sector is 0.08–0.09 (0.04) in Quebec and 0.13–0.16 (0.06–0.8) in the rest of Canada between 1980 and 1995. For females the statistics are 0.01 (0.00–0.01) in Quebec and 0.2–0.4 (0.01) in the rest of Canada.

21. All earnings forecasts were made by applying a real growth rate of zero percent per year to the average of an individual's observed earnings in the three years preceding the retirement year.

22. Average Pensionable Earnings is the average earnings over an individual's earnings history used to calculate their CPP/QPP entitlement. To capture potential nonlinear relationships between earnings and retirement decisions, we also included a full set of interactions between the cubics in $EARN_{it}$ and APE_{it}, and $SPEARN_{it}$ and $SPAPE_{it}$.

Table 2.1   **Retirement probits—Males sample**

	Peak value model		Option value model	
	Linear age	Age dummies	Linear age	Age dummies
ISW	0.077	0.022	0.067	0.012
	(0.003)	(0.004)	(0.004)	(0.004)
$10,000 change*	1.60	0.45	1.38	0.23
ACCRUAL	−0.577	−0.345	−0.284	−0.315
	(0.017)	(0.018)	(0.011)	(0.009)
$1,000 change*	−1.11	−0.67	−0.56	−0.61
RPP	0.124	0.123	0.124	0.126
	(0.013)	(0.013)	(0.013)	(0.013)
MARRIED	−0.454	−0.173	−0.411	−0.110
	(0.020)	(0.022)	(0.021)	(0.023)
TENURE	−0.034	−0.033	−0.030	−0.029
	(0.002)	(0.002)	(0.002)	(0.002)
TENURESQ	0.002	0.002	0.002	0.002
	(0.0001)	(0.0001)	(0.0001)	(0.0001)
TENURE CENS	0.028	0.027	0.034	0.032
	(0.006)	(0.007)	(0.006)	(0.007)
EXP	−0.018	−0.018	−0.014	−0.015
	(0.002)	(0.002)	(0.002)	(0.002)
EXP SQ	0.000	0.000	0.000	0.000
	(0.0001)	(0.0001)	(0.0001)	(0.0001)
SPOUSE EXP	−0.029	−0.029	−0.027	−0.028
	(0.003)	(0.003)	(0.003)	(0.003)
SPOUSE EXPSQ	0.001	0.001	0.001	0.001
	(0.0001)	(0.0001)	(0.0001)	(0.0001)
AGE	0.033		0.039	
	(0.001)		(0.001)	
AGEDIFF	0.001	−0.003	−0.001	−0.004
	(0.001)	(0.001)	(0.001)	(0.001)
AGE56		−0.036		−0.050
		(0.011)		(0.001)
AGE57		−0.059		−0.095
		(0.012)		(0.012)
AGE58		−0.015		−0.079
		(0.012)		(0.012)
AGE59		0.021		−0.071
		(0.012)		(0.013)
AGE60		0.189		0.101
		(0.013)		(0.013)
AGE61		0.162		0.066
		(0.014)		(0.014)
AGE62		0.179		0.074
		(0.015)		(0.015)
AGE63		0.203		0.089
		(0.016)		(0.016)
AGE64		0.353		0.227
		(0.017)		(0.018)

Table 2.1   (continued)

	Peak value model		Option value model	
	Linear age	Age dummies	Linear age	Age dummies
AGE65		1.028		0.928
		(0.019)		(0.019)
AGE66		0.658		0.555
		(0.021)		(0.020)
AGE67		0.338		0.229
		(0.023)		(0.022)
AGE68		0.262		0.148
		(0.024)		(0.024)
AGE69		0.238		0.118
		(0.026)		(0.025)
Pseudo R^2	0.100	0.115	0.099	0.116

Notes: ISW = income security wealth. AGEDIFF is the difference in ages between the individual and his spouse (coded 0 for singles). Asterisk indicates reported statistic is the percentage point change in the probability of retirement for the indicated change in ISW or accrual. Other control variables are 11 industry dummies, dummies for 6 categories of establishment size, province and year effects, a cubic in both own and spouse's predicted earnings and APE, and a full set of interactions between these cubics. The estimated parameters on these additional variables are not reported.

requirements, or the CPP/QPP dropout provisions for time spent rearing young children. Finally, our model does not incorporate the behavioral responses of any spouses. We simply assume that any spouse begins to collect each component of IS at the earliest possible age. While this may lead to an underestimation of a family's behavioral response to policy, this assumption was necessary to keep our model tractable.

Various measures of *ACC* were considered in the estimation. For the policy simulations that follow we use estimates based on two forward-looking specifications of accrual—*peak value* and *option value.* Peak value is defined as the difference between current *ISW* and the peak or maximum of expected *ISW* along its lifetime profile. For ages after the peak is reached, the peak value takes a value equal to the year-over-year difference in *ISW.* Option value is an analogous calculation, but is expressed in terms of utility and incorporating the value of leisure. Here the accrual is the difference between the utility of retiring today versus the optimal retirement date that maximizes the expected stream of utility, sometime in the future. We adopted the original specification of the indirect utility function used by Stock and Wise (1990), but directly parameterized it rather than jointly estimating its parameters. A complete description of our specification is contained in Baker, Gruber, and Milligan (2004).

The estimates that form the basis of our policy simulations are presented in tables 2.1 and 2.2 for males and females, respectively. For each measure

Table 2.2   **Retirement probits—Females sample**

	Peak value model		Option value model	
	Linear age	Age dummies	Linear age	Age dummies
ISW	0.082	0.030	0.076	0.017
	(0.005)	(0.005)	(0.005)	(0.006)
$10,000 change*	1.74	0.61	1.63	0.34
ACCRUAL	−0.306	−0.089	−0.116	−0.138
	(0.022)	(0.022)	(0.018)	(0.018)
$1,000 change*	−0.61	−0.18	−0.24	−0.28
RPP	0.160	0.158	0.157	0.159
	(0.016)	(0.017)	(0.016)	(0.017)
MARRIED	−0.247	−0.114	−0.238	−0.070
	(0.020)	(0.021)	(0.021)	(0.022)
TENURE	−0.012	−0.008	−0.012	−0.007
	(0.002)	(0.002)	(0.002)	(0.002)
TENURESQ	0.001	0.001	0.001	0.001
	(0.0001)	(0.0001)	(0.0001)	(0.0001)
TENURE CENS	−0.033	−0.032	−0.030	−0.031
	(0.008)	(0.008)	(0.008)	(0.008)
EXP	−0.039	−0.038	−0.038	−0.037
	(0.002)	(0.002)	(0.002)	(0.002)
EXP SQ	0.001	0.001	0.001	0.001
	(0.00004)	(0.00004)	(0.00004)	(0.00004)
SPOUSE EXP	−0.009	−0.009	−0.009	−0.010
	(0.007)	(0.007)	(0.007)	(0.007)
SPOUSE EXPSQ	0.000	0.000	0.000	0.000
	(0.0002)	(0.0002)	(0.0002)	(0.0002)
AGE	0.030		0.037	
	(0.002)		(0.002)	
AGEDIFF	0.010	0.003	0.009	0.002
	(0.001)	(0.001)	(0.001)	(0.001)
AGE56		−0.010		−0.015
		(0.013)		(0.013)
AGE57		−0.012		−0.023
		(0.013)		(0.013)
AGE58		−0.001		−0.017
		(0.014)		(0.014)
AGE59		0.049		0.028
		(0.014)		(0.015)
AGE60		0.234		0.214
		(0.015)		(0.015)
AGE61		0.157		0.136
		(0.016)		(0.017)
AGE62		0.183		0.161
		(0.018)		(0.018)
AGE63		0.204		0.180
		(0.019)		(0.020)
AGE64		0.294		0.268
		(0.021)		(0.021)

Table 2.2   (continued)

	Peak value model		Option value model	
	Linear age	Age dummies	Linear age	Age dummies
AGE65		0.970		0.947
		(0.022)		(0.022)
AGE66		0.598		0.572
		(0.024)		(0.024)
AGE67		0.324		0.292
		(0.027)		(0.027)
AGE68		0.222		0.184
		(0.029)		(0.029)
AGE69		0.232		0.188
		(0.031)		(0.031)
Pseudo R^2	0.104	0.116	0.104	0.116

Note: See table 2.1 notes.

of accrual we report results from specifications that alternatively include linear controls for age or age dummies. We also report the impact of a $10,000 change in ISW, or a $1,000 change in the accrual measure. For males, the results are uniformly supportive of an important role for IS incentives in determining retirement. There is a consistent positive and significant coefficient on ISW and a negative and significant coefficient on the accrual measure. Conditional on linear age, a $10,000 rise in ISW raises the odds of retirement by 1.4 to 2 percentage points, from a base of 14.8 percent. When, alternatively, age dummies are included, the effect of ISW falls considerably, by $10,000, now raising retirement rates by 0.23 to 0.51 percentage points. This drop in the ISW coefficient will be important for understanding the following simulation results. The estimates of ACC are also smaller when age dummies are included, but are less sensitive than ISW. The effects of a change in peak value are roughly half as large, while the estimates for option value are essentially invariant to the inclusion of age dummies.

For females, the estimates for ISW display the same magnitudes and patterns across specifications as the results for men. The estimates of ACC are generally smaller than the results for males, but again display the same patterns across specifications.

The estimated coefficients of the age dummies for both males and females display a distinct pattern, rising through the early 60s and peaking at age 65. One possibility is that these dummies are capturing an age-specific pattern of retirement that is due to nonlinear changes in the taste for leisure with age, or institutions such as mandatory retirement that are not otherwise captured in our model. An alternative is that the dummies capture responses to the IS system that are not captured by ISW and ACC. In the latter case, we are underestimating the effects of the IS system. As we discuss in the following, which of the alternatives better capture actual behavior has important implications for the interpretation of our simulation results.

2.4 Simulation Methodology

The goal of our analysis is to examine the response of older workers to different counterfactual retirement income systems, and the overall fiscal implications of these responses for the government budget. To do this, we follow the retirement decisions and retirement income of a cohort of workers from age 55 through the rest of their life under different institutional arrangements. In this section, we first describe the selection of our cohort. Next, we describe the methodology for the calculation of the IS flows, followed by the construction of the labor market exit probabilities. The penultimate subsection discusses our strategy for incorporating spousal response into the analysis. Finally, we describe in detail the structure of the two reforms we consider.

2.4.1 Cohort Selection

We select the cohort of men and women who were age 55 in 1991 from our full dataset. This includes all of the 55-year-old men from 1991, as well as the 55-year-old single females. Married females must be excluded to avoid double counting of individuals, as our sample of married men will account for their IS behavior. The spouses of our married men are taken without regard to their age. So, the cohort can be defined as a representative sample of Canadian 55-year-old workers in 1991 and their spouses.[23] To clarify the discussion that follows, we refer to those in the original sample as *cohort members* and the spouses of the cohort members as *spouses.*

Descriptive statistics appear in table 2.3. The sample includes 12,058 cohort members, of which 5,050 are married men, 3,662 single men, and 3,346 single women. The average age of the women married to our sample men is 51.5, which is 3.5 years less than the age of the sample men. The men have higher lifetime average pensionable earnings (APE) than the women do, as well as more job tenure, labor market experience, and a higher probability of employment-based pension coverage.

2.4.2 Calculating the Flows of Benefits and Taxes

We begin our analysis by calculating the benefit and tax flows that will be received and paid by cohort members and their spouses from the age of 55 until age 102. Our interest in the IS benefits is obvious—we wish to com-

---

23. Our sample excludes those in primary industries and the self-employed, so it is only representative of the population outside these sectors.

Table 2.3   Cohort characteristics

	All observations	Males		Females
		Married	Single	Single
Cohort members	12,058	5,050	3,662	3,346
Age	55	55	55	55
	(0)	(0)	(0)	(0)
Age of spouse	51.5	51.5	n.a.	n.a.
	(3.9)	(3.9)		
APE at age 55	19,337	21,717	20,597	14,364
	(7,072)	(5,696)	(6,311)	(7,850)
APE of spouse at age 55	5,782	13,807	n.a.	n.a.
	(8,820)	(8,820)		
RPP probability	0.537	0.578	0.570	0.439
	(0.266)	(0.258)	(0.255)	(0.263)
Labor market experience	12.5	13.0	12.7	11.4
	(3.4)	(3.0)	(3.2)	(3.9)
Labor market experience of spouse	11.4	11.4	n.a.	n.a.
	(6.3)	(6.3)		
Tenure	8.4	9.1	8.3	7.6
	(5.1)	(5.0)	(5.2)	(5.1)

Notes: Spousal characteristics averaged only over families with spouses. APE is expressed in 2001 euros.

pare the value of benefits paid out to the cohort under the base and reform IS systems. We account for taxes in order to show the full fiscal impact of the reformed IS systems. If a reform induces workers to stay in the labor force longer, then these workers will pay more in income taxes, payroll taxes, and consumption taxes. These tax effects can have a substantial impact on government balances, as will be shown in our results.

Taxes pay for public expenditures other than IS benefits, so the *level* of tax revenue has no meaningful comparison with the *level* of IS benefits. Instead, the inferences we draw come from the *difference* in tax revenue under different reforms. Presumably, any extra work induced by the reforms would have little impact on other demands for government spending, and so would be a windfall gain to the government's budget.

The IS and taxation system we consider is the one that prevailed in 1991. The methodology we employ assumes that this system remains constant in real terms into the future. Since 1991, the structure of the IS system remains largely unchanged, although some program parameters have changed.[24] This may have some impact on the *levels* of the IS calculations

24. The 1997 reform of the CPP/QPP system implemented several incremental changes in the calculation of benefits, but kept the core structure of actuarially adjusted earnings-related benefits replacing about 25 percent of preretirement earnings for average workers.

we make, but our inferences about how IS reform would change retirement behavior are relevant so long as the structure of the IS system takes the same basic form.

We calculate the three types of taxes in the following way. First, our treatment of income taxes includes both provincial and federal income taxes. Income taxes depend on the level of CPP/QPP benefits, OAS benefits, labor market income, and nonlabor income assigned to each individual in the family under a particular IS system. Payroll taxes are calculated based on labor market income. We account for the CPP/QPP payroll tax and the Employment Insurance payroll tax.[25] Both the employer and the employee portions are counted. Finally, for consumption taxes, we calculate a consumption tax factor that relates the proportion of consumption taxes to disposable income.[26] This factor is applied to the calculated after-tax income of our cohort families to estimate the proportion of their income that will end up as consumption tax revenue.

The assumptions about the impact of changes in work on government revenue are necessarily imperfect. For example, we do not treat the impact that an increase in labor supply might have on corporate profit and the resulting taxation of profit. As well, our treatment of consumption taxes is relatively crude. For these reasons, the resulting calculations should be interpreted only as illustrative of the effect changes in the IS system could have on tax revenues.

The benefit and tax flows must be calculated for forty-eight different states of the world, representing the different possible modes of exit from the labor market as described immediately following. The flows will be combined with the probabilities of being in each state to arrive at a value for the PDV of future benefit and tax flows for each family in our selected cohort.

Our point of departure is the observation that each member of the cohort will leave the labor force at some age between 55 and 78. This exit may take place by an exit to retirement or by an exit to death. These differing modes and ages for exit therefore comprise forty-eight different states of the world. From the point of exit forward, a DNPV calculation of future IS flows can be made to arrive at the *ISW* associated with each particular labor market exit state. If the probability for each state is known, then the total DNPV of all future IS flows from the point of view of the original

25. In 1991, the CPP/QPP payroll tax was 2.3 percent of earned income between $3,050 and $30,500. This 2.3 percent rate was levied both on employers and on employees, so the total tax rate was 4.6 percent. The Employment Insurance payroll tax was set for 1991 at $2.52 per $100 of earnings up to a cap of $35,360 for employees, and $3.53 on the same base for employers.

26. Personal Disposable Income from the national accounts for 1991 was $473,918 million (CANSIM II series V691803). Total consumption taxes at all levels of government for fiscal year 1991/1992 was $59,554 million (CANSIM II series V156262). Personal Disposable Income is reported net of indirect taxes, so the calculated consumption tax factor is [$59,554 million/($473,918 million − $59,554 million)] = 0.1115.

cohort when they are 55 can be calculated as an average of the state-specific *ISW,* using the probabilities as weights in an expected-value calculation.

The first task is to calculate the flow of IS payments, income taxes, and CPP/QPP premiums associated with each of the forty-eight states. We implement this by calculating, for each age between 55 and 102, the IS flows for both the cohort member and the spouse. All future IS flows are discounted back to age 55 for time preference at a real 3 percent rate. For ages past age 55, we project forward earnings as constant in real terms from age 55.

The flows we calculate are conditional upon the state under consideration. For example, consider the "exit to retirement at 67" state. We assume that the worker is in the labor force until age 66 and then retires at age 67. We account for benefits and taxes both before and after age 67—income taxes, CPP/QPP premiums, and GIS payments may occur in years prior to reaching age 67. We also assume that the worker is alive until at least age 67. In other words, benefits and taxes are received and paid with probability 1 until age 67, then using the life tables conditional on having reached age 67 for ages beyond 67. The probability of the worker dying before having reached age 67 will be accounted for in the construction of the probability of being in the "exit to retirement at age 67" state. The output of these calculations is the family level of IS payments, income taxes, and CPP/QPP premiums from the point of view of age 55 corresponding to each of the forty-eight states.

2.4.3   Calculating the Probabilities

To arrive at the expected value of future IS flows from age 55, we must average the flows received in each state using the probabilities associated with each state. The calculation of the flows associated with each state has been described previously. The probabilities can be calculated using the output of the models discussed in section 2.3. For each member of the cohort, we take the member's observed characteristics (age, province, tenure, etc.) and combine them with the estimated parameters displayed in tables 2.1 and 2.2 to generate a predicted probability of labor market exit. The key component of this calculation is the set of IS incentive variables. We must calculate the IS incentive variables for each potential age of exit, from age 55 to 78. The IS incentive variables can then be combined with the member's observed characteristics and the parameter estimates from our retirement model to obtain the predicted probability of labor market exit at each age from 55 to 78.

Predicting retirement after age 69 presents a challenge. Our empirical model estimated the retirement behavior of workers from age 55 to 69. For ages past 69, we therefore use the conditional probability of exit at age 69 for all ages from 69 on. This assumption has little impact on our overall fiscal measurements, since the probability of remaining in the labor force until age 69 is typically less than 1 percent in our simulations. This means that little weight is placed on these labor market exit states.

In our data, we cannot distinguish between death and retirement—individuals are observed as long as they receive T-4 forms. To decompose our predicted probability of labor market exit into a probability of exit to retirement and a probability of exit to death, we draw upon the age-contingent life tables. At each age we subtract the actuarial probability of death at that age from the predicted probability of labor market exit to obtain the predicted probability of retirement for that age.

The next step in computing the state probabilities is to transform the conditional age-specific exit rates to unconditional probabilities for each state. Starting with 100 percent probability of survival at age 55, the conditional probabilities of exit to retirement and to death at each age are multiplied by the remaining probability of survival. For example, if the probabilities for exits to death and to retirement are 0.02 and 0.05 at age 55, then those probabilities are multiplied by the probability of survival to age 55 (which is 1.0) to arrive at the probabilities for the age-55 states. For age 56, the conditional probabilities for exit at age 56 are multiplied by 0.93, which is the probability that the cohort member survived to age 56 (1.0–0.02–0.05). This delivers the state probabilities for age 56. Continuing in this way, the state probabilities for each age to 78 can be calculated.

2.4.4 Spouses

Spouses add a complication to these calculations. In our previous analysis, we held the spouse's retirement decision fixed at the first age of eligibility for retirement benefits, in order to avoid the complexity of modeling joint retirement decisions. For the simulation calculations we take a similar approach, assuming that any spouse retires at the age of first pension eligibility. As a check on this decision, we investigated a more flexible approach on a small subsample. We averaged each of the forty-eight state probabilities and flows over the forty-eight possible labor market exit states of the spouse. These simulations showed little change in the retirement incentives of our cohort members, compared to simulations with the fixed date of spousal retirement. This reflects two features of our situation. First, there is not a great deal of interspousal dependence of benefits in Canada. Second, the assumption of retirement at the date of first eligibility is a good approximation of average spousal behavior. Given this evidence, we proceeded with the use of the fixed spousal retirement assumption.

2.4.5 Reforms

In addition to performing these calculations for Canada's existing IS system, we also use this methodology to examine the impact of changes to the IS system. The motivation for analyzing these reforms is not to advocate for a particular structure for Canada's IS system, but instead to demonstrate the magnitude and shape of the fiscal effects of reforms. We contemplate two possible reforms. The first reform increases all age-specific entitlement ages by three years. The second involves a shift to a common system that is the same across all countries in the project.[27]

Three-Year Reform

Eligibility for all components of Canada's IS system is at least partly determined by age. In the Three-Year Reform, we raise the key entitlement ages by three years. For the CPP/QPP, this means that the first possible age of receipt of early retirement benefits is increased to 63, and the normal retirement age is increased to 68. The age of GIS and OAS entitlement also shifts up to 68. Finally, the Allowance is available to qualifying individuals between the ages of 63 and 67.

The Three-Year Reform should affect the level of *ISW*. Removing three years of eligibility from a worker's future benefit flows decreases the total value of future flows, meaning a lower level of *ISW*. Because our models predict a positive wealth effect on retirement decisions, this should lead to a shift toward later retirements.

The effects of this reform on dynamic incentives are both obvious and subtle. The obvious effect is a three-year shift in the age-dependent incentives of the IS system. For example, each dollar of labor market earnings reduce GIS entitlements by 50 cents (single) or 25 cents (married). Under the Three-Year Reform, this large disincentive for continued work is delayed until age 68. Similarly, the dynamic incentives at age 60 due to the availability of early retirement benefits is now delayed to age 63.

More subtly, the Three-Year Reform should also attenuate the magnitude of all dynamic incentives. Any change in the future yearly flow of pension entitlements caused by an extra year of work will have an impact over fewer years of pension receipt. This suggests that both retirement-inducing and retirement-delaying incentives will be smaller. Combined with the predictions about the effect of the reform on the level of *ISW*, we expect that the Three-Year Reform will lead to a substantial shift toward later retirements.

Common Reform

The second reform imposes a common program structure on each country in this project. We therefore refer to it as the *Common Reform*. It involves a single, earnings-related public pension. The pension is based on average real lifetime earnings calculated over the best forty years. We only have twenty-six-year earnings histories for our cohort when we first observe them at age 55,[28] so the average is constructed over the number of

27. Other countries in this project also simulated a reform with actuarially adjusted benefits. For the case of Canada, the actuarial adjustment reform replicated exactly the existing Canadian income security system, rendering these simulations uninformative for Canada.

28. Our data include earnings histories constructed back to the onset of the CPP/QPP programs in 1966. Our selected cohort is 55 in 1991, meaning that we have only twenty-six years of earnings for these workers.

years of work until they reach forty years of work, and then the best forty years thereafter. Wages are converted to constant dollars using a real-wage index.[29] The amount of the normal pension is set at 60 percent of the calculated average lifetime earnings. The normal age of retirement in the Common Reform is age 65. Early retirement benefits are available from age 60, subject to an actuarial adjustment of 6 percent per year. A survivor benefit is paid, equal to the worker benefit. However, a person is not entitled to both a survivor benefit and a retirement pension at the same time—only the larger of the two is received.

Relative to Canada's current IS system, the Common Reform eliminates the GIS, Allowance, and OAS benefits. The benefit structure is very similar, however, to that of the CPP/QPP, although with a much larger replacement rate. Because there is no cap to pensionable earnings, high earners should receive a much higher pension than they do under the existing Canadian system. In contrast, low earners will do poorly under the Common Reform, as all benefits become earnings dependent, in contrast to the existing Canadian system with its earnings-independent demogrants.

The effects of the Common Reform on retirement incentives are not as straightforward as for the Three-Year Reform. The level of ISW may increase for high earners but decrease for low earners. With the higher earnings replacement rate, the incentive for extra years of work should be larger than in the existing CPP/QPP, where the replacement rate is 25 percent and capped for high earners. The early and normal retirement ages, as well as the early retirement adjustment of 6 percent per year, coincide exactly with the structure of the CPP/QPP. Finally, the elimination of the income-tested benefits will remove their dynamic retirement incentives.

2.4.6   The Effects of Age

In section 2.3, we noted the difficulties in interpreting the estimates of the age-dummy variables in our empirical models. The ambiguity is potentially very important for our simulations of the Three-Year Reform, in which we change the age structure of the IS incentives. As a consequence, we implement two strategies that imply very different interpretations in investigating this reform. In the first, we do not shift the age dummies as the entitlement ages increase. Here we assume that any age-specific propensities for retirement, as captured by the age dummies, are independent of the parameters of the IS system. In the second strategy, we instead shift the age dummies three years forward in parallel with the shift in program eligibility ages. The estimated coefficient on the age-55 dummy becomes the dummy for age 58, the age-56 dummy becomes the dummy for age 59, and

---

29. The real wage index was created using the Industrial Composite Wage from 1966 to 1984, followed by the Industrial Average Wage from 1984 to 1998, along with the Consumer Price Index. These are derived from Statistics Canada (1983) and Statistics Canada (2000).

so on.[30] Here we allow the possibility that the age dummies capture latent effects of the IS system, and so are sensitive to the age parameters of the IS system.

2.4.7   Decomposition

The total effect of reforms to Canada's retirement income system can be decomposed into two effects. To show this, we first express the total effect of the reform as the difference of the "reform" IS flows and the "base" IS flows:

$$\text{Total effect} = \sum_{s=1}^{48} P_s^R ISW_s^R - \sum_{s=1}^{48} P_s^B ISW_s^B$$

The superscripts R and B index the reform case and the base case. The labor market exit states are indexed by s. For each state s, there is a probability P_s and a discounted flow of IS payments, ISW_s.

We decompose the total effect by adding and subtracting a term that combines the reform IS payments and the base probabilities:

$$\text{Total effect} = \left(\sum_{s=1}^{48} P_s^R ISW_s^R - \sum_{s=1}^{48} P_s^B ISW_s^R \right) + \left(\sum_{s=1}^{48} P_s^B ISW_s^R - \sum_{s=1}^{48} P_s^B ISW_s^B \right)$$

The second bracketed term we call the *mechanical effect*. It measures the difference in the discounted flows between the new and the old IS systems, holding retirement behavior constant. This is the cost to the treasury of increased (or decreased) pension payments, with an assumption of static behavior. The first bracketed term we call the *fiscal implications of the behavioral effect*. Here, holding ISW constant, we measure the effect of the change in the timing of retirement induced by the reform.

2.5   Results

We present three simulations for each of two measures of retirement incentives. The first simulation is based on the estimates for the empirical model with the linear control for age. The second is based on the estimates for the model with age dummies, but assumes that the effect of age as captured by the estimates of the dummies does not shift in tandem with the reforms (as discussed in section 2.4.6). Finally, in the third we again use the age dummy model, but assume the effects of age shift upward by three years in the Three-Year Reform. Finally, for each of these simulations we present both peak value and option value results.

The main results appear in tables 2.4 and 2.5. Going down each table, the six panels correspond to the six simulations outlined previously. Going

---

30. For ages 55 to 57, we apply the estimated coefficient on the age-55 dummy, as coefficients on dummy variables from earlier ages were not estimated.

Table 2.4   **Total fiscal impact of reform**

	Present discounted value			Total change relative to base (%)	
	Base	Three-Year	Common	Three-Year Reform	Common Reform
Peak value—linear age					
Benefits	111,106	91,328	192,515	−17.8	73.3
Taxes					
Payroll	15,202	17,446	14,952	14.8	−1.6
Income	81,687	88,243	104,174	8.0	27.5
Consumption	37,595	37,878	43,529	0.8	15.8
Total	134,485	143,567	162,655	6.8	20.9
Peak value—age dummies (no shift)					
Benefits	110,720	91,062	192,179	−17.8	73.6
Taxes					
Payroll	14,886	15,788	15,824	6.1	6.3
Income	80,334	81,294	111,991	1.2	39.4
Consumption	37,296	36,388	44,530	−2.4	19.4
Total	132,516	133,470	172,345	0.7	30.1
Peak value—age dummies (with shift)					
Benefit	110,720	91,182	192,179	−17.6	73.6
Taxes					
Payroll	14,886	16,564	15,824	11.3	6.3
Income	80,334	84,542	111,991	5.2	39.4
Consumption	37,296	37,099	44,530	−0.5	19.4
Total	132,516	138,205	172,345	4.3	30.1
Option value—linear age					
Benefit	111,084	91,491	187,796	−17.6	69.1
Taxes					
Payroll	15,182	16,821	12,537	10.8	−17.4
Income	81,313	85,075	93,608	4.6	15.1
Consumption	37,540	37,265	41,314	−0.7	10.1
Total	134,034	139,161	147,459	3.8	10.0
Option value—age dummies (no shift)					
Benefits	110,698	91,218	189,449	−17.6	71.1
Taxes					
Payroll	15,029	15,666	14,503	4.2	−3.5
Income	80,746	80,427	106,679	−0.4	32.1
Consumption	37,394	36,245	43,370	−3.1	16.0
Total	133,170	132,338	164,552	−0.6	23.6
Option value—age dummies (with shift)					
Benefits	110,698	91,332	189,449	−17.5	71.1
Taxes					
Payroll	15,029	16,216	14,503	7.9	−3.5
Income	80,746	82,646	106,679	2.4	32.1
Consumption	37,394	36,747	43,370	−1.7	16.0
Total	133,170	135,609	164,552	1.8	23.6

Notes: All values reported in 2001 euros. The first three columns show the PDV of benefits and taxes under the base plan and under the two illustrative reforms. The last two columns show the change relative to the base, for benefits and taxes. Each of the six panels down the table shows the results from a different simulation model.

Table 2.5   **Decomposition of the total effect of reform**

| | Change in present discounted value | | | | | |
| | Three-Year Reform | | | Common Reform | | |
	Mechanical	Behavioral	Total	Mechanical	Behavioral	Total
	Peak value—linear age					
Benefits	−19,481	−297	−19,778	78,881	2,528	81,409
Taxes: Total	−4,784	13,866	9,083	36,115	−7,944	28,171
Net change	−14,697	−14,163	−28,860	42,766	10,472	53,238
Change as % of						
base benefits	−13.2	−12.7	−26.0	38.5	9.4	47.9
	Peak value—age dummies (no shift)					
Benefit	−19,524	−134	−19,658	78,008	3,451	81,459
Taxes: Total	−4,762	5,716	954	35,684	4,145	39,829
Net change	−14,762	−5,850	−20,613	42,323	−693	41,630
Change as % of						
base benefits	−13.3	−5.3	−18.6	38.2	−0.6	37.6
	Peak value—age dummies (with shift)					
Benefits	−19,524	−14	−19,538	78,008	3,451	81,459
Taxes: Total	−4,762	10,451	5,689	35,684	4,145	39,829
Net change	−14,762	−10,464	−25,227	42,323	−693	41,630
Change as % of						
base benefits	−13.3	−9.5	−22.8	38.2	−0.6	37.6
	Option value—linear age					
Benefits	−19,459	−134	−19,593	79,151	−2,438	76,713
Taxes: Total	−4,778	9,905	5,127	36,231	−22,806	13,425
Net change	−14,681	−10,039	−24,720	42,920	20,368	63,287
Change as % of						
base benefits	−13.2	−9.0	−22.3	38.6	18.3	57.0
	Option value—age dummies (no shift)					
Benefit	−19,452	−28	−19,480	78,502	250	78,751
Taxes: Total	−4,753	3,921	−832	35,955	−4,572	31,383
Net change	−14,699	−3,949	−18,648	42,547	4,822	47,369
Change as % of						
base benefits	−13.3	−3.6	−16.8	38.4	4.4	42.8
	Option value—age dummies (with shift)					
Benefit	−19,452	86	−19,366	78,502	250	78,751
Taxes: Total	−4,753	7,192	2,440	35,955	−4,572	31,383
Net change	−14,699	−7,106	−21,805	42,547	4,822	47,369
Change as % of						
base benefits	−13.3	−6.4	−19.7	38.4	4.4	42.8

Notes: All values reported in 2001 euros. The table shows the total effect of the reform (shown in table 2.4) decomposed into mechanical and behavioral components. The first row shows the change in benefits. The second row shows the change in all taxes. The third row shows the net change (the change in benefits minus the change in taxes). The fourth row shows the net change as a percent of base benefits (shown in table 2.4).

across table 2.4, we present the simulated levels of benefits and taxes under the base system as well as the reform systems. Going across table 2.5, the total change is decomposed into its behavioral and mechanical components. Within each panel, we show the total PDV of benefits and taxes separately. In table 2.4, the tax total is broken down into its payroll, income, and consumption components. All values have been converted to 2001 Euros, using the December 31, 2001, exchange rate of C$1.4185 = €1.00.

2.5.1 Base System Results

In the first column of table 2.4 we present the base IS system results. For the peak value—linear age simulation, the PDV of benefits totals €111,106 per working family. The payroll tax total of €15,202 is lower than may be the case for other countries, reflecting Canada's relatively low rates of payroll tax. To put this in context, a single worker earning the average industrial wage in 1991 would have generated payroll tax revenue for the government in the 1991 fiscal year of about €2,704. The PDV of income taxes for the average family in our cohort is €81,687. Taking the difference of taxable income and the taxes paid by the cohort families, we estimate a total PDV of after-tax income of €337,225. When multiplied by the consumption tax factor of 0.1115, we arrive at the estimate for the PDV of consumption tax revenues of €37,595. The total PDV of the three sources of tax revenue generated by the cohort families from age 55 on is €134,485.

While the total tax revenue is larger than the future benefits, it must be recalled that tax revenue funds other government spending in addition to the IS system. As well, the tax revenue generated by the family before age 55 is not included in this calculation. For these reasons, no inferences about the sustainability of Canada's IS system can be drawn from these totals.

Looking down the six panels in table 2.4, there is little variation in the calculations across simulations. The age dummy simulations with and without the shift are identical for the base case because the age dummies do not shift in calculating the base case exit probabilities.

2.5.2 Three-Year Reform

The Three-Year Reform raises all of the critical entitlement ages in the IS system by three years. Figures 2.1 and 2.2 show the age profile of the PDV of benefits and taxes, respectively. Two observations are noteworthy. First, the age profile of IS benefits is quite flat. This reflects the actuarial adjustment made to CPP/QPP benefits, and the fact that OAS and GIS benefits are paid independent of participation in the labor market. In contrast, the age profile of taxes slopes steeply upward. Lifetime taxes are higher for those exiting the labor market at older ages, because they have more years of labor market earnings that are subject to income and payroll taxes. The second observation relates to the differences between the base case and

Fig. 2.1   Income security wealth by age of labor force exit, Three-Year Reform

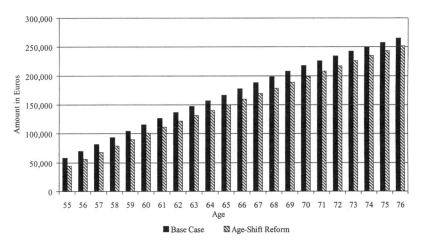

Fig. 2.2   Total taxes by age of labor force exit, Three-Year Reform

Three-Year Reform. The gap between the base case and the reform case diminishes with age. This is generated by the fewer years of expected future pension receipt for those retiring later.

The peak value—linear age panel of table 2.4 reveals that this reform would cut benefit levels to €91,328, which is 17.8 percent less than the base IS system level of benefits. However, all three types of tax revenue for the government would increase under the reform, with the total rising by 6.8 percent. This increase is driven by a large increase in payroll tax and income tax revenues.

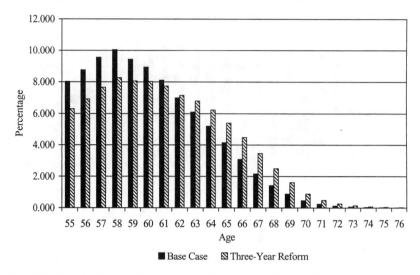

Fig. 2.3   Distribution of retirement ages: Three-Year Reform, option value—linear age

Underlying these increases in tax revenues is an increase in work generated by the reform. This can be clearly seen in figure 2.3. The distribution of retirement ages shifts out to the right, as the reform provides incentives to spend more years in the labor force. The incentive is provided both by the wealth effect of lower lifetime IS benefits and by an increase in the average peak value dynamic incentive measure, as the age at which peak benefits are reached moves to older ages.

In table 2.5, the total changes are broken down into the mechanical effect and the behavioral effect. Benefits drop mostly because of the mechanical effect. With no change in behavior, the government will save money by paying three fewer years of pension benefits. The small behavioral effect reflects the approximate actuarial fairness of the CPP/QPP system. Even though workers are retiring later, the PDV of their benefits changes little.

The extra work generated by the reform has a larger impact on tax revenues. Overall, tax revenues increase by €9,083. The mechanical effect is negative, as taxable income falls with the decrease in lifetime IS benefits. However, the behavioral effect captures the increase in government revenues generated by the increased work under the reform.

The importance of considering tax revenues is made clear in figure 2.4. We graph the total effect by age, for both the gross ISW benefits and the net of taxes ISW. The gross ISW in the darker bars is negative through age 63, reflecting the mechanical savings and the behavioral savings as retirement shifts later. However, starting at age 64, the total effect on gross IS benefits

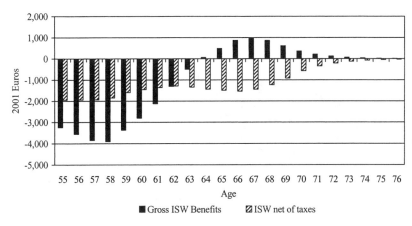

Fig. 2.4   Total effect by age of retirement: Three-Year Reform, option value—linear age

becomes positive. This is generated by the behavioral effect. Under the reform, there is now more retirement at later ages than under the base case. This increases the cost of IS benefits to the government for those retiring at later ages.

The light bars in figure 2.4 show the PDV of IS benefits less the PDV of taxes. Even when the gross IS benefits show a cost to the government after age 63, the light bars still show an overall decrease in the government's fiscal outflow. The difference is the extra work that is generated by the reform. Those who are shifting to retirement at later ages now work more years, which generates more tax revenue for the government. So, even though the actuarially adjusted IS benefits of later retirees costs the government more, the taxes they pay until they retire overcompensates for the increased IS benefit cost.

Overall, the net fiscal balance of the government under the Three-Year Reform changes by €28,860 per family, or 26 percent of the base level of benefits. Importantly, almost half of the 26 percent change is accounted for by the behavioral effect. In other words, an analysis that assumes static retirement behavior would underestimate the fiscal effects of the Three-Year Reform by about half.

The age-dummy simulations are quite informative for the Three-Year Reform. Looking first at table 2.4, the predicted benefit level for peak value in the age-dummy simulations is approximately the same as for the linear age simulation. The taxes, however, show some differences. For the no-shift simulation, the total taxes increase by only 0.7 percent, compared to 6.8 percent for the linear age simulation. The with-shift simulation shows an increase of 4.3 percent in tax revenues.

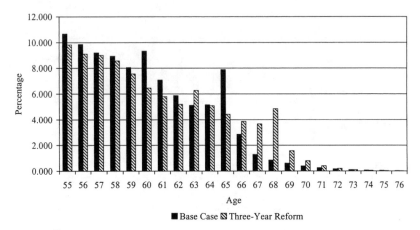

Fig. 2.5   Distribution of retirement ages: Three-Year Reform, option value—age dummies (with shift)

An explanation for these tax revenue differences can be found in table 2.5. The mechanical effect for the two dummy-shift simulations is identical, as expected. In the no-shift simulation, the behavioral effect is driven only by the changes in IS incentives. Here, the behavioral effect on taxes is smaller than in the linear age case at €5,716. However, for the with-shift simulation, the behavioral effect is nearly twice as large, at €10,451. This suggests that the shift in the age dummies generates only half of the behavioral effect. In other words, even with the seemingly strong assumption that age-related retirement propensities do not change when the normal retirement age changes, we still generate a substantial behavioral effect for taxes of €5,716 per family.

In figures 2.5 and 2.6, the age dummy simulations are graphed. These figures follow similar trends as the linear age graphs, but less smoothly, as particular ages have stronger effects. For example, there is a spike in pre-reform retirement at age 65 that moves to age 68 in the with-shift age dummy graph in both figure 2.5 and figure 2.6.

The overall net fiscal savings for government implied by the two age-dummy simulations is 18.6 percent of base benefits for the no-shift case and 22.8 percent for the with-shift case. The two biggest contributors to these changes are the mechanical effect on benefits as workers are entitled to fewer years of benefit receipt, and the behavioral effect on taxes as workers have higher lifetime earnings.

The option-value simulations in the bottom three panels of tables 2.4 and 2.5 show a similar pattern as the peak-value simulations for the Three-Year Reform. The overall change in net benefits as a percent of base benefits is 22.3 percent for the linear age simulation. For the age-dummy simu-

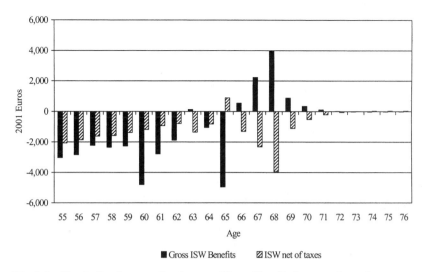

Fig. 2.6   Total effect by age of retirement: Three-Year Reform, option value—age dummies (with shift)

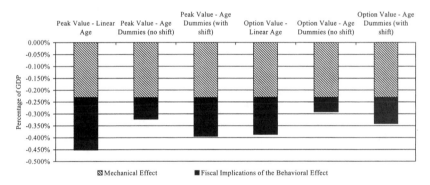

Fig. 2.7   Fiscal implications of reform as a percent of GDP: Three-Year Reform

lations, the no-shift case shows a smaller behavioral effect than the with-shift case.

We present the mechanical and behavioral effects for all six simulations graphically as a percentage of 2001 GDP in figure 2.7. Our sample is based on a 10 percent sample of the Canadian labor force outside the primary sector, so we arrived at the totals by summing over all 12,058 cohort members and multiplying by ten. The behavioral effect totals €1.7 billion and the mechanical effect totals €1.8 billion for the peak value—linear age simulation. Together, the two effects sum to about 0.45 percent of Canada's €770 billion GDP in 2001.

For both peak value and option value, the largest behavioral effect is found in the linear age specification. In both cases, this is caused by a larger wealth effect driven by a higher estimated ISW coefficient. The second and third bars show the difference between the age-dummies results with and without the age-dummy shift. As these two cases represent the two extreme assumptions for the treatment of the age dummies, they therefore bound the magnitude of the behavioral effect in the age-dummies simulations.

2.5.3   Common Reform

The Common Reform gives workers a benefit based on 60 percent of the average of their best forty years of lifetime earnings. Table 2.4 reveals that this reform has a large wealth effect. For the peak value linear age simulation, the level of benefits increases by 73.3 percent. The extra taxable income generated by the higher benefits leads to increases in income tax revenue and consumption tax revenue. However, payroll tax revenue declines under the reform. This suggests that the reform decreases the amount of work—that it leads to earlier retirement.

Figures 2.8 and 2.9 explore the Common Reform graphically. First, figure 2.8 shows the dramatic increase in IS benefits under the reform. Figure 2.9 shows the shift to earlier ages of retirement in the distribution of retirement ages under the option value–linear age specification. We now look into the source of this large shift to earlier retirement ages.

In table 2.5 we decompose the total effect of the Common Reform into the behavioral and mechanical effect. For benefits, the mechanical effect is much larger than the behavioral effect. The benefits paid under the Common Reform, at 60 percent of lifetime earnings, replace a higher proportion of earnings than the existing Canadian IS system. Like the Three-Year Reform, the larger behavioral effects can be seen in tax revenue. For the

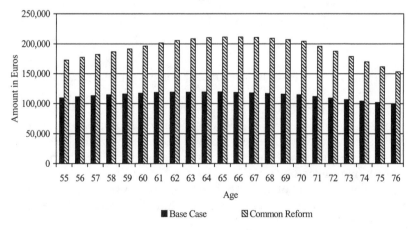

Fig. 2.8   Income security wealth by age of labor force exit, Common Reform

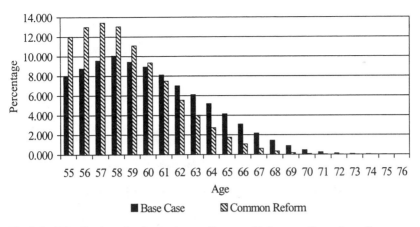

Fig. 2.9   Distribution of retirement ages: Common Reform, option value—linear age

peak value–linear age simulation, tax revenue falls by €7,944 per family because of the behavioral effect. With the age-dummy simulation, however, the drop in tax revenue is reversed.

The explanation for this difference lies in the relative strengths of the wealth effect and the dynamic incentive effect. The average value for peak value over our sample in the base case was €779. With the Common Reform, this increased to €4,370. Given the negative coefficient on peak value in tables 2.1 and 2.2, this implies a shift toward later retirement. In contrast, the wealth effect of the Common Reform shifts retirement in the other direction, as more wealth leads to a desire to retire earlier. However, as can be seen in tables 2.1 and 2.2, the magnitude of the coefficient on *ISW* falls dramatically between the linear age and the age-dummy estimates, from 0.077 to 0.022 for males and similarly for females. So, the wealth effect of the Common Reform dominates the dynamic effect for the linear age simulation, but with the small estimated coefficient on *ISW* for the age-dummy simulation, the dynamic incentive effect is able to dominate the wealth effect and retirement pushes later.

For the option value simulations, the decrease in work under the reform is stronger. Again, the wealth effect of *ISW* leads to earlier retirement. However, in contrast to the peak value case, the dynamic incentive of the option value is not able to overcome the wealth effect. So, the net effect is a larger decrease in work. The difference between the linear age and age-dummy simulations for option value are driven by the same factor as for peak value—the change in the *ISW* coefficient in tables 2.1 and 2.2.

In figure 2.10 we summarize the total impact of the Common Reform as a percent of GDP. In all six cases, the large increase in benefits under the Common Reform leads to a very large mechanical effect that increases the cost of the retirement income security system. The fiscal implications of

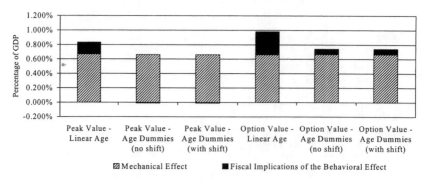

Fig. 2.10   Fiscal implications of reform as a percent of GDP: Common Reform

the behavioral effect, however, are positive only in the cases for which the wealth effect, inducing earlier retirement, outweighs the dynamic incentive effect. Overall, this reform would result in a large increase in the size of the retirement income system in Canada.

2.6   Distribution

In addition to looking at the shifts in behavior and the fiscal costs of IS reform, we can use our simulation models to examine how the two reforms affect the distribution of IS payments. We split our cohort families into quintiles based on the average lifetime income index described previously for the Common Reform. For married families, we use the sum of husband and wife income. For single cohort members, we use only the member's income. We rank the families based on this income measure separately for married and single families, so that an equal proportion of married and single families is in each quintile. The highest-income quintile of the single group is combined with the top one fifth of families from the married group to comprise quintile 1. Quintiles 2 through 5 are formed in a similar way, progressing to the lowest-income households in quintile 5.

Table 2.6 presents the distributional analysis for the option value–linear age simulations, and table 2.7 the option value–age dummy (with shift) simulations. The five quintiles appear in the five panels of each table. Across the table, we present the levels of the PDV of benefits and taxes as well as the changes relative to the base for each reform.

The linear age simulations in table 2.6 show that the base PDV of benefits is remarkably stable across quintiles. This stability reflects several aspects of Canada's IS system. First, only earnings up to the YMPE are insured by the CPP/QPP pensions. Since the YMPE is set close to median earnings, this means that lifetime earnings above the median will result in no additional CPP/QPP benefits. Second, the only part of the Canadian system that is related to lifetime earnings is the CPP/QPP component—

Table 2.6   **Distribution analysis: Option value—linear age**

	Present discounted value			Change relative to base PDV	
	Base	Three-Year	Common	Three-Year Reform	Common Reform
Quintile 1 (highest)					
Benefits	117,795	96,466	311,682	−21,329	193,888
Taxes: Total	239,146	252,177	253,924	13,032	14,778
Net change				−34,360	179,110
Change as % of base benefits				−29.2	152.1
Quintile 2					
Benefits	119,857	98,303	248,739	−21,554	128,882
Taxes: Total	134,394	140,252	158,074	5,858	23,680
Net change				−27,411	105,203
Change as % of base benefits				−22.9	87.8
Quintile 3					
Benefits	116,664	95,717	187,970	−20,946	71,306
Taxes: Total	117,619	121,447	133,518	3,828	15,898
Net change				−24,774	55,408
Change in % of base benefits				−21.2	47.5
Quintile 4					
Benefits	109,254	90,276	129,602	−18,978	20,348
Taxes: Total	105,408	107,734	114,728	2,326	9,320
Net change				−21,304	11,028
Change as % of base benefits				−19.5	10.1
Quintile 5 (lowest)					
Benefits	91,843	76,002	60,987	−15,841	−30,856
Taxes: Total	73,622	74,216	77,069	594	3,447
Net change				−16,435	−34,303
Change as % of base benefits				−17.9	−37.3

Note: All values reported in 2001 euros. The first three columns show the PDV of benefits and taxes under the base plan and under the two illustrative reforms. The last two columns show the change relative to the base, for benefits and taxes. Each of the five panels down the table shows the results for a different lifetime income quintile, from highest to lowest.

and it replaces a smaller share of the total IS system than do earnings-related benefits in other countries. Third, the income-tested components of the IS system tend to compensate those with lower lifetime earnings. Finally, higher-income individuals will be subject to higher rates of income taxation as well as potentially face the clawback of OAS benefits. Combined, these factors make the profile of IS benefits very flat with respect to changes in lifetime earnings.

Taxes, on the other hand, show a progressive pattern. The larger tax

Table 2.7   Distribution analysis: Option value—age dummies (with shift)

	Present discounted value			Change relative to base PDV	
	Base	Three-Year	Common	Three-Year Reform	Common Reform
		Quintile 1 (highest)			
Benefits	117,647	97,205	313,903	−20,442	196,256
Taxes: Total	236,465	243,786	301,467	7,321	65,003
Net change				−27,764	131,253
Change as % of base benefits				−23.6	111.6
		Quintile 2			
Benefits	119,630	97,971	253,096	−21,659	133,466
Taxes: Total	133,067	135,948	181,308	2,881	48,241
Net change				−24,540	85,225
Change as % of base benefits				−20.5	71.2
		Quintile 3			
Benefits	116,343	95,419	190,649	−20,924	74,306
Taxes: Total	116,907	118,519	146,348	1,613	29,441
Net change				−22,536	44,865
Change as % of base benefits				−19.4	38.6
		Quintile 4			
Benefits	108,572	90,108	129,795	−18,464	21,223
Taxes: Total	105,572	106,224	118,983	652	13,410
Net change				−19,116	7,812
Change as % of base benefits				−17.6	7.2
		Quintile 5 (lowest)			
Benefits	91,294	75,956	59,802	−15,339	−31,492
Taxes: Total	73,857	73,587	74,676	−269	819
Net change				−15,069	−32,311
Change as % of base benefits				−16.5	−35.4

Note: See table 2.6 notes.

levels in the higher-income quintiles reflect higher levels of CPP/QPP benefits, labor income while still in the labor force, and nonlabor income. As we move down the table to the lower-income quintiles, these sources of income are replaced with nontaxable Guaranteed Income Supplement (GIS) and Spouse Allowance (SPA) benefits.

The Three-Year Reform does not dramatically alter this pattern of distribution. Benefits are relatively flat across the earnings distribution, while taxes increase sharply with lifetime earnings. The net benefits drop in all quintiles. The percentage decrease follows a monotonic pattern, with the highest decrease in the first quintile and the lowest decrease in the fifth quintile. This suggests that a reform to delay benefit receipt by three years may be progressive.

The Common Reform has a very different impact on distribution. First-quintile households have their insurable earnings capped at a much higher level under the Common Reform than is the case in the status quo CPP/QPP, resulting in much higher benefits. The first-quintile households have almost no changes in their taxes, however. This result stems from the huge wealth effect on retirement implied by the large estimated income security wealth (ISW) coefficient combined with the large change in ISW. Government tax revenue does not increase, because they lose income and payroll taxes on the labor that is no longer provided by this quintile. Overall, the effect on the first quintile is a net increase of 156.2 percent over base benefits.

Further down the income distribution, the effect of the Common Reform is far less generous. For the fifth quintile, the replacement of the income-tested benefits and the OAS demogrant by a pure earnings-related benefit decreases the average level of benefits by one third. This has a wealth effect on their labor supply, causing them to work more. This generates more income and payroll tax revenue for the government than in the base case for this quintile. These households suffer a drop of 37.8 percent of base benefits under this reform.

The distribution analysis is repeated for the option value–age dummy simulations in table 2.7. The patterns are very similar to those in table 2.6, using peak value. The primary difference lies in the smaller magnitudes of the responses to the reforms across all income quintiles. Overall, the conclusions drawn from the distributional analysis in table 2.6 seem insensitive to alternative specifications.

2.7   Conclusions

In this paper we study the fiscal implications of reforms to Canada's retirement income security system. There are three major findings. First, any reform has both mechanical and behavioral fiscal effects, and we find that the behavioral effects are important. In some of our models, the behavioral effect represents almost half of the total effect of the reform. Second, reforms that shift retirement to later years improve government balances through increases in tax revenue generated by the increase in work among the elderly. Any analysis that does not consider the dynamic response to reforms will miss this channel, through which reform has an impact on government budgets. Finally, reforms to the mix of earnings-related benefits, demogrants, and income-tested benefits can have important distributional implications.

Two important caveats affect the interpretation of our results. First, our treatment of some aspects of the model is crude. For example, our assumption of fixed spousal labor supply and our treatment of consumption taxation ignore many important channels of adjustment to retirement income and incentives. Second, the reforms we consider are not balanced budget reforms and therefore set aside important general equilibrium and public finance considerations. In light of these caveats, it is important to interpret our results as illustrative of how behavioral responses to retirement incentives can affect all aspects of the government budget, rather than definitive estimates of the benefits of reform.

As future governments in Canada and other countries contemplate reforms of their retirement income systems, we conclude that consideration of the full fiscal and distributive impact of behavioral responses to the reform can significantly improve the analysis of proposed reforms.

References

Baker, Michael. 2002. The retirement behaviour of married couples: Evidence from the spouse's allowance. *Journal of Human Resources* 37 (Winter): 1–34.
Baker, Michael, Jonathan Gruber, and Kevin Milligan. 2004. Income security programs and retirement in Canada. In *Social security programs and retirement around the world: Micro estimation,* ed. J. Gruber and D. Wise, 99–154. Chicago: University of Chicago Press.
Gruber, Jonathan. 2000. Disability insurance benefits and labour supply. *Journal of Political Economy* 108:1162–83.
Milligan, Kevin. 2002. Tax-preferred savings accounts and marginal tax rates: Empirical evidence on RRSP participation. *Canadian Journal of Economics* 35: 436–56.
Office of the Superintendent of Financial Institutions. 1998. *Canada Pension Plan: 17th Actuarial Report as at December 31, 1997.* Ottawa: Department of Finance.
Picot, Garnett, and Zhengxi Lin. 1997. Are Canadians more likely to lose their jobs in the 1990s? Analytical Studies Branch Research Paper no. 96. Ottawa: Statistics Canada.
Statistics Canada. 1983. *Historical statistics of Canada,* 2nd ed. Catalogue no. E86-103. Ottawa: Statistics Canada.
Statistics Canada. 1998. *Permanent layoffs, quits and hirings in the Canadian economy.* Catalogue no. 71-539-XIB. Ottawa: Statistics Canada.
Statistics Canada. 1999. *Pension plans in Canada.* Catalogue no. 74-401-XPB. Ottawa: Statistics Canada.
Statistics Canada. 2000. *Employment, earnings, and hours.* Catalogue no. 72-002-XIB. Ottawa: Statistics Canada.
Stock, James H., and David A. Wise. 1990. Pensions, the option value of work, and retirement. *Econometrica* 58 (5): 1151–80.

3

Fiscal Implications of Reforms in Retirement Systems in Denmark

Paul Bingley, Nabanita Datta Gupta, and
Peder J. Pedersen

3.1 Introduction

Like most other OECD countries, Denmark faces a demographic
change of major dimensions in the coming decades. The expected change
in Denmark is, however, among the smallest among the OECD countries—that is, on the same level as expected in the United States and much
lower than the expected increase in some of the countries in southern Europe and Japan. Based on the most recent projection of the population by
age, the share of people 65 and older relative to the number of people 20 to
64 years old is expected to go up from 24 percent currently to about 40 percent 40 years from now (Statistics Denmark 2002, Economic Council
1998). This is not the first jump in the share, as it went up from 13 percent
in the years immediately after World War II to 26 percent in 1990. This development was, however, more easily absorbed by the economy. For one
thing, the initial burden of providing for the elderly was lower. Second, this
first jump in the share was accompanied by a strong increase in female labor force participation, to a level close to what is found for men. This, obviously, cannot be repeated during the expected future jump in the share of

Paul Bingley is associate professor at the Aarhus School of Business, Nabanita Datta
Gupta is research professor at the Danish National Institute of Social Research and an Institute of Labor Studies (IZA) research fellow, and Peder J. Pedersen is professor of economics
at the University of Aarhus and at the Danish National Institute of Social Research and IZA
research fellow. All three authors are affiliated with the Center for Integration and Marginal-
isation (CIM), Aarhus, and Bingley and Datta Gupta are members of the Center for Corporate Performance (CCP), Aarhus School of Business.

Financial support from the Danish Social Science Research Council (grants 24-02-0064
and 24-03-0268), the Danish National Research Foundation and the University of Aarhus
Research Fund is gratefully acknowledged.

people 65 years and older, as the current female labor force participation is close to that of men.

The demographic change has been accompanied by a change in retirement behavior, implying a significant decrease in the actual average retirement age. Comparing estimates from the mid-1970s to behavior in the late 1990s, before current reforms of the early retirement programs were enacted, the average retirement age for men has gone down from about 66 years to 61 to 62 years. For women, the average retirement age has gone down by about one year since the late 1980s. Women retire on average earlier than men, but the more moderate decline in the retirement age among women reflects the net effect of cohorts of married women with increasing labor market participation along with a decrease in the average retirement age (Economic Council 1998). Over this period, the official retirement age, defined as the age at which individuals are entitled to National Old Age Pension, has remained unchanged at 67 years. The decline in the actual average retirement age has occurred along with the introduction during the last 23 years of new public-sector subsidized programs for early retirement. At the same time, private pension plans and arrangements that typically contain options for early retirement, beginning at age 60, have become relevant for many people.

The projected changes in the age composition of the population along with changes in retirement behavior have potentially large consequences for public sector finances. In the Danish context, in a number of recent studies the full impact on the tax-to-GNP ratio has been estimated to be between 4 and 9 percent (Socialkommissionen 1993, Finansministeriet 1996, Finansrådet 1998, Economic Council 1998).

In this chapter, we quantify the impact of reforms to the social security system on the government's solvency situation for a particular cohort of workers aged 50 in 1995. The set of reforms considered are selected mainly for their comparability across OECD countries, and are not necessarily the most desirable or politically feasible in the context of Denmark. Nonetheless, the exercise is expected to yield some useful insights into the net effects on the government budget of changing social security provisions. The set of reforms we consider are compared to the system that was in place in 1995, the base year for our simulations, and include a mandatory increase in program eligibility ages, a move to an actuarially fair system, and the implementation of a simple unified system that is common across countries.

In the second section, we provide evidence on the decreased labor supply activity among the elderly in Denmark by surveying the main trends in the labor force participation of men and women over 45 years of age. We also review the basic institutional elements of the Danish retirement system. The Danish retirement system is a complex mix of pay-as-you-go-financed old-age pension, tax-financed social disability pension, with eligibility depending on a mix of health and social criteria, early retirement as part of labor market policy, funded labor market pensions, and a broad range of private pension arrangements. We emphasize the retirement incentives inherent in this broad range of programs and consider their impacts on retirement behavior. Finally, we review implications for the fiscal position of the growing dependency burden. Section 3.3 presents the basic model used for the simulations of the impact of reforms in retirement systems on the net fiscal contribution of older workers. Section 3.4 describes the simulation methodology and the particular issues that arise in its implementation in the Danish case, section 3.5 presents the findings from the simulation exercise on the main fiscal impacts of proposed policy reforms, in terms of expected changes in the present discounted value of tax receipts and benefit payments, and section 3.6 concludes.

3.2 Labor Supply of Older Workers and Retirement Systems in Denmark

3.2.1 Work Behavior of the Elderly

The very big changes in industrial structure along with changes in retirement programs and pension options for different groups have shaped the long-term development in participation rates. Another factor with a big impact, especially in the Nordic countries, has been the long-run trend toward increasing labor force participation among married women.

Figure 3.1 shows the trend in labor force participation since 1960 among men older than 44 years. The observation for 1975 is the first year with high unemployment in the graph. The first three observations refer to years of full employment in a period of big structural changes. There was a large move out of agriculture, implying a reduction in the share of self-employed men in these age groups. People in independent business have always had a relatively high retirement age, so this structural shift in the economy is part of the explanation for the declining participation rates in the beginning of the period covered in figure 3.1.

After 1975 there follows 20 years of high and mostly increasing unemployment until the mid-1990s. The participation rates among men 45 to 59 years old decline further, reflecting, among other things, an easier entry to Social Disability Pension (SDP) during a high unemployment period. It is evident, however, that the really large changes occur in the age group 60 and older, and especially so among people in the first half of their 60s. This reflects primarily the introduction in 1979 of a labor-market-related program for early retirement at the age of 60. The program, called the Post-Employment Wage (PEW) was intended for unskilled workers with many years of hard physical work behind them, but it turned out to become much more broadly popular than initially expected. We return to the details of the program in the following.

For women 45 years and older, figure 3.2 presents a quite different pic-

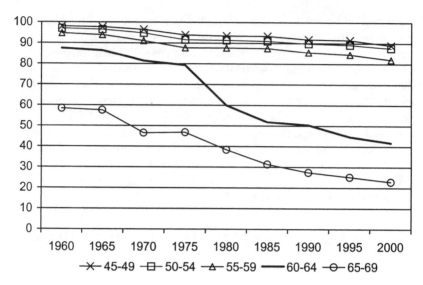

Fig. 3.1   Participation rates for men 45 years and older, 1960–2000

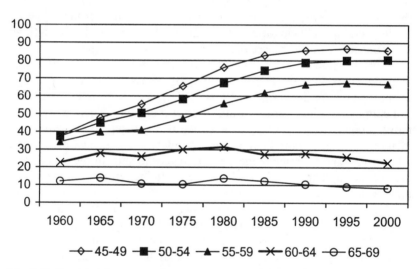

Fig. 3.2   Participation rates for women 45 years and older, 1960–2000

ture. The difference obviously relates to the strong increase in labor market participation among married women, which did not level out until the late 1980s.

The increase in participation in age groups up to 59 years until the mid-1990s reflects cohort effects. For those 60 years and older, the cohort effects are counteracted by the possibility of entry into the PEW program and

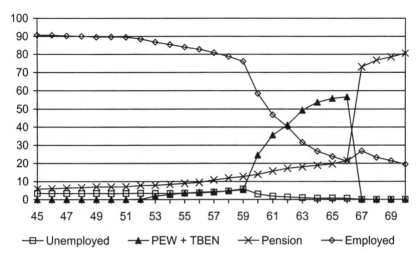

Fig. 3.3   **The distribution of men on activities, 45–70 years, 2000**

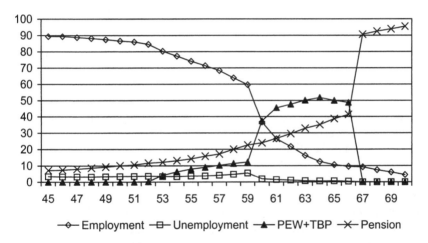

Fig. 3.4   **The distribution of women on activities, 45–70 years, 2000**

from extended possibilities to enter the SDP. The decline in participation rates is much smaller among men, but note that the participation rate among women 60 and older never reached near the initial level among men in this age group. For people up to the age of about 50, figures 3.1 and 3.2 show, on the other hand, a near complete convergence between the participation rates for women and men from the mid-1980s.

For the year 2000, figures 3.3 and 3.4 further illustrate the distribution of men and women according to a number of activities. For both women and men there is a distinct kink in the share in employment from age 60,

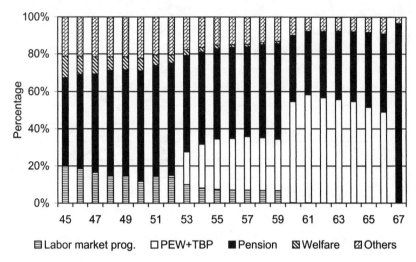

Fig. 3.5   Distribution of women 45–67 years old outside the labor force on different states in 2000

when a major part of the labor force becomes eligible for PEW. A corresponding decrease occurs in the share in unemployment from age 60. For women, there is a stronger decline in the employment share from age 50 to age 59 than among men. More women (52 and older) are in a temporary benefit program for early retirement, called the TBP program, which is described later. More important is the fact that the share of women with SDP in their late 50s is nearly double the level found among men. Fewer women than men fulfill the eligibility criteria for PEW. As a reflection of this, we note that the share of women with SDP at age 66, after which everyone becomes eligible to old age pension, is double the level found for men. From age 67, old-age pension takes over as the dominant state. Still, however, there is a gender difference here, as about 20 percent of the men still have a market income as the dominant income source at age 70.

While figures 3.3 and 3.4 include individuals in the labor force and in retirement programs, figures 3.5 and 3.6 concentrate on the distribution on different states of individuals outside the labor force between 45 and 67 years old.

Individuals in labor market programs and individuals on welfare benefits may return to the labor force. The other states included in figures 3.5 and 3.6 are approximately absorbing.

Most individuals outside the labor force have an income from a labor market program, from welfare, or from one of the early retirement programs. The ages of eligibility are clearly visible; that is, in 2000 it was 53 for the TBP program and 60 for the PEW program. In principle, people older

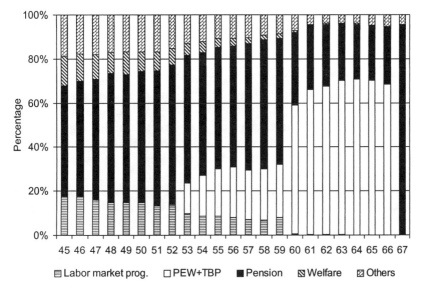

Fig. 3.6   Distribution of men 45–67 years old outside the labor force on different states in 2000

than 60 are not cut off from labor market programs or from being eligible for welfare. In practice, however, figures 3.5 and 3.6 demonstrate that alternative states become completely dominant from that age.

3.2.2   Retirement Programs in Denmark

By international comparison, the official retirement age in Denmark is high. Until 1998 it was, at 67, one of the highest in the OECD countries. Along with a reform in 1999 of a major early retirement program, the PEW, the official pension age was reduced to 65 years, effective from 2004.

The structure in the Danish pension and retirement system consists of a number of public-sector programs and private arrangements. The major public sector-financed programs consist of the National Old Age Pension (OAP, Folkepension), Social and Disability Pension (SDP, Førtidspension [until 1984 Disability pension]), and pensions to certain groups of public employees in permanent positions—the Public Employees Pension scheme (PEP, Tjenestemandspension).

There are two important mixed public/private sector arrangements. The biggest is a labor-market-related program open for people 60 to 66 years old, called the Post Employment Wage (PEW, Efterløn). Another is the ATP program, to which employed persons and their employers, both public and private, contribute.

Private-sector arrangements cover a broad range, from mature pension funds, other funds in the blue collar part of the labor market still in a build-up phase, and fully individual arrangements, of which most are tax subsidized. We describe the different programs briefly in the following.[1]

3.2.3   National Old Age Pension (OAP, Folkepension)

The OAP is in principle a universal program in the sense that eligibility depends only on age and on the duration of stay in Denmark. Thus, it is not dependent on labor market experience or former earnings. Depending on the level and the type of other income, a person is entitled from the age of 67 to a base amount and to pension supplements. The base amount is, however, means tested against earnings from work. Until the 1999 reform, the pension age was 67 years and the base amount was reduced, with 60 percent of eventual earnings from work in excess of an amount roughly corresponding to earnings in a fulltime job during the whole year at the minimum wage.[2]

The *reduction* of the official pension age in 1999 from 67 to 65, effective from 2004, appears as slightly paradoxical in relation to current policy discussions in most OECD countries of *increasing* the retirement age. The intention in the 1999 reform was, however, exactly to result in an *increase* in the *average* actual retirement age (currently around 61.5 years) at the same time as the official pension age was reduced. It was part of a policy package primarily directed toward the PEW. We return to complete this picture later. The reduction in the official pension age regarding the OAP was accompanied by more liberal rules regarding means testing of the base pension amount against earnings from work. In the future, the reduction percentage will be 30 percent of income from work in excess of annual earnings, corresponding roughly to the average annual income from an unskilled job. The impact from this change on retirement behavior is difficult to estimate in isolation, as by now people who are still in the labor force when they are 65 and older will typically have incomes well above the relevant part of the income scale regarding means testing. The eventual impact should be seen, however, in conjunction with the impact on retirement behavior and attitudes from changes in the PEW proposed in 1998 and enacted in 1999; see the following.

In addition to the base amount in the OAP, which as described is means tested against income from work, there is a pension supplement that is means tested against all other income, that is, also capital income. The rules regarding means testing of the pension supplement were not changed as part of the 1999 reform.

---

1. A discussion of the ongoing policy reforms in this area can be found in OECD (2000).

2. Actually, this is a description of the rule until the mid-1990s. During the last few years, until the 1998 reform, the free earnings maximum (the exemption) before reduction of the base amount was gradually increased.

3.2.4   Social Disability Pension (SDP, Førtidspension)

The main principles behind the rules for the SDP were enacted through a major reform in 1984 of the public sector programs regarding early retirement. The SDP was intended to replace a number of earlier programs. The biggest among these was the disability pension, which could be granted on three levels according to health criteria. Other programs, which were included into the SDP, were a public-financed program for widows' pension and a program for early OAP for persons whose (older) spouses were already receiving the OAP.

SDP on medical or social criteria can be granted on three levels. The highest level is applicable to persons younger than 60 whose work capacity has been (or always was) reduced to almost nothing. The intermediate-level SDP is open for those younger than 60 with a work capacity reduced to one-third of the normal level and to people 60 to 66 years old with almost no remaining work capacity. Eligibility for the highest and the intermediate-level SDP is decided on medical criteria. Finally, eligibility for the lowest level, the so-called ordinary-level SDP depends on work capacity having been reduced to below half the normal level. The evaluation of this is based on health criteria or on a combination of health and social criteria. Recipients of the ordinary-level SDP who are younger than 60 are entitled to a supplementary amount. Granting of the ordinary-level pension is dependent on rehabilitation having been considered or tried without success.

In principle, award of SDP depends on an application being decided on relative to a set of medical and social criteria. SDP is thus not an individual option like eligibility—for example, labor-market pension from a specific age. SDP consists of a number of components. Parallel to OAP, it includes a base amount and an additional pension amount. Furthermore, SDP can include supplementary amounts, depending on the level of the SDP that has been granted. A Work Inability Amount is granted to people on the highest SDP level. People in that group, along with people granted the intermediate-level SDP, receive further a Disability Amount, while— as mentioned earlier—persons younger than 60 granted the ordinary-level SDP receive a supplementary, so-called Compensating Amount. The SDP system is quite complex, as the rules differ regarding tax treatment and regarding means testing of the different components and amounts. In 2003 a reform was enacted that made the program simpler.

3.2.5   Post-Employment Wage (PEW, Efterløn)

In contrast to the SDP the PEW scheme, introduced in 1979, provides the possibility of early retirement without having to fulfill any health criteria. It was intended to be a labor-market policy instrument with the purpose of creating jobs for young people by reducing the retirement age for older workers. The PEW can be entered both from employment and from unemployment. To be eligible, a person must be between sixty and sixty-six years, have been a member of an unemployment insurance (UI) fund for 20 of the previous twenty-five years, and be eligible for UI benefits. If a person enters directly from a job, benefits in the PEW system are equal to the amounts to which she or he would be entitled in case of unemployment. This is for a maximum of 2.5 years, after which period benefits in the program are reduced to 82 percent of the UI benefits until reaching eligibility for the OAP. The only difference in the situation for a person who is entering PEW from unemployment is a reduction of the period with full UI benefits by the length of the spell of unemployment, which became terminated by entry into the program. Participants in the program are only allowed paid work up to a maximum of 200 hours per year. The benefits in the PEW program are not means tested against the income of other family members, but income from pension schemes from previous employers are deducted from the PEW benefits. The SDP cannot be collected at the same time as PEW. Finally, it should be mentioned that the PEW was introduced as a no-regret system, in the sense that a participant returning to the labor force could not reenter PEW at a later date.

In 1999 a fairly complicated reform of the PEW was enacted. In the following we describe the main features of this reform. A number of transitory arrangements are not covered. The age of eligibility is still at 60, but incentives were introduced to postpone entry until the age of 62 or later. At the same time, as part of the reform, the eligibility age for the old-age pension was reduced from 67 to 65. To become eligible for PEW after the reform, an individual is required to have been in an unemployment insurance fund for 25 out of the last 30 years, and to have paid an early retirement benefit contribution during this period.

If PEW is entered before the age of 62, benefits are reduced not only against actual income from other pension schemes but also against an actuarial calculation of the current value of the income stream from private pensions, which are postponed. Before age 62 benefits are 91 percent of the maximum unemployment benefits.

Entry from age 62 results in higher benefits and more favorable rules regarding means testing against other pension incomes. Furthermore, postponing retirement for two years or more from age 62 implies a tax discount maximized at a little above 100,000 Danish Kroner (13,800 €). Finally, the rules have been changed, making it more attractive to continue working at the same time as collecting PEW. The reform has so far resulted in a decline in the takeup of PEW for those 60 to 61 years old (see Economic Council 2002). The initial impact on retirement is analyzed using microdata by Danø, Ejrnaes, and Husted (2000) and Quaade (2001). The impact from a minor reform in 1992 is analyzed in Larsen (2005).

3.2.6   Transitional Benefits Program (TBP, Overgangsydelse)

This program was introduced in 1992. Eligible persons for entry were initially 55- to 59-year-old members of unemployment insurance funds who had been unemployed for at least 12 out of the most recent 15 months. Benefits were set at 82 percent of maximum unemployment insurance benefits and the maximum duration was until transition to PEW at the age of 60. From the beginning of 1994 the program was extended to cover the age group 50 to 54 years, with the same labor market criteria as for the 55- to 59-year-old group. Entry to the program was terminated at the beginning of 1996. Entry to the program surpassed projections, as was also the case when the PEW was introduced, in 1979.

3.2.7   Public Employees Pension Scheme (PEP; Tjenestemandspension)

The PEP is a program covering many employees in the public sector. The pension is considered to be part of a lifetime wage contract, and consequently is unfunded. The pension amount is calculated as a function of the wage, depending on seniority and position.

3.2.8   Labor-Market Pensions (LMP)

There is a wide and expanding coverage of LMP programs. The building up of pension funds began some 40 years ago for fairly small, highly educated groups. Coverage has since broadened; during the last decade a major part of the labor market for blue collar workers has also been covered with pension plans. Typically, the pension funds build on defined contributions of either 15 percent (high-wage groups) or 9 percent (industrial workers) of their annual earnings.

3.2.9   Other Programs

The General Labour Market Pension (ATP) is a small, supplementary program to OAP. It was introduced in 1964 and is being funded by contributions, which depend on hours of work. Finally, there is a broad coverage with private pension plans, mostly into some broad categories of savings arrangement, which until recently have been treated quite favorably by the tax rules.

3.2.10   Fiscal Implications of the Growing Dependency Burden

As reported in section 3.1, in the coming years the dependency ratio in Denmark is expected to go from the current four persons in the active age group per senior citizen (65 or over), to about 2.5 in 2040. Further, the proportion of very old persons (80 years and above) is expected to double in the years to come, from its current 5 percent of the working-age population to about 10 percent. The Economic Council (1998) has calculated the economic implications of the growing number of senior citizens, using a general equilibrium model. The findings show that expenditures on public pensions, nursing homes, and so on are expected to increase considerably. The decrease in the labor force will affect production and decrease the tax base. However, at the same time, tax revenue will increase due to greater taxable income being paid out from labor market and private pension schemes. Projections show that overall taxes must increase by 9.4 percent of GDP for the period 2005 to 2035. Other studies (Socialkommissionen [1993], Finansministeriet [1996], Finansrådet [1998]), find significantly lower increases in the tax/GDP ratio; that is, between 4 and 6 percentage points. While the calculations in the Economic Council (1998) take into account the changing demographic profile of future generations, and the growing importance of labor market pension schemes in future pensioners' income, no attempt is made to model retirement behavior, and all persons are assumed to leave the labor market at the age of 62 and to receive PEW income until the age of 67, when they start to receive old-age pension and income from pension funds. The most recent projection is made by the Velfaerdskommissionen (Welfare Commission [2004]), illustrating the importance of the assumptions regarding expected lifetime in the future. The base projection, assuming an expected lifetime increase, in accordance with the experience in recent decades and assuming no behavioral changes, results in a necessary increase in the basic income tax of 8.7 percentage points for fiscal policy to be long-run sustainable. Assuming instead, unrealistically, that no further increase occurs in expected lifetime, the necessary increase in the tax rate is only 1.6 percentage points.

In contrast, the approach taken here is to use the predictions arising out of a behavioral model of the retirement decision in which workers make forward-looking comparisons of the advantages of retirement at alternative ages in the future to the value of present retirement and update that information as they age. These predictions are then used to simulate the effects of strategic reforms of the pension system on the net fiscal contribution of older workers to retirement income finances. Of course, the analysis is limited to the implications of reform for a given (recent) cohort of older persons, and the given structure of the Danish pension and retirement system, in which old-age pensions from the government are the primary source of income for pensioners. In the future, most pensioners are expected to receive the greater part of their income from labor-market pension schemes. This will imply both higher mean income and a greater expected level of income dispersion among future pensioners. The Economic Council's (1998) calculations suggest that the median income of future pensioners will be around 40 percent higher than the income of today's pensioners. At the same time, however, a relatively large group of future pensioners will be without a private pension scheme and will have the same income level as today's pensioners. Those pensioners who were employed full-time throughout their careers are expected to make up the higher end of the income distribution, while people who were periodically unemployed or held part-time employment during their working life will constitute the middle of the income distribution, and those with only a loose attachment to the labor market will make up the lower end of the retirement income distribution.

With this background of the Danish pension and retirement system in mind, we turn in the next section to the exercise in which we focus on the retirement decisions of a recent cohort of older workers, simulate the effects of changes in plan provisions on the retirement decisions of these workers, and then track how changes in retirement patterns affect the fiscal balance sheet of retirement income for the current generation of older workers.

3.3   The Base Model for the Simulations

The data set used in the analysis is a 2 percent sample drawn from the Integrated Database for Labour Market Research (IDA), which covers the population of residents of Denmark. All information in the IDA data, which is compiled and made available by Statistics Denmark, is based on administrative registers and therefore has no survey component to it. We focus on a single-year birth cohort, that is, the 1945 birth cohort that is observed to be aged 50 in 1995, thereby controlling for both time and age effects in the analysis. Although early retirement eligibility begins first at age 60, we start our analysis at 50, as this is the age at which public or private retirement income for disability or illness can first be expected for those in the labor market. We condition on labor force attachment before 50, as most of the population in Denmark is employed at that age. Our sample sizes for the simulations are 1,533 individual workers. Each of the workers of age 50 in our sample represents 50 workers in the population of public and private sector workers born in 1945.

For each of the workers at age 50, we predict earnings forward for each year until age 70. Age 70 is the age at which all workers still in the labor force are assumed to exit the labor force permanently through retirement. On the basis of predicted earnings, we can then project each worker's social security wealth (SSW) at each possible future retirement age until age 100. As exit from the labor force can also occur through death, we account for mortality by applying the probability of dying taken from the age-gender life tables in 1995 for the total population. Workers in our sample can exit the data either through retirement, death, or attrition. We can identify when the first two types of exits occur, but cannot identify the reason behind the third type of exit (i.e., death or out-migration). Therefore, we use external population mortality rates in order to adjust the statistical sample for death. In equation form, we have, then:

$$\text{prob(exit)} - \text{prob(death)} = \text{prob(retirement)}$$

As our overall goal is to simulate the impact of reforms to retirement systems on the retirement behavior of older workers, and then to calculate the effects of changed labor supply behavior on the net contribution of older workers to retirement income finances, we start by presenting our estimates from an option value behavioral model of retirement, in which workers make forward-looking comparisons of the advantages of retirement at alternative ages in the future to the value of present retirement and update that information as they age (see Gruber and Wise [2004] for details on that model).

The option value model was operationalized by a simple probability model of retirement (for example, probit):

$$\text{Prob(retire in year } t) = \Pr[\alpha + \beta G_t(r^*) + \delta \mathbf{X}_t + \varepsilon_t > 0],$$

in which the dependent variable is binary and takes the value 1 if retired, 0 if not, and where $G(\cdot)$ is the option value of postponing retirement (in other cases, the peak value or the accrual measure) calculated under the assumed parameter values, and $\mathbf{X}$ is a vector of additional variables, including SSW.

In tables 3.1 and 3.2, we present model estimates of β and the coefficient of SSW (included in $\mathbf{X}$) for samples of male and female older workers drawn from the IDA. Each regression is run in two ways, with age entered either linearly or captured by a full set of dummies, for each of the three incentive measures mentioned earlier, accrual (one-year change in SSW), peak value (the financial option value) and option value.

Model estimates from the sample of males are shown in table 3.1. The

Table 3.1   **Estimates from the retirement probit—males sample**

	Accrual incentive		Peak value incentive		Option value incentive	
	Linear age	Age dummies	Linear age	Age dummies	Linear age	Age dummies
SSW	0.0023437	0.0000568	0.0021998	0.0009605	0.0020257	0.0009254
	(0.000122)	(0.0001361)	(0.0001238)	(0.0001306)	(0.0001252)	(0.0001325)
	0.001838	**4.12E-06**	**0.0001363**	**0.000075**	**0.0001235**	**0.0000716**
Incentive	0.0036759	−0.0355246	−0.0159361	−0.0050171	−0.0112939	−0.0041719
measure	(0.000608)	(0.0008928)	(0.0002211)	(0.000312)	(0.0001574)	(0.0002204)
	0.0002882	**−0.0025742**	**−0.0009874**	**−0.0003915**	**−0.0006887**	**−0.0003228**
Pseudo R^2	0.29	0.3658	0.3104	0.321	0.3117	0.3217
Log likelihood	−44,879.02	−40,085.73	−44,763.012	−44,077.778	−43,327.098	−42,699.919

Note: For each incentive measure, we report the estimated coefficient, its estimated standard error in parentheses, and the marginal effect in bold.

Table 3.2   **Average retirement ages in simulations—males and females**

		Simulated reform			
	Baseline	Three-Year Reform	Difference from baseline	Common Reform	Difference from baseline
Males					
Accrual—S1	60.44432	60.28469	−0.15963	60.38432	−0.06000
Accrual—S2	60.27340	60.64349	+0.37009	60.95542	+0.68202
Accrual—S3	60.27340	62.28802	+2.01462	59.60625	−0.66715
Peak value—S1	60.76490	62.12958	+1.36468	61.18836	+0.42346
Peak value—S2	60.68337	61.23892	+0.55555	61.08496	+0.40159
Peak value—S3	60.68337	62.57302	+1.88965	60.09098	−0.59239
Option value—S1	60.77458	62.16372	+1.38914	61.23221	+0.45763
Option value—S2	60.69852	61.32813	+0.62961	61.13278	+0.43426
Option value—S3	60.69852	62.59626	+1.89774	60.14049	−0.55803
Females					
Accrual—S1	60.44432	60.28469	−0.15963	60.38432	−0.06000
Accrual—S2	60.27340	60.64349	+0.37009	60.95542	+0.68202
Accrual—S3	60.27340	62.28802	+2.01462	59.60625	−0.66715
Peak value—S1	60.76490	62.12958	+1.36468	61.18836	+0.42346
Peak value—S2	60.68337	61.23892	+0.55555	61.08496	+0.40159
Peak value—S3	60.68337	62.57302	+1.88965	60.09098	−0.59239
Option value—S1	60.77458	62.16372	+1.38914	61.23221	+0.45763
Option value—S2	60.69852	61.32813	+0.62961	61.13278	+0.43426
Option value—S3	60.69852	62.59626	+1.89774	60.14049	−0.55803

level of SSW, which captures the wealth effects of retirement income, significantly positively affects the retirement probability, while in all but one case (accrual-linear age), the relevant incentive measure that measures the incentive to continue working significantly negatively affects the odds of retiring. In general, the age dummy specification fits the data a little better than the specification in which age is entered linearly. Specifications that employ forward-looking incentive measures (peak value and option value) fit the data better than using the one-year accrual incentive measure. Thus, observed retirement behavior is better explained by incentive measures that take into account the potential future benefits of continuing work. Similar results are obtained for the sample of females (not shown here).

Based on these model estimates, we map each worker's actual characteristics into a probability of retirement. Then, we simulate the impacts of three strategic reforms of the retirement system on the predicted probabilities of retirement. The first, the Three-Year Reform, involves a three-year delay in the early and normal ages of retirement. Thus, the age of first eligibility of postemployment wage (PEW) and early retirement through the Public Employee's Pension (PEP) is increased by three years (from 60 to 63), and the age of first eligibility of Transitional Benefit Program UI (TBP) is also delayed by three years, from 55 to 58. The normal old-age pension (OAP) retirement age is increased by three years. The age-gender-specific probability of disability for those aged 60 to 62 is assumed to be that probability observed in the data at age 59, and for those aged 63 to 70 the age-gender-specific probabilities are those observed in the data for individuals three years younger.[3]

The second, the Common Reform, is intended to apply a unified system in each country, in which the early retirement age is set at 60, the normal retirement age at 65, and in which benefits are set equal to 60 percent of (capped) lifetime earnings and are reduced actuarially 6 percent per year if taken before 65, and increased actuarially 6 percent per year if taken after 65. No other retirement program is assumed to be in effect alongside.

The third reform, the Actuarial Reform, implies a move to an actuarially fair system without changing the early or normal retirement ages or the replacement rate and without removing coexisting means-tested programs such as disability or public employers' pension. Thus, this reform is a compromise between the Three-Year Reform and the Common Reform and should thereby be useful in understanding the full impact of the Common Reform. Under this reform, the benefit at NRA is kept at its existing level and adjusted 6 percent per year actuarially away from this level, as in the common case.

In each case, we specify a model with age-specific dummy variables, doing the simulation in each of three ways: S1 is the simulation method in which a linear-age term is included in the estimation only; S2 is the simulation method in which the age dummies are included in the estimation but not in the simulation, and S3 is the simulation method in which age indicators are both used in the estimation, and the estimated coefficients on these indicators are used to simulate retirement under program changes. The resulting baseline and simulated average retirement ages in the Danish case are presented in table 3.2.

Average retirement ages for the male sample in table 3.2 show that the three-year eligibility delay under the Three-Year Reform increases the average age of retirement by nearly two years in Denmark for all incentive measures using S3 assumptions. Comparing across simulation methods S1, S2, and S3, we find that in general (except for the accrual case), the increase in the average retirement age is greatest under S3 and smallest under S2, while S1 falls in the middle. It is to be expected that S3 will predict later retirement than S2 and S1, as S3 includes both age-indicator effects and program incentive effects. For the Common Reform, in the Danish case the average retirement age is lowered under S3 assumptions, most likely due to the relative generosity of the Common Reform compared to the existing system. Again, S3 predicts a bigger decrease in the retirement

---

3. At the same time, we adjust the age at which the supplement for delayed retirement to PEW is effective from 63 to 66.

age than S2 and S1 for the reasons stated previously. Findings for females are nearly the same as seen in the bottom rows of table 3.2.

3.4 Simulation Methodology

Based on the predicted retirement rates generated under the current system and under each reform, our goal is to compute the associated tax revenue and benefit payments corresponding to the retirement patterns under the baseline, and then compare that to the projected tax revenue and benefit expenditure for each hypothetical change in plan provision. Thus, the key policy parameter will be the percentage change in the net cost of the retirement program for a representative individual (aged 50 in 1995) drawn from our sample of workers.

Note that in the implementation of this exercise, we do not use actual data for the workers in our sample, because this is the only way we can obtain a clean comparison of the expected outcome under the current system and the expected outcome under a change in pension plan provision. We merely take our sample of workers and apply to them the estimated retirement probabilities generated from our option value analysis, and use these as the starting point for producing a time series that tracks the evolution of this cohort of workers between age 50 and 100, the assumed date of death of the last remaining individual in the sample. Note that we do not keep track of survivors or dependents in the analysis. This is because the Danish retirement income and taxation calculation is purely individual based, so that accounting for dependents' and survivors' income is not a relevant issue.[4]

The presence of multiple retirement programs in the Danish context, however, introduces some complexity, which is solved by assuming that individuals take the most financially lucrative path by constructing a weighted incentive measure, in which the weights are the probabilities that the person is eligible for each program.[5] When simulating the reforms, the issue of eligibility to programs such as unemployment and disability needs to be addressed. While we increase all other eligibility ages (PEW, OAP, PEP, and TBP) by three years under the first reform, as disability benefits are available at every age in Denmark, we adjust the age-gender-specific probabilities of disability receipt so that they are the same as the observed probabilities of individuals three years younger. In the case of the Actuarial Reform, we retain the probabilities of disability receipt at each age but

---

4. The only element of joint taxation present in the Danish tax system is in the treatment of capital income, for which data is not available. Other than that, we account for allowances that vary by marital status, but do not need to use actual spousal income for computing individual tax or benefit amounts.

5. A more detailed description of the algorithm used to construct this weighted-average SSW can be found in the appendix to the introduction in Gruber and Wise (2004).

adjust the disability benefit 6 percent per year actuarially away from the NRA (67). In the Common Reform, we eliminate access to any other (including disability) programs.

The focus of the analysis will be to distinguish the effects on fiscal balances of the labor-supply response to the reform, which we label *fiscal implications of behavioral effect,* from the effects on fiscal balances that arise purely out of a change of benefit entitlements, holding constant any labor-supply response, which we term the *mechanical* effect. The total fiscal impact is then the sum of both effects. That is, if *i* denotes individual and *s* denotes state (exit to death or retirement at each age) and *B* is base and *R* is reform,

$$\text{base SSW} = \sum_{i=1}^{N} \sum_{s=1}^{40} P_{is}^{B} SSW_{is}^{B},$$

$$\text{reform SSW} = \sum_{i=1}^{N} \sum_{s=1}^{40} P_{is}^{R} SSW_{is}^{R},$$

$$\text{total effect of reform} = \sum_{i=1}^{N} \sum_{s=1}^{40} P_{is}^{R} SSW_{is}^{R} - \sum_{i=1}^{N} \sum_{s=1}^{40} P_{is}^{B} SSW_{is}^{B},$$

$$\text{mechanical effect} = \sum_{i=1}^{N} \sum_{s=1}^{40} P_{is}^{B} SSW_{is}^{R} - \sum_{i=1}^{N} \sum_{s=1}^{40} P_{is}^{B} SSW_{is}^{B},$$

$$\text{behavioral effect} = \sum_{i=1}^{N} \sum_{s=1}^{40} P_{is}^{R} SSW_{is}^{R} - \sum_{i=1}^{N} \sum_{s=1}^{40} P_{is}^{B} SSW_{is}^{R}.$$

Note that in our case, potential retirement ages go from 50 to 69, giving $2 \times 20 = 40$ possible states.

3.5   Results

The expected present discounted value (PDV) of tax payments and benefit payments for our sample of workers is computed from age 50 to age 100.[6] Results are based on the forward-looking incentive measures only (peak and option value) in this study, although in Gruber and Wise (2004), a set of results for one-year accrual in SSW were also generated. For most countries, it was found that accrual and peak value produced similar results. Also, in this study, we mainly discuss the findings arising out of the two simulation methodologies S1 (linear age) and S3 (age dummies included in the model and shifted in the simulation), although results for S2 are presented in the tables. These results appear in appendix figures 3A.1 to 3A.8, figure 3.7, and tables 3.3 and 3.4.

Consider first the set of figures labeled figure 3A.1, panels A–C (S1OV), which describe the option value, linear age specification results under the

6. All pension flows and tax payments are discounted back to age 50 by a 3 percent real rate of interest.

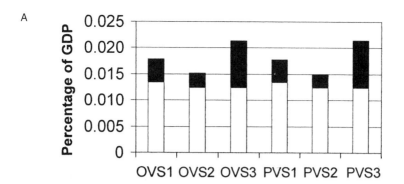

A

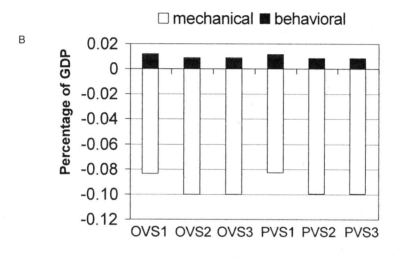

B

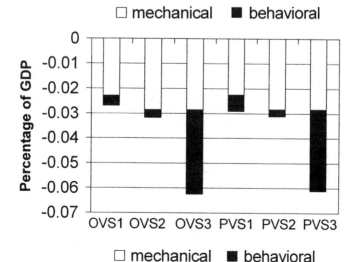

C

Fig. 3.7 *A,* Fiscal impact of Three-Year Reform; *B,* Fiscal impact of Actuarial Reform; *C,* Fiscal impact of Common Reform

three reforms. From figure 3A.1, panel A (S1OV), it appears that the gross SSW profile changes little under the Three-Year Reform, as entitlements do not change, only the age at which they can be first received. In figure 3A.1, panel B (S1OV), for the Actuarial Reform, note that gross SSW peaks at age 60 (age of first eligibility of early retirement) under the baseline and declines thereafter, though flattening out from age 66 and over. The decline in gross SSW under the baseline clearly reflects the actuarial unfairness of the benefits system, as gains in earnings from postponing retirement are largely offset by losses in future social security benefits. Gross SSW is considerably lowered for all ages up to 64 under the Actuarial Reform, and is higher thereafter compared to the baseline. Thus, the reform is more actuarially fair than the existing system at older ages. Gross SSW is particularly lowered at early retirement ages, both by the low level of benefits away from the NRA of 67, which are in turn weighted by the (low) probability of disability receipt at these ages. A similar profile to gross SSW is generated under the Common Reform, although benefits are not penalized nearly as much if retirement is taken early, because the NRA is now brought forward to 65 and access to disability is removed. Figure 3A.2, panels A–C (S1OV) present the PDV of tax collections under the baseline and for each of the three reforms. As evidenced in these figures, the PDV of tax is close to the baseline in the case of the Three-Year Reform, and slightly lowered in the 56 to 63 age group compared to baseline and higher than baseline in the 67-and-up age group in the case of the other two reforms. This would indicate that as the two latter reforms essentially make early retirement much less generous at early ages, less is collected by way of taxes on benefits. By the same argument, more would be collected at higher ages relative to baseline because the benefit profile becomes more actuarially fair. Of course, if retirement is delayed, people work longer and thereby pay taxes on income (although wages are not high on average for elderly workers), but as we shall see later, behavioral responses are relatively smaller in the Danish case, so changes to the tax profile are also dominated by changes in entitlements. From figure 3A.3, panel A (S1OV), there is no appreciable change in the postreform retirement hazard in the Three-Year Reform case, largely because the linear age specification fails to adequately capture the full behavioral effects of the change in the age of eligibility induced by the reform and because of the adjustment made to the age-gender-specific probabilities of disability, in which workers have the option of going on disability-based retirement even when all other programs' eligibility ages are shifted three years. In the case of the two other reforms, figures 3A.3, panels B–C, there appear to be significant delaying effects of retirement until the age of 60 as compared to the baseline, with the retirement hazard now peaking between 62 and 64 instead of between 60 and 62. This occurs also in the case of the Common Reform where the NRA is brought forward to 65, indicating the importance of early retirement in Denmark.

The next figure, figure 3A.4, panels A–C (S1OV), shows the total fiscal effect (gross and net) by age of labor force exit under the three reforms. The total effect is the sum of the mechanical and the behavioral effect and measures the reform SSW minus the base SSW. The gross total fiscal effect is positive and increasing up to 65 (the maximum about 9,000 euros per person) and declining thereafter (but still positive), under the Three-Year Reform. This reflects, (compare figure 3.2) that net SSW is higher at ages 60 and up compared to the baseline, because of the fact that by delaying eligibility to retirement programs by 3 years, the government is forced to pay out more to the (costly) disability program instead as disability continues to be available up to 63 now (previously only up to 60). The net effect is somewhat mitigated by increased collection of taxes on disability benefits and work for those who delay retirement. The gross total effect of the Actuarial Reform, figure 3A.4, panel B is considerably negative between ages 50 and 65 (nearly 80,000 euros per person in this age range) and moderately positive thereafter (20,000 euros). The considerable savings in the 50 to 65 age range are due to the removal of the costly PEW program, which offers a high replacement rate to those who take it up (skilled, blue collar workers), and therefore removing this program constitutes a considerable fiscal saving for the government. Plus, although disability is available in principle, the low probability of takeup in this age interval combined with the low earnings (age 67 NRA benefits actuarially adjusted at 6 percent per year) if disabled represents a big saving compared to the previous disability benefits paid out. Nearly the same gross total effect is seen in the case of the Common Reform, in figure 3A.4, panel C, except that the gains in the 50 to 65 age group are a bit less than half (30–35,000 Euros per person) of what they were under the Actuarial Reform. This is because access to disability is now removed, and instead people are paid the full actuarially adjusted retirement benefit for early retirement rather than a small fraction of it, depending on probability of disability. On the other hand, by bringing the NRA forward to 65 (from 67), more is paid out by way of normal retirement. However, the first effect still dominates, so that the net effect is still a total saving, despite the replacement rate under the Common Reform being more generous than the existing old-age pension system.

How do these results change when we change the way age is specified in the model? We expect larger fiscal implications of the behavioral effects, particularly in the Three-Year Reform, because the age dummies were highly significant in the Danish case. Figure A.5, panels A–C (S3OV) examines the impact of each reform on baseline SSW under S3 assumptions for the option value incentive measure. Looking first at the Three-Year Reform, figure A.5, panel A in contrast to the linear specification, gross SSW increases over the baseline at all retirement ages, but particularly in the 54 to 62 interval, indicating the move to disability for those no longer entitled to PEW at age 60. Gross SSW in the Actuarial Reform and Common

Reform, figure 3A.5, panels B–C, are not changed much under S3 assumptions. In figure 3A.6, panels A–C (S3OV), the PV of taxes also display nonmonotonicities and differ more from the baseline now, with the PV of tax collection peaking at 60 and 67 under the baseline, and now peaking at 68 as workers are induced to stay longer in the labor market under the Three-Year Reform (figure 3A.6, panel A). In both the Actuarial and Common case, figure 3A.6, panels B–C, the tax profile becomes much more nonmonotonic and concentrated around 67 indicating the higher taxes on earnings and consumption of those who are induced to continue working at older ages. In figure 3A.7, panel A (S3OV), Three-Year Reform, retirement hazards are no longer smooth functions of age (which they are by definition under S1) but show spikes at ages 60, 62, and 68 under the baseline, age 60 being the age of first eligibility of PEW, and age 62 possibly indicating the actuarial adjustment effect present in PEW if taken at 62 instead of 60 and the peak at 68 representing the mass of retirement that takes place around the age of first eligibility of the old-age pension, which is 67. The effect of the reform is a clear move to the right of the retirement hazard, so that the spikes now appear between 64 and 68, representing the behavioral response to the reform, which the S1 method failed to capture. The behavioral response is more moderate in the actuarial case, figure 3A.7, panel B, although there is evidence of delayed retirement, with spikes at 62 and 68 being more pronounced and less at earlier ages. In figure 3A.7, panel C (S3OV), the Common Reform redistributes the mass at 68 by inducing retirement to take place between 62 and 65, more clearly evidenced under S3 assumptions.

This indicates that when age dummies are introduced in the analysis, they clearly reflect the effect that people retire earlier (from 67 to 65) under the Common Reform, and this produces much larger fiscal implications of the behavioral effect in this age range.

In figure 3A.8, panels A–C (S3OV), the total effect (gross and net) of the reforms is largely the same under S1 and S3 for the Actuarial and Common Reforms. However, a big change is seen for the Three-Year Reform, in which the total effect is now (in both gross and net terms) considerably larger and nonmonotonic. The profile also peaks at 57 now instead of at 66. However, the total effect is still positive for this reform, even though the labor supply response was to delay retirement. The explanation must therefore lie in the alternative available to workers in the 60 to 62 age group, which is the expensive disability option.

Figure 3.7, panels A–C, summarizes the previous observations, by presenting both the behavioral effect and the mechanical effect together on the same diagram, for each reform, for each type of assumption (S1, S2, S3), and for each incentive measure (peak and option value).

In each case, as peak and option value results are nearly identical, only the option value results are discussed. For the Three-Year Reform, both mechanical and behavioral effects are positive, although mechanical effects are relatively larger, except under S3 assumptions, where both are roughly of the same magnitude. Both type of effects are, however, relatively small (less than 0.015 percent of GDP). In the actuarial case, in figure 3.7, panel B, mechanical effects are negative and relatively stronger than under the Three-Year Reform case (–0.1 percent of GDP). Behavioral effects are positive but small, so that the total effect is still a savings to the government of about 0.1 percent of GDP, which is not insignificant. That is, under the Actuarial Reform, it is largely changes in program rules that determine the overall fiscal picture, and the overall effect is a reduction in net SSW. In the case of the Common Reform (figure 3.7, panel C), both mechanical and behavioral effects are negative and reinforce each other, representing overall fiscal savings, particularly in the case of S3, to the tune of –0.06 percent of GDP. Thus, the biggest savings come from the Actuarial Reform, while the Three-Year Reform actually decreases the fiscal budget.

Tables 3.3 and 3.4 break out the fiscal impacts on the government budget of these three reforms into the effect on benefits and the effect on income and value added taxes, on average, for our sample.[7] Table 3.3 is in terms of levels of PDV, while table 3.4 in changes in the PDV. The monetary units are 2001 Euros. The numbers in the tables refer to an average per person. The results presented in these tables summarize and reinforce the figures. In table 3.3, option value S3 (the model that produced the best fit in the Danish case), the Three-Year Reform produces an average increase of benefits by 12.9 percent relative to baseline, while the Actuarial and Common Reform generate a benefits savings of 21 percent and 16 percent, respectively. After-tax income goes up 1.1 percent in the first case, and goes down 7.1 percent and 6 percent in the latter two reforms. The total tax collection, however, increases by 7.6 percent in the Three-Year Reform case and decreases between 0.9–2.7 percent in the other two cases. Thus, the Actuarial and Common Reforms produce a real savings for the government, despite the small drop in taxes. Looking at table 3.4, the row of interest is the "Change as a percent of base benefits," which shows that the change in PDV relative to base is greatest in the actuarial case, a drop of almost 20 percent in S2 and S3 assumptions and 17 percent in S1. The drop in the common program is about 7–13 percent. In the Three-Year Reform case, the increase is from 3–5 percent. Mechanical effects are relatively much larger in the Actuarial and Common Reforms, almost all the savings arising from changes in program rules, while in the Three-Year Reform, mechanical and behavioral effects are roughly of the same magnitude.

---

7. In the Danish case, retirement benefits are financed through overall taxes, not through a system of payroll taxes. The VAT factor = 0.3 and is derived from the national estimates of VAT taxes and specific taxes on goods over private consumption, 2002 data.

Table 3.3   Total fiscal impact of reform (VAT factor = 0.301803)

| | Present discounted value | | | | Total change relative to base (%) | | |
	Base	Three-Year Reform	Actuarial Reform	Common Reform	Three-Year Reform	Actuarial Reform	Common Reform
			Option value—S1				
Benefits	136	143	114	125	5.3	−16.4	−8.1
After-tax income	233	238	226	233	1.8	−3.3	−0.3
Taxes							
Payroll	0	0	0	0			
Income	85	86	88	84	1.1	3.3	−1.7
VAT	70	72	68	70	1.8	−3.3	−0.3
Total	156	158	156	154	1.4	0.3	−1.1
			Option value—S2				
Benefits	138	145	110	125	4.7	−20.7	−9.7
After-tax income	220	224	205	217	1.7	−7.1	−1.3
Taxes							
Payroll	0	0	0	0			
Income	80	81	83	78	1.5	4.3	−2.7
VAT	66	68	62	66	1.7	−7.1	−1.3
Total	146	149	145	143	1.6	−0.9	−2.1
			Option value—S3				
Benefits	138	156	110	116	12.9	−20.7	−15.9
After-tax income	220	223	205	207	1.1	−7.1	−6.0
Taxes							
Payroll	0	0	0	0			
Income	80	90	83	80	13.0	4.3	0.0
VAT	66	67	62	62	1.1	−7.1	−6.0
Total	146	158	145	142	7.6	−0.9	−2.7
			Peak value—S1				
Benefits	136	143	114	124	5.3	−1.64	−8.9
After-tax income	234	238	225	231	1.8	−3.5	−0.9
Taxes							
Payroll	0	0	0	0			
Income	85	86	88	84	1.1	3.2	−2.2
VAT	70	72	68	70	1.8	−3.5	−0.9
Total	156	158	156	153	1.4	0.2	−1.6
			Peak value—S2				
Benefits	138	145	109	125	4.6	−20.8	−9.6
After-tax income	220	224	204	217	1.7	−7.5	−1.4
Taxes							
Payroll	0	0	0	0			
Income	80	81	83	78	1.5	4.0	−2.8
VAT	66	68	61	65	1.7	−7.5	−1.4
Total	146	149	145	143	1.6	−1.2	−2.2
			Peak value—S3				
Benefits	138	156	109	117	13.0 ·	−20.8	−15.2
After-tax income	220	223	204	201	1.1	−7.5	−8.7
Taxes							
Payroll	0	0	0	0			
Income	80	90	83	80	13.0	4.0	0.5
VAT	66	67	61	61	1.1	−7.5	−8.7
Total	146	158	145	141	7.6	−1.2	−3.7

Table 3.4   **Decomposition of the total effect of reform**

	Change in present discounted value								
	Three-Year Reform			Actuarial Reform			Common Reform		
	Mechanical	Behavioral	Total	Mechanical	Behavioral	Total	Mechanical	Behavioral	Total
	Option value—S1								
Benefits	6	1	7	−29	7	−22	−12	1	−11
After-tax income	5	−1	4	−29	22	−8	−8	7	−1
Taxes									
Payroll	0	0	0	0	0	0	0	0	0
Income	1	0	1	0	3	3	−4	2	−1
VAT	1	0	1	−9	7	−2	−2	2	0
Total	3	0	2	−9	9	0	−6	5	−2
Net change	3	2	5	−20	−2	−23	−6	−4	−9
Change as % of									
base benefits	2.4	1.3	3.7	−15.0	−1.8	−16.8	−4.1	−2.7	−6.9
	Option value—S2								
Benefits	6	1	6	−35	6	−29	−15	1	−13
After-tax income	4	−1	4	−35	20	−16	−10	7	−3
Taxes									
Payroll	0	0	0	0	0	0	0	0	0
Income	1	0	1	0	3	3	−5	2	−2
VAT	1	0	1	−11	6	−5	−3	2	−1
Total	3	0	2	−10	9	−1	−8	5	−3
Net change	3	1	4	−25	−3	−27	−7	−3	−10
Change as % of									
base benefits	2.2	0.8	3.0	−17.7	−2.0	−19.8	−5.1	−2.4	−7.5
	Option value—S3								
Benefits	6	12	18	−35	6	−29	−15	−7	−22
After-tax income	4	−2	2	−35	20	−16	−10	−3	−13
Taxes									
Payroll	0	0	0	0	0	0	0	0	0
Income	1	9	10	0	3	3	−5	5	0
VAT	1	−1	1	−11	6	−5	−3	−1	−4
Total	3	8	11	−10	9	−1	−8	4	−4
Net change	3	4	7	−25	−3	−27	−7	−11	−18
Change as % of									
base benefits	2.2	2.7	4.9	−17.7	−2.0	−19.8	−5.1	−8.0	−13.0
	Peak value—S1								
Benefits	6	1	7	−29	7	−22	−12	0	−12
After-tax income	5	−1	4	−29	21	−8	−8	6	−2
Taxes									
Payroll	0	0	0	0	0	0	0	0	0
Income	1	0	1	0	3	3	−4	2	−2
VAT	1	0	1	−9	6	−2	−2	2	−1
Total	3	0	2	−9	9	0	−6	4	−3
Net change	3	2	5	−20	−2	−23	−6	−4	−10
Change as % of									
base benefits	2.4	1.2	3.6	−14.9	−1.7	−16.6	−4.1	−3.0	−7.1
	Peak value—S2								
Benefits	6	1	6	−35	6	−29	−15	1	−13
After-tax income	4	−1	4	−35	18	−17	−10	7	−3
Taxes									
Payroll	0	0	0	0	0	0	0	0	0
Income	1	0	1	0	3	3	−5	2	−2
VAT	1	0	1	−11	6	−5	−3	2	−1
Total	3	0	2	−10	9	−2	−8	4	−3

(*continued*)

Table 3.4   continued

	Change in present discounted value								
	Three-Year Reform			Actuarial Reform			Common Reform		
	Mechanical	Behavioral	Total	Mechanical	Behavioral	Total	Mechanical	Behavioral	Total
Net change	3	1	4	−24	−3	−27	−7	−3	−10
Change as % of									
base benefits	2.2	0.8	3.0	−17.7	−1.9	−19.5	−5.0	−2.3	−7.3
			Peak value—S3						
Benefits	6	12	18	−35	6	−29	−15	−7	−21
After-tax income	4	−2	2	−35	18	−17	−10	−9	−19
Taxes									
Payroll	0	0	0	0	0	0	0	0	0
Income	1	9	10	0	3	3	−5	5	0
VAT	1	−1	1	−11	6	−5	−3	−3	−6
Total	3	8	11	−10	9	−2	−8	2	−5
Net change	3	4	7	−24	−3	−27	−7	−9	−16
Change as % of									
base benefits	2.2	2.7	4.9	−17.7	−1.9	−19.5	−5.0	−6.3	−11.4

It may appear counterintuitive that the effect of the Three-Year Reform on PDV under the age-dummy specification results in more benefits paid out in spite of delayed eligibility to retirement programs, that is, a 6,000 Euro increase due to the mechanical effect in table 3.4. However, this finding can be explained by (1) retirement taking place through PEW at ages 63 or older after the Three-Year Reform means more years of PEW entitlement (extended to age 69), which is more generous than the previously entitled OAP and (2) that retirement taking place between 60 and 62 now means receipt of disability instead of PEW at these ages, which more than makes up for the loss of OAP between 67 and 69. Thus, (1) and (2) could lead to larger gross SSW under the Three-Year Reform, particularly as the loss of OAP under (2) occurs in the future and is small, due to discounting and mortality probabilities, while on the other hand expected DI payments are generous enough to offset these losses, even given the low probabilities of disability in this age range. However, a mitigating factor is that tax collections also rise because of delayed retirement, and the net effect is that PDV of benefits increases 12.9 percent, the change in PDV being about 5 percent of base level. While in the Common and particularly in the Actuarial Reform case, the generosity of benefits is significantly reduced by the 6 percent actuarial reduction of the NRA benefits, which is particularly taxing in the instance where the NRA is still retained at 67. This is because these reforms essentially eliminate the costly PEW early retirement program. This, in turn, has a strong effect on consumption and earnings, so that taxes also go down, but the net effect is still a large saving.

3.6   Conclusions

We study the fiscal implications for the government's budgetary situation resulting from a set of reforms to the social security system, traced through a particular cohort of workers aged 50 in 1995. Compared to the system that was in place in 1995, the reforms involve either a mandatory increase in program eligibility age, a move to an actuarially fair system, or the implementation of a simple unified system that is common across countries. Although future demographic changes in Denmark are projected to be smaller than in other OECD countries, they are expected nonetheless to have potentially big consequences for public-sector finances, as labor-force participation is already at high levels. Therefore, it becomes imperative to consider alternative ways to delay retirement and to gain an understanding of the implied fiscal consequences thereof. Our results show that the biggest savings are obtained under the Actuarial Reform, which, by replacing the PEW (existing early retirement) program by an actuarially fair benefits system, implies a large fiscal saving for the government. In the Danish case, changes in program rules largely drive the fiscal implications of the reforms, and behavioral effects are in general relatively smaller. However, small behavioral effects are to be expected, because disability continues to be a possible exit route from the labor market, even with reduced access and program generosity.

Appendix

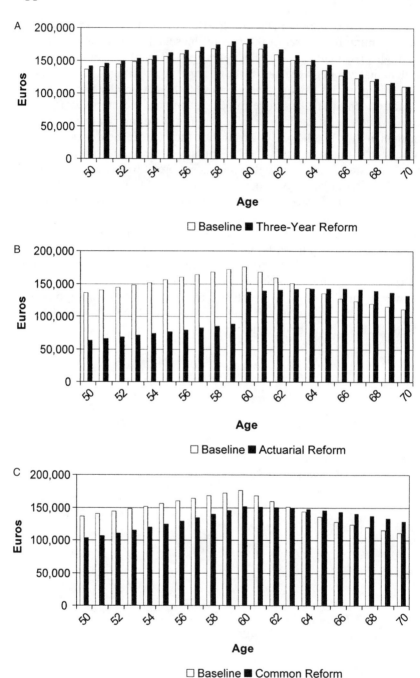

Fig. 3A.1 (S1OV) Gross social security wealth (SSW)

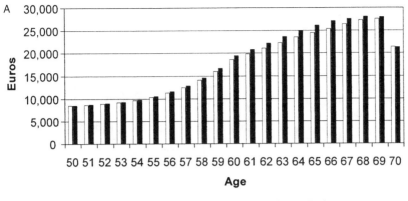

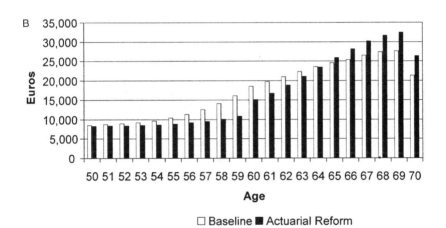

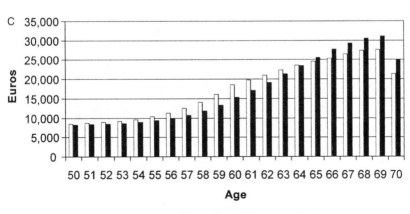

Fig. 3A.2 (S1OV) Peak value (PV) of taxes

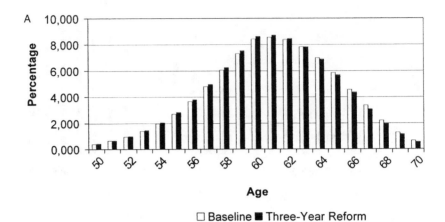

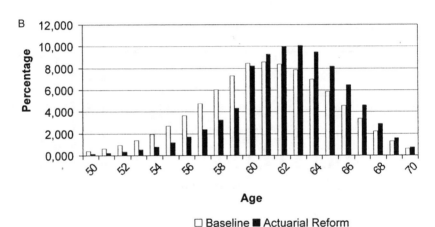

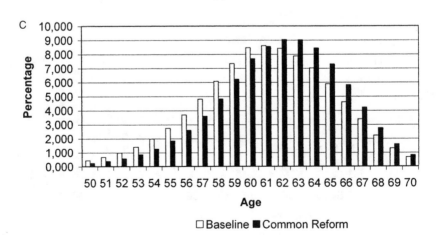

Fig. 3A.3   (S1OV) Retirement rates by age

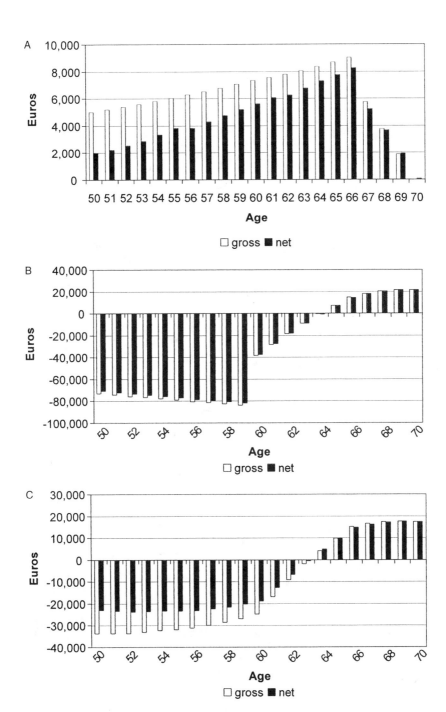

Fig. 3A.4 (S1OV): *A*, Total effect of Three-Year Reform; *B*, Total effect of Actuarial Reform; *C*, Total effect of Common Reform

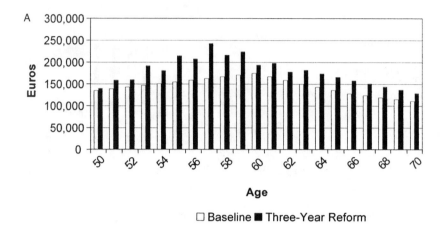

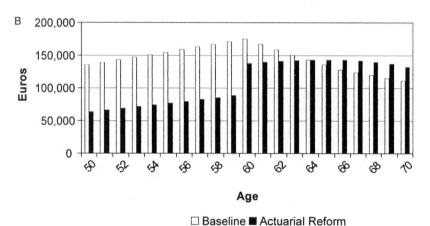

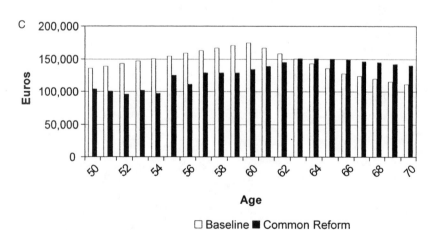

Fig. 3A.5   (S3OV) Gross social security wealth (SSW)

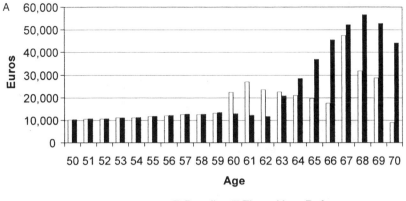

□ Baseline ■ Three-Year Reform

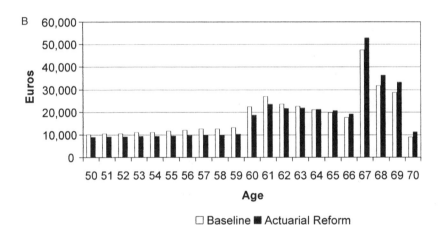

□ Baseline ■ Actuarial Reform

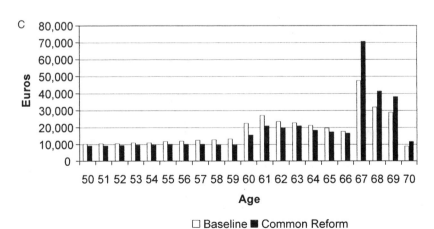

□ Baseline ■ Common Reform

Fig. 3A.6 (S3OV) peak value (PV) of taxes

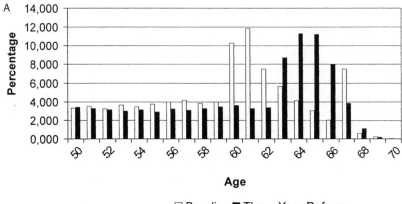

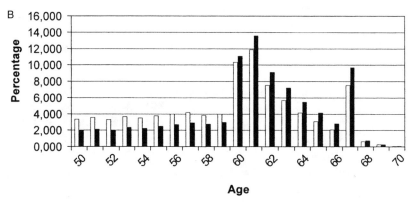

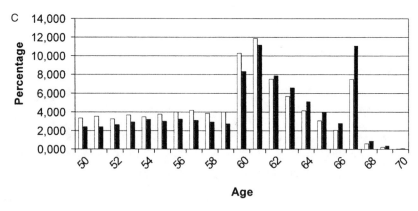

Fig. 3A.7   (S3OV) Retirement rates by age

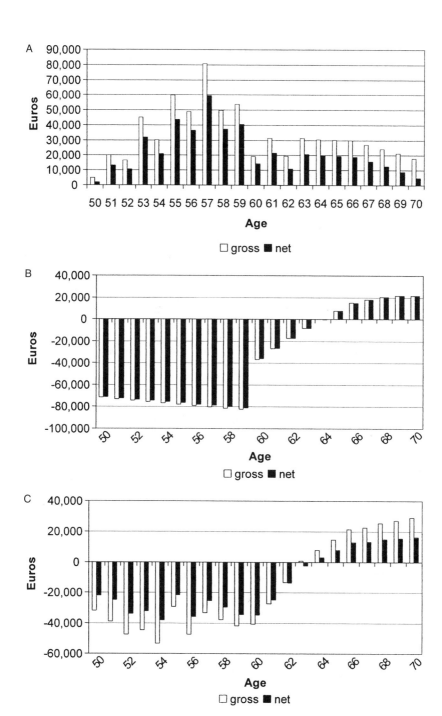

Fig. 3A.8   (S3OV): *A,* Total effect of Three-Year Reform; *B,* Total effect of Actuarial Reform; *C,* Total effect of Common Reform

References

Danø, A. M., M. Ejrnæs, and L. Husted. 2000. Hvordan påvirker efterlønsreformen de ældres tilbagetrækningsalder? (How does the reform of the PEW influence the retirement age?) *Nationaløkonomisk Tidsskrift* 138 (2): 205–21.

Economic Council. 1998. *The Danish economy: Autumn 1998* [in Danish]. Copenhagen: The Economic Council.

———. 2002. *The Danish economy: Autumn 2002.* Copenhagen: The Economic Council.

Finansministeriet. 1996. *Finansredegørelse 1996.* (Fiscal Report 1996.) Copenhagen: Ministry of Finance.

Finansrådet. 1998. *Opsparing og fremtidig velfærd.* (Savings and future welfare.) Copenhagen: Financial Council.

Gruber, J., and D. Wise. 2004. *Social security and retirement around the world: Microestimation.* Chicago: University of Chicago Press.

Larsen, M. 2005. The effect of the '92-reform of the voluntary early retirement pension on retirement age. A natural experiment. *Nationaløkonomisk Tidsskrift* 143 (2): 168–88.

Organisation for Economic Co-operation and Development (OECD). 2000. *Economic Surveys: Denmark.* Paris: OECD.

Quaade, T. 2001. Tilbagetrækning fra arbejdsmarkedet. (Retirement from the labor force.) Copenhagen: Socialforskningsinstituttet.

Socialkommissionen. 1993. *De ældre—En belysning af ældregenerationens forsørgelse.* (An analysis of the provision for the elderly.) Copenhagen: Danish Government Social Commission.

Statistics Denmark. 2002. Data bank. Copenhagen: Statistics Denmark.

Velfærdskommissionen. 2004. *Fremtidens velfærd kommer ikke af sig selv.* (Future welfare is not guaranteed.) Copenhagen: The Welfare Commission.

Simulating Retirement Behavior
The Case of France

Emmanuelle Walraet and Ronan Mahieu

4.1 Introduction

The pension debate in France has essentially focused, until recently, on ways of financing retirement, with a strong opposition between supporters of maintaining the quasi-exclusivity for pay-as-you-go (PAYG) financing and supporters of a progressive introduction of funded pensions, on top of existing PAYG basic and complementary schemes.

Attention has, however, recently shifted toward another variable of adjustment to the new demographic context, which is the age at retirement or, more widely, the age at exit from the labor force. The mean age at retirement in France is in the lower tail of the European distribution, and has been diminishing for the past twenty years for two main reasons:

- The incentive structure of the pension system itself, especially since the introduction of the *retraite à 60 ans:* until 1982, the first age of eligibility to social security (SS) benefits was 65. It was shifted to 60 for all wage earners in 1983. Retirement before reaching a total tenure of 37.5 years remained strongly penalized in the *régime général,* which covers about 65 percent of wage earners, but this constraint did not apply to most older male workers (since they often began to work about age 15) and thus did not prevent a continuous decline in participation rates.
- The relative generosity of unemployment benefits or early retirement provisions before age 60. As unemployment rose in the 1970s, the gen-

Emmanuelle Walraet is an economist and is currently in charge of regional studies at the French National Institute of Statistics and Economic Studies (INSEE). Ronan Mahieu is an economist and is currently head of the economic analysis department at the French Ministry of Labor.

erosity of these schemes was expanded to allow people between 60 and 65 to retire. When the early retirement age was set at 60, unemployment or early retirement provisions were targeted on people aged 55 to 59, whose participation rates also sharply decreased.

Age at retirement appears to be one variable on which there is potential room for large adjustments. Some steps have been made into this direction by one reform of the *régime général,* in 1993, which planned a progressive strengthening of the conditions giving access to normal (full-rate) retirement at age 60: the pre-1993 condition was to totalize at least 150 quarters (or 37.5 years) of contribution to pension schemes. This threshold will progressively increase to reach 160 quarters (i.e., forty years) from 2003. One of the propositions discussed in the Charpin Report (1999), ordered by the current prime minister, is to go further along this same direction, raising this threshold to 170 quarters.

Of course, modifying this state of affairs raises many problems. The low age at retirement or early retirement is itself a response to an employment shortage, and it is often feared that a less permissive policy may result in a worsened situation in the labor market; conversely, policies of early withdrawal from the labor force were never proved to be of any help in mitigating employment problems. The question can also be raised as to what is the best way to induce people to leave the labor force later. One possibility is coercion. The other is to rely (preferably) on incentives, with the idea of compensating the desired increase of the average retirement age by the introduction of more flexibility in this retirement age. This is the option specifically proposed by the Charpin Report, which suggests compensating the strengthening of conditions necessary to get a normal pension by a reduction of penalties associated with either the anticipation or postponing of retirement. The French system is characterized by a strong deviation from marginal actuarial fairness, and the proposition is made to bring it closer to this rule.

This context calls for a closer inspection of what determines retirement behavior, from both demand and supply sides, and also for an assessment of the financial implications of modifications of the retirement incentives. In this respect, the reforms studied in this chapter are not being proposed as feasible reforms for France. They are only chosen in order to illustrate the impact of behavioral effects and, of course, in order to proceed to cross-country comparisons. The following analysis will essentially focus on supply-side effects, although we shall try, systematically, to remind the reader of the importance of the demand side.

This chapter closely follows Mahieu and Blanchet (2002), which provided estimates of the effect of retirement incentives on labor participation. We performed new estimations of similar probit models of the retirement decision, which now include survivor benefits, which was not the case before. We then used these estimates to simulate the effect of possible reforms on both participation rates and older workers' net fiscal contributions to retirement income finances. These simulations include the impact of reforms on early retirement and unemployment provisions.

4.2   Basic Facts about the French Pension System

4.2.1   The Different Schemes

The French system is complex, but its structure can nevertheless be summed up quite simply.

- For a large part of the population (wage earners in the private sector), pensions rely on two pillars:

    1. The basic general scheme (Social Security), which offers benefits corresponding to the share of gross wages below a Social Security ceiling (€2,352 per month in 2002). In 1992, 70.5 percent of people over 60 received a pension from this general scheme. On the contributors' side, in the same year, the general scheme gathered 64.8 percent of the labor force.

    2. Complementary schemes, organized on an occupational basis. They consist of a large number (about 180) of specific schemes that are federated in two main organisms, ensuring interscheme demographic compensation: the executives' pension scheme general association (AGIRC) for executive workers and only for the fraction of their wages over the Social Security ceiling, and the wage earners' mandatory complementary pension schemes association (ARRCO) for other workers and executives' wages below the ceiling. In 1972, contributing to a complementary scheme became compulsory. Today, complementary schemes provide 40 percent of retirement pensions for wage earners in the private sector.

- Besides this simple two-pillar structure, the complexity of the French system, in fact, is essentially due to the existence of a large number of exceptions to this general rule of organization. These exceptions are the result of two factors. When Social Security was created, in 1945, people who already benefited from more generous dispositions refused to join the new system (for instance, civil servants or people employed in state-owned companies). Conversely, some categories chose to adopt cheaper systems offering lower protection because they thought that a large part of their retirement needs was likely to be covered by other sources, such as professional capital for the self-employed. Besides the two-pillar system constituted by the general scheme and ARRCO/AGIRC, there are therefore a multiplicity of specific schemes (civil servants, the self-employed) applying specific rules. For instance, there are about 120 first-pillar retirement schemes other than the general scheme. In particular, it must be observed that civil servants are not really covered by an autonomous pension system, since their pensions are directly paid by the state budget.

For all categories of people, there is a system of old-age minimum allowance (*minimum vieillesse*), which is a means-tested allowance available for people aged 65 or more. The population benefiting from this minimum pension has regularly declined in the past, due to the increasing maturity of normal pensions. It is now slightly below 1 million, against 2.55 million in 1959 (Commissariat Général du Plan 1995).

The following analysis will deal with two subpopulations: wage earners from the private sector and civil servants. We now give more details about the computation of pensions for these two categories.

4.2.2 Wage Earners in the Private Sector

General Regime

The basic general scheme offers contributory benefits corresponding to the share of wages below the Social Security ceiling. The principle is that the pension is proportional to the number of quarters of contribution to the system (truncated to N_{max} quarters), and to a reference wage, which, until 1993, has been the average wage of the D best years of the pensioners' career (past nominal wages being reevaluated at time of liquidation according to a set of retrospective coefficients). The equation giving the initial pension level is therefore:

$$(1) \qquad \text{Pension} = \alpha \times \left(\frac{N \text{ of quarters, truncated to } N_{max}}{N_{max}} \right)$$

$$\times \text{ (average wage of the } D \text{ best years),}$$

the proportionality coefficient α being itself modulated. It is maximal when the pensioner leaves at age 60, with a number of quarters of contributions of at least $\overline{N}$ to all pension schemes: in that case, its value is set at 50 percent, and this ensures a replacement rate of the reference wage (not necessarily the last wage) equal to 50 percent. The same value of α also applies whatever the number of contributed years when the individual leaves at age 65. In all other cases, the coefficient is reduced (table 4.1).

1. Either by 1.25 percentage points for each missing quarter to reach the value of $\overline{N}$ quarters.
2. Either by 1.25 percentage points for each missing quarter to reach age 65.

The adjustment actually applied is the one that leads to the most favorable outcome for the pensioner (see table 4.1).

Table 4.1   Value of α depending on age at receipt of first benefit and N, number of quarters of contribution to the general regime (%)

N	Age					
	60	61	62	63	64	65
32.5	25	30	35	40	45	50
33.5	30	30	35	40	45	50
34.5	35	35	35	40	45	50
35.5	40	40	40	40	45	50
36.5	45	45	45	45	45	50
≥37.5	50	50	50	50	50	50

For cohorts born before 1934, $\overline{N} = N_{max} = 150$.

Access to the full rate is also possible before 65 for people totalizing less than 150 quarters if they are considered disabled or suffer from handicap.

Values of $\overline{N}$ and D are currently changing, while N_{max} remains set to 150. As mentioned in the introduction, the value of $\overline{N}$ should reach 160 quarters when the 1993 reform fully produces its effects (cohorts born after 1943). The same reform also scheduled a progressive increase of D, up to twenty-five years (to be reached for cohorts born after 1948). But for the cohorts we are going to consider here, the rules are those that prevailed between 1983 (when the possibility of retiring at age 60 was generalized) and 1993, that is, $\overline{N} = 150$ (37.5 years) and $D =$ ten years.

This system means that the number of years of contribution affects the pension level in two ways, which may imply, in some cases, a very strong dependency between the age at retirement and the level of the pension. To provide a full understanding of this interaction, table 4.2 shows the consequences of this system, with pre-1993 parameters for three reference cases with individuals arriving at age 60 with, respectively, twenty-five, thirty, and thirty-five years of contribution.

- The first individual had to wait until age 65 to get retirement at a full rate α (50 percent). Even then, however, his or her pension was reduced by the fact that he or she only totaled 120 quarters of contribution at this age. The replacement ratio was therefore only equal to 120/150 of the maximum replacement ratio, which is equal to 50 percent. Note that, at each age lower than 60, the downward adjustment of α is here computed on the basis of the number of years missing to reach age 65 rather than the number of quarters missing to reach a value of N equal to 150, since the rule consists of applying the most advantageous of the two adjustments.
- The second individual also had to wait until age 65 to get the full rate α, but benefited at this age of a higher replacement rate, equal to 140/150 of the maximum replacement ratio of 50 percent. In this case, the

Table 4.2   Replacement rate provided by the general regime and the civil servants regime for three reference cases (%)

Age	Tenure (years)	α (general regime without complementary schemes) (1)	α (civil servants) (2)	No. of years/37.5 (3)	Replacement ratio, general regime (1) × (3)	Replacement ratio, civil servants (2) × (3)
			Individual A			
60	25	25	75	0.667	16.7	50.0
61	26	30	75	0.693	20.8	52.0
62	27	35	75	0.720	25.2	54.0
63	28	40	75	0.747	29.9	56.0
64	29	45	75	0.773	34.8	58.0
65	30	50	75	0.800	40.0	60.0
			Individual B			
60	30	25	75	0.800	20.0	60.0
61	31	30	75	0.827	24.8	62.0
62	32	35	75	0.853	29.9	64.0
63	33	40	75	0.880	35.2	66.0
64	34	45	75	0.907	40.8	68.0
65	35	50	75	0.933	46.7	70.0
			Individual C			
60	35	37.5	75	0.933	35.0	70.0
61	36	42.5	75	0.960	40.8	72.0
62	37	47.5	75	0.987	46.9	74.0
63	38	50	75	1.000	50.0	75.0
64	39	50	75	1.000	50.0	75.0
65	40	50	75	1.000	50.0	75.0

downward adjustment before age 65 is again based on the number of years missing to reach age 65.

- The third person will not have to wait until age 65. He or she will benefit from the maximum replacement rate as soon as he or she reaches a cumulated number of years of contributions equal to 150, that is, at age 62.5. If he or she decides to leave between age 60 and 62.5, the downward adjustment will now be computed according to the number of years missing to reach the total of 150 contributed years, rather than the number of years missing to reach age 65, since the first rule is now the most generous. Note also that, for this person, working past the age of 62.5 does not bring any further advantage in terms of the basic pension level.

Some additional observations must be added to this presentation of the general scheme:

- Some people were successively affiliated with different schemes, especially in older generations: for instance, people transiting from agriculture or self-employment to the status of wage earner in industry or in services. These people will cumulate two basic pensions, one from their initial scheme and one from the general scheme. The latter one will be proportional to the number of years spent in this scheme, according to equation (1), yet coefficient α will be evaluated taking into account the *total* number of years contributed, whatever the scheme. Reductions of α, furthermore, do not apply in a certain number of cases: veterans, disabled workers, female workers with 24 contributed years, and having raised three children.
- Equation (1) also implies that pensions, at the time they are claimed, are computed in current French francs. They are then reevaluated each year on a discretionary basis. During the 1970s and early 1980s, the general policy was to overindex these pensions (with respect to the average gross wage) in order to make up for the initial gap between standards of living of workers and pensioners. Since the mid-1980s, the practice has rather consisted of an indexation on prices. This practice has been confirmed by the 1993 reform.
- When the average wage (D best years) falls below a floor, it is raised to the level of that floor (about €12,000 in 2000) for individuals who can claim a full-rate pension. These provisions (the *minimum contributif*) mainly concern women who had part-time jobs or whose careers were short and whose annual earnings are thus very low. They involve an additional strong incentive to postpone retirement until the full rate.
- For women, $N_{\max}$ and $N'_{\max}$ are increased by two years for each child they raised. Moreover, people (either men or women) who raised at least three children enjoy a 10 percent increase in their basic pension.

Complementary Schemes

These schemes are almost fully contributory and are organized in a defined-contribution way (although they are not funded). Workers accumulate *points* during their careers, which are the pension's basic unit of calculation:

1. Points are accumulated during workers' careers in proportion to their contributions: the contribution rate is fixed, and 1 franc contributed in year t is considered equivalent to the formal buying of $1/PP_t$ points, where PP_t is the purchase price of one point (the official term for this purchase price is *salaire de référence*).

2. The pension is then equal to the total number of points accumulated over the pensioner's career, multiplied by a coefficient V (*valeur du point*), which is fixed every year.

The pension level at time t can therefore be written for a pensioner who started working at time t_0 and stopped at time t_1 as:

$$(2) \qquad \text{pension} = V(t) \cdot \sum_{t'=t_0}^{t_1} \frac{\tau(t')w(t')}{PP(t')},$$

where $\tau(t')$ and $w(t')$ are, respectively, the contribution rate and the worker's wage at time t'. As explained previously, only a fraction of the wage is taken into account for computing contributions and points accumulated each year:

1. For executives, contributions are collected by ARRCO for the part of the wage below the ceiling, and by AGIRC for the segment of the wage that is comprised between one and four ceilings.

2. For nonexecutives, the wage is truncated to three times the social security ceiling, and contributions are collected by ARRCO.

Concerning retirement age in these complementary schemes—normal retirement theoretically remains at age 65, even after the 1983 reform, which introduced retirement at age 60 in the *general scheme*. For retirement below 65, a quasi-actuarial adjustment is supposed to be applied. But, since the 1983 reform, this adjustment is not applied to people who fulfill the conditions for a basic retirement at full rate (more than 37.5 years of contribution).

4.2.3   Civil Servants

Civil servants have a unique pension scheme, directly financed from the state budget. As a general rule, pension claiming is possible at age 60, if people have at least fifteen years of service. A rather large minority can, however, leave at age 55: primary school teachers, policemen, and prison officers. For women who have raised at least three children, the age condition is completely relaxed. The benefit formula is:

$$(3) \quad \text{Pension} = 0.75 \times \left[\frac{\text{Number of quarters, truncated to } N_{\text{max}}}{N_{\text{max}}} \right]$$

$$\times \text{(last gross wage, excluding bonuses)}$$

The pension is a proportion of the last gross wage. Note that this gross wage excludes bonuses, which represent, on average, 15 percent of the total net income (and up to 50 percent for some specific categories). These bonuses remain insignificant for most civil servants working for the Education Department, which is the largest employer, but can reach 50 percent of the total net income for some specific categories, those with the highest incomes.

The key variable is the number of years a civil servant worked. Each year entitles him or her to a 2 percent annuity (table 4.2), the sum being truncated to 75 percent. Once this basic annuity is computed, some other periods may be taken into account: the most important provision is the additional year given to women for each child they raised. Each additional year also yields an additional 2 percent annuity, which may increase the basic annuity up to 80 percent. Finally, people (men or women) who raised at least three children enjoy a substantial increase in their pension. This increase is 10 percent if they have raised three children, and an extra 5 percent for every additional child. These provisions are roughly the same as in the private sector.

Note that this system strongly differs from the *general regime* as regards incentives to retire early: let us consider the example of people reaching the legal minimum age of retirement with only 32.5 contributing years, who decide to immediately claim their benefits. The civil servant's replacement rate is 65 percent (instead of 75 percent for a complete career). The private-sector wage earner's replacement rate (basic pension only) is 21.7 percent (instead of 50 percent for a complete career).

4.2.4 Survivor Benefits

Civil servants' as well as private-sector wage earners' widowers or widows may enjoy survivor benefits. The computation of these benefits is rather complex and we will give only their main features here, since our data prevent us from precisely computing these benefits (regarding the lack of information on spouses, see the following).

In the late 80s and early 90s (when our cohorts effectively retired), survivor benefits were far more generous for women than men: a civil servant's widow could enjoy survivor benefits (typically 50 percent of her husband's pension entitlements) whatever her age, whereas a civil servant's widower had to wait until 60. Moreover, benefits were capped at a relatively low level for widowers, which was not the case for widows. In the private sector, women could enjoy spouse benefits from age 55, whereas widowers had to wait until 65, and benefits were means tested. Gender discrimination was removed from the private sector in the late 90s, but the situation has remained unchanged for civil servants' widows or widowers.

4.2.5   Other Regulations Concerning Age at Retirement: Mandatory Retirement and Eligibility to Early Retirement Benefits

It is only for civil servants or in special schemes that mandatory retirement exists as such. The age for mandatory retirement is generally 65, with some exceptions either below that age (i.e., the armed forces) or above (very limited categories are allowed to work until age 68, such as academics).

In the private sector, a firm is not allowed to lay off a worker according to any age criterion. Yet it is allowed to do so when this worker reaches the conditions to get a full-rate SS pension. Given the employment context of the 1990s—and the relatively large wage gap between elder and younger workers—it is quite likely that firms will quasi-systematically make use of this possibility. A consequence, which will be recalled later when interpreting results, is that decisions to retire at the age when people get the full rate may be interpreted as demand-side as well as supply-side decisions.

Supply- and demand-side aspects are also strongly intertwined for all forms of early retirement. Early retirement developed in several steps in France. We will only describe the rules enacted after the 1983 reform, that is, after the generalization of possibilities to retire at age 60. There are two main paths to early exit from the labor force.

- One is through unemployment insurance. People falling into unemployment are entitled to a compensation for a limited period of time; the level of unemployment benefits, since 1992, is decreasing with the duration of unemployment. But these rules do not apply to people losing their jobs past a certain age (57 until mid-1993, now raised to 58), who can benefit from a full compensation until they are able to benefit from a normal SS pension at a full rate. This system is not officially described as an early retirement system, and people cannot enter into it completely freely: they can do so only if they have been explicitly laid off by their employers. Yet this system is more or less equivalent to an early retirement scheme.
- The second path for early exit is the *Fonds National pour l'Emploi* (FNE [National Fund for Employment]). The level of early retirement benefits is roughly similar to the level of unemployment benefits. People benefiting from this system can leave the labor force at around 58, with benefits maintained until they have access to a full-rate pension in the general regime. The difference from the former path is that this system is under direct control of the state: access to the FNE only concerns workers laid off in the context of a social plan, negotiated between the firm and the state, with some compensations offered by the firm (for instance, a commitment to hire young workers).

4.2.6   Labor Market Participation among Older Workers

Participation of men aged 50 and over sharply decreased over the past twenty years. The share of men employed at ages 55, 60, and 65 decreased from 83.4 percent, 47.0 percent, and 14.7 percent in 1983 to 78.5 percent, 32.1 percent, and 4.9 percent in 1998. The figures are somewhat different for women—52.2 percent, 29.1 percent, and 9.4 percent in 1983, 57.9 percent, 25.9 percent, and 5.9 percent in 1998—since cohort effects (the long-run increase of female labor supply) partly offset the effect of both economic difficulties (with growing exits through unemployment or early retirement) and the decrease to 60 of the minimum age to get SS benefits. Nonetheless, the regular decrease in male participation rates appears to have slowed down since 1997, due to the economic recovery.

In 1998 (table 4.3) employment rates reached 75 percent for people aged 50 to 54, but sharply decreased thereafter: 53 percent for the 55 to 59 age group, and only 12.4 percent (most of them being self-employed) for the 60 to 64 age group. Participation rates are close to zero after 65. Very few self-employed retire before 60. However, exit rates are high from 55 onward for wage earners.

About 8 percent of the population received public benefits (mainly unemployment benefits) between 50 and 54 in 1998 (table 4.4). This figure reaches 23.7 percent between 55 and 59, due to unemployment or early retirement (in the private sector) or SS benefits (for a sizeable minority of

Table 4.3   **Labor market participation by age group**

Age	Cohort	Employed			Not working
		Public sector	Private sector	Self-employed	
50–54	1944–48	22.6	33.4	18.8	25.2
55–59	1939–43	13.3	21.9	18.0	46.8
60–64	1934–38	2.5	3.5	6.4	87.6
65–69	1929–33	0.0	0.3	1.2	98.5

Source: Financial Assets Survey, Insee (1998).

Table 4.4   **Part of the population receiving public benefits by age group**

Age	Cohort	SS benefits	Preretirement benefits	Unemployment benefits	Total
50–54	1944–48	1.3	0.0	7.2	8.5
55–59	1939–43	9.4	6.0	8.3	23.7
60–64	1934–38	68.9	1.4	2.4	72.7
65–59	1929–33	86.2	0.0	0.0	86.2

Source: Financial Assets Survey, Insee (1998).

civil servants). Between 60 and 64, 72.7 percent of the population receive public benefits (now mainly SS benefits).

Research Background

Previous research on retirement behavior in France is relatively scarce, partly because economists lacked appropriate data until the *échantillon inter-régime de retraités* (EIR) was built. Moreover, individuals were so heavily constrained by SS incentives that explaining actual behaviors did not require a sophisticated approach (in econometric terms, for instance). In the first part of this project, Blanchet and Pelé (1999) showed that incentives to retire at the full rate were very strong. Pelé and Ralle (1999), using a life cycle model (based on an intertemporal budget constraint), demonstrated that retiring at the full rate was consistent with a rational utility-maximizing behavior.

Of course, retirement cannot entirely be explained by SS incentives: analyzing early retirement behaviors in France as a three-player game (the firm, the employee, and the government) may be of great interest, but once again, the lack of appropriate, firm data did not allow for a comprehensive analysis of individual behavior concerning early retirement.

4.3   Data Description

4.3.1   The Dataset

Few systematic datasets exist in France concerning the economic situation of retired people. Income surveys only give instantaneous and imperfect pictures of transfer incomes benefiting to retirees: they do not allow the reconstitution of past labor income, which would permit the evaluation of what these transfers would have been if the pensioners had made other choices concerning their age at retirement.

Some other specific surveys were also realized to analyze the transition between activity and retirement (e.g., a questionnaire on this topic was added to the regular Labor Force Survey in 1996). These surveys are especially useful for analyzing the variety of institutional paths from full-time activity to retirement (Caussat and Roth [1997], Burricand and Roth [2000]) and provide some interesting information on standards of living before retirement. But these surveys do not provide precise information on past wages and thus do not allow us to compute financial incentives to retirement.

In practice, the only large-scale survey that is available and that is suited for the current study is a specific panel, the EIR. This permanent survey (whose origin goes back to 1984[1]) matches administrative data collected from all pension schemes that exist in France. This strategy revealed itself

---

1. The operation has been initially organized by the SESI, the statistical unit within the ministry of social affairs, in connection with the INSEE. Since 1998, the SESI has been absorbed in a new direction within the Ministry of Social Affairs, the *Direction de la Recherche, des Etudes, de l'Evaluation et des Statistiques* (DREES).

to be the only way to overcome problems raised by the multiplicity of pension schemes in France. The other possibility—relying directly on pensioners' declarations—would have been necessarily partial and incomplete (given the limited knowledge these pensioners may themselves have of these various schemes).

The survey was organized as follows. For the first run, in 1988, four cohorts of pensioners were selected: those born in 1906, 1912, 1918, and 1922. A sample totaling 20,000 people belonging to these four cohorts was drawn by the Institut National de la Statistique et des Études (INSEE). Their national identification numbers were transmitted by INSEE to all existing pension schemes (more than 120 basic schemes and about 180 complementary schemes). All these pension schemes then had to search for these individuals in their records. If they were present, the information about their pension entitlements was then transmitted to the statistics, studies and information systems department, ministry of Social Affairs and Solidarity (SESI), who then carried out the matching, for all individuals of the sample, of the information returned by all existing pension schemes. Note that this matching, by the SESI, has been made according to an identification number that was different from the national identification number, in order to preserve the anonymity of final data.

The survey was renewed in 1993 and 1997. Each time, the same samples were redrawn for the cohorts included in the previous studies (and enlarged to compensate for mortality), and new cohorts added to the panel: cohort 1926 in 1993, cohorts 1930, 1932, 1934, 1936, 1938, 1940, and 1942 in 1997 (table 4.5). Since 1990, an additional matching has also been introduced, with information from other administrative sources:

Table 4.5   **Descriptive statistics on the sample**

Variable	Mean value
Sex (Male = 0, Female = 1)	0.439
Age	57.4
Married	0.753
Widowed	0.113
Single	0.125
Wage (euros)	20,095
Executive (private)	0.126
Technician (private)	0.154
Employee (private)	0.215
Skilled blue-collar (private)	0.189
Unskilled blue-collar (private)	0.105
Category A (public)	0.119
Category B (public)	0.055
Category C (public)	0.037
Total tenure (years)	36.4

Note: Sample size = 10,572 observations corresponding to 2,352 individual paths.

1. The Annual Declarations of Social Data (DADS), made each year by firms, which allow one to retrieve wages of people of the sample over the years before retirement, if these people were wage earners in the private sector or employed in state-owned companies.

2. The wage files from the State Service, for former civil servants.

3. Files from the National Professional Union for the Employment in Industry and Trade (UNEDIC), the French system of unemployment insurance, for people in unemployment before retirement (allowing, therefore, for the incorporation of the form of early retirement offered by the UNEDIC and the French National Employment Fund (FNF), as previously discussed).

This matching, however, does not allow a full reconstitution of past careers for these pensioners. DADS, in particular, generally do not go back further than 1985, with one additional missing year in 1990. This matching, for this reason, has not been done for cohorts 1906, 1912, and 1918, for whom it would have been irrelevant.

Given the structure of data available in the panel, our question has been to explore how these data could be best used for the estimation of a model of retirement behavior for France. The choices that have been made resulted from two constraints.

1. The need to have people for whom the situation before retirement has been observed over a significant period, in order to be able to extrapolate what their standard of living would have been in case they would have retired later than they actually did.

2. The need, conversely, to limit ourselves to cohorts for whom entry into retirement can be considered as fully completed. As detailed in the next subsection, our method for reconstructing individual pension entitlements under alternative retirement ages relies essentially on the pension level obtained at the *actual* retirement age. Of course, one possibility would have been, for people not yet retired, to evaluate entitlements on the basis of past working records. But the length of our wage records was too short for such a reconstitution, and for this population our files did not provide any proxy at all for the key variable, which is the number of quarters of past contribution.

The first constraint clearly ruled out cohorts 1906 to 1922. We also considered that wage data were too short, on average, for cohort 1926 (only two years of wages being observed for an individual of this cohort retiring in 1986). The second constraint, at the opposite end, ruled out cohorts 1934 to 1942. Even if a significant share of these cohorts was retired in 1997, we would have missed the fraction retiring at 65, which is precisely the fraction that brings the variance necessary to identify models. We considered that the same problem existed for workers from the private sector in cohort 1932. So, for this category, we finally restricted ourselves to cohort 1930. For civil servants, however, we decided to use both cohorts 1930 and 1932, in order to increase somewhat the sample size, considering that the selection bias on cohort 1932 was lower than for the private sector, given an average age at retirement that is lower in the public than in the private sector.

Concerning the key question of the definition of retirement, our data provided us with two possible choices: either the age when people definitely leave the labor market, or the age when people claim SS benefits. But this latter definition is not the most interesting from an economic point of view, since a huge majority of people in the private sector claim SS benefits as soon as they reach the full rate. It is more interesting to analyze the impact of SS provisions (and, if possible, early retirement or unemployment provisions) on the decision to definitely leave the labor market. We therefore decided to model the last year of recorded past employment using DADS data. This, of course, implies a restriction to people who are in paid employment in 1985, which limits a bit further our sample.

4.3.2 Reconstructing Wages, Taxes, and Pension Levels

Our data yield net wages (gross wages minus SS contributions) for all wage earners still employed at age 55. We assume that wages then increase, like the Consumer Price Index (CPI), for people employed in the private sector. For civil servants, we assume that wages increase from age 55, like the so-called "civil service point" that has been roughly following the CPI evolutions for more than fifteen years.

We compute income taxes assuming that people in our sample have only wage or pension income or are single (or, equivalently, married with their spouse earning the same income) with no children. This assumption is, of course, excessive, but we lack additional information on nonwage and nonpension income. Concerning indirect taxes, the normal VAT rate in France was 18.6 percent in the late 1980s and early 1990s, but some specific products were taxed at a 5.5 percent reduced rate. We compute an apparent VAT factor based on national accounts. This factor is defined as the share of indirect taxes (VAT, taxes on tobacco and alcohol, etc.) in personal disposable income. We thus assume an apparent VAT rate of 13.9 percent.

Social security payroll taxes do not really exist for civil servants, since pensions are directly paid on the state budget. We therefore compute pseudo-contributions for civil servants by assuming that the total SS payroll tax rate is the same for civil servants as for people employed in the private sector.

4.3.3 Other Data

Computing the actual value of future pension benefits required some additional information: information on people's own mortality risk, and information on the presence of a spouse and this spouse's mortality risk, assuming that individual evaluations of benefits include the evaluation of survival benefits if the individual dies before his or her spouse.

Mortality rates for people in the sample that was used are differentiated by sex and age but not by socioprofessional group, as in step 2. One point must be noted here: since the sample is conditioned on surviving until age 64 or 66 (depending on the cohort), a selection bias may result if there is a correlation between mortality and the retirement decision. If people with bad health status and a higher mortality risk tend to more frequently anticipate the claiming of their benefits, there will be a tendency to overestimate the actual age at retirement. However, judging from the mortality rates, this phenomenon should have a limited impact, as 14 percent of men and 5.4 percent of women die between 55 and 65.

The final sample consists of 10,572 observations (table 4.5) corresponding to 2,352 individuals still employed at 55 (who are thus observed, on average, between four and five years before they retire). Seventy-five percent of them are employed in the private sector (with a majority being men). Note that the average tenure at 55 is pretty high (over thirty-six years) and close to the tenure required to reach the full rate at 60: this reflects the fact that most people from the sample are entitled to full SS benefits as soon as age 60.

Analyzing pathways to retirement is straightforward for civil servants (they have no other choice than waiting until the minimum age to claim SS benefits, unless they choose to consume their savings). In the private sector (table 4.6), about 60 percent of people still working at 55 do not receive public benefits other than SS benefits. The remaining 40 percent are roughly equally divided between people retiring through unemployment and early retirement schemes.

Table 4.7 provides information on the level of the parameter α. A very tiny minority of men (0.3 percent) claim SS benefits are reduced rate, whereas the figure grows to 4.4 percent for women. About 4 percent of men and women are considered as disabled and are thus allowed to claim full-

Table 4.6   **Pathways to retirement in the sample**

	Retiree category			
	Private sector			Civil servants
Pathway	Men	Women	Total	Total
Directly to SS	57.4	60.8	58.7	100.0
Preretirement then SS	20.7	18.4	19.8	0.0
Unemployment then SS	21.9	20.8	21.5	0.0

Source: EIR, 1930 cohort, people still working at 55.

Table 4.7   **Level of the pension rate (α) when people claim SS benefits (private sector; %)**

	Men	Women
Full rate		
Normal conditions	92.0	81.0
Unfit for a job	3.7	10.7
Disabled	4.0	3.9
Reduced rate	0.3	4.4

rate SS benefits from 60 (even if their tenure is below 150 quarters) is 3.7 percent of men and 10.7 percent of women. The percentage that are unfit to hold a job and thus benefit from a full-rate pension from age 60. Others (over 80 percent of the sample) reach the full rate in normal conditions. In the public sector, there is no such incentive to postpone claiming SS benefits after the minimum age (mostly 60), since α is set to 0.75 whatever the total tenure. Nonetheless, it is worthwhile noting that the retirement rate for civil servants who reach age 60 with 150 quarters or more is 69 percent, whereas it drops to 53 percent for those who reach age 60 with less than 150 quarters. Moreover, the mean wage of civil servants who keep on working after 60 is €32,000 (instead of €23,400 for those who quit at 60). Others (over 80 percent of the sample) reach the full rate in normal conditions. In the public sector, there is no such incentive to postpone claiming SS benefits after the minimum age (mostly 60), since α is set to 0.75 whatever the total tenure. Nonetheless, it is worthwhile noting that the retirement rate for civil servants who reach age 60 with 150 quarters or more is 69 percent, whereas it drops to 53 percent for those who reach age 60 with less than 150 quarters. Moreover, the mean wage of civil servants who keep on working after 60 is €32,000 (instead of €23,400 for those who quit at 60). Remember that highly paid civil servants have—on average—lower replacement rates, since a large part of their wage consists in bonuses. At first glance, civil servants also seem sensitive to SS incentives (despite their weakness). But these preliminary observations must be confirmed by a deeper analysis.

4.3.4   Spouse Issues

This chapter differs from our previous work since we take survivor benefits into account. An ideal solution would have been to calculate an expected survivor benefit for each married individual of the sample, conditioned on the spouse characteristics (particularly his or her SS entitlements). However, we do not have such information. A solution would be to match married males with every married female of the sample or with a typical inactive woman, to compute survivor benefits for each of these would-be couples and deduce an average survivor benefit using appropriate weights. However, our data provide no relevant information on the way individual characteristics affect the individual process (for example, do educated men marry educated women? Moreover, we have no information on educational achievements). We thus eliminated this time-consuming solution and considered the survivor benefit of an average would-be spouse.

Married women in our sample are arbitrarily matched with a would-be man with average male SS benefits. Married men are matched with a would-be woman with average female SS benefits (with weight 0.8) and with zero SS benefits (with weight 0.2). In these elderly cohorts, about 20 percent of women never worked and thus cannot enjoy SS benefits when they reach age 60. We assume an age difference of two years between the spouses, which matches what is commonly observed in French data.

4.4   A Descriptive Analysis of Incentives to Retire

4.4.1   Definition of Incentive Variables

Two kinds of model will be applied to the analysis of labor force participation rates of older workers. In a first step, we introduce simple measures of SS incentives to retire in probit models to describe the choice to retire at age t for individuals still in the labor force at this age. For an individual aged t, we first compute social security wealth at age t. The value of this SSW will depend on the age $t' \geq t$ at which this individual will decide to retire. $B_s(t')$ is the probability of surviving up to age s for an individual aged t, and if T, at last, is the maximal age at death, we write:

$$SSW_{t,t'} = \sum_{s=t'}^{T} \beta^{s-t} \pi\left(\frac{s}{t}\right) B_s(t')$$

If, when he or she is 55, an individual is married and his or her spouse is alive, we add to this value the social security wealth corresponding to the spouse's would-be survivor pension if the spouse outlives the studied individual. In terms of social security wealth, the survivor pension is recorded for the spouse who dies first and is thus at the origin of this survivor benefit. If $SB_s(t')$ is the expected level of survivor pension at age s if the individual retires at age t'; if $\pi_{spouse}(s/55)$ is the probability that the spouse survives up to age $s\pm2$ (according to gender) conditioned on being alive at 55, as we assume here an age difference of two years between the spouses. The SSW of the studied individual is:

$$SSW_{t,t'} = \sum_{s=t'}^{T} \beta^{s-t} \pi\left(\frac{s}{t}\right) B_s(t') + \sum_{s=t'}^{T} \beta^{s-t}\left[1 - \pi\left(\frac{s}{t}\right)\right]\pi_{spouse}\left(\frac{s}{55}\right) SB_s(t')$$

From this value, we derive the pension accrual at age t, which is the algebraic increase in SSW that results, at age t, from the postponement of retirement by one year, that is,

$$\text{Accrual}_t = \text{SSW}_{t,t+1} - \text{SSW}_{t,t}.$$

The accrual will be our first measure of SS incentives. The tax rate is directly derived from the accrual. It captures the fact that a negative accrual involves an implicit tax on continued work: a part of the expected wage (if the individual postpones retirement) is taxed through the decrease in the SSW. The tax rate thus writes:

$$\text{Tax rate}_t = -\frac{\text{Accrual}_t}{E_t w_{t+1}}$$

An alternative measure is also directly derived from the definition of SSW. This variable is the peak index, which is the difference between the maximum of the SSWs associated to all possible ages at retirement beyond the current year, and SSW in case of an immediate retirement.

$$\text{Peak}_t = \underset{s \geq t+1}{\text{Max}}[\text{SSW}_{t,s}] - \text{SSW}_{t,t}$$

It assumes a less myopic behavior by the individual, who considers not only the potential gain in SSW resulting from delaying retirement by one year, but also gains that may be derived from retiring in any subsequent year. However, as with all measures derived from SSW, a limitation of this index is that it does not take into account the comparison that the individual can make between pension benefits and the level of his or her labor income. It assumes that the retirement decision is only affected by variations of pension entitlements. This limitation will be corrected in the following estimation by the introduction of wages as covariates in probit models, but it is more satisfactory to introduce incentive measures that introduce this comparison between benefit and wage levels in a less ad hoc way.

This is the case if we start from a model that fully includes expected flows of utility derived either from labor or retirement income. The model used will be the Stock and Wise (1990) option value model. Let us consider again an individual still in the labor force at age t. If he or she expects to retire at age r, he or she can expect a flow of labor incomes of $(Y_t, \ldots Y_{r-1})$ until retirement, and then a flow of pension benefits $[B_r(r), B_{r+1}(r), \ldots, B_s(r), \ldots]$. It is assumed that this individual derives an indirect utility U_w from his or her labor income and an indirect utility U_r from pension benefits. Time discounting occurs at rate β. For an age at retirement equal to r, the expected utility at age t is therefore:

$$V_t(r) = \sum_{s=t}^{r-1} \beta^{s-t} E_t[U_w(Y_s)] + \sum_{s=r}^{T} \beta^{s-t} E_t\{U_r[B_s(r)]\},$$

with

$$U_w(Y_s) = Y_s^{\gamma}$$
$$U_w(B_s) = (kB_s)^{\gamma}.$$

Note that this specification does not consider the possibility of smoothing income flows through private savings, an assumption that will essentially be valid for low- or medium-income workers. Given this definition of utility, we assume that the individual decides to retire if the resulting expected utility is higher than the maximum value of utilities expected for all other possible choices $r > t$. If we write

$$G_t(r) = V_t(r) - V_t(t),$$

the individual chooses to remain in the labor force if $G_t(r^*) > 0$, where

$$r^* = Arg \operatorname*{Max}_{r \geq t+1} V_t(r).$$

Therefore, $G_t(r^*) > 0$ is called the option value of postponing retirement to express that, given the irreversibility of retirement, remaining in the labor force offers the option to leave the labor force at a later age under better conditions. Stock and Wise (1990) performed a full maximum-likelihood estimation of the model on American data, which yielded $\beta = 0.97$, $\kappa = 1.25$, and $\gamma = 0.6$. Our own estimation of the model on French data led us to adopt the following parameterization: $\beta = 0.97$, $\kappa = 1.6$, and $\gamma = 0.25$. These values imply some risk aversion and a moderate preference for leisure: in the context of a one-period model, a value of κ equal to 1.6 means that an individual would demand a leisure income equal to 62.5 percent of his or her labor income to accept retirement.

4.4.2 Including Incentives Linked to Unemployment and Early-Retirement Benefits

We performed simulations of retirement decisions based on previous estimations. The main issue raised by our estimation process is the possibility offered to a number of workers to leave the labor market before the minimum age required to claim SS benefits: these workers receive unemployment or early retirement benefits that may *both* be viewed as early retirement benefits. This would not be a critical issue if we controlled for the eligibility to these programs. Unfortunately, this is not the case: this would require firm data providing some information on who had the possibility to get early retirement or unemployment benefits and who decided to retire.

We took account of these possible pathways in the following manner: assume, as a first step, that an individual is actually free to choose one of these means of early exit from the labor force. We can therefore compute three values for the SSW: the one computed earlier on the basis of normal pension entitlements only, the ones if we assume that the individual begins by spending a few years in unemployment or in the early retirement scheme and then moves on to normal retirement once he or she is entitled to the social security full rate. For instance, for an individual aged 55, we compute the following values, depending on age t, at which he or she will leave the labor force:

$$SSW1_{55,t} = \sum_{s=60}^{T} \beta^{s-t} \pi\left(\frac{s}{t}\right) B_s^{Pension}(t)$$

if the individual only relies on his or her normal pension;

$$SSW2_{55,t} = \sum_{s=t}^{59} \beta^{s-t} \pi\left(\frac{s}{t}\right) B_s^{une}(t) + \sum_{s=60}^{T} \beta^{s-t} \pi\left(\frac{s}{t}\right) B_s^{Pension}(t)$$

for a transition through unemployment insurance;

$$SSW3_{55,t} = \sum_{s=t}^{59} \beta^{s-t} \pi\left(\frac{s}{t}\right) B_s^{pre}(t) + \sum_{s=60}^{T} \beta^{s-t} \pi\left(\frac{s}{t}\right) B_s^{Pension}(t)$$

for a transition through early retirement.

Benefits B_s^{une} and B_s^{pre} are computed as a fraction of the last wage by direct application of official rules.

We then compute a weighted average of these three SSWs. Weights are a function of the sector of activity and reflect take-up probabilities. We tested other covariates, like gender or professional status (executives versus blue collar versus white collars), but their coefficients are mostly insignificant if sector dummies are included. This strategy is consistent with the results of previous studies that show that the sector of activity predicts access to early retirement or unemployment schemes far better than job skills or social group (Colin, Iéhlé, and Matieu 2000). As a general rule, the probability of facing a period of unemployment or early retirement at the end of one's career is markedly higher (at least for cohorts born around 1930) in industry. In particular, it is the automobile industry that concentrates the highest risks: at 55, there was a 60 percent probability of entering into unemployment or early retirement for a wage earner in the automobile industry. The reason is that around 1985, some sectors (including the automobile industry) benefited from exceptions, allowing for a lower age at entry in Allocation spéciale du Fonds national de l'emploi (ASFNE; fifty-five years instead of fifty-six years, two months).

These weights are conditional final probabilities: for a worker with a given age (e.g., 57) in a given sector (e.g., industry) we use the observed probability for this worker of this sector to retire through early retirement provisions (either early retirement or unemployment benefits) *conditional on still participating at that age (here 57) and whatever his or her actual age of retirement.* Note that this dependency on age is crucial, since eligibility to these programs typically changes with age. For the considered cohorts, exit probabilities through early retirement or unemployment benefits were rather high at 55 or 56, and then sharply decreased for those who remained in the labor market (there were types of window plans for workers aged 55 to 56 in the mid-80s in France). We finally compute incentives (Accrual, PV, and OV) with this weighted SSW.

4.4.3   Spouse Issues

The incentive variables are computed here for individuals; they include, nevertheless, survivor benefits. A household SSW would be defined as the sum of the SSW of the two spouses. But as we have explained previously, the only way to generate households is to simulate an average spouse. The spouse characteristics (wages, retirement ages, etc.) depend only on gender, and do not result from any matching criterion. As a consequence, for all the individuals of a given gender, the spouse's SSW is a constant. Therefore, in our case, the household SSW would only differ from the individual SSW by a constant and would not add any information to incentive variables.

4.4.4   Descriptive Results and Econometric Analysis

Descriptive Statistics

Table 4.8 yields the median values of each incentive distinguished by age. The results given here are quite different from those of the second step, but several changes in our simulation method (especially the fact that we include survivor benefits in the computation of incentives) may account for these discrepancies.

The tax rate incentive variable is defined as the opposite of the ratio between the accrual incentive and the expected wage if the worker postpones retirement. It may be considered as a tax rate since, if it is positive, the SSW decreases and part of the expected labor income is lost through social security mechanisms.

Average SSW levels in these tables may differ substantially from those in other country studies. Two main limitations in our data may explain these large figures.

1. We excluded the self-employed from our analysis, which induces an upward bias on SSW, since the self-employed in the aftermath of World War II voluntarily chose less generous pension schemes to avoid paying large social security contributions.

2. Concerning civil servants, our data exclude those employed by local governments or hospitals. Civil servants working for hospitals or local governments are, on average, less skilled and thus lower paid than those

Table 4.8 **Median values of incentives**

Age	NB	SSW	Accrual	Tax	Peak	Option
			A. Men, private sector			
55	1,182	240,585	−3,361	0.23	−1,929	32.22
56	914	233,193	−3,647	0.26	−1,143	29.72
57	755	229,450	−1,399	0.12	3,034	26.26
58	647	232,680	913	−0.05	4,948	20.15
59	547	232,423	3,633	−0.21	3,660	11.61
60	512	235,690	−9,783	0.64	−9,783	−0.11
61	169	227,101	−8,436	0.53	−8,436	0.81
62	109	244,038	−8,308	0.47	−8,308	1.48
63	74	222,876	−9,025	0.52	−9,025	0.71
64	56	203,996	−8,467	0.53	−8,467	0.55
65	41	183,713	−7,966	0.56	−7,966	0.11
			B. Men, civil servants			
55	188	352,388	5,390	−0.25	10,244	55.05
56	160	353,343	3,223	−0.15	8,624	45.41
57	134	352,614	5,182	−0.25	9,132	35.04
58	131	358,863	3,045	−0.15	3,543	23.48
59	129	354,606	450	−0.02	450	12.06
60	125	359,480	−18,792	0.84	−18,942	−1.01
61	48	376,017	−21,324	0.86	−21,323	−1.06
62	35	360,196	−20,457	0.79	−20,457	−0.85
63	24	379,089	−25,094	0.91	−25,094	−1.29
64	19	372,915	−22,437	0.84	−22,437	−1.09
65	13	385,788	−28,404	0.91	−28,404	−14.09
			C. Women, private sector			
55	742	137,989	−2,123	0.18	1,332	37.73
56	584	133,732	−1,829	0.15	3,285	34.26
57	505	130,543	−721	0.06	4,234	30.27
58	427	129,559	19	0.00	4,342	23.59
59	361	129,716	2,819	−0.33	3,356	15.40
60	337	134,022	−3,340	0.30	−3,340	4.01
61	136	103,908	−1,011	0.12	−623	8.78
62	115	103,403	−1,237	0.13	1,316	8.39
63	92	98,107	−747	0.09	3,101	6.90
64	77	102,401	3,833	−0.45	3,909	4.28
65	62	107,266	−3,619	0.39	−3,619	0.76
			D. Women, civil servants			
55	240	331,980	−379	0.03	−379	12.25
56	189	316,266	2,059	−0.14	4,532	41.29
57	159	291,850	3,987	−0.25	9,360	32.63
58	149	286,929	2,727	−0.17	6,283	22.25
59	140	282,897	4,047	−0.27	4,047	11.63
60	135	281,714	−12,133	0.74	−12,133	−0.54
61	43	310,768	−12,865	0.61	−12,865	−0.23
62	32	293,548	−12,520	0.66	−12,520	−0.34
63	18	270,546	−15,484	0.86	−15,484	−1.12
64	11	226,657	−13,239	0.80	−13,239	−0.84
65	6	223,162	−14,359	0.90	−14,359	−11.97

directly employed by the central government. We thus overestimate the average civil servant's pension.

Econometric Analysis

The econometric estimations are performed with two different specifications of age: method S1 is based on a linear specification of the age variable, whereas age dummies (from age 55 to 65) are used with method S3. For each age specification (S1 or S3) two estimations are performed: one with the peak variable (PV) and another with the option variable (OV).

Coefficients on incentives variables are significant at the 5 percent level, with the expected sign in all simulations (see table 4.9). The coefficient is larger with the S1 simulation, since incentives related to ages of first eligibility to (early) retirement programs are better captured by age dummies than by the linear age variable or the incentive variables. The coefficient on SSW is not significant in all estimations and never has the expected (positive) sign: this result may stem from a positive correlation between SS entitlements and employees' productivity. Assume that a firm employs two types of old-age workers: the first group consists of highly paid, highly productive employees, and the second of low-paid workers, whose productivity is declining. Since the firm cannot decrease wages, this second group is overpaid—although paid less than the first group. It is costly to fire these workers, so the firm will wait until they can benefit from early retirement or other retirement programs, and then ask them to leave. As a result, this may create a negative correlation between the level of SSW and the likelihood to retire.

Age dummies are strongly significant. We may distinguish three groups of ages, ordered by increasing coefficients: the first age group contains ages 57 to 59 and 61 to 64. At those ages, very few people decide to claim SS benefits (either they claim benefits as early as possible—60 for the private sector, 55 for some civil servants—or they decide to wait until 65), and very few people leave their job to get early retirement benefits (for most, exits to early-retirement programs occur at ages 55 or 56). The second group contains ages 55 and 56: there are some exits to early retirement or even retirement for a minority of civil servants. The third group contains ages 60 and 65, the age of first eligibility to full-rate SS benefits for the huge majority of people in our sample.

The coefficient on the linear age variable is counterintuitive—since negative—with the OV specification: this may stem from unobserved heterogeneity in the preference for leisure in our sample: consider two populations that differ only in their preference for leisure. Those who have a high preference for leisure quit early, say at 60. At 61, the OV measure of the remaining population is lower than the OV measure of the whole population at 60 (there remain fewer years of potential continued work) but is underestimated (since the computation does not account for the endogenous se-

Table 4.9   **Probit model of retirement**

	Peak S1	Peak S3	Option S1	Option S3
Men				
SSW	–0.012	–0.005	–0.018	–0.013
	0.003	0.002	0.003	0.003
PV/OV	–0.267	–0.094	–0.053	–0.035
	0.020	0.020	0.003	0.003
Wage	0.074	0.020	0.277	0.174
Wage square	0.0025	0.0009	–0.0015	–0.0009
Age linear	0.077		–0.138	
Age				
55		Ref		Ref
56		–0.101		–0.188
57		–0.248		–0.445
58		–0.191		–0.608
59		–0.659		–1.360
60		1.262		0.280
61		0.473		–0.543
62		0.437		–0.621
63		0.171		–0.928
64		0.300		–0.840
65		1.440		0.233
Women				
SSW	–0.002	0.006	–0.019	–0.011
	0.006	0.006	0.006	0.007
PV/OV	–0.319	–0.195	–0.039	–0.028
	0.027	0.026	0.003	0.003
Wage	0.008	–0.169	0.380	0.175
Wage square	0.0053	0.0186	–0.0238	–0.0092
Age linear	0.088		–0.057	
Age				
55		Ref		Ref
56		–0.252		–0.329
57		–0.199		–0.408
58		–0.192		–0.556
59		–0.658		–1.224
60		1.129		0.448
61		–0.028		–0.745
62		0.266		–0.494
63		0.098		–0.703
64		0.188		–0.662
65		2.094		1.201

lection on the preference for leisure). Nonetheless, the observed retirement rate will be lower at 61 than at 60, since the considered population has a low preference for leisure. If the econometrician does not observe the preference for leisure, the coefficients of linear age variables will be significantly negative.

4.5   Methodology of the Simulation of Reforms

In order to assess the financial implications of the retirement incentives and also to proceed to cross-country comparisons, four reforms are simulated.

- Three-Year Reform: the minimum age to claim SS benefits is shifted to 63. The full rate is obtained if people have worked at least 162 quarters (instead of 150) or if they are 68. Access probabilities to unemployment or early retirement schemes are shifted by three years (access to these schemes is therefore impossible before 58).
- Common Reform: people may claim SS benefits from 60 (ERA). Claiming SS benefits at 65 (NRA) provides a 60 percent replacement rate. The pension is decreased (respectively, increased) by 6 percent per year below (respectively above 65). Access to early retirement or unemployment schemes is now impossible. The complementary schemes are also removed.
- Actuarial Reform: full-rate SS benefits may still be claimed from 65[2] or from 60 for persons who have worked at least 150 quarters, as with the current legislation. The early retirement age (ERA) is maintained identical to the current one, that is, at 60. But penalties associated with anticipated retirement are decreased to 6 percent for each year missing to reach 65 or 150 validated quarters (instead of 12 percent), whereas SS benefits are increased by 6 percent for each year worked beyond the full rate *and* after age 60. With our assumptions, the NRA is defined individually as the age when a person reaches the full rate (150 quarters or the age of 65). It thus depends on the number of quarters validated. The level of early benefits is also reduced for persons who start receiving these benefits before the age of 60: the reduction is 6 percent if they leave their job at 59, 12 percent at 58, and so forth.
- Charpin Reform: we assess the impact of the reform proposed in the *Charpin* report in 1999. It consists first in increasing the total number of quarters of contributions required to claim full-rate SS benefits to 170 quarters. Second, this reform would involve a decrease in penalties associated with anticipated retirement for workers in the private sector: in the benefit formula for the general regime, the coefficient α is reduced by 0.6 percentage point missing to reach either 170 quarters or age 65. For civil servants, the reform would simultaneously involve an increase from 150 to 170 in the number of quarters required to claim full-rate SS benefits at age of first eligibility to SS benefits (55 to 60). Penalties associated with anticipated retirement (currently close to zero) would increase: the coefficient α (currently 75 percent for

2. Or from 60, for the civil servants who were entitled to their pension from the age of 55.

everybody) is reduced by 0.9 percentage point missing to reach either 170 quarters or age 65 (respectively, 60) for people whose age of first eligibility to SS benefits is 60 (respectively, 55).

In essence, the Actuarial Reform is a halfway point between the current system and the full Common Reform: the Common Reform is based on a 6 percent actuarial adjustment and a replacement rate of 60 percent at the normal retirement age (NRA), whereas the NRA replacement rate in the Actuarial Reform is the same as with the current system (i.e., larger than 60 percent). A specific difficulty for France (in comparison with other countries) stems from the fact that the NRA is individual specific. For most people (those who have worked at least 150 quarters) the NRA is 60: the NRA is then identical to the ERA. But for a minority with short careers the NRA will be larger (up to 65) and different from the ERA.

We simulate changes in retirement behavior following these reforms and assess their financial impact. This assessment deals with the whole government fiscal impact, not just Social Security. Indeed, the taxes taken into account include payroll taxes, income taxes, and consumption taxes (VAT). We distinguish the *mechanical* impact of reforms from their *behavioral* impact: the mechanical impact is the expected change for public net expenditure if we assume that no one changes his or her retirement behavior. The behavioral impact is the difference between the total financial impact (simulated with the estimates of the previous section) and the mechanical impact.

Concerning the implementation of the Common Reform, the 60 percent replacement rate is applied to an average wage computed over the whole career. This average wage replicates the forty best yearly wages of a worker, including zeros when the worker worked less than forty years. As wages before 55 are not available in our data, we simulate a trend for real wages along a career, taking into account a fixed return per year of seniority, consistent with the magnitude of previous estimates on French data (Lolliver and Payen 1990). We apply this trend to the last known wages, including the effect of the tenure, to get an average of yearly wages for the best forty years. These real lifetime earnings are deflated using the average net wage index.

For these four reforms, we compute the incentives for individuals aged 55 to 66, taking into account possible retirement up to age 68. Since retirement after 66 remains minor, all workers leaving after 66 are gathered with workers leaving at 66.

A key issue in our simulations is how to deal with age dummies in specifications of type S3. Estimated age dummies are likely to capture age of first eligibility effects—eligibility to either early retirement or retirement benefits. Thus, these effects are a serious matter of concern.

- In the Three-Year Reform, the eligibility to all programs is raised by three years.

- In the Actuarial Reform—as well as in the Charpin Reform—ages of eligibility to different programs remain unchanged: we thus keep the same coefficient levels.
- In the Common Reform, people are no longer eligible for early retirement programs.

Our first concern was to determine as precisely as possible the appropriate level of coefficients on age dummies when people are not eligible to any (early) retirement program: a no-eligibility coefficient. We chose the mean of estimated coefficients on age dummies at 58 and 59: in our sample, most exits to early retirement in the private sector occurred at ages 55 and 56, and very few at ages 58 and 59. Moreover, the age of first eligibility to SS benefits is 60 for most people (except 55 for a minority of civil servants [but those who are eligible to SS benefits at 55 usually either quit at 55 or 56, or postpone retirement until they reach age 60]).

In the Three-Year Reform, we multiply the age 58 dummy by the estimated age 55 coefficient (here zero, since age 55 was the reference), the age 59 dummy by the estimated age 56 coefficient, and so on. For ages 55 to 57, since there is no open early retirement program, we multiply the age dummies by the no-eligibility coefficient.

In the Common Reform, we keep the estimated coefficients for ages 60 and 65, since 60 or 65 were already ages of eligibility to normal SS benefits for all workers in the sample. For ages 55 to 59, since there is no open retirement program, we multiply the age dummies by the no-eligibility coefficient. For ages 61 to 64, we also use the no-eligibility coefficient, as it reflects retirement behavior between the early retirement age (55) and the normal retirement age (60 to 65). Eventually, for age 66, we use the average of the estimated coefficients between age 61 and 64, as they stand for retirement after the first normal retirement age.

Expected Effects

The Three-Year Reform should induce a rather large increase in the retirement age, since eligibility to *all* retirement pathways (including early retirement) is postponed by three years. Since the level of annual pensions does not fundamentally change (the average pension should slightly increase, since workers have longer careers), total SS entitlements should decrease by a large amount.

The Actuarial Reform should have a positive effect on the average level of SSW. Its impact on the mean age of retirement is not straightforward: the decrease of penalties should include earlier retirement. But increasing pensions when people claim SS benefits with more than 150 quarters has a priori mixed effects: on the one side, it induces people to postpone their retirement through a price effect; on the other side, it increases the level of people who already leave with more than 150 quarters, and could induce them to anticipate retirement through a wealth effect.

In France, for the cohorts considered, the Common Reform involves a sharp decrease in replacement rates: for a normal career, replacement rates (including complementary schemes for the private sector) were close to 75 percent of the last wage. With the Common Reform, the pension would amount to 60 percent of the real lifetime earnings, as previously defined, which are likely to be smaller than the last wages. Associated with the elimination of early retirement programs (before age 60), this may create an incentive to postpone retirement. However, most of the effect of the reform on total SS entitlements should be more mechanical than behavioral, since the Common Reform dramatically lowers the level of the average pension.

The Charpin Reform should have far smaller effects on retirement behavior and aggregate SS entitlements than the Three-Year Reform or the Common Reform: the tenure required to claim full-rate SS benefits at age 60 increases by five years, but ages of eligibility to retirement programs remain unchanged.

4.6   Results of the Simulations

Tables 4.10 and 4.11, figures 4.1, 4.2, 4.4, and 4.6 yield average SSWs or PDVs of benefits per worker, in euros. Table 4.12 yields total PDV for each quintile in euros. Figure 4.7 yields variations in the total PDV of benefits (with a distinction between mechanical and behavioral effects) in percentage of GDP: we multiplied average amounts per worker (in euros) by the number of retired people we consider here, and then divided by GDP. Our number of retired people excludes people who stopped working before age 55, given our sample restrictions: our figures thus underestimate the total effect of reforms, since these people get reduced (respectively, increased) benefits if the simulated reform consists in a reduction (respectively, an increase) in SS benefits.

4.6.1   PDV of Gross Benefits by Age of Retirement

Figure 4.1 presents the present discounted value (PDV) of the gross social security wealth (SSW) by age of retirement. With the current rules, the values are decreasing with the age of retirement because, when retirement is delayed by one year, the loss of one year of pension is not compensated by a much higher level of pension. The decreasing slope is stronger after 60, as the pension level is far more important than the average replacement income in case of a retirement before 60.

The Three-Year Reform shifts this profile to the right, with a loss in the level of SSW before 63. This loss is much higher between 55 and 57 due to the suppression of the early retirement and unemployment schemes. But, after 63, the difference in the SSW with the current rules and with the three-year shift almost vanishes.

With the Common Reform, the PDV of the gross SSW does not depend on the age of retirement (given the quasi-perfect actuarial adjustment) and

Table 4.10   Total fiscal impact of reform

	Present discounted value (in euros)					Total change relative to base (%)			
	Base	Three-Year	Actuarial	Common	Charpin	Three-Year Reform	Actuarial Reform	Common Reform	Charpin Reform
	Peak value—S1								
Benefits	277,488	230,797	316,098	102,175	248,604	-17	14	-63	-10
Taxes									
Payroll	55,794	68,224	43,394	63,378	61,681	22	-22	14	11
Income	38,390	38,334	36,462	17,860	37,017	0	-5	-53	-4
VAT	60,176	53,558	66,313	30,615	55,586	-11	10	-49	-8
Total	154,360	160,117	146,169	111,854	154,285	4	-5	-28	0
	Peak value—S2								
Benefit	278,144	229,697	311,546	99,680	250,884	-17	12	-64	-10
Taxes									
Payroll	54,936	62,041	47,334	56,555	57,954	13	-14	3	5
Income	38,245	36,852	37,826	16,773	35,890	-4	-1	-56	-6
VAT	60,262	52,594	65,488	29,655	55,838	-13	9	-51	-7
Total	153,443	151,486	150,647	102,982	149,681	-1	-2	-33	-2
	Peak value—S3								
Benefits	278,144	226,775	311,546	99,906	250,884	-18	12	-64	-10
Taxes									
Payroll	54,936	72,976	47,334	66,058	57,954	33	-14	20	5
Income	38,245	39,135	37,826	19,214	35,890	2	-1	-50	-6
VAT	60,262	52,700	65,488	30,858	55,838	-13	9	-49	-7
Total	153,443	164,812	150,647	116,130	149,681	7	-2	-24	-2

				Option value—S1					
Benefits	278,147	216,423	310,262	249,128	103,365	−22	12	−63	−10
Taxes									
Payroll	55,720	91,090	49,879	60,063	92,752	63	−10	66	8
Income	38,473	43,736	38,617	36,088	27,713	14	0	−28	−6
VAT	60,323	51,713	65,493	55,607	34,023	−14	9	−44	−8
Total	154,517	186,540	153,989	151,759	154,488	21	0	0	−2
				Option value—S2					
Benefits	278,679	220,370	309,727	250,674	100,951	−21	11	−64	−10
Taxes									
Payroll	54,970	83,199	49,640	57,722	81,055	51	−10	47	5
Income	38,264	42,346	38,786	35,463	25,354	11	1	−34	−7
VAT	60,389	52,069	65,369	55,791	32,796	−14	8	−46	−8
Total	153,622	177,614	153,795	148,977	139,206	16	0	−9	−3
				Option value—S3					
Benefits	278,679	225,116	309,727	250,674	101,242	−19	11	−64	−10
Taxes									
Payroll	54,970	81,380	49,640	57,722	86,452	48	−10	57	5
Income	38,264	42,271	38,786	35,463	26,789	10	1	−30	−7
VAT	60,389	53,076	65,369	55,791	33,422	−12	8	−45	−8
Total	153,622	176,727	153,795	148,977	146,663	15	0	−5	−3

Table 4.11   Decomposition of the total effect of reform

| | Change in present discounted value | | | | | | | | | | | |
| | Three-Year Reform | | | Actuarial Reform | | | Common Reform | | | Charpin Reform | | |
	Mechanical	Behavioral	Total	Mechanical	Behavioral	Total	Mechanical	Behavioral	Total	Mechanical	Behavioral	Total
				Peak value—S1								
Benefits	-47,978	1,287	-46,691	29,559	0	38,610	-177,855	2,542	-175,312	-27,429	-1,455	-28,884
Taxes: Total	-13,529	19,285	5,756	9,972	-18,164	-42,507	-51,958	9,451	-42,507	-8,965	8,889	-76
Net change	-34,449	-17,998	-52,447	19,587	18,164	37,751	-125,897	-6,909	-132,805	-18,464	-10,344	-28,808
Change as % of base benefits	-12.4	-6.5	-18.9	7.1	6.5	13.6	-45.4	-2.5	-47.9	-6.7	-3.7	-10.4
				Peak value—S2								
Benefits	-49,850	1,403	-48,447	28,683	4,718	33,402	-179,176	712	-178,464	-26,886	-374	-27,261
Taxes: Total	-13,845	11,888	-1,957	9,686	-12,482	-50,461	-52,115	1,654	-50,461	-8,759	4,997	-3,762
Net change	-36,005	-10,485	-46,490	18,997	17,201	36,198	-127,062	-942	-128,003	-18,127	-5,371	-23,499
Change as % of base benefits	-12.9	-3.8	-16.7	6.8	6.2	13.0	-45.7	-0.3	-46.0	-6.5	-1.9	-8.4
				Peak value—S3								
Benefits	-49,850	-1,519	-51,369	28,683	4,718	33,402	-179,176	938	-178,239	-26,886	-374	-27,261
Taxes: Total	-13,845	25,214	11,368	9,686	-12,482	-37,313	-52,115	14,802	-37,313	-8,759	4,997	-3,762
Net change	-36,005	-26,732	-62,737	18,997	17,201	36,198	-127,062	-13,864	-140,925	-18,127	-5,371	-23,499
Change as % of base benefits	-12.9	-9.6	-22.6	6.8	6.2	13.0	-45.7	-5.0	-50.7	-6.5	-1.9	-8.4

						Option value—S1						
Benefits	−47,844	−13,880	−61,724	28,252	3,863	32,115	−178,918	4,136	−174,782	−27,504	−1,515	−29,019
Taxes: Total	−12,467	44,491	32,024	9,602	−10,129	−29	−51,577	51,548	−29	−8,932	6,174	−2,758
Net change	−35,377	−58,371	−93,748	18,650	13,992	32,642	−127,341	−47,412	−174,753	−18,572	−7,690	−26,261
Change as % of base benefits	−12.7	−21.0	−33.7	6.7	5.0	11.7	−45.8	−17.0	−62.8	−6.7	−2.8	−9.4
						Option value—S2						
Benefits	−49,862	−8,446	−58,308	27,676	3,373	31,049	−179,864	2,136	−177,727	−27,248	−757	−28,005
Taxes: Total	−13,338	37,330	23,992	9,385	−14,416	−51,977	37,561	−14,416	−8,845	4,200	−4,645	−2,758
Net change	−36,524	−45,776	−82,300	18,291	12,585	30,876	−127,886	−35,425	−163,311	−18,403	−4,957	−23,360
Change as % of base benefits	−13.1	−16.4	−29.5	6.6	4.5	11.1	−45.9	−12.7	−58.6	−6.6	−1.8	−8.4
						Option value—S3						
Benefits	−49,862	−3,700	−53,562	27,676	3,373	31,049	−179,864	2,427	−177,436	−27,248	−757	−28,005
Taxes: Total	−13,338	36,443	23,105	9,385	−9,212	−6,959	−51,977	45,018	−6,959	−8,845	4,200	−4,645
Net change	−36,524	−40,143	−76,667	18,291	12,585	30,876	−127,886	−42,591	−170,477	−18,403	−4,957	−23,360
Change as % of base benefits	−13.1	−14.4	−27.5	6.6	4.5	11.1	−45.9	−15.3	−61.2	−6.6	−1.8	−8.4

Table 4.12 Distributional analysis: Option value—linear age (S1)

	Present discounted value					Change relative to base PDV			
	Base	Three-Year	Actuarial	Common	Charpin	Three-year Reform	Actuarial Reform	Common Reform	Charpin Reform
				Quintile 1 (highest)					
Benefits	209,697,209	164,681,193	238,116,614	93,858,974	188,250,564	-45,016,016	28,419,405	-115,838,235	-21,446,645
Taxes									
Payroll	64,666,928	99,310,017	52,397,681	91,496,876	70,141,689	34,643,089	-12,269,247	26,829,948	5,474,761
Income	59,510,041	68,662,650	54,316,181	46,528,054	57,783,757	9,152,609	-5,193,860	-12,981,987	-1,726,284
VAT	48,763,182	43,253,694	52,826,113	31,748,493	45,454,115	-5,509,488	4,062,931	-17,014,689	-3,218,067
Total	172,940,151	211,226,360	159,539,975	169,773,423	173,470,561	38,286,209	-13,400,176	-3,166,728	530,410
Net change						-83,302,225	41,819,581	-112,671,507	-21,977,055
Change as % of base benefits						-39.7	19.9	-53.7	-10.5
				Quintile 2					
Benefits	162,379,589	126,258,531	172,882,161	55,793,639	138,137,154	-36,121,058	10,502,572	-106,585,960	-24,242,435
Taxes									
Payroll	22,903,156	38,928,440	24,097,844	43,553,482	25,361,407	16,025,285	1,194,688	20,650,327	2,458,251
Income	15,623,047	16,816,461	17,870,200	9,685,589	13,284,928	1,193,415	2,247,153	-5,937,458	-2,338,118
VAT	33,461,519	28,136,932	35,213,870	17,280,449	29,424,117	-5,324,588	1,752,351	-16,181,070	-4,037,403
Total	71,987,722	83,881,834	77,181,914	70,519,520	68,070,452	11,894,112	5,194,192	-1,468,201	-3,917,270
Net change						-48,015,170	5,308,380	-105,117,749	-20,325,165
Change as % of base benefits						-29.6	3.3	-64.7	-12.5

Quintile 3									
Benefits	122,617,443	93,768,747	134,716,504	40,967,282	111,116,584	−28,848,696	12,099,061	−81,650,160	−11,500,859
Taxes									
Payroll	18,225,934	32,444,348	17,818,879	37,384,039	19,649,651	14,218,414	−407,055	19,158,105	1,423,716
Income	8,548,878	9,622,183	10,012,247	5,506,406	7,713,588	1,073,305	1,463,370	−3,042,471	−835,290
VAT	25,760,864	21,480,676	27,829,737	13,439,247	23,817,753	−4,280,189	2,068,873	−12,321,617	−1,943,111
Total	52,535,676	63,547,206	55,660,864	56,329,692	51,180,991	11,011,530	3,125,188	3,794,016	−1,354,685
Net change						−39,860,225	8,973,874	−85,444,176	−10,146,174
Change as % of base benefits						−32.5	7.3	−69.7	−8.3
Quintile 4									
Benefits	91,804,600	70,789,365	103,967,661	30,154,320	84,957,965	−21,015,235	12,163,061	−61,650,280	−6,846,636
Taxes									
Payroll	14,268,471	25,203,090	13,125,195	26,919,366	14,974,801	10,934,619	−1,143,276	12,650,895	706,330
Income	4,361,567	5,056,629	5,322,191	2,506,209	3,942,306	695,062	960,624	−1,855,358	−419,262
VAT	19,518,004	16,448,220	21,635,008	10,119,785	18,354,688	−3,069,783	2,117,005	−9,398,218	−1,163,316
Total	38,148,042	46,707,939	40,082,395	39,545,361	37,271,795	8,559,897	1,934,353	1,397,319	−876,247
Net change						−29,575,133	10,228,708	−63,047,599	−5,970,389
Change as % of base benefits						−32.2	11.1	−68.7	−6.5
Quintile 5 (lowest)									
Benefits	68,259,693	53,962,005	80,674,305	22,547,775	63,984,981	−14,297,689	12,414,612	−45,711,918	−4,274,712
Taxes									
Payroll	11,100,669	18,540,847	9,975,719	18,984,399	11,261,518	7,440,178	−1,124,950	7,883,731	160,849
Income	2,522,767	2,797,651	3,383,266	1,009,954	2,226,321	274,884	860,499	−1,512,813	−296,446
VAT	14,497,153	12,413,752	16,666,654	7,501,556	13,758,378	−2,083,401	2,169,501	−6,995,597	−738,775
Total	28,120,589	33,752,250	30,025,638	27,495,909	27,246,217	5,631,661	1,905,049	−624,679	−874,371
Net change						−19,929,350	10,509,563	−45,087,239	−3,400,340
Change as % of base benefits						−29.2	15.4	−66.1	−5.0

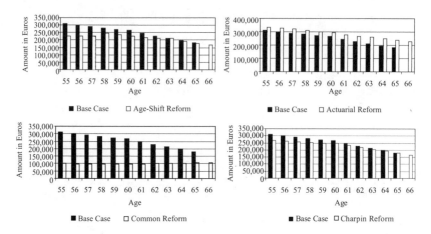

Fig. 4.1   Peak value of social security benefits by age of retirement

the level of SSW is very low compared to the current rules, due to the dramatic decrease in the average replacement rate.

The Actuarial Reform provides higher levels of SSW than the current situation, whatever the age of retirement. The results exhibit a more regular decrease with age than in the base case. However, this case is a halfway point between the current situation (with a strong deviation from actuarial fairness) and pure actuarial provisions. The age profile of SSW is thus not flat (contrary to the Common Reform).

The Charpin Reform induces a small loss in SSW for all ages of retirement. Because the new rules disadvantage early retirement, and also because of the discounting hypothesis, this loss decreases with the age of retirement.

4.6.2   PDV of Taxes by Age of Retirement

Figure 4.2 shows the PDV of the taxes paid by age of retirement. Consistent with our intuition, the PDV of taxes increases with the age of retirement with the current rules. Indeed, working one more year implies paying taxes on one more year of labor income and also earning a better SS pension, which will result in higher taxes for each year of retirement.

For the Three-Year Reform, the strong loss in SSW for retirement before 63 appears through a smaller level of PDV of taxes paid for those ages.

In like manner, for the Actuarial Reform, the better SSW for all ages of retirement appears through a higher level of PDV of taxes paid than with the current rules, particularly for later retirements.

With the Common Reform, the taxes paid remain lower than with the current rules. However, the evolution of the PDV of taxes with the age of retirement is much quicker than with the current rules. Indeed, the gap be-

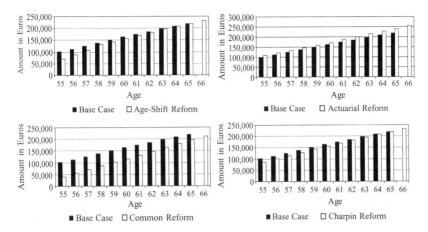

Fig. 4.2   Peak value of taxes by age of retirement

tween taxes paid with the current rules and with the Common Reform is due to the smaller level of pension with the Common Reform. The part of the taxes on pensions in the total of the taxes paid decreases with the age of retirement. As a result, the gap between the PDV of taxes paid with the current rule sand with the Common Reform decreases with the age of retirement.

The Charpin Reform generates slightly smaller levels of PDV of taxes, in particular for early retirement.

4.6.3   Age of Retirement

The results from the OV-S1 method display an average retirement postponement greater than three years, which is doubtful. This may stem from the negative sign for the coefficient on the linear age variable, which contradicts the expected increase of the utility of leisure with age (section 4.4). We shall not comment in detail on the results induced by this method (figures 4.3 and 4.4), but shall concentrate on the OV-S3 results.

Figure 4.5 shows the distributions of the ages at retirement with the OV-S3 modeling. The distributions of the ages at retirement evidence a strong delay in retirement ages with the Three-Year Reform, with an average increase of 2.4 years with the OV-S3 method. The retirement ages profile is close to what is expected, with new retirements before 58 and two peaks at 58 and 63.

Introducing more actuarial fairness hardly changes the distribution of the ages of labor force exit. We observe a slight decrease in the average age at retirement: the decrease in penalties associated with retirement before reaching the full rate are decreased and some people decide to quit earlier.

For the Common Reform, the average delay in the age at retirement is even higher than the one observed with the Three-Year Reform (3.6 years).

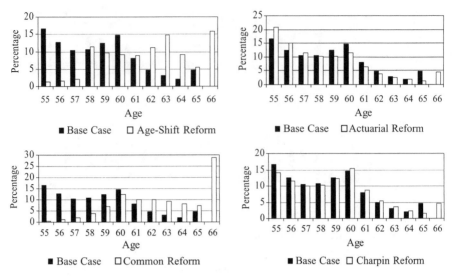

Fig. 4.3   Labor participation effects of reforms—Distribution of the age at retirement, OV-S1 method

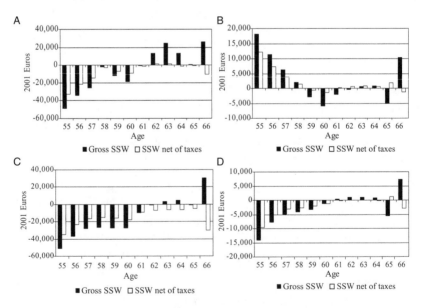

Fig. 4.4   Distribution of total effect, OV-S1 method: Total Effect by Age of Retirement (OV S1 Model); *A,* Age-Shift Reform; *B,* Actuarial Reform; *C,* Common Reform; *D,* Charpin Reform

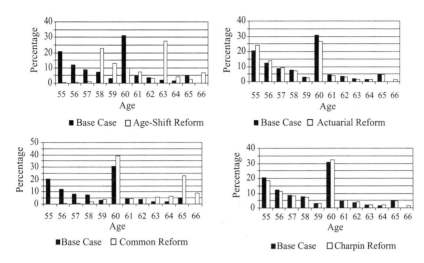

Fig. 4.5   Labor participation effects of reforms—Distribution of the age at retirement, OV-S3 method

The ages profiles show almost no retirement before 60, a large peak at 60, and a smaller one at 65.

For the Charpin Reform, the average delay is smaller (0.3 years). Retirement rates slightly decline before age 60 because fewer people reach the new target of 170 quarters of contributions.

4.6.4   Fiscal Effects: Mechanical versus Behavioral

Figures 4.6 and 4.7 show the impact of the different reforms on the gross and net present discounted value of Social Security benefits and present a decomposition of the total net effect between mechanical and behavioral components.

The Three-Year Reform induces a significant decrease (between 0.5 percent and 0.8 percent of GDP) in the net present discounted value (NPDV) of SS benefits (see figure 4.7). More than 50 percent of this decrease (i.e., 0.4 percent of GDP) results from simulated behavioral effects according to the OV method. Behavioral effects are smaller if we focus on PV simulations, but OV simulations take the future flows of wage income into account better than PV simulations. The future flows of income here are important, since continuing to retire at 60 now means no income until age 63 for people who do not qualify for early retirement benefits. The decrease in the NPDV of SS benefits is especially significant at ages 55 to 57 (see figure 4.6), since the age of first eligibility to early retirement benefits is now 58 and at age 60, since the age of first eligibility to normal SS benefits is now 63.

The Actuarial Reform induces a smaller increase in the NPDV (about 0.3 percent of GDP) and behavioral effects range from 0.1 percent to 0.2

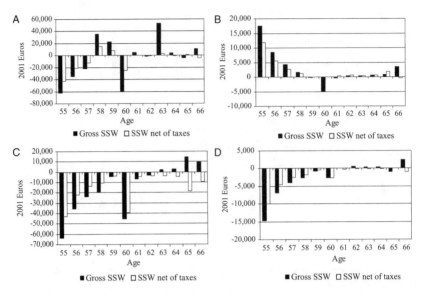

Fig. 4.6   Distribution of total effect by age of retirement, OV-S3 method: *A,* **Age-Shift Reform;** *B,* **Actuarial Reform;** *C,* **Common Reform;** *D,* **Charpin Reform**

percent of GDP. The increase is the largest at ages 55 and 56, since people who decide to leave at those ages without reaching the full rate face reduced penalties when they claim SS benefits.

The Common Reform exhibits a large decrease in the NPDV of SS benefits: about 1.7 percent of GDP. We prefer, again, OV specifications, since PV simulations (where the behavioral effect is negligible) do not capture the sharp decrease at all in the replacement rate of wage income by SS benefits at each age. The mechanical effect is very large: about 1.3 percent of GDP, and the behavioral effect is estimated to be 0.4 percent of GDP.

The Charpin Reform shows a small decrease in the NPDV of SS benefits (about 0.2 percent of GDP), less than half of which results from behavioral effects. This decrease is sharp at ages 55 to 57: people who qualified for early retirement benefits at these ages, and thus retired before 60, could claim full-rate SS benefits at 60 with the full rate since they had worked 150 quarters or more. This is no more the case for a large part of them because, in the reform, full-rate SS benefits at 60 are only available for those who worked 170 quarters or more.

4.6.5   Distributional Issues

Let us now consider distributional issues (see tables 4.12 and 4.13). The age-shift reform has a negative impact for all quintiles, since the age of first eligibility to SS benefits increases by three years for all people. But this

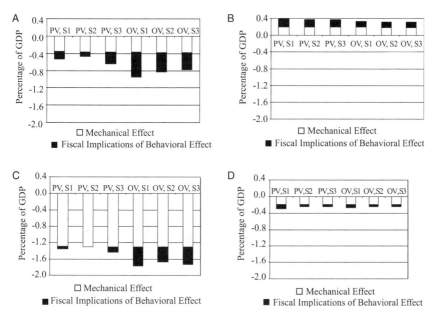

Fig. 4.7   Fiscal implications of reforms (percent of GDP): *A,* **3-year increase in ERA/NRA;** *B,* **Actuarial Reform;** *C,* **Common Reform;** *D,* **Charpin Reform**

effect is larger for the highest quintile: this does not stem from the effect of the reform on the gross PDV of SS benefits (the evolution is more or less the same for all quintiles) but on taxes, especially income taxes. Since people retire later and the level of pensions is clearly below the level of wages, people pay higher income taxes. This effect is large on the highest quintile but small for other quintiles (a large majority of people in the third-lowest quintiles pay zero income tax in France).

The Actuarial Reform has a positive impact for all quintiles, but the effect is larger for the extreme quintiles: in the lowest quintile, people often faced liquidity constraints that led a significant number of them to claim reduced benefits at 60, although it would have been better for them to wait until 65, given the strength of penalties. These people take advantage of the decrease of penalties. In the highest quintile, a number of people already worked after 60, although they did not expect any increase in SS benefits (perhaps because their replacement rate was rather low). They take advantage of the possibility to get higher SS benefits for people who postpone retirement after the full rate.

The Common Reform has a negative impact for all quintiles, given the sharp decrease in replacement rates, but the effect is larger for low quintiles: the replacement rate in the base case decreases with wage income and

Table 4.13 Distributional analysis: Option value—S3

	Present discounted value					Change relative to base PDV			
	Base	Three-Year	Actuarial	Common	Charpin	Three-Year Reform	Actuarial Reform	Common Reform	Charpin Reform
				Quintile 1 (highest)					
Benefits	210,826,547	173,350,742	237,628,955	91,910,828	190,113,094	-37,475,806	26,802,408	-118,915,719	-20,713,453
Taxes									
Payroll	63,242,882	88,495,737	52,322,038	86,112,825	66,590,386	25,252,855	-10,920,844	22,869,943	3,347,504
Income	58,951,696	66,175,743	54,768,867	45,802,338	56,478,326	7,224,047	-4,182,829	-13,149,358	-2,473,370
VAT	48,893,316	44,446,017	52,726,310	31,253,780	45,719,799	-4,447,298	3,832,995	-17,639,535	-3,173,517
Total	171,087,894	199,117,498	159,817,215	163,168,943	168,788,511	28,029,604	-11,270,678	-7,918,950	-2,299,382
Net change						-65,505,410	38,073,086	-110,996,769	-18,414,071
Change as % of base benefits						-31.1	18.1	-52.6	-8.7
				Quintile 2					
Benefits	161,943,994	129,411,886	172,819,678	54,325,693	138,621,659	-32,532,108	10,875,683	-107,618,301	-23,322,335
Taxes									
Payroll	22,833,029	35,254,768	23,510,317	40,490,503	24,512,929	12,421,740	677,288	17,657,475	1,679,901
Income	15,634,038	16,486,832	17,784,180	9,034,624	13,181,632	852,794	2,150,141	-6,599,414	-2,452,407
VAT	33,377,417	28,636,453	35,164,409	16,941,058	29,469,056	-4,740,964	1,786,992	-16,436,359	-3,908,361
Total	71,844,484	80,378,054	76,458,905	66,466,186	67,163,617	8,533,570	4,614,421	-5,378,298	-4,680,867
Net change						-41,065,678	6,261,262	-102,240,003	-18,641,468
Change as % of base benefits						-25.4	3.9	-63.1	-11.5
				Quintile 3					
Benefits	122,782,770	97,595,711	134,575,925	39,964,806	111,682,445	-25,187,059	11,793,155	-82,817,965	-11,100,325
Taxes									
Payroll	18,067,627	28,530,856	17,657,897	33,692,745	19,000,067	10,463,229	-409,729	15,625,119	932,440
Income	8,564,462	9,281,226	9,993,090	4,952,254	7,655,115	716,764	1,428,628	-3,612,207	-909,347
VAT	25,791,767	22,145,500	27,790,870	13,077,357	23,901,968	-3,646,267	1,999,103	-12,714,411	-1,889,799

Total	52,423,856	59,957,582	55,441,857	51,722,356	50,557,150	7,533,726	3,018,001	−701,499	−1,866,706
Net change						−32,720,785	8,775,153	−82,116,465	−9,233,619
Change as % of base benefits						−26.6	7.1	−66.9	−7.5

Quintile 4

Benefits	91,963,844	73,789,282	103,617,373	29,816,676	85,385,849	−18,174,562	11,653,529	−62,147,168	−6,577,995
Taxes									
Payroll	14,156,715	22,275,187	13,230,984	24,931,029	14,586,242	8,118,472	−925,732	10,774,314	429,527
Income	4,373,002	4,830,080	5,344,158	2,298,518	3,925,136	457,078	971,156	−2,074,484	−447,866
VAT	19,546,620	16,970,320	21,569,197	9,957,817	18,422,391	−2,576,300	2,022,576	−9,588,804	−1,124,230
Total	38,076,338	44,075,587	40,144,338	37,187,364	36,933,768	5,999,249	2,068,001	−888,973	−1,142,569
Net change						−24,173,811	9,585,528	−61,258,195	−5,435,425
Change as % of base benefits						−26.3	10.4	−66.6	−5.9

Quintile 5 (lowest)

Benefits	68,492,327	55,776,399	80,456,425	22,306,475	−12,715,929	11,964,098	−46,185,852	−4,209,222	
Taxes									
Payroll	11,098,934	17,011,221	10,131,733	18,280,225	11,188,279	5,912,287	−967,201	7,181,291	89,345
Income	2,549,384	2,731,710	3,410,845	973,388	2,240,536	182,326	861,461	−1,575,996	−308,848
VAT	14,545,814	12,743,339	16,628,472	7,446,308	13,819,894	−1,802,475	2,082,658	−7,099,506	−725,919
Total	28,194,132	32,486,270	30,171,050	26,699,921	27,248,710	4,292,138	1,976,919	−1,494,211	−945,422
Net change						−17,008,067	9,987,179	−44,691,642	−3,263,800
Change as % of base benefits						−24.8	14.6	−65.3	−4.8

is 60 percent for all (whatever the level of wage income) in the Common Reform. The loss is thus larger for low-paid people.

With the Charpin Reform the effects are rather small, and nothing appears clear concerning distributional issues.

4.7   Conclusion

This analysis focuses on the steady-state impact of reforms of retirement rules on an age-55 cohort. We rely on a previous assessment of the sensitivity of individual retirement behavior to the structure of Social Security incentives (Mahieu and Blanchet 2002). This enables us to measure the fiscal implications of changes in individual retirement decisions and thus to decompose the financial impacts of simulated reforms between this behavioral component and a mechanical component. However, the analysis does not incorporate any general equilibrium effect that may occur.

We simulate several reforms so as to assess the impact of the behavioral component on the total amount of Social Security benefits paid. The results exhibit a large impact of behavioral responses to modifications in SS provisions. For example, a reform that introduces a unique normal replacement rate of 60 percent at age 65 and a strictly actuarial adjustment involves a sharp increase in the average retirement age. This behavioral component is estimated to reduce the net present discounted value of SS benefits for the 1930 cohort by as much as 0.4 percent of GDP.

References

Blanchet, D., and L. P. Pelé. 1999. Social security and retirement in France. NBER Working Paper no. 6214. Chicago: University of Chicago Press.
Burricand, C., and N. Roth. 2000. Les parcours de fin de carrière des générations 1912–1941: l'impact du cadre institutionnel. *Economie et Statistique* 335: 63–79.
Caussat, L., and N. Roth. 1997. De l'emploi à la retraite: Générations passées et futures. *Revue Française des Affaires Sociales* (October 1997 special issue): 177–204.
Charpin, J. M., C. Zaidman, and J.-M. Aubert. 1999. L'avenir de nos retraites. Retrieved from ladocumentationfrançaise.fr/
Colin, C., V. Iéhlé, and R. Mahieu. 2000. Les trajectoires de fin de carrière des salariés du secteur privé. *Dossiers Solidarité et Santé* 3 (July–September 2000): 9–27.
Commissariat Général du Plan. 1995. *Perspectives à long terme des retraites.* Retrieved from ladocumentationfrançaise.fr/
Gruber, J., and D. Wise. 1997. Social security programs and retirement around the world. NBER Working Paper no. 6134.
Lollivier, S., and G. Payen. 1990. L'Hétérogénéité des carrières individualles mesurée sur données de panel. In La Formation des salaires: De la "loi du marché" aux stratégies des acteurs. *Economie et Prévision* 92–3:87–95.
Mahieu, R., and D. Blanchet. 2002. Estimating models of retirement behavior on

French data. In *Social security programs and retirement across the world: Micro-estimation,* eds. Jonathan Gruber and David A. Wise, 235–84. Chicago: University of Chicago Press, 2004.

Pelé, L. P., and P. Ralle. 1999. Les choix de l'âge de la retraite: Aspects incitatifs des règles du régime général et effets de la réforme de 1993. *Economie et Prévision* 2–3 (138–39): 163–77.

Rust, J., and C. Phelan. 1997. How Social Security and Medicare affect retirement behavior in a world of incomplete markets. *Econometrica* 65 (4): 781–831.

Stock, J., and D. Wise. 1990. Pensions, the option value of work, and retirement. *Econometrica* 58 (5): 1151–80.

5

The Budget Impact of Reduced Early Retirement Incentives on the German Public Pension System

Axel Börsch-Supan, Simone Kohnz, and
Reinhold Schnabel

5.1 Introduction

The public pension system is the single largest item in Germany's social budget. In 2000, public pension expenditures amounted to some 200 billion euro, representing 21 percent of public spending and 11.8 percent of gross domestic product (GDP). It is the second largest pension budget in the Organization for Economic Cooperation and Development (OECD) surpassed only by Italy (14.2 percent of GDP). It is more than 2.5 times as expensive as the U.S. Social Security system (4.4 percent of GDP; OECD 2001). This paper argues that this large pension budget can be significantly reduced by neutralizing the strong incentives in the German pension system to retire early.

The generosity of the German public pension system is considered a great social achievement and has been a model for many social security systems around the world. It has been successful in providing a reliable level of retirement income over the past 100 years. It is considered one of the pillars of societal stability in Germany. It has survived, albeit under severe modifications, through World Wars I and II, the Great Depression, and, most recently, the German unification.

Axel Börsch-Supan is a professor of economics and director of the Mannheim Research Institute of the Economics of Aging and Statistics, University of Mannheim, and a research associate of the National Bureau of Economic Research (NBER). Simone Kohnz is a PhD student at the Munich Graduate School of Economics. Reinhold Schnabel is a professor of economics at the University of Essen.

Financial support was provided by the National Institute on Aging through the NBER and by the Deutsche Forschungsgemeinschaft (DFG) through Sonderforschungsbereich 504. We are also grateful for financial support by the State of Baden-Württemberg and the German Insurers' Association (GDV). The first author enjoyed the hospitality of Dartmouth College while this paper was produced.

The aging of Germany's population, however, is threatening the very core of its pension system. All industrialized countries are aging, but Germany, together with Italy and Japan, will experience a particularly dramatic change in the demographic structure of its population. The severity of the demographic transition has two causes: a quicker increase in life expectancy than elsewhere, partly due to a relatively low level still in the 1970s, and a more incisive baby boom/baby bust transition (e.g., relative to the United States) to a very low fertility rate of 1.3 children per woman, only a bit higher than the rock-bottom fertility rate of 1.2 in Italy and Spain. Consequently, the ratio of elderly to working-age persons—the old-age dependency ratio—will increase steeply. According to the latest OECD projections, the proportion of elderly (aged 65 and above) will exceed a quarter of the population in 2030, and the German old-age dependency ratio will almost double, from 24.0 percent in 2000 to 43.3 percent in 2030.[1]

The increase in the dependency ratio has immediate consequences for a pay-as-you-go social insurance system because fewer workers must finance the benefits of more recipients. The German social security contribution rate, in 2003 at 19.5 percent of gross income, was projected in the mid-1990s to exceed 30 percent of gross income at the peak of population ageing in 2035 if the accustomed replacement rates were maintained.[2] This led to major pension reforms in 1999 (a failed first attempt) and 2001 (now successful). This reform bade farewell to the pure pay-as-you-go system and introduced a multipillar pension system with a small, but in the eyes of many Germans, revolutionary funded pillar.

The reform did not, however, touch the early and normal retirement age, which are age 60 and 65. This may come as a surprise, since in the light of a prolonged life span, increasing its active part appears to be a rather natural reform option. This option is particularly attractive as increasing the retirement age simultaneously increases the number of contributors and decreases the number of beneficiaries. Moreover, Germans retire quite early. Average retirement age is about 59.5 years, half a year younger than the earliest eligibility age for old-age pensions and more than five years younger than the so-called "normal" retirement age in Germany.[3] Hence, a substantial increase in the retirement age seems to be a reasonable policy option, particularly because age-specific morbidity rates appear to have shifted in line with mortality (Cutler and Sheiner 1998).

The politics of shifting the retirement age, however, are not favorable. According to survey results by Boeri, Börsch-Supan, and Tabellini (2001,

---

1. Organization for Economic Cooperation and Development (OECD). 2001. The OECD dependency ratio relates persons age 65 and older to persons between ages 15 and 64.

2. See Börsch-Supan (1998, 2000c) and Schnabel (1998) for descriptions of the problems, and Birg and Börsch-Supan (1999) and Börsch-Supan (2002) for concrete reform proposals.

3. See Börsch-Supan and Schnabel (1998).

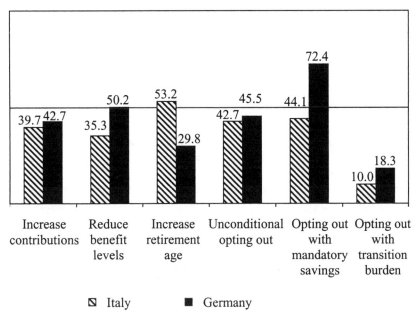

Fig. 5.1   **Popularity of pension reform options**

2002, and 2005), raising the retirement age is one of the most unpopular pension reform options in Germany (see figure 5.1). An interesting result of this survey, however, is that this option is particularly unpopular among those who are least informed about the costs of the current pension system. Hence, while early retirement is a well-appreciated social achievement among Germans, awareness of the costs of early retirement may moderate the opposition to increasing the retirement age. A rough back-of-the-envelope calculation may make the point. Since life expectancy at age 60 is about eighteen years, each year of early retirement corresponds to about 5.5 percent of pension expenditures. Hence, making the normal retirement age also the mean retirement age would cut pension expenditures by about 28 percent and would reduce the government projection of the contribution rate in 2020 from 22 percent to below 16 percent.

This chapter's aim is to produce a more sophisticated estimate of the budget effects of an increase in the retirement age. This is the third stage of an international research project on the causes for, and the effects of, early retirement. In the first stage (Gruber and Wise 1999), we described and quantified the incentives to retire early in the form of implicit taxes on continued work.

The second stage (Gruber and Wise 2003) provided econometric estimates of the strength of incentive effects on old-age labor supply, using several specifications of incentive variables. These highly significant and large estimates were used to simulate labor force participation responses to several policy changes. For instance, introducing (almost) actuarially fair adjustments (6 percent per year of delay) would increase the average retirement age of German men by about three years and two months. The effects are about half that size for women.

This third stage uses these estimates and converts them into budget effects on the German public pension system. We simulate the impact of several stylized reform plans on older workers' net fiscal contributions to the finances of the German public pension system. Such reform plans will have two effects on the budget of the pension system: first, a direct effect, by changing contributions and benefits for a given work history (we refer to this effect as the *mechanical* effect) and, second, an indirect effect through labor supply responses to the reform (the *behavioral* effect). We estimate the fiscal implications of both the mechanical and the behavioral effect, using the econometric retirement models from the second stage to predict labor supply responses. The result will be an estimate of the steady-state impact of the reforms on the financial balance sheet of the German public pension system.

More precisely, using a cohort of preretirement-age workers, we first estimate the probability that each worker will exit the labor force via death or retirement at each future age and the net present discounted value (PDV) of retirement program contributions and benefits associated with each type of labor force exit. The resulting weighted average social security wealth (SSW) will be the base for comparison. We will then reestimate the exit probabilities, contributions, and benefits under several reforms to obtain new social security wealth estimates. The key numbers will be the percentage changes in social security wealth, including and excluding a behavioral response to the reform. The difference between these numbers measures the extent to which labor supply responses amplify the effect of reforms on program solvency.

The paper is structured as follows: sections 5.2 and 5.3 describe the institutional background for private sector and civil servants' pensions.[4] Section 5.4 presents data and variable specifications, section 5.5 contains our simulation results, and section 5.6 concludes.

5.2   Private Sector Pensions

In this section we describe the German public retirement insurance (*Gesetzliche Rentenversicherung;* GRV), which covers about 85 percent of the German workforce. Most of these are private sector workers, but the GRV also includes those public sector workers who are not civil servants. Civil servants, about 7 percent of the workforce, have their own pension

---

4. These sections are updated versions of Börsch-Supan et al. (2002).

system, described in section 5.3. The self-employed, about 9 percent of the work force, are mainly self-insured, although some also participate in the public retirement insurance system. For the average German worker, occupational pensions do not play a major role in providing old-age income. Neither do individual retirement accounts, but there are important exceptions from this general picture. Broadly speaking, the German system is monolithic.

The following descriptions focus on the institutional rules that applied during the period 1984–97, because this is the sample period of the underlying econometric estimates (dubbed "1972 legislation," although there have been several administrative adjustments since). There have been two major pension reforms, in 1992 and 2001. They had, however, only negligible effects on the persons in the estimation sample, since generous grandfathering schemes applied. The last subsection briefly sketches the implications of the two major reforms.

5.2.1 Coverage and Contributions

The German pay-as-you-go public pension system features a very broad mandatory coverage of workers. Only the self-employed and, until 1998, workers with earnings below the official minimum earnings threshold (i.e., *Geringfügigkeitsgrenze,* 15 percent of average monthly gross wage; below this threshold are about 5.6 percent of all workers) are not subject to mandatory coverage.

Roughly 70 percent of the budget of the German public retirement insurance is financed by contributions that are administered like a payroll tax, levied equally on employees and employers. Total contributions in 2000 were 19.3 percent of the first DM8,600 of monthly gross income (upper earnings threshold, *Beitragsbemessungsgrenze,* about 180 percent of average monthly gross wage).[5] Technically, contributions are split evenly between employees and employers. While the contribution rate has been fairly stable since 1970, the upper earnings threshold has been used as a financing instrument. It is anchored to the average wage and has increased considerably faster than inflation.

Private sector pension benefits are essentially tax free. Pension beneficiaries do not pay contributions to the pension system and/or to unemployment insurance. However, pensioners have to pay the equivalent of the employees' contribution to the mandatory medical insurance. The equivalent of the employers' contribution to health insurance is paid by the pension system.

The remaining approximately 30 percent of the social security budget is financed by earmarked indirect taxes (a fixed fraction of the value-added

---

5. West Germany only, DM 7,200 in East Germany (one DM has a purchasing power of approximately $0.50).

tax and the new eco-tax on fossil fuel) and a subsidy from the federal government. The subsidy is also used to fine tune the pay-as-you-go budget constraint, which has a minimal reserve of one month worth of benefits.

5.2.2   Benefit Types

The German public retirement insurance provides *old-age pensions* for workers aged 60 and older, *disability benefits* for workers below age 60, which are converted to old-age pensions latest at age 65, and *survivor benefits* for spouses and children. In addition, preretirement (i.e., retirement before age 60) is possible through several mechanisms, using the public transfer system, mainly unemployment compensation. We begin by describing old-age pensions.

5.2.3   Eligibility for Benefits and Retirement Age for Old-Age Pensions

Eligibility for benefits and the minimum retirement age depend on which type of pension the worker chooses. The German public retirement insurance distinguishes five types of old-age pensions, corresponding to normal retirement and four types of early retirement (see table 5.1).

This complex system was introduced by the 1972 social security reform. One of the key provisions was the introduction of flexible retirement after age 63, with full benefits for workers with a long service history. In addition, retirement at age 60 with full benefits is possible for women, the unemployed, and older disabled workers. "Older disabled workers" refers to those workers who cannot be appropriately employed for health or labor market reasons and are age 60 or older. There are three ways to claim old-age disability benefits. One has to (1) be at least 50 percent physically disabled, (2) pass a strict earnings test, or (3) pass a much weaker earnings test. The strict earnings test is passed if the earnings capacity is reduced below the minimum earnings threshold for any *reasonable* occupation (about 15 percent of average gross wage; *erwerbsunfähig;* EU). The weaker earnings test is passed when no vacancies for the worker's *specific* job description are available and the worker has to face an earnings loss of at least 50 percent when changing to a different job (*berufsunfähig;* BU). As opposed to the disability insurance for workers below age 60 (see the following), full benefits are paid in all three cases.

Figure 5.2 shows the uptake of the various pathways,[6] including the disability pathway described subsequently, (adding to 100 percent on the vertical axis) and their changes over time (marked on the horizontal axis), mostly in response to reforms, benefit adjustments, and administrative rule changes, in particularly the tightening of the disability screening process. This figure shows the multitude of possible pathways. A major undertaking of this chapter is to take account of this diversity.

Through the 1992 social security reform and its subsequent modifica-

---

6. See Jacobs, Kohli, and Rein (1990) for this concept.

Table 5.1   **Old-Age pensions (1972 legislation)**

Pension type	Retirement age	Years of service	Additional conditions	Earnings test
A Normal	65	5		No
B Long service life ("flexible")	63	35		Yes
C Women	60	15	10 years of those after age 40	Yes
D Older disabled	60	35	Loss of at least 50% earnings capability	Yes
E Unemployed	60	15	1.5 to 3 years of unemployment (has changed several times)	Yes

Note: This legislation was changed in the reform of 1992. It has been effective until the year 1998.

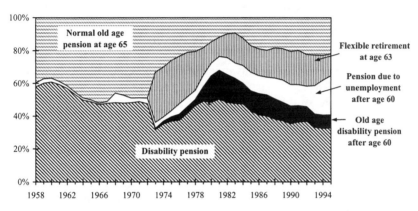

Fig. 5.2   Pathways to retirement (males), 1960–95

tions, the age limits of the various types of early retirement will gradually be raised to age 65. These changes will be fully phased in by the year 2004. The only distinguishing feature of types B and C of early retirement will then be the possibility to retire up to five years earlier than age 65 if a sufficient number of service years (currently thirty-five years) has been accumulated. As opposed to the pre-1992 regulations, benefits will be adjusted to a retirement age below age 65 in a manner that will be described later.

5.2.4   Benefits

Benefits are strictly work related. The German system does not have benefits for spouses, as in the United States.[7] Benefits are computed on a lifetime basis and are adjusted according to the type of pension and retirement age. They are the product of four elements: (1) the employee's relative earnings position, (2) the years of service life, (3) adjustment factors for pension type and (since the 1992 reform) retirement age, and (4) the aver-

7. There are, of course, survivor benefits.

age pension. The first three factors make up the personal pension base, while the fourth factor determines the income distribution between workers and pensioners in general.

The employee's relative contribution position is computed by averaging her or his annual relative contribution positions over the entire earnings history. In each year, the relative contribution position is expressed as a multiple of the average annual contribution (roughly speaking, the relative income position). A first element of redistribution was introduced in 1972, when this multiple could not fall below 75 percent for contributions before 1972, provided a worker had a service life of at least thirty-five years. A similar rule was introduced in the 1992 reform: for contributions between 1973 and 1992, multiples below 75 percent are multiplied by 1.5 up to the maximum of 75 percent, effectively reducing the redistribution for workers with income positions below 50 percent.

Years of service life are years of active contribution plus years of contribution on behalf of the employee and years that are counted as service years even when no contribution was made at all. These include, for instance, years of unemployment, years of military service, three years for each child's education for one of the parents, some allowance for advanced education, and so forth, introducing a second element of redistribution. The official government computations, such as the official replacement rate (*Rentenniveau*) assume a forty-five-year contribution history for what is deemed a normal earnings history (*Eckrentner*). In fact, the average number of years of contributions is about thirty-eight years. Unlike the United States, there is neither an upper bound of years entering the benefit calculation nor can workers choose certain years in their earnings history and drop others.

Since 1992, the average pension is determined by indexation to the average net labor income. This solved some of the problems that were created by indexation to gross wages between 1972 and 1992. Nevertheless, wage rather than cost of living indexation makes it impossible to finance the retirement burden by productivity gains.

The average pension has provided a generous benefit level for middle-income earnings. The net replacement rate for a worker with a forty-five-year contribution history is 70.5 percent in 1998. For the average worker with thirty-eight years of contributions, it is reduced to 59.5 percent. Unlike the United States, the German pension system has only little redistribution, as is obvious from the benefit computation.[8] The low replacement rates for high incomes results from the upper limit to which earnings are subject to social security contributions—they correspond to a proportionally lower effective contribution rate.

Before 1992, *adjustment of benefits to retirement age* was only implicit via years of service. Because benefits are proportional to the years of service,

---

8. See Casmir (1989) for a comparison.

Table 5.2 **Adjustment of public pensions by retirement age (pension as a percentage of the pension that one would obtain if one had retired at age 65)**

Age	Germany		United States		
	Pre-1992[a]	Post-1992[b]	Pre-1983[c]	Post-1983[d]	Actuarially fair[e]
62	100.0	89.2	80.0	77.8	80,5
63	100.0	92.8	86.7	85.2	86,3
64	100.0	96.4	94.4	92.6	92,8
65	100.0	100.0	100.0	100.0	100,0
66	107.2	106.0	103.0	105.6	108,1
67	114.4	112.0	106.0	111.1	117,2
68	114.4	118.0	109.0	120.0	127,4
69	114.4	124.0	112.0	128.9	139,1

Source: Börsch-Supan and Schnabel (1999).
[a] GRV 1972–92.
[b] GRV after 1992 reform has fully phased in.
[c] U.S. Social Security (OASDHI) until 1983.
[d] U.S. Social Security after 1983 Social Security Reform has fully phased in.
[e] Evaluated at a 3% discount rate, 1992–94 mortality risks of West German males and an annual increase in net pensions of 1%.

a worker with fewer years of service will get lower benefits. With a constant income profile and forty years of service, each year of earlier retirement decreased pension benefits by 2.5 percent, and vice versa.

The 1992 social security reform changed this by the year 2004. Age 65 will then act as the pivotal age for benefit computations. For each year of earlier retirement, up to five years, and if the appropriate conditions in table 5.1 are met, benefits will be reduced by 3.6 percent (in addition to the effect of fewer service years). The 1992 reform also introduced rewards for *later* retirement in a systematic way. For each year of retirement postponed past the minimum age indicated in table 5.1, the pension is increased by 6 percent in addition to the natural increase by the number of service years.

Table 5.2 displays the retirement-age-specific adjustments for a worker who has earnings that remain constant after age 60. The table relates the retirement income for retirement at age 65 (normalized to 100 percent) to the retirement income for retirement at earlier or later ages, and compares the implicit adjustments after 1972 with the total adjustments after the 1992 social security reform is fully phased in. As references, the table also displays the corresponding adjustments in the United States and actuarially fair adjustments at a 3 percent discount rate.[9]

While neither the German nor the American system were actuarially fair

9. The actuarially fair adjustments equalize the expected social security wealth for a worker with an earnings history starting at age $S = 20$. A higher discount rate yields steeper adjustments.

prior to the reforms, the public retirement system in Germany as enacted in 1972 was particularly distorted. There was less economic incentive for Americans to retire before age 65 and only a small disincentive to retire later than at age 65 after the 1983 reform, while the German social security system tilted the retirement decision heavily toward the earliest applicable retirement age. The 1992 reform has diminished but not abolished this incentive effect.

5.2.5   Disability and Survivor Benefits

The contributions to the German retirement insurance also finance *disability benefits* to workers of all ages and *survivor benefits* to spouses and children. In order to be eligible for disability benefits, a worker must pass one of the two earnings tests mentioned earlier for the old-age disability pension. If the stricter earnings test is passed, full benefits are paid *Erwerbsunfähigkeitsrente,* EU). If only the weaker earnings test is passed and some earnings capability remains, disability pensions before age 60 are only two-thirds of the applicable old age pension (*Berufsunfähigkeitsrente,* BU). In the 1970s and early 1980s, the German jurisdiction has interpreted both rules very broadly, in particular the applicability of the first rule. Moreover, jurisdiction also overruled the earnings test (see the following) for earnings during disability retirement. This lead to a share of EU-type disability pensions of more than 90 percent of all disability pensions. Because both rules were used as a device to keep unemployment rates down, their generous interpretation has only recently led to stricter legislation.[10]

Survivor pensions are 60 percent of the husband's applicable pension for spouses that are age 45 and over or if children are in the household (*große Witwenrente*), otherwise 25 percent (*kleine Witwenrente*). Survivor benefits are a large component of the public pension budget and of total pension wealth, as will be shown in section 5.3. Certain earnings tests apply if the surviving spouse has her or his own income, that is, her or his own pension. This is only relevant for a very small (below 10 percent) share of widows. Only since recently are male and female survivors treated equally. As mentioned before, the German system does not have a married couple supplement for spouses of beneficiaries. However, most wives acquire their own pension by active and passive contribution (mostly years of advanced education and years of child education).

5.2.6   Preretirement

In addition to benefits through the public pension system, transfer payments (mainly unemployment compensation) enable what is referred to as *preretirement.* Labor-force exit before age 60 is frequent: about 45 percent

---

10. See Riphahn (1995) for an analysis of disability rules.

of all men call themselves "retired" at age 59. Only about half of them retire because of disability; the other 50 percent make use of one of the many official and unofficial preretirement schemes.

Unemployment compensation has been used as preretirement income in an official scheme that induced very early retirement. Before workers could enter the public pension system at age 60, they were paid a negotiable combination of unemployment compensation and a supplement or severance pay. At age 60, a pension of type E (see table 5.1) could start. As the rules of pensions of type E and the duration of unemployment benefits changed, so did the unofficial retirement ages. Age 56 was particularly frequent in West Germany because unemployment compensation is paid up to three years for elderly workers; it is followed by the lower unemployment aid. Earlier retirement ages could be induced by paying the worker the difference between the last salary and unemployment compensation for three years; and in further years, the difference between the last salary and unemployment aid—it all depended on the so-called *social plan*, which a firm would negotiate with the workers before restructuring the workforce.

In addition, early retirement at age 58 was made possible in an official preretirement scheme (*Vorruhestand*), in which the employer received a subsidy from the unemployment insurance if a younger employee was hired. While the first (and unofficial) preretirement scheme was very popular, and a convenient way to bypass the strict German labor laws, few employers used the official second scheme.

5.2.7   Retirement Behavior

The average retirement age in 1998 was 59.7 for men and 60.7 for women. These numbers refer to West Germany. In the East, retirement age was 57.9 for men and 58.2 for women. The fraction of those who enter retirement through a disability pension has declined; see figure 5.2, and was 29 percent in 1998. Only about 20 percent of all entrants used the normal pathway of an old-age pension at age 65. The most popular retirement age is 60.

5.2.8   Pension Reform

During and since the estimation sample period, there have been two major pension reforms—1992 and 2001—and many smaller adjustments in between. The main changes in the 1992 reform were to anchor benefits to net rather than to gross wages. This has implicitly reduced benefits, since taxes and social security contributions have increased, reducing net relative to gross wages. This mechanism is particularly important as the population's aging accelerates. The other important changes in 1992 were the introduction of adjustments to benefits in some (not all) cases of early retirement and a change in the normal retirement age for women. They have been described in subsection 5.2.4. They will be fully effective in 2009 and will reduce the incentives to retire early, although they are still not actuarially fair, even at very low discount rates.[11]

The 1999 pension reform, which was supposed to lower the replacement rate according to a prespecified so-called demographic factor, was revoked after a change of government. A side effect of this reform, which was not revoked, is a gradual change of eligibility ages for pensions for women and unemployed (types C and E in table 5.1) from age 60 to age 65. This change will be fully implemented by 2017 and will effectively leave a window of retirement for only those who have at least thirty-five years of service.

The 2001 reform was a major change in the system. It will change the monolithic German system of old-age provision to a genuine multipillar system. Benefits will gradually be reduced by about 10 percent, lowering the replacement rate with respect to the average net earnings from 72 percent in 1997 to 64 percent in 2030. The effective benefit cuts are even larger, since the credit of earnings points for education and training will be greatly restricted. On the other hand, a redefinition of the official replacement rate minimizes the perception of these cuts, because the so-defined new replacement rate will be 67 percent with respect to a smaller net earnings base. The resulting pension gap of slightly less than 20 percent of the current retirement income is supposed to be filled with occupational and individual pensions. This new pillar is not mandatory, but the required private savings will be subsidized or tax privileged. The 2001 reform did not change the normal retirement age or the adjustment factors with respect to early retirement age that provide the large incentives to retire early, the main subject of this project.

5.3   Public Sector Pensions

There are two types of workers in the public sector: civil servants and other public sector workers. As already mentioned, the latter are part of the same system as the private sector workers described in the previous section. In addition, they participate in a supplemental system that resembles occupational pensions elsewhere and raises the pensions of public sector workers to the level of civil servants.

Civil servants do not pay explicit contributions for their pensions, as do the other employees in the private and public sectors.[12] Instead, the gross wage for civil servants is lower than the gross wage of other public sector employees with a comparable education. Civil servants acquire pension claims that are very generous compared to workers in the private sector.

---

11. Not even at zero.

12. Civil servants are also exempt from unemployment insurance contributions, since civil servants have a lifetime job guarantee. The government pays a certain percentage of health expenses of the civil servant and his or her dependents (ranging from 50 to 80 percent). The rest has to be covered by private insurance.

5.3.1   Eligibility: Pathways to Retirement for Civil Servants

There are three pathways for civil servants: the standard, the early, and the disability retirement option. The standard retirement age is 65. Before July 1, 1997, the early retirement age for civil servants was 62, one year less than the early retirement age in the social security system. In 1997, the early retirement age was raised to 63. Discount factors for early retirement are phased in linearly between the years 1998 and 2003, and will reach 0.3 percentage points per month of early retirement, the same as in the private sector and substantially smaller than is actuarially fair. Since our sample covers the years 1984 to 1997, these changes of rules do not play a role in our analysis.[13]

Filing for disability is a third pathway to retirement for civil servants. In the case of disability, a civil servant receives a pension that is based on his or her previous salary. The replacement rate depends on the number of service years reached before disability retirement and the number of service years that could potentially have been accumulated, up to age 60. For those who did not reach the maximum replacement rate before disability, one additional year of service raises the replacement rate by only 0.3 percentage point per year.

5.3.2   Computation of Pensions

The standard pension benefit for civil servants is the product of three elements: (1) the last gross earnings level, (2) the replacement rate as a function of service years, and (3) the new adjustment factors to early retirement. As described earlier, this third component does not affect our sample. There are three crucial differences between civil servants' pensions and private sector benefits. First, the benefit base is gross rather than net income. In turn, civil servants' pensions are taxed like any other income. Finally, the benefit base is the last salary, rather than the lifetime average.

In the following, we concentrate on describing how the system worked for the sample period 1984–97. Benefits are anchored to the earnings in the last position and then updated annually by the growth rate of the net earnings of active civil servants. If the last position was reached within the last two years before retirement, the pension is based on the previous, lower position. Due to the difference in the benefit base, gross pensions of civil servants are approximately 25 percent higher (other things being equal) than in the private sector.

The maximum replacement rate is 75 percent of *gross* earnings, which is considerably higher than the official replacement rate of the private sector system, which is around 70 percent of *net* earnings. The replacement rate depends on the years of service. High school and college education,

---

13. Very specific rules apply to some civil servants. For example, the regular retirement age for police officers is 60; for soldiers it is even lower, depending on their rank.

military service, and other work in the public sector are also counted as service years. For retirement after June 1997 the college education credit is limited to three years.

Before 1992, the replacement rate was a nonlinear function of service years. The replacement rate started at a value of 35 percent for all civil servants with at least five years of service. For each additional year of service between the 10th and the 25th year the increment was 2 percentage points. From the 25th to the 35th year the annual increment was 1 percent. Thus, the maximum replacement rate of 75 percent was reached with thirty-five service years under the old rule. This is much more generous than the private sector replacement rate of 70 percent, which requires forty-five years of service.

For persons retiring after January 1, 1992, the replacement rate grows by 1.875 percent points for each year of service. Thus, the maximum value is reached after forty years of service. However, there are transitional modifications to that simple rule. First, civil servants who reach the standard retirement age (usually age 65) before January 1, 2002, are not affected at all. Second, for younger civil servants, all claims that have been acquired before 1992 are conserved. These persons gain 1 additional percentage point per year from 1992 on. All persons who have acquired twenty-five service years before 1992 have reached 65 percentage points and would also have gained only 1 additional point per year under the old rule. Only persons with less than twenty-five service years in 1991 can be made worse off by the reform. The new proportional rule only applies if it generates a higher replacement rate than the transitional rule. Our calculations of pension wealth use these institutional changes, but only a few special cases are affected.

The generosity of gross pensions received by civil servants vis-à-vis the private sector workers is only partially offset by the preferential tax treatment of private sector pensions. Since civil servants' pensions are taxed according to the German comprehensive income taxation, the net replacement rates of civil service pension recipients depends on their position in the highly progressive tax schedule. In general, the net replacement rate with respect to the preretirement net earnings is higher than 75 percent, and thus considerably more generous than in the private sector.

5.3.3 Incentives to Retire

In the estimation sample, most civil servants have reached the maximum replacement rate by the age of 54. Persons who have started to work in the public sector before the age of 23 have reached a replacement rate of 75 percent when taking into account the disability rules. This also holds for civil servants, who—like professors—receive lifetime tenure late in their life cycle. For those groups, the starting age is usually set to 21. Additional years of service beyond the age of 54 increase pensions only if the civil servant is promoted to a position that has a higher salary. Retirement incentives therefore strongly depend on promotion expectations.

For persons who cannot expect to be promoted after age 54 the pension accrual is zero or very small. For those who have already reached the replacement rate of 75 percent, the accrual of the present discounted pension wealth is negative. Since the replacement rate is 75 percent of the gross earnings in the last position before retirement, the negative accrual of postponing retirement by one year is simply 75 percent of the last gross earnings. This is equivalent to a 75 percent tax on earnings.

For persons who expect to climb another step in the hierarchy the gross wage increase is, on average, 10.5 percent. This raises the pension by approximately 10 percent. In order to cash in the higher pension, the civil servant has to defer retirement by at least one year.[14] In this extreme case, the social security wealth increases 10 percent through the effect of higher pensions and decreases by 5 percent through the effect of pension deferral. In this extreme case, the pension accrual is positive. If the civil servant has to wait several years for the next promotion (or for the promotion to have an effect on pension claims) the accrual of working becomes negative.

The dependency on promotion expectations makes modeling the incentive effects for civil servants very hard, since the researcher needs information on the career prospects of the respondent. We do not have such information in our data and must therefore ignore the effect of potential promotions.

5.3.4   Retirement Behavior

The retirement behavior of civil servants reflects the German pension system's very generous disability and early retirement rules. The average retirement age for civil servants in the year 1993 was 58.9, about one year lower than in the private sector (see section 5.2.7). Disability is the most widely used pathway to retirement for civil servants: 40 percent of those who retired in the year 1993 used disability retirement. Almost one third used the early retirement option at the age of 62. Only about 20 percent of civil servants retired at the regular retirement age of 65.

5.4   **Data and Base Model**

Our microsimulation model is based on a computation of social security wealth for a large sample of German workers, drawn from the German Socio-Economic Panel (GSOEP). It is the same sample that we used in our

---

14. For the higher earnings to take effect on pensions it is usually required to work several years after the promotion.

second-stage paper (Börsch-Supan et al. 2003) to estimate the elasticities of labor supply with respect to the incentives toward early retirement. Our simulations then focus on a single cohort, namely all males born in 1942 (age 55 in 1997) and their spouses. Additional aggregate information was taken from data compiled by the German retirement insurance organization (Verband deutscher Versicherungträger [VDR]) and the German Department of Labor (Bundesministerium für Arbeit und Sozialordnung [BMA]). These data include annual statistics on average earnings, pension system entries and exits, retirement age, and so on (VDR 2002) and system parameters (BMA 1997). This section describes the data, the construction of social security wealth, the definition of incentive variables, and then briefly discusses the base estimates from our stage-two econometric estimation.

5.4.1 The German Socio-Economic Panel

The German Socio-Economic Panel (GSOEP) is an annual panel study of some 6,000 households and some 15,000 individuals. The data are gathered by the German Institute for Economic Research (DIW). The GSOEP is a panel survey of private households. Its design closely corresponds to the U.S. Panel Study of Income Dynamics (PSID).[15] The GSOEP includes carefully designed household weights that match the data with the German *Mikrozensus*. The panel started in 1984. We use 14 annual waves, through 1997.

In 1997, the GSOEP had four subsamples: (1) West German citizens (9,000 persons in 1984); (2) Foreign workers from Spain, Italy, Greece, Turkey, and the former Yugoslavia, residing in West Germany (3,000 persons in 1984, oversampled); (3) East German citizens (4,000 persons sampled from 1991 on); and (4) Germans who have remigrated (mainly from Romania and the former USSR; 1,000 persons sampled in 1995). We draw our working sample from samples 1 and 2, since the labor supply patterns of East Germans and remigrants are substantially different from residents in West Germany—such that pooling these samples is not warranted.[16]

We constructed a both-sided unbalanced panel of all persons aged 55 through 70 from subsamples 1 and 2 for which earnings data are available.[17] This panel includes 2,223 individuals, with 14,401 observations.

---

15. Wagner, Burkhauser, and Behringer (1993) provide an English-language description, code books, and links to an internationally accessible GSOEP version. Börsch-Supan (2000a) discusses the merits and limits of the GSOEP data for studies of retirement behavior.
16. Schmähl (1991) provides a narrative of the transition.
17. We excluded East Germany because retirement patterns in the East are dominated by the transition problems to a market economy. See Börsch-Supan and Schmidt (1996) for a comparison.

Average observation time is 6.5 years. The panel is left-censored, as we include only persons who have worked at least one year during our window in order to reconstruct an earning history. There is only a slight right censoring due to missing interviews. Specifically, foreign workers often leave Germany after retirement. However, since this affects only a few cases, we did not model this censoring. The sample contains private sector workers, civil servants and other public sector workers, and self-employed.

The GSOEP data provide a detailed account of income and employment status. Since the GSOEP performs personal interviews with each member aged 17 and over in the households, we have the same information on husbands and spouses. The personal information includes labor market status, gross and net income, hours worked, education, and marital status, but only a subjective indicator of health (plus disability status and number of doctor and hospital visits). The GSOEP also has a very detailed labor market calendar that provides monthly information on the labor market status (full time, part time, retired, unemployed, education) and its corresponding income for each sample person. This detailed information is augmented during the sample period by a retrospective history of labor force participation that starts with age 15. It carries the annual labor market status (full time, part time, unemployed, out-of-labor force, etc.) but has no retrospective earnings information. Our second-stage paper (Börsch-Supan et al. 2002) describes in detail how we reconstruct the earnings history of each sample person.

Table 5.3 presents the descriptive statistics of the most common socioeconomic variables in our working sample.

Table 5.3   **Descriptive statistics of main variables**

Variable	Valid observations	Mean	Standard deviation	Minimum	Maximum
Age	14,401	59.77	4.88	53	70
Health	14,401	8.09	3.05	0	10
Married	14,401	86%	34%	0	1
College	14,401	11%	31%	0	1
Skilled	14,401	86%	58%	0	2
Homeown	14,398	52%	50%	0	1
No wealth	14,312	11%	31%	0	1
Financial assets	14,401	22%	42%	0	1
Experience	14,401	450.29	96.01	0	646
Former self-employed	14,401	9%	29%	0	1
Former civil service	14,359	8%	27%	0	1
Children in household	14,401	33%	47%	0	1

Source: GSOEP, working sample of males, 1984–97.

5.4.2 Handling of Multiple Retirement Programs

A worker at age 55, at least theoretically has the choice between three retirement programs:

- old-age pensions, starting at age 60
- disability pensions
- preretirement schemes

The set of choices is actually larger, because some of these programs have several branch programs (within old-age pensions: unemployment, long-service life, etc.) as was depicted in figure 5.2. We refer to these choices as *pathways,* as we have done in figure 5.2. It is important to notice that all of these pathways pay the same benefit, once a person is eligible.[18]

In practice, there is no free choice, since most of these pathways are subject to eligibility criteria. Among those, we distinguish between strict eligibility rules that are tied to objective variables such as age, gender, and previous contribution history, and soft eligibility rules, which are subject to discretionary decisions, notably the determining of a worker's disability status.[19]

In the construction of social security wealth and the incentive variables (see the following), we need to compute expected pension benefits, which depend on the choice of pathway. In the computation of this expected value, we use the observed frequencies as weights. Let's suppose that the observed frequency of disability status at age 59 is 33 percent, and the sample person is not eligible for any other pathway at that age. Then, expected benefits at age 59 for this person will be a third of the (common) benefit level. Börsch-Supan (2001) provides an instrumental variables interpretation of this method and explores the sensitivity with respect to a more sophisticated choice of instruments.

5.4.3 Construction of Social Security Wealth

A key statistic in our computation of budget impacts is the change in the net present value of all future benefits when retirement is postponed. In a slight misuse of terminology, we call the net present value of all future benefits *social security wealth* (SSW) for both private sector and civil servants' pensions.

We define social security wealth as the expected present discounted value of benefits ($YRET$) minis applicable contributions that are levied on gross earnings ($c \cdot YLAB$). Seen from the perspective of a worker who is S years old and plans to retire at age R, social security wealth (SSW) is

---

18. Strictly speaking, preretirement programs can have any benefit level, because they are negotiated between workers and employers. In practice, however, the outcome of these negotiations is guided by public insurance benefits.

19. *Disability* depends on health as well as labor market characteristics.

$$SSW_S(R) = \sum_{t=R}^{\infty} YRET_t(R) \cdot a_t \cdot \delta^{t-S} - \sum_{t=S}^{R-1} c \cdot YLAB_t \cdot a_t \cdot \delta^{t-S},$$

with

SSW	net present discounted value of retirement benefits
S	planning age
R	retirement age
$YLAB_t$	gross labor income at age t
$YRET_t(R)$	net pension income at age t for retirement at age R
c_t	contribution rate to pension system at age t
a_t	probability to survive at least until age t, given survival until age S
δ	discount factor $= 1/(1 + r)$.

We choose the usual discount rate of 3 percent. Conditional survival probabilities are computed from the standard life tables of the German Bureau of the Census (*Statistisches Bundesamt*). SSW depends also on the *joint* survival probabilities of spouses through survivor pensions. We assume independence of survival of spouses to compute the joint probability.

5.4.4 Specification of Incentive Variables

The *behavioral effect,* which represents the labor supply response to the simulated reform plans as explained in the introduction, is determined by the elasticity of labor supply with respect to the incentives in the pension system. We use two different forward-looking incentive measures:

- *PEAKVAL:* the maximum of future SSW over all possible retirement ages minus the SSW for immediate retirement
- *OPTVAL:* the option value of postponing retirement by 1 year.

The *peak value* suggested by Coile and Gruber (2000) takes the difference between SSW today and SSW in the year in which the expected value of SSW is maximized:

$$PEAKVAL_S(R) = SSW_S(R) - \max_{T>R}[SSW_S(T)]$$

This measure therefore captures the tradeoff between retiring today and working until a year with a much higher SSW. In years beyond the year in which SSW peaks, this calculation collapses to a simple one-year accrual variable.

The peak value captures only the financial aspects of the retirement decision. Alternatively, one might consider the consumption utility of net earnings and pension benefits and also account for the utility aspects of the labor-leisure tradeoff. To this end, we employ as a second incentive variable the option value to postpone retirement (Stock and Wise 1990; Börsch-Supan 2000b). This value expresses for each retirement age the trade-off between retiring now (resulting in a stream of utility that depends on this retirement age) and keeping all options open for some later retirement date (with associated streams of utility for all possible later retirement ages).

Let $V_t(R)$ denote the expected discounted future utility at age t if the worker retires at age R, specified as follows:

$$V_t(R) = \sum_{s=t}^{R-1} u(YLAB_s^{\mathrm{NET}}) \cdot a_s \cdot \delta^{s-t} + \alpha \sum_{s=R}^{\infty} u[YRET_s(R)] \cdot a_s \cdot \delta^{s-t},$$

with

$YLAB_s^{\mathrm{NET}}$	after-tax labor income at age s, $s = t \ldots R-1$
$YRET_s(R)$	pension income at age s, $s > R$
R	retirement age
α	marginal utility of leisure, to be estimated
a	probability to survive at least until age s
δ	discount factor $= 1/(1 + r)$.

Utility from consumption is represented by an isoelastic utility function in after-tax income, $u(Y) = Y^\gamma$. Remember that pension income in Germany is effectively untaxed. To capture utility from leisure, utility during retirement is weighted by $\alpha > 1$, where $1/\alpha$ is the marginal disutility of work.

The option value for a specific age is defined as the difference between the maximum attainable consumption utility if the worker postpones retirement to some later year minus the utility of consumption that the worker can afford if the worker would retire now. Let $R^*(t)$ denote the optimal retirement age if the worker postpones retirement past age t, that is, $\max[V_t(r)]$ for $r > t$. With this notation, the option value is

$$G(t) = V_t[R^*(t)] - V_t(t).$$

The option value captures the economic incentives created by the pension system and the labor market, because the retirement income $YRET_s(R)$ depends on retirement age, according to the adjustment factors and on previous labor income by the benefit rules summarized in sections 5.2 and 5.3.

We compute the peak and option values for every person in our sample, using the applicable pension regulations and the imputed earning histories. The parameters chosen are a discount rate δ of 3 percent, a curvature parameter γ of 1.0, and a relative utility parameter α of 2.8; see our second-stage paper.

5.4.5   Base Model Estimates

The *behavioral effect* is based on the probit estimates obtained in the second stage of this project. See Börsch-Supan et al. (2002) for a detailed discussion. The probit estimations regressed old-age labor force status on one

Table 5.4   **Marginal effect of incentive variables**

	Option value: Age			Peak value: Age		
	Linear	Quadratic	Dummies	Linear	Quadratic	Dummies
Males						
Without SSW	-0.00023237	-0.0020934	-0.0024276	-0.0012644	-0.00107072	-0.00292954
	(-5, 5)	(-5, 0)	(-5, 5)	(-3, 8)	(-3, 2)	(-5, 7)
With SSW	-0.00030332	-0.00027806	-0.0003286	-0.00126031	-0.00105993	-0.00293449
	(-6, 1)	(-5, 6)	(-6, 2)	(-3, 7)	(-3, 2)	(-5, 7)
Females						
Without SSW	-0.00005129	-0.00006159	-0.00010106	-0.00133364	-0.00159996	-0.00270272
	(-3, 4)	(-3, 1)	(-3, 1)	(-5, 1)	(-5, 0)	(-4, 2)
With SSW	-0.00005499	-0.00006957	-0.00013015	-0.00155703	-0.00189241	-0.00384073
	(-3, 7)	(-3, 4)	(-3, 7)	(-5, 2)	(-5, 1)	(-4, 6)

Source: GSOEP, working sample, 1984–97.

Note: $\partial P/\partial x$ and t-statistics (in parentheses).

of the two incentive variables—peak value and option value—just described, and a set of other explanatory variables: an array of socioeconomic variables such as age, gender, marital status, wealth (indicator variables of several financial and real wealth categories), and a self-assessed health measure ranging from 0 for poor to 10 for excellent health.

Table 5.4 summarizes the base estimation results from 24 different models.[20] We use two different incentive variables (option value and peak value). For each of these incentive variables, we run probit regressions with three age specifications (linear, quadratic, and a full set of age dummies) and with and without including social security wealth. We pool public and private workers, but have separate regressions for males and females.

All incentive variables have the correct sign and are highly significant. They are very robust across all the different specifications, including inclusion of other covariates, sample selection, and definition of retirement (not shown in table 5.4). Including age dummies yields larger marginal effects and better precision, while including SSW has a very small weakening effect.

Among the other covariates, self-reported health is highly significant: healthier workers retire substantially later than those who report poor health. The effect of a college degree on retirement age is also very strong—independent of wealth and income effects. The wealth variables are barely significant: persons with higher wealth (homeownership, financial assets) afford an earlier retirement. Also, higher labor income weakens labor force attachment. The self-employed tend to work longer, while civil servants retire earlier.

20. The estimates differ slightly from those in Börsch-Supan et al. (2002) due to various changes in the common definitions' template.

5.5   Simulation Results

We now apply these estimated coefficients to simulate the budget effects of pension reforms. We first describe the design of the simulations. Second, we sketch the behavioral responses to the reforms, namely the changes in retirement age. Third, we present the budget effects, both in summary and disaggregated by age, by behavioral and mechanical effects, and by benefits and taxes/contributions. We end this section by discussing distributional issues.

5.5.1   Design of Simulations

All simulations are based on the 1942 cohort of preretirement workers (age 55 in 1997). We include (a) all male workers and their spouses (if any) and (b) all single female workers of this cohort.

Since this leaves us with a rather small sample, we augment this original cohort by thirteen additional cohorts, born between 1929 and 1941, by synthetically de-aging them to the more youthful 1942 cohort. This is done by assigning the persons in the earlier cohorts the earnings history and other characteristics (including age) they would have had at age 55. This procedure is possible because we have constructed complete earnings histories.

Based on this synthetic cohort, we first estimate the probability that each worker will exit the labor force via death or retirement at each future age and the net present discounted value of retirement program contributions and benefits associated with each type of labor force exit. The resulting weighted average social security wealth is our base for comparison. We then reestimate the exit probabilities, contributions, and benefits under several reforms in order to obtain new social security wealth estimates. Our key result is the percentage change in social security wealth, including and excluding a behavioral response to the reform, as the difference between these numbers measures the extent to which labor supply responses amplify the effect of reforms on program solvency.

We use three hypothetical reform scenarios (Three-Year Reform, Actuarial Reform, and Common Reform, explained in more detail later) and apply them systematically to several variants of our estimated models of retirement. These variants include the option value and the peak value model, each of which is estimated using a linear and a dummy-variable age specification. In the latter case and in combination with the Three-Year Reform, we introduce yet another two variants: keeping the dummy variables at their original ages (fixed dummies specification), or shifting them along with the shift in the incentive variables (shifted dummies specification). These latter variants are designed to bracket possible behavioral effects that are embedded in the age dummies; in particular, habitual effects associated with age 65 as a psychological anchor for retirement decisions.

The Three-Year Reform increases the age of early and normal retirement by three years relative to the status quo; it also shifts the corresponding adjustment factors, if applicable. The Actuarial Reform introduces a 6 percent per year actuarial adjustment, pivoted at age 65, roughly doubling the value that was legislated by the 1992 reform in Germany. The Common Reform changes all national systems to a common system with an early retirement age of 60 years, a normal retirement age of 65 years, a 60 percent replacement rate at age 65, and a 6 percent per year actuarial adjustment, pivoted at age 65. For Germany, this adds a reduction in the replacement rate of some 10 percentage points to the effect of the Actuarial Reform.

Even without a behavioral reaction, that is, without a response in labor supply, these reforms have an automatic effect on fiscal contributions by changing contributions and benefits for a given work history. We call this the *mechanical* effect of a reform. For instance, a shift in the early retirement eligibility age from age 60 to age 61 will leave those who retire at age 60 without benefits for a year, substantially reducing pension benefits.

Labor supply, however, is likely to respond to the shift in the early retirement age. This is the behavioral effect. Following up on our example, most of these early retirees will now work one additional year, adding the payroll contributions to the budget of the public pension system. The fiscal impact of this behavioral effect depends on two factors: first, on the strength of the labor force response as estimated in the previous section, and second, on the fiscal implications of the shift in retirement patterns. If a pension system is actuarially fair, a change in the average retirement age will not have any fiscal effect, provided that the discount rate used to define actuarial fairness equals the discount rate used to compute fiscal implications.[21]

There is actually a third effect, namely, the macroeconomic feedback effect of these reforms on the level of taxes and contributions. For instance, if a reform implies lower benefits, the government might lower the contribution rate to the pay-as-you-go budget. We do not model such feedback effects; our simulations are in this sense static simulations that exclude dynamic budget effects.

We simulate both the mechanical and the behavioral effect, using the econometric retirement models from the second stage to predict labor supply responses. The result is an estimate of the steady-state impact of the reforms on the financial balance sheet of the German public pension system.

---

21. We assume the same discount rate of 3 percent to define actuarial fairness and to compute intertemporal budget effects. One might argue that one should use a higher discount rate for actuarial fairness, reflecting the real rate of return on the capital market, and a lower discount rate for budget calculations, reflecting the low implicit rate of return of the pay-as-you-go system (Schnabel 1998, 1999).

Table 5.5   **Expected retirement age**

Model	Men	Women
Sample		
Sample frequencies	61.87	61.76
Base simulation		
Option value model, linear age	62.00	62.01
Option value model, dummies	61.87	61.79
Peak value model, linear age	62.00	62.01
Peak value model, dummies	61.88	61.79
Three-Year Reform		
Option value model, linear age	61.37	61.91
Option value model, dummies fixed	61.14	61.63
Option value model, dummies shifted	64.37	64.28
Peak value model, linear age	61.91	61.93
Peak value model, dummies fixed	61.75	61.68
Peak value model, dummies shifted	64.63	64.54
Actuarial Reform		
Option value model, linear age	65.28	63.86
Option value model, dummies fixed	64.92	63.92
Option value model, dummies shifted	64.96	64.14
Peak value model, linear age	63.53	64.08
Peak value model, dummies fixed	64.38	63.81
Peak value model, dummies shifted	64.34	64.01
Common Reform		
Option value model, linear age	65.42	62.77
Option value model, dummies fixed	65.02	62.69
Option value model, dummies changed	65.04	62.93
Peak value model, linear age	63.19	62.82
Peak value model, dummies fixed	64.05	62.71
Peak value model, dummies changed	63.97	62.93

Note: Expected value is taken over distribution truncated at age 72.

5.5.2   Behavioral Effects and Their Fiscal Implications

We begin with the behavioral effect, then describe its implications on the budget, and finally add the mechanical effect to obtain the total budget impact. We first summarize the behavioral effects of the hypothetical pension reforms on old-age labor supply as a change in the mean retirement age (see table 5.5) and then present detailed results in a set of graphs.[22]

The Three-Year Reform has little effect in the linear age and dummies-fixed specifications, and actually changes it insignificantly in the wrong direction. This may come as a surprise, but it is easy to explain. Since we

22. Figures differ from Börsch-Supan et al. (2003), since they refer to different reform implementations.

model the Germany disability insurance as a perfect substitute for old-age pensions, there is no effective early retirement age. Since there are no actuarial adjustments, shifting the normal retirement age has no economic implications as well (although there may be a psychological effect—this is modeled in the shifted-dummy specification following). The only difference of the Three-Year Reform is a shift of the bonus for retiring at age 66 or 67 to 69 and 70—but since most people have retired long before these ages, the reform undoes the minor incentive at the ages 66 and 67, and therefore shifts the average retirement age slightly forward. If we assume in the shifted-dummies specification, however, that the entire retirement behavior shifts by three years for psychological reasons related to the signaling effect of the normal retirement age, we more or less tautologically see such change.

In contrast, the other two reform policies shift the retirement age quite substantially, by between two and four years. Considering the overall length of retirement in Germany, which is currently about 18 years, the orders of magnitude are quite significant.

Figure 5.3 gives a more detailed description of the behavioral effect by looking on the impact of reforms by age of labor force exit. The figure has eighteen panels, corresponding to the eighteen simulation results in table 5.5. For each of the three reforms, we present six simulation variants. These variants include the option value and the peak value model, each of which is estimated using a linear and a dummy-variable age specification (see table 5.4). We split the latter specification in two treatments of the set of dummy variables, indicating age when we simulate the reform impact: (a) keeping the dummy variables at their original ages, and (b) shifting them along with the shift in the incentive variables. These two treatments are designed to bracket possible behavioral effects that are embedded in the age dummies; in particular, habitual effects, associated with age 65 as a psychological anchor for retirement decisions. Treatment (a) assumes that this anchor stays constant in spite of the three-year shift in retirement age in our first reform option, and the actuarial adjustment in the second reform option. Treatment (b) shifts the anchor according to the shift in the so-called normal retirement age.

We begin with figure 5.3, panel A. The linear age model does not capture the spikes typical for retirement behavior. They are clearly visible in the second and third panel, where dummy variables describe the effect of age on retirement. As previously described, the Three-Year Reform does not matter much in the German system unless the entire set of dummies is shifted by three years as well, modeling a shift in the perceived normal retirement by three years—see the third panel. In this case, not surprisingly, the spikes shift about three years later.

Panels B and C of figure 5.3 show the behavioral effects of the Actuarial

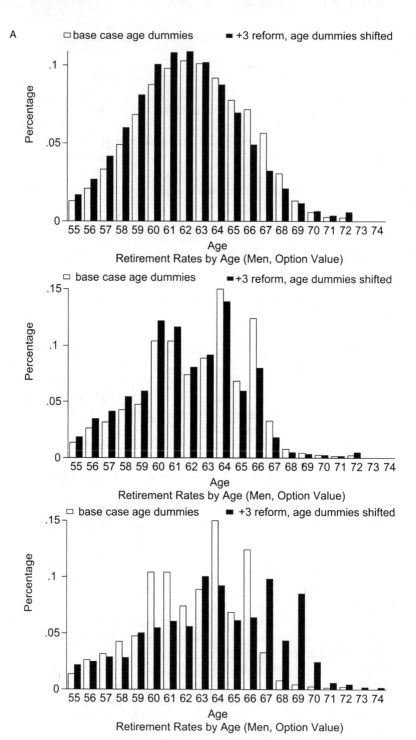

Fig. 5.3   Distribution of retirement rates: *A,* Three-Year Reform, option value; *B,* Actuarial Reform, option value; *C,* Common Reform, option value; *D,* Three-Year Reform, peak value; *E,* Distribution of retirement rates: Actuarial Reform, peak value; *F,* Common Reform, peak value

B

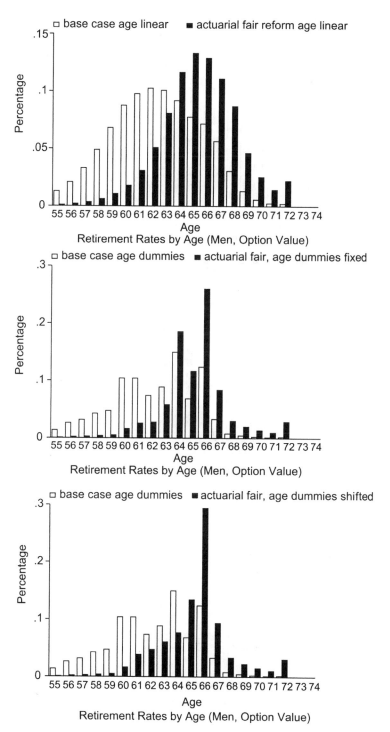

Fig. 5.3   (cont.)

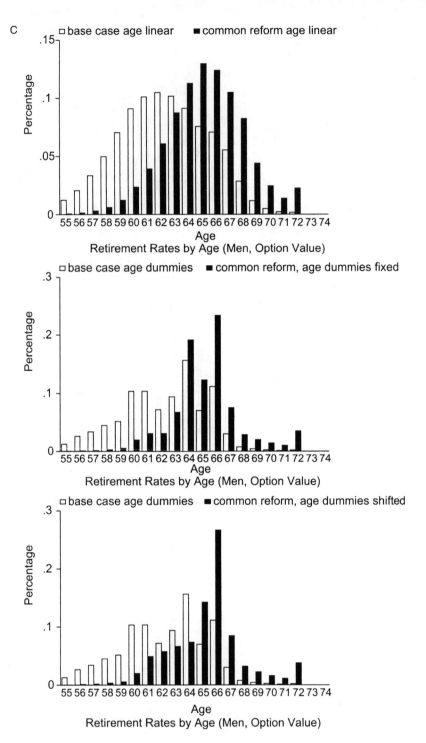

Fig. 5.3 (cont.) Distribution of retirement rates: *A*, Three-Year Reform, option value; *B*, Actuarial Reform, option value; *C*, Common Reform, option value; *D*, Three-Year Reform, peak value; *E*, Distribution of retirement rates: Actuarial Reform, peak value; *F*, Common Reform, peak value

D

Fig. 5.3   (cont.)

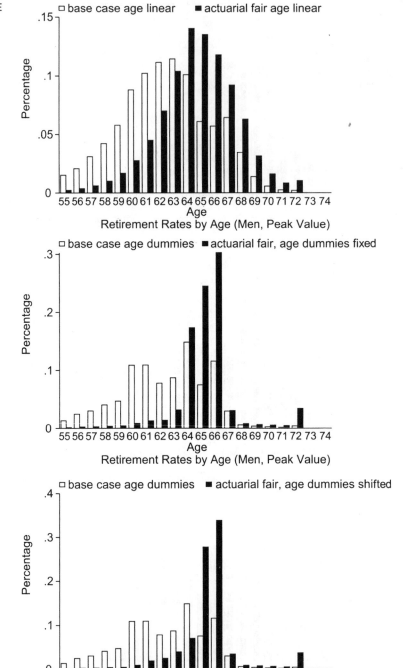

Fig. 5.3 (cont.) Distribution of retirement rates: *A,* Three-Year Reform, option value; *B,* Actuarial Reform, option value; *C,* Common Reform, option value; *D,* Three-Year Reform, peak value; *E,* Distribution of retirement rates: Actuarial Reform, peak value; *F,* Common Reform, peak value

F

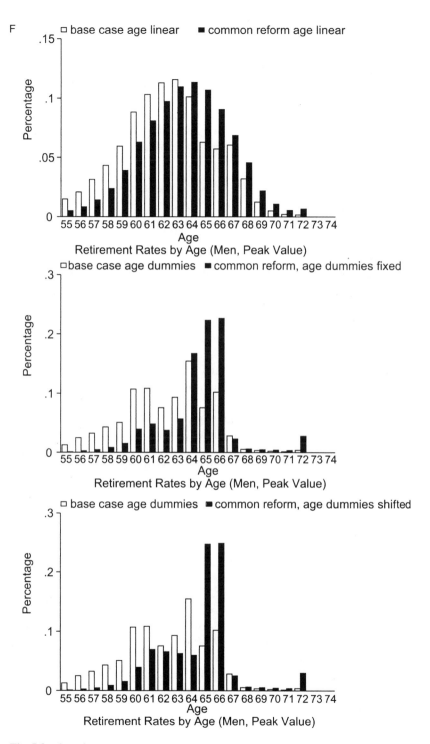

Fig. 5.3 (cont.)

Reform and the Common Reform, which are quite similar. Modal retirement age increases by four years in the linear specifications and by about two years in the dummy-variable specifications. Note that early retirement before age 63 is greatly reduced due to the actuarial adjustment.

Figure 3, panels *D–F* repeat the exercise, using the peak value estimates rather than the option value estimates. The estimated behavioral effects are qualitatively similar but somewhat smaller than in the option value model.

5.5.3   Budget Effects

Together with the mechanical effects of the reforms, the changing retirement patterns have substantial budget effects. Table 5.6 shows how they emerge.

The Three-Year Reform eliminates the incentives to retire at age 66 and 67, thereby very slightly reducing benefits (except panel B). Through the induced earlier retirement age, work-related taxes and contributions also decrease by about 8 percent according to the option value model, and between 1 and 2 percent in the peak value model. If we enforce a shift in the entire retirement distribution (panels C and F) in the shifted-dummies specification, benefits decrease a bit more, but the main budget effect is created by a substantial increase in taxes and contributions of about 25 percent.

The Actuarial Reform and the Common Reform postpone retirement by two to four years. This reduces benefits and increases taxes and contributions in a similar fashion as the Three-Year Reform in the dummies-shifted specification (benefits by some 10 percent, taxes and contribution by some 30 percent). While the behavioral effects are similar for the Actuarial Reform and the Common Reform (see figure 5.3), the additional mechanical effect of reducing the replacement rate in the Common Reform reduces benefits quite dramatically, by more than 30 percent.

Table 5.7 decomposes the budget effect into mechanical and behavioral effects. Note that the denominator of the percentage change in the last row of each panel is now the baseline PDV of benefits. The introduction of a 6 percent per year actuarial adjustment in the Actuarial Reform implies a reduction of pension expenditures for our 1942 cohort by 18 percent in direct benefit reductions and by an additional 26 percent through labor supply responses. The introduction of the hypothetical common pension system, used as a yardstick in all country chapters of this volume, which features an early retirement age of 60 years, a normal retirement age of 65 years, a 60 percent replacement rate at age 65, and a 6 percent per year actuarial adjustment, pivoted at age 65, will reduce pension expenditures by 37 percent directly and by about 26 percent through labor supply responses, relative to the pre-1992 system in Germany. This system has a steeper actuarial adjustment and a deeper pension cut than introduced by the actual 1992 and 2001 reforms.

Figure 5.4 converts these percent changes relative to baseline benefits

Table 5.6 Fiscal impact of pension reform (euros per worker)

	Present discounted value				Change relative to base (%)		
	Base	Three-Year	Actuarial	Common	Three-Year	Actuarial	Common
Option value—S1							
Benefits	203.542	203.013	184.237	140.221	-0.3	-9.5	-31.1
Contributions	45.609	42.067	62.541	61.185	-7.8	37.1	34.2
Income taxes	63.409	58.750	86.109	84.432	-7.3	35.8	33.2
Other social security	59.407	55.232	78.786	76.504	-7.0	32.6	28.8
VAT	37.892	35.260	49.861	48.222	-6.9	31.6	27.3
Taxes: Total	206.317	191.309	277.297	270.343	-7.3	34.4	31.0
Option value—S2							
Benefits	203.207	203.708	184.495	140.645	0.2	-9.2	-30.8
Contributions	45.229	41.050	62.245	60.999	-9.2	37.6	34.9
Income taxes	62.920	57.412	85.729	84.209	-8.8	36.3	33.8
Other social security	58.959	54.029	78.428	76.278	-8.4	33.0	29.4
VAT	37.607	34.501	49.632	48.073	-8.3	32.0	27.8
Taxes: Total	204.715	186.992	276.034	269.559	-8.7	34.8	31.7
Option value—S3							
Benefits	203.207	184.914	184.829	140.763	-9.0	-9.0	-30.7
Contributions	45.229	57.782	62.788	61.471	27.8	38.8	35.9
Income taxes	62.920	79.596	86.413	84.807	26.5	37.3	34.8
Other social security	58.959	73.672	79.057	76.831	25.0	34.1	30.3
VAT	37.607	46.823	50.032	48.426	24.5	33.0	28.8
Taxes: Total	204.715	257.873	278.289	271.535	26.0	35.9	32.6

(continued)

Table 5.6 (continued)

| | Present discounted value | | | | Change relative to base (%) | | |
	Base	Three-Year	Actuarial	Common	Three-Year	Actuarial	Common
			Peak value—S1				
Benefits	203.287	200.521	175.487	133.037	-1.4	-13.7	-34.6
Contributions	46.138	45.646	54.481	52.863	-1.1	18.1	14.6
Income taxes	64.668	64.014	75.940	74.182	-1.0	17.4	14.7
Other social security	60.508	59.907	69.590	67.265	-1.0	15.0	11.2
VAT	38.579	38.197	44.043	42.383	-1.0	14.2	9.9
Taxes: Total	209.894	207.764	244.054	236.693	-1.0	16.3	12.8
			Peak value—S2				
Benefits	203.452	202.119	181.720	138.116	-0.7	-10.7	-32.1
Contributions	45.176	44.185	59.208	57.553	-2.2	31.1	27.4
Income taxes	63.601	62.234	82.362	80.648	-2.1	29.5	26.8
Other social security	59.535	58.293	75.331	73.061	-2.1	26.5	22.7
VAT	37.961	37.174	47.658	46.038	-2.1	25.5	21.3
Taxes: Total	206.273	201.886	264.559	257.300	-2.1	28.3	24.7
			Peak value—S3				
Benefits	203.452	184.376	181.658	137.851	-9.4	-10.7	-32.2
Contributions	45.176	58.734	59.325	57.465	30.0	31.3	27.2
Income taxes	63.601	81.656	82.502	80.520	28.4	29.7	26.6
Other social security	59.535	75.470	75.466	72.956	26.8	26.8	22.5
VAT	37.961	47.945	47.747	45.974	26.3	25.8	21.1
Taxes: Total	206.273	263.804	265.042	256.915	27.9	28.5	24.6

Note: "Other social security" includes health insurance, long-term care insurance, and unemployment insurance.

Table 5.7   Decomposition of the total impact (euros per worker)

	Change in present discounted value								
	Three-Year Reform			Actuarial Reform			Common Reform		
	Mechanical	Behavioral	Total	Mechanical	Behavioral	Total	Mechanical	Behavioral	Total
Option value—S1									
Benefits	-3.299	2.770	-528	-39.947	20.643	-19.304	-78.912	15.592	-63.320
Taxes and contributions	-0.018	-11.448	-11.466	-1.867	55.915	54.048	-3.420	51.870	48.450
Net change	-3.281	17.761	14.479	-38.080	-52.205	-90.284	-75.493	-51.853	-127.346
Change as % of base benefits	-1.61	8.73	7.11	-18.71	-25.65	-44.36	-37.09	-25.48	-62.56
Option value—S2									
Benefits	-2.543	3.044	501	-39.590	20.878	-18.712	-78.560	15.998	-62.563
Taxes and contributions	-0.010	-13.534	-13.544	-1.871	56.175	54.303	-3.431	52.505	49.074
Net change	-2.532	20.757	18.225	-37.719	-52.312	-90.031	-75.129	-52.278	-127.407
Change as % of base benefits	-1.25	10.21	8.97	-18.56	-25.74	-44.30	-36.97	-25.73	-62.70
Option value—S3									
Benefits	-15.856	-2.437	-18.293	-39.590	21.212	-18.378	-78.560	16.116	-62.444
Taxes and contributions	-0.467	41.071	40.604	-1.871	57.887	56.015	-3.431	54.010	50.578
Net change	-15.389	-56.061	-71.450	-37.719	-54.233	-91.952	-75.129	-54.135	-129.264
Change as % of base benefits	-7.57	-27.59	-35.68	-18.56	-26.69	-45.25	-36.97	-26.64	-63.61
Peak value—S1									
Benefits	-3.382	616	-2.766	-39.290	11.490	-27.800	-77.864	7.614	-70.250
Taxes and contributions	-0.019	-1.618	-1.637	-1.871	27.688	25.817	-3.369	23.443	20.074
Net change	-3.363	2.726	-637	-37.419	-24.541	-61.961	-74.495	-22.554	-97.049
Change as % of base benefits	-1.65	1.34	-0.31	-18.41	-12.07	-30.48	-36.65	-11.09	-47.74

(continued)

Table 5.7 (continued)

	Three-Year Reform			Actuarial Reform			Common Reform		
	Mechanical	Behavioral	Total	Mechanical	Behavioral	Total	Mechanical	Behavioral	Total
Peak value—S2									
Benefits	-2.350	1.017	-1.332	-40.063	18.331	-21.732	-78.398	13.062	-65.336
Taxes and contributions	-0.010	-3.385	-3.396	-1.870	46.124	44.254	-3.366	42.016	38.650
Net change	-2.339	5.393	3.054	-38.193	-41.826	-80.019	-75.032	-41.331	-116.363
Change as % of base benefits	-1.15	2.65	1.50	-18.77	-20.56	-39.33	-36.88	-20.32	-57.19
Peak value—S3									
Benefits	-15.858	-3.218	-19.076	-40.063	18.269	-21.794	-78.398	12.797	-65.601
Taxes and contributions	-0.467	44.439	43.973	-1.870	46.490	44.620	-3.366	41.719	38.353
Net change	-15.391	-61.216	-76.607	-38.193	-42.370	-80.563	-75032	-41.211	-116.243
Change as % of base benefits	-7.57	-30.09	-38.32	-18.77	-20.83	-39.60	-36.88	-20.26	-57.14

Change in present discounted value

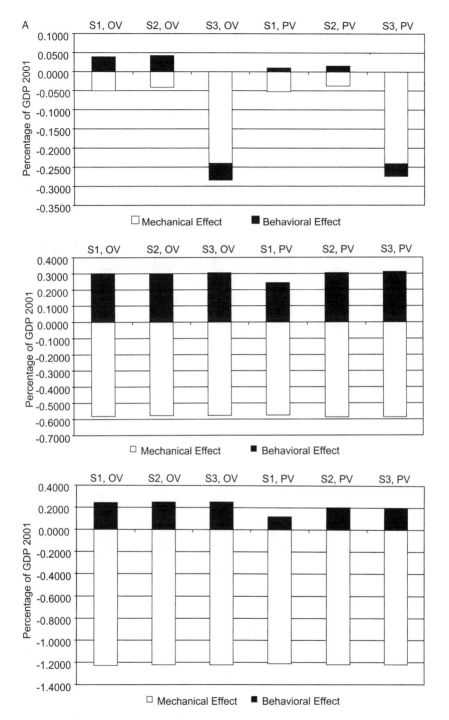

Fig. 5.4   Behavioral, mechanical, and total budget impact of pension reform: *A*, Gross Benefits; *B*, Benefits net of taxes and contributions

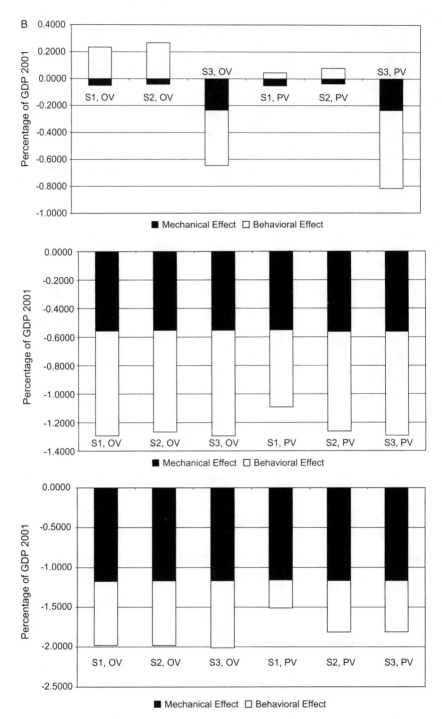

Fig. 5.4 (cont.) Behavioral, mechanical, and total budget impact of pension reform: *A,* Gross Benefits; *B,* Benefits net of taxes and contributions

into percent of GDP. Panel A of figure 5.4 only looks at changes in pension benefits, while panel B adds changes in taxes and contributions. The largest effect occurs, as we have seen, in the common form, which combines a replacement rate cut with a later retirement age and saves pension expenditures of up to 2 percent of GDP.

Finally, we disaggregate the total effect by age of entry into retirement. This is shown in figures 5.5 and 5.6. Figure 5.5 shows the total effect, while figure 5.6 looks only at benefits. Note that the amount of taxes and contributions collected for a given age of retirement remains unchanged, due to the static definition of our hypothetical reforms. Of course, the total amount of taxes and contributions changes considerably under the reforms, because the weight for each retirement age is changed. All figures relate to the option value estimation with linear age dummies.

Figures 5.5 and 5.6 show that the Three-Year Reform has very little impact, and only on retirement around age 67 and 68, due to the somewhat awkward jump in the replacement rate at ages 66 and 67, which is shifted by the reform to ages 69 and 70. Note the scale: the effects are relatively small.

The Actuarial Reform and the Common Reform have a clear-cut pattern: negative effects for early retirement (before age 65), and positive effects for late retirement. Since the latter are smaller in the aggregate than the former, the overall effect is a reduction in the budget, as we have seen earlier.

5.5.4 Distributional Considerations

Tables 5.8 and 5.9 show the financial implications of the reforms by quintiles of lifetime earnings. Lifetime earnings are defined on a family basis and incorporate the forty highest income years of both spouses. We chose cutoff points for married and single persons separately such that the lowest quintile, for example, contains 20 percent of the poorest couples and 20 percent of the poorest singles. The figures shown correspond to the 1942 cohort.

The first column of each table displays the net present value of benefits, contributions, and taxes paid by the ith quintile. The lowest earnings group makes up approximately 7.5 percent of the entire net PDV, while the highest earnings group covers around 33.5 to 34 percent.

The second column reports the percentage changes in the net PDV of the social security wealth (SSW) by quintile: $(\Sigma_{i \in \text{quintile}} SSW_i(R) - \Sigma_{i \in \text{quintile}} SSW_i(BC))/\Sigma_{i \in \text{quintile}} SSW_i(BC)$ where R stands for reform and BC for base case.

In all three reforms, the percentage change from the base case is negative for all quintiles, except for the Three-Year Reform in the constant dummies specification, where the reform, as we have emphasized earlier, is essentially ineffective. In every quintile, pension expenditure decreases.

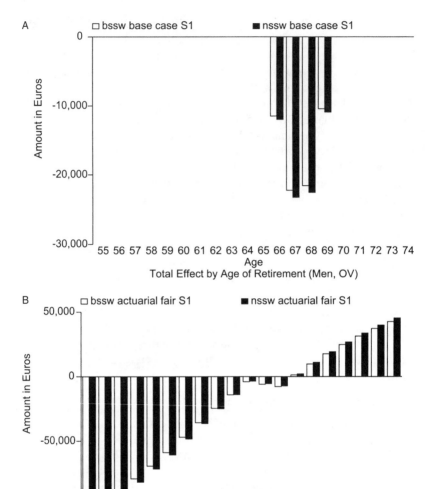

Fig. 5.5   Fiscal impact of total effects: *A*, Three-Year Reform, option value; *B*, Actuarial Reform, option value; *C*, Common Reform, option value; *D*, Three-Year Reform, peak value; *E*, Actuarial Reform, peak value; *F*, Common Reform, peak value.

C

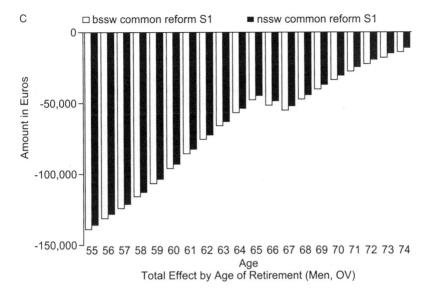

Total Effect by Age of Retirement (Men, OV)

D

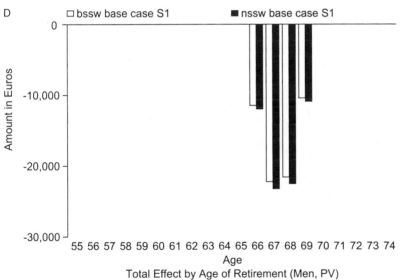

Total Effect by Age of Retirement (Men, PV)

Fig. 5.5   (cont.)

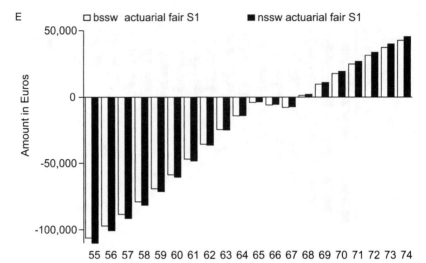

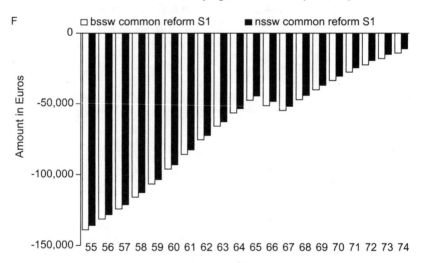

Fig. 5.5   (cont.) Fiscal impact of total effects: *A,* Three-Year Reform, option value; *B,* Actuarial Reform, option value; *C,* Common Reform, option value; *D,* Three-Year Reform, peak value; *E,* Actuarial Reform, peak value; *F,* Common Reform, peak value.

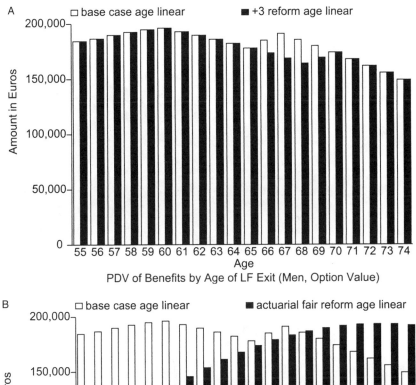

Fig. 5.6 Present discounted value of social security wealth benefits: *A*, Three-Year Reform, option value; *B*, Actuarial Reform, option value; *C*, Common Reform, option value; *D*, Three-Year Reform, peak value; *E*, Actuarial Reform, peak value; *F*, Common Reform, peak value

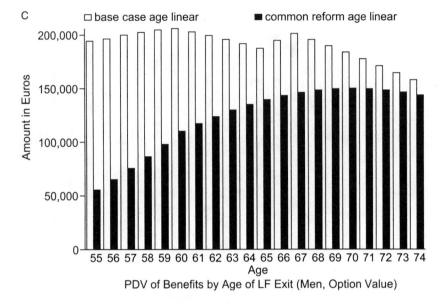

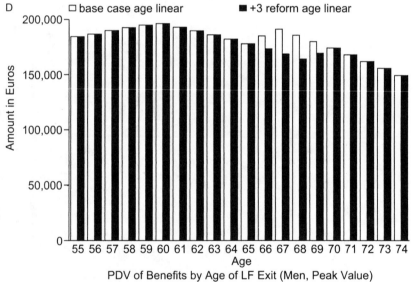

Fig. 5.6 (cont.) Present discounted value of social security wealth benefits: *A,* Three-Year Reform, option value; *B,* Actuarial Reform, option value; *C,* Common Reform, option value; *D,* Three-Year Reform, peak value; *E,* Actuarial Reform, peak value; *F,* Common Reform, peak value

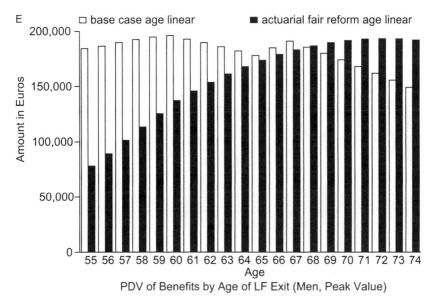

E

□ base case age linear   ■ actuarial fair reform age linear

PDV of Benefits by Age of LF Exit (Men, Peak Value)

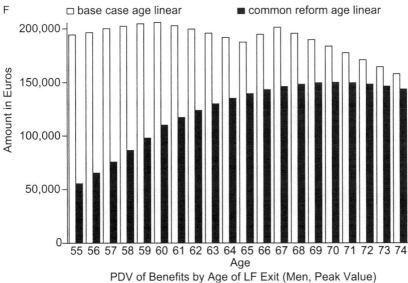

F

□ base case age linear   ■ common reform age linear

PDV of Benefits by Age of LF Exit (Men, Peak Value)

Fig. 5.6   (cont.)

Table 5.8   Distributional analysis (Option value—S1, euros per worker)

	Base case	Present discounted value			Change relative to base PDV		
		Three-Year	Actuarial	Common	Three-Year	Actuarial	Common
Highest quintile (1)							
Benefits	339.019	337.415	311.220	288.080	-1.605	-27.799	-50.939
Contributions	72.908	68.089	104.617	101.175	-4.819	31.709	28.267
Tax	121.125	114.185	170.295	165.723	-6.940	49.170	44.598
Insurance	116.403	110.204	158.165	152.042	-6.199	41.762	35.638
VAT	74.666	70.762	100.403	96.019	-3.903	25.737	21.354
Net change					20.257	-176.177	-180.797
Percent change					6.0	-52.0	-53.3
Quintile 2							
Benefits	271.570	271.382	250.790	182.445	-.212	-20.780	-89.124
Contributions	61.374	54.789	85.157	83.306	-6.585	23.783	21.932
Tax	81.766	73.337	111.829	109.691	-8.429	30.063	27.925
Insurance	75.589	68.017	101.483	98.885	-7.572	25.894	23.296
VAT	48.158	43.380	64.214	62.400	-4.779	16.056	14.242
Net change					27.577	-116.576	-176.518
Percent change					10.2	-42.9	-65.0
Quintile 3							
Benefits	220.432	219.935	197.471	137.570	-.497	-22.960	-82.862
Contributions	48.763	44.954	65.843	64.866	-3.809	17.080	16.103
Tax	64.430	59.528	86.201	85.059	-4.902	21.771	20.629
Insurance	63.134	58.735	81.188	78.632	-4.399	18.054	15.498
VAT	40.656	37.881	51.663	49.657	-2.775	11.007	9.001
Net change					15.389	-90.872	-144.092
Percent change					7.0	-41.2	-65.4

Quintile 4

Benefits	173.751	173.325	157.046	108.488	-.426	-16.705	-65.263
Contributions	37.623	34.571	51.503	50.249	-3.052	13.879	12.626
Tax	49.464	45.515	67.210	65.656	-3.949	17.746	16.192
Insurance	45.119	41.583	60.486	58.670	-3.536	15.367	13.551
VAT	28.615	26.287	38.166	36.911	-2.228	9.550	8.296
Net change					12.339	-73.247	-115.927
Percent change					7.1	-42.2	-66.7

Lowest quintile (5)

Benefits	110.112	109.509	97.764	75.875	-.603	-12.347	-34.237
Contributions	27.211	25.800	35.558	35.460	-1.411	8.347	8.249
Tax	36.292	34.424	47.236	47.140	-1.868	10.944	10.848
Insurance	32.456	30.787	41.958	41.815	-1.669	9.501	9.358
VAT	20.432	19.380	26.343	26.238	-1.052	5.911	5.807
Net change					5.396	-47.052	-68.500
Percent change					4.9	-42.7	-62.2

Table 5.9   Distributional analysis (Option value—S3, euros per worker)

	Base case	Present discounted value			Change relative to base PDV		
		Three-Year	Actuarial	Common	Three-Year	Actuarial	Common
Highest quintile (1)							
Benefits	338.753	309.298	311.182	288.236	−29.455	−27.571	−50.517
Contributions	71.597	91.278	104.435	100.898	19.682	32.838	29.301
Tax	119.194	149.559	169.853	165.253	30.365	50.660	46.059
Insurance	114.657	141.152	157.790	151.610	26.495	43.133	36.952
VAT	73.561	90.081	100.172	95.745	16.520	26.610	22.184
Net change					−122.517	−180.813	−185.013
Percent change					−36.2	−53.4	−54.6
Quintile 2							
Benefits	281.063	246.935	251.012	182.817	−24.129	−20.051	−88.246
Contributions	60.850	76.918	85.100	83.411	16.067	24.249	22.561
Tax	81.163	101.545	111.765	109.854	20.382	30.602	28.690
Insurance	75.028	93.099	101.427	99.023	18.071	26.399	23.995
VAT	47.499	59.142	64.179	62.485	11.343	16.380	14.686
Net change					−89.992	−117.682	−178.178
Percent change					−33.2	−43.4	−65.7
Quintile 3							
Benefits	219.984	199.587	198.203	138.214	−20.397	−21.781	−81.770
Contributions	48.633	61.471	66.191	65.353	12.838	17.558	16.720
Tax	64.293	80.649	86.648	85.693	16.356	22.355	21.399
Insurance	63.003	77.264	81.589	79.197	14.262	18.586	16.194
VAT	40.571	49.460	51.916	50.012	8.890	11.345	9.441
Net change					−72.742	−91.626	−145.525
Percent change					−33.1	−41.7	−66.2

				Quintile 4			
Benefits	173.385	157.748	157.743	109.088	-15.637	-15.642	-64.297
Contributions	37.432	48.435	51.883	50.646	11.002	14.451	13.213
Tax	49.245	63.232	67.717	66.188	13.987	18.472	16.943
Insurance	44.914	57.395	60.934	59.139	12.481	16.020	14.226
VAT	28.484	36.339	38.446	37.206	7.855	9.963	8.722
Net change					-60.962	-74.547	-117.401
Percent change					-35.2	-43.0	-67.7
				Lowest quintile (5)			
Benefits	109.905	99.878	98.363	76.386	-10.027	-11.543	-33.519
Contributions	26.969	34.829	35.764	35.740	7.860	8.794	8.771
Tax	35.994	46.234	47.522	47.527	10.240	11.528	11.533
Insurance	32.187	41.310	42.208	42.152	9.123	10.021	9.965
VAT	20.261	26.000	26.500	26.449	5.738	6.238	6.187
Net change					-42.988	-48.125	-69.976
Percent change					-39.1	-43.8	-63.7

Moreover, the absolute magnitude of the change increases with increasing quintiles.

5.6 Conclusions

This chapter shows that the very large public pension budget in Germany can be reduced significantly by neutralizing its strong incentives to retire early. Our simulations show a large response of old-age labor force participation to two reforms, the introduction of an actuarial adjustment (Actuarial Reform) and the introduction of a system with an early retirement age of 60 years, a normal retirement age of 65 years, a 60 percent replacement rate at age 65, and a 6 percent per year actuarial adjustment, pivoted at age 65 (Common Reform). These reforms combine elements of the actual 1992 and 2001 reforms in Germany. However, both hypothetical reforms have steeper actuarial adjustments than introduced by the actual 1992 reform, and the Common Reform has a deeper pension cut than introduced by 2001 reform.

Mean retirement age will increase by between two and four years in both reform scenarios. And since the German system is far from actuarially fair, these labor supply responses translate into large fiscal effects. These effects are augmented by the mechanical effects when the eligibility age for pension benefits is changed.

The introduction of a 6 percent per year actuarial adjustment implies a reduction of pension expenditures for a typical cohort born in 1942 (and thus still mainly governed by the pre-1992 pension rules) by 18 percent in direct benefit reductions and by an additional 26 percent through labor-supply responses. The introduction of the hypothetical common pension system, used as a yardstick in all country chapters of this volume, which features an early retirement age of 60 years, a normal retirement age of 65 years, a 60 percent replacement rate at age 65, and a 6 percent per year actuarial adjustment, pivoted at age 65, will reduce pension expenditures by 37 percent directly and by about 26 percent through labor-supply responses, relative to the pre-1992 system in Germany.

References

Birg, H., and A. Börsch-Supan. 1999. *Für eine neue Aufgabenteilung zwischen gesetzlicher und privater Altersversorgung.* Berlin: German Insurers' Association.

Boeri, T., A. Börsch-Supan, and G. Tabellini. 2001. Would you like to shrink the welfare state? The opinions of European citizens. *Economic Policy* 32:9–50.

———. 2002. Would you like to reform the pension system? The opinions of European citizens. *American Economic Review* 92 (2): 396–406.

———. 2005. How would you like to reform your pension system? The opinions of German and Italian citizens. In *The Politics and Finance of Social Security Reform,* ed. R. Brooks and A. Razin, 333–52. New York: Cambridge University Press.

Börsch-Supan, A. 1998. Germany: A social security system on the verge of collapse. In *Redesigning social security,* ed. H. Siebert, 129–59. Tübingen, Germany: J. C. B. Mohr (Paul Siebeck).

———. 2000a. *Data and research on retirement in Germany.* Washington, DC: National Academy of Sciences.

———. 2000b. Incentive effects of social security on labour force participation: Evidence in Germany and across Europe. *Journal of Public Economics* 78 (1–2): 25–49.

———. 2000c. A model under siege: A case study of the German retirement insurance system. *The Economic Journal* 110 (461): F24–45.

———. 2001. Incentive effects of social security under an uncertain disability option. In *Themes in the economics of aging,* ed. D. A. Wise, 281–310. Chicago: University of Chicago Press.

———. 2002. Blaupause für eine nachhaltige Rentenreform. MEA Discussion Paper Series 001-02, University of Mannheim.

Börsch-Supan, A., and P. Schmidt. 1996. Early retirement in East and West Germany. In *Employment policy in the transition to free enterprise: German integration and its lessons for Europe,* ed. R. Riphahn, D. Snower, and K. Zimmermann, 83–102. Berlin: Springer-Verlag.

Börsch-Supan, A., and R. Schnabel. 1998. Social security and declining labor force participation in Germany. *American Economic Review* 88 (2): 173–78.

———. 1999. Social security and retirement in Germany. In *Social security and retirement around the world,* ed. J. Gruber and D. A. Wise, 135–80. Chicago, London: University of Chicago Press.

Börsch-Supan, A., R. Schnabel, S. Kohnz, and G. Mastrobuoni. 2003. Micromodelling of retirement choices in Germany. In *Incentive effects of public pension systems,* ed. J. Gruber and D. Wise, 285–344. Chicago: University of Chicago Press.

Bundesministerium für Arbeit und Sozialordnung (BMA). 1997. *Statistics taschenbuch.* Bonn: Bundespresseamt.

Casmir, B. 1989. *Staatliche rentenversicherungssysteme immigration internationalen vergleigh.* Frankfurt: Lang.

Coile, Courtney, and Jonathan Gruber. 2000. Social security and retirement. NBER Working Paper no. 7830. Cambridge, MA: National Bureau of Economic Research, August.

Cutler, D., and L. M. Sheiner. 1998. Demographics and medical care spending: Standard and non-standard effects. NBER Working Paper no. 6866. Cambridge, MA: National Bureau of Economic Research, December.

Gruber, J., and D. A. Wise eds. 1999. *Social security and retirement around the world.* Chicago: University of Chicago Press.

Gruber, J., and D. A. Wise eds. 2003. *Incentive effects of public pension systems.* Chicago: University of Chicago Press.

Jacobs, K., M. Kohli, and K. Rein. 1991. Germany: The diversity of pathways. In *Time for retirement: Comparative studies of early exit from the labor force,* ed. M. Kohli, M. Rein, A.-M. Guillemard, and H. van Gunsteren, 181–221. New York: Cambridge University Press.

Organization for Economic Cooperation and Development (OECD). 2001. *Ageing and income: Financial resources and retirement in 9 OECD countries.* Paris: OECD.

Riphahn, Regina T. 1995. Disability retirement among German men in the 1980s.

Münchner Wirtschaftswissenschaftliche Beiträge, No. 95-20. Munich: Ludwig Maximilians Universität.

Schmähl, W. 1991. Alterssicherung in der DDR und ihre Umgestaltung im Zuge des deutschen Einigungsprozesses—Einige verteilungspolitische Aspekte. In *Sozialpolitik im vereinten Deutschland,* ed. G. Kleinhenz, 50–95. Berlin: Duncker & Humblot.

Schnabel, Reinhold. 1998. Rates of return of the German pay-as-you-go pension system. *Finanzarchiv* 55 (3): 374–99.

———. 1999. Opting out of social security: Incentives and participation in the German public pension system. SFB504-Discussion Paper no. 99-42. Mannheim, Germany: University of Mannheim.

Stock, J. H., and D. A. Wise. 1990. The pension inducement to retire: An option value analysis. In *Issues in the economics of aging,* ed. D. A. Wise, 205–30. Chicago: University of Chicago Press.

Verband deutscher Rentenversicherungsträger (VdR). 2002. *Die rentenversicherung in zeitreihen.* Frankfurt am Main, Germany: Aktion Demokratische.

Wagner, G. G., R. V. Burkhauser, and F. Behringer. 1993. The English language public use file of the German Socio-Economic Panel. *Journal of Human Resources* 28:413–15.

Fiscal Implications of Pension Reforms in Italy

Agar Brugiavini and Franco Peracchi

6.1 Introduction

Italy has seen a flurry of reforms during the 1990s, and economists and policymakers are still struggling to assess their immediate results as well as their long-term effects. Many analysts argue that the overall design of the recent Italian reforms is probably good, yet more steps need to be taken to speed up the reform process and reap the benefits, which, due to the adverse demographic trends, could easily evaporate.

In this chapter, we contribute to the current debate on the Italian pension system by analyzing the impact of social security reforms, in terms of both their budgetary implications and their distributional effects. This is done by simulating the effects of three hypothetical reforms, plus the effects of the 1995 reform of the Italian pension system (the so-called Dini reform). Our approach relies on the use of a semistructural econometric model to predict retirement probabilities under different policy scenarios, so as to properly take into account the behavioral effects of the reforms. On the basis of the estimated retirement model, we develop a complete accounting exercise that includes not only changes in gross future benefits due to policy changes, but also changes in social security contributions, income taxes, and value-added taxes. Thus, our results provide not only estimates of the workers' gains or losses, but also an exhaustive evaluation of the gains and losses for the government budget.

We find that the reforms, particularly the Dini reform (once fully phased in), have a substantial impact on individuals' retirement decisions and

Agar Brugiavini is a professor of economics at the University Ca' Foscari, Venice. Franco Peracchi is a professor of econometrics at the University Tor Vergata, Rome.

their net social security wealth, as well as substantial gains for government finances.

6.2   An Overview of the Italian Pension System and Its Reforms

Before turning to the analysis of different social security reforms, it is useful to briefly describe the reform process that has taken place in Italy, and the recent developments in the political arena. The growing concern of the European Union (EU) with meeting the targets imposed by the Stability and Growth Pact has stimulated a debate on the effects of the recent reforms and the need for further reforms. It should be mentioned that Italy, along with the other member states of the EU, committed itself to a five-year increase of the effective retirement age by the year 2010. Specific targets have also been set on participation rates of older workers.

Many argue that the changes introduced during the 1990s may be inadequate in the light of future demographic trends, and that it is imperative to raise the effective retirement age. Empirical work carried out on the issue shows that there is a strong relationship between the tax incentives to retire and the age at which men are observed to actually retire in different countries.[1] For Italy, we still observe a substantial number of early retirees.[2] Therefore, an evaluation of the impact and efficacy of the reforms, which has already started with the 2001 Ministerial Committee[3] appointed by the Italian Welfare Ministry, is of crucial importance.

The reforms of the 1990s have tackled several aspects of the Italian social security system, but three are particularly relevant: (1) benefit computation rules, (2) indexation rules, and (3) retirement age and eligibility criteria.[4] It is useful to recall that the vast majority of the population is insured with the National Institute for Social Security (INPS), and since this chapter focuses attention on the most important fund administered by the INPS, the Private Sector Employees Fund (FPLD), our description of the reforms will mainly focus on the changes affecting private sector employees.

A first reform (known as the Amato reform) was passed by Parliament in 1992. Once phased in, it would reduce pension outlays and iron out major differences between various sectors and occupations. However, this reform only marginally changed the rules governing early retirement and, according to many, did not produce the much-needed savings in the budget. Hence the second reform (the so-called Dini reform) of 1995. This reform totally

---

1. The concept of an implicit tax was introduced by Gruber and Wise (1999).
2. See Brugiavini and Peracchi (2004) and Brugiavini, Peracchi, and Wise (2003).
3. Relazione Finale della Commissione Ministeriale di "Verifica del sistema previdenziale ai sensi della legge 335/95 e successivi provvedimenti, nell'ottica della competitività, dello sviluppo e dell'equità."
4. For a description of the Italian social security system before 1992, see Brugiavini (1999), Brugiavini and Peracchi (2004), and Franco (2002).

changed some of the basic rules for granting benefits to future retirees, and tried to harmonize the actuarial rates of return for early and late retirees. Table 6.1 summarizes some of the key features of three regimes: the regime prevailing before the Amato reform (denoted as pre-1993 regime), the one prevailing during the transition (currently in place), and the one prevailing with the Dini reform fully in place (post-1995 regime). However, both the Amato and the Dini reforms are characterized by a very long transitional period affecting all cohorts of post-1992 retirees: the provisions for the transitional periods involve a pro rata method of establishing eligibility and benefit computation criteria on the basis of seniority.

6.2.1 The Dini Reform and Recent Assessments of the Reform Process

The Dini reform adopts a notionally defined-contribution method of benefit calculation. The initial pension amount is the annuity equivalent to the present value (at retirement) of past payroll taxes, capitalized by means of a five-year moving average of nominal GDP growth rates. The relevant payroll tax rate is 33 percent, and an age-related actuarial adjustment factor is applied to the resulting figure.[5] In this case, too, capping is applied on the present value of contributions, rather than on pensionable earnings. The 1995 reform introduced—at the steady state—a window of pensionable ages with an associated actuarially based adjustment of pensions. This window spans age 57 to 65, with actuarial adjustment factors of 4.720 percent and 6.136 percent, respectively. These coefficients make the present value of future benefits equal to capitalized contributions for people with survival probabilities equal to those in the 1990 life tables. They should be revised every ten years on the basis of changes in life expectancy and a comparison of the rates of growth of GDP and taxable earnings. It should be noted that, even at the steady state, the system will not achieve complete age-neutrality, given the mortality prospects of Italian workers.[6]

Minimum contribution requirements changed from the initial fifteen years to just five years after 1995, while payroll taxes increased to 32.7 percent of gross earnings (to be split between employer and employee), up from approximately 27 percent in 1995.

The implementation of the reform was (and still is) extremely gradual. Workers with at least eighteen years of contributions in 1995 will receive a pension computed on the basis of the rules applying before 1992. Those with less than eighteen years of contributions in 1992 will be subject to a pro rata regime: the 1995 reform will apply only to the contributions paid after 1995.[7] Only individuals who began working after 1995 will receive a

---

5. Hence the benefit is: 33 percent × adjustment factor × present value of SS taxes.
6. See Barbi (2001).
7. The benefits paid to individuals in the pro rata regime will be computed on the basis of two components: the pre-1995 contributions and the contributions paid from 1995 onward.

Table 6.1   Key features of the pre-1993 regime, the transitional phase, and the 1995 reform (at the steady state)

	Pre-1993 regime	Transition	1995 reform
Normal retirement age	60 (men) 55 (women)	Gradually, from 60 to 65 (men) and from 55 to 60 (women)	Any age after 56 (for both men and women)
Transition period			Until about 2035
Pensionable earnings	Average of last five years of real earnings (converted to real values through price index)	Gradually, average of last six to ten years' earnings (converted to real values through price index + 1%)	Career contributions (capitalized using a five-year moving average of GDP growth rate)
Pension benefit	2% (pensionable earnings) × (t), where t is years of tax payments (at most 40)	2% × (pensionable earnings) × (t), where t is years of tax payments (at most forty)	Proportional to capitalized value of career contributions, the proportionality factor increasing with age at retirement (from .04720 at age 57 to .06136 at age 65)
Pension indexation	Cost of living plus real earnings' growth	Cost of living	Cost of living
Survivor's pension	60% to spouse 20% to each child 40% to each child (if no spouse)	Same	Same
Early retirement provision	Any age if contributed to SI for thirty-five years or more, no actuarial adjustment	Gradually ages between 54 and 58 if contributed to SI for thirty-five years or more, no actuarial adjustment	None
Total payroll tax	24.5% of gross earnings	Gradually, to 32.7% of gross earnings	32.7% of gross earnings

pension computed only on the basis of the new rules. Hence the length of the transition phase, as well as other aspects of the reform, may significantly reduce its expected benefits.

A first round of evaluations of the reforms became available throughout the 1990s. Some of these evaluations were based on generational accounting. For example, it was estimated that in order to ensure the long-term sustainability of public finances, a 5 percent increase in taxes paid by all generations would be required. Without the pension reforms introduced in the 1990s, the required tax increase would have been 9 percent. About 40 percent of those employed in 1999 could fully retire under the pre-1992 regime. For these people, the incentive to retire early was actually increased by expectations that the retirement conditions might be tightened (Franco 2002).

The Report of the Ministerial Committee (2001) shows that the savings obtained between 1996 and 2000 were essentially due to changes in the indexation rules and curtailing early retirement. The difficulty in building a complete evaluation model that incorporates behavioral responses to the reforms relies on the availability of good data and on the overall approach. Brugiavini and Peracchi (2004) provide an econometric model that focuses on dynamic incentives but does not address fiscal implications, while other recent studies[8] carry out accounting exercises that neglect the impact of policy changes on the retirement decisions of individuals.

6.3   The Retirement Model

The simulation exercise carried out in the present chapter relies on an econometric model of the retirement decisions of Italian workers based largely on the work of Gruber and Wise (2004) and already applied to the Italian case by Brugiavini and Peracchi (2004). In the present chapter, we limit our description of the econometric work to the main features of our modeling strategy and to the data. An important difference with respect to Brugiavini and Peracchi (2004) is the fact that the availability of a new release of the data, characterized by a larger sample size, allows us to follow a novel approach. Therefore, the underlying empirical work also deserves attention.

6.3.1   The Data

The retirement decision is analyzed through a reduced-form model, estimated on a random sample of administrative records from the Istituto Nazionale di Previdenza Sociale (INPS) archives.[9] The sample is drawn

---

8. See Ministero dell'Economia (Ragioneria Generale dello Stato) 2001 and Fornero-Castellino 2001.

9. This is a subsample of workers born either on March 1st or on October 1st of any possible year contained in the archive.

from the so-called INPS Workers-Archive (Archive O1M), which contains records on all private sector employees insured with INPS. The information on each employee is entered by the employer on a standard form. Our data consists of a random sample of about 200,000 workers entering the archive at any time during the period 1973–1997, and was followed continuously until they leave the sample. Employment spells can last any number of years, and individuals who leave the sample may enter again in any subsequent year. The panel is therefore highly unbalanced.

The main advantages of using these data are that they span a fairly long time period and contain information on gross earnings, which form the basis for the calculation of social security benefits. However, there are several shortcomings.

1. The dataset only covers private sector employees, leaving out public sector employees and the self-employed. Even for private sector employees, however, coverage is not full, and a small fraction of them is not included.

2. The reason a worker drops off the archive is not known: in addition to retiring, workers could die, become self-employed or public sector employees, or simply stop working.

3. Important covariates (e.g., education level, spousal information, and other family background variables) are missing. As a result, we have very few demographic controls available, we do not know about marital status, and we cannot say much about differential mortality.

4. There is no information on receipt of disability or other types of benefits.

The initial sample selection is as follows. We focus on workers between 18 and 70 years of age who work at least 28 days a year. We exclude from the analysis workers belonging to special INPS funds (nursery-school teachers, local authorities employees, etc.).[10]

6.3.2   Earnings Projection and Transitions to Retirement

The specification of a model for the age-earnings profile represents an essential step in the estimation of social security wealth at the individual level. This is especially important in Italy, as the process of social security reform involves moving from a final salary type of benefit formula (pre-1993 system) to a formula based on the value of lifetime contributions (1995 reform).[11] In the following we describe additional hypothetical reforms, which also involve extending the benefit calculation period.

---

10. We could include these observations to add variability across funds, but these workers represent only a small number (less than 100 observations) and tend to exhibit many gaps in their careers.

11. In this and the following sections we only describe results for the 1995 reform (results for the other cases are available on request from the authors).

In order to estimate earnings profiles and eventually measure social security wealth, we further select the sample by including only workers who are present in the sample for an uninterrupted period of at least five years (workers often appear for one year and then disappear from the sample for a long spell). The five-year minimum requirement is activated by the fact that this corresponds to the minimum contributive period under the 1995 reform. We only keep workers who do not have substantial gaps (more than ten years missing) in their records. This is because we cannot say whether in that time span they were engaged in other labor market or non-labor market activities (such as maternity leaves, or undertaking further education). The choice of a ten-year interval is arbitrary, and is based on a preliminary inspection of the data.[12]

The information available to model age-earnings profiles in the INPS sample is somewhat limited, for it consists only of age, gender, occupation, sector of employment, and region of working activity.[13]

The earnings-modeling strategy is as follows: individual real age-earnings profiles are modeled with individual fixed effects in order to fill gaps of one or two years in workers' careers. The earnings profile is assumed to be completely flat after the last year of observed earnings. This corresponds to the assumption that, at the individual level, the real earnings process is a random walk, with no drift. In practice, the jump-off point for the earnings projections is taken to be the average of the last three years of observed earnings. This jump-off point pins down the level of the age-earnings profile for each individual.[14] Note that this might lead to underestimating future earnings growth, particularly for younger cohorts. However, since our "sample at risk" (as defined in the following) consists mainly of older cohorts, the problem may not be too severe.[15] Furthermore, for

12. It should be noted that in order to gain variability in social security benefits, we did experiment with a larger sample that included almost all workers, regardless of the existence of gaps in their careers. However, this did not add valuable information, as the majority of workers with substantial spells out of the private sector would end up qualifying for minimum benefits (the level of which is fixed by legislation each year) or for an old-age income guarantee (*pensione sociale*). Hence there would be very little correlation between earnings histories and pension benefits for these individuals, and the effects of potential reforms in changing the incentives to retire would be negligible (these workers would basically qualify for the minimum benefit under all regimes). Therefore these cases would end up blurring the results rather than adding variability to be exploited. Finally, our choice of the ten years' threshold and the requirement of a minimum of five years' presence in the archive give us an estimated sample percentage of minimum benefit recipients that is not too far from what was observed in the universe of pension awards as recorded by the INPS Administration.

13. This is actually the region where the firm is located. Hence a comparison with the SHIW and national accounts data reveals that there seems to be a higher number of workers located in the northwest, where many large firms have their headquarters.

14. When going backward, the jump-off point corresponds to the average of the first three observations available for each individual.

15. The cohorts at risk are defined according to year of birth: for the oldest cohort these are between 1918 and 1926, for the next cohort 1927–36, and for the youngest cohort, 1937–44.

those above 50, earnings are lower on average and are very noisy, possibly because of part-time work or the coexistence of early retirement benefits and working activities. If one looked backward, using a flat earnings profile would grossly overestimate the level of earnings at earlier ages and grossly underestimate real earnings growth. To avoid this problem, individual earnings are assumed to grow at the annual growth rate of aggregate earnings, for the years when this information is available, and at a constant real rate of 1.5 percent otherwise.[16]

Notice that, although our first data point is in 1973, we need to go back to the 1930s for some of our workers in order to complete their working history. Hence, we are forced to use a procedure that makes use of aggregate growth rates when projecting backward into the distant past. Also, in projecting earnings forward, individuals are assumed to form expectations by using the model. In other words, for each age we only use actual earnings up to that age, and project earnings from that age forward according to the forecasting model.

Our data contain no information on the reasons why workers leave the archive. Thus, in order to use the data, we make the strong assumption that every exit from the archive is due to retirement. In fact, rather than retiring, a worker could have died, or moved from private sector employment to public sector employment or to self-employment. Our identifying assumption is that, over the range of ages that we consider (age 50 to 65), exit from the INPS archive is due to retirement, not to other reasons. This assumption is not in contrast with what we observe in an alternative sample provided by the Bank of Italy (Survey of Household Income and Wealth [SHIW]), where we have the full set of information available concerning the occupational status of individuals in each year.[17] As for mortality, in the simulation we purge the exits of the component that can be attributed to differential mortality by age, sex, and cohort.

For Italian workers, the only relevant alternative escape route from the labor force is disability. Although other bridging plans exist, they would all fall in the category of preretirement or early retirement and, in our data, would effectively correspond to retirement. We argue that exits via disability are not particularly relevant to our sample because, after the changes legislated in 1984, the importance of this escape route has greatly diminished and, in the age range that we consider (50 to 70), the number of disability pensions is negligible relative to old-age pensions.[18]

---

16. Aggregate earnings are equal to the earnings series put together by Rossi, Sorgato, Toniolo (1993) for the years before 1970 and to national account statistics for subsequent years up to 1999.

17. In the SHIW sample, different definitions of pensioner are available, based on self-reported occupational status, on earnings, and on benefits receipts. However, no marked difference in the distribution of retired people by age emerged from adopting different definitions.

18. See Brugiavini and Peracchi (2004) for a more detailed discussion.

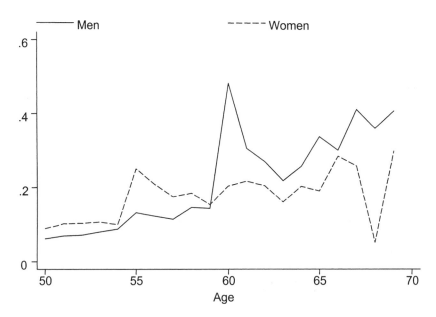

Fig. 6.1   Empirical hazard from the INPS sample

Figure 6.1 presents the nonparametric retirement hazard based on the INPS sample for men and women. For men there is an important spike at age 60, but the hazard is not flat at younger ages, whereas for women there are several important ages at which the conditional probability of leaving the labor force peaks.

6.3.3   Definition of Social Security Wealth and Incentive Measures

Key elements of our econometric model are the concepts of social security wealth and related dynamic incentives. It is useful to briefly recap these concepts.

For a worker of age a, we define social security wealth (SSW) in case of retirement at age $h \geq a$ as the expected present value of future pension benefits

$$SSW_h = \sum_{s=h+1}^{S} \rho_s B_s(h),$$

where S is the age of certain death (110 years), $\rho_s = \beta^{s-a} \pi_s$ is a discount factor that depends on the rate of time discount β and the survival probability π_s at age s conditional on being alive at age h, and $B(h)$ is the pension benefit expected at age $s \geq h + 1$ in case of retirement at age h. Pension benefits are the net of income taxes. Given SSW, we define three incentive measures for a worker of age a.

1. *Social security accrual (SSA)* is the difference in SSW due to postponing retirement from age a to age $a + 1$.

$$SSA_a = SSW_{a+1} - SSW_a = \sum_{s=a+2}^{S} \rho_s[B_s(a + 1) - B_s(a)] - \rho_{a+1}B_{a+1}(a).$$

The SSA is negative if the expected present value of pension benefits forgone by postponing retirement by one year is greater than $\sum_{s=a+2}^{S} \rho_s[B_s(a + 1) - B_s(a)]$, the expected present value of the increment in the flow of future pension benefits. The rescaled negative accrual $\tau_a = -SSA_a/W_{a+1}$, where W_{a+1} are expected net earnings at age $a + 1$ based on the information available up to age a, is called the implicit tax/subsidy of postponing retirement from age a to age $a + 1$.

2. *Peak value:* $PV_a = \max_h(SSW_h - SSW_a), h = a + 1, \ldots, R$, where R is the mandatory retirement age (the latter does not exist in Italy, but given the retirement evidence we find it reasonable to put $R = 70$). Thus, the peak value is the maximum difference in SSW between retiring at future ages and retiring at the current age.

3. *Option value:* $OV_a = \max_h(V_h - V_a), h = a + 1, \ldots, R$, where

$$V_a = \sum_{s=a+1}^{S} \rho_s[kB_s(h)]^\gamma$$

is the intertemporal expected utility of retiring at age a, while

$$V_h = \sum_{s=a+1}^{h} \rho_s W_s^\gamma + \sum_{s=h+1}^{S} \rho_s[kB_s(h)]^\gamma$$

is the intertemporal utility of retiring at age $h > a$. Thus, the option value is the maximum utility difference between retiring at future ages and retiring at age a. We parameterize the model by assuming $\gamma = 1$ and $k = 1.25$. Under these assumptions, $V_a = 1.25SSW_a$ and

$$V_h = \sum_{s=a+1}^{h} \rho_s W_s^\gamma = 1.25SSW_h.$$

If expected earnings are constant at W_a (as assumed in our earnings model), then

$$V_h - V_a = W_a \sum_{s=a+1}^{h} \rho_s + 1.25(SSW_h - SSW_a).$$

That is, the peak value and the option value are proportional to each other, except for the effect due to the term $\sum_{s=a+1}^{h} \rho_s$.

In the actual calculation of SSW, we assume a time discount factor of 1.5 percent ($\beta = .985$). Benefits are defined in real terms, and the indexation rules prevailing under each legislation are implemented (e.g., in the baseline we apply indexation to both price inflation and real wages). We also assume that real earnings growth after 1997 (the last year of the INPS sample) is constant at 1.5 percent.

Estimation of SSW is carried out separately for men and women. Household social security wealth is set equal to the man's social security wealth when the wife does not work. In estimating the model, we must deal with the fact that the actual age of entry into the labor market is not always known. We used the information on the initial occupational level to get a reasonable proxy for educational attainments. This is then used to impute an initial age for a worker's contributive history.

Eligibility and benefit computation rules prevailing under each regime are rather complex (see section 6.2), and some shortcuts were made. Finally, we computed social security wealth net of income tax, by subtracting income tax from gross pension benefits.

6.3.4   The Reduced-Form Retirement Model: Methodology and Estimation Results

In this section, we present the results of modeling exit into retirement using probit models that include, in addition to a standard set of covariates (such as age, occupation, and sector of employment), the incentive measures discussed in the previous section.

The response variable is a binary indicator, representing exit from the INPS sample between the year t and the year $t + 1$. The population at risk consists of workers aged between 50 and 70 in any of the relevant years. The sample used for estimation includes all consecutive pairs of years from 1980 to 1981 through 1996 to 1997. We restrict the analysis to individuals at risk after 1980. The reason is twofold: first, it is very hard to capture the behavior of workers, taking into account all of the institutional changes affecting the various cohorts over a long time span. The period 1980–1992 has the advantage of being relatively stable in terms of policy changes. Second, because in some cases we have to model earnings profiles going back fifty years, given the existing limitations on aggregate wage data it is reasonable to limit the time horizon to recent years. In this way, our oldest worker is aged 70 in 1980, and we only need to back-cast earnings to the year 1930.[19]

The social security regime is assumed to be the transitional one introduced in 1992 (see table 6.1). This is the relevant regime for the workers in our sample, who would not yet experience the changes introduced by the 1995 reform through the sample period. Overall, using the pre-1993 rules would lead to negligible differences in terms of social security wealth and

19. Retirement is not mandatory. Given that we assume an individual at risk up to age 70, and given that we cannot exclude that she or he started working at age 20, we cannot rule out the possibility that this individual worked for fifty years.

eligibility. This is because, as already mentioned, the rights of workers near retirement were changed only marginally by the 1992 reform: according to seniority, most workers at risk would fully retire under the pre-1993 rules.

For each incentive measure, two basic specifications are considered, for a total of six estimated models. The incentive variables are the accrual, the peak value, and the option value, whereas the dependence of the retirement hazard on age is modeled either through a simple linear age term or through a full set of age dummies. All specifications include a set of sectoral and regional indicators and a set of earnings measures relevant for the retirement choice. Different from our previous work, and from other countries that contribute to this project, we only use two resource measures, capturing, respectively, the level of social security wealth and the trade-off between benefits and labor earnings: net social security wealth and pensionable earnings.[20] The additional variable, measuring future earnings, which we included in previous studies, is left out, because in the Italian case a multicollinearity problem emerges under the baseline and the transitional period.[21] The problem is caused by the way benefits are computed: pensionable earnings, which form the basis of our social security wealth estimate, are equal to average earnings in the last five years, and in many cases they take the same value of (or a very close value to) one-step-ahead projected earnings.

Results for the specification with age dummies are summarized in table 6.2: each column refers to a particular incentive variable and we report only the estimated coefficients of the variables of interest. It should be noted that our purpose here is not to produce a good fit, but rather to create a basis for the simulation exercise by adopting a parsimonious specification.[22] The use of age dummies increases the fit relative to the model with a linear age term, but only marginally. This suggests that age is an important determinant of retirement decisions but, despite the presence of spikes in the hazard, we obtain only marginal gains by making use of a fully parameterized model. Hence, these spikes may be less important than first appears in explaining the age-retirement process, as most of the movement comes from the exits taking place between age 50 and age 60. As shown in table 6.2, the social security wealth variable and the incentive variables have, by and large, the correct sign: of the three incentive variables, the accrual and option value have the correct sign and are significantly different from zero.

---

20. To be more precise, we use a quadratic polynomial in pensionable earnings. All continuous variables enter in the form of deviation from the mean.

21. For brevity, we do not report the estimates of regressions of the future earnings variable against social security wealth, pensionable earnings, and all the relevant covariates. This regression shows the clear symptoms of multicollinearity; for example, an extremely high t-statistics for the two variables under investigation.

22. For example, if we used year-of-birth cohorts, results improve dramatically.

Table 6.2   **Probit models of retirement decisions (with age dummies)**

	Accrual		Peak value		Option value	
	Estimated coefficient	Standard error	Estimated coefficient	Standard error	Estimated coefficient	Standard error
		Male: 20,092 observances				
Social security						
wealth	0.00058	0.00025	0.00060	0.00028	0.00027	0.00028
Incentive	−0.00103	0.00065	−0.00031	0.00063	−0.00099	0.00036
Constant	−1.29995	0.04415	−1.32031	0.04738	−1.27715	0.04400
R^2	0.0836		0.0835		0.0840	
Log-likelihood	−7054.7301		−7055.8927		−7052.1504	
		Female: 5,165 observances				
Social security						
wealth	0.00063	0.00083	0.00157	0.00094	0.00002	0.00097
Incentive	−0.00480	0.00474	0.00443	0.00312	−0.00210	0.00137
Constant	−1.18974	0.06768	−1.209801	0.06881	−1.15935	0.07085
R^2	0.0314		0.0316		0.0317	
Log-likelihood	−2029.3559		−2028.872		−2028.6804	

6.4 Simulating Policy Changes

The aim of this section is to simulate the total fiscal implications of pension reforms. The hypothetical reforms, described later, contain some useful elements for the debate currently taking place in Italy. For example, the reform that we indicate as "actuarial adjustment" represents a change of the current Italian system in line with what many experts and policy makers advocate. We also simulate the steady-state effects of the actual reform introduced in 1995 (the so-called Dini Reform).

6.4.1 Social Security Regimes

The baseline or reference regime ($R0$) is the social security system prevailing before 1992; the various successive regime changes are evaluated against this regime.[23] As for the reforms considered, a brief description is useful.

R1: Three-Year Reform

This reform preserves all the features of the system but increases by three years the normal retirement age. Since in Italy all ages before the normal

23. As we already pointed out, the econometric model that predicts retirement is estimated on the sample of workers observed between 1974 and 1997, hence experiencing the transitional period. In the estimation, we evaluate social security wealth and the incentive variables according to the rules of the transitional phase, because these are the incentives actually faced by individuals. However, in the simulation we look at changes occurring between steady states.

retirement age are potentially an early retirement age (conditional on seniority), the entire hazard is effectively shifted by three years. The seniority rule is preserved in its original format (see also table 6.1).

R2: Actuarial Reform

This reform should achieve an actuarially fair system without changing any other feature of the program (i.e., no change in basic benefit calculation rules, in means testing and eligibility to minimum benefits, and in indexation). The normal retirement age is the same as the base case, and the rules in place are unchanged at that age (hence, the replacement ratio is the same at that age). The reform introduces an actuarial adjustment of 6 percent for each year past the normal retirement age. Thus, benefits becoming available before the normal retirement age are reduced by 6 percent per year, while benefits becoming available after the normal retirement age are increased by 6 percent per year.

R3: Common Reform

This reform is common to all countries considered in this volume. The crucial feature is that, different from the other cases, this reform envisages an ideal system, the same for all countries, which represents a complete departure from the systems currently in place in many countries (Italy is one example). This simulation features an early retirement age of 60 and a normal retirement age of 65. It provides a retiree with a benefit that replaces 60 percent of her or his projected earnings when she or he turns 65. It applies an actuarial reduction of 6 percent per year for early claiming and an actuarial increase of 6 percent per year for later claiming. It essentially makes early retirement costly and introduces age neutrality in retirement choices.

R4: The 1995 Reform

The 1995 reform adopts a notionally defined contribution method of benefit calculation. The initial pension amount is the annuity equivalent to the present value (at retirement) of past payroll taxes, capitalized by means of a five-year moving average of the nominal GDP growth rate. The value of the annuity is an increasing function of the age at retirement. It is equal to 4.72 percent of the present value of past payroll taxes for people retiring at age 57, and to 6.136 percent for people retiring at age 65 or older.[24] Capping is applied (on the present value of contributions, rather than on pensionable earnings).

6.4.2 Simulation Methodology

For each of the five policies described previously (four regime changes plus the baseline) and for each worker in our final sample, we estimate the

---

24. Hence the benefits is: 33 percent × adjustment factor × present value of SS taxes.

social security wealth variable and the incentive measures. For each worker we also observe a number of covariates, such as age, occupational status, and so on. We simulate retirement decisions of these workers on the basis of the econometric model described in section 6.3, using the social security wealth variable and the incentive measures specific to each regime. All other covariates are identical across simulations. In this way, retirement probabilities change in response to changes in the policy variables according to the estimated parameters (shown also in table 6.2). However, a few adjustments are needed in order to adapt the estimates to the policy environment. One of these adjustments concerns the age dummies. To recap, we make use of two econometric models: one where age enters linearly and is not affected by the reform changes (S1), and one where age enters through a set of age dummies (S3). The coefficients on the age dummies of this model are bound to be affected by the reforms, over and above the changes implied by any modification in eligibility rules. For example, in Italy, the hazard for men has a spike at age 60, which is the normal retirement age for men under the baseline ($R0$). If the normal retirement age is shifted by three years (regime $R1$), then the age effect observed at age 60 should be felt at age 63, and the whole hazard should reflect the policy change.

Simulations are carried out in two steps: the first step generates retirement probabilities under the different scenarios, whereas the second step computes the fiscal implications of the changes. In order to carry out the exercise, we initially focus on a homogeneous group of workers by drawing a simulation sample of 699 individuals (men and women) born in 1938, 1939, and 1940 from the original INPS sample.[25] We disregard time differences between these three cohorts and simply assume everybody to be age 50 in 1990. For these individuals, we have all the relevant information for all ages between 50 and 70; that is, we follow them through these ages even if some of them have effectively retired in the original sample. The intuition behind this procedure is to compute the direct fiscal effects of the reforms (the mechanical effects) and the fiscal effects due to changes in retirement behavior (the behavioral effects) as seen from the perspective of an individual who reaches age 50 in 1990 and is considering whether to retire at any future age.

6.4.3 Basic Assumptions

Unlike most other countries in this project, we assume that men are married to women who do not work, while working women are single. Hence, social security wealth of men can be thought of as a household's social security wealth (men are head of the household). This assumption is introduced

---

25. There are 235 workers in the 1938 cohort, 223 in the 1939 cohort, and 241 in the 1940 cohort.

because our data contain no information on workers' marital status, and in the Italian legislation the only major difference between a single worker and a married worker is eligibility to survivors' pension (there is no dependent-spouse benefit[26]). We did not attempt an imputation procedure to assign spouses to workers because this would generate a significant amount of noise while not adding much to the results.[27]

Disability benefits have not been taken into account because multiple exit routes are not relevant in the Italian case. Also, we do not account for the lump-sum benefit occurring at any separation between employer and employee (the so-called TFR) because, as shown in Brugiavini (1999), this lump-sum benefit does not alter dynamic incentives and would not essentially be affected by the reforms.

To complete the simulation we need information on mortality rates and labor force participation in the population. A full set of mortality rates for each sex–age–cohort combination has been constructed by fitting a grouped-logit model with cohort fixed effects to the sex–age–cohort mortality rates kindly provided by professor Graziella Caselli, of the University of Rome "La Sapienza," and spanning the period 1974 to 1994. On the basis of the mortality rates obtained in this way, and the projected probabilities of exit from the labor force projected for each regime, we infer retirement probabilities at each age between 50 and 70. We then apply to our results an inflation factor that takes into account the fact that we initially normalize the size of the cohort to 100 workers aged 50 in 1990. The inflation factor has been computed using data from the Italian Labor Force Survey, distinguishing workers by age and sex.[28]

Finally, total fiscal effects are evaluated, both as a percentage of gross benefits under the baseline regime (obtained directly from the simulation exercise) and as a percentage of the gross domestic product (GDP) of the private sector. In the second case, since our sample is confined to private sector employees, we first gross up the results obtained (total gain/loss

26. There is a difference in the rebates on income tax and in the calculation of minimum benefit, particularly in the way means testing is carried out.

27. We have assigned to men a wife who is three years younger, so that in case of death she is entitled to survivors' benefits. Doing so, and further assuming that women are single, leads to three sources of errors: (a) we overestimate benefits to survivors when workers are men, as in reality some are single; (b) we underestimate household social security wealth, by assuming that wives never work, and (c) we underestimate benefits to survivors of working women. We estimated from the SHIW survey that the probability of being married for a man of age 50 is 88 percent. Of these, only 35 percent have a working wife; hence we hope that the combination of overestimation and underestimation may cancel each other out. In any case, it should be noted that none of the reforms changes the basic features of survivors' benefits.

28. This step is necessary in order to produce the total gain/loss. More precisely, in 1990 our sample contains 699 workers born in 1938 to 1940, an average of 233 workers per annual cohort. According to the Labor Force Survey, the population of these cohorts is about 193,000 workers, of which 75 percent are men. Thus, one worker in our sample represents 193,000/233 = 828 workers in the population. We then multiply our results by the inflation factor in order to produce the effects for the whole population.

from the reform) for a single representative individual of the cohort, by multiplying by the number of employees (men and women) in the private sector belonging to that cohort.[29] The result of this calculation is the aggregate effect of the reform, which is then divided by the level of GDP observed in the year 2001 in the private sector (approximately 994 billion euros). It should be noted that GDP in the private sector represents more than 80 percent of Italian GDP.

6.4.4   Computing Expected Benefits and Fiscal Effects

Fiscal effects of the reforms are evaluated by computing the net present value of pension expenditures for the cohort of people who are aged a in year t (in our case, age 50 in 1990). We study an initial sample of workers (whose number, N, is normalized to be 100) who can leave the labor force through retirement or death. The whole exercise hinges on the definition of expected total gross benefit payments:

$$TGSW_i = \sum_{s=a}^{S}[p_{si}^R(X)SSW_{si} + p_{si}^D(X)SSW_{si}^D]$$

for $i = 1, \ldots N$, where p_{si}^R and p_{si}^D are, respectively, the conditional probability of retirement and death at age a for individual i. In a general model, both these probabilities would depend on observable characteristics X, but in our model the retirement probability is individual specific (projected), while the probability of death is imputed from external data and depends only on sex and age. The terms SSW and SSW^D represent the discounted sum of future benefits that would accrue to a worker if he or she was alive and retired at each future age a, or to her or his survivor in case of death.[30] Both are discounted at a 3 percent real discount rate.

A full evaluation of the fiscal effects of the reforms requires a more general approach to the social security budget than can be achieved by looking at the Social Security Administration in isolation. Therefore, a more general approach is required, both from the point of view of the workers belonging to the cohort of interest and from the point of view of fiscal authorities. As for the former, any change to the social security rules would imply a change in retirement/labor supply decisions, which in turn may affect income tax revenue. The latter is easily explained by bearing in mind that the Italian pension system is financed on a pay-as-you-go (PAYG) basis, and is systematically running a deficit. Also, different sources of

---

29. As we said, we deal with the three year-of-birth cohorts as if the workers all belonged to the same cohort. The number of employees in the private sector of the 1940 cohort (in fact, an average of the 1938, 1939, and 1940 cohorts) is 193,000.

30. It should be noted that while in the econometric exercise we make use of net social security wealth (net of income taxes), in the simulation we proceed in two steps; first, we compute gross social security wealth, and then take off all taxes when aggregating for all individuals.

revenue should be taken into account, because pension outlays are financed partly through current contributions and partly through taxation at large. Therefore, we cannot identify a specific item of the government revenue to be earmarked to finance the social security budget deficit. For this reason, we compute the present value of future taxes that each worker would pay conditional on work, retirement, or death.[31] Looking from the perspective of a worker of age 50: for any future year that she works, she pays social security contributions plus income taxes plus VAT; if she retires, she pays income tax on gross benefits and VAT; if she dies, her spouse will pay income tax and VAT on survivors' benefits. Therefore, for any additional year of work, the value of contributions typically grows (due also to a progressive income tax schedule), while the value of gross benefits may increase or decrease depending on eligibility and the rules of the system.

After computing the present value of gross benefits and total taxes for each individual, we select the proper weights (which are based on labor force data and depend on individuals' age and sex) and obtain total projected benefits and taxes for that cohort. Hence we can easily compute total net expected benefits.

These calculations are carried out for each regime. The final step is to compute gains and losses by taking the difference of total net benefits between each different regime ($R1$, $R2$, $R3$, and $R4$) and the baseline ($R0$). The simple difference between the two net quantities provides the total effects of the reform:

$$\text{Total effect} = \sum_{i=1}^{N} \sum_{s=a}^{S} P_{is}^{R1} NTSW_{is}^{R1} - \sum_{i=1}^{N} \sum_{s=a}^{S} P_{is}^{R0} NTSW_{is}^{R0},$$

where $R1$ stands for the first regime (or any of the reforms), $R0$ stands for the baseline regime, and $NTSW$ indicates the present value of total net benefits. We can also compute the mechanical effect and the behavioral effect of the reforms as follows:

$$\text{Mechanical effect} = \sum_{i=1}^{N} \sum_{s=a}^{S} P_{is}^{R0} NTSW_{is}^{R1} - \sum_{i=1}^{N} \sum_{s=a}^{S} P_{is}^{R0} NTSW_{is}^{R0}$$

$$\text{Behavioral effect} = \sum_{i=1}^{N} \sum_{s=a}^{S} P_{is}^{R1} NTSW_{is}^{R1} - \sum_{i=1}^{N} \sum_{s=a}^{S} P_{is}^{R0} NTSW_{is}^{R1}$$

The mechanical effect freezes the retirement probabilities at the prereform values, so that the only changes are due to changes of the social security rules. The behavioral effect maintains the same value for the net expected benefits (values after the reform), but changes the probabilities according to the regime under evaluation.

---

31. A detailed description of the assumptions regarding the tax base and tax rates is given in the appendix.

6.5   Results

Results are better described by looking separately at each regime change, so that we can discuss the simulation strategy implemented in each specific case. An overall summary of the results is provided in table 6.3 and table 6.4. The former shows the total fiscal impact of the three reforms, $R1$, $R2$, and $R3$, whereas the latter decomposes these total effects into mechanical and behavioral effects. It should be noted that, although the results are presented as total effects for workers born between 1938 and 1940, the unit of analysis is really the household. To be more precise, given our assumptions on marital status, we essentially describe a stylized economy of married male workers (in which case we have household social security wealth) and single female workers. For brevity, in this section we only comment on results obtained using the option value as the incentive variable. The full set of results can be found in tables 6.3 and 6.4, and in the corresponding figures (figure 6.3 through 6.28). The total effects given in these tables have been obtained by aggregating the individual with weights given by the inflation factors described previously in section 6.4. Because, as we shall argue, the econometric specification based on the linear term does not provide a good representation of the behavior of Italian workers, we focus our attention on the model based on age dummies.[32]

R1: Three-Year Reform

This reform entails a shift of the hazard by three years, while all other features of the social security system are preserved as under the baseline. The reform has a direct effect on the hazard and an indirect effect on benefits through eligibility. It should be noted that when using the linear age model, the projected age profile of labor force exits does not accurately capture the empirical hazard (figures 6.1 and 6.2): exits are evenly distributed over ages, and there is a hump around age 55 (figure 6.3). Instead, the empirical hazard shows higher variability and marked spikes at ages 55 and 60 (figure 6.1). Furthermore, the age distribution by age of retirement rates is essentially unaffected by the reform (figure 6.3). This is because the linear term does not pick up any of the policy changes, and as a result the behavioral effect is negligible.

For the model with a linear age term, the present value of benefits is reduced by 11.40 percent relative to the baseline value. Because taxes are also reduced by the reform, the total net change is –9.5 percent (table 6.3). Most of the impact of the reform is due to the mechanical effect (–9.6 percent).

32. Also, it should be noted that after age 66 there are very few workers left in the dataset, so that the estimated hazard is very volatile. We decided to set the hazard of exits (for retirement or death) equal to 0.5 after age 66 and equal to 1 at the latest age (69). The value 0.5 emerges as the estimated value at age 65, which is the last age that we have a reasonable sample size available.

Table 6.3   Total fiscal impact of reforms

		Present discounted value			Total change relative to base (%)		
	Base	Three-Year Reform	Actuarial Reform	Common Reform	Three-Year Reform	Actuarial Reform	Common Reform
		Peak value—Linear age					
Benefits	168,752	148,332	141,059	62,376	−12.10	−16.41	−63.04
Taxes							
Payroll	31,869	31,481	32,562	33,379	−1.22	2.17	4.74
Income	25,301	23,464	20,812	12,806	−7.26	−17.74	−49.39
VAT	16,873	15,425	15,299	10,128	−8.58	−9.33	−39.98
Total	74,042	70,370	68,673	56,313	−4.96	−7.25	−23.94
		Peak value—Age dummies					
Benefits	168,016	141,632	142,282	63,683	−15.70	−15.32	−62.10
Taxes							
Payroll	32,398	37,133	33,375	33,549	14.62	3.02	3.55
Income	25,847	25,771	22,083	13,686	−0.29	−14.56	−47.05
VAT	16,879	15,731	15,448	10,186	−6.80	−8.48	−39.65
Total	75,124	78,635	70,906	57,422	4.67	−5.61	−23.56
		Option value—Linear age					
Benefits	168,002	148,856	142,463	61,972	−11.40	−15.20	−63.11
Taxes							
Payroll	32,730	32,555	32,874	32,876	−0.53	0.44	0.45
Income	25,607	23,955	21,044	12,415	−6.45	−17.82	−51.52
VAT	16,959	15,633	15,457	10,031	−7.82	−8.86	−40.85
Total	75,296	72,143	69,375	55,322	−4.19	−7.86	−26.53
		Option value—Age dummies					
Benefits	166,778	142,067	145,207	65,357	−14.82	−12.93	−60.81
Taxes							
Payroll	33,387	38,048	35,399	35,079	13.96	6.03	5.07
Income	26,214	26,271	24,031	14,747	0.22	−8.33	−43.74
VAT	16,949	15,905	15,907	10,515	−6.16	−6.15	−37.96
Total	76,549	80,223	75,337	60,341	4.80	−1.58	−21.17

Note: Values in 2001 euros.

The behavioral effect, albeit very small, runs opposite to what one would expect (0.1 percent), because retirement probabilities are higher at younger ages after the reform, and precisely at those ages losses would be greater (table 6.4 and figure 6.4). As for distributional effects, table 6.5 shows that losses are evenly spread over the population: people next to the highest quintile (quintile 4) suffer most from the reform, but the loss in terms of net present value of benefits is not much higher than for the population at large.

For the model with age dummies, which is documented in figures 6.5 through 6.9, retirement probabilities are much closer to the empirical hazard; this is clearly shown by the age distribution of labor force exits (figure

Table 6.4 Decomposition of the total effect of the reforms

Change in present discounted value

	Three-Year Reform			Actuarial Reform			Common Reform		
	Mechanical	Behavioral	Total	Mechanical	Behavioral	Total	Mechanical	Behavioral	Total
Peak value—Linear age									
Benefits	−19,304	−1,116	−20,420	−28,348	655	−27,693	−107,342	966	−106,376
Taxes: Total	−2,860	−812	−3,672	−6,816	1,446	−5,369	−19,824	2,095	−17,729
Net change	−16,444	−304	−16,748	−21,532	−791	−22,324	−87,518	−1,129	−88,647
Change as % of base benefits	−9.7	−0.2	−9.9	−12.8	−0.5	−13.2	−51.9	−0.7	−52.5
Peak value—Age dummies									
Benefits	−18,878	−7.506	−26,384	−26,564	830	−25,734	−105,682	1,349	−104,333
Taxes: Total	−2,796	6,307	3,511	−6,317	2,100	−4,218	−19,897	2,195	−17,702
Net change	−16,082	−13,813	−29,895	−20,247	−1,270	−21,516	−85,785	−846	−86,631
Change as % of base benefits	−9.6	−8.2	−17.8	−12.0	−0.8	−12.8	−51.1	−0.5	−51.6
Option value—Linear age									
Benefits	−18,931	−215	−19,146	−26,305	766	−25,539	−106,237	207	−106,030
Taxes: Total	−2,810	−342	−3,153	−6,224	303	−5,921	−19,788	−185	−19,974
Net change	−16,121	127	−15,993	−20,081	463	−19,618	−86,449	392	−86,056
Change as % of base benefits	−9.6	0.1	−9.5	−11.9	0.3	−11.6	−51.5	0.2	−51.2
Option value—Age dummies									
Benefits	−18,345	−6,365	−24,711	−24,311	2,741	−21,571	−104,053	2,633	−101,421
Taxes: Total	−2,731	6,405	3,674	−5,670	4,458	−1,212	−19,846	3,638	−16,208
Net change	−15,614	−12,770	−28,385	−18,641	−1,717	−20,359	−84,207	−1,005	−85,213
Change as % of base benefits	−9.4	−7.7	−17.0	−11.0	−1.0	−12.1	−50.5	−0.6	−51.1

Note: Values in 2001 euros.

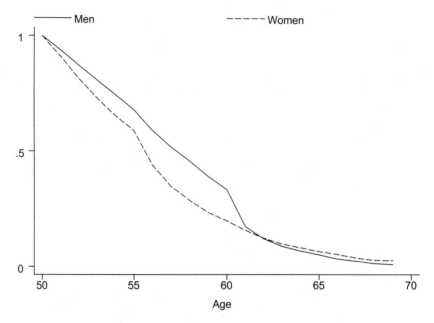

Fig. 6.2   Empirical survival curve in the INPS sample

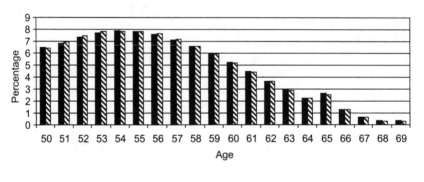

Fig. 6.3   Three-Year Reform—Option value, distribution of age of labor force exit (OV linear age)

Note: Figures in percentage terms.

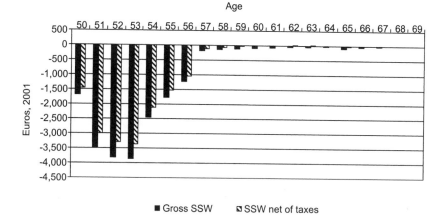

Fig. 6.4   Three-Year Reform—Option value, total effect by age of retirement (OV linear age)
Note: Values in euros of 2001.

6.5).[33] The reform clearly affects retirement behavior: the distribution of retirement rates is shifted toward older ages, and the spikes are observed to occur with three years' delay. This implies that while a substantial fraction of losses are suffered at ages 50 to 57, they tend to be very high at ages 55 and 60 (the normal retirement age of women and men under the baseline). Older retirees would instead gain from the reform, because of the increase in benefits at older ages.

When the econometric model allows for age dummies, we not only observe a decline in benefits (−14.82 percent relative to the baseline), but also an increase in the overall fiscal impact (4.80 percent), so that the total net effect is −17.0 percent (table 6.3 and figures 6.8 and 6.9). This is largely due to the mechanical effect, although, as shown in table 6.4 and figure 6.7, a nonnegligible role is played by the behavioral effect (−7.7 percent). Note that figure 6.7 reports the results as a percentage of private-sector GDP: these are small (the total effect is approximately −0.5 percent), but one should bear in mind that social security spending is approximately 14 percent of total GDP in Italy. In this sense, the implied saving for the budget may be nonnegligible. The distributional effects of the reform are significant, with the highest quintile of social security wealth suffering a loss of approximately 20 percent against a 12.4 percent loss at the lowest quintile (table 6.6). Hence, according to this model, a reform that shifts the retirement age by three years in Italy would be effective in reducing outlays and would also be progressive.

---

33. Besides changing the eligibility rules, we increment all age dummies by three years, so that the normal retirement age is effectively increased by three years.

Table 6.5   Distribution analysis: Option value—Model with linear age

	Present discounted value				Change relative to base PDV		
	Base	Three-Year	Actuarial	Common	Three-Year Reform	Actuarial Reform	Common Reform
			Quintile 5 (highest)				
Benefits	13,163	11,516	10,583	4,628	−1,647	−2,580	−8,535
After-tax income	11,883	10,486	10,096	5,162	−1,396	−1,787	−6,721
Taxes							
Payroll	3,478	3,448	3,415	3,386	−30	−64	−92
Income	4,194	3,929	3,356	2,301	−264	−837	−1,893
VAT	1,338	1,230	1,200	825	−108	−139	−514
Total	9,010	8,607	7,971	6,512	−403	−1,040	−2,499
Net change					−1,244	−1,540	−6,036
Change as % of base benefits					−9.45	−11.70	−45.86
			Quintile 4				
Benefits	10,603	9,281	8,336	3,081	−1,322	−2,268	−7,522
Taxes: Total	4,378	4,161	3,893	3,009	−217	−485	−1,369
Net change					−1,105	−1,783	−6,153
Change as % of base benefits					−10.43	−16.81	−58.03
			Quintile 3				
Benefits	8,466	7,543	7,240	2,786	−923	−1,226	−5,680
Taxes: Total	2,788	2,693	2,737	2,119	−95	−51	−670
Net change					−828	−1,175	−5,011
Change as % of base benefits					−9.78	−13.88	−59.19
			Quintile 2				
Benefits	6,006	5,435	5,613	2,550	−572	−393	−3,457
Taxes: Total	1,779	1,734	1,855	1,454	−45	75	−325
Net change					−526	−469	−3,132
Change as % of base benefits					−8.76	−7.80	−52.14
			Quintile 1 (lowest)				
Benefits	3,763	3,441	3,849	2,455	−322	86	−1,308
Taxes: Total	887	859	906	752	−28	19	−135
Net change					−293	68	−1,173
Change as % of base benefits					−7.80	1.80	−31.17

Note: Values in 2001 euros.

R2: Actuarial Reform

The basic idea of this reform is to preserve the status quo in several respects as well as to introduce an actuarial adjustment in order to guarantee neutrality of the system with respect to the retirement age. Before describing the results in detail, it is useful to remind the reader that the

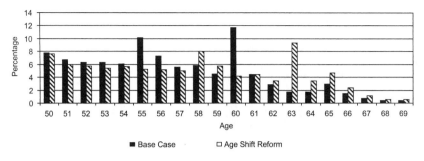

Fig. 6.5   Three-Year Reform—Option value, distribution of age and labor force exit (OV age dummies)

Note: Figures in percentage terms.

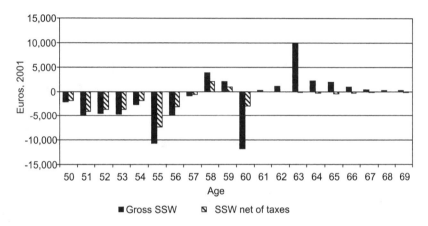

Fig. 6.6   Three-Year Reform—Option value, total effect by age of retirement (OV age dummies)

Note: Values in euros of 2001.

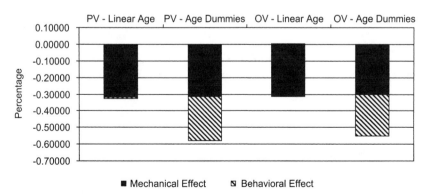

Fig. 6.7   Three-Year Reform—Option value, fiscal implications of Three-Year Reform as a percentage of GDP

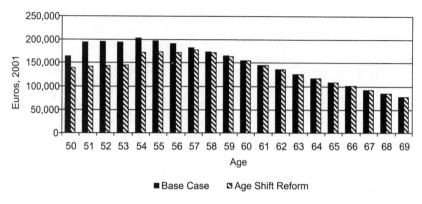

Fig. 6.8   Three-Year Reform—Option value, SSW by age of labor force exit (OV age dummies)

Note: Values in euros of 2001.

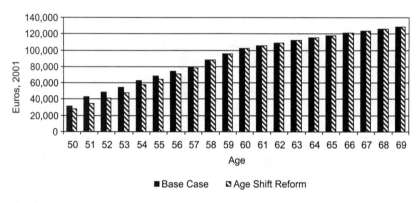

Fig. 6.9   Three-Year Reform—Option value, taxes by age of labor force exit (OV age dummies)

Note: Values in euros of 2001.

baseline (pre-1993) is very far from being actuarially fair, as no actuarial penalties are envisaged for early retirement (and no bonus for late retirement).

As we already argued, the linear case is not very interesting for the Italian system. This can be easily understood by looking at figures 6.10 and 6.11, where a very smooth age profile of exit probabilities is shown, which is quite different from the observed hazard.

Focusing one's attention on figure 6.12, one can see that the Actuarial Reform has some effect on the age distribution of retirement probabilities. In fact, although their basic pattern is unchanged after the reform, exits from the labor force are lower at younger ages and higher at older ages.

Table 6.6   **Distribution analysis: Option value—model with age dummies**

	Present discounted value				Change relative to base PDV		
	Base	Three-Year	Actuarial	Common	Three-Year Reform	Actuarial Reform	Common Reform
Quintile 5 (highest)							
Benefits	13,185	11,078	11,100	5,344	−2,107	−2,085	−7,841
After-tax income	11,839	9,936	10,255	5,585	−1,904	−1,584	−6,255
Taxes							
Payroll	3,550	4,103	3,879	3,980	553	329	430
Income	4,283	4,304	3,927	2,884	21	−356	−1,399
VAT	1,348	1,283	1,281	942	−65	−67	−406
Total	9,181	9,690	9,087	7,805	509	−94	−1,376
Net change					−2,616	−1,991	−6,465
Change as % of base benefits					−19.84	−15.10	−49.04
Quintile 4							
Benefits	10,429	8,753	8,449	3,161	−1,677	−1,980	−7,269
Taxes: Total	4,474	4,638	4,166	3,118	164	−308	−1,356
Net change					−1,841	−1,672	−5,912
Change as % of base benefits					−17.65	−16.03	−56.69
Quintile 3							
Benefits	8,344	7,159	7,271	2,777	−1,185	−1,073	−5,567
Taxes: Total	2,840	2,981	2,855	2,084	141	15	−757
Net change					−1,326	−1,088	−4,810
Change as % of base benefits					−15.90	−13.03	−57.65
Quintile 2							
Benefits	5,970	5,212	5,613	2,559	−758	−356	−3,410
Taxes: Total	1,785	1,873	1,865	1,387	88	80	−397
Net change					−846	−436	−3,013
Change as % of base benefits					−14.18	−7.31	−50.47
Quintile 1 (lowest)							
Benefits	3,769	3,319	3,875	2,509	−450	106	−1,260
Taxes: Total	876	894	883	713	18	6	−163
Net change					−468	99	−1,097
Change as % of base benefits					−12.41	2.64	−29.11

Note: Values in 2001 euros.

Coupled with the actual reduction of benefits that the reform envisages for younger retirees (figure 6.13), this implies that gross benefits are reduced (−12.93 percent). Since total taxes are also marginally reduced (−1.58 percent), the net effect is −12.1 percent of baseline gross benefits (table 6.3 and table 6.4). The effect is largely due to the actual reduction in benefits; that

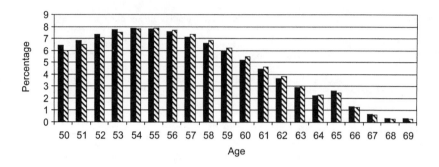

Fig. 6.10   Actuarial Reform—Option value, distribution of age of labor force exit (OV linear age)

Note: Values in percentage terms.

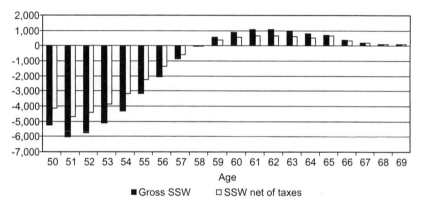

Fig. 6.11   Actuarial Reform—Option value, total effect by age of retirement (OV linear age)

Note: Values in euros of 2001.

is, the mechanical component is prevalent (–11 percent), although the behavioral effect goes in the expected direction (table 6.4 and figure 6.14). In terms of private sector GDP, the revenue gains are of the order of 0.4 percentage points. The distributional effects are interesting, both in terms of age distribution and of welfare. Losses are concentrated in the age group 50 to 57, while gainers are retirees aged 58 to 69 (figure 6.15). A clear ranking also emerges in terms of wealth distribution: the highest losses are suffered by rich retirees (–15.1 percent and –16 percent respectively for the 5th and 4th quintiles of social security wealth), while the poor retirees gain from this reform (table 6.6).

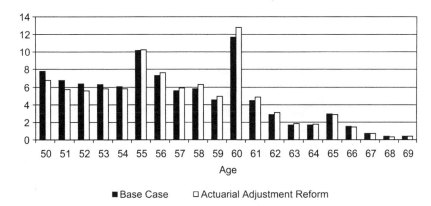

Fig. 6.12   Actuarial Reform—Option value, distribution of age of labor force exit (OV age dummies)

Note: Values in percentage terms.

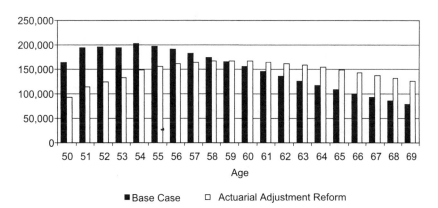

Fig. 6.13   Actuarial Reform—Option value, SSW by age of labor force exit
Note: Values in euros of 2001.

R3: Common Reform

The Common Reform is a hypothetical reform that introduces very different rules from the ones currently in place in Italy. On average, benefits are lower: the gross replacement rate for a fully eligible Italian worker is 80 percent at age 60 under the baseline, but would become 60 percent at age 65 under the Common Reform. Penalties for early retirement are non-existent under the baseline, but would be substantial under R3. One further important difference is the indexation rule: in the pre-1993 system, benefits were indexed to nominal wages, while the Common Reform (as well as the post-1993 regime) only indexes benefits to prices. It should be

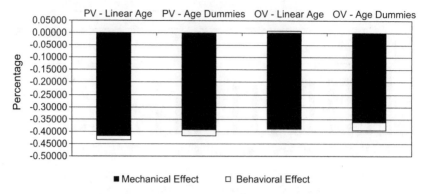

Fig. 6.14 **Actuarial Reform—Option value, fiscal implications of Actuarial Reform as a percentage of GDP**

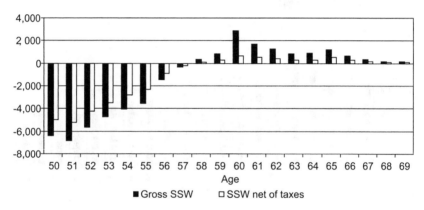

Fig. 6.15 **Actuarial Reform—Option value, total effect by age of retirement (OV age dummies)**

noted that in order to identify which specific feature of the reform produced the most important changes, we kept the legislation concerning capping and eligibility to minimum benefits unchanged with respect to the baseline (figures 6.16–6.18).

Figure 6.19 shows the distribution of labor force exits by age when use is made of the model with age dummies.[34] This reform reduces the exit rates at younger ages and shifts their distribution toward older ages. Gross benefits are much lower at all ages, in particular between 50 and 60. Table 6.3

34. The effect of the age dummies estimated in the hazard of exits (to retirement and to death) is slightly modified in this simulation to take account of the fact that we have implicitly moved the normal retirement age forward. Therefore, the age effect observed at age 60 should be felt at age 65 after the reform. The change is done through a smoothing procedure.

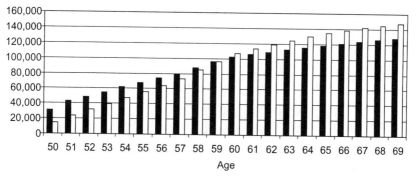

Fig. 6.16   Actuarial Reform—Option value, taxes by age of labor force exit
Note: Values in euros of 2001.

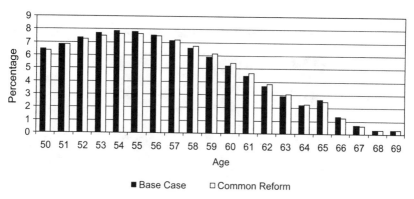

**Fig. 6.17   Common Reform—Option value, distribution of age of labor force exit
(OV linear age)**
Note: Values in percentage terms.

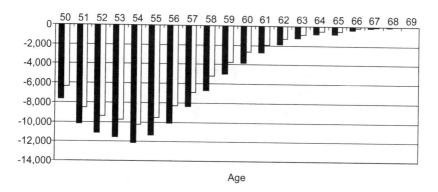

**Fig. 6.18   Common Reform—Option value, total effect by age of retirement (OV
linear age)**
Note: Values in euros of 2001.

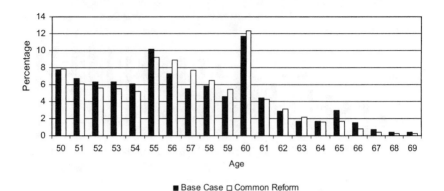

Fig. 6.19   Common Reform—Option value, distribution of age in labor force exit (OV age dummies)

Note: Values in percentage terms.

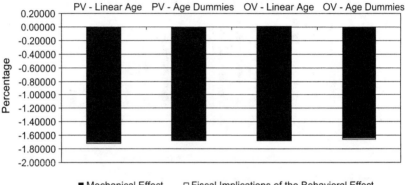

Fig. 6.20   Common Reform—Option value, fiscal implications of Common Reform as a percent of GDP

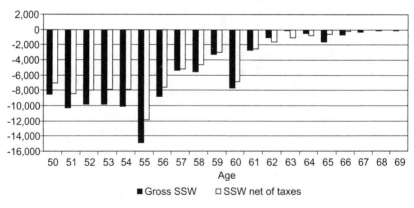

Fig. 6.21   Common Reform—Option value, total effect by age of retirement (OV age dummies)

Note: Values in euros of 2001.

Table 6.7   **Decomposition of the effects of the Dini Reform**

| | Change in present discounted value | | |
| | Three-Year Reform | | |
	Mechanical	Behavioral	Total
	Peak value—Age dummies		
Benefits	−68,054	−1,890	−69,944
Taxes: Total	−13,953	27,045	13,093
Net change	−54,101	−28,935	−83,037
Change as % of base benefits	−32.2	−17.2	−49.4
	Option value—Age dummies		
Benefits	−67,114	−2,142	−69,256
Taxes: Total	−13,895	26,326	12,431
Net change	−53,219	−28,468	−81,687
Change as % of base benefits	−31.9	−17.1	−49.0

shows that, for all the reasons given earlier, the total impact on gross benefits is huge (−60.8 percent). However, taxes are also lower, particularly income tax, so that the total net effect with respect to baseline benefits is −51.1 percent. This is almost completely explained by the mechanical effect that swamps the small gain due to delayed retirement (table 6.4). As shown in figure 6.20, the total effect is quite sizeable in terms of GDP: the fiscal authorities would gain approximately 1.6 percent of private sector GDP.

The largest losses are suffered by workers retiring at ages 55 and 60, which are the normal retirement ages under the baseline. In general, the bulk of the fiscal saving for the government comes from the age group 50 to 60 (figure 6.21). In terms of wealth distribution everyone loses from the reform, but the median retiree (3rd quintile) appears to lose more, whereas retirees placed at the lowest quintile suffer the smallest loss (table 6.7).

R4: The Dini Reform

This is the actual reform enacted in 1995 by the Dini government. As described in sections 6.2 and 6.3, at the steady state this reform would represent a radical departure from the baseline in all respects. By introducing a notionally defined contribution method of calculation of benefits, it implies a potential reduction in the present value of benefits for many workers. It also introduces actuarial principles in the benefit computation formula, as well as indexation to prices. The rules that this reform envisages (we stress, at the steady state) are not dissimilar from those proposed by the common reform (R3). Results are shown in figures 6.22–6.28.

Figure 6.24 shows the age distribution of exit probabilities. These are all shifted to older ages, both because we impose that people cannot retire before age 57 and because incentives are such that it is optimal to postpone retirement. The reduction in gross benefits is substantial at ages 50 to 60

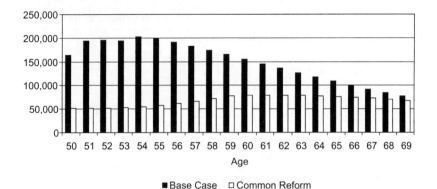

Fig. 6.22   Common Reform—Option value, SSW by age of labor force exit (OV age dummies)

Note: Values in euros of 2001.

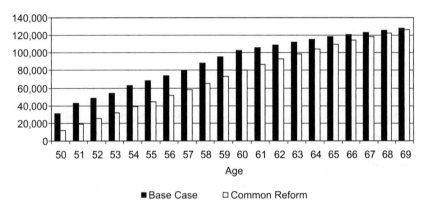

Fig. 6.23   Common Reform—Option value, taxes by age of labor force exit (OV age dummies)

Note: Values in euros of 2001.

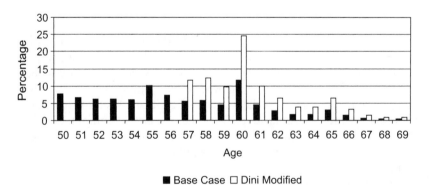

Fig. 6.24   1995 Reform (Dini Reform)—Option value, distribution by age of labor force exits (OV age dummies)

Note: Values in percentage terms.

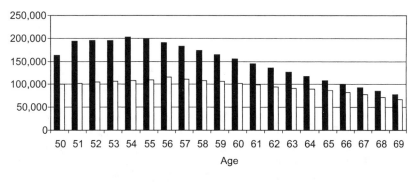

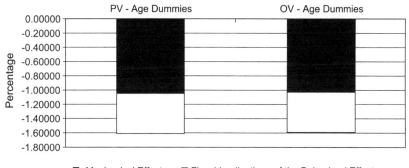

Fig. 6.25   1995 Reform (Dini Reform)—Option value, SSW by age of labor force exit

Note: Values in euros of 2001.

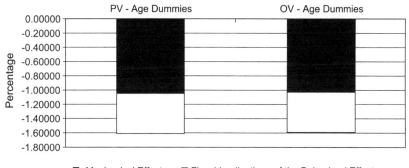

Fig. 6.26   1995 Reform (Dini Reform)—Option value, fiscal implications of Dini Reform as a percentage of GDP

Note: Values in euros of 2001.

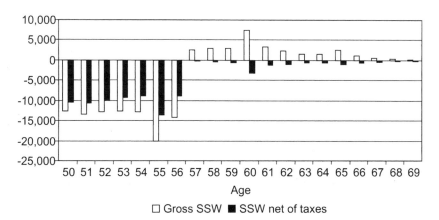

Fig. 6.27   1995 Reform (Dini Reform)—Option value, total effect by age of retirement (OV age dummies)

Note: Values in euros of 2001.

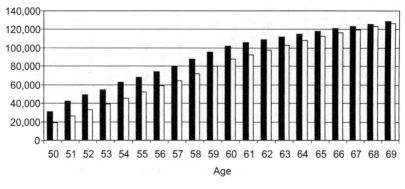

50 51 52 53 54 55 56 57 58 59 60 61 62 63 64 65 66 67 68 69

Fig. 6.28   1995 Reform (Dini Reform)—Option value, taxes by age of labor force exit

Note: Values in euros of 2001.

Table 6.8   Total fiscal impact of the Dini Reform

	Present discounted value		Total change relative to base (%)
	Base	Dini Reform	Dini Reform
Peak value—Age dummies			
Benefits	168,016	98,072	−41.63
Taxes			
Payroll	32,398	49,780	53.65
Income	25,847	23,411	−9.43
VAT	16,879	15,026	−10.98
Total	75,124	88,217	17.43
Option value—Age dummies			
Benefits	166,778	97,522	−41.53
Taxes			
Payroll	33,387	50,309	50.69
Income	26,214	23,617	−9.91
VAT	16,949	15,054	−11.18
Total	76,549	88,980	16.24

(figure 6.25). As a result, gross benefits are reduced by 41.53 percent and taxes increase by 16.24 percent (table 6.8). This is due both to a substantial mechanical effect (−31.9 percent) and to a marked behavioral effect (−17.1 percent), which produce a net effect of −49 percent of benefits. The bulk of the losses is concentrated in the age group 50 to 56, while the older group experiences a gain in terms of gross benefits, largely offset by an increase in taxes (figure 6.27). In terms of private sector GDP, this reform would imply a gain for the government budget of approximately 1.6 percent.

Table 6.9	Distributional analysis of the Dini Reform model with age dummies		
	Present discounted value		Change relative to base PDV
	Base	Dini Reform	Dini Reform
	Quintile 5 (highest)		
Benefits	13,185	8,759	−4,426
After-tax income	11,839	8,013	−3,826
Taxes			
Payroll	3,550	5,133	1,583
Income	4,283	4,346	63
VAT	1,348	1,298	−51
Total	9,181	1,323	−7,858
Net change			3,432
Change as % of base benefits			26.03
	Quintile 4		
Benefits	10,429	5,362	−5,067
Taxes: Total	4,474	1,226	−3,248
Net change			−1,820
Change as % of base benefits			−17.45
	Quintile 3		
Benefits	8,344	4,466	−3,879
Taxes: Total	2,840	591	−2,249
Net change			−1,629
Change as % of base benefits			−19.53
	Quintile 2		
Benefits	5,970	3,373	−2,597
Taxes: Total	1,785	258	−1,527
Net change			−1,070
Change as % of base benefits			−17.92
	Quintile 1 (lowest)		
Benefits	3,769	2,435	−1,334
Taxes: Total	876	74	−802
Net change			−532
Change as % of base benefits			−14.12

The distributional impact of the reform is somewhat perverse in our simulation, as the highest social security wealth quintile gains from the reform while all the rest of the cohort suffers a loss, particularly the median group (table 6.9).

6.6   Conclusions

The reform process that many advocate for the Italian social security system has rarely been analyzed with microdata. On the other hand, the few econometric studies available do not consider the total budgetary implications of the proposed pension reforms. In this chapter, we offer a novel approach to evaluating reforms that derives the entire range of fiscal implications by taking behavioral effects into account.

Our work builds on the econometric estimates in Brugiavini and Peracchi (2004), based on a longitudinal sample of private sector employees provided by the Italian Social Security Administration (INPS). A new release of the data allows us to employ a richer model, also briefly described in this chapter.

The simulation exercise considers three hypothetical reforms plus the actual reform introduced in Italy in 1995 (the so-called Dini Reform). These reforms are evaluated against a baseline represented by the pre-1992 system. The hypothetical reforms range from marginal variation of the status quo to an ideal system. The first regime change ($R1$) is a shift of three years in all retirement ages, the second ($R2$) proposes an actuarial adjustment to benefits such that early retirement is discouraged while providing incentives to delay exits. A reform common to all countries participating to the project ($R3$) allows us to evaluate the effects of a regime change that is quite radical in the Italian case, as it implies a sharp benefit cut, an actuarial adjustment, and a change in the indexation rules. Finally, a full application of the Dini Reform ($R4$) changes many features of the current system. In particular, it introduces a notionally defined contribution method of benefits computation. In several dimensions, this actual reform shows similarities with the hypothetical Common Reform.

The simulations are carried out by focusing on the cohorts of workers born in the years 1938, 1939, and 1940. For these workers, we construct measures of all the variables of interest, including projected probabilities of retirement under each policy regime.

Analyzing the three hypothetical reforms against the baseline, we find that even a modest change in the *effective* retirement age would imply nonnegligible effects. Measured as a percentage of prereform gross benefits, losses for the workers in our cohorts are approximately 17 percent. Grossing up to the population size of the cohorts considered, and measuring as a percentage of the Italian output, this change is equivalent to approximately 0.5 percent of the GDP produced in 2001 by the private sector. The losses for retirees represent savings for the government budget that come through a reduction in benefit outlays and increases in social security contributions, income tax revenue, and VAT revenue.

The Actuarial Reform and the Common Reform are particularly interesting for the Italian case. The former introduces in the baseline (pre-1993) regime an actuarial adjustment, leaving unaffected all other aspects of the social security system. This change has some effects on the age distribution of retirement rates, as workers tend to delay retirement. Coupled with the actual reduction of benefits that the reform envisages for younger retirees, we obtain a net total effect of –12.1 percent of baseline gross benefits. In terms of GDP, the revenue gains are of the order of 0.4 percentage points.

The Common Reform reduces the probability of exit at younger ages and shifts the distribution of retirement rates toward older ages. Gross benefits are much lower at all ages, particularly at ages 50 to 60. The total impact on gross benefits is huge, but due to a reduction in the total tax burden, the overall net effect is a loss to workers of 51.1 percent relative to the baseline case. This is almost completely explained by the mechanical effect, which swamps the small gain due to delayed retirement. The total effect is quite sizeable in the aggregate: fiscal authorities would gain approximately 1.6 percent of GDP.

Finally, the Dini Reform of 1995 also introduces radical changes in the Italian pension system. In our simulations, this reform is evaluated at its steady state. The age distribution of retirement rates is shifted toward older ages, both because workers cannot retire before age 57 and because incentives are such that it is optimal to postpone retirement. The reduction in gross benefits, leading to an almost uniform distribution of benefits under the new regime, is substantial at ages 50 to 60. Overall, the net effect is a 49 percent benefit loss for workers in the chosen cohorts. If fully implemented in 2001, this reform would imply a gain for the government budget equal to about 1.6 percent of private sector GDP.

The general conclusion is that, in Italy, there is still room for reforms able to generate nonnegligible savings for the government budget. Some of these reforms would also have desirable properties in terms of redistribution between generations, and between rich and poor retirees. Further research is needed to assess the effects of these reforms for a larger number of cohorts and to analyze the distributional impact of the regime changes in several dimensions.

Appendix

The Treatment of Taxes and Contributions

We have made use of four different types of taxes. These are estimated for the years 1973 to 1996 (the period in which we observe the real labor force exit) and then projected twenty years forward.

First we use contributions (or payroll taxes) paid by both the employee and the employer. The source is INPS (www.inps.it/Doc/Professionista/aliquote/aliquote.htm) for the years 1991 to 2000. For the years between 1973 and 1990 we refer to "Relazione Generale sulla Situazione Economica del Paese," published by Ministero della Programmazione Economica e del Tesoro. The contribution rate paid by employees increases every year, from 0.0635 of gross earnings in 1973 to 0.0889 in 1999. The rate paid by employers increases from 0.1345 to 0.2381 in 1999.

Next we use income taxes, both for earnings and for pensions. In Italy, there are several income brackets attracting different tax rates (see "Testo Unico delle Imposte sui Redditi"). From 1974 to 1982 we could count 32 income brackets, which we grouped into nine groups in order to compare with the legislation of the 1990s. We also modify the tax rates accordingly (these range from 10 percent to approximately 60 percent). In this dataset we have also included rates to calculate the deductions for employees and pensioners. There are different deduction values for every income bracket and for every year.

The third type of taxes are Value Added Taxes (VAT), which would be collected on expenditures. There are mainly four VAT tax rates, which apply to different goods and services. We create a basket of goods and services with a related price index. From this we infer an average VAT rate to be applied on expenditures. This has been changing every year: the order of magnitude is 0.09089 in 1982; 0.09521 in 1983; 0.10763 until 1993, and then it decreases slightly. As we only observe earnings in our data, we calculate the total value of this tax as a percentage of earnings, taking account of the average propensity to consume. This is approximately 70 percent of income, which is about 55 percent of earnings.

References

Barbi, E. 2001. Aggiornamento ed analisi delle caratteristiche strutturali dei coefficienti di trasformazione previsti dalla legge 335/1995. In *Completezza e qualità delle informazioni statistische utilizzabili per la valutazione della spesa pensionistica,* Rapporti di Ricerca, no. 1, ed. F. Peracchi, E. Barbi, A. Brugiavini, T. Tamborrini, and E. Viviano, 8–26. Rome: Presidenza del Consiglio dei Ministri, Commissione per la Garanzia dell'Informazione Statistica (CGIS).

Brugiavini, A. 1999. Social security and retirement in Italy. In *Social security and retirement around the world,* ed. J. Gruber and D. Wise, 181–237. Chicago: University of Chicago Press.

Brugiavini, A., and F. Peracchi. 2004. Micro-modeling of retirement behavior in Italy. In *Social security programs and retirement around the world: Microestimation,* ed. J. Gruber and D. A. Wise, 345–99. Chicago: University of Chicago Press.

Brugiavini, A., F. Peracchi, and D. Wise. 2003. Pensions and retirement incentives: A tale of three countries: Italy, Spain and the U.S.A. *Giornale degli Economisti e Annali di Economia* 61 (2): 131–70.

Fornero, E., and O. Castellino. 2001. *La riforma del sistema previdenziale Italiano.* Bologna: Il Mulino.

Franco, D. 2002. Italy: A never-ending pension reform. In *Social security pension reform in Europe,* ed. M. Feldstein and H. Siebert, 251–60. Chicago: University of Chicago Press.

Gruber, J., and D. A. Wise. 1999. *Social security and retirement around the world.* Chicago: University of Chicago Press.

Gruber, J., and D. Wise. 2004. *Social security programs and retirement around the world: Micro-estimation.* Chicago: University of Chicago Press.

Ministero dell'Economia. 2001. *Aggiornamento del modello di previsione del sistema pensionistico della RGS: le previsioni '00,* June. Unpublished paper.

Rossi, N., A. Sorgato, and G. Toniolo. 1993. I conti economici italiani: Una ricostruzione statistica, 1890–1990. *Rivista di Storia Economica* 10:1–47.

Financial Implications of Social Security Reforms in Japan

Akiko S. Oishi and Takashi Oshio

7.1 Introduction

As in other OECD countries, public pension insolvency is now one of the most serious problems that an aging society poses for the Japanese economy. The proportion of people aged 65 and above—19.5 percent in 2004, which is close to the OECD average—is expected to grow faster than in any other advanced country. The latest official population projections, published in December 2006, expect the share of elderly to rise to 30.5 percent in 2025 and 39.6 percent in 2050. These projections assume that the fertility rate will remain low at 1.26 by 2050, expecting no substantial recovery from 1.26 in 2005.

Rapid population aging is a big challenge to the sustainability of the social security system, which relies heavily on future generations. Under strong demographic pressures, the government announced a pension reform plan in 1999, which has been implemented since April 2000. Since Japan's public pension program is basically a pay-as-you-go system, the government must reduce benefits and/or increase contributions in order to keep the programs financially sustainable. To finance pension benefits promised in the 1994 Reform, the contribution rate must eventually increase to 34.5 percent, which seems unacceptable. The 2000 Reform thus incorporates measures to hold down the burden on future generations by making eligibility conditions and benefit schemes less generous than previously scheduled.

Still, the chance that the 2000 reform will fail to solve insolvency problems is very high, since it is still based on seemingly overestimated popu-

Akiko S. Oishi is an associate professor of economics at Chiba University. Takashi Oshio is a professor of economics at the Graduate School of Economics, Kobe University.

lation growth[1] and rosy macroeconomic forecasts. Indeed, several analysts show that the public pension fund would be exhausted by 2050, even with several changes called for by the 2000 Reform. Net pension liabilities are estimated to be 550 trillion yen, about 108 percent of net GDP, at the end of fiscal year 1999 and will probably keep increasing.

It should be noted, however, that the typical approach to the financial liabilities often ignores the effect of policy changes on the labor supply of elderly people. It is important to understand retirement incentive effects in order to assess the full impact of pension reforms on the financial liabilities of the systems. Those effects will be critical in Japan, since postwar baby-boomers will become eligible for public pension benefits in the next few years. The reform that raise labor supply among the elderly can improve the fiscal position of the social security system and other public sector, but the fiscal implications will depend much on the provisions of the system.

This chapter aims to illustrate how social security reforms affect the financial balance sheet of retirement income systems through a change in retirement decisions by elderly workers. The reforms considered in this chapter are chosen for the purpose of cross-country comparisons and are not proposed as desirable or politically feasible in Japan. It should be also noted that the reforms are being compared to the pre-2000 Reform system, not necessarily to a solvent system. In addition, the incentive measures in this article are calculated based on the social security schemes as of the year 1996 when the data we use were surveyed. However, the basic structure of the social security programs remains the same after the Reform, and main messages and policy implications in this chapter are still relevant.

The structure of the paper is as follows. Section 7.2 provides a brief picture of retirement programs in Japan. Section 7.3 presents the base model used for analysis. Section 7.4 describes the simulation methodology and issues that arise in Japan, section 7.5 presents simulation results and discusses their policy implications, and section 7.6 concludes.

7.2   Institutional Background

7.2.1   Public Pension Plans

The principal program for private sector employees in Japan is the *Kosei-Nenkin-Hoken* (KNH), which covers about 85 percent of all employees. Government employees, private school teachers, and employees in agriculture/forestry/fishing organizations are covered by special programs

---

1. The 2000 Reform was based on 1998 population projections, which unrealistically expected the fertility rate to smoothly recover to 1.61 by 2050.

provided by *Kyosai-Kumiai* (mutual aid associations), but those programs have almost the same structure as the KNH. Thus, our analysis of public pensions in this paper mainly focuses on the KNH, and treats *Kyosai-Kumiai* members as KNH members.

The KNH operates a two-tier system. One pays flat-rate Basic Pension (*Kiso Nenkin*) benefits, which are applied to all residents: not only employees, but also the self-employed and unpaid family workers. Full Basic Pension benefits paid to those with 40-year contributions are about 67,000 yen per month. The other pays earnings-related benefits, which are only for private and public employees. Those benefits are calculated as the career average monthly earnings × the number of contribution years × the actuarial rate (which differs by birth year). Both benefits are inflation-indexed every year in terms of consumer prices, and adjusted for wage growth every five years.[2]

The normal eligibility age for full KNH benefits—both flat-rate and earnings-related components—had been 65 until 1999, but one could get full benefits at age 60 if he or she retired and stopped working at that age. Since 2001, however, the eligibility age for the flat-rate benefits is raised by one year every three years. And beginning in 2013, the eligibility age for the earnings-related benefits will also be raised by one year every three years. These two steps of increasing the eligibility age have been called for by the 1994 and 2000 Reforms. If they are implemented as scheduled, men who were born in 1961 and later and women who were born in 1966 and later will receive no pension benefits until age 65.

It should be also noted that a KNH recipient, who keeps working during ages 60 and 64, can receive reduced KNH benefits subject to an earnings test. This scheme, which is called the *Zaishoku* Pension, is roughly equivalent to the early retirement system in many other OECD countries. If the total of monthly earnings and KNH benefits exceed 280,000 yen, the marginal tax rate is 50 percent. For high-salaried elderly workers who earn more than 480,000 yen a month, the marginal tax rate is 100 percent. One has to pay KNH contributions as long as he or she keeps working, although he or she can expect an increase in future pension benefits.

Contributions are based on the employee's monthly standard earnings and are shared equally by the employee and employer. The total contribution rate for the KNH Pension—covering both the flat-rate and earnings-related components—is currently 14.642 percent, meaning that an employee and employer contribute 7.321 percent each. A female employee pays premiums at the same contribution rate, while a dependent housewife does not need to contribute.

---

2. This wage indexation was abolished in the 2000 Reform. The current system has only the price indexation.

7.2.2   Other Income Support

Unemployment insurance (UI) adds temporary income support to retired employees. In many cases, an individual who reaches age 60 leaves the firm where she or he has been working, and starts to receive KNH benefits. At the same time, it is normal to apply for UI benefits when quitting one's previous job, regardless of one's wish to find a new job. Unemployment insurance benefits for those of age 60 to 64 replace 45 to 80 percent of wage earnings at age 60, for 240 days at most. There had been many cases where the total replacement rate—adding KNH and UI benefits together—was effectively more than 100 percent of income at the first retirement age, probably reducing the incentive to work. Under a new law, effective April of 1998, however, an individual cannot receive UI and KNH benefits at the same time; as long as one is receiving UI benefits, one has to postpone receipt of KNH benefits.

Another income support that potentially interacts with public pension programs is the wage subsidy (WS) to elderly workers. This program was introduced in 1994 as a part of the public employment insurance scheme to replace the aforementioned UI benefits. The WS, which is equivalent to 15 percent of the current wage, is provided to an employee—subject to a certain wage ceiling—on condition that he or she is 60 to 64 years old and his or her wage earnings are less than 75 percent lower than his or her preretirement wage at age 60.

This WS program is independent from the public pension scheme, but its economic implications are similar to those of the *Zaishoku* Pension. Both programs are applicable to the same age group (60–64) and subject to certain earnings criteria. The WS can be treated as a negative premium in calculating social security incentives. The WS equivalent to 15 percent of wage earnings can exceed the employee's share of KNH contributions (7.321 percent). The combination of the WS and pension premium thus would add to an individual's net pension wealth, although it may not be enough to offset the negative effect from postponing receipt of pension benefits.

7.2.3   2000 Pension Reform

The 2000 Reform incorporated measures to lower contributions paid by future generations, making it inevitable that the eligibility conditions and benefit system would become less generous than scheduled in the 1994 Pension Reform. In particular, the 2000 Reform called for:

- a 5 percent reduction in earnings-related benefits
- a gradual increase in the eligible age of the earnings-related benefits to 65, from 60 since 2013 (in addition to the already-scheduled increase of the eligibility age to 65, from 60 during 2000 and 2013, called for by the 1995 Pension Reform)

- abolishing the wage indexation for pension benefits
- applying an earnings test for KNH benefits to high-salaried workers who are 65 years old and above
- a rise in the ratio of the subsidy from the central government to one-half, from the current one-third of Basic Pension benefits (without referring to any specific tax reform).

If these proposals are implemented as scheduled, the final contribution rate for KNH will be eventually pushed up to 25 percent, in contrast to the previously scheduled 34.5 percent. And the pension fund, which amounts to 144 trillion yen at the end of fiscal 1999, will not be exhausted over the next fifty years and more.

However, the risk that this 2000 Reform fails to raise sustainability of the overall social security scheme is high, because the reform depends on the seemingly optimistic estimations of population growth and rosy macroeconomic forecasts. Indeed, several simulations conducted by private think tanks and researchers show that the pension fund is likely to turn into a deficit by 2050, with more realistic assumptions about fertility rates, interest rates, and inflation rates.

7.3 Base Model

7.3.1 Data Source

Our analysis is based on the *Survey on Labor Market Participation of Older Persons* (*Konenreisha Shugyo Jittai Chosa*), which was conducted in October 1996 and published in December 1997 by the Ministry of Labor. The survey covers men and women aged 55 to 69 who were employees, company executives, self-employed, or not working. Our analysis centers on those who were employed at age 55 and had been working until 1996. The size of the sample we use for analysis is 4,141, out of 21,219 in the survey.

A major problem is that the data from this survey are cross-sectional, not longitudinal. What we know from the survey is an individual's age, current working status, wage income, pension benefits, and so on at the survey date. The survey asks each individual what kind of firm (industry and size) he or she was working for at age 55, whether and when he or she would face mandatory retirement, and when he or she wants to retire (if working at the time of the survey). However, any other longitudinal information, including wage profiles and the actual date of retirement, is not available: what we know from the survey is just whether an individual was retired or still working in the survey year of 1996. Moreover, data on an individual's background, such as education and family situation, are limited.

The most important quantitative information available from the survey relates to an individual's current wage earnings and his or her social security and other benefits, on which our incentive calculations are based. It is, however, difficult to capture the diversity of incentives in employer-based pension policies, and information about lump-sum retirement benefits is not available. Moreover, answers regarding the category and amount of benefits seem at times to be unreliable, probably due to inaccurate and/or limited knowledge among respondents about social security programs. We estimate the theoretical value of social security benefits based on projected wage profiles, and make some adjustment if the discrepancy between theoretical and actual figures is too large to be ignored.

7.3.2   Cohorts in Focus

To estimate the impact of pension reforms on retirement decisions and assess its financial implications, we limit our sample to those who were working at age 55. We use multiple birth cohorts: that is, fifteen birth cohorts of ages 55 to 69 in the survey year 1996. This is because the sample size of a single birth cohort is very small (around 400). Individuals who are older than age 55 in 1996 are de-aged back to age 55 by being given the projected earnings history (which is discussed in the next section) and other characteristics they had at age 55 (which are known from the survey).

Two things should be mentioned about spousal issues. The first is how to obtain spousal information, which is needed to calculate family social security wealth (SSW) and other incentives to retire. Matching can be completely made if a spouse is 55 to 69 years old, since she or he is included in the sample and her or his information is available from the survey.[3] If a spouse's age is below 55 or above 69, however, we cannot know anything about her or him. We exclude the latter type of individual—whose age tends to be close to 55 or 69 in most cases—from the sample. We believe that this adjustment has no substantial impact on the results, because we de-age the observations aged 56 years and over back to age 55; the average age difference between husbands and wives is in accordance with the national average.

The second issue is how to avoid spousal double counting. If both a husband and his wife are included in the sample cohort, we would have their SSW twice in the sum. We solve this problem by including only men and single women in the analysis and incorporating all benefits received by married women (both from their own work and their husbands) in the cal-

---

3. The question sheets of the survey are sent to randomly selected households that have at least one household member aged between 55 and 69; everyone aged 55 to 69 in the surveyed households is requested to fill in the sheet and send it back to the office. Thus, for example, in the case of a couple with a husband aged 65 and wife 63, both are included in the survey, whereas in the case of a husband 55 and wife 53, only the husband is included. We exclude the latter type of couples from the sample.

culations for the husbands.[4] The sample, after adjustment, consists of 8,101 people—3,489 couples, 548 single male workers, and 575 single female workers.

7.3.3   Earnings Projections

Backward and forward projections of wage earnings are required to analyze the impact of social security incentives on retirement decisions. With limited longitudinal information, our projections of the age-earnings profiles depend largely on the cross-sectional data. Also, we use information from the Wage Census (*Chingin Sensasu*) to complement reported individual characteristics observed in the survey. To summarize our methodology, we use: (1) current wage earnings as a benchmark, (2) average age-wage profiles obtained from the survey for the ages 55 to 69, and (3) cohort-specific age-earnings profiles in backward projections, starting at age 55 and below, obtained from the Wage Census.

For earnings projections for ages 55 to 69, we rely on average wage growth rates observed from the survey, because cohort-specific information is not available. To calculate average wage growth, we regress the logarithm of monthly earnings (for males and females, separately) on an individual's age, experience of mandatory retirement, job categories, firm size at the employee's age of 55, whether a private or public employee at 55, and residential areas. All independent variables are dummies.

Based on this regression, we create each sample's earnings profile for the ages 55 to 69, using the reported current wage earnings as a benchmark. The wage growth rate is thus set to be the same for each individual: it is calculated by taking the difference in parameters on the two subsequent age dummies. The timing of mandatory retirement, which in most cases is 60 years old, is important in projecting the earnings profile. We assume that one will face mandatory retirement at 60, regardless of her or his desire to go to secondary labor markets.

To construct earnings histories before age 55, we use age-earnings data from the Wage Census, which is conducted and published every year by the Ministry of Health, Labor, and Welfare. The Wage Census provides average age-wage profiles by industry, firm size, and educational background. We project wage earnings backward, using estimated earnings at 55 as a benchmark and also using the cohort-specific wage curve.

Based on those earnings projections, we compute SSW (Social Security Wealth) and two kinds of incentive measures: PV (Peak Value) and OV (Option Value) at each age for each individual.[5] The technical problem

4. We also exclude women whose husbands are assumed to be deceased.
5. See Stock and Wise (1990) and Coile and Gruber (2000a) for the definition and implications of the option value, and see Coile and Gruber (2000a, 2000b) and Gruber and Wise (2003) for those of the peak value.

here is how to deal with multiple retirement income programs: KNH, UI, and *Zaishoku* benefits. In the previous study (Oshio and Oishi 2004), we captured the role of multiple retirement programs by creating weighted average incentive measures that incorporated all possible pathways to retirement. We cannot allocate workers across multiple programs based on these weights, since benefits are linked to their wage profiles. Instead, we use the weights to compute the weighted average of each program's benefits.

7.3.4   Model Estimates

In this section, we describe the empirical framework for regression analysis on the impact of social security on retirement. We first have to estimate each sample's previous working/retirement status, since our survey tells us only whether each sample is retired in the survey year of 1996. Hence, we first explain how to build up the quasi-longitudinal data; then we address the reduced-form models of retirement decisions.

To estimate models for incentive measures we select from the survey the individuals who were working at age 55 *and* are expected to have kept working until 1995, one year before the survey year. We apply the probit models to them to explain their retirement decisions in 1996: whether to keep working or to retire. The main problem of our analysis is that we cannot exactly identify those who were working in 1995, due to a lack of longitudinal information. Hence, we first assume that those who were working in 1996 were also working in 1995. And for those who were already retired, we only use those whose age of retirement can be identified from their reported answers about mandatory retirement and subsequent job experience. Thus, 2,629 men and 1,075 women out of the total sample are estimated to have been working in 1995—whose statistical characteristics are summarized in table 7.1.

For baseline simulations, we compute the projected work and retirement trajectory for our cohorts under the pre-2000 Reform scheme, using the two models with PV and OV. We use models that have controls for earnings, demographics, and sectors. Each model includes SSW. For ages, we have two types of methodologies: one with linear ages, the other with age dummies. Earnings controls consist of projected earnings for next year, average lifetime earnings, and the squares of each. Other controls include property income, dummies for health conditions, new occupational dummies, dummies for four categories of firm size at age 55, and eight dummies of residential areas.

Table 7.2 summarizes estimation results for men and women, respectively. For men, the coefficients on PV and OV are negative and significant in both S1 models, while in S3 models we find negative and insignificant impact of incentive measures on retirement. For women, the coefficient on PV is negative and significant in both cases of S1 and S3, while it is insignificant in OV models. For both men and women (supporting intuitive

Table 7.1   **Summary statistics for the estimation sample**

	Mean	Standard deviation	Min.	Max.
Males (sample size = 2,629)				
Retired	0.132	0.339	0.000	1.000
SSW (billion yen)	32.748	9.412	6.100	74.558
SSA (billion yen)	−0.050	2.476	−7.212	6.130
Peak value (billion yen)	1.844	3.761	−7.212	13.319
Option value (billion yen)	63.417	43.952	1.125	396.407
Property income (10 thousand yen)	2.099	13.850	0.000	500.000
Health condition: not well	0.151	0.358	0.000	1.000
Health condition: bad or sick	0.035	0.183	0.000	1.000
Projected earnings (billion yen)	3.393	2.264	0.100	14.417
Average lifetime earnings (billion yen)	3.486	1.792	0.799	7.080
Square of PE	16.635	25.715	0.010	207.860
Square of ALE	15.359	14.765	0.639	50.126
Age	61.324	3.660	55.000	69.000
Lives with spouse	0.858	0.349	0.000	1.000
Females (sample size = 1,075)				
Retired	0.186	0.389	0.000	1.000
SSW (billion yen)	33.633	14.838	9.057	80.908
SSA (billion yen)	0.239	1.626	−6.512	6.185
Peak value (billion yen)	1.909	3.003	−6.512	12.761
Option value (billion yen)	106.208	66.216	1.218	442.930
Property income (10 thousand yen)	0.804	3.836	0.000	66.000
Health condition: not well	0.148	0.355	0.000	1.000
Health condition: bad or sick	0.032	0.175	0.000	1.000
Projected earnings (billion yen)	1.957	1.270	0.120	12.000
Average lifetime earnings (billion yen)	1.985	1.163	0.799	7.080
Square of PE	5.440	10.762	0.014	144.000
Square of ALE	5.292	7.928	0.639	50.126
Age	59.309	3.378	55.000	69.000
Lives with spouse	0.735	0.442	0.000	1.000

explanations of income and substitution effects) average lifetime earnings tend to increase disincentives to work, while projected earnings tend to decrease them. The coefficient on SSW is positive in all cases, although insignificant in some, suggesting the existence of the wealth effect of SSW on retirement; a reduced SSW is expected to encourage people to keep working.

7.3.5   Predicted Probabilities of Retirement and Pension Reform

We can predict a probability of retirement at each age beyond 55, based on the previously-mentioned models and projected earnings. We first compute baseline hazard rates, assuming no policy change from the pre-2000 Reform schemes. Then we consider the following four policy changes, the last of which is specific to Japan:

Model	PV—S1	PV—S3	OP—S1	OP—S3
	A. Male sample (N = 2,623)			
SSW	0.000	0.001	0.031	0.004
	(0.006)	(0.006)	(0.006)	(0.009)
Incentive measure	−0.119	−0.071	−0.006	−0.001
	(0.013)	(0.042)	(0.002)	(0.002)
Property income	0.007	0.007	0.007	0.007
	(0.004)	(0.004)	(0.004)	(0.004)
Health condition: not well	0.287	0.299	0.278	0.303
	(0.088)	(0.090)	(0.087)	(0.091)
Health condition: bad or sick	1.075	1.133	1.084	1.158
	(0.154)	(0.167)	(0.150)	(0.152)
Projected earnings	−0.240	−0.227	−0.990	−0.274
	(0.406)	(0.485)	(0.399)	(0.494)
Average lifetime earnings	0.781	0.793	1.374	0.847
	(0.381)	(0.447)	(0.397)	(0.458)
Square of PE	0.009	0.009	0.048	0.011
	(0.021)	(0.025)	(0.020)	(0.025)
Square of ALE	−0.097	−0.099	−0.127	−0.102
	(0.024)	(0.027)	(0.025)	(0.027)
Age	−0.038		−0.068	
	(0.019)		(0.021)	
Age 55		0.509		0.524
		(0.364)		(0.358)
Age 56		0.207		0.420
		(0.385)		(0.369)
Age 57		−0.247		−0.099
		(0.416)		(0.404)
Age 58		0.225		0.429
		(0.392)		(0.397)
Age 59		0.537		1.336
		(0.609)		(0.398)
Age 60		0.871		1.406
		(0.496)		(0.396)
Age 61		0.023		0.545
		(0.512)		(0.427)
Age 62		0.312		0.839
		(0.516)		(0.431)
Age 63		0.128		0.651
		(0.529)		(0.454)
Age 64		0.606		1.029
		(0.471)		(0.428)
Age 65		0.174		0.576
		(0.479)		(0.449)
Age 66		0.099		0.507
		(0.521)		(0.491)
Age 67		−0.247		0.156
		(0.545)		(0.487)
Age 68		−0.077		0.322
		(0.548)		(0.543)
Pseudo R^2	0.175	0.208	0.135	0.207
Other controls	Yes	Yes	Yes	Yes

Table 7.2   **Retirement probits**

Table 7.2 (continued)

Model	PV—S1	PV—S3	OP—S1	OP—S3
	B. Female sample (N = 1,075)			
SSW	0.010	0.010	0.014	0.007
	(0.004)	(0.004)	(0.006)	(0.006)
Incentive measure	−0.137	−0.163	−0.001	0.001
	(0.026)	(0.067)	(0.002)	(0.002)
Property income	0.056	0.056	0.058	0.057
	(0.017)	(0.017)	(0.018)	(0.017)
Health condition: not well	0.138	0.194	0.152	0.209
	(0.132)	(0.134)	(0.130)	(0.135)
Health condition: bad or sick	1.230	1.242	1.129	1.255
	(0.231)	(0.238)	(0.229)	(0.238)
Projected earnings	−0.288	−0.535	−0.794	−0.664
	(0.461)	(0.485)	(0.440)	(0.482)
Average lifetime earnings	0.330	0.626	0.766	0.618
	(0.536)	(0.539)	(0.536)	(0.540)
Square of PE	0.043	0.061	0.068	0.065
	(0.033)	(0.033)	(0.033)	(0.033)
Square of ALE	−0.095	−0.121	−0.118	−0.110
	(0.071)	(0.065)	(0.072)	(0.066)
Age	−0.029		0.036	
	(0.022)		(0.024)	
Age 55		0.321		0.432
		(0.238)		(0.234)
Age 56		0.067		0.554
		(0.309)		(0.252)
Age 57		0.418		0.843
		(0.286)		(0.247)
Age 58		0.060		0.607
		(0.324)		(0.271)
Age 59		−0.142		1.253
		(0.601)		(0.279)
Age 60		0.225		1.270
		(0.469)		(0.284)
Age 61		0.044		1.117
		(0.490)		(0.317)
Age 62		−0.433		0.656
		(0.515)		(0.365)
Age 63		−0.675		0.454
		(0.521)		(0.380)
Age 64		0.275		1.314
		(0.494)		(0.391)
Age 65		−0.216		0.795
		(0.542)		(0.454)
Age 66		−0.276		0.759
		(0.607)		(0.759)
Age 67		−0.981		0.182
		(0.544)		(0.418)
Age 68		−0.283		0.699
		(0.725)		(0.616)
Pseudo R^2	0.151	0.172	0.125	0.168
Other controls	Yes	Yes	Yes	Yes

Notes: Other control variables are 9 occupational dummies, dummies for 4 categories of establishment size, and 8 regional dummies. The estimated parameters on these variables are not reported. Numbers in parentheses show robust standard errors.

- The Three-Year Reform calls for a three-year increase in the ages of early and normal retirement age (ERA and NRA hereafter). In Japan, this means shifting the ERA to 63 from 60 and the NRA to 68 from 65. In this reform, we assume that the spouse retires at the original ERA, both before and after the reform.
- The Actuarial Reform implements a 6 percent annual actuarial adjustment per year away from the NRA, without changing the ERA, NRA, or replacement rate. In this reform, we assume that benefits become available at the existing ERA level and keep benefits at the NRA the same as in the current system.
- The Common Reform calls for a common system, with (1) the ERA of 60, the NRA of 65, (2) a benefit equal to 60 percent of the lesser of average indexed lifetime earnings and the 90th percentile of the wage distribution for men, (3) a 6 percent per year actuarial adjustment, and (4) a survivor benefit equal to 100 percent of her or his spouse's benefit.[6] We assume that if a person retires before age 60 she or he still receives benefits starting at age 60, and that taxation of benefits is the same as in the base case.
- The JP 2000 Reform calls for an NRA of 65, with no ERA, and a 5 percent reduction in earning-related benefits, reflecting the final stage implied by the Pension Reform.

For all of these four reforms, we consider three methodologies regarding ages to check the sensitivity of the results to the treatment of ages in the estimated models: S1, based on the models with linear ages; S2, based on the models with age dummies, leaving them unchanged; and S3, based on and incrementing the models with age dummies. We perform these simulations by taking the estimated retirement model, plugging in new incentive measures and possibly new retirement ages, and estimating for each individual a new probability of retirement. Also, it should be remembered that the Japanese system already has an ERA of 60 and an NRA of 65, and that the JP 2000 Reform calls for no benefit at all before age 65.[7]

7.4   Simulation Methodology

7.4.1   Methodology

The goal of our simulation is to estimate the impact of pension reforms on older workers' net fiscal contributions to retirement income finances.

6. In Japan, a widow can receive the maximum of (a) three-fourths of her husband's worker benefit, (b) the full amount of her own benefit, and (c) half of her husband's worker benefit and half of her own worker benefit, in addition to her Basic Pension benefit. The first option is chosen in most cases, since womens' wage income is much lower than mens', and women work shorter years than men. A widower cannot receive the survivor benefit.

7. Disability pension benefits are available, but they are strictly targeted to accidentally handicapped people, not used for transitory income support until the normal eligibility age.

Such reforms will have two effects: (1) an automatic effect on fiscal contributions, by changing contributions and benefits for a given work history, and (2) an additional effect, through labor supply responses to the reform. We will estimate the fiscal implications of both, using the retirement model. It should be noted, however, that the result is an estimate of the steady-state impact of the reforms, with the transitory path neglected for simplicity.

The steps that we take are summarized in what follows. First, we project each worker's wage earnings forward (based on the predicted wage earnings) and backward (based on the Wage Census), as well as his or her SSW and incentive measures at each age.

Second, we obtain his or her estimated probability of exit at each age by multiplying incentive measures (and other time-independent variables augmented for the current age and year) by the estimated coefficients in the probit functions and plug through the normal distribution. We also explicitly account for the probability of dying at each age from the official mortality tables—to know whether he or she remains in the labor force, retires, or dies.

Third, we calculate net SSW at each age for those exiting the labor force to retirement and those exiting it to death, corresponding to the social security system that is applied to them. For couples, we calculate the SSW values, assuming that the spouse retires at the ERA. Net SSW is calculated for the entire family's SS payroll taxes and other taxes at each age, paid by both spouses.

Fourth, we get the expected net SSW of those exiting the labor force at each age, by multiplying the probabilities of entering retirement and of death by the net SSW associated with these states.

Fifth, we add the expected net SSW across all potential states, to calculate the average SSW that the individual is expected to receive under a given social security scheme. From the government's viewpoint, this average SSW is the net payment to the individual who leaves the labor force. The difference of the level between the baseline case and alternative reform scenarios quantitatively shows the financial implications of the reforms.

Finally, we separate out the fiscal effects of the reforms that automatically arise due to changes in program rules and those that arise due to labor supply responses. We call the former the *mechanical* effect and the latter the *behavioral* effect. We compute the mechanical effect by simulating the paths of taxes and benefits without assuming any change in retirement behavior: that is, taking the baseline path of exiting the labor market and applying this path to the new taxes/benefits structure. We then obtain the fiscal implications of the behavioral effect as the difference between the total effect and the mechanical effect.

7.4.2   Issues That Arise in Japan

The methodology discussed in the previous section is largely applicable to Japan, but there are some minor issues that more particularly arise for Japan. First, we have to ignore the survivor pension benefit for dependent children, for simplicity. We have little information about an individual's family members, and survivor pension benefits for dependent children are generally strict, especially if they are older than 18. We also ignore the possibility of divorce after age 55.

Second, in calculating taxes, we include all payroll taxes (SS contributions paid by both employees and employers), personal income taxes, and consumption taxes (VAT), to assess the magnitude of a change in tax revenues at both the SS budget and total government budget. The consumption tax rate is currently 5 percent in Japan, and we roughly estimate consumption tax revenues by multiplying personal disposable income by the consumption-tax factor, which is calculated so that for the economy as a whole VAT revenues = consumption tax factor × personal disposable income in the national accounts.[8]

Third, there is a risk that we may overestimate the impact on older workers' labor supply in Japan, since there are limited chances to get a full-time job after age 60. We cannot rule out the case that a substantial part of policy incentives to stimulate. working will be induced to firms rather than older workers through a reduction in wage. Our methodology assumes that additional labor supply, which is stimulated by pension reforms, can be smoothly realized without a reduction in wage.

7.5   Simulation Results

7.5.1   Main Results

Table 7.3 shows the present discounted values of gross and net SS benefits for the four reforms—the Three-Year, Actuarial, Common, and JP 2000 Reforms—in comparison with the base case. For each, the effect of the reform on tax revenues is broken down into payroll taxes (SS contributions), income taxes, and consumption taxes. The calculations are based on PV and OV models and methodologies S1, S2, and S3—that is, six types of combination. The numbers are reported in euros per worker.[9]

This table indicates that the financial implications depend on the type of

---

8. The tax rate was 3 percent in the survey year 1996, but we use the current 5 percent to assess the impact of the reforms on consumption tax revenues. The consumption tax factor is assumed to be equal to 0.0397, which is implicitly calculated from national accounts and tax statistics.

9. We use the CPI to put values in 2001 yen, and translate them to euros using the December 31, 2001, euro/yen exchange rate (117.32).

Table 7.3   **Total fiscal impact of reform**

	Present discounted value (in euros)					Total change relative to base (%)			
	Base	Three-Year Increment	Actuarial	Common	JP2000	Three-Year Increment	Actuarial	Common	JP2000
				Peak value—S1					
Benefits	249,744	219,839	206,612	240,321	194,463	-12.0	-17.3	-3.8	-22.1
After-tax income	208,521	214,765	211,485	180,744	213,511	3.0	1.4	-13.3	2.4
Taxes									
Payroll	37,478	44,432	37,760	34,630	38,458	18.6	0.8	-7.6	2.6
Income	10,621	10,740	10,635	9,102	10,703	1.1	0.1	-14.3	0.8
Consumption	8,269	8,516	8,386	7,167	8,467	3.0	1.4	-13.3	2.4
Total	56,369	63,689	56,781	50,899	57,628	13.0	0.7	-9.7	2.2
Net change (in euros)		-37,225	-43,544	-3,954	-56,541				
Change as % of base benefits		-14.9	-17.4	-1.6	-22.6				
				Peak value—S2					
Benefits	243,678	215,322	200,309	234,580	190,789	-11.6	-17.8	-3.7	-21.7
After-tax income	201,983	206,443	203,914	188,694	205,897	2.2	1.0	-6.6	1.9
Taxes									
Payroll	36,509	43,082	36,496	34,898	37,041	18.0	0.0	-4.4	1.5
Income	10,336	10,401	10,330	9,525	10,396	0.6	-0.1	-7.8	0.6
Consumption	8,010	8,186	8,086	7,483	8,165	2.2	1.0	-6.6	1.9
Total	54,854	61,670	54,912	51,905	55,602	12.4	0.1	-5.4	1.4
Net change (in euros)		-35,172	-43,426	-6,149	-53,637				
Change as % of base benefits		-14.1	-17.4	-2.5	-21.5				

(continued)

Table 7.3 (continued)

		Present discounted value (in euros)				Total change relative to base (%)			
	Base	Three-Year increment	Actuarial	Common	JP2000	Three-Year Increment	Actuarial	Common	JP2000
				Peak value—S3					
Benefits	243,678	219,182	200,309	234,580	188,208	-10.1	-17.8	-3.7	-22.8
After-tax income	201,983	242,905	203,914	188,694	236,078	20.3	1.0	-6.6	-16.9
Taxes									
Payroll	36,509	47,529	36,496	34,898	41,038	30.2	0.0	-4.4	12.4
Income	10,336	11,915	10,330	9,525	11,569	15.3	-0.1	-7.8	11.9
Consumption	8,010	9,632	8,086	7,483	9,362	20.3	1.0	-6.6	16.9
Total	54,854	69,077	54,912	51,905	61,968	25.9	0.1	-5.4	13.0
Net change (in euros)		-38,719	-43,426	-6,149	-62,584				
Change as % of base benefits		-15.5	-17.4	-2.5	-25.1				
				Option value—S1					
Benefits	250,012	220,642	203,991	245,195	187,853	-11.7	-18.4	-1.9	-24.9
After-tax income	209,029	224,215	207,124	205,310	221,921	7.3	-0.9	-1.8	6.2
Taxes									
Payroll	38,108	46,623	37,695	37,631	39,444	22.3	-1.1	-1.3	3.5
Income	10,583	11,121	10,379	10,291	10,940	5.1	-1.9	-2.8	3.4
Consumption	8,289	8,891	8,213	8,142	8,800	7.3	-0.9	-1.8	6.2
Total	56,980	66,635	56,288	56,064	59,185	16.9	-1.2	-1.6	3.9
Net change (in euros)		-39,025	-45,329	-3,901	-64,363				
Change as % of base benefits		-15.6	-18.2	-1.6	-25.8				

Option value—S2

Benefits	243,651	217,996	200,372	236,168	192,243	-10.5	-17.8	-3.1	-21.1
After-tax income	202,114	206,151	204,245	202,965	205,020	2.0	1.1	0.4	1.4
Taxes									
Payroll	36,519	43,463	36,526	36,414	36,916	19.0	0.0	-0.3	1.1
Income	10,342	10,438	10,345	10,299	10,415	0.9	0.0	-0.4	0.7
Consumption	8,015	8,175	8,099	8,049	8,130	2.0	1.1	0.4	1.4
Total	54,876	62,076	54,970	54,761	55,461	13.1	0.2	-0.2	1.1
Net change (in euros)						-32,855	-43,374	-7,368	-51,993
Change as % of base benefits						-13.2	-17.4	-3.0	-20.8

Option value—S3

Benefits	243,651	213,762	200,372	236,168	182,237	-12.3	-17.8	-3.1	-25.2
After-tax income	202,114	254,556	204,245	202,965	254,697	25.9	1.1	0.4	26.0
Taxes									
Payroll	36,519	48,335	36,526	36,414	43,271	32.4	0.0	-0.3	18.5
Income	10,342	12,322	10,345	10,299	12,180	19.2	0.0	-0.4	17.8
Consumption	8,015	12,322	8,099	8,049	10,100	53.7	1.1	0.4	26.0
Total	54,876	72,979	54,970	54,761	65,550	33.0	0.2	-0.2	19.5
Net change (in euros)						-47,993	-43,374	-7,368	-72,089
Change as % of base benefits						-19.2	-17.4	-3.0	-28.9

reform, and that their extent relies heavily on the combination of models and methodologies. We find that net benefits decline in all cases, although the magnitude of reduction relies much on the type of reform and the combination of models and methodologies. First, the Three-Year Reform saves net benefits by 13.2 percent to 19.2 percent, with S3 reducing them more than S1 and S2. The Actuarial Reform turns to be somewhat more effective than the Three-Year Reform in saving the benefits, suggesting that the current system is more generous than actuarially fair. In sharp contrast to these two reforms, the Common Reform fails to significantly reduce net benefits. To be sure, the proposed actuarial adjustment incorporated in this reform should reduce the benefits, as suggested in the case of the Actuarial Reform. This effect seems to be, however, mostly offset by the proposed benefit at 65 (equal to 60 percent of the average indexed lifetime earnings) and the survivor benefit (equal to 100 percent of her or his spouse's benefit)—both of which are more generous than in the current system. Actually, we find little change in gross benefits from the base case. Finally, the JP 2000 Reform, which reduces net benefits by 20.8 percent to 28.9 percent, is more effective than the other three reforms, mainly because it pays no pension benefits until age 65 and incorporates a 5 percent reduction of earnings-related benefits.

In addition, dividing the impact into the changes in gross benefits and taxes, we find that reforms other than the Common Reform succeed in reducing gross benefits, with the Three-Year Reform raising tax revenues most. This result suggests that the Three-Year Reform is more effective in postponing exit from labor force (see the following).

Table 7.4 divides the impact into the mechanical effect and the fiscal implications of the behavioral effect. In all cases, most of the financial effect can be attributed to the mechanical effect; the fiscal implications of the behavioral effect are relatively small, even positive in some models. This probably reflects two factors: (1) limited responsiveness of retirement to incentive measures, which is implied by small coefficients on them, as reported in tables 7.2, panels A and B, and (2) the actuarial adjustment already incorporated in the current scheme (especially for the earnings-related component).[10] The effects of the proposed reforms thus center on the eligibility conditions and benefit payment scheme, rather than changes in the working/retirement behavior of the elderly.

The results in tables 7.4, 7.5, and 7.6 also depend greatly on the model specifications and estimation methodologies. We find that OV tends to produce a greater reduction in net benefits than PV, while S3 tends to produce a larger reduction than S1 and S2. The estimated impact is the biggest for the combination of OV and S3 and is the smallest for the combination of PV and S2, with some exceptions.

---

10. In addition, older workers receive WS, which is a subsidy equivalent to 15 percent of wage income, although this scheme has not been widely used to date.

Table 7.4 Decomposition of the total effect of reform (in euros)

	Three-Year Increment			Actuarial			Common			JP2000		
	Mechanical	Behavioral	Total	Mechanical	Behavioral	Total	Mechanical	Behavioral	Total	Mechanical	Behavioral	Total
					Peak value—S1							
Benefits	-27,049	-2,857	-29,905	-44,676	1,544	-43,131	-8,836	-587	-9,423	-52,669	-2,612	-55,281
After-tax income	1,938	4,306	6,244	2,182	782	2,964	1,687	-29,464	-27,777	743	4,247	4,990
Taxes												
Payroll	7,002	-48	6,954	0	281	281	0	-2,848	-2,848	429	551	980
Income	0	119	119	0	13	13	0	-1,519	-1,519	0	82	82
Consumption	77	171	248	87	31	118	67	-1,168	-1,101	29	168	198
Total	7,079	242	7,320	87	326	412	67	-5,536	-5,469	458	802	1,260
Net change	-34,127	-3,098	-37,225	-44,762	1,219	-43,544	-8,903	4,949	-3,954	-53,127	-3,414	-56,541
Change as % of base benefits	-13.7	-1.2	-14.9	-17.9	0.5	-17.4	-3.6	2.0	-1.6	-21.3	-1.4	-22.6
					Peak value—S2							
Benefits	-26,130	-2,226	-28,356	-43,328	-41	-43,369	-7,066	-2,032	-9,098	-50,847	-2,043	-52,890
After-tax income	1,843	2,617	4,460	2,065	-134	1,931	1,601	-14,890	-13,289	852	3,062	3,914
Taxes												
Payroll	6,666	-93	6,573	0	-14	-14	0	-1,612	-1,611	190	343	532
Income	0	65	65	0	-6	-6	0	-811	-811	0	60	60
Consumption	73	104	177	82	-5	77	63	-590	-527	34	121	155
Total	6,739	76	6,815	82	-24	57	64	-3,013	-2,949	224	524	748
Net change	-32,869	-2,302	-35,172	-43,409	-17	-43,426	-7,130	981	-6,149	-51,070	-2,567	-53,637
Change as % of base benefits	-13.5	-0.9	-14.4	-17.8	0.0	-17.8	-2.9	0.4	-2.5	-21.0	-1.1	-22.0

Change in present discounted value (spanning header over Actuarial, Common, JP2000 groups)

(continued)

Table 7.4 (continued)

	Change in present discounted value											
	Three-Year Increment			Actuarial			Common			JP2000		
	Mechanical	Behavioral	Total	Mechanical	Behavioral	Total	Mechanical	Behavioral	Total	Mechanical	Behavioral	Total
					Peak value—S3							
Benefits	−26,130	1,633	−24,496	−43,328	−41	−43,369	−7,066	−2,032	−9,098	−50,847	−4,623	−55,470
After-tax income	1,843	39,079	40,922	2,065	−134	1,931	1,601	−14,890	−13,289	852	33,244	34,096
Taxes												
Payroll	6,666	4,354	11,020	0	−14	−14	0	−1,612	−1,611	190	4,339	4,529
Income	0	1,579	1,579	0	−6	−6	0	−811	−811	0	1,233	1,233
Consumption	73	1,550	1,623	82	−5	77	63	−590	−527	34	1,318	1,352
Total	6,739	7,483	14,222	82	−24	57	64	−3,013	−2,949	224	6,890	7,114
Net change	−32,869	−5,850	−38,719	−43,409	−17	−43,426	−7,130	981	−6,149	−51,070	−11,513	−62,584
Change as % of base benefits	−13.5	−2.4	−15.9	−17.8	0.0	−17.8	−2.9	0.4	−2.5	−21.0	−4.7	−25.7
					Option value—S1							
Benefits	−28,749	−621	−29,370	−44,874	−1,147	−46,021	−4,510	−306	−4,817	−53,751	−8,408	−62,159
After-tax income	2,087	13,099	15,186	2,379	−4,284	−1,905	1,792	−5,511	−3,719	654	12,238	12,892
Taxes												
Payroll	7,333	1,182	8,515	0	−413	−413	0	−477	−477	685	651	1,336
Income	0	538	538	0	−204	−204	0	−292	−292	0	357	357
Consumption	83	519	602	94	−170	−76	71	−219	−147	26	485	511
Total	7,416	2,239	9,655	94	−786	−692	71	−987	−916	711	1,494	2,205
Net change	−36,165	−2,860	−39,025	−44,968	−361	−45,329	−4,581	681	−3,901	−54,462	−9,901	−64,363
Change as % of base benefits	−14.5	−1.1	−15.6	−18.0	−0.1	−18.1	−1.8	0.3	−1.6	−21.8	−4.0	−25.7

Option value—S2

Benefits	-26,096	441	-25,655	-43,294	15	-43,279	-7,077	-406	-7,483	-50,810	-597	-51,408
After-tax income	1,846	2,191	4,037	2,067	63	2,130	1,603	-752	851	854	2,052	2,906
Taxes												
Payroll	6,661	283	6,944	0	7	7	0	-105	-105	190	207	397
Income	0	96	96	0	3	3	0	-43	-43	0	73	73
Consumption	73	87	160	82	3	84	64	-30	34	34	81	115
Total	6,734	466	7,201	82	12	94	64	-178	-115	224	362	586
Net change	-32,830	-26	-32,855	-43,376	2	-43,374	-7,141	-227	-7,368	-51,034	-960	-51,993
Change as % of base benefits	-13.5	0.0	-13.5	-17.8	0.0	-17.8	-2.9	-0.1	-3.0	-20.9	-0.4	-21.3

Option value—S3

Benefits	-26,096	-3,794	-29,889	-43,294	15	-43,279	-7,077	-406	-7,483	-50,810	-10,604	-61,414
After-tax income	1,846	50,596	52,441	2,067	63	2,130	1,603	-752	851	854	51,729	52,583
Taxes												
Payroll	6,661	5,154	11,815	0	7	7	0	-105	-105	190	6,562	6,752
Income	0	1,980	1,980	0	3	3	0	-43	-43	0	1,838	1,838
Consumption	73	2,006	2,080	82	3	84	64	-30	34	34	2,051	2,085
Total	6,734	9,141	15,875	82	12	94	64	-178	-115	224	10,451	10,675
Net change	-32,830	-12,935	-45,965	-43,376	2	-43,374	-7,141	-227	-7,368	-51,034	-21,055	-72,089
Change as % of base benefits	-13.5	-5.3	-18.8	-17.8	0.0	-17.8	-2.9	-0.1	-3.0	-20.9	-8.6	-29.6

Table 7.5 Distributional analysis (OV—S1)

		Present discounted value				Change relative to base			
	Base	Three-Year Increment	Actuarial	Common	JP2000	Three-Year Increment	Actuarial	Common	JP2000
		Quintile 1 (highest)							
Benefits	335,041	295,519	269,756	402,395	249,898	−39,522	−65,285	67,354	−85,142
After-tax income	394,134	411,898	383,865	385,330	406,366	17,763	−10,269	−8,804	12,232
Taxes									
Payroll	54,945	65,575	54,239	54,047	58,587	10,630	−706	−898	3,643
Income	29,648	31,073	29,081	28,823	30,490	1,425	−567	−825	841
Consumption	15,629	16,334	15,222	15,280	16,114	704	−407	−349	485
Total	100,222	112,981	98,542	98,150	105,191	12,759	−1,680	−2,072	4,969
Net change						−52,281	−63,604	69,426	−90,112
Change as % of base benefits						−15.6	−19.0	20.7	−26.9
		Quintile 2							
Benefits	277,682	245,859	224,759	279,766	207,877	−31,823	−52,923	2,084	−69,805
After-tax income	241,606	252,157	235,207	236,206	248,904	10,550	−6,400	−5,401	7,298
Taxes									
Payroll	44,233	53,179	43,689	43,531	46,002	8,947	−544	−702	1,769
Income	9,455	9,967	9,271	9,199	9,847	512	−184	−256	392
Consumption	9,581	9,999	9,327	9,367	9,870	418	−254	−214	289
Total	63,269	73,146	62,287	62,097	65,720	9,877	−981	−1,171	2,451
Net change						−41,700	−51,941	3,255	−72,256
Change as % of base benefits						−15.0	−18.7	1.2	−26.0

Quintile 3

Benefits	245,695	216,424	199,933	232,467	184,085	−29,272	−45,763	−13,119	−61,610
After-tax income	189,163	197,954	184,389	184,890	195,569	8,791	−4,773	−4,273	6,406
Taxes									
Payroll	36,671	44,900	36,272	36,208	37,928	8,229	−399	−463	1,257
Income	6,662	7,033	6,532	6,481	6,948	372	−130	−181	286
Consumption	7,501	7,850	7,312	7,332	7,755	349	−189	−169	254
Total	50,834	59,783	50,116	50,020	52,631	8,949	−718	−813	1,797
Net change						−38,221	−45,045	−12,415	−63,407
Change as % of base benefits						−15.6	−18.3	−5.1	−25.8

Quintile 4

Benefits	214,549	188,910	177,186	187,450	162,407	−25,640	−37,364	−27,099	−52,142
After-tax income	145,567	152,758	142,168	142,157	151,008	7,190	−3,400	−3,410	5,441
Taxes									
Payroll	31,217	38,835	30,930	30,935	31,860	7,619	−287	−281	643
Income	4,903	5,169	4,807	4,768	5,095	266	−96	−135	192
Consumption	5,772	6,058	5,638	5,637	5,988	285	−135	−135	216
Total	41,892	50,062	41,375	41,340	42,943	8,170	−517	−552	1,051
Net change						−33,810	−36,846	−26,548	−53,193
Change as % of base benefits						−15.8	−17.2	−12.4	−24.8

Quintile 5

Benefits	177,224	156,616	148,423	124,121	135,095	−20,608	−28,801	−53,103	−42,130
After-tax income	84,445	88,790	82,956	82,407	88,106	4,345	−1,488	−2,037	3,662
Taxes									
Payroll	23,502	30,654	23,373	23,461	22,873	7,152	−129	−41	−629
Income	2,261	2,376	2,218	2,198	2,336	115	−43	−63	75
Consumption	3,349	3,521	3,290	3,268	3,494	172	−59	−81	145
Total	29,111	36,550	28,881	28,927	28,703	7,439	−231	−184	−408
Net change						−28,048	−28,570	−52,919	−41,722
Change as % of base benefits						−15.8	−16.1	−29.9	−23.5

Table 7.6 Distributional analysis (OV—S3)

		Present discounted value				Change relative to base			
	Base	Three-Year Increment	Actuarial	Common	JP2000	Three-Year Increment	Actuarial	Common	JP2000
				Quintile 1 (highest)					
Benefits	326,889	286,895	265,548	388,612	243,460	−39,993	−61,340	61,723	−83,428
After-tax income	381,113	465,541	379,436	380,855	463,858	84,429	−1,677	−258	82,745
Taxes									
Payroll	53,095	70,200	53,107	52,933	65,864	17,105	12	−163	12,769
Income	29,011	34,203	29,019	28,887	33,671	5,192	8	−124	4,660
Consumption	15,113	18,461	15,046	15,103	18,394	3,348	−66	−10	3,281
Total	97,219	122,864	97,172	96,922	117,929	25,645	−47	−297	20,710
Net change						−65,638	−61,294	62,020	−104,139
Change as % of base benefits						−20.1	−18.8	19.0	−31.9
				Quintile 2					
Benefits	271,160	238,228	221,418	270,109	201,620	−32,932	−49,743	−1,052	−69,541
After-tax income	233,746	284,924	232,622	233,565	284,033	51,178	−1,124	−181	50,286
Taxes									
Payroll	42,735	55,653	42,744	42,599	50,660	12,918	9	−136	7,925
Income	9,213	11,133	9,216	9,176	11,076	1,920	3	−37	1,863
Consumption	9,269	11,299	9,225	9,262	11,263	2,029	−45	−7	1,994
Total	61,218	78,084	61,185	61,038	72,999	16,867	−33	−180	11,782
Net change						−49,799	−49,710	−872	−81,322
Change as % of base benefits						−18.4	−18.3	−0.3	−30.0

					Quintile 3				
Benefits	239,460	209,542	196,413	223,739	178,455	−29,918	−43,047	−15,721	−61,005
After-tax income	182,653	224,279	181,987	182,449	224,012	41,625	−666	−205	41,359
Taxes									
Payroll	35,138	46,390	35,145	35,036	41,564	11,252	7	−102	6,426
Income	6,494	7,884	6,495	6,467	7,842	1,391	2	−26	1,348
Consumption	7,243	8,894	7,217	7,235	8,883	1,651	−26	−8	1,640
Total	48,874	63,168	48,857	48,738	58,289	14,294	−18	−136	9,414
Net change						−44,212	−43,029	−15,585	−70,420
Change as % of base benefits						−18.5	−18.0	−6.5	−29.4
					Quintile 4				
Benefits	208,950	182,833	173,779	179,976	157,288	−26,117	−35,171	−28,974	−51,662
After-tax income	140,347	173,185	140,081	140,093	173,213	32,838	−266	−254	32,866
Taxes									
Payroll	29,656	39,435	29,661	29,578	34,528	9,779	5	−78	4,872
Income	4,786	5,772	4,788	4,767	5,726	985	1	−20	940
Consumption	5,565	6,868	5,555	5,555	6,869	1,302	−11	−10	1,303
Total	40,008	52,074	40,004	39,900	47,122	12,066	−4	−108	7,115
Net change						−38,184	−35,167	−28,866	−58,776
Change as % of base benefits						−18.3	−16.8	−13.8	−28.1
					Quintile 5				
Benefits	171,928	151,424	144,803	118,621	130,458	−20,503	−27,125	−53,307	−41,470
After-tax income	81,287	100,762	81,565	81,089	101,369	19,475	278	−198	20,082
Taxes									
Payroll	21,999	30,029	22,001	21,951	23,775	8,030	3	−48	1,776
Income	2,217	2,635	2,218	2,208	2,600	417	1	−9	382
Consumption	3,223	3,996	3,234	3,216	4,020	772	11	−8	796
Total	27,439	36,659	27,454	27,375	30,394	9,220	14	−65	2,955
Net change						−29,723	−27,139	−53,242	−44,425
Change as % of base benefits						−17.3	−15.8	−31.0	−25.8

7.5.2 Interpreting the Results

Figures 7.1 to 7.7 are useful in interpreting the simulation results discussed in the previous section. We focus on the Three-Year Reform, based on the OV model, to save space.

Figure 7.1 indicates how the reform changes gross SSW by age of retirement from the base case. The reform reduces gross SSW at each age, probably encouraging people to work via the negative wealth effect, while the gap with the base case becomes the narrowest at age 65, which is the NRA. By contrast, the reform raises taxes from the base case at each age, as indicated in figure 7.2. This is mainly because increased eligibility ages make people pay more taxes (mostly payroll taxes) while working, as indicated in table 7.4.

Figure 7.3 shows how the distribution of the retirement age changes from the base case. The reform does not change the spike at age 60, and it raises the probability of labor-force exit for people aged 62 and above and lowers it for younger people, suggesting a rise in the average retirement age. People aged 68 and above show little response to the reform. These results point to relatively small behavioral effect, which is again consistent with the results in table 7.4.

Figure 7.4 depicts the distribution of the total effect of the reform in terms of gross and net SSW. This figure shows that the reform succeeds in reducing SSW substantially for people aged 62 and younger but raises SSW between ages 63 and 67, in line with a change in the distribution of the retirement age, shown in figure 7.3. In addition, we observe no substantial impact beyond age 68, which is the new NRA.

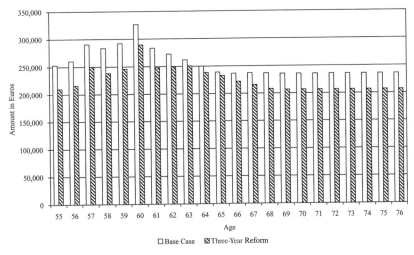

Fig. 7.1 SSW by age of labor force exit

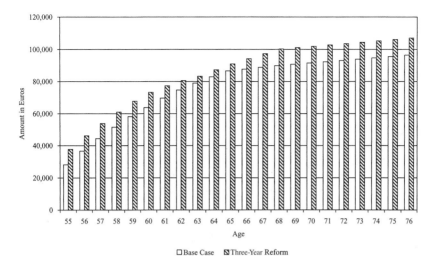

Fig. 7.2   Taxes by age of labor force exit

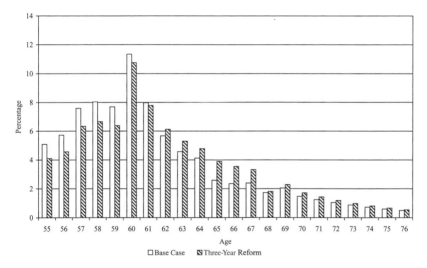

Fig. 7.3   Distribution of age of labor force exit (OV-S1 Model)

Figures 7.5 and 7.6 show how the previously-mentioned results change if we use the S3 model instead of the S1 model. Figure 7.5 shows a clear rightward shift in the spike of retirement age, probably reflecting a rise in age dummies incorporated in S3. Correspondingly, the total effect shows a sharp contrast at old and new spikes of labor-force exit: both gross and net SSW decline sharply at ages 60 and 61, while they jump at 63 and 64, reflecting an increase in the early retirement age.

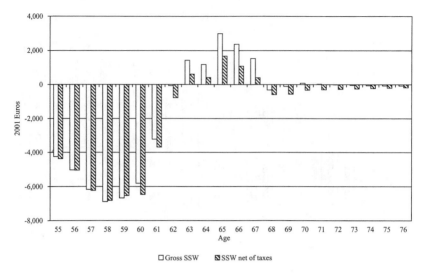

Fig. 7.4   Total effect by age of retirement (OV-S1 Model)

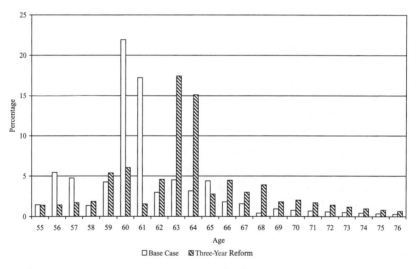

Fig. 7.5   Distribution of age of labor force exit (OV-S3 Model)

Finally, figure 7.7 summarizes the fiscal implications of the Three-Year Reform under the combinations of PV/OV and S1/S2/S3. This figure shows the results in terms of a share of nominal GDP to assess the magnitude of the impact for the whole economy and enable comparisons across countries. Our sample consists of only private-sector employees, who are mostly KNH members. Public-sector employees are covered by *Kyosai-Kumiai,* which has almost the same structure as KNH but is independent. Also,

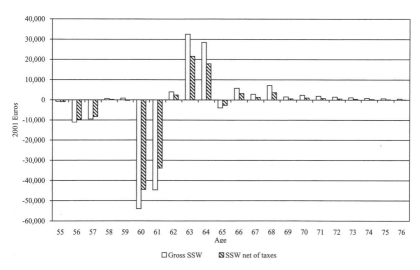

Fig. 7.6   Total effect by age of retirement (OV-S3 Model)

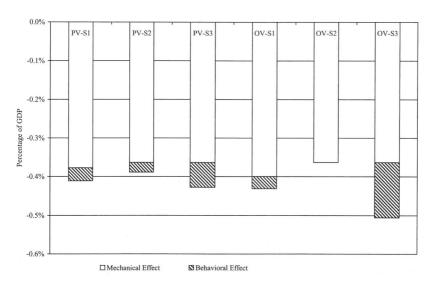

Fig. 7.7   Fiscal implications of reform as a percent of GDP

self-employed workers receive only Basic Pension benefits and pay the flat-rate contributions. Thus, we scale up the results for private-sector employees, estimating what percentage of people aged 55 are covered by KNH.

Two things should be noted about this figure. First, the size of the total impact of reforms is around 0.4 percent of nominal GDP, which is not substantial, but cannot be neglected, especially given the lower growth potential in Japan. Second, and more interestingly, the mechanical effect dominates fiscal implications of the behavioral effect in all cases, as is already suggested by a change in the distributions of the retirement age and of the total effect.

7.5.3   Distributional Issues

The proposed pension reforms seem to have different effects on different income groups. For considering distributional issues, we divide the sample into quintiles according to real family average lifetime earnings, and show how a change in net benefit is distributed by lifetime income group.

The results are summarized in table 7.5, panels A and B, for the combinations of OV-S1 and OV-S3, respectively. Table 7.5, panel A shows that: (1) the Three-Year Reform affects each quintile almost equally, (2) the Actuarial and JP 2000 Reforms are more favorable for people with lower income than people with higher income, reducing net benefits somewhat more for people with higher income, and (3) the Common Reform increases net benefits for people with higher income and reduces them for those with a lower income. The regressive feature of the Common Reform can be explained by its increase in the survivor benefit, which is favorable for rich couples.

However, the progressiveness of other reforms is also limited, reflecting the doubledecker feature of the KNH, which has the flat-rate basic benefit as well as the earnings-related benefit. The proposed increase in the eligibility age is biased toward a reduction in the basic benefit component over one's lifetime, which is relatively harmful to poor workers. To richer workers, on the other hand, the longer period of contributions incorporated by the reforms adds to earnings-related benefits, which partly (or more) offset a reduction in the basic benefit.

7.6   Conclusions

Our analysis has several limitations. First, it is an analysis about the steady-state impacts on some specific cohorts, not about the transition to the new steady state. And the proposed pension reforms cannot be implemented immediately; they have to incorporate many adjustments for cohorts in transition. Second, it does not incorporate any general equilibrium effects that might occur. Third, we neglect how firms will respond to an increase in labor supply of the elderly; they might reduce wage and absorb some of the impact from reforms.

However, our policy simulations show that the proposed pension reforms can mitigate strong pressures on social security finances from aging. We find, especially, that postponing eligibility ages can significantly reduce net SS payments, mainly through the mechanical effect that arises automatically due to changes in program rules. The fiscal implications of behavioral effects are relatively small, because of limited responsiveness of retirement to incentive measures and the actuarial adjustment already incorporated in the current scheme. Simulation results heavily depend on model specifications and estimation methodologies, but they clearly suggest that encouraging work in older age should be an effective way to help mitigate aging-related pressures on the government budget.

References

Coile, C., and J. Gruber. 2000a. Social security incentives for retirement. In *Themes in the economics of aging,* ed. D. Wise, 311–41. Chicago: University of Chicago Press.

———. 2000b. Social security and retirement. NBER Working Paper no. W7830.

Gruber, J., and D. A. Wise. 2004. Introduction and summary. In *Social security programs and retirement around the world: Micro-Estimation,* ed. J. Gruber and D. Wise, 1–40. Chicago: University of Chicago Press.

Oshio, T., and A. S. Oishi. 2004. Social security and retirement in Japan: An evaluation using micro-data. In *Social security programs and retirement around the world,* ed. J. Gruber and D. A. Wise, 399–460. Chicago: University of Chicago Press.

Stock, J. H., and D. A. Wise. 1990. Pensions, the option value of work and retirement. *Econometrica* 58 (5): 1151–80.

8

Simulation of Pension Reforms in The Netherlands

Arie Kapteyn and Klaas de Vos

8.1 Introduction

Broadly speaking, in The Netherlands all individuals aged 65 or over are entitled to the same Basic State Pension (Social Security—AOW in Dutch—abbreviated to SS throughout this chapter). Most other public benefits (e.g., disability insurance [DI], unemployment insurance [UI], welfare) expire when one turns 65. In addition, for those both above and below 65, next to the public entitlement programs guaranteed by law, a relatively large percentage of people who stop working are entitled to other private benefits, for example, occupational pensions supplementing SS for individuals over 65 and early-retirement (ER) benefits for individuals below 65.

Like most other developed countries, The Netherlands is faced with an increasing share of elderly in its total population. The share of the population over 65 has grown from 8 percent in 1950 to 14 percent in 2000 and is expected to rise to 24 percent by the year 2035. If nothing else changes, this will cause a considerable increase in SS expenditures. Faced with this prospect, the government has recently come up with policy measures to maintain its sustainability. Furthermore, recent developments in the stock market have caused concern about the sustainability of the fully funded occupational pensions supplementing SS, most of which are characterized by defined benefits.

An additional problem for the Dutch economy is the low labor force participation rate of individuals below 65 combined with the costs of the programs providing income to the individuals in this age group who have left the labor force. This concerns public programs, such as DI, but also private

Arie Kapteyn is a senior economist at RAND. Klaas de Vos is a senior researcher at CentERdata, Tilburg University.

ER schemes. During the 1980s and 1990s these programs have induced almost all employees to retire before reaching the age of 65. All of this has led to highly increased costs, both for the public DI and UI programs and for the employer-financed ER schemes. In reaction, eligibility conditions for DI and UI benefits have been tightened, and, increasingly, ER schemes are replaced by flexible retirement programs offering less attractive and actuarially fair (or fairer) pensions. In addition, the earlier pressure on elderly employees to vacate one's job for a younger job seeker has decreased dramatically with the spectacular reduction in unemployment. It remains to be seen to what extent all these phenomena will actually contribute to a reversal of the trend of decreasing labor market participation of the elderly.

In this chapter, we use model specifications developed in our earlier work (de Vos and Kapteyn 2004) to simulate the effect of three policy reforms on retirement patterns and on the benefits and taxes individuals pay after the age of 50. Notably, these reforms have been chosen for the purpose of cross-country comparisons, and are not being proposed as desirable or politically feasible reforms in The Netherlands. The remainder of the chapter is structured as follows. In section 8.2 we sketch the institutional framework within which people retire in The Netherlands. Section 8.3 describes the data and the way in which we use them for our analysis. Section 8.4 is devoted to the construction of incentive measures that are used in the estimation of the retirement equations. These equations are specified according to a common model, which is by and large used for all countries represented in this study. Section 8.5 presents the estimation results for the common model. Section 8.6 describes the three reforms, section 8.7 gives results of the policy simulations based on the estimated common model, and section 8.8 concludes.

8.2   Institutional Background

Social security (SS) guarantees a sufficient income to virtually all individuals 65 or over. Basically, SS is a flat-rate benefit equal to half the statutory minimum wage (after tax) with supplements for single individuals and for individuals with a spouse aged younger than 65 with a low income. Social security is financed largely as pay-as-you-go by a payroll tax on taxable income of individuals aged below 65. The associated tax rate is currently 17.9 percent (as of 2003), levied on taxable income up to a maximum (of €28,850 per annum). In 2001, SS benefits amounted to more than €20 billion, or 5 percent of GDP. Currently, about one in every five households in The Netherlands receives SS. The entitlement to SS does not require retirement from the labor force.

8.2.1   Other Public Programs

A number of arrangements exist that enable individuals to stop working before turning 65. The main ones are: DI, UI, and various ER schemes.

Disability insurance (DI) covers all employees against loss of earnings due to long-term sickness and disability. Currently, DI guarantees employees who lost more than 80 percent of their earnings capacity a benefit equal to 70 percent (80 percent before 1985) of their daily wage (up to a maximum). The benefit falls to a lower level after a certain period (both the length of this period and the percentage depend on age), and terminates at age 65. Most employees have taken out an additional insurance to cover the risk of a DI benefit falling below 70 percent of their previous earnings.[1]

In the 1980s, the DI program became a very popular arrangement, which employers could use to shed less productive elderly employees. Severe legal obstacles existed (and still exist) to lay off employees, while DI benefits were more generous than UI benefits. As a result, both employers and employees had a preference for the disability route to unemployment. The ensuing rise in costs of DI has induced the government to limit eligibility for it by tightening entry conditions and reducing benefit levels. Moreover, individuals receiving disability benefits are now subject to a more rigorous screening of their loss of earnings capacity.

The main reason why UI is less attractive than DI is that unemployment benefits are only paid for a limited period (depending on the number of years worked before unemployment). However, most people aged 60 or above who become unemployed can expect to receive unemployment benefits equal to 70 percent of their previous earnings up to age 65.[2]

All public benefits for individuals younger than 65 are paid only if an individual is not employed.[3]

8.2.2 Private Transfers

Next to SS, a majority of the population over 65 is entitled to a supplementary occupational pension. In general, if an employer offers a pension scheme, then participation in such a scheme is compulsory. Until recently, more than 99 percent of the pension schemes were of the defined-benefit type, most of them being defined on the basis of final pay. Typically, occupational pensions—(PP [private pensions])—supplement SS to 70 percent of final pay for individuals who have worked 40 years. After tax, the replacement rate is usually substantially higher.

Most large firms have their own pension fund; smaller firms usually participate in sector-wide pension funds. Usually, these private pension

---

1. It should be noted that for single earners who lost more than 80 percent of their earnings capacity, disability benefits are always at least as high as the relevant social assistance (welfare) level (ABW/RWW), which, for a couple, is approximately equal to the after-tax minimum wage. In contrast to the entitlement to social assistance, household wealth is not taken into account when determining eligibility.

2. Similar to the case for disability benefits, if necessary the unemployment benefit is supplemented by welfare benefits to reach the social assistance level without taking household wealth into account. Hence, for single earners with low wages, the replacement rate can be almost 100 percent.

3. For individuals in part-time employment, benefits may supplement their earnings.

arrangements require that people leave the job in which they accumulate pension rights at age 65 at the latest. There is no earnings test, however, and people may consider looking for secondary jobs once they retire.

Early retirement (ER) has become increasingly common during the 1980s, and was viewed as a means of reducing unemployment. Typically, the ER schemes guarantee an employee a benefit equal to 70 or 80 percent of previous earnings up to the age of 65. In after-tax terms, replacement rates are even higher. Furthermore, while being in ER, one often keeps accumulating pension rights, though possibly at a lower rate than when one would be working.

Early retirement may be organized via the pension funds, which also provide the occupational pensions, or via the employer. Moreover, in contrast to pensions, ER is mostly financed as pay-as-you-go. Early retirement usually requires ten years of employment with the same employer before the ER date, whereas old-age pension rights remain valid if the worker changes jobs. The receipt of ER pensions usually requires a complete withdrawal from the labor market.

In recent years, costs of ER have increased considerably, and many firms are currently trying to reduce these costs. In particular, as mentioned in the introduction, instead of the original arrangements, which provided incentives to retire as soon as one was eligible, more and more programs are being introduced that offer flexible ER pensions, of which the level depends on the retirement age.

Despite these developments, the general conclusion remains that an elaborate system of income-replacing transfers exists in The Netherlands, which can be expected to act as incentives to leave the labor force on one's 65th birthday at the latest. Moreover, it should be noted that whereas rather strict laws are in force that prevent employers from laying off younger employees, reaching age 65 is a legal reason for dismissal, and social insurance protecting against loss of earnings as a result of sickness, disability, or unemployment only cover employees younger than 65.

8.3 The Data

Most of the results presented in this chapter are obtained using The Netherlands Socio-Economic Panel (SEP). The SEP is a longitudinal survey administered by Statistics Netherlands (CBS), consisting of approximately 5,000 households. The survey is representative of the Dutch population, excluding those living in special institutions like nursing homes. The SEP was launched in April 1984. The same households were interviewed in October 1984 and then twice a year (in April and October) until 1989. Since 1990, the survey has been conducted once a year (in May). In order to address the problem of sample attrition, Statistics Netherlands regularly adds new households to the SEP. Information is collected at the respondent

level on socioeconomic characteristics, income, and labor market participation, and on a wide range of assets and liabilities at the household level.
For this paper, data have been used for the period 1984 to 1996.

In the analysis, we include men and unmarried women aged 50 to 64 who
had positive earnings in 1984. Individuals are added in later years (until
1994) as they turn 50, subject to positive earnings at age 50. For all individuals, we observe whether they retire during the next year, and if so,
whether they receive (early) retirement pensions, disability or unemployment insurance benefits, or no benefits at all. In addition, we observe education level, labor market sector, number of hours worked, and so on. For
the purpose of this analysis we restrict the sample to working males (with
or without partner) and working females without a partner. Individuals
are in our sample for all the years they are working plus the first year they
enter retirement. Retirement is assumed to be absorbing, so after an individual enters retirement, he or she is no longer followed. All information
available for the individual is also available for his or her partner. In addition, we have information on assets and income from capital received by
the household. However, this information is fairly unreliable and is not
used in our analyses. Table 8.1 presents the means of the most important
variables used in estimation. The meaning of option value (OV) and peak
value (PV) is explained in the following. Social security wealth (SSW) comprises the present value of both SS and other benefits one receives in retirement.

As we are trying to model the individual retirement decision, we are limited by a lack of information on the eligibility for the various exit routes out
of the labor force. In particular, we don't know whether and at which age
individuals can take ER. We also don't know whether they might be entitled to DI benefits—and we have insufficient health information to be
used as a proxy (although health would not present the full picture of DI

Table 8.1   **Sample statistics of the variables used in estimation**

Variable	Mean	Standard deviation
Retired (%)	11.8	
Social security wealth	218,021	98,635
Option value	12,201	6,849
Peak value	35,228	26,488
After-tax earnings	20,724	10,499
After-tax earnings partner	2,704	9,078
Age	54.5	3.5
Two-earner family (%)	28.1	
Partner present (%)	82.7	
Female head (%)	10.9	

Note: Number of observations = 3,922; money amounts in 2001 euros.

eligibility anyway). Therefore, the incentives for the individual to retire have been approximated as a weighted average of the incentives provided by the various exit routes, where the weight for a particular exit route is determined by the proportion of individuals in the age group observed to ultimately retire taking the exit route in question. The incentive to retire through ER is calculated as a weighted average of the incentive to retire through ER, given eligibility at a certain age. For this eligibility age for ER we have used information based on one wave of an alternative panel, the CentERpanel,[4] in which employed individuals were asked whether they were participating in an occupational pension plan, and at which age that would allow them to retire. The eligibility age distribution for ER is differentiated by sector of employment (see de Vos and Kapteyn 2004, table 5).

8.4   Construction of Incentive Measures

As SS is a flat-rate benefit, whereas ER, DI, and UI benefits and occupational pensions are (usually) based on final pay, information on earnings histories is not needed to determine social security wealth (the actuarially discounted sum of future benefits; the benefits include not only SS benefits but also ER, PP, DI, and UI benefits wherever appropriate). Only information on the number of years in pensionable employment, together with information on the final earnings, would be sufficient to determine the benefit level to which the individual is entitled. The number of years in pensionable employment is generally unknown, but in the Dutch system this number, although clearly affecting SSW, generally has only a marginal effect on most of the incentive variables to be included in the retirement decision (peak value and option value, defined later): the effect of working an additional year is by and large constant over a rather wide interval of years.

As the jump-off point for the forward projections we use actual earnings, assuming constant real earnings. We do not calculate three-year averages, because this would limit the number of observations that could be included in the analysis.

In our calculations we do not distinguish UI benefits from DI benefits (both are received until the age of 65), and assume that, like SS (received after age 65), benefits do not depend on the age of retirement. After becoming unemployed or disabled, the older worker can expect to keep the same level of benefits up to age 65. After age 65, SS is independent of work history. Hence, the only way in which an employee's future income (after the coming year) may be affected by retiring one year earlier is via his or her private pension. Retiring before the age of 65 may affect the level of private pension to be received after age 65 by reducing the number of years

---

4. The CentERpanel comprises about 2,000 households and is run by CentERdata, a survey research institute affiliated with Tilburg University.

counting toward pension benefits. Moreover, if an employee were to retire before his or her ER age he or she would no longer be eligible for ER benefits.

In this section we describe how SSW, option values, and peak values are calculated. As mentioned previously, SSW is calculated as the actuarially discounted sum of future benefits. In our incentive calculations we distinguish the following cases:

1. Eligibility for (early) retirement at a certain age between 55 and 65. Eligible individuals will receive a private pension in addition to SS once they turn 65.
2. Eligibility for disability/unemployment benefit upon retirement before age 65, receipt of a private pension in addition to SS as of age 65.
3. Eligibility for SS only (as of age 65).

For all entitlements, we assume zero growth in real terms after 1995.[5] For survival probabilities we use sex- and/or age-specific survival tables of Statistics Netherlands (1992). We assume independence between the mortality rates of the worker and his or her spouse. We use a real discount rate of 3 percent. To compute net benefit and pension levels we subtract payroll and income taxes. For the years after 1995 we use the tax schedule for 1995, keeping tax rates and brackets fixed in real terms. For individuals with working spouses, we assume that the spouse will stop working at age 65. In our calculations, we take into account that if an individual retires before age 65 and is not entitled to any benefit or pension, his or her spouse (if older than 65) may be entitled to a supplement to his or her SS benefit.

The option value of postponing retirement (Stock and Wise 1990) is approximated as

$$(1) \qquad G_t(r^*) = V_t(r^*) - V_t(t),$$

where $V_t(t)$ represents the utility of retiring now and $V_t(r^*)$ represents the highest feasible utility (obtained by retiring at age r^*). $V_t(r)$ is calculated as

$$(2) \qquad V_t(r) = \sum_{s=t}^{r-1} \beta^{s-t} Y_s^\gamma + \sum_{s=r}^{S} \beta^{s-t} [k B_s(r)]^\gamma,$$

where Y_s represents earnings in the years before retirement and $B_s(r)$ represents benefits received in the years after retirement at age r. We use $k = 1.5$, $\beta = 0.97$, and $\gamma = 0.75$.

The peak value, as proposed by Coile and Gruber (2000), is defined as the difference between the highest possible SSW when retiring at some point in the future and SSW when retiring now.

As mentioned earlier, the incentive measures used in the estimations in

---

5. For disability, SS, and unemployment benefits, this is more or less in line with current government policy.

the next section are weighted averages of the incentives for the various exit routes (DI, ER, SS only), where the weights are determined by the proportions of persons ultimately retiring in the various programs, differentiated by age. Notably, in these calculations, the fact that persons may become eligible for ER at different ages is taken into account by using the probabilities for eligibility by age based on results of the CentERpanel, as described earlier, multiplied by the empirical take-up rate of ER. In this way, the weighted SSW-measure of individuals aged 60, for example, is calculated as:

$$(3) \quad SSW_{60} = p_{DI,60} SSW_{DI,60} + p_{exit,60} SSW_{SSonly,60} + p_{ER,60}(p_{ER,60\,60} SSW_{ER,60}$$
$$+ p_{ER,61\,60} SSW_{ER,61} + p_{ER,62\,60} SSW_{ER,62} + p_{ER,63\,60} SSW_{ER,63}$$
$$+ p_{ER,64\,60} SSW_{ER,64} + p_{ER,65\,60} SSW_{ER,65}),$$

where $p_{ER,60}$, $p_{DI,60}$ and $p_{exit,60}$ are empirical proportions of persons ultimately retiring on the various programs, and $p_{ER,60\,60}$, $\cdots$, $p_{ER,65\,60}$ represent sector-specific eligibility probabilities (for ER at age 60 through 65, given eligibility for private pension and having reached age 60, respectively), based on the CentERpanel data. The same weighting scheme is used for the calculation of option and peak values. Notably, this weighting scheme differs from the one used in the previous volume.

8.5   Estimation Results for Two Model Versions

Table 8.2 presents the estimation results of the retirement probits for four variants. Two variants use peak value as an incentive variable (columns [1] and [3]) and either represent age by means of separate dummies or a quadratic in age. The two remaining variants are similar, but with peak value replaced by option value as an incentive variable.

We observe that in columns (1) and (3), peak value is insignificant. In the other columns, option value is highly significant. Social security wealth has a significant positive influence on the probability of exit out of the labor force. The presence of a partner, whether one lives in a two-earner family, and being female all have a negative effect on the probability of exit, although the coefficients of these variables generally are not significant. Age has a positive effect on the likelihood of labor-force exit. The age dummies exhibit peaks at ages 59, 60, and 64. Ages 59 or 60 are, in most cases, the early retirement age. The normal retirement age is 65.

8.6   Description of Reforms

We consider three incentive changes and their effects on retirement probabilities. The reforms and their implications for retirement are discussed consecutively.

Table 8.2 Estimation results of probit equations

Variable	Variant 1 Peak value, age dummies	Variant 2 Option value, age dummies	Variant 3 Peak value, quadratic age	Variant 4 Option value, quadratic age
Social security wealth	3.76e-07	2.90e-07	2.59e-07	2.87e-07
	(2.89)***	(2.82)***	(2.08)**	(2.77)***
Peak value	−6.16e-07		2.95e-08	
	(1.53)		(0.08)	
Option value		−0.0000101		−9.49e-06
		(4.66)**		(4.46)***
Net income	−2.19e-06	2.24e-06	−2.56e-06	2.15e-06
	(2.00)**	(1.56)	(2.32)**	(1.50)
Net income squared	−2.50e-12	−1.73e-11	−1.28e-12	−2.07e-11
	(0.20)	(1.34)	(0.11)	(1.59)
Include partner	3.83e-06	4.25e-06	3.96e-06	4.41e-06
	(0.90)	(1.02)	(1.03)	(1.08)
Include partner squares	−1.30e-10	−1.35e-10	−1.02e-10	−1.25e-10
	(0.78)	(0.82)	(0.71)	(0.78)
Age				
51	−0.025	−0.028		
	(1.09)	(1.29)		
52	−0.009	−0.017		
	(0.37)	(0.79)		
53	0.016	−0.002		
	(0.64)	(0.07)		
54	0.101	0.061		
	(3.57)***	(2.40)**		
55	0.067	0.023		
	(2.45)**	(0.96)		
56	0.188	0.110		
	(5.85)***	(3.82)***		
57	0.175	0.079		
	(5.30)***	(2.67)***		
58	0.293	0.155		
	(7.85)***	(4.44)***		
59	0.437	0.255		
	(10.31)***	(5.97)***		
60	0.453	0.234		
	(9.11)***	(4.69)***		
61	0.302	0.111		
	(5.58)***	(2.37)**		
62	0.132	−0.003		
	(2.47)**	(0.07)		
63	0.229	0.035		
	(3.85)***	(0.78)		
64	0.637	0.332		
	(8.29)***	(4.19)***		
Two earners	−0.023	−0.021	−0.028	−0.024
	(1.08)	(1.01)	(1.34)	(1.15)

(*continued*)

Table 8.2   (continued)

Variable	Variant 1 Peak value, age dummies	Variant 2 Option value, age dummies	Variant 3 Peak value, quadratic age	Variant 4 Option value, quadratic age
Partner	−0.019	−0.009	−0.008	−0.009
	(0.92)	(0.48)	(0.38)	(0.47)
Female	−0.025	−0.022	−0.020	−0.020
	(1.50)	(1.37)	(1.14)	(1.20)
Age			0.010	0.136
			(2.57)**	(4.01)***
Age²			−0.001	−0.001
			(1.99)**	(3.59)***
No. of observations	3,922	3,922	3,922	3,922

Note: Absolute value of z statistics in parentheses.
***Significant at 1 percent.
**Significant at 5 percent.

8.6.1   Reform 1. A Three-Year Increment in Eligibility Ages (the Three-Year Reform)

Since eligibility is not directly observed and the computation of incentives is based on actual retirement behavior, there are different ways in which one can implement such a reform in the context of the model as presented so far. We choose a particularly straightforward approach by calculating for every individual in the sample (and his or her partner, if any) the incentive variables as if this individual were three years younger. That is, we assign the weights as well as the amounts of benefits to be received (but not mortality rates) as if the individual is three years younger and then recalculate the incentive variables. However, for ages 51 to 53, we assume that the weights for ER and DI are zero. The working spouse is assumed to retire at the original retirement age of 65. We present two different sets of simulation results. The first simulation (S1) simply uses the retirement equations with age and age-squared and replaces the incentive variables by the new ones, based on delayed eligibility. Regarding the model with age dummies, the S3 simulation shifts the age dummies backward by three years. That is, for ages 51, 52, and 53, the age dummies are set equal to zero. The new age dummy for age 54 is set equal to the estimated age dummy for age 51, the new age dummy for age 55 is set equal to the estimated age dummy for age 52, and so on.

8.6.2   Reform 2. The Common Reform

The Common Reform involves the possibility of early retirement at age 60 and normal retirement at age 65. The replacement rates depend on age. The (before-tax) replacement rate at age 65 is equal to 60 percent of average lifetime earnings during the 40 best years (assumed to be 75 percent of current earnings). At other ages, an actuarial adjustment of 6 percent is applied.[6] That is, when retiring at age 60 an individual receives 70 percent of the pension receivable upon retirement at age 65, when retiring at age 61 the individual receives 76 percent, and so on. This also applies to retirement ages higher than 65. For instance, when retiring at age 70, an individual receives 130 percent. Widows receive the maximum of their own pension and the pension of the spouse. Again, two sets of simulation results are presented: S1, using the retirement equation with age and age-squared and replacing the incentive variables with the ones calculated for the Common Reform, and S3, using the retirement equation with age dummies, where the same incentive variables are used, and where the dummies for ages above 64 are assumed to be similar to the age dummy for age 64.

8.6.3   Reform 3. Actuarial Reform

In this reform we stay as close as possible to the current benefit system, but adjust benefits such that these change with the age of retirement in an approximately actuarially fair way. In particular, ER and DI benefits are assumed to depend on the age of retirement. Moreover, recipients of these benefits keep receiving the same level of benefits upon reaching age 65, rather than shifting to SS + PP. The (full) ER replacement rate is assumed to be equal to the PP replacement rate of 70 percent, but recipients of DI and ER no longer pay SS payroll taxes. In keeping with the current system, all persons who did not retire earlier are assumed to retire at age 65. As was the case previously, we present the results of simulations S1 and S3, obtained by replacing the incentive variables by the ones implied by the reform.

8.6.4   Simulation Cohort

The fiscal effects in terms of costs (pension benefits) and benefits (payroll taxes, occupational pension contributions, income taxes, and VAT) for the base case and the three pension reforms have been simulated for a cohort of age-50 workers, on the basis of the retirement probabilities estimated earlier. In order to increase the number of observations, this cohort has been augmented by including workers aged 51 to 55 who have been de-aged to age 50, and by pooling these observations from the years 1990 to 1994. In the de-aging process, the age of the spouse has been adapted accordingly, but all other variables are assumed to remain the same. The following reported monetary values are always present discounted values of annual money flows discounted back to age 50.

---

6. In contrast to the earlier volume, persons retiring before age 60 are assumed to receive a pension when reaching age 60. Average lifetime earnings are corrected to take into account the number of years not worked between the retirement age and 60.

8.7   Results

We will first discuss a selection of the simulation results by means of a number of graphs. After that, we consider the quantitative effects on taxes and benefits by means of a number of tables. For the graphs we consider only the OV models.

8.7.1   Results by Age

Figures 8.1 and 8.2 present the distributions of retirement ages under four regimes for the models, with and without age dummies. We should note that for each scenario, the hazard of leaving the labor force has been set equal to 1 in the final year of the simulation. This explains the spikes that one observes in these final years: observations with very low predicted hazards during the simulation period, by construction have a very high likelihood of exiting the labor force in the final year. Clearly, the reforms induce later labor force exits. The Three-Year Reform scenario tends to draw out the distribution of labor force exits toward later ages. Compared to the Three-Year Reform, the Common Reform has its greatest effect in the age range below 60, and around the early and normal retirement age, as one would expect. The effects of the Actuarial Reform are somewhat more modest than those of the other two reforms. Effects in the model with age dummies tend to be more dramatic, due to the shift in dummies, than in the model with quadratic age. Regarding figure 8.2, we should note that for the Common Reform the density of retiring at ages 69 and 70 is not zero; values of less than 1 percent have been rounded off to zero.

Figure 8.3 presents the distribution of social security benefits by age of retirement for the model with age dummies. As elsewhere, the social security benefits represent present discounted values (discounted back to age 50) of benefits to be collected as of the date of retirement. Thus, for each age in the figure, we calculate the SSW of each individual in the sample if he or she were to retire at that age. We next weight that individual's SSW with the probability that the individual will retire at that age.

Figure 8.3 reveals an artifact of the simulations at the final age for each reform. As mentioned, under each scenario, the hazard of leaving the labor force has been set equal to 1 in the final year of the simulation. It turns out that there are four observations for which the value of the explanatory variables is such that the hazard of leaving the labor force predicted by the model is essentially zero. In particular, the partner's income turns out to be very high. These four observations have a high SSW. Since by construction their probability of exiting in the final year is very high, these four observations get a very high weight in the final year relative to the other observations. This then inflates the average SSW of people exiting in this year. One should note that when looking at total effects across all ages, these observations become less influential, so that the calculation of total effects is not unduly influenced.

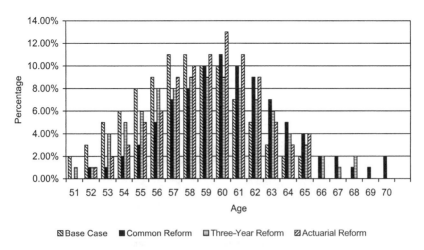

Fig. 8.1 Distribution of retirement age (OV-S1 Model)

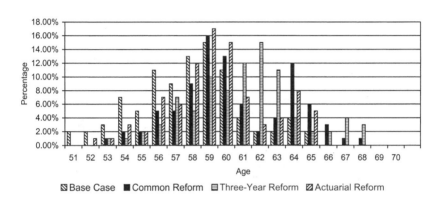

Fig. 8.2 Distribution of retirement age (OV-S3 Model)

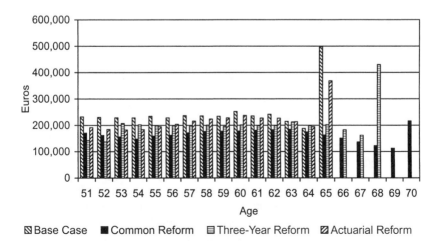

Fig. 8.3 Social security benefits by age of retirement (OV-S3 Model)

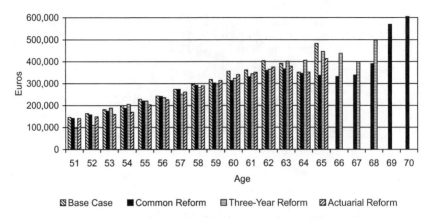

Fig. 8.4   Taxes by age of retirement (OV-S3 Model)

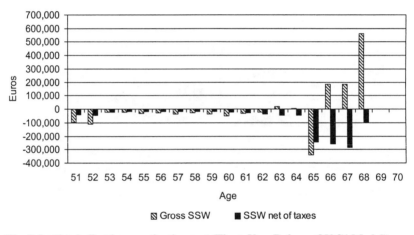

Fig. 8.5   Total effect by age of retirement (Three-Year Reform, OV-S1 Model)

Figure 8.3 illustrates that the reforms make it less attractive from a benefit point of view to retire early. Particularly at younger ages, benefits are substantially lower if one were to retire under the reforms than under the current system.

Figure 8.4 shows the flip side of figure 8.3 in that it presents the total taxes paid by individuals by age of retirement. We observe that the Three-Year Reform scenario shifts the taxes to later ages of exit.

Figures 8.5 and 8.6 show total effects for the Three-Year Reform. We show both the change in total benefits if one moves from the base case to the Three-Year Reform and the change in benefits net of taxes. Both models produce fairly similar pictures. Gross benefits fall before age 65, but after age 65 benefits increase, for the simple reason that under the base case scenario there are no people retiring after age 65, so that benefits are zero

Fig. 8.6   Total effect by age of retirement (Three-Year Reform, OV-S3 Model)

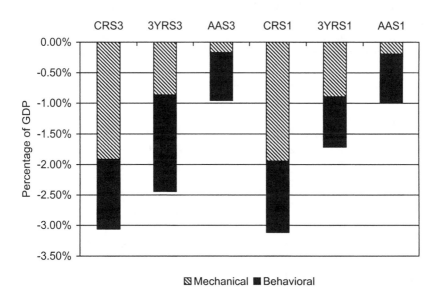

Fig. 8.7   Fiscal implications of reforms as a percentage of GDP

for these age categories. When looking at benefits net of taxes, we see that these fall across all ages, but particularly after age 65.

8.7.2   Fiscal Effects

Figure 8.7 decomposes the total effects (total benefits net of taxes) into a mechanical effect and a behavioral effect for all three reforms (Common Reform [CR], Three-Year Reform [3YR], and Actuarial Reform [AA]) and for the models with dummies (S3) and for the models with quadratic age effects (S1). The mechanical effect assumes that there are no behavioral responses to the change in benefits. The behavioral response is the difference between the total effect and the mechanical response. We observe that the total effects are biggest for the Common Reform scenarios (more than 3 percent of GDP) and smallest for the Actuarial Reform (less than 1 percent of GDP). However, the behavioral effects are biggest in the three-year increment scenarios, particularly for the model with dummies (S3). As a percentage of the total effect, the behavioral effects are biggest in the actuarial scenarios.

Table 8.3 provides more detail about the total effects on taxes and benefits for various models and scenarios. We concentrate our discussion of the table on the columns with percentages, as these are relatively easiest to interpret. We note that the outcomes for benefits are quite similar for the peak value models and the option value models. For taxes, however, we observe that the peak value models indicate a slight reduction for the Common Reform, whereas the option value models indicate an increase; the same is true for the Actuarial Reform. For the Three-Year Reform scenarios, the peak and option value models produce outcomes that are more similar. Qualitatively, all models show a reduction in benefits as a result of the reforms. The reduction is on the order of 30 percent for the Common Reform, 15 percent for the Three-Year Reform, and 7 percent for the Actuarial Reform. In all cases, we observe that pension payments increase substantially. This is, of course, not surprising, given that the reforms induce people to work longer. Income taxes mostly increase, due to the progressivity of the tax system. The high earners, in particular, work longer and hence pay more income taxes. Obviously, all these results depend crucially on the assumption that tax rates as well as pension contribution rates remain the same after the reforms.

Table 8.4 presents a decomposition of the fiscal effects in a mechanical component and a behavioral component. We see once again that for the option value model the behavioral component is relatively more important in the Three-Year Reform scenario than under the Common Reform. The peak value model mimics this pattern for the model with age dummies, but less so for the model with quadratic age. The effects under the Actuarial Reform are relatively more modest.

8.7.3   Distributional Effects

For the option value model with quadratic age, table 8.5 presents fiscal effects by income quintile. Income here is total after-tax household earnings at age 55. In percentage terms, the distributional effects appear to be minor. For instance, under the Common Reform the reduction in benefits net of taxes as a percentage of base benefits is 48 percent for the lowest quintile and 41 percent for the highest quintile. For the Three-Year Reform scenario, the reduction is 16 percent for the lowest quintile and 27 percent for the highest quintile. For the Actuarial Reform, the reduction ranges from 9 percent to 16 percent. Table 8.6 presents the same analysis for the

Table 8.3   Total fiscal effect of reform

Cost or revenue item	Present discounted value				Total change relative to base (%)		
	Base	Three-Year Reform	Actuarial Reform	Common Reform	Three-Year Reform	Actuarial Reform	Common Reform
Peak value—Quadratic age (PV-S1)							
Benefits	240,379	209,125	223,640	164,580	-13.0	-7.0	-31.5
Taxes: Payroll	136,691	140,542	130,428	126,996	2.8	-4.6	-7.1
Taxes: Income	87,601	86,877	86,309	84,720	-0.8	-1.5	-3.3
Pension payments	28,133	29,654	28,534	38,199	5.4	1.4	35.8
Taxes: VAT	33,477	32,174	32,969	29,360	-3.9	-1.5	-12.3
Taxes: Total	285,902	289,247	278,240	279,275	1.2	-2.7	-2.3
Peak value—Age dummies (PV-S3)							
Benefits	239,639	202,383	224,659	166,198	-15.5	-6.3	-30.6
Taxes: Payroll	137,384	156,424	132,943	129,602	13.9	-3.2	-5.7
Taxes: Income	88,300	99,980	87,330	84,969	13.2	-1.1	-3.8
Pension payments	28,620	34,371	29,238	38,602	20.1	2.2	34.9
Taxes: VAT	33,612	34,849	33,345	29,772	3.7	-0.8	-11.4
Taxes: Total	287,915	325,623	282,857	282,945	13.1	-1.8	-1.7
Option value—Quadratic age (OV-S1)							
Benefits	240,807	208,567	224,647	171,754	-13.4	-6.7	-28.7
Taxes: Payroll	136,640	148,409	142,401	146,583	8.6	4.2	7.3
Taxes: Income	88,747	95,207	94,350	94,135	7.3	6.3	6.1
Pension payments	28,274	32,153	30,968	43,698	13.7	9.5	54.6
Taxes: VAT	33,541	33,629	34,911	32,528	0.3	4.1	-3.0
Taxes: Total	287,202	309,398	302,630	316,944	7.7	5.4	10.4
Option value—Age dummies (OV-S3)							
Benefits	239,844	203,667	224,832	172,319	-15.1	-6.3	-28.2
Taxes: Payroll	137,570	158,454	143,565	147,655	15.2	4.4	7.3
Taxes: Income	89,113	101,798	94,499	94,378	14.2	6.0	5.9
Pension payments	28,730	34,904	31,329	43,901	21.5	9.0	52.8
Taxes: VAT	33,686	35,235	35,025	32,699	4.6	4.0	-2.9
Taxes: Total	289,099	330,391	304,418	318,632	14.3	5.3	10.2

Notes: The first four columns show the PDV of benefits and taxes under the base plan and under each of the three illustrative reforms. The last three columns show the change relative to the base, for benefits and for taxes.

Table 8.4   Decomposition of total effect of reform, change in present discounted value

	Three-Year Reform			Actuarial Reform			Common Reform		
	Mechanical	Behavioral	Total	Mechanical	Behavioral	Total	Mechanical	Behavioral	Total
	Peak value—Quadratic age (PV-S1)								
Benefits	−35,647	4,393	−31,254	−17,128	389	−16,739	−76,549	750	−75,799
Total taxes	−7,411	10,757	3,346	−11,112	3,451	−7,661	−15,139	8,513	−6,626
Net change	−28,237	−6,364	−34,601	−6,016	−3,062	−9,078	−61,410	−7,763	−69,173
Change as % of base benefits	−11.7	−2.6	−14.4	−2.5	−1.3	−3.8	−25.5	−3.2	−28.8
	Peak value—Age dummies (PV-S3)								
Benefits	−33,722	−3,534	−37,256	−15,663	683	−14,980	−75,288	1,847	−73,441
Total taxes	−6,287	43,995	37,708	−10,288	5,230	−5,058	−14,633	9,662	−4,971
Net change	−27,436	−47,528	−74,964	−5,374	−4,548	−9,922	−60,655	−7,815	−68,470
Change as % of base benefits	−11.4	−19.8	−31.3	−2.2	−1.9	−4.1	−25.3	−3.3	−28.6
	Option value—Quadratic age (OV-S1)								
Benefits	−34,869	2,630	−32,239	−17,163	1,003	−16,160	−76,575	7,522	−69,053
Total taxes	−6,588	28,785	22,197	−11,145	26,573	15,428	−15,061	44,803	29,742
Net change	−28,280	−26,156	−54,436	−6,018	−25,571	−31,589	−61,514	−37,282	−98,796
Change as % of base benefits	−11.7	−10.9	−22.6	−2.5	−10.6	−13.1	−25.5	−15.5	−41.0
	Option value—Age dummies (OV-S3)								
Benefits	−33,076	−3,102	−36,178	−15,564	552	−15,012	−75,062	7,537	−67,525
Total taxes	−5,714	47,006	41,292	−10,236	25,555	15,319	−14,457	43,991	29,534
Net change	−27,362	−50,108	−77,470	−5,328	−25,003	−30,331	−60,605	−36,454	−97,059
Change as % of base benefits	−11.4	−20.9	−32.3	−2.2	−10.4	−12.6	−25.3	−15.2	−40.5

Notes: The table shows the total effect of the reform (shown in table 8.3) decomposed into mechanical and behavioral components. The first rows show the change in benefits. The second rows show the change in all taxes. The third rows show the net change (the change in benefits minus the change in taxes). The fourth rows show the net change as percent of base benefits (shown in table 8.3).

Table 8.5   Distributional analysis: Option value—Quadratic age (OV-S1)

Cost or revenue item	Present discounted value				Total change relative to base		
	Base	Three-Year Reform	Actuarial Reform	Common Reform	Three-Year Reform	Actuarial Reform	Common Reform
			Quintile 1 (highest)				
Benefits	396,097	339,113	375,157	289,331	-56,984	-20,940	-106,766
After-tax income	675,227	686,338	694,977	666,818	11,111	19,750	-8,409
Taxes: Payroll	202,673	220,778	206,435	214,514	18,105	3,762	11,841
Taxes: Income	263,296	283,300	275,239	277,973	20,004	11,943	14,677
Pension payments	78,625	87,944	82,614	109,409	9,319	3,989	30,784
Taxes: VAT	56,719	57,652	58,378	56,013	933	1,659	-706
Taxes: Total	601,313	649,674	622,666	657,909	48,361	21,353	56,596
Net change					-105,345	-42,293	-163,362
Change as % of base benefits					-26.6	-10.7	-41.2
			Quintile 2				
Benefits	252,067	217,602	232,480	201,119	-34,465	-19,587	-50,948
After-tax income	432,229	433,924	453,769	437,951	1,695	21,540	5,722
Taxes: Payroll	160,302	174,450	167,046	176,954	14,148	6,744	16,652
Taxes: Income	88,993	96,102	97,138	97,807	7,109	8,145	8,814
Pension payments	27,507	32,071	31,200	47,633	4,564	3,693	20,126
Taxes: VAT	36,307	36,450	38,117	36,788	142	1,809	481
Taxes: Total	313,109	339,073	333,501	359,182	25,963	20,391	46,073
Net change					-60,428	-39,978	-97,021
Change as % of base benefits					-24.0	-15.9	-38.5
			Quintile 3				
Benefits	213,253	185,704	196,466	161,185	-27,549	-16,787	-52,068
After-tax income	360,647	360,693	379,686	355,228	46	19,039	-5,419

(continued)

Table 8.5 (continued)

Cost or revenue item	Present discounted value				Total change relative to base		
	Base	Three-Year Reform	Actuarial Reform	Common Reform	Three-Year Reform	Actuarial Reform	Common Reform
Taxes: Payroll	140,442	152,773	148,337	152,587	12,331	7,895	12,145
Taxes: Income	51,812	55,626	57,172	56,656	3,814	5,360	4,844
Pension payments	18,204	21,167	21,165	32,279	2,963	2,961	14,075
Taxes: VAT	30,294	30,298	31,894	29,839	4	1,599	−455
Taxes: Total	240,752	259,864	258,568	271,361	19,112	17,815	30,609
Net change					−46,661	−34,602	−82,677
Change as % of base benefits					−21.9	−16.2	−38.8
Quintile 4							
Benefits	189,524	166,380	174,963	126,942	−23,144	−14,561	−62,582
After-tax income	306,204	303,799	321,071	287,150	−2,405	14,867	−19,054
Taxes: Payroll	114,998	124,281	122,555	121,636	9,283	7,557	6,638
Taxes: Income	27,694	28,704	29,875	28,724	1,010	2,181	1,030
Pension payments	12,181	14,002	14,258	20,274	1,821	2,077	8,093
Taxes: VAT	25,721	25,519	26,970	24,121	−202	1,249	−1,601
Taxes: Total	180,594	192,506	193,658	194,755	11,912	13,064	14,160
Net change					−35,056	−27,625	−76,742
Change as % of base benefits					−18.5	−14.6	−40.5
Quintile 5 (lowest)							
Benefits	152,197	133,290	143,311	79,402	−18,907	−8,886	−72,795
After-tax income	221,654	215,735	226,965	187,260	−5,919	5,311	−34,394
Taxes: Payroll	64,326	69,258	67,183	66,718	4,932	2,857	2,392
Taxes: Income	13,841	13,805	14,283	10,812	−36	442	−3,029
Pension payments	4,583	5,277	5,321	8,511	694	738	3,928
Taxes: VAT	18,619	18,122	19,065	15,730	−497	446	−2,889
Taxes: Total	101,369	106,462	105,852	101,771	5,093	4,483	402
Net change					−24,000	−13,369	−73,197
Change as % of base benefits					−15.8	−8.8	−48.1

Table 8.6   Distributional analysis: Option value—Age dummies (OV-S3)

Cost or revenue item	Present discounted value				Total change relative to base		
	Base	Three-Year Reform	Actuarial Reform	Common Reform	Three-Year Reform	Actuarial Reform	Common Reform
			Quintile 1 (highest)				
Benefits	395,150	334,607	375,683	290,051	-60,543	-19,467	-105,099
After-tax income	676,678	709,289	695,389	668,383	32,611	18,711	-8,295
Taxes: Payroll	203,415	229,752	207,133	215,490	26,337	3,718	12,075
Taxes: Income	263,370	298,548	274,525	277,666	35,178	11,155	14,296
Pension payments	79,237	92,162	82,933	109,423	12,925	3,696	30,186
Taxes: VAT	56,841	59,580	58,413	56,144	2,739	1,572	-697
Taxes: Total	602,863	680,042	623,004	658,723	77,179	20,141	55,860
Net change					-137,722	-39,608	-160,959
Change as % of base benefits					-34.9	-10.0	-40.7
			Quintile 2				
Benefits	250,984	211,963	232,958	201,781	-39,021	-18,026	-49,203
After-tax income	434,490	456,214	455,282	440,952	21,724	20,792	6,462
Taxes: Payroll	161,365	185,836	168,303	178,285	24,471	6,938	16,920
Taxes: Income	89,882	105,352	97,730	98,578	15,470	7,848	8,696
Pension payments	28,194	35,856	31,764	48,072	7,662	3,570	19,878
Taxes: VAT	36,497	38,322	38,244	37,040	1,825	1,747	543
Taxes: Total	315,938	365,366	336,041	361,975	49,428	20,103	46,037
Net change					-88,449	-38,129	-95,240
Change as % of base benefits					-35.2	-15.2	-37.9
			Quintile 3				
Benefits	212,134	180,128	196,550	161,765	-32,006	-15,584	-50,369
After-tax income	362,622	380,418	381,229	357,453	17,796	18,607	-5,169
Taxes: Payroll	141,566	164,629	149,855	153,947	23,063	8,289	12,381
Taxes: Income	52,330	60,934	57,674	57,099	8,604	5,344	4,769
Pension payments	18,700	23,983	21,613	32,571	5,283	2,913	13,871

(continued)

Table 8.6 (continued)

Cost or revenue item	Present discounted value				Total change relative to base		
	Base	Three-Year Reform	Actuarial Reform	Common Reform	Three-Year Reform	Actuarial Reform	Common Reform
Taxes: VAT	30,460	31,955	32,023	30,026	1,495	1,563	-434
Taxes: Total	243,056	281,501	261,165	273,643	38,445	18,109	30,587
Net change					-70,451	-33,693	-80,956
Change as % of base benefits					-33.2	-15.9	-38.2
Quintile 4							
Benefits	188,531	160,993	174,893	127,437	-27,538	-13,638	-61,094
After-tax income	307,843	321,084	322,726	289,212	13,241	14,883	-18,631
Taxes: Payroll	116,051	135,475	124,004	122,773	19,424	7,953	6,722
Taxes: Income	27,941	31,030	30,118	27,360	3,089	2,177	-581
Pension payments	12,522	16,062	14,588	20,473	3,540	2,066	7,951
Taxes: VAT	25,859	26,971	27,109	24,294	1,112	1,250	-1,565
Taxes: Total	182,373	209,538	195,819	194,900	27,165	13,446	12,527
Net change					-54,703	-27,084	-73,621
Change as % of base benefits					-29.0	-14.4	-39.0
Quintile 5 (lowest)							
Benefits	151,527	129,893	143,216	79,769	-21,634	-8,311	-71,758
After-tax income	222,941	228,807	228,547	188,616	5,866	5,606	-34,325
Taxes: Payroll	64,996	76,075	68,086	67,271	11,079	3,090	2,275
Taxes: Income	13,938	14,676	14,392	10,892	738	454	-3,046
Pension payments	4,726	6,140	5,464	8,582	1,414	738	3,856
Taxes: VAT	18,727	19,220	19,198	15,844	493	471	-2,883
Taxes: Total	102,387	116,111	107,140	102,589	13,724	4,753	202
Net change					-35,358	-13,064	-71,960
Change as % of base benefits					-23.3	-8.6	-47.5

model with age dummies. For the Common Reform and the Actuarial Reform, the effects in table 8.6 are quite similar to the effects reported in table 8.5. For the Three-Year Reform, the model with dummies yields bigger reductions in benefits than the model with quadratic age: the reduction varies from 23 percent in the lowest quintile to 35 percent in the highest quintiles.

8.8   Conclusions

The Netherlands has a relatively generous system of pensions, social security benefits, early retirement arrangements, and unemployment and disability benefits, which for most people provide incentives to retire from the labor market well before the age of 65. In view of the increasing proportion of elderly, the sustainability of this system is a problem, and sooner or later, reforms will be unavoidable. In this paper, we compare the budget effects of three possible reforms, having modeled transitions into retirement on the basis of microdata from The Netherlands Socio-Economic Panel (SEP). Notably, these reforms have been devised for the purpose of cross-country comparisons, and are not being proposed as desirable or politically feasible reforms in The Netherlands. Furthermore, it should be noted that the simulations have been performed on a particular cohort of individuals, and results need not be the same for other cohorts. Bearing these limitations in mind, we find that the reforms would have considerable (favorable) budget effects. In general, the Common Reform has the strongest effects, a major part of which would be mechanical rather than behavioral. The effects of the second reform, which delay eligibility for three years, depend largely on the retirement model chosen. The Actuarial Reform has the smallest effects.

References

Coile, C., and J. Gruber. 2000. Social security and retirement. NBER Working Paper no. 7830. Cambridge, MA: National Bureau of Economic Research.

de Vos, K., and A. Kapteyn. 2004. Incentives and exit routes to retirement in the Netherlands. In *Social security and retirement around the world: Micro-Estimation,* ed. Jonathan Gruber and David Wise, 461–98. Chicago: University of Chicago Press.

Statistics Netherlands. 1992. *Life tables for the Netherlands,* 1986–1990. The Netherlands: Voorburg/Heerlen.

Stock, J. H., and D. A. Wise. 1990. Pensions, the option value of work and retirement. *Econometrica* 58:1151–80.

9

Evaluating Spanish Pension Expenditure Alternative Reform Scenarios

Michele Boldrin and Sergi Jiménez-Martín

9.1 Introduction

In this chapter we evaluate the quantitative impact that a number of alternative reform scenarios may have on the total expenditure for public pensions in Spain. We consider five scenarios: the first three are common to the other countries considered in this volume, while the second two correspond to specific reforms adopted by the Spanish government in 1997 and 2002.

Each reform scenario consists of changes to one or more of the constitutive elements of a public pension system: retirement age, replacement rate as a function of the number of contributive years, penalization for early retirement, and contribution rate. The kind of reforms considered here, similar to those debated in many advanced countries, would have been politically unthinkable twenty or thirty years ago, when most of the current work force began its contributive careers. Hence, the changes considered, should they be implemented, would certainly take most contributors off guard and would engender, for given contributive histories and wage profiles, substantial changes in their net position toward the social security administration. While workers are likely to react to the change of rules by modifying their behavior when a reform takes place, it is also clear that a completely satisfactory reaction is feasible only for workers who are

Michele Boldrin is a professor of economics at Washington University in St. Louis. Sergi Jiménez-Martin is an associate professor of economics at Universitat Pompeu Fabra.

We are grateful to the National Science Foundation, the University of Minnesota Grant-in-Aid program, the BEC2002-04294-C02-01 and SEC2005-08783-C04-01, and the Fundación Banco Bilboa Vizcaya Argentaria (FBBVA) for financial support.

at the very beginning of their contributive histories. In other words, reforming pension systems will mechanically affect expenditure by changing the relationship between past work histories, contributions, and expected benefits in such a way that it cannot be undone by the reaction of the economic agents. We call this the *mechanical* effect, to distinguish it from the *behavioral* one. The latter is meant to measure the variation in expenditure brought about by the changing behavior of the workers facing a different incentive system. Our evaluation aims at providing a separate quantitative evaluation of these two effects.

To accomplish this, we strive to model the behavioral response of different individuals to the changing incentives provided by each reform scenario. We use the results from previous microeconometric studies of Spanish retirement patterns (especially Boldrin, Jiménez-Martín and Peracchi [2004]) to capture the behavioral responses of different individuals. Such behavioral responses have been estimated by means of a family of reduced-form models of retirement behavior in which various financial measures of the incentive to retirement are used.

In keeping with the tradition of this series, we consider both common scenarios, which apply equally to each country in the group, and national scenarios, which are meant to capture hypotheses of reform historically relevant for the specific country under examination. In the case of Spain, we simulate the impact of the 1997 reform (which was fully implemented at the end of 2002) and of the 2002 amendment to the same reform; from now on, respectively, the reform and the amendment. See table 9.1 for a summary description of these measures.

Our quantitative findings can be summarized in two sentences. For all the reforms considered, the financial impact of the mechanical effect is order of magnitudes larger than the behavioral impact. For the two Spanish reforms, we find once again that their effect on the outstanding liability of the Spanish social security system is negligible: neither the mechanical nor the behavioral effect amounts to much for the 1997 reform, and they amount to very little for the 2002 amendment.

The reason for the first finding is, quite simply, that the underlying behavioral model, which is meant to map changes in financial incentives into changes in retirement patterns, explains a very small proportion of the measured variability in actual retirement behavior and, of that small portion, the part that is captured by the financial incentives is just a fraction. Hence, changing financial incentives does not seem to make much of a difference (at least according to our sample) to the behavioral model adopted in these studies and to the estimation we have performed. The reason for the second finding is that, given the structure of the current Spanish labor force and given the contributive histories of its members, the reform and the amendment make little difference: for most individuals, the social security wealth calculations give very similar numbers with both the old and the new rules. Further, as the new rules change incentives to retirement only very slightly, we predict that people's behavior will also only very slightly change. If the reforms had been introduced to reduce public pension expenditure, then our conclusion is that they are very ineffective and badly designed. If they had been introduced to pretend something was being done without doing anything, then they can be declared a success.

9.2   Background of the System

9.2.1   Public Programs for Old-Age Workers

We provide here a brief description of the pre-1997 social security system reform. Changes introduced by the reform and the amendment are noted later. For more details on the Spanish social security system, we refer the reader to Boldrin, Jiménez-Martín, and Peracchi (1999, 2001).

Table 9.1 summarizes the programs available after age 50. Leaving aside private pensions, there are three public programs that affect the behavior of old age workers: unemployment benefits, disability benefits, and retirement pensions.

Unemployment benefits are generally conditional on previous periods of contributions and are available only for workers in the General Regime (RGSS) of the Spanish social security (S3) system.[1] There are two continuation programs for those who have exhausted their entitlement to contributory unemployment benefits: one for those aged over 45 (UB45+ program) and the other for those aged over 52 (UB52+ program). The latter is a special subsidy for unemployed people who are older than 52, lack other income sources, have contributed to unemployment insurance for at least six years in their life and, except for age, satisfy all requirements for an old-age pension.

The S3 system provides insurance against both temporary and permanent illness or disability. Contributory disability (DI) benefits are far more generous than any other old-age program, since they are not subject to penalties for young age or insufficient years of contribution.[2] Disability insurance benefits are subject to approval by a medical examiner (notoriously, the tightness of admissibility criteria used by examiners varies over time and

---

1. People enrolled in any of the special regimes (RESS) either have no access to unemployment benefits (self-employed and household employees) or have special unemployment programs (farmers and fishermen).

2. For a discussion of noncontributory disability pensions and other marginal insurance schemes (which are not relevant to the following analysis and have little or no impact on the retirement decisions of the workers we are considering) see Boldrin, Jiménez-Martín, and Peracchi (1999).

Table 9.1   **Public programs at older ages**

Age	Unemployment insurance	Disability insurance	Private pension plan	Social security benefits[a]
50	Cont. from 45+	Cont./Non-cont.	Yes	[b]
52	Cont. from 52+	Cont./Non-cont.	Yes	[b]
55	Cont. from 52+	Cont./Non-cont.	Yes	[b]
60	Cont.	Cont./Non-cont.	Yes	ER: Cont.
65			Yes	NR: Cont./Non-cont.

Notes: Cont. = contributory; Non-cont. = noncontributory; 45+ and 52+ = Special UI program for 45+ and 52+ workers enrolled in the RGSS; ER = early retirement; NR = normal retirement.

[a]All public programs provide benefits for dependants.

[b]There are age bonuses for certain professions, allowing for retirement before 60.

across regions) and, since the early 1990s, they have become harder to obtain at older ages. In fact, and contrary to the practice prevailing during the 1980s, it is now uncommon to access permanent DI benefits after age 55. This has been achieved mainly by tightening the disability evaluation process for the temporary illness program (*Incapacidad Laboral Transitoria*), which, in the past, was most often used as a bridge to retirement.

Both the unemployment and the disability plans offer, as we will subsequently argue, a pathway-to-early-retirement alternative to the official one (the latter consisting of early retirement at 60 and of normal retirement at 65). Such alternative pathways are taken into account in our estimation and simulation procedures.

The retirement program we label official (or regular) offers two options: early retirement and normal retirement. Early retirement is possible from age 60, but it only applies to workers who started their contributive career before 1967. The normal retirement age is 65, although some professional groups have lower normal retirement ages (e.g., miners, military personnel, policemen, fishermen). Collective wage settlements often impose mandatory retirement at age 65, facilitate retirement at 64 with full benefits, or encourage retirement between 60 and 63 through lump-sum payments.

9.2.2 Social Security Regimes and Their Rules

Under current legislation, public contributory pensions are provided by the following programs.

- The General Social Security Scheme (*Régimen General de la Seguridad Social,* or RGSS) and the Special Social Security Schemes (*Regímenes Especiales de la Seguridad Social,* or RESS) cover, respectively, the private-sector employees as well as self-employed workers and professionals. The RGSS also covers the members of cooperative firms, the employees of most public administrations other than the central governments, and all unemployed individuals who comply with the minimum number of contributory years upon reaching 65. The RESS include five special schemes:

1. Self-employed (*Régimen Especial de Trabajadores Autónomos* [RETA]).
2. Agricultural workers and small farmers (*Régimen Especial Agrario* [REA]).
3. Domestic workers (*Régimen Especial de Empleados de Hogar* [REEH]).
4. Sailors (*Régimen Especial de Trabajadores del Mar* [RETM]).
5. Coal miners (*Régimen Especial de la Minería del Carbón* [REMC]).

• The scheme for government employees (*Régimen de Clases Pasivas* [RCP]) includes public servants employed by the central government and its local branches. In this study we do not consider this regime.

Legislation approved by the Spanish parliament in 1997 established the progressive elimination of all the special regimes but RETA by the end of year 2001. At the moment, however, this piece of legislation has not been implemented, and the special regimes are still active.

9.2.3   Rules of the RGSS

This subsection describes the rules, since 1985, governing the old-age and survivors' pensions in the RGSS. The changes introduced by the 1997 reform (R97) and the 2002 (A02) amendment will be illustrated as we progress. A summary of the basic technical aspects of the pre- and post-1997 systems can be found in table 9.2.

Financing and Eligibility

The RGSS is a pure pay-as-you-go scheme. Contributions are a fixed proportion of covered earnings, defined as total earnings, excluding payments for overtime work, between a floor and a ceiling that vary by broadly defined professional categories. Eleven categories are currently distinguished, but the effective number of ceilings and floors for covered earnings is only four.

The current RGSS contribution rate is 28.3 percent, of which 23.6 percent is attributed to the employer and the remaining 4.7 percent to the employee. A tax rate of 14 percent is levied on earnings from overtime work.

Entitlement to an old-age pension requires at least fifteen years of contributions. As a general rule, recipiency is conditional on having reached age 65, and is incompatible with income from any kind of employment requiring affiliation with the Social Security system.

Table 9.2   Pension provisions, institutions, and systems

Institutions	RGSS system 1985–96	RGSS system after 1997
A. Basic ingredients	*Provisions affecting all individuals*	
A1. The benefit base formula	$\dfrac{1}{96}\left(\displaystyle\sum_{j=1}^{24} BC_{t-j} + \sum_{j=25}^{96} BC_{t-j}\,\dfrac{I_{t-25}}{I_{t-j}}\right)$	$\dfrac{1}{180}\left(\displaystyle\sum_{j=1}^{24} BC_{t-j} + \sum_{j=25}^{180} BC_{t-j}\,\dfrac{I_{t-25}}{I_{t-j}}\right)$
Contribution period	8 years	15
Fraction actualized	6 years	13
A2. Fiscal system		
Income tax	[progressive]	id.
Labor tax	linear (regime and group specific)	id.
B. Replacement rates		
Function of contributive years	$\begin{cases} 0, & \text{if } n<15, \\ .6+.02(n-15), & \text{if } 15\le n<35, \\ 1, & \text{if } 35\le n. \end{cases}$	$\begin{cases} 0, & \text{if } n<15, \\ .5+.03(n-15), & \text{if } 15\le n<25, \\ .8+.02(n-25), & \text{if } 25\le n<35, \\ 1, & \text{if } 35\le n. \end{cases}$
Function of age	$\begin{cases} 0, & \text{if } a<60, \\ .6+.08(a-60), & \text{if } 60\le a<65, \\ 1, & \text{if } 65\le a. \end{cases}$	exception for $n\ge 40$: $\begin{cases} 0, & \text{if } a<60, \\ .65+.07(a-60), & \text{if } 60\le a<65, \\ 1, & \text{if } 65\le a. \end{cases}$
	Provisions affecting particular individuals	
C. Income tax exemptions		
Max. pension exempted	∝ minimum wages	id.
Max. income exempted	∝ minimum wages	id.

D. Min./Max. contributions		
Min. level of contribution	(specific for 12 group)	id.
Max. level of contribution	(specific for 12 group)	id.
E. Min. and Max. pensions		
Min. pension	∝ minimum wages and family specific	id.
Max. pension	4.3 minimum wage (in 1995)	id.
F. Age bonuses	Yes (occupation specific)	id.
G. Survivor benefits	$0.45 \times$ (benefit base)	id.
H. Dependant benefits	18, 20 (means tested)	18, 23 (means tested)
Eligibility	2 years contributed last 10 years	2 out of last 15 years
Pension computation	$b_t = \max(\min\{\tilde{b}_t[n, e, BR(BC, I)], \bar{b}_t\}, \underline{b}_t)$	

where $\tilde{b}_t$ is the pension in A + B and $\bar{b}_t$ and $\underline{b}_t$ are respectively the maximum and minimum pension.

2002 Amendment

Scheme for early retirement	$\alpha_n = \begin{cases} 0, & \text{if } a < 61, \\ 1 - \kappa(a-60) & \text{if } 61 \le a < 65, \\ 1 & \text{if } 65 \le a. \end{cases}$	where $\kappa = \begin{cases} 0.08 & \text{if } n = 30 \\ 0.075 & \text{if } 31 \le n \le 34 \\ 0.07 & \text{if } 35 \le n \le 37 \\ 0.065 & \text{if } 38 \le n \le 39 \\ 0.06 & \text{if } 40 \le n. \end{cases}$
Premium for late retirement	$\alpha_n = 1 + 0.02\,(a - 65)$ iff $n \ge 30$	
Social Security contributions	No contributions for workers 65+, provided $n \ge 35$	
Survivor benefits	$0.46 \times$ (benefit base)	

Note: RGSS = Régimen General de la Seguridad Social.

Benefit Computation

When eligibility conditions are met, a retiring worker receives an initial monthly pension P_t equal to

$$P_t = \alpha_n BR_t,$$

where the benefit base (*base reguladora*) BR_t is a weighted average of covered monthly earnings over a reference period that consists of the last eight years before retirement:

$$BR_t = \frac{1}{112}\left(\sum_{j=1}^{24} W_{t-j} + \sum_{j=25}^{96} W_{t-j}\frac{I_{t-25}}{I_{t-j}}\right),$$

where W_{t-j} and I_{t-j} are earnings and the consumer price index is in the j-th month before retirement. Pensions are paid in fourteen annual installments, hence the division by 112 in the previous formula.

The replacement rate α_n depends on the age of the retirees and on the number of years of contribution. When age is below 60, $\alpha_n = 0$ for all n. For age equal or larger than 65, α_n is equal to

$$\alpha_n = \begin{cases} 0, & \text{if } n < 15, \\ .6 + .02\,(n-15), & \text{if } 15 \le n < 35, \\ 1, & \text{if } 35 \le n. \end{cases}$$

In the case of early retirement, that is, for ages between 60 and 65, α_n is determined by the previous formula multiplied by a penalization factor. The latter is equal to .6 at 60, and increases .08 each year until reaching the value of 1.0 at age 65.

Beginning in 1997, the number of reference years used for computing BR_t has been increased by one every year until 2003, to reach a total of fifteen years. The formula for computing α_n has been changed to the following:

$$\alpha_n = \begin{cases} 0, & \text{if } n < 15, \\ .5 + .03\,(n-15), & \text{if } 15 \le n < 25, \\ .8 + .02\,(n-25), & \text{if } 25 \le n < 35, \\ 1, & \text{if } 35 \le n. \end{cases}$$

The penalization factors have, basically, remained the same, an exception made for workers with forty or more years of contributions (details in the next subsection).

The A02 amendment allows for the possibility of α_n being greater than one when people are above age 65, that is,

$$\alpha_n = 1 + .02(a - 65), \quad \text{if } 65 \le a \text{ and } n \ge 35.$$

In all of our simulations we use the pre-1997 formula, which was in place over the relevant sample period. We consider the impact of the 1997 reform and the 2002 amendment when examining alternative policies (see, respectively, R97 and A02 in section 9.7).

Outstanding pensions are fully indexed to price inflation, as measured by the consumer price index. Until 1986, pensions were also indexed to real wage growth.

Early Retirement

The normal retirement age is 65, but early retirement at age 60 is permitted as a general rule for those who became affiliated with the Social Security system (*Mutualidades Laborales*) before 1967. The replacement rate for early retirees is reduced by 8 percentage points for each year under age 65. Starting from 1997, workers who retire after age 60 with forty or more contributive years are charged a penalty of only 7 percent for each year under age 65. The 2002 amendment has further modified the rules determining the replacement rate. It now reads as follows:

$$\alpha_n = \begin{cases} 0, & \text{if } a < 61, \\ 1 - \kappa(65 - a), & \text{if } 61 \leq a < 65, \\ 1, & \text{if } 65 \leq a, \end{cases}$$

where

$$\kappa = \begin{cases} 0.08 & \text{if } n = 30, \\ 0.075 & \text{if } 31 \leq n \leq 34, \\ 0.07 & \text{if } 35 \leq n \leq 37, \\ 0.065 & \text{if } 38 \leq n \leq 39, \\ 0.06 & \text{if } 40 \leq n. \end{cases}$$

Unless a collective labor agreement prescribes mandatory retirement, individuals may continue working after age 65. Before 2002, there were no incentives to work past age 65. As mentioned, the 2002 legislation now allows for

$$\alpha_n = 1 + .02(a - 65), \quad \text{if } 65 \leq a \text{ and } n \geq 35,$$

and eliminates social security contributions for workers meeting the eligibility criteria for full normal retirement ($a \geq 65$ and $n \geq 35$) who continue working.

About 10 percent of the workers enrolled in the RGSS are actually exempt from reduction in the replacement rate in case of early retirement. This applies to a number of privileged categories (bullfighters, employees of railroads, airlines, and public transportation, for example), or to workers who were laid off during cases of industrial restructuring regulated by special legislation. These exemption rights are portable in proportion to the number of years spent working in the privileged sector.

Maximum and Minimum Pension

Pensions are subject to a ceiling, legislated annually and roughly equal to the ceiling on covered earnings. The 2000 ceiling corresponds to about 4.3 times the minimum wage (*salario mínimo interprofesional* [SMI]) and about 1.6 times the average monthly earnings in the manufacturing and service sectors. If the initial old-age pension, as previously computed, is below a minimum, then the minimum pension is paid. The latter is also legislated annually. Other things being equal, minimum pensions are higher for those who are older than 65 or who have a dependent spouse.

In the last decade, minimum pensions grew at about the same rate as nominal wages, whereas maximum pensions grew at the rate of inflation. The ratio between the minimum old-age pension and the minimum wage has been increasing steadily from the late 1970s (it was 75 percent in 1975) until reaching almost 100 percent in the early 1990s. The percentage of RGSS retirees receiving a minimum pension has been declining steadily, from over 75 percent in the late 1970s to 27 percent in 1995.

Family Considerations

A pensioner receives a fixed annual allowance for each dependent child who is younger than 18 or is disabled. In 2000, this allowance was equal to 48,420 pesetas for each child under 18, and to 468,720 pesetas (45 percent of the annualized minimum wage) for each disabled child.

Survivors (spouse, children, other relatives) may receive a fraction of the benefit base of the deceased if the latter was a pensioner or died before retirement after contributing for at least 500 days in the last five years. The benefit base is computed differently in the two cases. If the deceased was a pensioner, the benefit base coincides with the pension. If the deceased was working, it is computed as an average of covered earnings over an uninterrupted period of two years, chosen by the beneficiary, among the last seven years immediately before death. If death occurred because of a work accident or a professional illness, then the benefit base coincides with the last earnings.

The surviving spouse gets 45 percent of the benefit base of the deceased (46 percent after the 2002 amendment, a fraction that will be further increased in forthcoming years). In case of divorce, the pension is divided between the various spouses according to the length of their marriage with the deceased. Such a pension is compatible with labor income and any other old-age or disability pension, but is lost if the spouse remarries.

Each of the surviving children gets 20 percent of the benefit base until the age of 18 (raised to 23 percent in 1997). An orphan who is the sole beneficiary may receive up to 65 percent of the benefit base. If there are several surviving children, the sum of the pensions to the surviving spouse (if any) and the children cannot exceed 100 percent of the benefit base.

A Spanish peculiarity is the pension in favor of family members. This pension entitles other surviving relatives (e.g., parents, grandparents, siblings, nephews) to 20 percent of the benefit base of the principal if they satisfy certain eligibility conditions (older than 45, do not have a spouse, do not have other means of subsistence, have been living with and depending economically upon the deceased for the last two years). To this pension, one may add the 45 percent survivors' pension if there is no surviving spouse or eligible surviving children.

9.2.4   Special Schemes

In this section we sketch the main differences between the general and the special schemes. Whereas rules and regulations for sailors and coal miners are very similar to the ones for the general scheme, special rules apply to the self-employed, farmers, agricultural workers, domestic helpers, and a few other categories not discussed here, such as part-time workers, artists, travelling salespeople, and bullfighters. Beside the differences in the SS tax rate and the definition of covered earnings, an important difference is the fact that affiliates of the special schemes have no early-retirement option (exceptions are made for miners and sailors).

The rest of this section focuses on the special schemes for self-employed workers (RETA) and farmers (REA), which together represent 93 percent of the affiliates of the special schemes, and 86 percent of the pensions they pay out.

Self-employed

While the SS tax rate is the same for the RETA and the general scheme (28.3 percent in 2000), covered earnings are computed differently, as the self-employed are essentially free to choose their covered earnings between a floor and a ceiling that are legislated annually. Not surprisingly, in light of the strong progressivity of Spanish personal income taxes, a suspiciously large proportion of self-employed workers report earnings equal to the legislated floor until they reach age 50. After that age one observes a sudden increase in reported covered earnings. This behavior exploits the finite memory in the formula for the calculation of the initial pension.

In 2000, the RETA contributive floor and ceiling were equal to 116,160 pesetas (pta) and 407,790 pta per month respectively, corresponding to 1.4 and 5 times the minimum wage, and to .5 and 1.9 times the average earnings in manufacturing and services. To reduce misreporting of earnings on the part of the self-employed, a different ceiling applies to self-employed aged over 50 who had not reported higher earnings in previous years. In

2000, the latter was only 219,000 pta per month, roughly equal to average monthly earnings.

A crucial difference with respect to the general scheme is that, under the RETA, recipiency of an old-age pension is compatible with maintaining the self-employed status. The implications of this provision for the retirement behavior of self-employed workers are discussed later.

Other important provisions are the following: RETA only requires five years of contributions in the ten years immediately before the death of the principal in order to qualify for survivors' pensions. Under RETA, the latter is 50 percent of the benefit base. If the principal was not a pensioner at the time of death, the benefit base is computed as the average of covered earnings over an uninterrupted period of five years, chosen by the beneficiary among the last ten years before the death of the principal.

Farmers

In this case, both the SS tax rate and the covered earnings differ with respect to the general scheme. Self-employed farmers pay 19.75 percent of a tax base that is legislated annually and is only weakly related to average earnings. In 2000, this was equal to 91,740 pta per month, corresponding to 1.24 times the minimum wage and about 40 percent of average monthly earnings in the manufacturing and service sectors.

Farm employees, instead, pay 11.5 percent of a monthly base that depends on their professional category and is also legislated annually. In addition, for each day of work, their employer must pay 15.5 percent of a daily base that also varies by professional category and is legislated annually.

9.3   Key Ingredients of the Retirement Models

In this section we review the main steps taken in order to estimate reduced-form retirement models. First, we describe the sample and the characteristics of the earning processes. Then we construct the various measures of social security incentives. In the last part we review the results from the estimated models.

9.3.1   The Sample

Our main microeconomic dataset is based on administrative records from the Spanish Social Security Administration (*Historiales Laborales de la Seguridad Social* [HLSS]). The sample consists of 250,000 individual work histories randomly drawn from the historical files of SS affiliates (*Fichero Histórico de Afiliados* [FHA]). The sample includes only individuals aged over 40 on July 31, 1998, the date at which the files were prepared. The sample contains individuals from the RGSS and the five special regimes—RETA, REA, REEH, RTMC, and RTMAR. As we mentioned earlier, civil servants and other central government employees are not covered by the SS administration and are not considered in this study.

The dataset consists of three files. The first file (the history file, or H) contains the work history of individuals in the sample. Each record in this file describes a single employment period of the individual. As we argue later, the work histories are very accurate for periods or histories that began after the mid-1960s. The second file (covered earnings file, or CE) contains annual averages of covered earnings (*bases de cotización*) from 1986 to 1995. The third file (benefits file, or B) contains information on the lifetime SS benefits received by individuals in the sample. Benefits are classified by function (retirement, disability, survival, etc.) and initial amount received. To be more precise, the benefits file contains the initial benefit amount and the length of the period during which the benefit was received. A fourth file (relatives file, or R) is also available; it reports some benefits paid to relatives of the individual while members of his or her household.

For each individual in the sample who contributed to SS during the 1986–1995 period, the CE file reports the annual average of covered earnings together with the contributions paid. For individuals enrolled in either the RGSS or the RTMC, covered earnings are a doubly censored (from above and below) version of real earnings. This is due to the existence of legislated ceilings and floors, as reported earlier. For people enrolled in SS regimes other than RGSS and RTMC, covered earnings are chosen by the individual within given ceilings and floors (see section 9.2 for details) and, consequently, in this case there is no clear link between covered and actual earnings.

For each employment spell in the HLSS-H file, we know age, sex, and marital status of the person, the duration of the period (in days), the type of contract (in particular, we can distinguish between part-time and full-time contracts), the social security regime, the contributive group, the cause for the termination of the period, the sector of employment (4-digits SIC), and the region of residence (52 Spanish provinces). For each individual in the H file who has received some benefits at any point, we know most of the information that the SS Administration uses to compute the monthly benefits to be paid. In particular, we know the initial and current pension, the benefit base (*base reguladora*), the number of contributive years, the current integration toward the minimum pension (*complementos por el mínimo*), the date pension was claimed, the date it was awarded, the type of benefits, and so on. See Boldrin, Jiménez-Martín, and Peracchi (2004) for a description of the demographic characteristics of the sample and the sample selection rules.

9.3.2 Earnings Distribution, Earnings Histories, and Projections

As commented in section 9.3.1, we do not observe earnings directly but only covered earnings. Covered earnings are a doubly censored version of earnings for workers in the RGSS or Regimen Trabajadores Mineria Carbon (RTMC), while they are very weakly related to true earnings for workers in the RETA because of the presence of both legislated tariffs and widespread tax fraud.

RGSS and RTMC

To deal with the top-censoring problem, we proceed as follows. First, we estimate a Tobit model for covered earnings. Then we use the estimated parameters to impute the earnings of the censored observations and to estimate an earning function using imputed earnings for those affected by the ceilings. Finally, we generate true earnings for all the individuals in the top censored groups, by using the estimated regression function and adding an individual, random noise component.

From the individual profile of covered earnings c_t between year $T-k$ and year T we impute the individual profile of true real earnings (w_t, $t = T-k$, . . . , T). Given this information, we project earnings forward and backward in the following way.

- Forward: here we assume zero real growth, hence $\hat{w}_{T+m} = w_T$ for $m = 1, \ldots, M$.
- Backward: $\hat{w}_{T-k-1} = w_{T-k} + g(a_{T-k-1})$ for $l = 1, \ldots, L$. The function $g(\cdot)$ corrects for the growth of log earnings imputable to age a and is defined as:

$$g(a_{T-k-l}) = \beta_1 \cdot a_{T-k-l} + \beta_2 \cdot a_{T-k-l}^2 - \beta_1 \cdot a_{T-k} - \beta_2 \cdot a_{T-k}^2.$$

The βs are the estimated coefficients from a fixed-effects earnings equation, the details of which are available upon request. The correction is specific for each combination of sex and contributive group.

We further correct backward the log of average earnings to control for the variation of the average productivity of the Spanish economy in the period 1960–1985, which is the time horizon of our backward projection.

RETA

As already pointed out, for individuals enrolled in the RETA, covered earnings are very weakly related to true earnings. The self-employed are free to choose their benefit base between an annual floor and ceiling, and practically all choose the floor. This implies that there is no way in which true earnings for the self-employed can be recovered from the HLSS dataset. We are therefore forced to assume that the earnings and the contributive profile coincide. Thus, we project (real) earnings given the observed profile of (real) contributions as follows:

- Backward: $w_{t-k-l} = c_{t-k}$, for $l = 1, \ldots, L$,
- Forward: $w_{t+m} = c_t(1 + g)^m$, for $m = 1, \ldots, M$ with $g = 0.005$.

In other words, we assume that contributions were constant up to the first time they are observed, while they grow at a constant annual rate of 0.5 percent thereafter.

It is important to recall, from section 9.2, that current Spanish legislation allows the self-employed to begin drawing retirement pensions without retiring, at least as long as they keep managing their own business. Hence, in the dynamic choice of the self-employed, the opportunity cost of retiring is not measured by the loss of future earnings but, instead, by the fact that contributions can no longer be accumulated to increase future pensions, and marginal income taxes must be paid on pensions. This implies that for the self-employed, maximization of the (net of taxes) Social Security payoff is a very reasonable, objective function.

9.3.3 Evaluation of Social Security Incentives

Assumptions

For every male worker in the wage sample who is enrolled either in the RGSS or in the RETA we assume that: (a) he is married to a nonworking spouse, (b) his wife is three years younger, and (c) his mortality corresponds to the baseline male mortality from the most recent available life tables (INE 1995).

For every female in the wage sample we assume that: (a) she is married to either a retiree or a worker entitled to retirement benefits, (b) her husband is four years older, and (c) her mortality is the baseline female mortality from the most recent available life tables (INE 1995).

For both men and women we further assume that (d) starting at age 55 and until age 65, there are three pathways to retirement: the UB52+ program, DI benefits, and early retirement. At each age, an individual has an age-specific probability of entering retirement using any of these three programs. However, the following restrictions are important in characterizing the actual usage of the three pathways to retirement.

1. No person has access to early retirement before age 60.
2. After age 60, a person cannot claim UB52+ and can only claim early retirement or DI benefits.
3. A self-employed person enrolled in RETA can never claim UB52+ benefits.

This implies that, in practice, pathways for retirement are relatively simple. For people in the RGSS, either they retire before 60 via the UB52+ or the DI benefits program or they retire after 60 via the DI (most unlikely, though, since 1992) or the retirement program. People in the RESS either go via the DI benefits or the retirement program, with the likelihood of the former being low and decreasing from age 60 onward.

Calculating SS Incentives

For a worker of age a, we define social security wealth (SSW) in case of retirement at age $h \geq a$ as the expected present value of future pension benefits.

$$\mathrm{SSW}_h = \sum_{s=h+1}^{S} \rho_s B_s(h)$$

Here S is the age of certain death, $\rho_s = \beta^{s-a}\pi_s$, with β denoting the pure time discount factor and π_s the conditional survival probability at age s for an individual alive at age a, and $B_s(h)$ the pension expected at age $s \geq h + 1$ in case of retirement at age h. Given SSW, we define three incentive variables for a worker of age a:

1. *Social security accrual* (SSA) is the difference in SSW from postponing retirement from age a to age $a + 1$

$$\mathrm{SSA}_a = \mathrm{SSW}_{a+1} - \mathrm{SSW}_a = \sum_{s=a+2}^{S} \rho_s[B_s(a + 1) - B_s(a)] - \rho_{a+1}B_{a+1}(a).$$

The SSA is positive if the expected present value $\sum_{s=a+2}^{S} \rho_s[B_s(a + 1) - B_s(a)]$ of the increment in the flow of pension benefits is greater than the expected present value $\rho_{a+1}B_{a+1}(a)$ of the pension benefit forgone by postponing retirement. If the increments $B_s(a + 1) - B_s(a)$ are small, as it is usually the case, then the SSA is negative. The rescaled negative accrual $\tau_a = -\mathrm{SSA}_a/W_{a+1}$, where W_{a+1} equals expected net earnings at age $a + 1$ based on the information available up to age a, is called the implicit tax/subsidy on postponing retirement from age a to age $a + 1$.

2. *Peak value* $\mathrm{PV}_a = \max_h(\mathrm{SSW}_h - \mathrm{SSW}_a)$, $h = a + 1, \ldots, R$, where R is a mandatory retirement age (which does not exist in Spain, but given the retirement evidence we find it reasonable to assume $R = 70$). Thus, the peak value is the maximum difference in SSW between retiring at any future age and retiring at age a.

3. *Option value* $\mathrm{OV}_a = \max_h(V_h - V_a)$, $h = a + 1, \ldots, R$, where

$$V_a = \sum_{s=a+1}^{S} \rho_s[kB_s(h)]^\gamma$$

is the total expected utility of retiring at age a, and

$$V_h = \sum_{s=a+1}^{h} \rho_s W_s^\gamma + \sum_{s=h+1}^{S} \rho_s[kB_s(h)]^\gamma$$

is the total expected utility of retiring at age $h > a$. Thus, the option value is the maximum utility difference between retiring at any future age and retiring at age a. We parameterize the model by assuming $\beta = .97$, $\gamma = 1$, and $k = 1.25$. Under our assumptions, $V_a = 1.25\,\mathrm{SSW}_a$ and

$$V_h = \sum_{s=a+1}^{h} \rho_s W_s + 1.25 \, \mathrm{SSW}_h.$$

If expected earnings are constant at W_a (as assumed by our earnings model), then

$$V_h - V_a = W_a \sum_{s=a+1}^{h} \rho_s + 1.25(\mathrm{SSW}_h - \mathrm{SSW}_a),$$

that is, the peak value and the option value are proportional to each other except for the effect due to the term $\Sigma_{s=a+1}^{h}\rho_s$.

The restrictions embodied in assumption (d) require us to combine the incentive measures I_j from the various programs (j = UB, DI, R, where UB denotes unemployment benefits, DI disability benefits, and R the retirement programs) as follows:

$$I = \begin{cases} p_a^{DI}I_{DI} + I_{UB}(1 - p_a^{DI}), & \text{if } 55 \le a < 60, \\ p_a^{DI}I_{DI} + I_R(1 - p_a^{DI}), & \text{if } 60 \le a < 65, \\ I_R, & \text{if } 65 \ge a, \end{cases}$$

where p_a^{DI} denotes the probability of observing a transition from employment into disability at age a. Since the self-employed have no access to UB52+ benefits, the combined incentives from age 55 to age 59 for members of this group change to

$$I = p_a^{DI}I_{DI} + I_R(1 - p_a^{DI}), \quad 55 \le a \le 59.$$

We have followed a regression-based approach to compute the unconditional probability of qualifying for a disability pension (see table 9.3; see also Boldrin, Jiménez-Martín, and Peracchi [2004] for a description).

9.3.4   The Reduced-Form Retirement Model

This section briefly illustrates the explanatory power of our incentive measures (accrual, peak value, and option value) for retirement behavior. The results reported here are distilled from the extensive econometric analysis conducted in Boldrin, Jiménez-Martín, and Peracchi (2004), to which the reader is referred for all relevant details.

We follow a regression-based approach to model the effect of social security wealth, incentive measure (either accrual, peak, or option value), and individual demographic characteristics on the decision to retire in 1995, conditional on being active at the end of 1994. Retirement probabilities are assumed to have the probit form

$$Pr(R_i = 1) = \Phi(\delta_1 \mathrm{SSW}_i + \delta_2 I_i + \delta_3' X_i),$$

where R is a binary indicator of retirement, Φ is the distribution function of a standard normal, I denotes the incentive measure, and X is a vector of

Table 9.3   Probit models of the 1995 retirement rates

	Accrual				Peak				Option value			
	M1		M2		M1		M2		M1		M2	
	Coef.	SE	Coef.	SE	Coef.	SE	Coef.	SE	Coef.	SE	Coef.	SE
	Male RGSS: 16,191 observations											
SSW	.00344	.00128	.00749	.00152	.00871	.00149	.01387	.00170	.01080	.00165	.00627	.00186
ME	.00033	.00012	.00071	.00014	.00087	.00015	.00136	.00017	.00109	.00017	.00161	.00018
Incentive	−.00906	.00430	−.00130	.00489	.00147	.00245	.00448	.00254	.00884	.00111	.01032	.00115
ME	−.00088	.00042	−.00012	.00046	.00015	.00024	.00044	.00025	.00089	.00011	.00102	.00011
Constant	−1.642	.50046	−1.197	.53053	−1.495	.49230	−1.273	.52863	−1.360	.49665	−1.262	.53657
R^2	.336		.373		.341		.380		.342		.381	
Log-likelihood	−3,791		−3,579		−3,766		−3,544		−3,758		−3,534	
	Female RGSS: 3,852 observations											
SSW	.00970	.00325	.01812	.00419	.01138	.00345	.02022	.00438	.01176	.00381	.02175	.00477
ME	.00090	.00030	.00162	.00038	.00107	.00033	.00185	.00040	.00111	.00036	.00199	.00044
Incentive	−.0092	.00710	−.00580	.00755	.00135	.00490	.00393	.00527	.00247	.00202	.00361	.00210
ME	−.00086	.00066	−.00053	.00068	.00013	.00046	.00036	.00048	.00023	.00019	.00033	.00019
Constant	−.4766	.64579	−.2204	.74217	−.3112	.64244	−.2072	.74880	−.3301	.64892	−.3375	.75922
R^2	.327		.355		.327		.356		.326		.356	
Log-likelihood	−897.8		−860.1		−897.7		−858.5		−897.9		−858.5	

Male RETA: 4,355 observations

SSW	.00870	.00496	.00726	.01174	-.00068	.00695	.00992	.01238	.00757	.00938	.00501	.01451
ME	.00117	.00067	.00096	.00155	-.00009	.00092	.00131	.00163	.00100	.00124	.00066	.00191
Incentive	-.04703	.01212	.01050	.01440	-.02915	.00900	.01432	.01056	-.00920	.00729	.00187	.00758
ME	-.00630	.00162	.00138	.00190	-.00385	.00119	.00188	.00139	-.00122	.00097	.00025	.00100
Constant	-2.079	.68022	-1.542	1.2772	-1.848	.72708	-1.6444	1.2819	-2.107	.70436	-1.324	1.283
R^2	.168		.252		.166		.253		.167		.253	
Log-likelihood	-1,201		-1,079		-1,203		-1,078		-1,202		-1,079	

Female RETA: 2,051 observations

SSW	.00316	.00643	-.00176	.01113	.00188	.00732	-.00248	.01119	.00342	.01334	-.01475	.01781
ME	.00047	.00095	-.00025	.00156	.00028	.00108	-.00035	.00157	.00051	.00199	-.00207	.00250
Incentive	.01813	.01096	.02538	.01207	.00849	.00979	.01824	.01039	.00241	.01448	.00739	.01736
ME	.00268	.00162	.00355	.00169	.00126	.00145	.00256	.00146	.00036	.00215	.00104	.00244
Constant	-3.358	3.5687	-3.678	3.7786	-3.175	3.5836	-2.457	3.8070	-3.259	3.6326	-1.876	3.9571
R^2	.142		.197		.141		.196		.140		.195	
Log-likelihood	-638.5		-597.9		-639.4		-598.5		-639.8		-598.9	

Notes: M1 = model with a linear age trend; M2 = model with age dummies; Coef. = coefficient; SE = standard error; ME = marginal effect; RGSS = Régimen General de la Seguridad Social; RETA = Régimen Especial de Trabajadores Autónomos.

predictors that include individual earnings and sociodemographic characteristics. The socioeconomic and earnings information is richer for the RGSS than for the RETA. This, coupled with the widespread misreporting of earnings that characterizes the affiliates to RETA, makes a quantitative analysis of their retirement patterns a very difficult task. Regression results for RETA, in fact, are much poorer than those for RGSS and, in any case, should be taken with caution.

For each one of the three incentive measures (accrual, peak, and option value) we have used the following specification for the set of predictors X. The latter contains an eligibility dummy for attainment of a minimum of fifteen years of contributions; three industry-specific variables: the fraction of collective wage settlements having a clause favoring early retirement, the presence of rules permitting retirement at age 64 without penalty, and the existence of mandatory retirement at age 65; different measures of seniority on the job and in the labor market (length of the current employment spell and its square, number of years of contribution and its square, number of years since first employment); dummies for schooling level and contributive group (only for people in the RGSS); dummies for part-time work and sector of occupation (only for people in the RGSS); the expected wage and our estimate of the lifetime earnings net present value and their squares; the net present value of expected wages until the year in which either the peak value or the option value reach their maximum.

A Summary of Estimation Results

The results obtained for each incentive measure are presented separately by sex and social security regime in table 9.3. In each case, we have considered two specifications for the age effect: a linear time trend (M1) and age-specific dummies (M2). The models have been fit to the observed transitions between 1994 and 1995. We show, for each combination of sex and regime, the estimates of the probit coefficients, their estimated standard errors, and the implied probability effect. Since we report the results from a large number of models, we concentrate on the variables of interest. The complete set of results is available from the authors upon request.

Quite obviously, M2 provides a uniformly better fit than M1 and, in particular, captures the hazard peaks at 60 and 65, which M1 fails to fit; on any other aspect, though, the qualitative as well as most of the quantitative performances of the two models are equivalent. Hence, the comments that follow apply, unless stated otherwise, to both specifications. The SSW term is positive and significant in all cases. Contradictory results are obtained instead for the three incentive variables. In fact, while the accrual usually shows the expected (negative) sign, both the peak and the option value show the wrong (positive) sign. Further, neither SSW nor the incentive variables are significant for people enrolled in RETA, indicating that the

SSW and the financial variables do not capture retirement incentives for individuals enrolled in RETA. Measures of fitness, such as the R^2, are either mediocre or poor, suggesting that a great deal of retirement variability cannot be captured by our incentive indicators. This is particularly true for people enrolled in the special regimes (RETA). These relatively poor results are discussed at length in Boldrin, Jiménez-Martín, and Peracchi (2004) and we will not go back to them here. They do suggest, though, that the quantitative impact that a change in the financial incentives may have on predicted retirement behavior is bound to be either negligible or small. The implied probability effects are minuscule, suggesting that only abnormally large variations in the incentive measures may be able to have a quantitatively sizable effect on early retirement. As a consequence of this fact, when evaluating the policy reforms we concentrate our attention mostly on changes in SSW and on the effect of variables other than the pure financial incentive variables. As the forthcoming analysis underlines, reforming the legislated early and normal retirement age appears to be the most reliable and effective way of altering existing retirement patterns.

9.4 Simulation Methodology

9.4.1 Policy Simulations

The main aim of this paper is to investigate the budgetary implications of pension system reforms. In the simulations we consider five policies, of which the last two are specific to the Spanish case:

R1: Three-Year Reform. A reform of the existing system, consisting of a three-year increase in both the early and the normal retirement age (ERA and NRA, respectively), while keeping all other aspects of the Spanish social security system unchanged.

R2: Actuarial Reform. This reform introduces the following change to the base Spanish pension system: a 6 percent annual actuarial adjustment per year away from the normal retirement age. Benefits become available at the existing ERA (60), and retirements after the NRA receive a positive 6 percent adjustment per year. This actuarial adjustment is also applied to disability benefits.

R3: Common Reform. This reform implies the following changes to the base system: (a) ERA at 60, (b) NRA at 65, (c) a replacement rate at age 65 equal to 60 percent of the gross (but net of the employers contributions) average lifetime earnings (on the best 40 earnings years before retirement or the first age of eligibility, whichever comes first), and an actuarial adjustment of 3.6 percent per year from age 60 to 70 (this implies a replacement rate of 42 percent at age 60 and 78 percent at age 70). Notice that (a) and (b) correspond to the current Spanish system, whereas the actuarial adjustment for retirement before age 65 is less favorable than the one currently used in Spain. Also, the current Spanish system is more generous for retirement at age 65 and has no actuarial adjustment for postponing retirement after that age.

R97: The retirement regime created by the 1997 Spanish reform.

A02: The previous regime, as altered by the amendment introduced in 2002.

We recall that the 1997 reform, described in section 9.2, implies the following changes in the basic benefit formula and in the penalties related to age and contributive history: (a) the number of years of contribution used to construct the benefit base is increased from eight, as prescribed by the 1985 legislation, to fifteen, (b) workers retiring after the age of 60 with 40 or more contributive years are charged an actuarial adjustment of only 7 percent (instead of 8 percent) for each year under age 65, and (c) the penalty for insufficient contributions is such that the replacement rate (ratio between pension and BR) is

$$
\alpha_n = \begin{cases} 0, & \text{if } n < 15, \\ .5 + .03(n - 15), & \text{if } 15 \le n < 25, \\ .8 + .02(n - 25), & \text{if } 25 \le n < 35, \\ 1, & \text{if } 35 \le n. \end{cases}
$$

The 2002 amendment has introduced the following changes, which are also illustrated in section 9.2: (a) a generalized penalization rule for early retirement, starting at age 61; (b) a new incentive scheme for those retiring after the age 65 with at least 35 years of contributions; (c) an increase in survivor benefits.

For each of the five policies we carry out the following simulations:

S1: Starting from the model with a linear trend (M1), we modify the SSW and incentive measures in accordance with the new policy. Specifically, in the calculation of SSW, we increase by three years the early and the normal retirement ages and shift by three years the age-specific probability of receiving DI-UI benefits.

S2: Starting this time from M2, we modify the SSW and incentive measures according to the assumed policy changes. We also change the probabilities of receiving DI benefits, by setting them to zero after age 60, but leave untouched the coefficients on the age dummies.

S3: Again using M2, in addition to the changes described in S2, we also shift the coefficients on the age dummies by three years, so that the entire age profile of the retirement hazard shifts forward by three years. Specifically, in the calculation of SSW, we increase by three years the early and the normal retirement ages, and shift by three years the age-specific probability of receiving DI-UI benefits.

9.4.2 Simulation Sample

We use individuals born in 1940 (aged 55 in 1995) extracted from the sample described previously, since the zero real-growth assumption seems to be very unrealistic for younger cohorts. We have concentrated on workers enrolled in either the general regime (RGSS) or the self-employed regime (RETA). These two groups cover practically 90 percent of the affiliates to the Spanish social security.

Given that the base sample (HLSS) is not completely representative of the regional distribution of Spanish employment, we have constructed a balanced random sample by sampling (with replacement) from the HLSS, using the population weights of the six territorial areas into which Spain is divided by the Labor Force Survey (EPA). The rebalancing procedure has been further refined by taking into account, within each of the six regions, the composition of the labor force by sex and by contributive regime. In a second step, weights have been assigned to each observation in order to replicate the population number of workers born in 1940 who were active in the labor market in 1995 (farmers and civil servants excluded).

9.4.3 Baseline Case and Family Assumptions

Our baseline case makes the same assumptions as in Boldrin, Jiménez-Martín, and Peracchi (2004) with regard to interest and mortality rates. The other assumptions are illustrated next.

Marital Status Assumptions

We have used family data from the Spanish Labor Force Survey to obtain information on the marital status of individuals born in 1940. The main findings, which we try to replicate in our simulations, are the following:

- Male: 95 percent married and 5 percent single. Among those married, 75.2 percent have a nonworking spouse and the rest a working spouse. In both cases the spouse was (on average), born in 1943 (aged 52).
- Female: 74 percent married and 26 percent single. Among those married, 34.5 have a nonworking spouse (presumably retired) and the rest a working spouse. In both cases the spouse (on average) was born in 1937 (aged 58).

Two remarks are relevant with respect to the way in which the benefits of survivorship are handled in the simulation exercises.

1. Since survivor and retirement benefits are fully compatible (up to the amount of the maximum pension) there is no necessity to correct for double counting in the Spanish case. Whenever the maximum pension ceiling is supposed to take effect, this is applied to the total pension payments accruing to the survivor.

2. Survivor benefits accruing to members of the 1940 cohort in force of

their having a working spouse are not accounted for (i.e., are not included in the computation of the SSW for a member of the 1940 cohort) since they are included in the computation of benefits for the cohort the spouse belongs to.

Dependant Assumptions

As noted previously, our dataset does not provide sufficient information on marital status or on the number and age of dependants. In our projections, we handle this inconvenience by using information extracted from the Spanish Labor Survey over the 1995–2001 period. From such data we compute the average number of dependants (per worker) in each of the six regions (Catalonia, South, Centre or Castilla, Madrid, East, and North). We also distinguish by the sex and age of the individual worker. In other words, we assume that the factors determining the number of dependants are age, sex, and region of residence. Then we regress the data so collected for each of the seven years comprised by the EPA sample, and for each region of residence and sex cell with respect to the age of the worker and its square. Next, we use these regressions to predict, for people born in 1940, the average number of dependants when they reach the age between 55 and 70. After that age we assume that the number of dependants (spouse excluded) drops to zero. In order to impute the benefits for dependants in the calculation of the SSW, we assume that all of them receive the legislated minimum (see Boldrin, Jiménez-Martín, and Peracchi [2004] for data and legislation).

9.4.4 Computing Expected Expenditure for Those Who Retire before Fifty-five

The goal here is to estimate the total expenditure for pension payments to those members of the 1940 cohort who retired before the year 1995 (i.e., before reaching the age of 55) and whose retirement behavior we will not try to model. While during the 1980s and early 1990s the number of Spanish workers retiring before age 55 was considerable, this practice has been dropping remarkably quickly during the last decade. As we have already pointed out, this is due to a substantial tightening of the requirements for accessing DI benefits and the sharp reduction in the usage of subsidized early retirement as an instrument for handling industrial restructuring.

The relevant information in our sample has the following form. We have information on the initial benefits for all the workers belonging to the 1940 cohort who retired before 1998 (age 58). This allows us to reconstruct the SSW of those workers in pesetas of the reference year (1995 in our case). To proceed further we need three additional assumptions.

1. Anyone retiring before age 55 did it through the DI program.
2. None of the five reforms being considered will affect the benefits of those workers who retire before age 55 by means of the DI program.

3. The marital status and the number of dependant entitled to benefits for people in this group are the same as for the average member of the co-hort.

This allows us to estimate the (after-income taxes) net present value, in millions of 2001 euros, of the SSW attributable to members of the 1940 co-hort who retired before the age of 55. This is euro 1,360.4 and 289.6, for male and females, respectively. These values are to be added to those obtained in tables 9.9 and 9.10.

9.4.5   Computing Expected Expenditure

Our aim is to compute the lifetime net present value (NPV) of the pension expenditure for a given cohort C aged a in year t. We are endowed with a sample of N observations from which we want to project expenditure for a working population of size M. There are two ways of leaving the labor force: retirement and death. Under such circumstances, the expected net present value of the benefits payments for person i of cohort C is given by:

$$NPVBP_i = \sum_{h=a}^{S}[\pi_{hi}(R; X)\,SSW_{hi} + \pi_{hi}(d; X)SSW_{hi}^d]; \, i = 1, \ldots, N,$$

where $\pi_{hi}(R; X)$ and $\pi_{hi}(d; X)$ are, respectively, the conditional probabilities (at age a) of retirement and death at age h. Both of them may depend—or not—on individual characteristics (X). In our exercise, the retirement probabilities do depend on individual characteristics and the probability of dying does not (except for the sex of the individual). Obviously, the retirement probabilities at each age depend on individual characteristics in accordance with the retirement probabilities estimated previously.

Selecting the adequate weights (which depend on individual characteristics) for each observation and summing up over individuals we obtain the projected benefits payments for a given cohort C:

$$NPVBP_C = \sum_{i=1}^{N} NPVPE_i \cdot W_i(X); \, i = 1, \ldots, N,$$

where $W_i(X)$ is the share of individuals of type i in the population, according to the vector of characteristics X.

The net present value of social security contributions is given

$$NPVTP_C = \sum_{i=1}^{N} NPVTP_i \cdot W_i(X); \, i = 1, \ldots, N,$$

where the net present value of social security contributions for an individual of type i in cohort C has been computed as

$$NPVTP_i = \sum_{h=a}^{S}[1 - \pi_{hi}(R; X) - \pi_{hi}(d; X)]C_{hi}^d,$$

Table 9.4   **Population factors for the 1940 cohort in 1995**

	Male		Female	
	Work force	Fraction	Work force	Fraction
RGSS				
Catalonia	2,427,278	.1920417	862,297	.1806272
South	2,655,976	.2101359	1,299,916	.2722962
Castilla	888,563	.0703015	476,717	.0998589
Madrid	2,441,918	.1932	71,427	.1496197
East	2,063,698	.163276	813,333	.1703706
North	2,161,893	.171045	607,372	.1272275
RETA				
Catalonia	623,986	.1615313	85,814	.0700625
South	989,671	.2561962	312,326	.2549975
Castilla	308,444	.0798469	148,902	.1215705
Madrid	497,341	.1287467	242,192	.1977368
East	767,909	.1987886	249,680	.2038504
North	675,591	.1748903	185,906	.1517823

and C_{hi}^d are the social security contributions paid at age h by an individual of type i. Finally, the projected expenditure (benefits–taxes) is given by

$$NPVPE_C = NPVBP_C - NPVTP_C.$$

9.4.6   Elevation to the Population

As noted previously (see Boldrin, Jiménez-Martín, and Peracchi [2004]), the HLSS data source is not completely representative of the Spanish population. In table 9.4 we present the set of population factors we have used in order to make our sample representative of the working population under study. The source of the weights is the second-quarter wave of the 1995 Spanish Labor Force Survey. We distinguish individuals according to two social security regimes (RGSS, RETA), six regions (Catalonia, South, Centre or Castilla, Madrid, East, and North) and by their sex, for a total of 24 different types.

9.4.7   Income Tax and Indirect Taxes

A full evaluation of the fiscal impact of a social security reform cannot be restricted to the impact that the latter may have on the budget of the Social Security Administration alone. While in many countries, Spain being one of them, the social security administration formally runs a separate budget distinct from that of the central government, such separation is only formal and is continuously violated in practical circumstances. So, for example, in the Spanish system, the employees of the central government belong to a pension system that is managed directly by the Spanish treasury and is financed by general taxation. While the RGSS has been running a current account surplus during the last few years, this was not the case in the past and, most likely, will not be the case again in the near future. In previous years, the annual deficits of the RGSS (and of the various regimes listed in the RESS) were covered by transfers from the central government. In fact, part of the current surplus of the RGSS is due to the fact that, progressively, since the 1985 reform, a number of functions originally pertaining to the RGSS have been transferred or are being financed directly by general taxation (Social Security social services [INSERSO], noncontributive pensions, part of the minimum pension payments, some disability payments, etc.). More generally, it is quite obvious that surpluses and deficits of the public pension system are surpluses and deficits of the central government, which guarantees the payment of future pensions via its power of taxation, and which considers the net present value of current and future pension entitlements as part of the public debt. This implies that a full picture of the fiscal effect of a reform can be achieved only by adding to the net present value calculations we just illustrated—the impact of changing work and retirement patterns on other sources of fiscal revenues.

Among the latter, income taxes take the lion's share. By retiring, an individual not only stops contributing to the pension system and starts drawing a pension; he or she also starts paying income taxes on a pension that is usually substantially smaller than the previous labor income. This effect is further magnified by the existence, in many countries, of a strongly progressive income taxation and a number of exemptions for low incomes, among which pensions loom large, at least in the case of Spain. Finally, moving from work to retirement also implies a number of changes in the consumption habits of an individual, which may also affect his or her exposure to other forms of taxation, such as VAT. While we do take this effect into account in our estimations, a word of caution should be added. Most of the VAT impact is due not so much to changes in the composition of consumption baskets (VAT rates are fairly homogenous) but to the lower income level of pensioners. One is therefore led to assume, as we do here, that a relatively stable relationship exists between income and sales/consumption taxes. While this may be a correct first-order approximation, it should be interpreted with care, as it may easily overestimate the reduction in indirect taxation that follows retirement. The reason is obvious: VAT is a consumption tax, hence the portion of disposable income that is saved is not burdened with VAT. Saving propensities drop substantially after retirement, which may imply that the amount of VAT paid, as a percentage of one's income or income taxes, does not stay constant but increases after retirement.

These caveats notwithstanding, we proceeded as follows. For each individual in the 1940 cohort, and for each age from 55 onward, we computed the total income taxes paid; that is, the sum of the income taxes paid as an active worker (assuming that our estimated labor income at that age, and in that year coincided with the totality of his or her income) and as a retiree (again, assuming the pension received coincided with her or his total income). Additionally, we have tried to impute the VAT taxes paid, starting from the income taxes and multiplying by a VAT factor defined as:

$$VAT = PT/T,$$

where PT consists of VAT plus other sales and consumption taxes, and T is total income taxes. The resulting VAT factor, using national accounts data for 1995–2001 is 0.92.[3]

The total tax receipts from a pension system, ignoring the general equilibrium effects, are therefore given by:

$$\text{Total Taxes} = \text{SS contribution} + (1 + VAT) \text{ Income Taxes.}$$

The difference between total taxes under the base case and under each of the five reforms quantifies the fiscal impact of that reform.

9.5   Results

Overall, the results are mixed, and in a sense, as we should make clear as we proceed with the discussion, not fully satisfactory. Recall our distinction (see introduction) between a mechanical and a behavioral effect of a policy reform. As we argued there, to the extent that individuals who are in the middle, or toward the end, of their working history are faced with a change of rules to which they cannot appropriately respond, the first effect is always present. The second will come about only if two conditions are simultaneously realized: (1) the reform affects the financial incentives to either retire or continue working, and (2) people respond strongly to variations in such financial incentives.

Basically, as one would have expected from the low ability of our reduced-form estimations to capture the variability of retirement behaviors, while the five reforms do affect the two incentive indicators, the latter do not induce strong behavioral responses on the part of workers. More precisely, the fraction of workers whom, we estimate, would postpone retirement age is quite small, and the number of years by which retirement is postponed is also small. As a consequence, the overall fiscal impact of the various reforms is due mostly to the mechanical component, with little being added by the change in workers' behavior. While this statement should (and will [see the analysis of individual reforms, regime by regime, in the rest of this section]) be qualified, we think it summarizes decently well the overall picture. We are inclined to say that, if our estimations of the behavior of Spanish workers past age 55 were to be taken at face value, then the most effective way of postponing retirement would be to simply legislate a

3. See the Bank of Spain web site, at www.bde.es.

shift in the early and normal retirement ages without bothering to modify the other rules.

9.5.1   Results by Regime and Gender

Since the results are fairly homogeneous across sexes, we present detailed results only for males. Results for females are available on request. However, our comments cover both groups without distinguishing between them. Obviously, as female labor-force participation is still substantially low in Spain, the actual magnitude involved is rather different between men and women.

RGSS

We begin our analysis of results from the RGSS. Figure 9.1 reports SSW by age for the S3 model. We have collected the five reforms in three groups, one for each panel; to allow for ease of comparison with the status quo, the latter is reported in each panel. In the first panel, we compare the status quo with the R1 reform in its two versions, S2 and S3. As S3 differs from S2 only in the retirement hazard, SSW estimates are identical. They are both lower than in the base case, especially at the crucial ages between 55 and 65. The reduction is substantial and, in particular, this reform also shifts forward the SSW age profile in such a way that the maximum is now

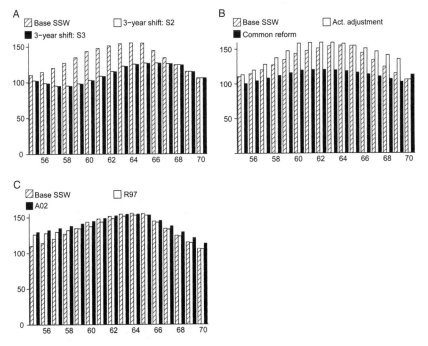

Fig. 9.1   SSW by age of labor force exit: *A,* RGSS; *B,* Option Value; *C,* S3 model

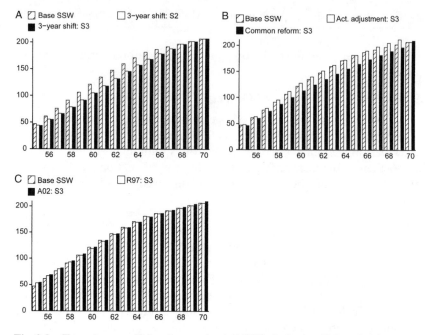

Fig. 9.2   Taxes by age of labor force exit: *A,* RGSS; *B,* Option Value; *C,* S3 model

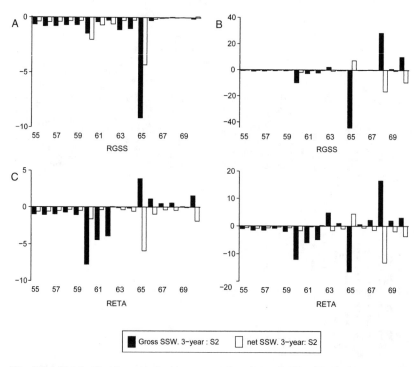

Fig. 9.3   Total effect by age of retirement and regime: *A,* Three-Year Reform; *B,* Option Value; *C,* S2 and S3 models

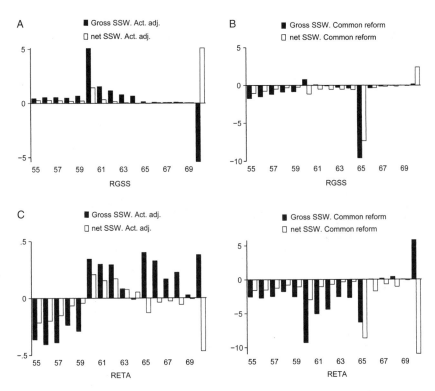

Fig. 9.4   Total effect by age of retirement and regime: *A*, Actuarial and Common Reforms; *B*, Option Value; *C*, S3 model

reached at a later age, around 65 to 67, instead of the current 63 to 65. A similar but somewhat less strong reduction in SSW is obtained by the Common Reform, R3, while the impact of the Actuarial Reform, R2, is small. Further, neither R2 nor R3 succeed at shifting forward the age at which SSW is maximized, thereby leaving this incentive to retirement basically unaltered. Things are even less satisfactory for the two Spanish reforms, R97 and A02, reported in the third panel: the age profile of SSW is left unchanged by these reforms. This behavior of the SSW indicator is reflected in that of (cumulated) taxes paid at each retirement age, which are reported in figure 9.2. The aggregate behavior seems simple enough to be understandable without comment. The disaggregation of the fiscal impact of reforms is discussed in the following. In the two upper panels of figures 9.3, 9.4, and 9.5 we report, by age and for each reform, the estimated total change in gross and net SSW. The reader should not be confused by the different scales used in the various panels. The top two panels of figure 9.3 show that the impact of R1 is much stronger on gross SSW under S3 than S2, while the result is mixed, or even reversed, for net SSW. As shown in figure 9.4, the impact of R2 is either irrelevant (as it reduces gross SSW

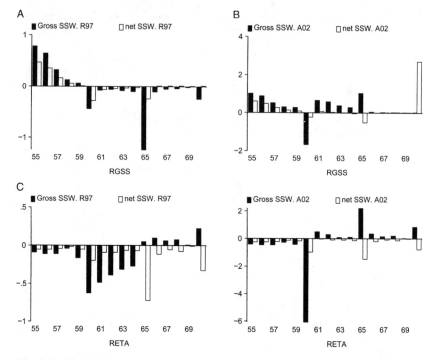

Fig. 9.5   Total effect by age of retirement and regime: *A,* **Spanish reforms;** *B,* **Option Value;** *C,* **S3 model**

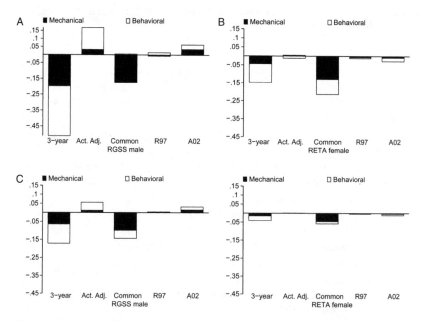

Fig. 9.6   Fiscal implications of reforms as a percentage of the GDP by gender and regime, S3 model

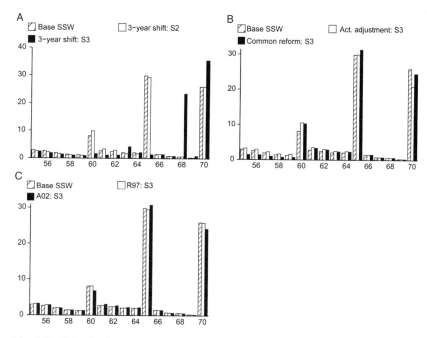

Fig. 9.7   **Distribution of age of labor force exit:** *A,* **RGSS;** *B,* **Option Value;** *C, S3* model

only for people retiring very late, while at the same time increasing their net SSW) or it goes in the wrong direction, slightly increasing SSW at earlier retirement ages. Reform R3, instead, does reduce SSW substantially at the normal retirement age and, by an almost negligible amount, at earlier dates (figure 9.6, top panels). Finally, in the top panels of figure 9.5, the two Spanish reforms seem to cause a negligible, and most of the time undesired, effect on SSW wealth at all retirement ages considered.

The impact of the five reforms on the distribution of retirement ages can be found in figure 9.7, which is also structured in three panels to facilitate comparison. Results are straightforward: R97 and A02 have no impact on retirement ages; both the Actuarial and the Common Reform shift the distribution only very mildly to the right, making the peak at age 65 more pronounced. The R1 reform has a much stronger impact, in the S3 version in particular, on the distribution of retirement ages. This is not very surprising. The current peaks at 60 and 65 are moved to 63 and 68, respectively, while the rest remain roughly the same.

Let us now closely consider the fiscal impact of the various reforms. This can be done by studying tables 9.5 and 9.6. A large amount of information is reported in these tables, hence we outline only the main features. In table 9.5 we have reported, for each reform, a breakdown of the different components of the total fiscal impact: reduction in benefits, increase in payroll

Table 9.5   **Fiscal impact of reforms by regime: Males in RGSS (in 10^6 2001 euros)**

	Present discounted value				Change relative to base		
	Base (A)	Three-Year (B)	Actuarial (C)	Common (D)	(B)/(A)	(C)/(A)	(D)/(A)
			Comparative reforms				
			Peak value: S1				
Benefits	11,700	9,989	12,147	7,987	−14.6	3.8	−31.7
Taxes							
Payroll	5,526	5,796	5,702	6,291	4.9	3.2	13.8
Income	2,257	1,903	2,389	1,548	−15.6	5.9	−31.4
VAT	1,757	1,540	1,804	1,279	−12.4	2.7	−27.2
Total	9,540	9,239	9,896	9,118	−3.2	3.7	−4.4
			Peak value: S2				
Benefits	12,000	10,061	12,280	8,032	−16.2	2.3	−33.1
Taxes							
Payroll	5,558	5,730	5,698	5,989	3.1	2.5	7.8
Income	2,341	1,902	2,426	1,529	−18.8	3.7	−34.7
VAT	1,791	1,553	1,830	1,293	−13.3	1.6	−27.8
Total	9,689	9,185	9,944	8,811	−5.2	2.6	−9.1
			Peak value: S3				
Benefits	12,000	9,730	12,280	8,032	−18.9	2.3	−33.1
Taxes							
Payroll	5,558	6,491	5,698	5,989	16.8	2.5	7.8
Income	2,341	1,968	2,426	1,529	−15.9	3.7	−34.7
VAT	1,791	1,478	1,820	1,293	−17.4	1.6	−27.8
Total	9,689	9,937	9,944	8,811	2.6	2.6	−9.1
			Option value: S1				
Benefits	11,507	9,995	12,432	8,023	−13.1	8.0	−30.3
Taxes							
Payroll	5,654	5,793	5,349	6,008	2.5	−5.4	6.3
Income	2,233	1,903	2,410	1,517	−14.8	7.9	−32.0
VAT	1,728	1,541	1,850	1,295	−10.8	7.0	−25.1
Total	9,615	9,237	9,609	8,820	−3.9	−0.1	−8.3
			Option value: S2				
Benefits	11,829	10,119	12,572	8,009	−14.5	6.3	−32.3
Taxes							
Payroll	5,654	5,658	5,303	5,516	0.1	−6.2	−2.4
Income	2,316	1,904	2,441	1,466	−17.8	5.4	−36.7
VAT	1,766	1,563	1,867	1,305	−11.5	5.8	−26.1
Total	9,735	9,125	9,611	8,287	−6.3	−1.3	−14.9
			Option value: S3				
Benefits	11,829	9,676	12,572	8,009	−18.2	6.3	−32.3
Taxes							
Payroll	5,654	6,494	5,303	5,516	14.9	−6.2	−2.4
Income	2,316	1,955	2,441	1,466	−15.6	5.4	−36.7
VAT	1,766	1,472	1,867	1,305	−16.6	5.8	−26.1
Total	9,375	9,920	9,611	8,287	1.9	−1.3	−14.9

Table 9.5   (continued)

	Present discounted value				Change relative to base		
	Base (A)	Three-Year (B)	Actuarial (C)	Common (D)	(B)/(A)	(C)/(A)	(D)/(A)
			Spanish-specific reforms				
	Base (A)	R97 (B)	A02 (C)		(B)/(A)	(C)/(A)	
			Peak value: S3				
Benefits	12,000	11,922	12,392		−0.6	3.3	
Taxes							
Payroll	5,5558	5,512	5,601		−0.8	0.8	
Income	2,341	2,302	2,454		−1.7	4.8	
VAT	1,791	1,783	1,832		−0.4	2.3	
Total	9,689	9,597	9,886		−1.0	2.0	
			Option value: S3				
Benefits	11,829	11,829	12,427		0.0	5.0	
Taxes							
Payroll	5,654	5,629	5,584		−0.4	−1.2	
Income	2,316	2,297	2,460		−0.8	6.2	
VAT	1,766	1,768	1,837		0.2	4.0	
Total	9,735	9,694	9,881		−0.4	1.5	

Notes: The first four columns show the PDV of benefits and taxes under the base case, the three comparative reforms and two Spanish-specific reforms: the 1997 reform and the 2002 amendment. The last three columns show the change relative to the base, for benefits and for taxes. RGSS = Régimen General de la Seguridad Social.

taxes, variation in income, and VAT taxes. The breakdown is calculated for three models (S1 to S3) and using two different financial measures of retirement incentives, the peak and option values. Table 9.6 summarizes the decomposition of the fiscal effects into the behavioral and the mechanical components, which were discussed earlier in the chapter. The main findings are strikingly simple. First, neither of the two Spanish reforms make any difference[4]—variations are of the same magnitude of rounding errors, and are completely accounted for by the sample uncertainty of our estimations. Among the other three reforms, the Common Reform is the one with the largest negative impact on both benefits paid to retirees and on tax revenues; the total effect on government revenues is positive because the drop in benefits is about three times larger than the drop in tax revenues (table 9.6). While the quantities estimated differ, both the option and the peak value indicators provide the same ranking of effects, and the estimated changes in government revenues and outlays are comparable. Next, in terms of total impact, comes the R1 reform under the S3 simulation procedure,

4. See Jiménez-Martín (1999) or Abío et al. (1999) for previous evaluations. In both cases the estimated effects are of small magnitude.

Table 9.6   Decomposition of the total effect by regime: Males in RGSS (in 10⁶ 2001 euros)

| | Change in present discounted value | | | | | | | | |
| | Three-Year | | | Actuarial | | | Common | | |
	Mechanical	Behavioral	Total	Mechanical	Behavioral	Total	Mechanical	Behavioral	Total
	Comparative reforms								
				Peak value: S1					
Benefits	-1,790	80	-1,710	549	-102	447	-3,727	14	-3,712
Taxes: Total	-628	327	-301	204	151	356	-1,228	807	-421
Net change	-1,162	-247	-1,410	345	-254	91	-2,498	-793	-3,291
Relative change	-9.9	-2.1	-12.0	2.9	-2.2	0.8	-21.4	-6.8	-28.1
				Peak value: S2					
Benefits	-1,944	5	-1,939	320	-40	280	-3,997	29	-3,968
Taxes: Total	-695	191	-504	115	140	255	-1,334	455	-878
Net change	-1,249	-186	-1,435	206	-180	25	-2,664	-426	-3,090
Relative change	-10.4	-1.5	-12.0	1.7	-1.5	0.2	-22.2	-3.5	-25.7
				Peak value: S3					
Benefits	-1,944	-325	-2,270	320	-40	280	-3,997	29	-3,968
Taxes: Total	-695	943	248	115	140	255	-1,334	455	-878
Net change	-1,249	-1,268	-2,518	206	-180	25	-2,664	-426	-3,090
Relative change	-10.4	-10.6	-21.0	1.7	-1.5	0.2	-22.2	-3.5	-25.7
				Option value: S1					
Benefits	-1,627	115	-1,512	499	426	925	-3,535	51	-3,484
Taxes: Total	-572	193	-378	185	-192	-6	-1,165	371	-794
Net change	-1,055	-79	-1,134	314	618	931	-2,370	-320	-2,690
Relative change	-9.2	-0.7	-9.9	2.7	5.4	8.1	-20.6	-2.8	-23.4

Table (rotated 90°). Panels decompose total effect into mechanical and behavioral components.

Option value: S2

	Mechanical	Behavioral	Total	Mechanical	Behavioral	Total	Mechanical	Behavioral	Total
Benefits	-1,814	103	-1,711	280	462	742	-3,829	8	-3,821
Taxes: Total	-649	39	-610	100	-224	-124	-1,276	-173	-1,448
Net change	-1,165	64	-1,100	181	686	867	-2,553	181	-2,372
Relative change	-9.8	0.5	-9.3	1.5	5.8	7.3	-21.6	1.5	-20.1

Option value: S3

	Mechanical	Behavioral	Total	Mechanical	Behavioral	Total	Mechanical	Behavioral	Total
Benefits	-1,814	-339	-2,153	280	462	742	-3,829	8	-3,821
Taxes: Total	-649	834	185	100	-224	-124	-1,276	-173	-1,448
Net change	-1,165	-1,173	-2,338	181	686	867	-2,553	181	-2,372
Relative change	-9.8	-9.9	-19.8	1.5	5.8	7.3	-21.6	1.5	-20.1

Spanish-specific reforms

R97

Peak value

	Mechanical	Behavioral	Total
Benefits	-56	-22	-78
Taxes: Total	-31	-62	-92
Net change	-25	40	14
Relative change	-0.2	0.3	0.1

Option value

	Mechanical	Behavioral	Total
Benefits	-37	37	0
Taxes: Total	-24	-18	-42
Net change	-13	54	42
Relative change	-0.1	0.5	0.4

A02

Peak value

	Mechanical	Behavioral	Total
Benefits	-37	430	393
Taxes: Total	34	163	197
Net change	-71	267	196
Relative change	-0.6	2.2	1.6

Option value

	Mechanical	Behavioral	Total
Benefits	143	454	597
Taxes: Total	-27	173	146
Net change	170	282	452
Relative change	1.4	2.4	3.8

Notes: The table shows the total effect of the reform (see table 9.5) decomposed into mechanical and behavioral components. The first and second row of each panel show the changes in benefits and taxes. The third row of each panel shows the net change (benefits minus taxes). The last row of each panel shows the net change as percent of base benefits (see table 9.5). RGSS = Régimen General de la Seguridad Social.

that is, assuming that retirement ages are effectively shifted three years down, pretty much by fiat. This reform also yields an important improvement of the government net position; most of it comes from a reduction in the net present value of benefits, with a small residual due to increase in total taxation. In particular, the substantial increase in payroll contributions generated by the longer worklife is almost completely balanced by the reduction in income and VAT revenues that the reform induces. Next, in terms of change in the fiscal position, is the R1 reform as estimated under the S2 hypothesis; directions of change are the same as in the S3 version but, obviously, the quantities are much smaller. Finally, R2 is predicted to have a negative impact on the fiscal position of government, as the small increase in tax revenues it induces is more than compensated by an increase in benefits paid, leading to a small but visible worsening of the government net position.

A second look at table 9.6 also shows that, as anticipated earlier, the behavioral impact of the reforms we consider is rather limited. Most of the savings comes from the mechanical aspects of the change; that is, the fact that by suddenly reducing benefits or lengthening working lives one captures the workers off guard, especially the older workers, and this leads to substantial savings for the public purse. For this reason, mechanical effects are orders of magnitude larger than the behavioral ones, uniformly across reforms and independently of the financial indicator adopted. Notice that, at least in the case of R3 and R1 + S3, the relative reduction of government net outlays is substantial, oscillating between –18.0 and –30.0 percent, depending on the financial indicator adopted.

RESS

Move next to estimates for workers enrolled in the special regimes, of which RETA is by far the most important, and upon which most of our data rely. Results here are dirtier, especially when it comes to forecasting the impact of each specific reform on retirement patterns by age. This is due, as discussed earlier, to the very low explanatory power of our financial measures of incentive to retirement, which in the case of the self-employed capture a small portion of the actual retirement patterns. In any case, the analysis proceeds in the same fashion as for the RGSS and results are organized likewise. However, we omit the corresponding SSW and tax figures.

The two lower panels of figures 9.3 to 9.5 contain the relevant information. In figure 9.3 we see that, similarly to RGSS, the impact of R1 on gross SSW is substantially stronger under S3 than S2, and that, contrary to RGSS, the same ranking of relative impact applies to net SSW. The impact of R2 is either irrelevant (as it reduces SSW only for people retiring either very early or very late) or it goes in the wrong direction, slightly increasing SSW at currently observed retirement ages (between 60 and 69). Reform R3, instead, does reduce SSW substantially and across the whole spectrum of possible retirement ages, with a somewhat stronger impact at 60 and 65

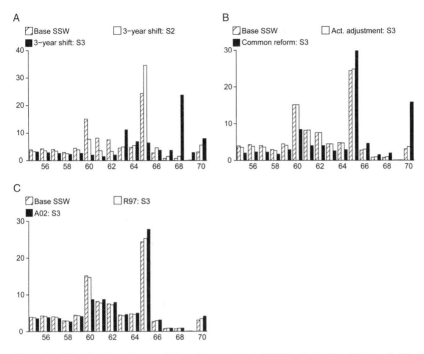

Fig. 9.8   Distribution of age of labor force exit: *A*, RETA; *B*, Option Value; *C*, S3 model

(figure 9.4, bottom panels). Finally, in the bottom panels of figure 9.5, the two Spanish reforms appear to have a small impact, in the correct direction, on the SSW of self-employed people, in particular before and around the normal retirement age of 65. It is important to notice, though, that the amounts involved in this case are quite small, and that the likely impact on retirement behavior is probably negligible.

The likely effect of the five reforms on the distribution of retirement ages can be found in figure 9.8. Results in this case seem to be slightly more positive than in the RGSS case, but only by small amounts. The two Spanish reforms, R97 and A02, appear to have some impact on retirement ages, which are pushed slightly to the right; the Actuarial Reform instead does not shift the distribution of retirement ages, while the Common Reform moves it visibly to the right, making the peak at age 65 even more pronounced than it already is. The R1 reform has a strong impact, in particular in the S3 version. Compared to the RGSS case of figure 9.7, the impact is weaker; still, it is the most substantial among those produced by the five reform scenarios.

Finally, we can see the disaggregation of the fiscal effects in tables 9.7 and 9.8. As before for the RGSS, in table 9.7 we have reported, for each reform, a breakdown of the different components of the total fiscal impact: reduction in benefits, increase in payroll taxes, variation in income and VAT taxes.

Table 9.7 **Fiscal impact of reforms by regime: Males in RETA (in 10⁶ 2001 euros)**

	Present Discounted Value				Change relative to base		
	Base (A)	Three-Year (B)	Actuarial (C)	Common (D)	(B)/(A)	(C)/(A)	(D)/(A)
			Comparative reforms				
			Peak value: S1				
Benefits	2,191	1,786	2,311	985	–18.5	5.5	–55.1
Taxes							
Payroll	773	865	775	852	11.9	0.3	10.3
Income	411	353	433	244	–14.0	5.6	–40.5
VAT	309	253	324	145	–17.9	4.9	–53.1
Total	1,492	1,471	1,532	1,241	–1.4	2.7	–16.8
			Peak value: S2				
Benefits	2,340	1,868	2,403	987	–20.2	2.7	–57.8
Taxes							
Payroll	591	629	603	687	6.3	1.9	16.2
Income	423	361	434	249	–14.5	2.8	–41.0
VAT	332	267	340	146	–19.5	2.4	–56.0
Total	1,346	1,257	1,377	1,082	–6.6	2.3	–19.6
			Peak value: S3				
Benefits	2,237	1,808	2,350	987	–19.2	5.1	–55.9
Taxes							
Payroll	719	812	717	789	12.9	–0.3	9.7
Income	413	354	433	246	–14.4	4.9	–40.5
VAT	316	257	331	146	–18.6	4.6	–53.9
Total	1,448	1,423	1,481	1,180	–1.7	2.2	–18.5
			Option value: S1				
Benefits	2,318	1,805	2,342	984	–22.1	1.0	–57.5
Taxes							
Payroll	660	875	684	856	32.5	3.5	29.5
Income	425	364	431	250	–14.5	1.4	–41.2
VAT	327	254	330	144	–22.3	0.8	–56.1
Total	1,413	1,493	1,445	1,250	5.7	2.2	–11.6
			Option value: S2				
Benefits	2,318	1,849	2,342	984	–20.2	1.0	–57.5
Taxes							
Payroll	660	766	684	856	16.0	3.5	29.5
Income	425	363	431	250	–14.8	1.4	–41.2
VAT	327	263	330	144	–19.8	0.8	–56.1
Total	1,413	1,391	1,445	1,250	–1.6	2.2	–11.6
			Option value: S3				
Benefits	2,318	1,805	2,342	984	–22.1	1.0	–57.5
Taxes							
Payroll	660	875	684	856	32.5	3.5	29.5
Income	425	364	431	250	–14.5	1.4	–41.2
VAT	327	254	330	144	–22.3	0.8	–56.1
Total	1,413	1,493	1,445	1,250	5.7	2.2	–11.6

Table 9.7   (continued)

	Present Discounted Value				Change relative to base		
	Base (A)	Three-Year (B)	Actuarial (C)	Common (D)	(B)/(A)	(C)/(A)	(D)/(A)
			Spanish-specific reforms				
	Base (A)	R97 (B)	A02 (C)		(B)/(A)	(C)/(A)	
			Peak value				
Benefits	2,340	2,272	2,243		–2.9	–4.1	
Taxes							
Payroll	591	594	632		0.4	6.8	
Income	423	411	414		–2.8	–2.0	
VAT	332	323	318		–2.7	–4.3	
Total	1,346	1,328	1,364		–1.3	1.3	
			Option value				
Benefits	2,318	2,245	2,205		–3.1	–4.9	
Taxes							
Payroll	660	672	699		1.8	5.8	
Income	425	413	413		–2.9	–3.0	
VAT	327	318	311		–2.9	–4.9	
Total	1,413	1,403	1,423		–0.7	0.7	

Note: See table 9.5 notes.

Again, the breakdown is calculated for three models (S1 to S3), and using two different financial measures of retirement incentives, the peak and option values. Similarly, in table 9.8 we report the decomposition between mechanical and behavioral components. There are quantitative, but not qualitative, differences with the RGSS case described earlier (tables 9.5 and 9.6). The two Spanish reforms now have a somewhat more visible impact on the fiscal position, which is predicted to improve slightly (see table 9.8). The magnitudes involved, though, are quite small (less than 5 percentage points) and may still be accounted for by the sample uncertainty of our estimates. Among the other three reforms, the Common Reform is the one with the largest negative impact on both benefits paid to retirees and tax revenues; the total effect on government revenues is substantially positive. In fact, the percentage variations involved are much larger (about twice the size) than those we estimated for the RGSS (see table 9.8). Next, in terms of total fiscal impact, comes the R1 reform under the S3 simulation procedure. This reform also yields an important improvement of the government net position; slightly more than half of it comes from a reduction in the net present value of benefits, with the rest coming from an increase in taxation, in particular a substantial increase in payroll contributions due to the longer worklife. Next is R1 under the S2 hypothesis; directions of change are the

Table 9.8   Decomposition of the total effect by regime: Male in RETA (in 10⁶ 2001 euros)

	Change in present discounted value								
	Three-Year			Actuarial			Common		
	Mechanical	Behavioral	Total	Mechanical	Behavioral	Total	Mechanical	Behavioral	Total
Comparative reforms									
Peak value: S1									
Benefits	-377	-28	-405	100	20	120	-1,209	2	-1,206
Taxes: Total	-107	86	-21	32	8	40	-327	77	-250
Net change	-270	-114	-384	68	12	80	-881	-74	-956
Relative change	-12.3	-5.2	-17.5	3.1	0.5	3.6	-40.2	-3.4	-43.6
Peak value: S2									
Benefits	-467	-5	-472	58	6	64	-1,366	13	-1,353
Taxes: Total	-124	36	-89	17	14	31	-357	93	-264
Net change	-342	-40	-383	40	-8	32	-1,009	-80	-1,089
Relative change	-14.6	-1.7	-16.4	1.7	-0.3	1.4	-43.1	-3.4	-46.6
Peak value: S3									
Benefits	-467	-38	-504	58	6	64	-1,366	13	-1,353
Taxes: Total	-124	163	39	17	14	31	-357	93	-264
Net change	-342	-200	-543	40	-8	33	-1,009	-80	-1,089
Relative change	-14.6	-8.6	-23.2	1.7	-0.3	1.4	-43.1	-3.4	-46.6
Option value: S1									
Benefits	-402	-27	-429	96	17	113	-1,254	4	-1,250
Taxes: Total	-112	87	-25	30	2	33	-335	67	-268
Net change	-290	-113	-404	66	15	81	-919	-63	-982
Relative change	-13.0	-5.1	-18.1	3.0	0.7	3.6	-41.1	-2.8	-43.9

Option value: S2

	Mechanical	Behavioral	Total	Mechanical	Behavioral	Total	Mechanical	Behavioral	Total
Benefits	−420	−49	−469	44	−20	24	−1,346	12	−1,334
Taxes: Total	−114	92	−22	14	18	32	−355	192	−164
Net change	−306	−141	−447	31	−38	−8	−991	−180	−1,170
Relative change	−13.2	−6.1	−19.3	1.3	−1.6	−0.3	−42.7	−7.7	−50.5

Option value: S3

	Mechanical	Behavioral	Total	Mechanical	Behavioral	Total	Mechanical	Behavioral	Total
Benefits	−420	−93	−513	44	−20	24	−1,346	12	−1,334
Taxes: Total	−114	194	80	14	18	32	−355	192	−164
Net change	−306	−287	−593	31	−38	−8	−991	−180	−1,170
Relative change	−13.2	−12.4	−25.6	1.3	−1.6	−0.3	−42.7	−7.7	−50.5

Spanish-specific reforms

Peak value

	R97			A02		
	Mechanical	Behavioral	Total	Mechanical	Behavioral	Total
Benefits	−67	−1	−68	−88	−8	−96
Taxes: Total	−21	3	−18	−22	40	18
Net change	−46	−4	−50	−66	−48	−114
Relative change	−2.0	−0.2	−2.1	−2.8	−2.1	−4.9

Option value

	R97			A02		
	Mechanical	Behavioral	Total	Mechanical	Behavioral	Total
Benefits	−69	−4	−73	−89	−25	−113
Taxes: Total	−22	11	−10	−23	33	10
Net change	−47	−15	−62	−66	−57	−123
Relative change	−2.0	−0.7	−2.7	−2.8	−2.5	−5.3

Notes: The table shows the total effect of the reform (see table 9.9) decomposed into mechanical and behavioral components. The first and second row of each panel show the changes in benefits and taxes. The third row of each panel shows the net change (benefits minus taxes). The last row of each panel shows the net change as percent of base benefits (see table 9.7). RETA = Régimen Especial de Trabajadores Autónomos.

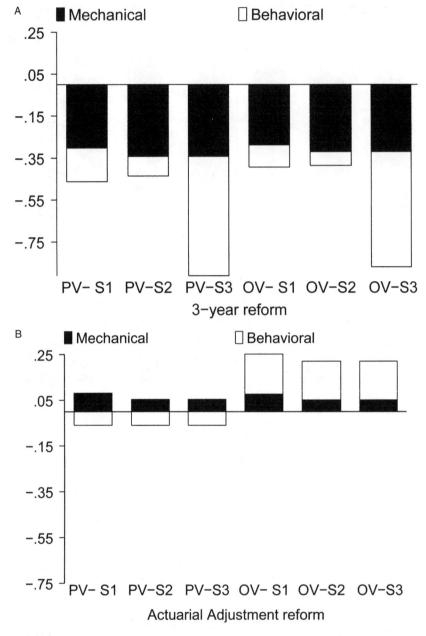

Fig. 9.9   Fiscal implications of comparative reforms as a percentage of the GDP, RGSS·and RETA: *A,* Three-Year Reform; *B,* Actuarial Reform; *C,* Common Reform

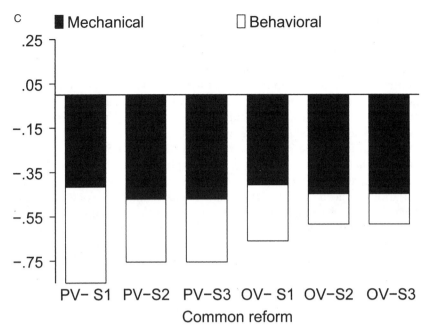

Fig. 9.9   (continued)

same as in the S3 version but, obviously, the quantitative impact is much smaller, as people are not forced to shift ahead three years of that part of their retirement behavior that is captured by age dummies. Finally, R2 is predicted to have a negative impact on the fiscal position of government, as the small increases in tax revenues it induces is more than compensated by an increase in benefits paid, leading to a small but visible worsening of the government net position.

9.5.2   1940 Cohort Results for RGSS and RETA

A second look at table 9.6 also shows that, as anticipated earlier, the behavioral impact of the reform scenarios we consider is rather limited. Most of the savings come from the mechanical aspect of the changes: reforms that unexpectedly reduce benefits (such as the Common Reform) do have a positive impact on the government fiscal position, while reforms that legally force workers to retire later, like the R1, especially in the R3 simulation, have a strong impact on retirement patterns and, consequently, benefits paid out. For this reason, mechanical effects are orders of magnitude larger than the behavioral ones, uniformly across reforms and independent of the financial indicator adopted. Notice that, at least in the case of R3 and R1 + S3, the relative reduction of government net outlays is substantial, oscillating between –18.0 and –30.0 percent, depending on the financial indicator adopted. These conclusions are summarized in figures 9.9 to

9.11. Figure 9.9 reports the fiscal effect of each reform by gender and regime, using simulation S3; figure 9.10 reports the total (RGSS plus RETA) fiscal effect of each reform for both simulations S1 and S3. We distinguish, in each case, between mechanical and behavioral effect. The same information is reported, in numerical form, in tables 9.9 and 9.10. All the quantities reported in these tables and figures, we recall, are relative to the 1940 cohort; that is to say, we compute the positive/negative variations in pension expenditure and tax revenues that are induced by applying each of the five reforms to the 1940s cohort only. At the same time, it should also be noted that the numbers we report are net present value estimations, that is, they correspond to the net present value, at the time of reform, of the variations induced by the reform itself over the remaining life of the cohort. They do not correspond, therefore, to variations in annual flows.

Our model predicts that the two Spanish reforms, R97 and A02, have a negligible total fiscal effect, that the Actuarial Reform (R2) would worsen the fiscal position of the government, and that, finally, the R1 and the Common Reform (R3) would improve it. The largest effect is predicted for the R1 reform under the S3 simulation scenarios, that is, when that portion of current retirement patterns that is captured by age dummies is shifted to the right of exactly three years. The net amount saved, in this case, is substantial: about 0.80 percentage points of GDP. In the other two cases (R1 without the impact of age dummies, and R3), the amounts saved are, respectively, around 0.35 and 0.55 percentage points of GDP. While these are large amounts, they are not so large in relation to either the annual expenditure for social security pensions (which is about 10 percentage points of GDP) or to the size of outstanding Spanish pension debt, which is estimated to range around 200 percentage points of GDP. Even by multiplying these quantities by a factor of fifty (that is, even assuming that savings of similar size can be achieved during the next fifty years for each cohort born between 1940 and 1990) we would still be projecting total savings equal to, at best, 20 percent of the outstanding pension debt. From this perspective, the savings that can be achieved via the reforms considered here are somewhat modest and, probably, still below the level that appears to be desirable. Finally, we should note that, in all cases but R2 + S3, most of the savings come from the mechanical aspect. Only R2 + S3 shows a large behavioral effect, which is due to the fact that, by shifting the age dummies to the right, we are in fact assuming that Spanish workers will voluntarily choose to translate their age-related retirement patterns forward three years. One should keep in mind that, once a reform is implemented, workers will adjust their behavior optimally (from their viewpoint) to the changed circumstances. After a few years, such adjustment is likely to eliminate or at least greatly reduce the savings that we estimate to accrue via the mechanical channel. This would leave, in the long run, only the impact of

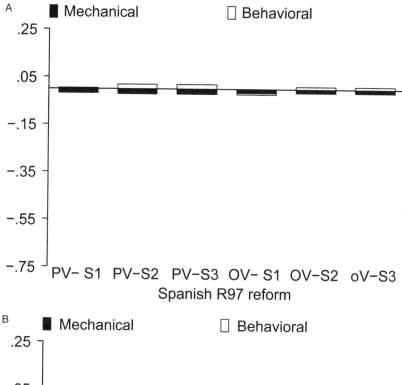

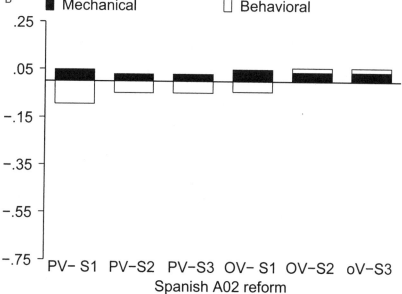

Fig. 9.10   Fiscal implications of Spanish reforms as a percentage of the GDP, RGSS and RETA: *A*, Spanish R97 reform; *B*, Spanish A02 reform

Table 9.9   **Total fiscal impact of reforms (in 10⁶ 2001 euros)**

	Present discounted value				Change relative to base		
	Base (A)	Three-Year (B)	Actuarial (C)	Common (D)	(B)/(A)	(C)/(A)	(D)/(A)
	Comparative reforms						
	Peak value: S1						
Benefits	18,842	15,990	19,606	11,967	−15.1	4.1	−36.5
Taxes							
Payroll	8,602	9,093	8,845	9,764	5.7	2.8	13.5
Income	3,588	3,035	3,797	2,381	−15.4	5.8	−33.6
VAT	2,809	2,441	2,894	1,910	−13.1	3.0	−32.0
Total	15,000	14,570	15,536	14,055	−2.9	3.6	−6.3
	Peak value: S2						
Benefits	19,441	16,195	19,900	12,027	−16.7	2.4	−38.1
Taxes							
Payroll	8,410	8,695	8,616	9,135	3.4	2.5	8.6
Income	3,716	3,044	3,846	2,363	−18.1	3.5	−36.4
VAT	2,885	2,478	2,935	1,929	−14.1	1.7	−33.1
Total	15,011	14,217	15,397	13,428	−5.3	2.6	−10.5
	Peak value: S3						
Benefits	19,441	15,704	19,900	12,027	−19.2	2.4	−38.1
Taxes							
Payroll	8,410	9,915	8,616	9,135	17.9	2.5	8.6
Income	3,716	3,138	3,846	2,363	−15.5	3.5	−36.4
VAT	2,885	2,368	2,935	1,929	−17.9	1.7	−33.1
Total	15,011	15,421	15,397	13,428	2.7	2.6	−10.5
	Option value: S1						
Benefits	18,647	16,026	20,045	12,016	−14.1	7.5	−35.6
Taxes							
Payroll	8,707	9,018	8,283	9,292	3.6	−4.9	6.7
Income	3,560	3,035	3,825	2,343	−14.8	7.4	−34.2
VAT	2,780	2,448	2,964	1,932	−11.9	6.6	−30.5
Total	15,047	14,501	15,072	13,566	−3.6	0.2	−9.8
	Option value: S2						
Benefits	19,221	16,301	20,247	11,997	−15.2	5.3	−37.6
Taxes							
Payroll	8,485	8,633	8,040	8,653	1.7	−5.3	2.0
Income	3,687	3,062	3,860	2,292	−17.0	4.7	−37.8
VAT	2,851	2,491	2,991	1,942	−12.6	4.9	−31.9
Total	15,023	14,186	14,891	12,887	−5.6	−0.9	−14.2
	Option value: S3						
Benefits	19,221	15,655	20,247	11,997	−18.6	5.3	−37.6
Taxes							
Payroll	8,485	9,889	8,040	8,653	16.5	−5.3	2.0
Income	3,687	3,128	3,860	2,292	−15.2	4.7	−37.8
VAT	2,851	2,360	2,991	1,942	−17.2	4.9	−31.9
Total	15,023	15,376	14,891	12,887	2.3	−0.9	−14.2

Table 9.9   (continued)

	Present discounted value				Change relative to base		
	Base (A)	Three-Year (B)	Actuarial (C)	Common (D)	(B)/(A)	(C)/(A)	(D)/(A)
	Spanish-specific reforms						
	Base (A)	R97 (B)	A02 (C)		(B)/(A)	(C)/(A)	
	Peak value						
Benefits	19,441	19,234	19,822		−1.1	2.0	
Taxes							
Payroll	8,410	8,351	8,524		−0.7	1.4	
Income	3,716	3,646	3,853		−1.9	3.7	
VAT	2,885	2,862	2,920		−0.8	1.2	
Total	15,011	14,859	15,296		−1.0	1.9	
	Option value						
Benefits	19,221	19,118	19,869		−0.5	3.4	
Taxes							
Payroll	8,485	8,467	8,426		−0.2	−0.7	
Income	3,687	3,644	3,861		−1.2	4.7	
VAT	2,851	2,841	2,925		−0.3	2.6	
Total	15,023	14,951	15,212		−0.5	1.3	

Notes: The first four columns show the PDV of benefits and taxes under the base case, the three comparative reforms and two Spanish-specific reforms: the 1997 reform and the 2002 amendment. The last three columns show the change relative to the base, for benefits and for taxes.

the behavioral channel. And, as we have seen, the savings one can obtain via the behavioral channel are estimated to be quite small for each and every one of the reforms we have considered in this chapter. It is in this sense that, as mentioned at the beginning, we find the quantitative results of our exercise unsatisfactory and, in some sense, worrying. To the extent that one can predict, using advanced econometric techniques, even serious and somewhat draconian reforms of the Spanish pension system, such as those considered here, are not likely to reduce pension expenditure of any significant amount in the long run.

9.6   Distributional Issues

Distributional issues always loom big in discussions about pension reforms. They also happen to be among the least simple to handle. To the extent that, given the historical circumstances, all reform proposals aim at either reducing benefits for future retirees or postponing the age of retirement—or both—it is clear that some redistribution away from future retirees is being planned. So much is clear, and the calculations reported in

Table 9.10   Decomposition of the total effect of reforms (in 10⁶ 2001 euros)

| | Change in present discounted value | | | | | | | | |
| | Three-Year | | | Actuarial | | | Common | | |
	Mechanical	Behavioral	Total	Mechanical	Behavioral	Total	Mechanical	Behavioral	Total
Comparative reforms									
Peak value: S1									
Benefits	-2,907	56	-2,852	872	-108	764	-6,902	27	-6,875
Taxes: Total	-985	555	-430	317	219	536	-2,158	1,214	-944
Net change	-1,922	-500	-2,421	555	-327	228	-4,744	-1,187	-5,931
Relative change	-10.2	-2.7	-12.9	2.9	-1.7	1.2	-25.2	-6.3	-31.5
Peak value: S2									
Benefits	-3,236	-9	-3,246	506	-47	459	-7,472	58	-7,414
Taxes: Total	-1,099	305	-794	177	209	386	-2,337	754	-1,583
Net change	-2,138	-314	-2,452	329	-256	73	-5,135	-696	-5,831
Relative change	-11.0	-1.6	-12.6	1.7	-1.3	0.4	-26.4	-3.6	-30.0
Peak value: S3									
Benefits	-3,236	-500	-3,737	506	-47	459	-7,472	58	-7,414
Taxes: Total	-1,099	1,509	410	177	209	386	-2,337	754	-1,583
Net change	-2,138	-2,009	-4,147	329	-256	73	-5,135	-696	-5,831
Relative change	-11.0	-10.3	-21.3	1.7	-1.3	0.4	-26.4	-3.6	-30.0
Option value: S1									
Benefits	-2,727	106	-2,621	801	596	1,398	-6,708	77	-6,632
Taxes: Total	-918	372	-546	290	-266	24	-2,086	605	-1,481
Net change	-1,809	-266	-2,075	511	862	1,373	-4,622	-528	-5,150
Relative change	-9.7	-1.4	-11.1	2.7	4.6	7.4	-24.8	-2.8	-27.6

Option value: S2

Benefits	−2,987	67	−2,920	434	591	1,025	−7,265	41	−7,224
Taxes: Total	−1,014	177	−837	152	−285	−133	−2,261	125	−2,136
Net change	−1,973	−110	−2,083	283	876	1,158	−5,004	−84	−5,088
Relative change	−10.3	−0.6	−10.8	1.5	4.6	6.0	−26.0	−0.4	−26.5

Option value: S3

Benefits	−2,987	−579	−3,567	434	591	1,025	−7,265	41	−7,224
Taxes: Total	−1,014	1,367	353	152	−285	−133	−2,261	125	−2,136
Net change	−1,973	−1,946	−3,920	283	876	1,158	−5,004	−84	−5,088
Relative change	−10.3	−10.1	−20.4	1.5	4.6	6.0	−26.0	−0.4	−26.5

Spanish-specific reforms

Peak value: S3

	R97			A02		
Benefits	−177	−31	−207	445	−63	382
Taxes: Total	−72	−80	−152	185	100	285
Net change	−104	49	−55	260	−163	97
Relative change	−0.5	0.3	−0.3	1.3	−0.8	0.5

Option value: S3

	R97			A02		
Benefits	−142	39	−103	483	165	647
Taxes: Total	−61	−11	−72	200	−11	189
Net change	−81	50	−31	283	176	469
Relative change	−0.4	0.3	−0.2	1.5	0.9	2.4

Notes: The table shows the total effect of the reform (see table 9.9) decomposed into mechanical and behavioral components. The first and second row of each panel show the changes in benefits and taxes. The third row of each panel shows the net change (benefits minus taxes). The last row of each panel shows the net change as percent of base benefits (see table 9.9).

Table 9.11   **Distributional analysis: Comparative reforms, Option value, S1 (in 10⁶ 2001 euros)**

	Present discounted value				Change relative to base		
	Base (A)	Three-Year Reform (B)	Actuarial Reform (C)	Common Reform (D)	(B)/(A)	(C)/(A)	(D)/(A)
Quintile 1 (highest)							
Benefits	5,439	4,649	5,868	4,638	−790	429	−801
Taxes							
Payroll	2,866	2,969	2,713	2,753	103	−153	−113
Income	1,287	1,119	1,374	1,089	−168	87	−197
VAT	805	706	861	716	−99	6.9	−89
Total	4,957	4,794	4,947	4,558	−163	−10	−400
Net change					627	439	−402
Change as % of							
base benefits					−11.5	8.1	7.4
Quintile 2							
Benefits	4,314	3,623	4,698	2,799	−691	384	−1,515
Taxes							
Payroll	2,025	2,125	1,908	2,281	100	−117	256
Income	864	721	939	548	−143	74	−316
VAT	636	549	686	446	−87	7.9	−190
Total	3,525	3,394	3,533	3,275	−131	8	−250
Net change					−560	376	−1,265
Change as % of							
base benefits					−13	8.7	29.3
Quintile 3							
Benefits	3,366	2,867	3,645	1,984	−499	279	−1,382
Taxes							
Payroll	1,567	1,625	1,491	1,751	58	−77	184
Income	594	495	645	329	−99	51	−264
VAT	501	438	538	325	−63	7.4	−177
Total	2,663	2,558	2,674	2,405	−104	11	−257
Net change					−395	268	−1,125
Change as % of							
base benefits					−11.7	8	−33.4
Quintile 4							
Benefits	2,993	2,594	3,202	1,591	−399	209	−1,402
Taxes							
Payroll	1,303	1,339	1,256	1,408	35	−48	104
Income	467	393	504	228	−74	37	−239
VAT	451	400	479	268	−51	6.2	−183
Total	2,222	2,131	2,238	1,904	−90	16	−318
Net change					−309	193	−1,085
Change as % of							
base benefits					−10.3	6.4	36.2

Table 9.11   (continued)

	Present discounted value				Change relative to base		
	Base (A)	Three-Year Reform (B)	Actuarial Reform (C)	Common Reform (D)	(B)/(A)	(C)/(A)	(D)/(A)
			Quintile 5 (lowest)				
Benefits	2,508	2,266	2,603	990	−242	95	−1,518
Taxes							
Payroll	940	955	911	1,093	15	−29	152
Income	344	303	359	145	−41	15	−199
VAT	383	351	396	175	−32	3.4	−208
Total	1,667	1,609	1,666	1,413	−58	−1	−254
Net change					−184	96	−1,263
Change as % of base benefits					−7.3	3.8	−50.4

Notes: For each quintile, the first four columns show the PDV of benefits and taxes under the base case, the three comparative reforms, and two Spanish-specific reforms: the 1997 reform and the 2002 amendment. The last three columns show the change relative to the base, for benefits and for taxes.

the previous section, especially at the very end, summarize the amount of redistribution planned, in the aggregate, from the retiring cohort to the rest of society. The natural question, at this point, is one of equal treatment within the retiring cohort: which group of workers, within the 1940s cohort, is going to foot the bill? Is the cut going to be uniform across sexes, educational levels, regime of affiliation, and so on?

It would be surprising if the kind of reforms we have been considering affect all workers in the same way and to the same extent. In fact, they do not. In order to provide an initial assessment of such differential impact, we have classified the individuals in our sample according to the quintile of the Spanish labor income distribution to which they belong. We have then used the simulated results from the various policy scenarios to estimate, in the usual manner, the impact that each reform would have on the average member of each quintile. We measure the impact on both benefits and taxes. The summary measure is the net impact of the reform in both absolute and relative terms. A summary of our findings is reported in tables 9.11 (S1 model) and 9.12 (S3 model) for the comparative reforms, and table 9.13 for the Spanish specific reforms (S3 model only).

Consider first R1-R3. The impression is striking. For all measures of financial incentives, the burden falls rather unevenly on different income groups. More importantly, different reforms affect different groups quite differently, so that some reforms are regressive (redistribute away from the poorest quintiles more than from the richest quintiles) and others are

Table 9.12   **Distributional analysis: Comparative reforms, Option value, S3 (in 10^6 2001 euros)**

		Present discounted value			Change relative to base		
	Base (A)	Three-Year Reform (B)	Actuarial Reform (C)	Common Reform (D)	(B)/(A)	(C)/(A)	(D)/(A)
Quintile 1 (highest)							
Benefits	5,510	4,554	5,888	4,599	−955	378	−911
Taxes							
Payroll	2,906	3,310	2,716	2,591	404	−190	−315
Income	1,320	1,146	1,390	1,063	−174	70	−257
VAT	810	681	861	713	−129	6.3	−97
Total	5,035	5,136	4,966	4,367	101	−69	−669
Net change					−1,056	447	−242
Change as % of							
base benefits					−19.2	8.1	−4.4
Quintile 2							
Benefits	4,438	3,551	4,731	2,816	−887	293	−1,622
Taxes							
Payroll	1,995	2,346	1,873	2,115	351	−122	120
Income	899	748	950	535	−151	51	−364
VAT	649	529	689	452	−120	6.1	−197
Total	3,544	3,623	3,513	3,102	79	−31	−441
Net change					−996	324	−1,180
Change as % of							
base benefits					−21.8	7.3	−26.6
Quintile 3							
Benefits	3,501	2,813	3,688	1,990	−689	187	−1,512
Taxes							
Payroll	1,504	1,758	1,436	1,622	254	−68	118
Income	619	514	649	320	−106	30	−299
VAT	519	424	545	328	−95	4.9	−191
Total	2,642	2,696	2,629	2,271	54	−13	−371
Net change					−742	200	−1,141
Change as % of							
base benefits					−21.2	5.7	−32.6
Quintile 4							
Benefits	3,151	2,543	3,272	1,597	−608	121	−1,554
Taxes							
Payroll	1,216	1,436	1,175	1,310	220	−41	94
Income	490	408	507	226	−82	17	−264
VAT	473	388	490	271	−85	3.6	−203
Total	2,179	2,231	2,172	1,807	52	−7	−372
Net change					−667	128	−1,182
Change as % of							
base benefits					−21.0	4.1	−37.5

Table 9.12   (continued)

	Present discounted value			Change relative to base		
	Base (A)	Three-Year Reform (B)	Actuarial Reform (C)	Common Reform (D)	(B)/(A)	(C)/(A)	(D)/(A)
			Quintile 5 (lowest)				
Benefits	2,602	2,167	2,647	984	−435	46	−1,618
Taxes							
Payroll	862	1,034	838	1,011	172	−24	148
Income	356	309	361	145	−47	5	−211
VAT	397	333	403	175	−63	1.7	−221
Total	1,615	1,676	1,602	1,331	62	−13	−283
Net change					−497	58	−1,334
Change as % of base benefits					−19.1	2.2	−51.3

Notes: See table 9.11 notes.

progressive (achieve the opposite). The following is a summary, reform by reform.

R1: The reduction in the absolute amount of benefits is monotone, increasing from the lowest to the highest quintile, and almost monotone as a percentage of current benefits. The same is true for the net change, which also takes into account the variations in contribution and taxes the reform would bring about. The percentage reduction for people in the highest quintile, though, is lower (about minus 10.0 percent) than for the second and third higher. From the 12 percent reduction for the second quintile the effect decreases to minus 9 percent for the lowest. When the S3 shift is added (the R1 + S3 case), then the reduction in gross and net benefits more than doubles. In this case, the progressivity, which was already very mild, disappears almost completely.

R2: The Actuarial Reform has a small but sizeable reverse effect on the net benefits, as on average the latter increase. It is also fairly regressive, as both the absolute value and the percentage by which benefits increase is actually decreasing with the level of earnings.

R3: As we pointed out, the Common Reform would imply a substantial cut of benefits in the case of Spain. While it changes retirement ages only mildly, it cuts initial benefits across the board, and of an amount equal to roughly 30 percent of current pension payments. Together with the forward shift in the early retirement age, which our model predicts as a consequence of the reform, R3 has the effect of drastically reducing the SSW of the lowest-paid individuals. The amounts involved are very large, and they appear most definitely unrealistic, at least from a socio-political point of view: a cut in net benefits of about 50 percentage points

Table 9.13 **Distributional analysis: Spanish reforms, S3 age dummies model (in 10^6 2001 euros)**

	Present discounted value			Change relative to base	
	Base (A)	R97 (B)	A02 (C)	(B) − (A)	(C) − (A)
Quintile 1 (highest)					
Benefits	5,510	5,526	5,864	16	354
Taxes					
Payroll	2,906	2,882	2,854	−24	−51
Income	1,320	1,313	1,416	−6	96
VAT	810	813	850	3	40
Total	5,035	5,009	1.7	−27	85
Net change				43	269
Change as % of					
base benefits				0.8	4.9
Quintile 2					
Benefits	4,438	4,425	4,637	−13	199
Taxes					
Payroll	1,995	1,991	1,977	−4	−18
Income	899	888	947	−11	47
VAT	649	649	673	−0	24
Total	3,544	3,528	1.5	−15	53
Net change				3	146
Change as % of					
base benefits				0.1	3.3
Quintile 3					
Benefits	3,501	3,487	3,618	−14	117
Taxes					
Payroll	1,504	1,504	1,498	−0	−5
Income	619	613	647	−6	28
VAT	519	518	533	−1	14
Total	2,642	2,634	1.4	−8	36
Net change				−7	81
Change as % of					
base benefits				−0.2	2.3
Quintile 4					
Benefits	3,151	3,111	3,183	−40	32
Taxes					
Payroll	1,216	1,220	1,219	4	3
Income	490	481	499	−9	9
VAT	473	468	477	−5	4
Total	2,179	2,169	0.7	−11	16
Net change				−30	16
Change as % of					
base benefits				−0.9	0.5

Table 9.13   (continued)

	Present discounted value			Change relative to base	
	Base (A)	R97 (B)	A02 (C)	(B) − (A)	(C) − (A)
		Quintile 5 (lowest)			
Benefits	2,602	2,551	2,546	−51	−56
Taxes					
Payroll	862	867	874	5	12
Income	356	345	349	−11	−7
VAT	397	390	389	−6	−8
Total	1,615	1,603	−0.2	−12	−3
Net change				−39	−53
Change as % of base benefits				−1.5	−2.0

Notes: For each quintile the first three columns show the PDV of benefits and taxes under the base case and the two Spanish-specific reforms: the 1997 reform and the 2002 amendment. The last two columns show the change relative to the base.

does not seem to be in the cards of any political coalition. Also, in this as in the previous case, the impact is regressive: higher-paid workers would bear a smaller burden, at least in percentage. In fact, the degree of regressivity that R3 displays is quite substantial.

The two Spanish reforms, as we already pointed out, have a practically insignificant impact on aggregate quantities. The same is true for the five quintiles.

R97: Besides doing little, which was already clear from the aggregate analysis, this is the only reform that affects almost all groups equally. If anything, it leans slightly more heavily on the lower wage groups, like all other reforms except R1. In either case, the variations are estimated to be of the order of plus or minus 1 percentage point of current benefits.

A02: In this case, the aggregate impact is somewhat larger and the distributional one becomes pronouncedly regressive. The total difference between the percentage gains of the highest-paid quintile (about 5 percentage points) and the losses of the lowest-paid one (minus 2 percent) is quite large and, in some sense surprising, as the A02 modification to the R97 reform was arranged and agreed upon, in some sense requested by, the Spanish trade unions.

9.7   Concluding Remarks

We summarize here the main findings, with an eye to policy implications and possible reforms. As pointed out in the main text, some of the quantitative estimates reported should be taken with (more than) the usual grain of salt, as they are based on estimations of reduced-form behavioral equations that appear to have only a limited power to capture observed retirement patterns. This caveat is particularly important for the affiliates to the RETA, for which none of the financial measures of retirement incentive seem to play a major role in affecting decisions. Once this is understood, our findings can be summarized, reform by reform, as follows.

The Actuarial Reform is probably the least effective among the three comparison reforms considered in the volume. This evaluation applies both in terms of expenditure, retirement patterns, and redistributional effect. Furthermore, most of the fiscal gains are accrued via the mechanical channel, which suggests that little would be gained in the long run by implementing the Actuarial Reform in Spain.

The Three-Year Reform may have an impact that is likely to become quite strong if, by changing legislation, one also affects in the same direction the behavioral component of retirement, which seems to be captured purely by age dummies. In other words, if legislating 68 as the common retirement age leads most people who now retire at 65 to retire at 68, then the gains in labor-force participation of the elderly, achievable via the R1 scenario, could be substantial. Correspondingly, the fiscal gains could be sizable even if, as we argued earlier, once we compare the magnitude of these fiscal gains to the outstanding implicit social security debt of Spain, the actual reduction would be likely to be around 15 percentage points at most. Further, some redistributional aspects of the R1 reform need to be adjusted to make it politically acceptable. The direction in which it redistributes wealth, from future retirees to the working population, is probably acceptable, but the distribution of that burden within the retiring cohorts seems much less acceptable, as it falls disproportionately on the lowest-earning groups. This is an aspect that deserves further examination.

The same goes for the Common Reform. The latter does not really shift retirement patterns uniformly but, rather, cuts in about half the exit rate at age 60 (which corresponds to early retirement in Spain), and which is mostly used by the lower wage earners. At the same time, it reduces benefits, and therefore outstanding SSW, quite drastically. Also, this reform, like the previous one, suffers from having a very regressive bias, which makes it politically unfeasible. The fiscal gains accrued entail drastic reductions in the SSW and in the yearly pension payments of workers belonging to the lower 60 percent of the wage distribution.

The two Spanish reforms are the least effective of the group. In both cases the total SSW varies very little, retirement patterns remain almost identical (a very mild shift to the right is predicted for the RETA affiliates), and the net fiscal effect is tiny. Also, these reforms are regressive when one looks at within-cohorts redistribution. The amount of regressivity is, naturally, limited by the small reduction in aggregate SSW. Still, and quite paradoxically, the 2002 Amendment seems to make the overall Spanish reform more regressive than it was after the 1997 change. In any case, there is no reason to believe that the very minor improvement in the government fiscal position that A02 engenders will be sufficient to contain the forthcoming Spanish pension deficit.

Appendix

Data and Variables

In this section we define the variables that have been employed in the specification of the reduced-form probit. The data source is the HLSS, unless stated otherwise.

Variables from HLSS

Experience, Education, and Occupation

- Period: length of the current period in the dataset.
- History: history in the dataset, that is, length of participation in the labor market.
- Part-time: indicator variable that takes the value 1 if the individual does not work full time.
- Fraction working: history divided by potential experience (time elapsed since first time observed in the dataset).
- Temporary illness: length of history spent in temporary illness.
- Sector: one-digit SIC industry classification.
- Contributive group: ten groups, from college to unskilled blue collar workers.
- Education: proxy for the level of education, constructed as follows: all individuals in contributive group 1 (i.e., college), are assigned to the college level of the educational variable. People belonging to contributive groups 2, 3, and 4 are assigned to the high school (*diploma*) category. People in all other contributive groups are assigned to a generic class labelled *less than high school.*
- Years of contributions: number of years contributed.
- Eligibility indicator: a dummy variable that takes the value 1 if the individual meets the contributive threshold (fifteen years of contributions); zero otherwise.

Earnings and Pension Variables

- Covered earnings or pensionable earnings: monthly amount upon which SS taxes are levied.

- Monthly earnings: methods of computation (for workers in RGSS) as described in section 9.3.2.
- Pension amount: see section 9.2 for a detailed description.
- Average life cycle earnings: constructed on the basis of a fixed-effect model for each contributive group.
- Expected earnings: see section 9.3.2 for a description.
- Expected earnings peak indicator: discounted sum of the expected earnings from the present to the year the peak is reached.
- Expected earnings OV indicator: discounted sum of the expected earnings from the present to the year the option value is maximized.
- Minimum pension indicator: a dummy variable that takes value 1 if the individual's expected retirement pension falls below the minimum retirement pension.
- Censoring earnings indicators: two dummy variables. The first takes value 1 if the individual's level of contributions falls below the minimum (mandatory) level of contributions. The second takes value 1 if the individual's level of contribution is greater than the maximum level of contributions.

Variables from the Collective Settlements Register (*Estadística de Convenios Colectivos* [ECC])

Since we do not have direct information about regulations affecting specific workers, we use the Spanish register of collective settlements in order to construct proxies for such regulations. In particular, using the ECC (see Jiménez-Martín [1998] for a brief description of the source) we have constructed three indicators of the coverage of early and mandatory retirement provisions for each (two-digit) industry.

- Early-retirement indicator: fraction (weighted by employment) of collective settlements, including a provision favoring early retirement.
- Retirement at 64: fraction (weighted by employment) of collective settlements, including a provision to facilitate retirement of workers aged 64 without incurring age penalty. This variable only applies to people aged 64 enrolled in RGSS.
- Mandatory retirement at 65: fraction (weighted by employment) of collective settlements, including a provision promoting mandatory retirement at 65. This variable only applies to people aged 65 enrolled in RGSS.

The Spanish Labor Force Survey (EPA)

EPA: a quarterly CPS-like survey of roughly 60,000 Spanish households. It contains fairly detailed information on labor-force status, education, and family background variables, but no information on wages and income. Publicly released cross-sectional files are available from 1976 onward. Starting with 1987, INE also releases the so-called *Encuesta de Poblacion Activa Enlazada* (EPAL), which is the panel version of EPA obtained by exploiting the rotating cross-section nature of the original survey. It contains fewer variables than EPA, but it permits the following of individuals for up to six consecutive quarters.

References

Abío, G., H. Bonin, J. Gil, and C. Patxot. 1999. El impacto intergeneracional de la reforma de las pensiones en España: Un enfoque de contabilidad generacional. *Cuadernos Económicos de ICE* 65:101–16.
Boldrin, M., S. Jiménez-Martín, and F. Peracchi. 1999. Social security and retirement in Spain. In *Social Security Programs and Retirement around the World,* ed. J. Gruber and D. Wise, 305–82. Chicago: Chicago University Press.
———. 2001. *Sistema de pensiones y mercado de trabajo en España.* Madrid: Fundación BBV.
———. 2004. Micro-modelling of retirement behavior in Spain. In *Social security and retirement around the world: Micro-estimation,* ed. J. Gruber and D. Wise, 499–578. Chicago: Chicago University Press.
Instituto Nacional de Estadística (INE). 1995. *Proyecciones de la población de España.* Madrid: Instituto Nacional de Estadística.
Instituto Nacional de Estadística (INE). *Encuesta de población activa. Microdata files from 1995-II to 2001-II,* various issues. Madrid: Instituto Nacional de Estadística.
Jiménez-Martín, S. 1998. Indexation and wage change settlements: Evidence from Spanish manufacturing firms. *Oxford Bulletin of Economics and Statistics* 60:449–84.
Jiménez-Martín, S. 1999. El impacto de la reforma de 1997 en los incentivos y la deuda implícita de la Seguridad Social. *Economistas* 84:200–208.

10

Financial Implications of Income Security Reforms in Sweden

Mårten Palme and Ingemar Svensson

10.1 Introduction

Like most other Western industrialized countries, Sweden will in the near future face the financial burden from the combined effect of large birth cohorts reaching retirement age, increased longevity, and a trend toward early retirement. An obvious way to ease this financial pressure is to increase labor supply among older workers by providing economic incentives to stay in the labor force. Although this was one of the main motives behind the recent major reform of Sweden's public old-age pension system, there are, to our knowledge, no previous studies examining the link between the economic incentives inherent in the income security system and the finances of the public sector in Sweden.

In this study we use an econometric model of the retirement decision developed in Palme and Svensson (2004) to simulate the public finance implications of three hypothetical reforms of Sweden's income security system. In these simulations the labor supply response to the reform among older workers is taken into account. Changes in total payments from the public income security system (including labor market insurance programs) and tax payments (including payroll taxes, value added tax [VAT], and income tax to the state and the municipalities) are considered separately in the simulations.

One of the study's emphases is to decompose the overall change in the finances of the public sector into a *mechanical* and a *behavioral* component. The mechanical component is defined as the change in the finances of the

Mårten Palme is a professor of economics at Stockholm University. Ingemar Svensson is a senior researcher at the Division for Research at the Swedish Social Insurance Agency.

public sector when individuals do not change their retirement behavior as a result of the reform. The behavioral effect is defined as the change that occurs as a result of changes in retirement behavior.

In the first hypothetical reform, the early and normal retirement ages (60 and 65, respectively, in the current system) are delayed by three years. This implies that the actuarial adjustments in the pension scheme and the probability of being eligible for benefits from a labor market insurance program (disability, sickness, or unemployment insurance) are delayed by three years. In the second reform, an actuarial adjustment of 6 percent per year of early withdrawal before the normal retirement age is applied to all income security programs. Although this adjustment is very similar to the actuarial adjustment in the current public pension scheme and some occupational pensions, the adjustment is also applied to the labor market insurance programs under the second reform policy regime. Finally, in the third reform, the current income security system is replaced by a pension benefit that replaces 60 percent of average earnings during the best forty years if the pension is claimed at the normal retirement age (65). The pension can be claimed from age 60 with an actuarial adjustment of 6 percent for each year of early withdrawal. Benefits from labor market insurance programs could no longer be used to finance early exit from the labor market.

Although these reforms were chosen for the purpose of the cross-country comparison in this volume, rather than being realistic policy alternatives for Sweden, we believe that the results have relevance for the current public policy debate on the income security system in Sweden. Sweden has recently implemented a reform of its public old-age pension system. One of the main features of the reformed system (see, for example, Palmer 2001 for an overview of the reform) is that benefits are indexed to follow the growth in the average nominal wage rate rather than consumer prices. This means that benefit levels will be reduced if the growth rate in the economy falls below the norm. Hence, the type of reductions in benefit levels considered as reforms in this study is automatic, rather than discretionary, under the postreform pension system in Sweden. Labor supply responses studied in this paper can, therefore, be an important stabilization of public finances under the new public pension system.

There are several issues related to reforms of income security systems that are excluded from the analysis and left for further research. We do not model changes in household savings behavior, which is likely to be an important response to benefit cuts in the income security system. We also ignore potentially important general equilibrium effects on different prices in the economy, which may, in turn, influence public finances.

The rest of the chapter is organized as follows. Section 10.2 gives a brief overview of Sweden's income security system. Section 10.3 describes the data, gives a short description of the empirical model, and presents results from the estimation of the empirical model. Section 10.4 presents the hypothetical reforms of the income security system and describes the simulation methodology. The results from the simulations are presented in section 10.5. Section 10.6 concludes.

10.2 Sweden's Income Security System

The income security system in Sweden consists of three parts: the public old-age pension system, the occupational pension schemes, and the compulsory labor market insurance programs. These programs are, to about the same extent, used for financing exits from the labor market. In this section, we give a brief description of how these programs are constructed.[1] We start with the public old-age pension programs and the occupational pension schemes. We then describe the disability, sickness, and unemployment insurance programs.

10.2.1 The Public Old-Age Pension System

Sweden's public old-age pension system consisted of two parts during the period studied: a basic pension and a supplementary pension (ATP).[2] All Swedish citizens are entitled to the basic pension, which is unrelated to previous earnings. The normal retirement age for this benefit is 65, but it can be claimed from age 60 with a permanent actuarial reduction of 0.5 percent for each month of early withdrawal. If the benefit is claimed beginning after age 65, the level is permanently increased by 0.7 percent for each month of delayed withdrawal up to age 70.

All social insurance programs in Sweden are indexed by the basic amount (BA), which follows the consumer price index (CPI) closely. In the year 2001, the level of one BA was 36,900 Swedish Kronor (SEK).[3] The level of the basic pension is 96 percent of a BA for a single pensioner and 78.5 percent for married. The basic pension also contains a survivor's pension.

The supplementary pension is related to a worker's previous earnings. The amount of the benefit is calculated using the following formula:

$$(1) \qquad Y_i = 0.6 \cdot AP_i \cdot \min\left[\left(\frac{N_i}{30}\right), 1\right] \cdot BA,$$

where AP_i is individual average pension points, BA is the basic amount, and N_i is the number of years an individual has recorded covered income greater than zero. The average of pension points is calculated as the average of annual earnings between 1 BA and the social security ceiling of 7.5 BA of the worker's fifteen best years. The normal retirement age for the supplemen-

---

1. For a more complete description, see Palme and Svensson (1999, 2004).
2. The description is based on the rules pertaining for persons covered in the study. Sweden introduced a reform of the public old-age pension system in the 1990s.
3. In 2001 the exchange rate was about 10 SEK/US$.

tary pension is 65. The actuarial adjustments for early and delayed withdrawal are the same as for the basic pension.

10.2.2 Occupational Pensions

Sweden has a highly unionized labor market. Around 95 percent of all employees are covered by central agreements between the unions and the employers' confederations. These agreements regulate pension programs and other insurance programs for the employees. There are four main agreements, each with its own pension scheme. The private sector has one scheme for blue collar and one for white collar workers. In the public sector, there is one scheme for employees in central government and one for employees in county and local governments.

The private sector blue collar workers included in our sample are under two different occupational pension schemes. Those born between 1927 and 1931 are covered by the STP scheme. The benefit in this scheme is 10 percent of the average annual earnings below the social security ceiling of the three best years of the five years between age 55 and 59. At least three years of earnings between 55 and 59 are required to be eligible for the pension. The benefits are paid out starting when the worker is aged 65. The STP plan is financed on a pay-as-you-go basis.

In 1996 the STP scheme was replaced by a fully funded scheme, covering workers born after 1940. The cohorts between 1938 and 1940 are covered by a transition scheme; those who were born between 1932 and 1937 can choose between STP and the transition scheme. The benefits in the transition scheme are calculated as 10 percent of annual earnings under the social security ceiling after age 30 plus the amount that the worker receives from the fully funded system. The contributions to the fully funded scheme were 2.0 percent of annual earnings between 1996 and 1999. The contribution rate was increased to 3.5 percent in 2000.

White collar workers in the private sector are, in general, covered by the ITP and ITPK schemes. The ITP pension replaces 10 percent of a worker's earnings the year before retirement up to the social security ceiling of 7.5 BA, 65 percent of earnings between 7.5 and 20 BAs, and 32.5 percent between 20 and 30 BAs. The normal retirement age for the ITP plan is 65, but the benefit can be claimed with an actuarial adjustment from age 60. ITPK is a fully funded scheme that was introduced in 1977. The contribution rate is 2 percent of gross annual earnings.

Until 1992, employees in central government were covered by a gross pension scheme that replaced 65 percent of annual earnings the year before retirement. This scheme was replaced with a net pension that is similar to the ITP scheme. However, the benefit is determined by the average of annual earnings during the five years preceding retirement. Employees in central government are also covered by a fully funded scheme that was introduced in 1992. The contribution rate in this scheme is 1.7 percent of the annual wage sum.

Finally, employees in county councils and local government are covered by a gross pension, which is determined by the average of annual earnings of the five best years of the seven years preceding retirement. It replaces 96 percent below 1 BA, 78.5 percent between 1 and 2.5 BA, 60 percent between 2.5 and 3.5 BAs, 64 percent between 3.5 and 7.5 BAs, 65 percent between 7.5 and 20 BAs, and 32.5 percent between 20 and 30 BAs. It can be claimed, with an actuarial adjustment, from age 60.

10.2.3 Labor Market Insurance Programs

There are three important labor market insurance programs: disability insurance (DI), sickness insurance (SI), and unemployment insurance (UI). Eligibility for disability insurance requires that the individual's capacity to work is permanently reduced by at least 25 percent. Full compensation requires that the capacity is completely lost. A physician determines work capacity in general, but eligibility for disability insurance is ultimately determined by the local social insurance administration. Between 1972 and 1991, disability insurance could be granted for labor market reasons, that is, no requirement of reduced work capacity was needed.

The disability benefits consist of a basic pension and a supplementary pension (ATP). The level of the basic pension is the same as for the old-age scheme; the supplementary pension is determined in the same way as for the old-age scheme with no actuarial reduction for early retirement. Assumed pension points are calculated for each year between the date of disability and age 64.

Sickness insurance replaces a share of lost earnings due to temporary illnesses, up to the social security ceiling. The replacement level has been changed on several occasions during the time period covered by this study. In a reform in 1987, the replacement level was set to 90 percent of the worker's insured income. Since then, the replacement has been decreased several times. The first was in a reform in 1991. In 1996 it was set to 75 percent of the insured income for long sickness spells, and in 1998 it was raised to 80 percent.

The unemployment insurance benefit consists of two parts: one basic part, which is unrelated to a worker's insured income, and one part that requires membership in an unemployment benefit fund and is related to a worker's insured income. Unemployed workers who actively search for a new job are eligible for compensation. The main difference between the benefit level in the unemployment and sickness insurance programs is the income ceiling. The ceiling in the sickness insurance is the same as for other parts of the social insurance system, while the ceiling in the unemployment insurance is subject to discretionary changes, and is lower than the ceiling for the sickness benefit. The replacement rate for unemployment insurance has also been changed on several occasions during the period analyzed in this empirical example. These changes have roughly followed the changes in the sickness insurance.

10.2.4 Income Taxes and Housing Allowances

Sweden went through a major income tax reform in 1991. Before the reform, all income was included in the same tax base and was taxed with a proportional local government tax (around 30 percent, depending on municipality) and a progressive national tax. The maximum marginal tax rate was set to 75 percent. The main feature of the tax reform was that the tax base was divided into capital income and earned income. Income from capital is taxed at the national level with a rate of 30 percent and earned income is subject to a local government tax, and above a certain break point, by a 20 percent national tax. The marginal tax rate was reduced considerably.

Old age, disability, and survivor's pensioners with low income are entitled to a housing allowance. In 1995, this allowance was at most 85 percent of the housing cost, up to a ceiling. About 30 percent of all old-age pensioners received housing allowances in 1995.

10.3 Empirical Model

We use an econometric model to predict the behavioral responses to the policy reforms considered in this paper. For the current purpose, we provide a brief overview of data sources, the specification of the empirical model, estimation results, and results from the prediction of the behavioral responses to the reform. A detailed description of these issues is given in Palme and Svensson (2004).

10.3.1 Data

The data come from the Longitudinal Individual Data panel dataset (LINDA). This dataset is a pure register sample, that is, no interviews were made when the data were collected. The three main registers used to obtain the LINDA panel are the Income and Wealth Register (Inkomst- och Förmögenhetsstatistiken [IoF]), Population Census (Folk- och Bostadsräkningen [FoB]),[4] and the National Social Insurance Board Registers for pension points (based on earnings).

The original sample for the LINDA panel is a random selection of about 300,000 individuals from the 1995 population register. The sampling pro-

---

4. The FoB exists for every fifth year between 1960 and 1990, and is obtained from mailed questionnaires. Everyone living in Sweden is included in the FoB, and participation in the census is compulsory.

cedure used to update the panel backward and forward from 1995 is designed so that each yearly cross-section of LINDA is also a random sample of the Swedish population, that is, each individual has the same probability of being included in the sample, irrespective of the type of household he or she is living in.

The LINDA panel also contains information on the spouse of each individual originally included in the sample. In general, the same variables as for the original individuals are also available for their spouses. There are two, somewhat different, definitions of spouse in LINDA. The first definition, used by the tax authorities, includes individuals who are either formally married or are cohabiting and having children together. The second definition refers to all spouses who, in the mailed questionnaire, have reported that they are living together, that is, they share housing. This information is only available for the years of the census (FoB). When calculating incentive variables for this analysis, we used the first definition, since it is available for all years.

In this study, we use two subsamples. In the first, used for the estimation, we select individuals born between 1927 and 1940. We further restricted the sample to employees at age 50; that is, we exclude those who were self-employed, unemployed, or out of the labor force at age 50. Table 10.1 shows the number of individuals remaining in the sample after different steps in the sample selection procedure. In the time dimension, we restrict the sample to the period 1983 to 1997. For this period we are able to observe the retirement behavior using the detailed income components available. The second sample is used for the policy simulations. This one is restricted to individuals born in 1940. In section 10.4 we describe this restricted sample.

We define a worker as retired the first year when income from work is permanently below one BA. We have also compared this definition of retirement with one where we define the year of retirement as the first year when an individual starts to receive less income from work than pension benefits. It turned out that the similarity between these definitions for the individuals in the sample was fairly good. However, since the former definition of retirement is more in accordance with the general definition of the

Table 10.1   **Number of individuals remaining after each step in the sample selection**

	Men	Women	Men and women
Individuals born 1927–40	22,375	21,948	44,323
Neither emigrated nor dead in 1983	22,055	21,798	43,853
Usable earnings histories	22,046	21,781	43,827
Not retired at age 50	20,364	19,576	39,940
Not retired in 1983	18,163	15,916	34,079
Employed in 1983	15,619	14,820	30,439

date when the worker leaves the labor force, we used that in the empirical analysis.

10.3.2 Empirical Specification

The following retirement model was estimated:

$$(2) \quad R_{it} = \delta_0 + \delta_1 ACC_{it} + \delta_2 ISW_{it} + \delta_3 AGE_{it} + \delta_4 PREARN_{it} + \delta_5 EARN_{it}$$
$$+ \delta_6 PREARN_{it} \cdot EARN_{it} + \delta_7 SPEARN_{it} + \beta' X_{it} + v_{it},$$

where R_{it} is a dummy variable that takes the value 1 if year t is individual i's last year in the labor force, where ACC_{it} is the measure of accrual at time t; ISW_{it} is the net present value of social security wealth discounted to time t; AGE_{it} represents the individual's age either by a linear variable or by indicators for each age; $PREARN$ is the individual's predicted earnings at time t and the square of this measure; $EARN$ is a measure of the individual's lifetime earnings and its square; $SPEARN$ is lifetime earnings of the spouse, its square and the spouse's net social security wealth discounted back to time t; X is a set of individual characteristics, including marital status, education level ($Educ1$–$Educ6$), socioeconomic group ($Occ1$–$Occ4$) and indicators for each of Sweden's twenty-five counties (compare section 10.4 for the construction of these variables).

The key variables are the measures of economic incentives described by income security wealth (ISW) and ACC. Income security wealth is measured for each individual for each potential retirement age as

$$(3) \qquad\qquad ISW(r, t) = \sum_{s=r}^{max\ age} \delta^{s-t} E_t B(s, r),$$

where δ is the discount factor and $E_t B(s, r)$ is the expected benefit at age s if the worker retires at age r, that is,

$$(4) \quad E_t B(s, r) = p(s\,|\,t)q(s\,|\,b)BM(s, r) + p(s\,|\,t)[1 - q(s\,|\,t)]BS(s, r)$$
$$+ [1 - p(s\,|\,t)]q(s\,|\,t)S(s, r, t)$$

where $BM(s, r)$ is the worker's pension benefit at age s if he or she is married and retires at age r; $BS(s, r)$ is the worker's pension benefit at age s if he or she is not married and retires at age r; $S(s, r, t)$ is the survivor's benefit when the worker would have been aged s and retired at age r; $p(s\,|\,t)$ is the probability of survival at time s conditional on survival at time t; $q(s\,|\,t)$ is the probability of the spouse surviving at age s conditional on survival at age t. $S(s, r, t)$ depends on the spouse at time t as well as the retirement age r, while $BM(s, r)$ and $BS(s, r)$ are not dependent on t, since we assume perfect foresight about wages. We also disregard the possibility of divorce.

Three alternative measures of ACC were used in the estimation. In the policy simulations we use *peak value* and *option value*. Peak value is defined as the difference between the current ISW and the maximum ISW the worker can expect in the future, provided that he or she stays in the labor force. It is forward looking, not only in the sense that it considers all future expected benefit payments, but also in the sense that it considers all future possible gains of staying in the labor force. This is also true for the option value measure, but this measure includes additional parameters for the subjective discount rate, the valuation of leisure, and a risk-aversion parameter. The accrual is then defined as the difference between the utility stream of retiring the current year versus at the optimal future date, that is, it measures the value of the option of staying in the labor force. Palme and Svensson (2004) describe how the additional parameters are estimated.

10.3.3   Estimation Results

Tables 10.2 and 10.3 show the estimates for the models that we use in the policy simulations for males and females, respectively. Each table contains four different specifications: for each of the two alternative accrual measures, one equation applies a linear specification in age and one uses dummy variables for each age.

The coefficient estimates for the variables measuring economic incentives—income security wealth for the sample individual and the spouse as well as the alternative accrual measures—are of key importance in the policy simulations. Table 10.2 shows that the coefficients estimate for each accrual measure have the expected (negative) sign and are significantly different from zero in both models. The estimates for ISW, both for the sample individual and the spouse, are, as expected, positive and significantly different from zero in all four models.

The estimates for the sample of women are, as can be seen in table 10.3, somewhat different. Again, the estimates for the accrual measures are significant with the expected sign in all specifications. However, the estimates of the ISW coefficient are only significant with the expected sign for the sample individual in the peak value specification with age dummies. The estimates for the husband's ISW are insignificant in all specifications, and the ISW coefficient for the sample individual in the option value models is significantly different from zero with the unexpected sign.

10.4   Simulation Methodology

The aim of the simulation exercise is to study the financial implications of three hypothetical reforms when taking the change in retirement behavior as a response to the reform into account. To do this, we will follow one particular birth cohort—those born in 1940, going through four alternative policy regimes: one following from the current Swedish income security system, and three following as a result of the hypothetical reforms of the system.

Table 10.2 **Results from probit regressions on individual retirement decision—men**

	Peak value		Option value	
	Linear age	Age dummies	Linear age	Age dummies
ACCR/10^6	−0.93	−0.92	−5.11	−6.74
	(−10.12)	(−9.94)	(−9.39)	(11.42)
ISW/10^6	0.34	0.35	0.31	0.24
	(6.41)	(6.43)	(5.50)	(4.16)
Lifetime earnings	−2.76	−2.80	−2.43	−2.55
	(−1.92)	(−1.92)	(−1.71)	(−1.76)
Lifetime earnings^2	0.11	0.11	0.10	0.12
	(1.45)	(1.39)	(1.31)	(1.58)
Predicted earnings	1.47	1.40	1.26	1.59
	(0.93)	(0.87)	(0.80)	(1.00)
Predicted earnings^2	−0.09	−0.09	−0.08	−0.10
	(−2.14)	(−2.16)	(−1.91)	(−1.94)
Lifetime · Predicted	0.13	0.15	0.12	0.08
	(0.91)	(0.96)	(0.83)	(0.53)
(Lifetime · Predicted)^2	−0.01	−0.01	−0.01	−0.01
	(−1.78)	(−1.77)	(−1.62)	(−1.33)
Education2	0.22	0.22	0.22	0.22
	(6.91)	(6.85)	(6.92)	(6.91)
Education3	0.18	0.18	0.18	0.19
	(11.19)	(10.99)	(11.23)	(11.24)
Education4	0.13	0.14	0.14	0.15
	(6.87)	(6.75)	(6.88)	(7.04)
Education5	0.12	0.12	0.12	0.12
	(4.71)	(4.44)	(4.75)	(4.73)
Education6	0.07	0.07	0.07	0.07
	(2.50)	(2.41)	(2.46)	(2.59)
Occupation2	−0.17	−0.17	−0.17	−0.17
	(−9.77)	(−9.53)	(−9.68)	(−9.16)
Occupation3	0.03	0.03	0.03	0.03
	(1.38)	(1.46)	(1.42)	(1.62)
Occupation4	−0.18	−0.19	−0.18	−0.19
	(−8.68)	(−8.78)	(−8.82)	(−8.90)
Age	0.11		0.11	
	(38.39)		(33.28)	
Married	−0.05	−0.06	−0.04	−0.02
	(−1.21)	(−1.29)	(−0.93)	(−0.47)
Lifetime earn, spouse	0.03	0.04	0.02	0.03
	(2.45)	(2.77)	(2.11)	(2.63)
Lifetime earn, spouse^2	−0.01	−0.01	−0.01	−0.01
	(−2.51)	(−2.83)	(−2.16)	(−2.68)
ISW, spouse/10^6	0.04	0.04	0.03	0.03
	(3.01)	(3.11)	(2.98)	(3.01)
Indicators for age	No	Yes	No	Yes
Indicators for counties	Yes	Yes	Yes	Yes
Pseudo R^2	0.1621	0.1841	0.1612	0.1844
Log likelihood	−24,571	−23,928	−24,599	−23,920

Notes: T-values are in parentheses. Number of individuals = 15,619; number of observations = 127,390.

Table 10.3 **Results from probit regressions on individual retirement decision—women**

	Peak value		Option value	
	Linear age	Age dummies	Linear age	Age dummies
ACCR/10⁶	–1.42	–1.29	–23.4	–24.0
	(–10.39)	(–9.69)	(–20.43)	(–21.67)
ISW/10⁶	0.07	0.13	–0.47	–0.48
	(1.27)	(2.16)	(–7.13)	(–7.14)
Lifetime earnings	–4.68	–4.60	–6.31	–6.22
	(–2.47)	(–2.34)	(–3.39)	(–3.25)
Lifetime earnings²	0.40	0.36	0.66	0.65
	(5.07)	(4.34)	(7.32)	(6.80)
Predicted earnings	5.94	6.02	5.53	8.82
	(3.50)	(3.38)	(3.56)	(3.56)
Predicted earnings²	–0.19	–0.22	–0.07	–0.08
	(–3.05)	(–3.20)	(–1.26)	(–1.47)
Lifetime · Predicted	–0.19	–0.12	–0.46	–0.46
	(–1.06)	(–0.66)	(–2.85)	(–2.68)
(Lifetime · Predicted)²	–0.00	–0.00	0.00	0.00
	(–0.37)	(–0.38)	(0.04)	(0.19)
Education2	0.06	0.05	0.09	0.08
	(2.27)	(1.80)	(3.44)	(2.96)
Education3	0.07	0.06	0.09	0.09
	(4.15)	(3.87)	(5.72)	(5.52)
Education4	0.07	0.06	0.11	0.09
	(2.23)	(1.70)	(3.32)	(2.78)
Education5	–0.00	–0.00	0.04	0.05
	(–0.07)	(–0.05)	(1.74)	(1.80)
Education6	–0.08	–0.09	–0.02	–0.04
	(–2.75)	(–3.04)	(–0.82)	(–1.10)
Occupation2	–0.11	–0.11	–0.03	–0.03
	(–5.12)	(–4.93)	(–1.48)	(–1.29)
Occupation3	–0.04	–0.04	–0.02	–0.01
	(–1.81)	(–1.52)	(–0.67)	(–0.42)
Occupation4	–0.13	–0.13	–0.21	–0.21
	(–7.27)	(–6.82)	(–11.34)	(–10.95)
Age	0.14		0.09	
	(50.07)		(24.64)	
Married	0.29	0.32	0.32	0.35
	(4.61)	(4.87)	(4.96)	(5.28)
Lifetime earn, spouse	0.01	0.00	0.00	0.00
	(0.30)	(0.12)	(0.27)	(0.04)
Lifetime earn, spouse²	–0.00	–0.00	–0.00	–0.00
	(–0.66)	(–0.48)	(–0.67)	(–0.43)
ISW, spouse/10⁶	–0.01	–0.01	–0.02	–0.02
	(–0.58)	(–0.68)	(–1.12)	(–1.23)
Indicators for age	No	Yes	No	Yes
Indicators for counties	Yes	Yes	Yes	Yes
Pseudo R²	0.1762	0.2004	0.1828	0.2083
Log likelihood	–23,540	–22,850	–23,351	–22,624

Notes: T-values are in parentheses. Number of individuals = 14,820; number of observations = 123,979.

Since the LINDA panel is a random sample of individuals,[5] our sample constitutes a random sample of individuals born in 1940, with the additional requirement that they should be employed or temporarily unemployed at age 55, that is, the self-employed and those who were not in the labor force were excluded. This selection resulted in a sample size of 2,148 (1,109 men and 1,039 women). Using the sampling weights of the dataset, it can be shown that this sample represents 66 percent of the 1940 birth cohort living in Sweden at age 55. In the calculations, as we will explain later, we will also use information from 1,561 spouses of the individuals in the sample.

10.4.1 Different States and IS Flows

We consider individual retirement behavior starting at age 56 up to age 79. In each year, an individual can exit from the labor force to either retirement, in most cases financed through the income security system, or to death. Since these alternative states have very different financial implications, we will consider the two alternative states (retired or dead) for each of the twenty-four years, that is, forty-eight different states, ex post, for each individual in the sample.

If the individual exits to retirement, there are, as we explained in section 10.2, different possibilities for financing retirement through the income security system. Ideally, it would have been desirable to consider all of the different paths to retirement and assign a probability to each of them. This would, however, as is explained in Palme and Svensson (2004), involve an unrealistic number of alternatives. Instead, as we did in the estimation of the retirement-choice models, we combine the paths that involve labor market insurance into one stylized path. This means that the retirement state is further divided into two pathways to retirement: the old-age and the labor market insurance pathway.

Each state has different financial implications for the public sector. To calculate these, we consider all expected income and payroll tax payments, VAT, and payments from the income security system between age 55 and 108. All future payments are discounted back to age 55 using a 3 percent real interest rate. For workers for whom we cannot observe labor earnings, we use a three-year average of earnings before the exit from the labor force to predict this missing information. In addition to that, for workers younger than age 55, we upgrade the earnings by the age-specific average increase in earnings.

10.4.2 Predicting the Probability for Each State

In order to predict the income streams we also need the probabilities for each individual to end up in each state. Since there are three different states at each age, these calculations have to be made stepwise.

---

5. The individual rather than the household is the sampling unit.

We use the estimated econometric model described in section 10.3 to predict individual retirement hazards at each age. That is, we use the characteristics of each individual and use the estimated probit equation to obtain the conditional probabilities. The covariates include the economic incentive variables; that is, we are able to predict the probability of exiting to retirement for alternative income security policies. Using the predicted retirement hazard and gender-specific life tables, we can calculate the probability of exiting to retirement or death at each age.

For the probability of financing the exit from the labor market by labor market insurance, rather than old-age pension, we assign the probability observed in the data to that path *conditional* on exiting from the labor market at a particular age. Note that this is different from the strategy we used in the estimation, where we used the probability of being granted benefits from a labor market insurance program *unconditional* on applying for such insurance or leaving the labor force. Both of these sets of probabilities are shown in figure 10.1. The base probabilities are also used for the Actuarial Reform and the Common Reform.

10.4.3 Handling Spouses in the Simulation

In the estimation of the retirement choice model, the economic position of the spouse was allowed to influence the retirement probability of the sample individual through lifetime income and social security wealth. On the other hand, we made the simplifying assumption that retirement *behavior* was fixed. Assuming fixed behavior of the spouse is obviously not satisfactory in simulations of financial implications of policy reforms, since some of the financial impact may come through behavioral changes of the spouses, through changes in the size of the sample individual's income security wealth.

In the Swedish income security system this interaction transpires only through survivor benefits and housing allowances. The income of the spouse does not influence income taxes paid by the individual. The rules for housing allowances are very complicated, and the overall importance of housing allowances for incentives and benefit flows is rather limited. For this reason we have treated them as if they were individual benefits, as part of a simplified model of housing allowances. Given this simplification, it is possible to calculate the taxes paid and the benefits received for our sample on an individual basis. We use information about the spouse (including predicted behavioral responses to reform) in order to estimate survivor benefit payments to the primary sample individual, but the estimate of financial effects is only based on the 1940 cohort primary sample. This strategy means that men and women are treated in the same way, which is desirable, since labor force participation for women in the 1940 cohort is almost the same as that for men.

To take this behavioral change into account, we follow a three-step

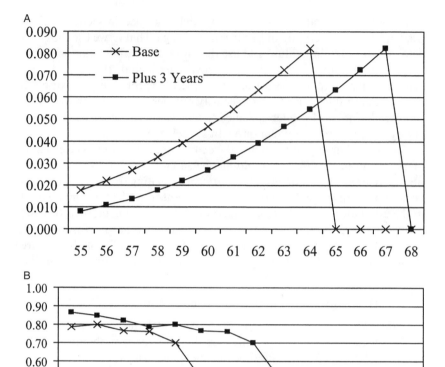

Fig. 10.1   Probability of access to the labor market insurance pathway and probability of using the labor market insurance pathway conditional on retirement age: *A*, Probability of access to the labor market insurance pathway by age; *B*, Probability of using the labor market insurance pathway conditional on retirement age

procedure. In the first step, we calculate the ISS flows for each age of the sample individual *conditional* on retirement of the spouse at each age between 55 and 70. In the second step, we predict retirement probabilities of the spouse, using the same model as for the sample individual. Finally, in the third step, for each age of the sample individual we average the ISS flows of the individual in the sample using the weights of the predicted retirement probabilities of the spouse.

10.4.4   Hypothetical Reforms of the Income Security System

We will simulate the financial implications of three hypothetical reforms of Sweden's income security system. The reforms are rather different in their design. The first reform delays eligibility of all pension benefits by three years. The second introduces an actuarial adjustment in the labor market insurance programs. All other rules of the baseline system, including eligibility ages, are retained. The third reform replaces the entire income security system with a pension that replaces 60 percent of average earnings during the best forty years. This reform is referred to as the *Common Reform*, since it allows for cross-country comparisons with results from the other chapters in this volume.

Reform 1: Delaying Eligibility by Three Years

As we explained in section 10.2, most Swedish old-age pension benefits have a normal retirement age at 65 but can be claimed from age 60. Also, the labor market insurance programs depend on age. The probability of being admitted DI increases with age, and the prevalence of older workers being admitted to long-term sickness as well as unemployment insurance is also greater than in younger age groups. In addition, rules on mandatory retirement age in the Swedish labor market will also affect the dependence between age and labor force participation rates.

Delaying eligibility ages in the old-age pension system, and the probability of being eligible for labor market insurance programs decreases the value of the ISW, since each worker can expect either fewer benefit payments or a larger actuarial adjustment compared to the current system. Since we estimated a positive effect of ISW on retirement probability, we expect the reform to delay retirement.

In simulating the effects of delaying the eligibility ages in the income security system, a key issue is how to separate the effects of economic incentives—both through the old-age pension programs and labor market insurance, through changes in the probability of being eligible for benefits—from the effects from mandatory retirement ages and latent retirement behavior specific to age. Our strategy to deal with this issue is to do a sensitivity analysis that produces a lower and an upper bound for the effect on retirement behavior from the reform.

To carry out this sensitivity analysis we do three different simulations. In the first simulation (S1), we use the model with a linear specification in age (M1). In the second one (S2), we use the model with age dummies (M2). In the third simulation (S3), we again use the M2 model, but now we shift the age dummies by three years. The S2 simulation constitutes a lower bound for the predicted effect of the reform, since it implicitly assumes that the over-parameterized dummy variable specification in age *only* reflects the latent retirement behavior by age and rules on mandatory retirement ages on the labor market. The S3 simulation constitutes an upper bound for the predicted effect by implicitly making the equally unrealistic assumption that the dummy variable specification *only* reflects the unmeasured economic incentives generated by the income security system.

Reform 2: Extension of the Actuarial Adjustment

In this reform, the actuarial adjustment is changed to 6 percent for each year of early withdrawal before the normal retirement age at 65. This means that the actuarial adjustment is maintained in the public pension system (for ages 60 to 64) as well as in the occupational pension schemes for white collar workers in the private sector and employed in the central government. Also, the pension plan for blue collar workers in the private sector is maintained, since it cannot be claimed before age 65.

The actuarial adjustment in the occupational pension system for employees in the municipalities is somewhat increased, and the actuarial adjustment in ages 66 to 70 in the public system is reduced from 8.4 percent per year. However, the major change implied by this reform is that an actuarial adjustment is applied also for the disability insurance and for those who exit from the labor market through the unemployment or sickness insurance. This change is likely to increase the accrual in individual income security wealth of staying in the labor force, and thereby increases the economic incentives of staying in the labor force.

Reform 3: Change to a Common System

In this reform, the entire income security system is replaced with a pension system where the benefit is calculated as 60 percent of average earnings during the best 40 years if the worker retires at a normal retirement age at 65. It can, however, be claimed from age 60 with a lifelong actuarial adjustment of 6 percent per year of early withdrawal, and delayed until age 70 with a symmetric actuarial adjustment. All labor market insurance programs are abolished in this hypothetical reform.

The effect of the reform on the economic incentives is less transparent compared to the Three-Year Reform. In general, most workers will experience a substantial reduction in their income security wealth, since the current system, in general—except for very high-income earners—has a higher replacement level, including the occupational pensions. There is also an effect from the abolition of the labor market insurance programs on income security wealth. The actuarial adjustments are very similar to those in the current old-age pension system. However, the abolition of the labor market insurance programs implies that we can expect an effect on the accrual measures as well.

10.4.5   Decomposition of the Total Financial Implication of the Reforms

To measure the total financial effect of a reform in the income security system we use the individual Income Security Wealth (ISW), as defined in equation (2). The total financial effect is then defined as the aggregate differences between the ISW under the prereform policy regime and the postreform regime, respectively. Within a given policy regime, the individual ISW depends in each period on whether the individual remains in the labor force and on survival. It is, however, possible to calculate ISW, conditional on that the individual is each of the forty-eight states and for the pre- and postreform policy regimes, respectively. In the sample, the total effect can be calculated as

$$
(5) \qquad Total\ effect = \sum_{i=1}^{N}\sum_{s=1}^{48} P_{is}^{R}ISW_{is}^{R} - \sum_{i=1}^{N}\sum_{s=1}^{48} P_{is}^{B}ISW_{is}^{B},
$$

where P_{is} denotes the probability of each of the forty-eight states between age 56 and 79 of being in the labor force, retired, or dead for a particular individual i. The superscripts B and R denote the pre- and postreform policy regimes, respectively. That is, at age 55 all members of the sample are alive and in the labor force. At age 56 each individual will have a probability of being dead and a probability of being in the labor force under the prereform policy regime, which is different from that in the postreform regime. This is true at age 57 and each age until 78. At age 79 we assume that all individuals have retired.

The total financial effect of a reform of the income security system can be decomposed in two components. We call the first component the *mechanical* effect. This is the predicted financial implication of the reform under the assumption that the workers do not change their labor supply behavior as a response to the reform. The second component, the *behavioral* effect, is the financial effect that can be referred to as the predicted change in the workers' labor supply behavior. This effect is ignored in financial predictions of reforms in the income security system that do not take labor supply considerations into account.

By adding and subtracting $\sum_{i=1}^{N}\sum_{s=1}^{48} P_{is}^{B}ISW_{is}^{R}$ to equation (3) we obtain the following decomposition:

$$
(6) \qquad Total\ effect = \left(\sum_{i=1}^{N}\sum_{s=1}^{48} P_{is}^{R}ISW_{is}^{R} - \sum_{i=1}^{N}\sum_{s=1}^{48} P_{is}^{B}ISW_{is}^{R} \right)
$$
$$
+ \left(\sum_{i=1}^{N}\sum_{s=1}^{48} P_{is}^{B}ISW_{is}^{R} - \sum_{i=1}^{N}\sum_{s=1}^{48} P_{is}^{B}ISW_{is}^{B} \right),
$$

where the first right hand side term within parenthesis is the behavioral effect and second term the mechanical effect. For the mechanical effect, the prereform-state probabilities, which reflect prereform labor supply behavior, are maintained, while the ISW in each state is calculated under the pre- and postreform regime, respectively. Conversely, for the behavioral effect, the ISW under the postreform is used for both terms, while the first term uses state probabilities for the postregimes and the second term uses prereform ones.

10.5   Results

The predictions of the overall financial implications of the hypothetical reforms are shown in tables 10.4 and 10.5. Table 10.4 shows the outcomes measured in expected present value per person in 1995, that is, at age 55 for the individuals in the sample. Throughout the analysis, we use a 3 percent discount rate. Euros per person in 2001 prices is used as currency unit.[6] Table 10.4 also shows the percentage change of the three different reforms relative to the current system.

Table 10.4 contains six main panels. Each panel shows the results from a combination of model specification, either the peak or option value accrual measure, and the three different simulation strategies explained in section 10.4. Each main panel contains results on six different simulated outcomes for the current system and for the three hypothetical reforms, respectively.

The first row shows the expected present value of all future benefits from the public pension system. The pension benefits from the occupational pension schemes, which are considered in the incentive calculations, since they contribute to net income after retirement, are deducted in order to focus on financial implications for the public sector. To also show the total financial implications for the average worker, the second row shows total benefits, including occupational pension benefits.

The third through the fifth row shows the average present value on different taxes paid directly or indirectly by the worker. The third row shows the payroll tax, the fourth the income tax, and the fifth the VAT and indirect taxes.[7] Finally, the sixth row shows the sum of all these taxes.

Table 10.5 shows the decomposition, explained in section 10.4.5, of the total financial implication of the reforms in a mechanical and a behavioral effect. As in table 10.4, the results in table 10.5 are divided into six main panels, depending on the combination of model specification and simulation strategy. Instead of the outcomes for the three different tax categories,

---

6. We have used the exchange rate between SEK and euro on January 1, 2001 (9.3175 SEK/ Euro).

7. To be able to estimate the effect of income changes on VAT and other indirect tax payments, we need a tax rate for the combined effect from these taxes. This is set to 22 percent and is obtained from the ratio between the aggregate sum of all indirect tax payments and household disposable income. We use data from the 2001 National Accounts for Sweden.

Table 10.4   Discounted expected value at age 55 of benefit and tax payments

	Present discounted value				Total change relative to base (%)		
	Base	Three-Year Reform	Actuarial Reform	Common Reform	Three-Year Reform	Actuarial Reform	Common Reform
Peak value—S1							
Benefits	167,147	158,050	138,769	134,688	−5.4	−17.0	−19.4
Benefits incl. occup.	190,242	173,187	162,066	134,688	−9.0	−14.8	−29.2
Taxes							
Payroll	64,627	68,208	64,767	68,964	5.5	0.2	6.7
Income	107,656	104,790	95,879	89,093	−2.7	−10.9	−17.2
VAT	55,216	54,279	51,691	49,704	−1.7	−6.4	−10.0
Total	227,499	227,276	212,337	207,761	−0.1	−6.7	−8.7
Peak value—S2							
Benefits	163,661	155,370	138,733	134,518	−5.1	−15.2	−17.8
Benefits incl. occup.	187,750	170,363	162,682	134,518	−9.3	−13.4	−28.4
Taxes							
Payroll	66,351	69,920	66,520	70,761	5.4	0.3	6.6
Income	108,424	105,444	98,009	90,890	−2.7	−9.6	−16.2
VAT	55,509	54,556	52,388	50,367	−1.7	−5.6	−9.3
Total	230,285	229,920	216,918	212,018	−0.2	−5.8	−7.9
Peak value—S3							
Benefits	163,661	139,474	138,733	134,518	−14.8	−15.2	−17.8
Benefits incl. occup.	187,750	158,406	162,682	134,518	−15.6	−13.4	−28.4
Taxes							
Payroll	66,351	82,105	66,520	70,761	23.7	0.3	6.6
Income	108,424	114,474	98,009	90,890	5.6	−9.6	−16.2
VAT	55,509	57,552	52,388	50,367	3.7	−5.6	−9.3
Total	230,285	254,130	216,918	212,018	10.4	−5.8	−7.9

(continued)

Table 10.4   (continued)

		Present discounted value			Total change relative to base (%)		
	Base	Three-Year Reform	Actuarial Reform	Common Reform	Three-Year Reform	Actuarial Reform	Common Reform
		Option value—S1					
Benefits	168,476	158,265	137,729	134,037	-6.1	-18.2	-20.4
Benefits incl. occup.	190,741	173,112	160,215	134,037	-9.2	-16.0	-29.7
Taxes							
Payroll	63,531	68,025	63,382	68,319	7.1	-0.2	7.5
Income	106,955	104,753	93,839	88,401	-2.1	-12.3	-17.3
VAT	54,982	54,274	51,052	49,444	-1.3	-7.1	-10.1
Total	225,468	227,052	208,273	206,164	0.7	-7.6	-8.6
		Option value—S2					
Benefits	167,432	158,670	138,163	134,187	-5.2	-17.5	-19.9
Benefits incl. occup.	190,066	172,809	160,563	134,187	-9.1	-15.5	-29.4
Taxes							
Payroll	62,686	67,123	62,528	67,540	7.1	-0.3	7.7
Income	105,414	103,218	92,731	87,175	-2.1	-12.0	-17.3
VAT	54,595	53,897	50,785	49,170	-1.3	-7.0	-9.9
Total	222,695	224,238	206,044	203,884	0.7	-7.5	-8.4
		Option value—S3					
Benefits	167,432	147,465	138,163	134,187	-11.9	-17.5	-19.9
Benefits incl. occup.	190,066	164,633	160,563	134,187	-13.4	-15.5	-29.4
Taxes							
Payroll	62,686	75,856	62,528	67,540	21.0	-0.3	7.7
Income	105,414	109,937	92,731	87,175	4.3	-12.0	-17.3
VAT	54,595	56,050	50,785	49,170	2.7	-7.0	-9.9
Total	222,695	241,843	206,044	203,884	8.6	-7.5	-8.4

Table 10.5   Change in discounted expected value at age 55 of benefit and tax payments

	Three-year increment			Actuarial Reform			Common Reform		
	Mechanical	Behavioral	Total	Mechanical	Behavioral	Total	Mechanical	Behavioral	Total
				Peak value—S1					
Benefits	-4,937	-4,160	-9,097	-28,334	-44	-28,378	-33,659	1,201	-32,459
Benefits incl. occup.	-14,426	-2,629	-17,055	-28,180	5	-28,175	-56,754	1,201	-55,553
Taxes: Total	-7,867	7,643	-223	-15,510	347	-15,163	-31,399	11,661	-19,738
Net change	2,930	-11,804	-8,873	-12,824	-391	-13,215	-2,260	-10,460	-12,720
Change as % of base benefits	1.8	-7.1	-5.3	-7.7	-0.2	-7.9	-1.4	-6.3	-7.6
				Peak value—S2					
Benefits	-4,129	-4,163	-8,292	-24,878	-51	-24,929	-29,964	821	-29,143
Benefits incl. occup.	-14,504	-2,883	-17,386	-25,075	7	-25,068	-54,052	821	-53,231
Taxes: Total	-7,923	7,558	-364	-13,793	426	-13,367	-30,018	11,751	-18,267
Net change	3,794	-11,721	-7,927	-11,085	-477	-11,562	54	-10,931	-10,876
Change as % of base benefits	2.3	-7.2	-4.8	-6.8	-0.3	-7.1	0.0	-6.7	-6.6
				Peak value—S3					
Benefits	-4,129	-20,058	-24,187	-24,878	-51	-24,929	-29,964	821	-29,143
Benefits incl. occup.	-14,504	-14,840	-29,344	-25,075	7	-25,068	-54,052	821	-53,231
Taxes: Total	-7,923	31,768	23,846	-13,793	426	-13,367	-30,018	11,751	-18,267
Net change	3,794	-51,827	-48,033	-11,085	-477	-11,562	54	-10,931	-10,876
Change as % of base benefits	2.3	-31.7	-29.3	-6.8	-0.3	-7.1	0.0	-6.7	-6.6

Change in present discounted value

(continued)

Table 10.5   (continued)

	Three-year increment			Actuarial Reform			Common Reform		
	Mechanical	Behavioral	Total	Mechanical	Behavioral	Total	Mechanical	Behavioral	Total
				Option value—S1					
Benefits	-4,771	-5,440	-10,210	-30,728	-19	-30,746	-35,989	1,550	-34,439
Benefits incl. occup.	-13,787	-3,842	-17,629	-30,498	-28	-30,526	-58,255	1,550	-56,705
Taxes: Total	-7,505	9,089	1,584	-16,783	-412	-17,195	-32,087	12,784	-19,304
Net change	2,734	-14,529	-11,795	-13,945	393	-13,552	-3,901	-11,234	-15,135
Change as % of base benefits	1.6	-8.6	-7.0	-8.3	0.2	-8.0	-2.3	-6.7	-9.0
				Option value—S2					
Benefits	-3,316	-5,447	-8,763	-29,301	31	-29,269	-34,926	1,680	-33,246
Benefits incl. occup.	-13,309	-3,948	-17,257	-29,529	25	-29,504	-57,560	1,680	-55,880
Taxes: Total	-7,240	8,782	1,543	-16,232	-419	-16,651	-31,691	12,880	-18,811
Net change	3,923	-14,229	-10,306	-13,069	451	-12,618	-3,235	-11,200	-14,435
Change as % of base benefits	2.3	-.5	-6.2	-7.8	0.3	-7.5	-1.9	-6.7	-8.6
				Option value—S3					
Benefits	-3,316	-16,651	-19,967	-29,301	31	-29,269	-34,926	1,680	-33,246
Benefits incl. occup.	-13,309	-12,124	-25,433	-29,529	25	-29,504	-57,560	1,680	-55,880
Taxes: Total	-7,240	26,388	19,148	-16,232	-419	-16,651	-31,691	12,880	-18,811
Net change	3,923	-43,039	-39,115	-13,069	451	-12,618	-3,235	-11,200	-14,435
Change as % of base benefits	2.3	-25.7	-23.4	-7.8	0.3	-7.5	-1.9	-6.7	-8.6

Change in present discounted value

each panel in table 10.5 contains two additional items. The first one, Net Change, measures the change in the benefits from the public income security system minus the changes in tax payment for each reform relative to the current system. The second item measures this as a percentage share of the benefits from the public income security system under the current regime.

In analyzing the results we will first look separately at the background of the results in table 10.4 and 10.5 for each of the three reforms. We then look at the decomposition of the total financial effects in a mechanical and a behavioral effect, as described in section 10.4. Finally, we analyze the income distribution implications by showing separately how the different quintiles in the distribution of lifetime income are affected by the reforms.

10.5.1 Three-Year Reform

Obtaining the predictions and the decomposition analysis presented in tables 10.4 and 10.5 involves several steps. To explain these steps, and to thereby give an assessment of the reliability of the predictions, we will first explain the mechanical effects of the age-shift reform—mechanical in the sense that the outcomes are measured assuming no change of labor force exit at different ages; that is, the behavioral responses are not taken into account. We then present the predictions of the behavioral changes implied by the reform; and, finally, we present the predictions of the financial outcome, that is, combining the predictions of the mechanical and behavioral changes.

Panel A of figure 10.2 shows the gross income security wealth, excluding occupational pensions, at age 55 by different ages of labor force exit for the current income security system and the policy implied by the Three-Year Reform, respectively. It can be seen that the average social security wealth is somewhat higher under the Three-Year Reform regime for most ages, up to age 62. This is due to the fact that the probability of using the labor market insurance programs conditional on age of labor force exit is higher for younger age groups. Since these probabilities are shifted by three years in the Three-Year Reform, the ISW at a given age of exit will be higher under the postreform regime. Between age 62 and 71, when most workers exit the labor market, the ISW is substantially higher under the current regime, due to the higher actuarial adjustment under the postreform rules.

For measuring the budget implications for the public sector of the reform, it is necessary to also consider all possible tax payments to the public sector. Panel B of figure 10.2 shows the changes in the present value of the total taxes by age of labor force exit. It can be seen that the taxes paid are markedly lower under the postreform regime between age 62 and

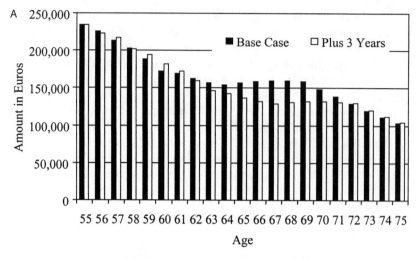

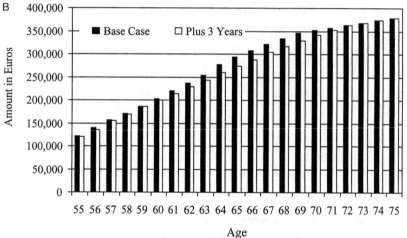

Fig. 10.2   Results for the Three-Year Reform: *A*, SSW by age of labor force exit; *B*, Taxes by age of labor force exit; *C*, Distribution of age of labor force exit, OV S1 model; *D*, Total effect by age of retirement, OV S1 model; *E*, Distribution of age of labor force exit, OV S2 model; *F*, Total effect by age of retirement, OV S2 model; *G*, Distribution of age of labor force exit, OV S3 model; *H*, Total effect by age of retirement, OV S3 model

71. This reflects the lower replacement and consumption levels under this regime.

The differences in pre- and postreform regimes conditional on age of labor force exit, shown in panels A and B of figure 10.2 weighted by the pre-reform-state probabilities sum up to the mechanical effect shown in table 10.5. It can be seen that the reform implies that both benefit payments and

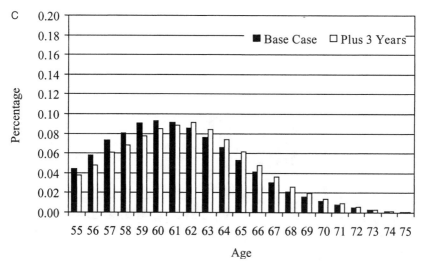

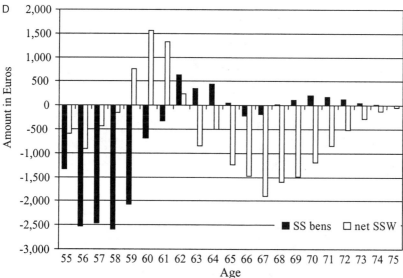

Fig. 10.2   (continued)

taxes decrease, which was also evident from the figures.[8] The net change, however, is positive, which implies that the tax decrease dominates and the

8. It can be seen in the second column of table 10.5 that this mechanical effect varies between the simulation where the linear specification in age is used and the two specifications with age dummies. This is due to the different weighting of the different states. Since the dummy variable specification provides weighting that is closer to the actual behavior under the prereform regime, this is probably a better prediction of the mechanical effect.

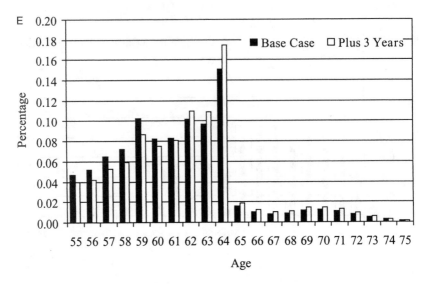

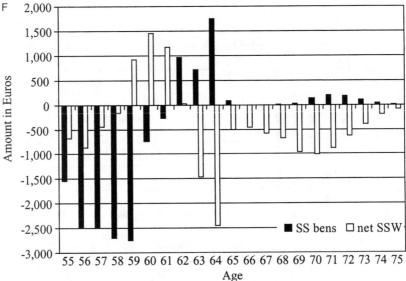

Fig. 10.2   (cont.) Results for the Three-Year Reform: *A,* SSW by age of labor force exit; *B,* Taxes by age of labor force exit; *C,* Distribution of age of labor force exit, OV S1 model; *D,* Total effect by age of retirement, OV S1 model; *E,* Distribution of age of labor force exit, OV S2 model; *F,* Total effect by age of retirement, OV S2 model; *G,* Distribution of age of labor force exit, OV S3 model; *H,* Total effect by age of retirement, OV S3 model

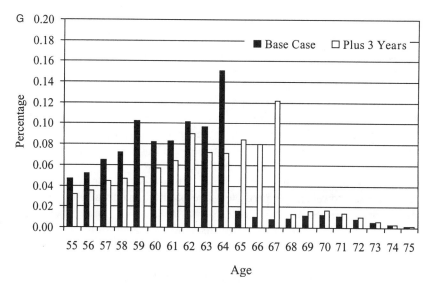

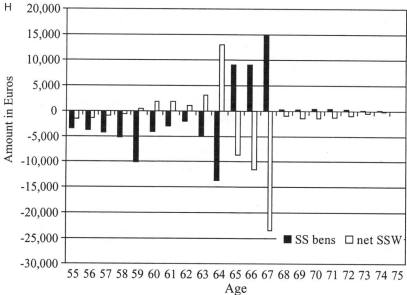

Fig. 10.2   (continued)

total mechanical effect of the reform represents a deficit for the public sector. This deficit is comparatively small—it corresponds to only 2.3 percent of the total benefits from the prereform public income security system.

The predictions of the behavioral response of the reform are shown in panels C, E, and G of figure 10.2 for the option value specification and the three different simulation strategies. Each figure shows retirement probabilities for the pre- and postreform regimes, respectively, for each age between 55 and 75. It is evident from these figures that all simulation strategies predict delayed retirement as a result of the reform. The peak value predictions are not shown in the figure, but the results are also quantitatively fairly robust with respect to choice of incentive measure (peak or option value). However, the predicted size of the behavioral effect is very different between S2 and S3.

In section 10.4.4, Reform 1, we discussed the methodological background of the three simulation strategies. One interpretation of the large difference between the S2 and S3 results is that there are important aspects of the economic incentives that are not measured by the incentive measures in the model, which, in turn, are caught by the over-parameterized dummy-variable specification. It is, however, also possible that the dummy variables reflect institutions in the labor market, like rules on mandatory retirement ages and social norms, which are likely to affect the retirement behavior but are omitted in the econometric model. For this particular reform, which includes increasing the ERA from 60 to 63 and reducing access to labor market insurance programs at each age, the large behavioral response predicted by the S3 strategy might be more plausible than for other conceivable reforms.

Table 10.5 shows that all models and simulation strategies predict a financial surplus for both the income security system and the entire public sector from the reform. However, as expected from the simulation of the retirement behavior, the magnitude of the surplus differs substantially between the S2 and S3 simulations. This difference is largest when the peak value measure is used for measuring economic incentives, where the difference in net change is almost five times as large in the S3 simulation, compared to about three times as large when the option value measure is employed. This difference follows from both a higher prediction of the S2 lower bound, about 14.2 thousand euros compared to the 11.7 for the option value measure and a higher prediction of the S3 upper bound, 43.0 thousand euros compared to 51.8. The prediction from the S1 simulation is, as expected from the simulation methodology explained in section 10.4.4, Reform 1, between the S2 and S3 lower and upper bounds, being very close, both in the peak and option value models, to the lower bounds.

The simulations of the behavioral effects also show that the greatest source of the surplus from the reform for the entire public sector (the net change) comes from greater tax payments. The share of the surplus that comes from more tax payments varies between 62 and 65 percent, depending on model and simulation strategy.

The last step in obtaining the financial implications of the reform is to combine the mechanical, financial predictions with the behavioral ones. Figure 10.2, panel D, F, and H show the total effect by age of retirement. The shaded bars show the total change in present value for all benefits (except occupational pensions) by age of labor force exit. The nonshaded ones give the corresponding information for the size of the total net effect. A negative outcome gives a surplus for the public sector from the reform corresponding to a particular age of labor force exit.

The total financial effect for the public income security system (benefits) and the total public sector (net change), respectively, shown in table 10.5, can be obtained by summing the two sets of bars over all ages of labor force exit. The net change row is also shown in figure 10.5. It is evident from the results in table 10.5 that the financial surplus from the behavioral effect of the reform is substantially larger than the mechanical. This result comes out in all combinations of specifications and simulation strategy.

To sum up, the results on the first reform show that there is large degree of uncertainty, depending on the choice of simulation strategy. Using the peak value measure, the net effect on the finances of the entire public sector compared to the current system is about five times as large when the second simulation strategy is used compared to the first one. The difference comes from both smaller benefit payments and larger tax contributions. All predictions, however, give substantial financial implications of the first reform. For the lowest estimate, the difference compared to the current system is about 5 billion SEK, which corresponds to about 0.2 percent of GDP in 2001.

10.5.2   The Actuarial Reform

The corresponding results to those shown in the previous section for the Three-Year Reform are obtained for the Actuarial Reform. As in the previous section, we start the analysis of the simulation results by looking at the mechanical effects. We then turn to the behavioral effects and, finally, to the total financial implications of the reform.

Figure 10.3, panel A shows the mechanical reform effect on benefit payments from the public income security system by age of exit from the labor market. The results here are very different compared to those obtained for the Three-Year Reform. As expected, the present value of the payments, conditional on labor force exit in young ages, the ages when the actuarial adjustment of the labor market insurance programs in the reform have a large effect, are substantially reduced compared to the current system. Also, after age 64, as the last year in the labor force, there are still slightly higher payments under the current system. This is due to the fact that the 0.7 percent per month (8.4 percent per year) actuarial increase for delaying

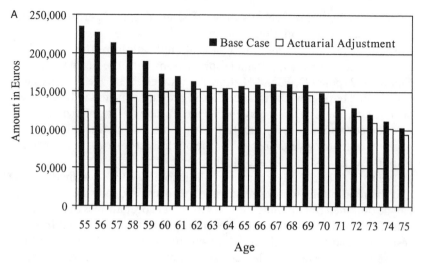

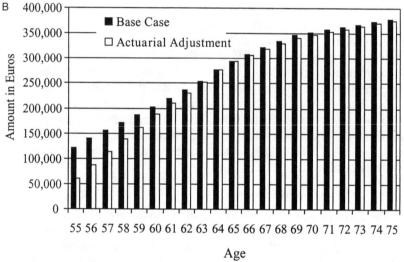

Fig. 10.3   Results for the Actuarial Reform: *A*, SSW by age of labor force exit;
B, Taxes by age of labor force exit; *C*, Distribution of age of labor force exit, OV S1
model; *D*, Total effect by age of retirement, OV S1 model; *E*, Distribution of age of
labor force exit, OV S3 model; *F*, Total effect by age of retirement, OV S3 model

retirement after age 65 under the current system is actually *higher* than the
6 percent actuarial adjustment implied by the reform.

Figure 10.3, panel B shows the corresponding results for tax payments.
As expected, tax payments decrease for all ages of labor force exit. The effect
is largest conditional on early ages of labor market exit, where the largest
effects on payments from the public income security system were located.

The mechanical effect is summarized in table 10.5. Comparing the re-

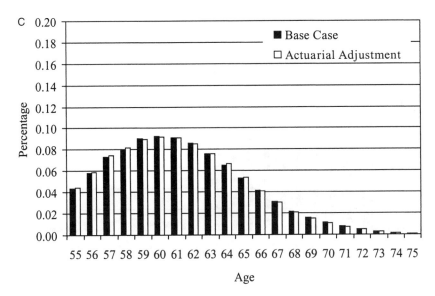

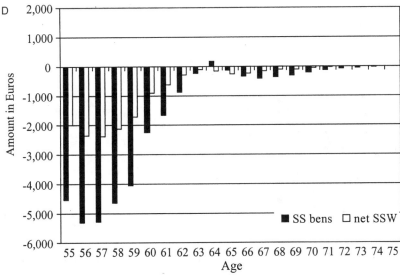

Fig. 10.3   (continued)

sults to those of the Three-Year Reform, it can be seen that the effects are
much larger for this reform—both for income security payments and taxes.
Unlike the previous reform, the reductions in income security payments
dominate the reduction in tax payments, resulting in a surplus for the entire public sector (net change) from the mechanical effect.

Turning to the behavioral effects, figure 10.3, panel C and E shows that
the effect toward delayed labor market exit is much smaller compared to

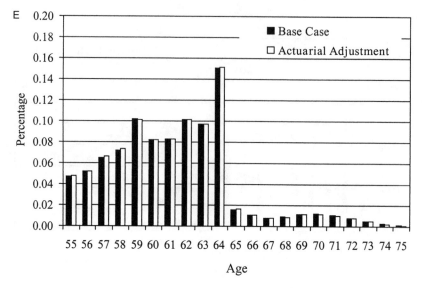

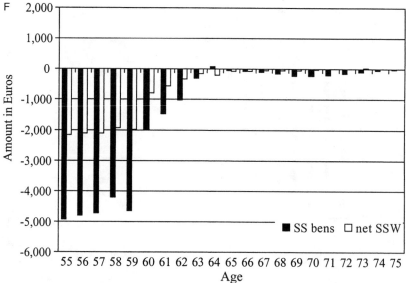

Fig. 10.3   (cont.) Results for the Actuarial Reform: *A*, SSW by age of labor force exit; *B*, Taxes by age of labor force exit; *C*, Distribution of age of labor force exit, OV S1 model; *D*, Total effect by age of retirement, OV S1 model; *E*, Distribution of age of labor force exit, OV S3 model; *F*, Total effect by age of retirement, OV S3 model

the Three-Year Reform. Since neither the ERA nor NRA are changed from the current income security system, S2 and S3 are identical, which means that we only need to consider four combinations of simulation strategy and model specification. Comparing the results in figure 10.3, panel C and E shows that the predicted effects on behavior are, in general, smaller when the dummy-variable specification is used.

Again, table 10.5 summarizes the behavioral effects. It is evident from these results that the financial implications from the behavioral effect can be ignored. The main explanation for this result is, of course, the small, predicted changes in retirement behavior. Also, in the age interval where any differences were predicted, the current system is very similar to that under the reform.

The total effect, shown in table 10.5 and figure 10.5, summarizes the results for the Actuarial Reform. These results show that the effect is somewhat larger than the predicted lower bound of the Three-Year Reform: around 7 percent compared to around 5 percent of the expected payments from public income security under the current system. However, compared to the upper bound of the Three-Year Reform, the effect of this reform is substantially smaller.

10.5.3   The Common Reform

The mechanical effects of the Common Reform have, as can be seen in figure 10.4 panel A and B, a similar pattern to those of the Actuarial Reform, discussed in the previous subsection; the results from the Common Reform are, however, somewhat stronger for young ages of labor market exit. This is due to the fact that the labor market insurance programs are abolished for these ages, while only actuarially reduced under the Actuarial Reform policy.

Again, the mechanical effects are summarized in table 10.5. These results confirm that the mechanical effects on payments from the public income security system are stronger in the Common compared to the Actuarial Reform. However, the largest difference between the mechanical effects of these reforms is on taxes: the reduction in tax payments is more than twice as large in the Common Reform compared to the Actuarial Reform. The background to this result is that the occupational pension is abolished in the Common Reform. Also, the payments from the income security system are capped at the 90th percentile of the income distribution. As a result, total benefit levels are substantially lower than under the actuarial adjustment and current policy regime, which can be seen from the second row of table 10.4. Benefits, including occupational pension benefits, are reduced by 29 percent, compared to 15 percent for the Actuarial Reform and 9 percent for the Three-Year Reform. Tax payments, especially from high-income retirees, are therefore reduced. The mechanical effect on the entire public sector is much smaller than for the Actuarial

A

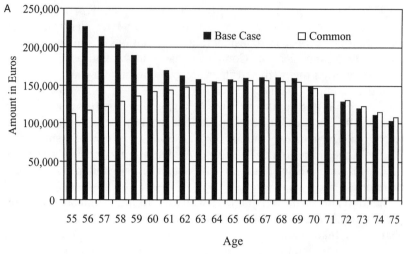

B

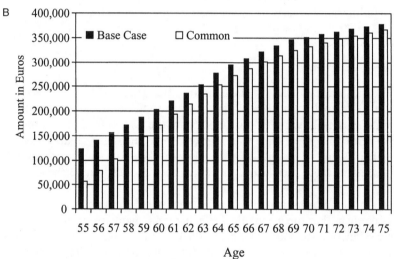

Fig. 10.4   Results for the Common Reform: *A*, SSW by age of labor force exit; *B*, Taxes by age of labor force exit; *C*, Distribution of age of labor force exit, OV S1 model; *D*, Total effect by age of retirement, OV S1 model; *E*, Distribution of age of labor force exit, OV S3 model; *F*, Total effect by age of retirement, OV S3 model

Reform, and is actually zero in the simulation with the peak value incentive measure and the dummy-variable specification.

Turning to the behavioral effects, figure 10.4, panel C and E show much stronger behavioral effects of the Common Reform compared to the Actuarial Reform. This is expected, since the Common Reform implies a more radical reduction of the income security benefits. This implies that the age

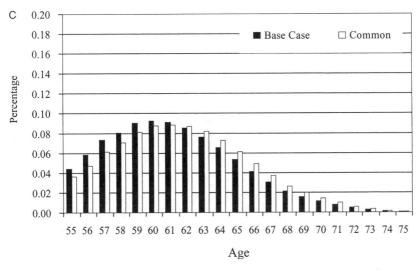

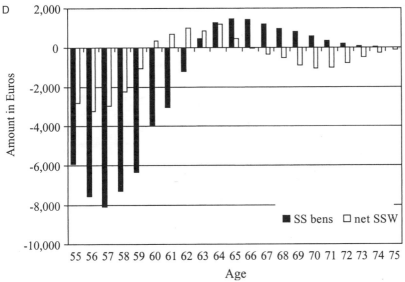

Fig. 10.4   (continued)

distribution of exit from the labor market shifts to ages when the present value of the payments from the income security system are larger, which, in turn, implies that the behavioral effect on benefits from the income security system is positive. This result can be seen for all four combinations of incentive measure and simulation strategies in table 10.5. However, this shift also implies that tax payments will increase, which induces a financial surplus for the entire public sector. As can be seen in table 10.5, this effect

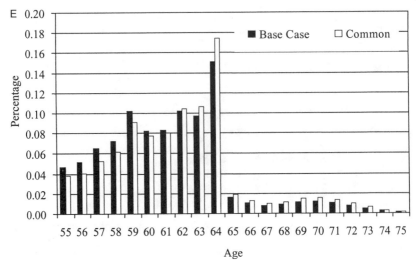

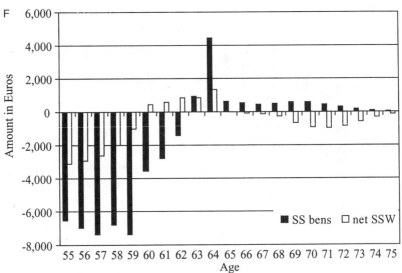

Fig. 10.4   (cont.) Results for the Common Reform: *A,* SSW by age of labor force exit; *B,* Taxes by age of labor force exit; *C,* Distribution of age of labor force exit, OV S1 model; *D,* Total effect by age of retirement, OV S1 model; *E,* Distribution of age of labor force exit, OV S3 model; *F,* Total effect by age of retirement, OV S3 model

dominates, and the net change is very close to that obtained for the Actuarial Reform.

For the Common Reform, the mechanical and behavioral effects work in the same direction. This implies that there will be a financial surplus from the reform. For the Actuarial Reform, almost the entire effect can be attributed to the mechanical effect, while the behavioral effect dominates for the Common Reform.

10.5.4 The Total Effect of the Reforms as Shares of GDP and the Relative Importance of Mechanical and Behavioral Effects

Figure 10.5, panels A–C show the decomposition of the total financial implications of the three hypothetical reforms as shares of Sweden's GDP for 2001. Relating the effects to GDP shows the economic importance of implementing the reforms for *the group of individuals that form the population of our sample.* As we described in section 10.4, we use a random sample of individuals who were born in 1940 and employees in 1995 at age 55.[9] This group corresponds to 66 percent of all born in 1940 and living in Sweden in 1995. The size of this group is about 64,000 individuals.

Panel A of figure 10.5 reveals that the net effect for the public sector finances corresponds to between 0.2 and 0.4 percent of GDP for the lower-bound prediction of the Three-Year Reform and all predictions for the Actuarial and Common reforms. Considering that the population under study corresponds to only about 1.5 percent of the total labor force, the effect must be considered to be of economic significance. Figure 10.5, panel A also shows that the upper-bound prediction of the effect of the Three-Year Reform gives a net effect between 1 and 1.3 percent of GDP. This is, however, likely to be an overestimate of the true effect.

Figure 10.5 also highlights the very different allocation between mechanical and behavioral effects between the reforms. An interesting result is that the behavioral effect is largest, even for the lower bound simulations, for the Three-Year Reform. The only reform for which the mechanical effects seem to be important is the Actuarial Reform.

10.5.5 Income Distribution Effects of the Hypothetical Reforms

The simulations of the three hypothetical reforms also allow us to look at distributional implications. To do that we use family lifetime income from labor[10] to split the cohort sample into five quintile groups. The first

9. In the labor force, not self-employed.
10. We use the sum of labor earning for the forty best years (highest earnings) since age 20. For married couples we sum earnings from both spouses. Information on family composition is obtained from 1995, and we assume that each individual has been married (or in consensual union) to the same individual his or her entire life. The sample is divided into separate quintiles for married and single and then merged together. This means that we get the same shares of married and single individuals in each quintile.

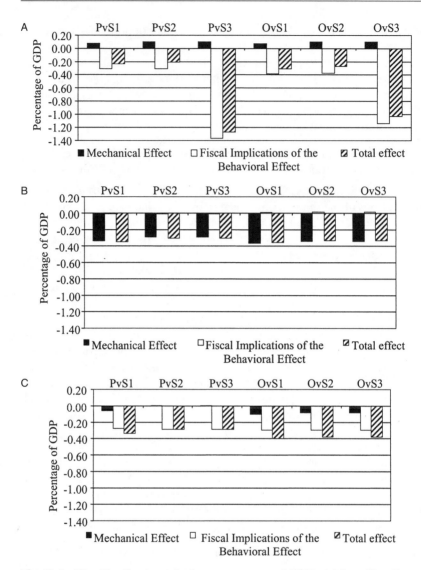

Fig. 10.5   Fiscal implications of reform as a percent of GDP: *A*, Three-Year Reform; *B*, Actuarial Reform; *C*, Common Reform

quintile constitutes the 20 percent richest households; the second includes households with lifetime income between the 60th and the 80th percentiles, and so on until the poorest 20 percent, which forms the fifth group.

The results are shown in tables 10.6 and 10.7. The S1 simulation strategy is used for obtaining the results in table 10.6 and S3 for the results in table 10.7. The option value (OV) accrual measure was used for both sets of results. The key result in these tables is the average change in net public sec-

Table 10.6   Distributional analysis: Option value—Linear age (S1)

	Present discounted value				Change relative to base			
	Base	Three-Year Reform	Actuarial Reform	Common Reform	Three-Year Reform	Actuarial Reform	Common Reform
			Quintile 1 (highest)				
Benefits	193,126	175,623	164,917	182,759	−17,504	−28,210	−10,368
Benefits incl. occup.	257,348	221,499	230,230	182,759	−35,849	−27,118	−74,589
Taxes: Total	381,011	385,989	366,917	372,501	4,978	−14,094	−8,511
Net change					−22,481	−14,115	−1,857
Change as % of base benefits					−11.6	−7.3	−1.0
			Quintile 2				
Benefits	181,545	169,163	150,307	148,254	−12,381	−31,238	−33,291
Benefits incl. occup.	201,977	182,327	170,896	148,254	−19,650	−31,081	−53,723
Taxes: Total	238,815	239,955	221,434	221,030	1,140	−17,381	−17,784
Net change					−13,522	−13,857	−15,506
Change as % of base benefits					−7.4	−7.6	−8.5
			Quintile 3				
Benefits	167,528	158,605	135,812	128,794	−8,923	−31,716	−38,734
Benefits incl. occup.	178,767	165,157	146,971	128,794	−13,610	−31,796	−49,972
Taxes: Total	192,534	193,224	174,317	171,290	691	−18,217	−21,244
Net change					−9,614	−13,500	−17,490
Change as % of base benefits					−5.7	−8.1	−10.4

(continued)

Table 10.6 (continued)

		Present discounted value			Change relative to base		
	Base	Three-Year Reform	Actuarial Reform	Common Reform	Three-Year Reform	Actuarial Reform	Common Reform
Quintile 4							
Benefits	159,599	151,767	128,337	117,416	-7,832	-31,262	-42,183
Benefits incl. occup.	168,940	157,121	137,551	117,416	-11,819	-31,389	-51,523
Taxes: Total	175,126	175,517	156,931	151,817	391	-18,195	-23,309
Net change					-8,223	-13,067	-18,874
Change as % of base benefits					-5.2	-8.2	-11.8
Quintile 5 (lowest)							
Benefits	140,712	136,271	109,411	93,164	-4,41	-31,301	-47,548
Benefits incl. occup.	146,908	139,631	115,666	93,164	-7,277	-31,242	-53,744
Taxes: Total	140,328	141,056	122,247	114,691	728	-18,081	-25,636
Net change					-5,170	-13,220	-21,912
Change as % of base benefits					-3.7	-9.4	-15.6

Table 10.7   Distributional analysis: Option value—Age dummies (S3)

	Present discounted value				Change relative to base		
	Base	Three-Year Reform	Actuarial Reform	Common Reform	Three-Year Reform	Actuarial Reform	Common Reform
Quintile 1 (highest)							
Benefits	193,020	164,725	165,713	183,124	-28,295	-27,307	-9,896
Benefits incl. occup.	257,363	215,389	230,112	183,124	-41,975	-27,251	-74,239
Taxes: Total	371,381	408,270	357,073	362,556	36,889	-14,308	-8,825
Net change					-65,184	-12,999	-1,071
Change as % of base benefits					-33.8	-6.7	-0.6
Quintile 2							
Benefits	180,847	157,621	150,659	148,075	-23,226	-30,188	-32,772
Benefits incl. occup.	201,587	173,233	171,168	148,075	-28,354	-30,419	-53,512
Taxes: Total	235,642	255,807	218,594	218,358	20,165	-17,048	-17,283
Net change					-43,391	-13,141	-15,489
Change as % of base benefits					-24.0	-7.3	-8.6
Quintile 3							
Benefits	166,474	147,006	136,146	128,899	-19,468	-30,329	-37,576
Benefits incl. occup.	178,144	155,332	147,464	128,899	-22,813	-30,681	-49,246
Taxes: Total	191,460	206,753	173,848	170,735	15,293	-17,612	-20,725
Net change					-34,761	-12,716	-16,851
Change as % of base benefits					-20.9	-7.6	-10.1

(continued)

Table 10.7 (continued)

	Base	Present discounted value			Change relative to base		
		Three-Year Reform	Actuarial Reform	Common Reform	Three-Year Reform	Actuarial Reform	Common Reform
Quintile 4							
Benefits	158,152	140,703	128,685	117,645	−17,449	−29,467	−40,507
Benefits incl. occup.	167,995	147,610	138,107	117,645	−20,385	−29,887	−50,350
Taxes: Total	174,673	188,007	157,372	152,221	13,334	−17,302	−22,452
Net change					−30,783	−12,165	−18,055
Change as % of base benefits					−19.5	−7.7	−11.4
Quintile 5 (lowest)							
Benefits	138,804	127,366	109,750	93,393	−11,438	−29,054	−45,411
Benefits incl. occup.	145,478	131,776	116,199	93,393	−13,702	−29,279	−52,084
Taxes: Total	140,775	150,885	123,793	116,037	10,110	−16,982	−24,738
Net change					−21,548	−12,072	−20,672
Change as % of base benefits					−15.5	−8.7	−14.9

tor payments in the quintile, measured as a share of the average present value of benefit payments in the current system. This amount measures how the burden of the decrease in public sector net payments is divided between different parts of the income distribution relative to their original share of expected payments from the public income security system. Note that the percentage change of expected discounted net income will be different, since they also include occupational pension payments.

Although the results in tables 10.6 and 10.7 are in some cases on somewhat different levels, they show a very similar pattern regarding how the burdens of the reforms are distributed. The Three-Year Reform is progressive in the sense that the upper quintiles in the income distribution experience a larger burden of the reform, as a proportion of the average present value of the expected payments from the income security system, than the quintiles with less average lifetime income. The results for the Common Reform, and to a less extent also for the Actuarial Reform show the opposite pattern: the low-income quintile groups suffer from a larger average burden of the reform than proportional to the average present value of their expected payments from the current income security system.

There are two main reasons for the simulation results for the Three-Year Reform. The first reason is differences in changes in benefit payments due to the reform. Individuals in the low-income group have higher retirement probabilities at relatively young ages. One part of the Three-Year Reform is that the probability of access to the labor market insurance benefits at each age and the probabilities of receiving benefits from a labor market insurance program, conditional on retirement at a particular age, are also shifted by three years (see figure 10.1). The net effect is that individuals in the low-income group will experience an increased probability of receiving benefits from a labor market insurance program, and the benefits from these programs are not affected by the reform. This is not true for the high-income group, who, on average, retire at a much older age and have a lower probability of being eligible for labor market insurance benefits and, therefore, will suffer more from the shift in the actuarial adjustment implied by the reform.

The second reason is that tax payments increase more in the high-income group. Tax payments have three main components in this analysis: VAT, income, and payroll taxes. Payments from income taxes and VAT will decrease with the S1 simulation strategy, since the benefit levels decrease as a result of the reform. For the S3 case, the behavioral effect is so large that it outweighs the negative mechanical effects on income taxes and VAT. However, payments through payroll taxes will always increase as a result of the delayed exit from the labor market, since payroll taxes are only paid by workers in the labor force. The payroll tax increase as a percent of public benefit payments will be large in the high-income group, due to a lower replacement rate and possibly also due to a larger behavioral response to the reform.

The result—that the Common Reform is regressive—also stems from differences in retirement behavior between different segments of the income distribution. Since the low-income group, on average, retire earlier and have a higher probability of being eligible for benefits from a labor market insurance program, they will, on average, suffer more when these programs are replaced by an old-age pension scheme under the Common Reform policy regime. This also applies to the Actuarial Reform, but to a much less extent, since the labor market insurance programs are only subject to an actuarial adjustment under this policy regime.

10.6   Conclusions

In this chapter we use a labor supply model for the retirement decision and a sample of workers born in 1940 to simulate the effect on net public sector payments of three hypothetical reforms of Sweden's income security system. The estimates of the magnitude of the effects, disregarding the upper bound of the Three-Year Reform, ranges between, on average, approximately 8,000 to 11,000 euros in present value of all future transactions for the Three-Year Reform, to about 13,000 euros for the Actuarial Reform, and to about 15,000 euros for the Common Reform. These average effects correspond to between about 0.2 and 0.4 percent of Sweden's GDP in 2001, for 66 percent of the 1940 cohort.

These total effects are achieved very differently between the reforms. For the Three-Year Reform, the entire effect comes from the behavioral effect. The mechanical effect actually works in the opposite direction. For the Actuarial Reform, the entire difference comes from the mechanical effect, while for the Common Reform the mechanical effect is close to zero and, again, the behavioral effect is the most important.

Also, the simulated effects on income distribution are very different between the reforms. The Three-Year Reform is progressive in the sense that a larger burden of the reform, measured as a share of the present value of expected payments from the income security system, is attributed to households with relatively high lifetime earnings. The opposite is true for both the other reforms, although to a larger extent for the Common Reform. The backgrounds to the results were found mainly in the fact that low-income workers, on average, exit earlier from the labor market and are more likely to be eligible for benefits from a labor market insurance program.

A general conclusion from the study is that both differences in retirement behavior between different groups of workers, in particular for the distribution analysis, and behavioral responses to the reforms, in particular for the total effect of both the Three-Year and the Common reforms, are very important for analyzing economic implications of reforms in the income security system.

References

Palme, Mårten, and Ingemar Svensson. 1999. Social security and occupational pensions in Sweden. In *Social security and retirement around the world,* ed. Jonathan Gruber and David Wise, 355–402. Chicago: University of Chicago Press.

———. 2004. Income security programs and retirement in Sweden. In *Social security and retirement around the world: Micro-estimation,* ed. Jonathan Gruber and David Wise, 579–641. Chicago: University of Chicago Press.

Palmer, Edward. 2001. Swedish pension reform—How did it evolve and what does it mean for the future? In *Coping with the pension crisis: Where does Europe stand?* ed. Martin Feldstein and Horst Siebert, 171–205. Chicago: University of Chicago Press.

Fiscal Effects of Reforming the UK State Pension System

Richard Blundell and Carl Emmerson

11.1 Introduction

In this chapter we evaluate the fiscal and distributive impact of social security reform in the United Kingdom. To examine this, we consider three reforms to the state pension system, all designed to increase the retirement age by changing the incentive structure underlying the pension system. We analyze both the mechanical fiscal effects of implementing the reforms without allowing for behavioral responses as well as the full effects that additionally account for an individual's altering his or her retirement decisions in light of the reformed pension system. To address the behavioral effects we use a transition model of retirement that is based on microdata from the UK Retirement Survey. This model is developed in Blundell, Meghir, and Smith (2001), and we adapt that specification in this paper to provide simulations on individual data of pension reforms. Before describing the reforms and the simulation model, we introduce this study with

Richard Blundell is the Ricardo Professor of Political Economy at University College, London, and Research Director of the Institute for Fiscal Studies. Carl Emmerson is a deputy director of the Institute for Fiscal Studies.

This paper forms part of the International Social Security project at the National Bureau of Economic Research (NBER). The authors are grateful to John Gruber, David Wise, and participants of that project, to seminar participants at the Institute for Fiscal Studies (IFS), and to Sarah Smith, whose work on the previous stage of this project contributed toward this analysis. The Department of Social Security is thanked for financing the primary analysis of the second wave of the Retirement Survey, and for making the data available. Both waves of the Retirement Survey are now deposited at the Economic and Social Research Council (ESRC) Data Archive at the University of Essex. This research is part of the program of research by the ESRC Centre for the Micro-Economic Analysis of Public Policy at IFS, and we are grateful to the Economic and Social Research Council for funding.

some background concerning the current situation regarding pension reform in the United Kingdom.

In line with other OECD countries, the United Kingdom will experience population ageing over the next few decades and a growth in the proportion of people aged 65 and over relative to the working-age population. However, this process is not likely to be as dramatic in the United Kingdom as it is predicted to be in Germany, Italy, or Japan. The financial sustainability of the state pension system is not a substantive issue. Indeed, under current pension rules, the burden of state pensions is projected by the government to fall slightly as a percentage of national income, from 5.1 percent in 2001–2002 to around 4.8 percent by 2050–2051. Figure 11.1 also shows that expenditure on the basic state pension is forecast to fall as a share of national income. Expenditure on the State Earnings-Related Pension Scheme (SERPS) and the State Second Pension is forecast to rise, but by far less than would have been the case under the initial SERPS, introduced in 1978. This is a consequence of a series of reforms to the pension system in the 1980s that dramatically reduced its generosity.[1] There is also an increase in forecast expenditure on the Minimum Income Guarantee and Pension Credit entitlement, both of which are means tested.[2]

In contrast, the trend in the 1970s was toward a more generous state pension system. The main element of the state pension system, the basic state pension, was increased each year, in line with the greater of the increase in earnings or prices. In 1978 a new second-tier earnings-related pension (SERPS) was introduced, which was originally intended to pay a pension worth 25 percent of an individual's best 20 years of earnings. However, SERPS was never a universal scheme for all employees. Workers who belonged to a defined-benefit occupational pension could opt out of SERPS (and pay lower rates of National Insurance) so long as their occupational scheme guaranteed at least the same pension as SERPS. (In fact, until 1988, employers were allowed to make membership of their occupational pension scheme a condition of employment). At the time that SERPS was introduced more than half of all employees, and more than two-thirds of male employees, were opted out of the state scheme.[3]

It is worth bearing in mind that spending on pensions represents only part of total government spending on benefits for older nonworkers. In the 1980s, there was a very large increase in the number of older nonworkers on disability benefits[4] (see Tanner 1998), and spending on these benefits has more than doubled in real terms since 1990. As the level of the basic state pension is below the level of means-tested benefits for pensioners,

1. See Emmerson and Johnson (2002) for more details.
2. This is discussed further in Clark and Emmerson (2003).
3. For more details of the contracting out of arrangements and their impact see, for example, Disney, Emmerson, and Smith (2003).
4. The main benefit was invalidity benefit, which was replaced by incapacity benefit in 1995.

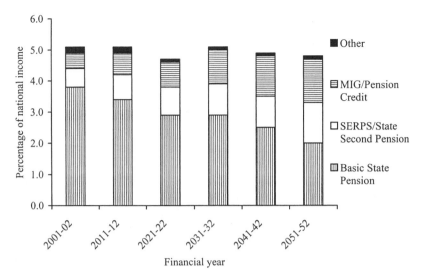

Fig. 11.1   **Projected state spending on pensions in the UK**

many pensioners are eligible for means-tested benefits on top of their state pension. By April 2003 more than half of families with an individual aged 60 or over were entitled to means-tested benefits.[5] Means testing is continuing to be an increasingly important element in state provision for pensioners, with the introduction of an earnings-indexed means-tested Pension Credit since October 2003.

Since the early 1980s, successive reforms have cut back the generosity of the state pension provision. The greater of growth in prices or earnings lasted only until November 1980, since when it has been formally indexed to prices and has fallen relative to average earnings. Reforms to SERPS introduced in 1986 and 1995 have reduced its generosity for anyone reaching the state pension age after 2000. Also, the state pension age for women, currently 60, is set to increase to 65 by 2020. These reforms were coupled with further encouragement for individuals to make private provision for their pension. The most important change was to give individuals the choice to opt out of SERPS into a defined contribution scheme from 1988 (or alternatively, to leave their employer's defined-benefit scheme and join either a defined-contribution pension or return to SERPS). In practice, this meant a growth in individual retirement accounts (personal pensions) and the development of defined-contribution occupational pensions. The growth in personal pensions was rapid. By the early 1990s they covered nearly one-quarter of employees and an even higher proportion of younger workers.

The UK government is currently considering further pension reform.

---

5. See table 4.2 of Banks, Blundell, Disney, and Emmerson (2002).

While the United Kingdom does not have a public finance problem in terms of future expected state expenditures (at least under the current settlement), there is concern that some individuals might not be making sufficient private provision for their retirement. The latest proposals are to preserve the average per-pensioner generosity of state pensions at roughly their current level. In part, this would be financed through an increase in the state pension age to 68 by the middle of this century, although the proportion of national income spent on transfer payments to pensioners would still be projected to rise by 1.5 percent of national income over the next fifty years. The government has also proposed defaulting all employees into a private pension scheme—with (unless they choose to leave the scheme) a compulsory employer contribution worth 3 percent of salary. Reforms aimed at increasing retirement ages, and therefore improving the adequacy of retirement provision, are also being implemented.[6]

In fact, like many other OECD countries, the United Kingdom has been experiencing a trend toward earlier labor market exits among older, particularly male, workers. The percentage of employed men aged 60 to 64 halved from 1968, when over 80 percent were employed, to a little over 40 percent in 1996.[7] The fall in the proportion of older men who were in *full-time* employment was even greater than the fall in the proportion in any form of employment, with a relative shift within the employed to self-employment and part-time employment. Female employment has not experienced the same downward trend—but this contrasts with rising participation among most other age groups of females across the same period.

Blundell, Meghir, and Smith (2001) looked at the extent to which these labor market trends might be explained by the financial incentives in the pension system that people faced when making their retirement decisions. In doing so, they focused not only on the pensions provided by the state, but also on employer-provided pensions and on other state benefits, such as invalidity benefit, both of which have played a crucial role in the United Kingdom. They found significant accrual and pension wealth effects, reflecting the substitution and wealth effects of pension systems on the incentive to retire.

Compared to many other European countries, the United Kingdom stands out as having a high level of coverage of private pensions and, at least in recent years, a trend toward less generous state pension provision. The models of retirement behavior estimated in the Blundell, Meghir, and Smith study fully account for the incentives underlying private occupational schemes, and those estimates are used in this chapter to analyze the fiscal impact of pension reform.

---

6. Proposals recently implemented are set out in *Department for Work and Pensions* (2002) and discussed in Emmerson and Wakefield (2003). The latest proposals are contained in *Department for Work and Pensions* (2006) and are discussed in Emmerson, Tellow, and Wakefield (2006).

7. See Banks, Blundell, Disney, and Emmerson (2002) or Disney and Hawkes (2003).

The plan of the chapter is as follows. The next section describes the UK pension system and the key elements that are likely to affect retirement behavior. Section 11.3 presents the basic empirical model we use to simulate the behavioral effects of pension reform. Section 11.4 describes the simulation methodology and the set of policy reforms. In section 11.5 the simulation results from three policy reforms designed to reduce the incentives for early retirement in the current pension system are presented. Section 11.6 concludes.

11.2   Institutional Features of the UK State Pension Scheme

The UK pension system is three-tiered. Figure 11.2 provides a summary diagram of these three tiers. A more detailed discussion can be found in Banks and Emmerson (2000). The first tier, provided by the state, consists of the basic state pension and a significant level of means-tested benefits (made more significant by the introduction of the Minimum Income Guarantee for those aged 60 and over in April 1999). The second tier, compulsory for all employees with earnings above a certain floor, is made up of the State Earnings-Related Pension Scheme[8] and a large and continually growing level of private provision. Finally, there is a third tier consisting of additional voluntary contributions and other private insurance.

11.2.1   The Basic State Pension

The basic state pension is a flat-rate contributory benefit payable to people aged over the state pension age (65 for men and 60 for women[9]) who have made sufficient contributions throughout their working lives.[10] In April 2003, the basic state pension was worth £77.45 a week for a single pensioner. Prior to 1978, married women could opt to pay a reduced rate of National Insurance, which meant they did not qualify for a basic state pension in their own right. Couples in which one partner does not qualify for the basic state pension receive a dependant addition, irrespective of whether they have ever worked. Since 1989 there has been no earnings test for receipt of the basic state pension.[11] Individuals who choose to defer their state pension currently receive an additional 1 percent for every seven

---

8. The State Second Pension replaced SERPS in April 2002. This is more generous to lower earners. For a discussion see, for example, Agulnik (1999) or Disney, Emmerson, and Tanner (1999).

9. The state pension age for women will be raised by six months each year from 2010 to 2020 so that equalization is achieved in 2020.

10. To qualify for the basic state pension, individuals need to have made or be credited with National Insurance contributions for 90 percent of their working lives. Credits are available for periods of illness, disability, or unemployment. Since the introduction of Home Responsibilities Protection in 1978, the number of years of contributions required can be reduced by time spent caring for children or another dependent.

11. See Disney and Smith (2002) for a discussion of the effects of the abolition of the earnings test on labor supply.

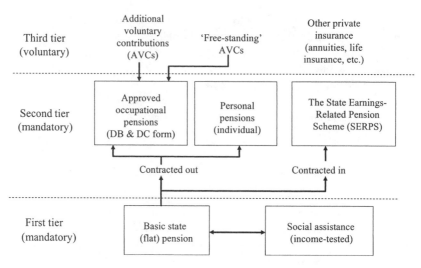

Fig. 11.2   The UK pension system, 1990

weeks of deferral, and from April 2006 this has been increased to 1 percent for every five weeks.

11.2.2   The State Earnings-Related Pension Scheme (SERPS)

The first part of the second tier of pension provision is the State Earnings-Related Pension Scheme. Introduced in 1978, this pays a pension equal to a fraction of an individual's qualifying annual earnings (above a specified lower earnings limit) each year since 1978. When it was introduced, SERPS was intended to pay a pension worth one quarter of an individual's best twenty years' earnings (up to a specified upper earnings limit). Subsequent reductions in the generosity of SERPS mean that it will eventually only be worth 20 percent of average lifetime earnings. Married women who opted to pay reduced-rate National Insurance contributions do not qualify for SERPS. Currently widows can claim their husbands' SERPS pensions in full if they receive no additional pension in their own right.[12] After retirement, the SERPS pension is uprated each year in line with price fluctuation.

11.2.3   Income Support and Invalidity Benefit

In addition to the basic state pension and SERPS, there are two other state benefits that are widely taken up by older nonworkers—income support and incapacity benefit (formerly invalidity benefit). Income support is

---

12. This was due to be reduced to half from April 2000. However, the failure of the government to properly inform individuals of the change in entitlement led to the reform being delayed.

a flat rate, noncontributory means-tested benefit. It is payable to those who are on low incomes and are not in paid employment. Unlike people in younger age groups, those aged 60 and over do not have to show that they are actively seeking work in order to qualify. From April 1999, income support for pensioners was renamed the Minimum Income Guarantee and made more generous with an increase in the level and a commitment to uprate in line with earnings, at least for the short-to-medium term. The generosity of means-tested benefits was extended further with the introduction of the pension credit in October 2003, which will be payable to lower-income individuals aged 65 or over.[13]

Incapacity benefit is a contributory benefit paid to the long-term sick and disabled. Incapacity benefit can only be received by individuals aged under the state pension age. In the case of invalidity benefit, an individual qualified on the basis of medical certificates from their doctor showing them to be incapable of work that was reasonable to expect them to do (given their age, qualifications, etc.). With the introduction of incapacity benefit in 1995 this was changed to the stricter all work test carried out by a doctor employed by the Benefits Agency Medical Service. The change from invalidity benefit to incapacity benefit was a response to very rapid growth in receipt of benefits during the 1980s. A key feature of incapacity benefit (and invalidity benefit) is that, before April 2001, it was not means tested and could be received in conjunction with private pension income (unlike income support). Since April 2001, it has been means tested against individual occupational pension income.

11.2.4   Occupational and Personal Pensions

Compared to most other European countries, the United Kingdom has a high level of coverage of private pensions, including both occupational pensions and individual retirement accounts, known in the United Kingdom as Personal Pensions. Any employee can choose to contract out of SERPS and into one of these two types of secondary private pension. (From April 2001, people have also been able to choose to opt out into a stakeholder pension, which is effectively a benchmarked individual retirement account.) Members of defined-benefit and defined-contribution occupational schemes pay a reduced rate of National Insurance, while those with personal or stakeholder pensions receive a National Insurance rebate paid directly into their fund.

In 2000, occupational pensions covered 10.1 million individuals, down from 11 million in the mid-1980s. They are typically defined-benefit schemes (see table 11.1), although since 1988 employees have also been allowed to opt out into defined-contribution occupational schemes, and

---

13. For an explanation of the pension credit, its impact on savings incentives, and the implications of earnings indexation to eligibility over time, see Clark and Emmerson (2003).

Table 11.1   Occupational schemes: Defined benefit versus defined contribution

	Private sector schemes	Public sector schemes	All schemes
Number of members (in millions):			
Defined benefit plans	4.6	4.5	9.1
Defined contribution planes	0.9	—	0.9
Hybrid schemes	0.1	—	0.1
Total	5.7	4.5	10.1
Percent of members in each type:			
Defined benefit plans	81	100	90
Defined contribution planes	16	—	9
Hybrid schemes	2	—	1
Total	100	100	100

Source: Table 3.2 of Government Actuary's Department (2003).

there has been a gradual shift from DB to DC schemes since then (see Disney and Stears 1996). The decline in coverage of occupational pension plans is due to a number of factors. It reflects changing employment patterns and a shift to employers who employ fewer workers. Also, it reflects increasing pension choice among individuals working for employers offering occupational pensions who, since 1988, can no longer be compelled to join the scheme.

Since 1988, individuals have been able to contract out of SERPS (and leave their occupational scheme) and take out a personal pension. To kickstart these schemes when they were introduced, a bonus National Insurance contribution of 2 percent was paid by the government, in addition to the contracted-out rebate. By the mid-1990s, around 6 million people (more than one quarter of all employees) had taken out a personal pension. Take-up was higher among younger workers, as would be expected. However, there is a serious issue over the number of older workers who were mis-sold personal pensions by financial advisers who wrongly advised them that they would be better off leaving their occupational pension plan.

Table 11.2 summarizes labor market participation and income receipt by age, using data from the Family Expenditure Survey of 1994–1995 (corresponding to the second wave of the Retirement Survey). It shows relatively high rates of labor market withdrawal among men before the state pension age. The two most important sources of income before state pension age are income from private (predominantly occupational) pensions and disability benefit. It is important to stress that these two sources of income are not always alternative preretirement income sources, but are typically received together by the same people. The fact that disability benefit was not means tested meant that it could be received in conjunction with other forms of income. Three-quarters of people in receipt of disability benefit income also received some money from a private pension.

Table 11.2   **Labor market participation and benefit receipt**

	Full time work	Part time work	Not working	Public pension	Private pension	Disability benefits	Disability benefits plus private	Other benefits
Men								
50–54	0.6447	0.2053	0.1500	0.0000	0.0947	0.0737	0.0237	0.0658
55–59	0.4620	0.1881	0.3598	0.0000	0.3432	0.1386	0.0825	0.0728
60–64	0.2680	0.1778	0.5533	0.0000	0.5395	0.2096	0.1478	0.1237
65–69	0.0213	0.0816	0.8972	0.8121	0.7411	0.1667	0.1312	0.0532
Women								
50–54	0.4667	0.2427	0.2907	0.0507	0.1040	0.0400	0.0133	0.0480
55–59	0.2936	0.2385	0.4679	0.0975	0.1988	0.0398	0.0061	0.0520
60–64	0.0909	0.1394	0.7697	0.7970	0.3606	0.0242	0.0152	0.0485
65–69	0.0156	0.0688	0.9156	0.9594	0.4125	0.0000	0.0000	0.0469

Source: Family Expenditure Survey, 1994–95.

11.3   The Basic Empirical Model

The simulated responses used in this chapter are based on the retirement model presented in Blundell, Meghir, and Smith (2002). This model was estimated using the UK Retirement Survey, and in this section we briefly review the model and specification of pension incentives. We also present the estimated model that is used in the simulations.[14]

11.3.1   The Data

The main data used for analyzing retirement behavior are drawn from the UK Retirement Survey (RS), a household panel survey collected by the Office for Population and Census Surveys on behalf of the Department for Social Security. This is the first large-scale panel dataset in the United Kingdom to focus on individuals around the time of their retirement. Two waves of data were collected on a national random sample of individuals born between 1919 and 1933. The first wave of the survey was conducted between November 1988 and January 1989, and collected information on 3,543 key respondents (aged 55 to 69). The key respondents include spouses if they were in the relevant age range. In addition, information was also collected on 609 spouses outside this age range. About two-thirds of the original sample were reinterviewed in 1994. Eleven percent of respondents disappeared in this interval due to mortality; the residual attrition is a combination of nonresponse and (perhaps) unreported mortality.[15]

---

14. For other studies of retirement behavior in the United Kingdom see, for example, Blundell and Johnson (1998, 1999), Disney, Meghir, and Whitehouse (1994) and Tanner (1998).

15. The high attrition rate is largely due to the fact that the survey was not originally intended to be a panel survey. Hence, little attempt was made to keep in touch with respondents after the first wave. Attanasio and Emmerson (2003) use the retirement survey to look at the impact of wealth on morbidity and mortality, and incorporate the possibility that attrition may be correlated with mortality.

The Retirement Survey offers a relatively large sample of people in the relevant age range, compared to more general panel surveys such as the British Household Panel Survey. It also offers very rich demographic, economic, and health information on individuals—and their spouses—in both waves. And it has employment history information and private pension history information dating right back to individuals' first jobs.[16] However, compared to the administrative datasets available in other countries, the sample in the Retirement Survey is relatively small (and is reduced by the high attrition rate between the two waves). Also, the survey does not collect earnings history information, which is needed to calculate exact pension entitlements for each individual. Instead, we impute earnings histories on the basis of employment history information.

11.3.2   The Pension Incentive Calculations

The Basic State Pension

Calculation of basic state pension entitlement is straightforward. It depends on the total number of years' contributions and, for a married woman, on whether she opted to pay reduced-rate National Insurance contributions. This latter piece of information is known directly from the Retirement Survey.

Although the basic state pension is flat rate, total wealth will vary among individuals because of the dependant's allowance and because of the fact that widows not entitled to a pension in their own right can claim their spouse's pension in full when their spouse dies. In these cases, we need to compute husbands' total pension wealth over the life of the couple, based on the age difference between the spouses. Obviously, the larger the age difference between husband and wife, the greater the husband's total pension wealth.

Calculating State Earnings-Related Pension Scheme Benefits

The precise formula for calculating an individual's SERPS pension is given by:

$$SERPS = \sum_{t=1978}^{R} (\tilde{W}_t \frac{Y_R}{Y_t} - LEL_{R-1}) \chi_{Rt}, \text{ where } \tilde{W}_t = \max(W_t, UEL_t).$$

Earnings up to the annual upper earnings limit (UEL) are revalued to the year of reaching state pension age (R) using an index of economy-wide average earnings (Y_R/Y_t). The lower earnings limit (LEL) in the year prior to the individual's reaching state pension age is deducted from each year's revalued earnings figure, and the net of LEL earnings are multiplied by an

---

16. For a good overview of information in the Retirement Survey see Disney, Grundy, and Johnson (1997).

accrual factor (χ_{Rt}).[17] For people retiring before 2000 the accrual rate was 1.25 percent a year. Details of earnings factors, upper and lower earnings limits, and accrual rates are given in Blundell, Meghir, and Smith (2001). Having calculated earnings profiles for each individual in the Retirement Survey, their SERPS entitlements are fairly straightforward to calculate. We assume zero SERPS pension for people who are in occupational pension plans and for married women who have opted to pay reduced-rate National Insurance contributions.

Accrual rates have changed since 2000, but this reform will not affect the cohort of individuals in the Retirement Survey, all of whom will have reached the state pension age before then. Finally, the fact that widows can claim their former husbands' SERPS pensions if they receive no pension in their own right means that, as with the basic state pension, men's marital status, and the age difference between them and their spouse, also affect their total pension wealth and accrual.

Invalidity Benefit

One possible way to treat entitlement to invalidity benefit would be to assume that only individuals who received the benefit were eligible, and that all those who satisfied the eligibility conditions received the benefit. However, given the potential for subjective evaluation of "incapacity for work" and "reasonable work" and in light of significant variation in the number of people receiving the benefit over time, as well as anecdotal evidence of differences between doctors in their willingness to certify individuals as being incapable of work, this assumption is inappropriate. Instead, we calculate an individual's invalidity benefit wealth on the basis of an assigned probability that he or she will receive the benefit. These probabilities are derived in Blundell, Meghir, and Smith (2001) from a probit model for receipt of invalidity benefit as a function of characteristics such as age, education, region, tenure, marital status, and spouse's employment status, which we estimate using data drawn from the Family Expenditure Survey from April 1988 to March 1994. We impute probabilities for individuals in the Retirement Survey on the basis of matched characteristics.

Occupational Pensions

The pension received in a defined-benefit occupational pension plan is typically determined by a formula of the type:

$$P = \chi(PE_R - \beta LEL_{R-1})N,$$

---

17. From April 2000 this formula has changed. Instead of uprating annual earnings and then subtracting the LEL from the year prior to retirement, the lower earnings limit from the year worked is subtracted from earnings first, then the difference is uprated in line with earnings growth. Since the LEL is annually uprated in line with the Basic State Pension, that is, with prices, this has the effect of reducing the generosity of SERPS.

where P is the annual occupational pension, χ is the scheme-specific accrual rate, PE_R is pensionable earnings at the time of retirement (which are typically the individual's average earnings in the last year, or last few years, before retirement), β is the integration factor, and N is the number of years that the individual has belonged to the scheme. From information in the Retirement Survey, we know N, the number of years the individual has belonged to the scheme. However, we have to make reasonable assumptions about χ_{Rt}, PE_R, and β.

The key distinction that we make is between individuals who work in the public sector versus those in the private sector. We assume that different typical schemes apply in the two sectors with different accrual rates, definitions of pensionable earnings, and integration factors. We assume an accrual rate of 1/60th for private sector and 1/80th for public sector. For pensionable earnings we take the best three out of the last ten years' earnings for individuals working in the private sector and the best year's earnings out of the last ten years for individuals working in the public sector. We assume an integration factor of 1 for private-sector schemes and 0 for public-sector schemes.

11.3.3   Total Pension Wealth and Pension Incentive Measures

In the analysis of the incentive effects of pensions on retirement presented in Blundell, Meghir, and Smith (2001), three different forward-looking measures of accrual were used. The first was simply the one-period accrual—that is, how much an individual can add to his or her total pension wealth by working this period. The second was peak value. This represents the difference between total pension wealth accumulated by the start of the period and the maximum total pension wealth an individual could accumulate looking forward across all future years. This is a more appropriate measure if it is assumed that labor market exits by older workers are irreversible. In this case, when someone leaves the labor market he or she is giving up all possible future additions to his or her pension and will therefore consider how much he or she could increase the pension by staying in the labor market not just this period, but in all future periods. By not retiring now, individuals retain an option to retire in the future and, thereby, to increase their pension. This is very similar in spirit to the option value (Stock and Wise 1990a, 1990b), which is the third measure used.

In the option value model, individuals are assumed to compare the value of retiring now to the maximum of the expected values of retiring at all future ages, where the value of retiring at future ages includes both possible pension additions and future earnings, that is,

$$OV = V_t(r^*) - V_t(t) \text{ where } V_t(r) = \sum_{s=t}^{r-1} \beta^{s-t} Y_s^\gamma + \sum_{s=r}^{T} \beta^{s-t}[kB_s(r)]^\gamma,$$

where Y_s is earnings and B_s is retirement benefits. The option value differs from the peak value by incorporating the future value of earnings until retirement and by incorporating utility parameters k, the differential value of income in leisure compared to earned income, and γ, the coefficient of relative risk aversion. In our calculation of option values we assume $k = 1.5$ and $\gamma = 0.75$. We assume a discount factor, β, of 0.97 throughout.

11.3.4 The Retirement Probability Model

A summary of the estimated retirement model results are presented in table 11.3. These are the estimated marginal effects from a probit model of transitions into retirement. A full set of results are presented in the Appendix. This model specification includes both an option value accrual term as well as separate terms for pension wealth. The wealth terms relate to the discounted present value of pension wealth for the individual whose retirement we are modeling and that of his or her spouse. Two specifications are considered in the simulations reported here. The first relates to a model in which there is a separate dummy variable for each age. The second simply includes a linear age trend. The specification of age dummies in a retirement transition model is clearly important. These two specifications provide a range of specifications over which to compare our simulation results.

In each specification, the coefficients on this wealth are always strongly significant and suggest that the restrictions underlying the standard option value model need to be relaxed to allow saving and borrowing against future pension wealth. If these wealth variables are excluded, the option

Table 11.3	Estimated retirement transition models, with a full set of time dummies and with a linear time trend only	
	Full set of time dummies	Linear time trend only
Total wealth	0.0608	0.0631
	(0.0164)	(0.0163)
Option value	–0.5145	–0.4446
	(0.3476)	(0.3426)
Spouse pension wealth	0.0280	0.0269
	(0.0108)	(0.0107)
No. of observations	1,998	1,998
Pseudo R^2	0.197	0.153
Log likelihood	–661.525	–697.758

Notes: Marginal effects are reported. Standard errors in parentheses. The full set of demographic controls include earnings (and earnings squared), education, health, job tenure, industry, proportion of time spent in full-time employment, whether individual has an occupational pension, housing tenure, financial wealth, age difference within couples, spouse's earnings, spouse's health, and whether spouse is retired. See table 11A.1.

value coefficient becomes much larger and significantly negative. For example, the coefficient becomes –0.903 (0.275) for the first model that contains a full set of time dummies.

In all cases, the pension wealth and option value variables are jointly significant. These results are consistent with the presence of both income and substitution effects in retirement decisions.[18] The positive coefficient on the total pension-wealth variable points to an income effect, whereby individuals who accumulate a lot in earlier years retire earlier. The impact of the option value reflects forgone future opportunities from stopping working now; the negative coefficient on this term indicates that the greater those forgone opportunities, the less likely individuals are to retire. Since the incentive variables are measured in €100,000, the coefficient of –0.5145 on the option value, for example, implies that a €10,000 rise in the option value (leaving pension wealth unaffected) reduces the probability of retirement by a little over 5 percentage points.[19]

The behavioral adjustments in the counterfactual simulations presented in the next section reflect these estimated marginal effects.

11.4   The Pension Policy Reforms and Simulation Methodology

As we have seen, each individual's total pension wealth and pension accrual measures are built up from combining four separate elements of the pension system—the basic state pension, the State Earnings-Related Pension Scheme, occupational pensions, and disability benefit.[20] Here we outline the nature of the pension reforms and the methodology used for simulation.

11.4.1   Reform 1 (Increased State Pension Age)

The first reform concerns an increase in the state pension age for everyone by three years. Hence, under this reform (the Three-Year Reform) the state pension age is 68 for men and 63 for women. This means that the basic state pension and SERPS will not be received until individuals reach this higher state pension age. As disability benefits can currently be received until the state pension age, we also increase the age until which individuals can claim these benefits by three years.

We also augment the normal occupational pension retirement ages by three years. There is clearly a correspondence in practice between the state

18. The option value and total pension wealth measures are in €100,000s while net earnings are in €1,000s.

19. It is worth noting that the option value is significant and slightly larger in size for men, as is also shown in the Blundell, Meghir, and Smith (2001) study. However, it is much less precisely estimated for women. In our simulations, we chose to use the combined sample results as presented in table 11.3.

20. We ignore income support, since it is a universal benefit.

pension ages and the normal retirement ages in occupational pension plans, so increasing the state pension could be expected to have such a knock-on effect on occupational pension plans. Moreover, the increases in life expectancy that, in part, might cause the government to reduce the generosity of the state pension system could have a similar effect on occupational schemes.

11.4.2   Reform 2 (Common Reform)

The second reform assumes a pension system of the following five components: (a) an early entitlement age of 60, (b) a normal retirement age of 65, (c) a 60 percent replacement rate at age 65, (d) a 6 percent actuarial adjustment from 60 to 70, and (e) no other pathways to retirement.

Under this reform we replace the current state pension system with this revised state pension system and remove the possibility of individuals retiring onto any other sources of income—that is, we remove means-tested support, disability benefits, and existing, private occupational pension schemes.

This system is considerably more expensive to the treasury than the existing UK state pension system. This can be shown by the fact that entitlement to a full basic state pension is worth approximately 15 percent of average earnings with entitlement to the SERPS at most around 30 percent of average earnings (since it provides 20 percent of earnings between a lower and an upper threshold, with the former worth about 15 percent of average earnings and the latter set at around 150 percent of average earnings[21]). However, it should be noted that this reformed system is not more generous to all individuals. This is because it removes the possibility of retiring onto means-tested income support or disability benefit (invalidity benefit). In the base system, those who reach retirement with no or little other income will be eligible for means-tested income support, which essentially tops-up their income to that of the social security safety net. In addition, those able to meet the health criteria will be able to receive the flat-rate invalidity benefit (which, prior to April 2001, was not means tested) on top of any other occupational pension income that they might have.

In addition, higher-income individuals might also lose from this reformed system, since it is assumed that the more generous state system will replace occupational pensions (both public and private). Hence, those whose occupational pension plan provides a replacement rate more generous than this reformed state scheme will lose out. For example, those in a private-sector occupational pension plan are assumed to have an accrual rate of 1/60—therefore, someone with 40 years of service would receive a

21. These are known as the Lower Earnings Limit (LEL) and the Upper Earnings Limit (UEL), respectively.

replacement rate of 40/60 = 2/3 (integrated with the basic state pension), which is greater than the 60 percent offered at age 65 under reform 2. Those who retire before 65 will be entitled to even less under the reformed system. Those in public-sector occupational pension plans were assumed to have an accrual rate of 1/80, but not integrated with the basic state pension. This means that whether someone with 40 years of service is better off under the reformed system will depend on whether the 60 percent replacement rate is greater than 50 percent of his or her final salary (i.e., 40/80) plus the basic state pension.

11.4.3   Reform 3 (Modified Common Reform)

The other chapters in this volume present an Actuarial Reform in addition to the Common Reform and the increase in the state pension age. The purpose of this is to investigate the fiscal implications of making the actuarial adjustment approximately fair without changing either the normal retirement age or the average generosity of the system. This proposed system is, however, not relevant to the United Kingdom, as the existing UK state pension system pays benefits from the state pension age regardless of whether the individual has retired. It is not possible to claim state pension benefits prior to the state pension age. Currently, individuals can choose to defer receiving benefits if they wish, but this decision is purely an investment decision, as it can be made independently of whether to undertake paid employment. Hence, rather than increasing the generosity of the deferral payment, we instead estimate the fiscal impact of an alternative reform that is strongly based on the Common Reform (reform 2), but modified to bring it slightly more into line with the base UK pension system.

Under this modified common reform the state pension system still offers a replacement rate of 60 percent at age 65 (with the same accrual structure as under reform 2), but it also has a floor on benefits equal to the basic state pension and a ceiling set at the higher threshold, above which additional employee National Insurance contributions are not paid.[22] In addition, both means-tested income support and disability benefit are retained until age 60. As a result, only high-income individuals can be worse off under reform 3 compared to reform 2 (due to the fact that under reform 3, maximum pension income is capped). Furthermore, the retention of means-tested income support will mean that low-income individuals cannot be worse off under reform 3 than they are under the base system, since retired low-income individuals will be able to receive means-tested income support until age 60 and then a state pension worth at least the basic state pension from this age onward.

22. Known in UK parlance as the Upper Earnings Limit.

11.5   Effect of Policy Reforms

This section uses the estimated retirement transition models described in section 11.3 to model the impact of each of the reforms set out in sections 11.4.1, 11.4.2, and 11.4.3 on retirement ages and the government's finances. This impact is then separated into the mechanical impact of the reform, namely, that which would arise if retirement ages were fixed, and the behavioral impact of the reform; that is, the fiscal implications of any modeled change in retirement ages. We then turn to examine the distributional impact of each of the reforms. Additional tables of results—directly comparable to those in other chapters—can be found in the Appendix (tables 11A.2, 11A.3, and 11A.4).

11.5.1   Retirement Ages and Fiscal Implications of Reform 1, Using a Retirement Model with a Full Set of Age Dummies

The effect of raising the state pension age is to reduce the median level of total pension wealth and to increase option values, compared to the existing pension system. The income and substitution effects work in the same direction; the combined effect is to reduce the conditional probability of retirement at younger ages. The precise magnitude of the effect of reforming the state pension system depends on which specification is used. When a full set of age dummies is included these tend to dominate any of the pension wealth and accrual incentives, and the effect of reforming the pension system appears to be very small. To the extent that the age dummies pick up the incentive effects, these would need to be adjusted to reflect the pivotal ages in the new system. Under the base system, with a full set of age dummies included, the mean retirement age is estimated at 63.1.

The first reform, which increases the state pension age for both men and women by three years, is estimated to increase this to 63.5 if the estimated age effects are assumed to be unchanged by the reform. Under the alternative assumption, that the reformed system would lead directly to a shift in the estimated age effects, this rises to 64.9. Figure 11.3, panel A, shows the estimated distribution of retirement ages under both of these assumptions compared to the estimated distribution in the base pension system. This shows that the distribution of retirement ages under the base system and under reform 1, when the estimated age effects are held constant, are very similar, although the reform does lead to slightly fewer retirements between 56 and 60 (inclusive) and more retirements occurring between 62 and 70 (inclusive). As expected, when the reform is also assumed to shift the estimated age effects, this leads to larger differences in the distribution of retirement ages. The spikes in the base system that occurred at 60 and 65 (which are the state pension ages for women and men, respectively) now occur at 63 and 68.

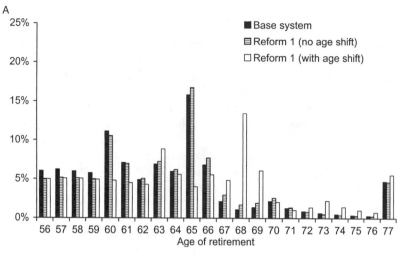

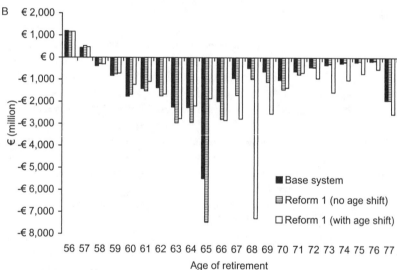

Fig. 11.3 *A,* The distribution of retirement ages under the base system and reform 1, using an option value model and a full set of age dummies; *B,* Net expenditure under the base system and reform 1, by age of retirement, using an option value model and a full set of age dummies; *C,* Gross expenditure under the base system and reform 1, by age of retirement, using an option value model and a full set of age dummies; *D,* Income tax, National Insurance Contribution, and VAT receipts under the base system and reform 1, by age of retirement, using an option value model and a full set of age dummies.

Note: For details of the specification of the retirement model, see section 11.3

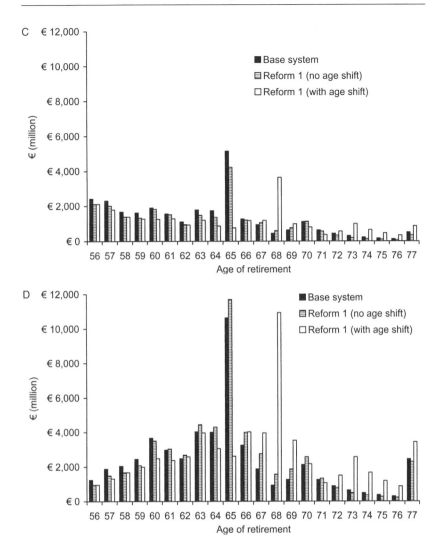

Fig. 11.3 (continued)

Increasing the state pension age would lead to a lower level of expenditure on the state pension. The increase in retirement ages would also lead to an increase in government revenues, arising from increased income tax and national insurance contributions. Both of these would lead to lower levels of government borrowing (or larger government surpluses) than under the base system. This impact, at least in part, will be offset by increased state spending on both means-tested income support and disability benefit. This is because these can both be received until the state pension age, and therefore under the reformed system can be received for up to three extra years.

Estimates of the government expenditure and government revenues from these sources under both the base system and under reform 1 are presented in table 11.4. Under the base system, expenditure on the state pension to this cohort of individuals is estimated to be €24.7 billion. Under the reformed system (assuming no change in the estimated age effects) this is reduced by 24.2 percent to €18.7 billion. As we will show later (in section 11.5.4) this comprises a slightly larger mechanical effect, arising from the increase in the state pension age, offset slightly by an increase in some individuals' entitlements to the SERPS, arising from the increased average retirement ages.

The net reduction in spending on the state pension is partially offset by a large increase in expenditure on disability benefit (invalidity benefit) of 40.7 percent and a tripling in expenditure on means-tested income support (an increase of 200.3 percent). Overall, state expenditures are still reduced by 12.1 percent. Under the alternative assumption, that the increase in the state pension age also shifts the estimated age effects, the savings from reduced expenditure on the state pension are reduced. This is because the larger upward shift in retirement ages leads to higher expenditure on the SERPS than when the age effects are held fixed. As a result, the reduction in net state pension spending is smaller than in the model when the age effects are not shifted by the full three years. The smaller reduction in state

Table 11.4   Total fiscal impact of reform 1—option value model with a full set of age dummies

	€ (in millions)			Percent change on base system	
	Base	Reform 1 (no age shift)	Reform 1 (age shift)	Reform 1 (no age shift)	Reform 1 (age shift)
State pension	24,733	18,741	19,739	−24.2	−20.2
Invalidity benefit	2,619	3,685	3,671	40.7	40.2
Income support	765	2,297	1,470	200.3	92.2
Total spending	28,117	24,723	24,881	−12.1	−11.5
Employee National Insurance	5,354	6,427	6,758	20.0	26.2
Employer National Insurance	7,045	7,457	8,261	5.8	17.3
Income tax	28,156	29,755	33,130	5.7	17.7
Value added tax	10,637	10,660	11,716	0.2	10.1
Total tax	51,192	54,299	59,866	6.1	16.9
Net expenditure	−23,075	−29,576	−34,985	28.2	51.6
Net change as % of gross base benefits	n.a.	n.a.	n.a.	−23.1	−42.4

Note: For details of the specification of the retirement model see section 11.3; n.a. = not applicable.

pension spending is almost entirely offset by a larger reduction in expenditure on means-tested income support. In particular, shifting the age effects by three years reduces the amount of additional spending on income support. Overall expenditure under the model with the shift in age effects is 11.5 percent lower than under the base case, compared to the 12.1 percent lower found when the age effects are held constant.

Turning to the impact of increasing the state pension age on government receipts: this reform will also have both a direct and an indirect impact. The direct impact will be through increased employee National Insurance contributions on earnings, as these will now be paid up to the higher state pension age (there is no corresponding direct impact on employers' National Insurance contributions, as these are levied on the earnings of individuals aged both below and above the state pension age). There will also be a direct effect that will lead to reduced income tax receipts levied on both state and private pension income due to the increase in the pension age. Similarly, there will be a direct impact from reduced VAT receipts, arising from the lower social security spending.[23] The indirect impact of reform 1 arises as a result of the increased average retirement age. This will increase income tax and employees' and employers' National Insurance contributions. Table 11.4 shows that in the base system, total government receipts from these taxes are estimated at €51.2 billion. This estimate comprises employees' National Insurance contributions of €5.4 billion, employers' National Insurance contributions of €7.0 billion, income tax receipts of €28.2 billion, and VAT receipts of £10.7 billion. The table shows that total revenues from these four taxes exceed total spending on means-tested income support, disability benefit, and state pension. This means that the excess revenues are essentially being used to pay for other items of public expenditure or to reduce public debt.

We find that under reform 1, assuming no change in the estimated age effects, employee national insurance is increased by 20.0 percent. The increase in employer national insurance is smaller, at 5.8 percent, which is not surprising, since this is only from the indirect impact of an increased average retirement age, discussed previously. The increase in income tax receipts is smaller still, at 5.7 percent. Increased income tax receipts under reform 1 show that the direct impact of lower receipts on pension income is more than offset by the impact of an increased average retirement age. Overall income tax, national insurance, and VAT revenues are estimated to be 6.1 percent higher.

Under the alternative assumption, that the increase in the state pension age would also shift the estimated age effects by a full three years, we find

---

23. The standard rate of VAT in the United Kingdom is currently 17.5 percent. But because some items, such as food, books, and newspapers are zero rated and domestic fuel is rated at 5 percent we set VAT equal to 10 percent of net incomes.

that government revenues from each of these three sources would be further increased. This is due to the larger increase in average retirement ages that occurs under this assumption. Overall, income tax, VAT, and national insurance revenues would be 16.9 percent higher than under the base system, compared to the 6.1 percent found earlier.

The overall impact on the government's finances from the items modeled is also presented in table 11.4. Under the base system, there is a net surplus of €23.1 billion. This is increased by 28.2 percent, to €29.6 billion under the model where the age effects are held fixed. It is increased by 51.6 percent, to €35.0 billion under the model where age effects are, by assumption, fully shifted by three years. In part, these percentages are inflated by the fact that they are being compared to the net surplus. However, the fiscal gains to the treasury are also large when compared to gross expenditures. Under the model with no shift in the estimated age effects, the increase in the net surplus of €6.5 billion represents 23.1 percent of gross expenditure. Under the model with a full three-year shift in the estimated age effects, the increase in the net surplus of €11.8 billion represents 42.4 percent of gross expenditure.

The reduction in net expenditure (increase in net surplus), disaggregated by age of retirement, is shown in figure 11.3, panel B. Under the base system, there is an overall net expenditure from the state on those who retire before age 58. This is because the expenditure and revenues are calculated over ages 56 to 77, and therefore taxes on earnings from those who retire this early will often be low (or for those who retire at 56, zero). Net expenditure peaks at age 65—this is not due to those retiring at this age being particularly expensive to the state, but due to the fact that 65 is the most common retirement age (as shown in figure 11.3, panel A). Under reform 1, the pattern of net expenditures varies by the assumption that is made to the interpretation of the age effects. Under the assumption that there is no shift in the estimated age effects, the pattern of net expenditure is quite similar to that observed in the base system, although there is, unsurprisingly, a particularly large reduction in net expenditure (i.e., an increase in the net surplus) among those who retire at age 65. Under the assumption that the estimated age effects are shifted by the full three years, the spike at 65 is shifted to age 68.

The estimated impact on the budget of an increase in the state pension age can also be disaggregated into the impact on gross expenditures and the impact on gross government revenues. This is shown in figures 11.3, panels C and D. The spike in gross expenditures occurring at age 65 is reduced under the assumption that the age effects are fixed, and is reduced and moved to age 68 under the assumption that reform leads to a shift in the age effects by three years. Turning to government revenues—under the first assumption, the revenue received from those retiring at age 65 is increased, and under the second assumption, it is both increased and shifted to age 68.

11.5.2   Retirement Ages and Fiscal Implications of Reforms 2 and 3, Using a Retirement Model with a Full Set of Age Dummies

Under both reform 2 and reform 3, the median level of total pension wealth is increased. The income effect from these reforms will therefore tend to reduce retirement ages. The substitution effect will tend to work in the opposite direction, with state pension rights being increased by 6 percent for each year of additional work between 60 and 70. This is in contrast to being employed under the base system, where the basic state pension and the State Earnings-Related Pension Scheme become payable at the state pension age regardless of whether an individual has actually retired. The option value effect is reinforced in reform 2 by the absence of any nonpension benefits (such as disability benefits) before retirement age under the simulated reform, which increases the incentive to stay in work. In both reform 2 and reform 3, the overall effect on retirement behavior is to lead to an increase in the average retirement age. Under the base system, this is estimated to be 63.1, under reform 2 it is estimated to be 64.6, and under reform 3 it is estimated to be 63.9. The fact that average retirement ages are closer in reform 3 to the base system than in reform 2 is perhaps not surprising, as the reform 3 system is, by design, closer to the base system.

The estimated distribution of retirement ages under both reform 2 and reform 3 are shown in figure 11.4, panel A, alongside those arising from the base system. Under all three systems, the most common retirement ages are 60 and 65. This corresponds to the state pension ages for women and men, respectively, in the base pension system. These spikes are the result of the estimated age effects from the base pension system and therefore could be expected to change under the reformed system. Reform 2 leads to lower retirement rates at all ages up to 63 (inclusive) and correspondingly higher retirement rates up to age 76. The large fall in retirements prior to age 60 is unsurprising, as under reform 2 they would receive no pension income until they reached 60. Turning to reform 3: for all ages between 56 and 73, the retirement rates under reform 3 are estimated to be between those under the base system and those under reform 2. Again, this is to be expected, given the design of the system.

Both reform 2 and reform 3 represent more generous and therefore more expensive state pension systems than the existing UK pension system. This is shown in table 11.5. Total state expenditure is estimated to be €73.5 billion under reform 2 and €81.8 billion under reform 3, compared to €28.1 billion under the base system. Under reform 2, this increase in spending is due to a large increase in spending on the state pension, which is partially offset by the fact that there is no spending on means-tested income support or disability benefit. Under reform 3, spending on state pensions is even higher than under reform 2. This shows that the cap on state pension

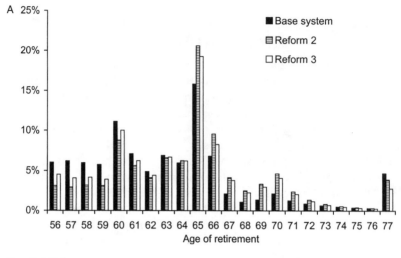

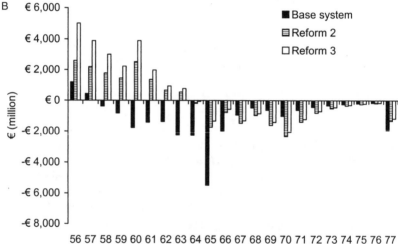

Fig. 11.4   *A,* **The distribution of retirement ages under the base system, reform 2 and reform 3, using an option value model and a full set of age dummies;** *B,* **Net expenditure under the base system, reform 2 and reform 3, by age of retirement, using an option value model and a full set of age dummies.**

income under reform 3 does not reduce spending sufficiently to finance the (re-) introduction of a floor on pension benefits equal to the basic state pension. In addition, under reform 3, disability benefit (invalidity benefit) and means-tested income support are retained for those who retire before age 60. This leads to lower disability benefit expenditure than in the base system (as under reform 3, men aged 60 to 64 will no longer be able to claim

Table 11.5   **Total fiscal impact of reforms 2 and 3—option value model with a full set of age dummies**

	€ (in millions)			Percent change on base system	
	Base	Reform 2	Reform 3	Reform 2	Reform 3
State pension	24,733	73,498	80,087	197.2	223.8
Invalidity benefit	2,619	0	731	–100.0	–72.1
Income support	765	0	954	–100.0	24.7
Total spending	28,117	73,498	81,772	161.4	190.8
Employee National Insurance	5,354	6,828	6,561	27.5	22.6
Employer National Insurance	7,045	8,546	8,128	21.3	15.4
Income tax	28,156	41,769	40,590	48.3	44.2
Value added tax	10,637	17,102	16,593	60.8	56.0
Total tax	51,192	74,245	71,872	45.0	40.4
Net expenditure	23,075	747	9,901	96.8	n.a.
Change as % of					
base benefits	n.a.	n.a.	n.a.	79.4	117.3

Notes: For details of the specification of the retirement model see section 3. Given the move from net surplus to a net deficit under reforms 2 and reform 3 it is not possible to express the change in net expenditure as a percentage. n.a. = not applicable.

it), but higher levels of means-tested income-support spending (which is due to those retiring before 60 having no other pension income and therefore falling onto income support, being enough to more than offset the fact that people will not be eligible from 60 onward.

Turning to government revenues, both reform 2 and reform 3 lead to higher levels of government receipts. Revenues from employers' national insurance are increased by 15.4 percent as a result of the increase in average retirement ages. Employees' National Insurance receipts are increased by 22.6 percent. This is higher than the estimated increase in employers' National Insurance receipts because of women in paid employment having to pay employees' National Insurance contributions up to age 65 under the reformed systems (compared to the state pension age for women of 60 under the base system). Income tax receipts are increased even more substantially—this larger increase being due to more income tax being paid on the more generous state pension system. The increase in revenues under reform 2 is larger than the increase under reform 3. This is due to the earlier average retirement age under reform 3 and the fact that the ceiling on taxable state pension benefits reduces receipts. The reintroduction of disability benefit and means-tested income support does not increase income tax receipts, as these sources of income are not taxable, while those who only receive a pension income equal to the floor of the basic state pension will also not have to pay any income tax (this is because their income will not be sufficient to take them above the income tax personal allowance). The increase in spending on the state pension, and the increase in retirement ages, also leads to a substantial increase in estimated VAT receipts.

The overall impact on the government's finances from the items modeled is also presented in table 11.5. Under the base system, there is a net surplus of €23.1 billion. Under reform 2, this leads to the system being just in balance (surplus of £0.7 billion), and under reform 3, a large deficit of €9.9 billion. The cost to the treasury of reform 2 would be €22.3 billion, or 79.4 percent of gross expenditure. The cost of reform 3 would be €33.0 billion, or 117.3 percent of gross expenditure.

A breakdown of net expenditure by the age at which individuals retire is provided in figure 11.4, panel B. Comparing reform 2 to the base system, we see that the reformed system is more expensive to the treasury at all retirement ages prior to age 67, with net expenditure being similar thereafter. Reform 2 is particularly more expensive at ages 60 and 65, as shown by the difference between the reform 2 and base system bars at these points. These are the modal retirement ages for women and men, respectively. Figure 11.4, panel B also shows that reform 3 has a greater budgetary cost than reform 2, at all retirement ages.

11.5.3   Retirement Ages and Fiscal Implications of Reforms 1, 2, and 3, Using a Retirement Model with a Linear Age Model

All of the analysis so far has looked at retirement ages and the fiscal impact of different reforms using a retirement model containing a full set of age dummies. This section performs the same analysis but with the more parsimonious retirement model that only allows for a linear age trend. The estimated retirement ages under the base system, and each of the three reforms, is shown in figure 11.5, panel A. Under the base system, the model retirement age is estimated to be 63 and the pattern of retirement ages differs substantially from the more flexible model that used a full set of age dummies (and was shown in figure 11.3, panel A). The changes in retirement ages caused by each of the reforms are all in the same direction as estimated in the model using a full set of age dummies. Under the base system, the average retirement age is estimated to be 63.2 (compared to 63.1 found under the model with a full set of age dummies). Reform 1 leads to an increase in average retirement age to 63.5, which is exactly the same as found using the previous model with no shift in the estimated age effects (using a model with an age shift led to an increase to 64.9). Reform 2 is estimated to increase the average retirement age to 64.2, while reform 3 is estimated to lead to a slightly smaller increase, to 63.7. These compare to the 64.6 and 63.9 ages found using the first retirement model.

The fiscal impact of these reforms, using the linear age retirement model, is summarized in table 11.6. Despite the very different distribution of retirement ages shown in figure 11.5, panel A, compared to 11.3, panel A, and 11.4, panel A, the estimated fiscal impacts are very similar to those ob-

A

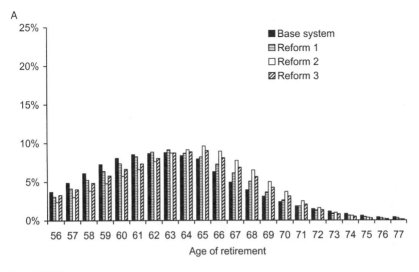

B

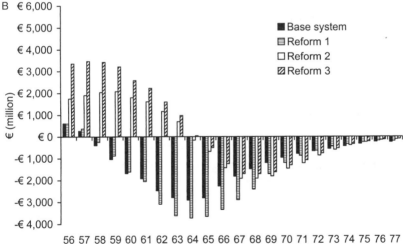

Fig. 11.5 *A,* The distribution of retirement ages under the base system, reform 1, reform 2, and reform 3, using an option value model and a linear age term; *B,* Net expenditure under the base system and reform 1, by age of retirement, using an option value model and a linear age term.

tained when using the retirement model with a full set of age dummies. Reform 1 is estimated to reduce total state spending by 13.4 percent and to increase government revenues by 4.7 percent. This compares to a saving of 12.1 percent and an increase of 6.1 percent found using a full set of age dummies and not shifting the age effects (presented in table 11.3). Under reform 2, expenditures are estimated to increase by 167.1 percent and tax

Table 11.6   **Total fiscal impact of reforms 1, 2, and 3—option value model with a linear age trend only**

	Percent change on base system		
	Reform 1	Reform 2	Reform 3
State pension	−24.0	194.7	220.1
Invalidity benefit	48.6	−100.0	−75.0
Income support	171.7	−100.0	32.2
Total spending	−14.4	167.1	195.7
Employee National Insurance	18.9	20.8	17.4
Employer National Insurance	4.4	14.6	10.3
Income tax	4.2	40.0	37.4
Value added tax	−1.1	54.3	51.2
Total tax	4.7	37.4	34.4
Net expenditure	24.0	n.a.	n.a.
Change as % of			
base benefits	−23.4	137.7	169.6

Note: Given the move from net surplus to a net deficit under reforms 2 and reform 3, it is not possible to express the percentage change in net expenditure. n.a. = not applicable.

revenues by 37.4 percent (compared to 161.4 percent and 45.0 percent shown in table 11.5), while under reform 3 expenditures are estimated to increase by 195.7 percent and tax revenues by 34.4 percent (compared to 190.8 percent and 40.4 percent, as shown in table 11.5).

Figure 11.5, panel B breaks down this net expenditure by the age of retirement. This does give a very different picture to that shown for reform 1 in figure 11.3, panel B and reforms 2 and 3 in figure 11.4, panel B. This is caused by the very different pattern of retirement ages estimated using a linear age trend (and shown in figure 11.5, panel A) compared to those found when using a full set of age dummies (and shown in figures 11.3, panel A and 11.4, panel B). The large cost of reforms 2 and 3 still arises from those retiring before age 67.

11.5.4   Decomposing the Fiscal Implications of Reforms 1, 2, and 3

The fiscal impact of each of the reforms that has been described in sections 11.5.1 to 11.5.3 can be broken down into two components. First, the fiscal impact that would arise if the reformed system were introduced but individuals did not change their retirement behavior (the mechanical effect). Second, the fiscal impact that arises due to individuals changing their retirement behavior (the behavioral effect). This section presents these two breakdowns for each of the three reforms and each of the two retirement models discussed so far.

The fiscal impact of the first reform is decomposed into these two effects in table 11.7. The first set of rows take the retirement model with a full set of age dummies and where the estimated age effects are held fixed. Under this model, reform 1 was estimated to reduce state expenditure by €3.4 billion. The mechanical effect is found to reduce spending by €3.9 billion, with the increase in retirement ages leading to a relatively small offset in expenditure of €0.5 billion. This small increase is mainly due to an increase in state pension spending, as individuals retire later and therefore accrue a larger entitlement to the SERPS. On tax receipts, it is the mechanical effect of the reform that is relatively small, at €0.1 billion. This is due to increased employee National Insurance receipts arising from the increase in the state pension age, which is slightly offset by lower income tax receipts on the reduced state pension benefits. The behavioral part of the fiscal impact works in the same direction as the mechanical effect, due to increased tax receipts from the increase in average retirement ages. This is estimated to increase revenues by €3.0 billion.

The second set of rows show the mechanical and behavioral effects using the retirement model with the full set of age dummies and shifting the estimated age effects by the full three years. By definition, the mechanical

Table 11.7   **Decomposition of the total effect of reform 1**

	Mechanical	Behavioral	Total
Full age dummies, no age shift			
Total expenditure (€)	−3,894	500	−3,394
Total taxes (€)	95	3,012	3,107
Net change (€)	−3,989	−2,512	−6,501
Net change as % of net			
base benefits	17.3	10.9	28.2
Net change as % of gross			
base benefits	−14.2	−8.9	−23.1
Full age dummies, with age shift			
Total expenditure (€)	−3,894	658	−3,236
Total taxes (€)	95	8,579	8,674
Net change (€)	−3,989	−7,921	−11,910
Net change as % of net			
base benefits	17.3	34.3	51.6
Net change as % of			
gross base benefits	−14.2	−28.2	−42.4
With linear age trend			
Total expenditure (€)	−3,976	247	−3,729
Total taxes (€)	132	2,522	2,654
Net change (€)	−4,108	−2,275	−6,383
Net change as % of net			
base benefits	15.7	8.7	24.4
Net change as % of gross			
base benefits	−14.8	−8.2	−23.0

Note: For details of the specification of the retirement model see section 11.3.

effect of this reform is exactly the same as under the previous model. The larger increase in retirement ages leads to larger behavioral effects. The increase in state expenditures from the behavioral response to the reform is still relatively small at just €0.7 billion. This is due to the fact that for many individuals, extra years of employment will not increase their entitlement to state pensions—for example, because they are opted out of the SERPS, or if the extra years of work do not add to their best twenty years. The behavioral component of the fiscal impact is estimated to be larger on tax receipts. This is because the larger increase in retirement ages increases receipts from National Insurance contributions, income tax, and VAT revenues. The third set of rows of table 11.7 show the decomposition using the retirement model with a linear age trend. These are quite similar to the model with no shift in the estimated age effects.

The decomposition of the fiscal impact of reforms 2 and 3 under each of the retirement models is presented in table 11.8. As with reform 1, the behavioral impact of the reforms is found to be relatively larger in the retirement model with the full set of age dummies than in the model that only uses a linear age trend. This is due to the estimated increase in retirement ages accruing under reforms 2 and 3, being larger in the former model.

Looking at state expenditure under reform 2, it is clear that the mechanical impact of the reform is only very slightly offset by its behavioral impact. The fact that the very large increase in the generosity of the state system implied by this reform is only slightly offset by individuals retiring slightly later is unsurprising. With tax receipts, the behavioral impact of the reforms is found to be relatively more important, and as with reform 1 they are found to both operate in the same direction—namely, to increase revenues.

Under reform 3, the mechanical component of the fiscal effect of the reform on both state spending and tax receipts is estimated to be larger than under reform 2. This reflects the fact that reform 3 is, on average, more generous than reform 2. The behavioral component of the fiscal effect on both state spending and tax receipts is estimated to be smaller. This reflects the smaller increase in average retirement ages occurring as a result of reform 3. Hence with regards to state expenditures, the behavioral components of the fiscal effect of reform 3 are very small relative to the mechanical component. On tax receipts, both effects are still very important, and continue to operate in the same direction.

11.5.5   Distributional Impact of Reforms 1, 2, and 3

The microdata used in this analysis can also be used to examine the distributional impact of each of these potential reforms. This data calculates each individual's total expected pension wealth under the base system and under each of the three reforms. An alternative calculation would be to take the individual's incomes in each of the three reforms. However, this seems inappropriate, since a reform such as an increase in the state pension

Table 11.8   **Decomposition of the total effect of reforms 2 and 3**

	Mechanical	Behavioral	Total
Reform 2, full age dummies			
Total expenditure (€)	47,807	–2,426	45,381
Total taxes (€)	10,642	12,411	23,053
Net change (€)	37,165	–14,837	22,328
Net change as % of net			
base benefits	–161.1	64.3	–96.8
Net change as % of gross			
base benefits	132.2	–52.8	79.4
Reform 2, with linear age trend			
Total expenditure (€)	47,994	–1,651	46,343
Total taxes (€)	11,173	6,847	18,020
Net change (€)	36,821	–8,499	28,322
Net change as % of net			
base benefits	–141.0	32.5	–108.5
Net change as % of gross			
base benefits	132.7	–30.6	102.1
Reform 3, full age dummies			
Total expenditure (€)	54,374	–719	53,655
Total taxes (€)	11,947	8,733	20,680
Net change (€)	42,427	–9,451	32,976
Net change as % of net			
base benefits	–183.9	41.0	–142.9
Net change as % of gross			
base benefits	150.9	–33.6	117.3
Reform 3, with linear age trend			
Total expenditure (€)	54,381	–111	54,270
Total taxes (€)	12,500	4,627	17,127
Net change (€)	41,881	–4,738	37,143
Net change as % of net			
base benefits	–160.4	18.1	–142.2
Net change as % of gross			
base benefits	151.0	–17.1	133.9

Note: For details of the specification of the retirement model see section 11.3.

age might lead to individuals remaining in work longer, and therefore receiving a higher income, but they would prefer the unreformed system, in which they could retire earlier.

Individuals are then placed in wealth quintiles on the basis of the wealth in the base system according to two different equivalence scales. The first assumes that to have the same standard of living, couples need two-thirds more wealth than a single individual. The second simply places one fifth of single individuals and one fifth of couples in each quintile. Essentially, this latter equivalence scale assumes that a couple at the 80th percentile of the wealth distribution of couples is as well off as a single person at the 80th percentile of the wealth distribution of single individuals.

The concern with this latter equivalence scale is that it might overstate the well-being of single individuals, since we know that, on average, older single people are poorer than older couples. However, as this section will show, the distributional results do not seem to be sensitive to the choice of either of these equivalence scales. Once individuals are placed in wealth quintiles according to their wealth and family size under the base system, the total amount of wealth in each quintile is estimated. This is then compared to the total amount of wealth in each base quintile under each of the reformed systems. Working out the distributional impact in this way, rather than taking the average change in wealth observed across individuals, is designed to make our results less sensitive to any outliers, which is a particular concern given our relatively small sample sizes.

The distributional impact of each of the reforms using the simple equivalence scale is presented in table 11.9. Table 11.10 shows the distributional results, assuming that one fifth of single individuals and one fifth of couples are in each quintile.

Reform 1, which increases the state pension age, unsurprisingly leads to lower levels of average pension wealth. Under the retirement model with a full set of age dummies without any shift in the estimated age effects, the reform leads to average losses across the top three wealth quintiles. This compares to no average loss in the poorest two wealth quintiles. This is caused by the availability of means-tested income support and disability benefit, compensating many of those who are out of work, who do not have a private pension.

Shifting the age effects leads to quite different distributional effects, with those in the poorest two quintiles suffering average losses. This is be-

Table 11.9   **Distributional impact of the reforms, measured by the percent change in pension wealth, using a simple equivalence scale**

System and retirement model	1 (poorest)	2	3	4	5 (richest)	All (%)
Reform 1						
Full age dummies, no age shift	−0.2	0.4	−5.3	−10.4	−6.7	−5.9
Full age dummies, with age shift	−13.5	−14.1	−13.6	−13.6	−9.9	−12.2
Linear age trend only	12.6	7.8	0.2	−8.0	−5.5	−2.2
Reform 2						
Full age dummies	202.8	35.3	19.2	−19.6	−5.9	13.7
Linear age trend only	209.7	48.3	18.9	−18.5	−8.0	15.0
Reform 3						
Full age dummies	261.0	65.1	38.4	5.2	−1.5	32.1
Linear age trend only	268.0	76.5	41.0	5.4	−3.3	33.6

Note: For details of the specification of the retirement model see section 11.3.

Table 11.10   **Distributional impact of the reforms, measured by the percent change in pension wealth, keeping one-fifth of singles and couples in each quintile**

System and retirement model	Quintile (%)					All (%)
	1 (poorest)	2	3	4	5 (richest)	
Reform 1						
Full age dummies, no age shift	0.9	−1.0	−4.6	−9.8	−7.0	−5.9
Full age dummies, with age shift	−14.4	−14.4	−12.9	−12.7	−10.5	−12.2
Linear age trend only	12.6	6.9	0.6	−7.8	−5.7	−2.2
Reform 2						
Full age dummies	188.6	37.3	16.9	−18.5	−6.9	13.7
Linear age trend only	199.3	44.6	18.6	−19.0	−7.8	15.0
Reform 3						
Full age dummies	239.2	68.2	36.3	6.0	−2.1	32.1
Linear age trend only	248.5	76.7	40.0	4.5	−2.7	33.6

Note: For details of the specification of the retirement model see section 11.3.

cause many individuals are now assumed to retire later as a result of the reform. This means that entitlements to means-tested income support and disability benefit will be reduced (which are included in the estimates of pension wealth, whereas earnings are not). The results from the retirement model that includes only a linear age trend are quite different. These suggest that in fact, on average those in the poorest two wealth quintiles will gain from the reform. However, this feature arises simply from the fact that under this model, many of these individuals estimated to be employed and under the reformed system will be able to continue to accrue an additional entitlement to the SERPS when the state pension is increased. In practice, this appears to be an unreasonable estimate, as demonstrated by the difference in estimated retirement rates shown in figures 11.3, panel A, and 11.5, panel A.

Table 11.9 and table 11.10 also show that under reform 2, individuals are, on average, better off than under the base system. This is due to large increases in the pension wealth of those in the poorest three wealth quintiles, and in particular, very large gains among those in the poorest quintile. Those in the top two wealth quintiles actually lose, on average. These differences are caused by the fact that individuals with higher pension wealth under the base system will be more likely to have a private pension, which they will lose under the reformed system. These distributional results are invariant to the choice of retirement model.

Under reform 3, the average gains across the whole population are larger than under reform 2. On average, all of the quintiles gain from this reform, compared to reform 2. This is because the retention of the basic state pension, means-tested income support, and disability benefit are worth more to each quintile than the fact that the earnings-related component of the state pension is now capped. On average, compared to the base system, the richest quintile still loses. Again, these distributional results are invariant to the choice of retirement model.

11.6   Summary and Conclusions

The focus of this chapter has been the evaluation of the fiscal and distributive impact of social security pension reform in the United Kingdom. We have considered three reforms to the state pension system that are all designed to increase the retirement age by changing the incentive structure underlying the pension system. The first increased the pension age by three years, the second introduced an actuarial adjustment to retirement before 65 and after 65, allowing deferral to age 70. It also eliminated all other pathways to retirement. The final reform adapted the second reform to include a cap and a floor so as to more closely mirror the existing state pension scheme in the United Kingdom.

The simulations show that increasing the state pension age would lead to a lower level of expenditure on the state pension. The increase in retirement ages would also lead to an increase in government revenues, arising from increased income tax and national insurance contributions. In particular, employee National Insurance receipts would increase, since they would be payable to new increased state pension age. The increase in receipts and reduction in state spending would lead to lower levels of government borrowing (or larger government surpluses) than under the base system. At least in part, this impact will be offset by increased state spending on both means-tested income support and disability benefit.

As age effects are so central to any microeconometric model of retirement transitions, the detailed simulation results were presented for different specifications. For reform 1, in which the state pension age is increased, the important contrast in these different specifications was whether the age dummies were held fixed or allowed to shift in line with the reform. For the first reform, the overall expenditure under the model with the shift in age effects is 11.5 percent lower than under the base case, compared to the 12.1 percent lower found when the age effects are held constant. We also find that, assuming no change in the estimated age effects, employee National Insurance is increased by 20.0 percent. Overall, income tax, national insurance, and VAT revenues are estimated to be 6.1 percent higher. Under the alternative assumption that the increase in the state pension age would also shift the estimated age effects by a full three years, we find that government revenues from each of these sources would be further increased. This is due to the larger increase in average retirement ages that occurs under this assumption. Overall, tax and National Insurance revenues would be 16.9 percent higher than under the base system, compared to the current 6.1 percent.

Both reform 2 and reform 3 represent considerably more generous and therefore more expensive state pension systems than the existing UK pension system. Under reform 2, this increase in spending is due to a large increase in spending on the state pension, which is partially offset by the fact that there is no spending on means-tested income support or disability benefit. Under reform 3, spending on state pensions is even higher than under reform 2. This shows that the cap on state pension income under reform 3 does not reduce spending sufficiently to finance the (re-) introduction of a floor on pension benefits equal to the basic state pension. In terms of government revenues, both reform 2 and reform 3 lead to higher levels of government receipts.

Appendix

Table 11A.1   **Retirement transition models, with a full set of time dummies and with a linear time trend only**

	Full set of time dummies		Linear time trend only	
Variable	Men	Women	Men	Women
Total wealth	0.0608		0.0631	
	(0.0164)		(0.0163)	
Option value	−0.5145		−0.4446	
	(0.3476)		(0.0326)	
Spouse pension wealth	0.0280		0.0269	
	(0.0108)		(0.0107)	
Net earnings	−0.0039		−0.0021	
	(0.0047)		(0.0046)	
Net earnings^2	0.0001		0.0001	
	(0.0001)		(0.0001)	
Partners net earnings	−0.0066		−0.0068	
	(0.0029)		(0.0029)	
Partner's net earnings^2	0.0002		0.0002	
	(0.0001)		(0.0001)	
Female dummy		0.1252		0.9176
		(0.1611)		(0.2186)
Age difference	−0.0042	−0.0065	−0.0038	−0.0064
	(0.0023)	(0.0039)	(0.0022)	(0.0039)
Job tenure	0.0000	0.0028	0.0005	0.0028
	(0.0014)	(0.0015)	(0.0014)	(0.0015)
Percent full-time employment	0.0535	0.0214	0.0461	0.0284
	(0.0380)	(0.0403)	(0.0377)	(0.0405)
Education dummy	−0.0210	−0.0088	−0.0188	−0.0191
	(0.0196)	(0.0248)	(0.0199)	(0.0235)
Health score	0.0228	0.0230	0.0196	0.0206
	(0.0094)	(0.0106)	(0.0095)	(0.0107)
Partner's health score	−0.0090	−0.0201	−0.0110	−0.0176
	(0.0067)	(0.0123)	(0.0068)	(0.0122)
				(*continued*)

Variable	Full set of time dummies		Linear time trend only	
	Men	Women	Men	Women
Renter	−0.0177	−0.0053	−0.0165	−0.0057
	(0.0223)	(0.0306)	(0.0225)	(0.0306)
Mortgage	−0.0357	−0.0293	−0.0366	−0.0289
	(0.0202)	(0.0226)	(0.0203)	(0.0229)
Industry				
Engineering	0.0525	−0.0382	0.0482	−0.0439
	(0.0433)	(0.0438)	(0.0423)	(0.0415)
Manufacturing	−0.0006	n.a.	0.0039	n.a.
	(0.0373)	n.a.	(0.0379)	n.a.
Distribution	−0.0053	0.0398	0.0059	0.0328
	(0.0343)	(0.0704)	(0.0365)	(0.0675)
Services	−0.0540	−0.0310	−0.0500	−0.0400
	(0.0246)	(0.0446)	(0.0259)	(0.0429)
Government	−0.0122	−0.0070	0.0090	−0.0176
	(0.0407)	(0.0597)	(0.0467)	(0.0551)
Spouse retired	0.0688	0.1170	0.0756	0.1069
	(0.0395)	(0.0550)	(0.0396)	(0.0534)
Occupational pension	0.6049	0.0290	0.060	0.0148
	(0.0252)	(0.0372)	(0.0245)	(0.0350)
£1–£3,000 wealth	0.0235	−0.0119	0.0246	−0.0016
	(0.0302)	(0.0307)	(0.0302)	(0.0328)
£3,000–£10,000 wealth	0.0358	0.0339	0.0361	0.0435
	(0.0371)	(0.0457)	(0.0369)	(0.0480)
>£10,000 wealth	0.0233	−0.0326	0.0325	−0.0226
	(0.0390)	(0.0330)	(0.0403)	(0.0366)
Missing wealth	0.0414	−0.0480	0.0672	−0.0445
	(0.0613)	(0.0373)	(0.0659)	(0.0401)
Linear age term	n.a.	n.a.	0.0305	0.0211
	n.a.	n.a.	(0.0042)	(0.0054)
Age				
57	0.0298	−0.0218	n.a.	n.a.
	(0.1187)	(0.0590)	n.a.	n.a.
58	0.0003	0.0010	n.a.	n.a.
	(0.0956)	(0.0642)	n.a.	n.a.
59	0.0134	−0.0096	n.a.	n.a.
	(0.1013)	(0.0592)	n.a.	n.a.
60	−0.0031	0.1961	n.a.	n.a.
	(0.0916)	(0.1102)	n.a.	n.a.
61	0.1024	0.1247	n.a.	n.a.
	(0.1001)	(0.1010)	n.a.	n.a.
62	0.0142	0.0713	n.a.	n.a.
	(0.1016)	(0.0937)	n.a.	n.a.
63	0.0980	0.1270	n.a.	n.a.
	(0.1420)	(0.1182)	n.a.	n.a.
64	0.1365	0.0997	n.a.	n.a.
	(0.1595)	(0.1256)	n.a.	n.a.

Table 11A.1   (continued)

Variable	Full set of time dummies		Linear time trend only	
	Men	Women	Men	Women
65	0.5369	0.4000	n.a.	n.a.
	(0.2002)	(0.1816)	n.a.	n.a.
66	0.2555	0.5152	n.a.	n.a.
	(0.2157)	(0.3772)	n.a.	n.a.
67	0.3585	n.a.	n.a.	n.a.
	(0.2382)	n.a.	n.a.	n.a.
68	0.2615	n.a.	n.a.	n.a.
	(0.2455)	n.a.	n.a.	n.a.
69	0.4353	n.a.	n.a.	n.a.
	(0.2655)	n.a.	n.a.	n.a.
70	0.7241	n.a.	n.a.	n.a.
	(0.2226)	n.a.	n.a.	n.a.
No. of observations	1,998		1,998	
Pseudo R^2	0.197		0.153	
Log likelihood	−661.525		−697.758	

Notes: Marginal effects are reported. Standard errors in parentheses. n.a. = not applicable.

***Significant at the 1 percent level.

**Significant at the 5 percent level.

*Significant at the 10 percent level.

Table 11A.2   Total fiscal impact of reform

		Present discounted value			Total change relative to base (%)		
	Base	Three-Year	Common	Modified	Three-Year Reform	Common Reform	Modified Reform
		Option value linear age (S1)					
Benefits							
State pension	25,134	19,094	74,080	80,446	−24.0	194.7	220.1
Invalidity benefit	1,754	2,606	0	439	48.6	−100.0	−75.0
Income support	5,679	2,309	0	1,123	−59.3	−100.0	−80.2
Total	32,567	24,009	74,080	82,008	−26.3	127.5	151.8
Taxes							
Employee National Insurance	5,679	6,752	6,858	6,666	18.9	20.8	17.4
Employer National Insurance	7,441	7,769	8,529	8,207	4.4	14.6	10.3
Income tax	29,706	30,959	41,579	40,819	4.2	40.0	37.4
VAT	11,023	10,905	17,003	16,667	−1.1	54.3	51.2
Total	53,849	56,385	73,970	72,359	4.7	37.4	34.4
		Option value—Age dummies (no shift) (S2)					
Benefits							
State pension	24,733	18,741	73,498	80,087	−24.2	197.2	223.8
Invalidity benefit	2,619	3,685	0	731	40.7	−100.0	−72.1
Income support	765	2,297	0	954	200.3	−100.0	24.7
Total	28,117	24,723	73,498	81,772	−12.1	161.4	190.8

Taxes							
Employee National Insurance	5,354	6,427	6,828	6,561	20.0	27.5	22.6
Employer National Insurance	7,045	7,457	8,546	8,128	5.8	21.3	15.4
Income tax	28,156	29,755	41,769	40,590	5.7	48.8	44.2
VAT	10,637	10,660	17,102	16,593	0.2	60.8	56.0
Total	51,192	54,299	74,245	71,872	6.1	45.0	40.4
Option value—Age dummies (with shift) (S3)							
Benefits							
State pension	24,733	19,739	73,498	80,087	−20.2	197.2	223.8
Invalidity benefit	2,619	3,671	0	731	40.2	−100.0	−72.1
Income support	765	1,470	0	954	92.2	−100.0	24.7
Total	28,117	24,881	73,498	81,772	−11.5	161.4	190.8
Taxes							
Employee National Insurance	5,354	6,758	6,828	6,561	26.2	27.5	22.6
Employer National Insurance	7,045	8,261	8,546	8,128	17.3	21.3	15.4
Income tax	28,156	33,130	41,769	40,590	17.7	48.3	44.2
VAT	10,637	11,716	17,102	16,593	10.1	60.8	56.0
Total	51,192	59,866	74,245	71,872	16.9	45.0	40.4

Table 11A.3   Decomposition of the total effect of reform

	Three-Year Reform			Common Reform			Modified Common Reform		
					Change in present discounted value					
	Mechanical	Behavioral	Total	Mechanical	Behavioral	Total	Mechanical	Behavioral	Total
				Option value linear age (S1)					
Benefits: Total	-8,806	247	-8,558	43,165	-1,651	41,513	49,552	-111	49,441
Taxes: Total	132	2,404	2,536	10,469	9,652	20,121	12,500	6,010	18,510
Net change	-8,938	-2,157	-11,094	32,696	-11,303	21,392	37,052	-6,121	30,931
Change as % of base benefits	-27.4	-6.6	-34.1	100.4	-34.7	65.7	113.8	-18.8	95.0
				Option value—Age dummies (no shift) (S2)					
Benefits: Total	-3,894	500	-3,394	47,807	-2,426	45,381	54,374	-719	53,655
Taxes: Total	599	2,485	3,084	7,080	9,508	16,588	8,009	6,714	14,724
Net change	-4,494	-1,985	-6,478	40,727	-11,934	28,793	46,364	-7,433	38,932
Change as % of base benefits	-16.0	-7.1	-23.0	144.8	-42.4	102.4	164.9	-26.4	138.5
				Option value—Age dummies (with shift) (S3)					
Benefits: Total	-3,894	658	-3,236	47,807	-2,426	45,381	54,374	-719	53,655
Taxes: Total	599	6,996	7,595	7,080	9,508	16,588	8,009	6,714	14,724
Net change	-4,494	-6,338	-10,831	40,727	-11,934	28,793	46,364	-7,433	38,932
Change as % of base benefits	-16.0	-22.5	-38.5	144.8	-42.4	102.4	164.9	-26.4	138.5

Table 11A.4   **Distributional analysis: Option value—Linear age (S1)**

	Present discounted value				Change relative to base		
	Base	Three-Year	Common	Modified	Three-Year Reform	Common Reform	Modified Reform
Quintile 1 (highest)							
After-tax income	13,512	12,748	12,463	13,141	−764	−1,049	−371
Change as % of base benefits					−5.7	−7.8	−2.9
Quintile 2							
After-tax income	7,848	7,232	6,360	8,199	−615	−1,487	352
Change as % of base benefits					−7.8	−19.0	4.9
Quintile 3							
After-tax income	6,217	6,254	7,371	8,705	37	1,155	2,488
Change as % of base benefits					0.6	18.6	39.8
Quintile 4							
After-tax income	4,340	4,640	6,275	7,667	300	1,934	3,327
Change as % of base benefits					6.9	44.6	71.7
Quintile 5 (lowest)							
After-tax income	2,290	2,579	6,853	7,981	289	4,563	5,691
Change as % of base benefits					12.6	199.3	220.7

Table 11A.5   Distributional analysis: Option value—Age dummies (with shift) (S3)

	Present Discounted Value				Change relative to base		
	Base	Three-Year	Common	Modified	Three-Year Reform	Common Reform	Modified Reform
			Quintile 1 (highest)				
After-tax income	13,440	12,029	12,510	13,161	−1,411	−930	−279
Change as % of base benefits					−10.5	−6.9	−2.3
			Quintile 2				
After-tax income	7,801	6,809	6,359	8,268	−993	−1,442	467
Change as % of base benefits					−12.7	−18.5	6.9
			Quintile 3				
After-tax income	6,270	5,461	7,329	8,545	−809	1,059	2,275
Change as % of base benefits					−12.9	16.9	41.7
			Quintile 4				
After-tax income	4,459	3,816	6,122	7,499	−643	1,663	3,039
Change as % of base benefits					−14.4	37.3	79.6
			Quintile 5 (lowest)				
After-tax income	2,295	1,965	6,624	7,785	−330	4,329	5,490
Change as % of base benefits					−14.4	188.6	279.4

References

Agulnik, P. 1999. The proposed state second pension. *Fiscal Studies* (20) 4:409–21.

Attanasio, O., and C. Emmerson. 2003. Mortality, health status and wealth. *Journal of the European Economics Association* 1 (4): 821–50.

Banks, J., R. Blundell, R. Disney, and C. Emmerson. 2002. Retirement, pensions and the adequacy of saving: A guide to the debate. *IFS Briefing Note 29* (October).

Banks, J., and C. Emmerson. 2000. Public and private pension spending: Principles, practice and the need for reform. *Fiscal Studies* 21 (1): 1–63.

Blundell, R., and P. Johnson. 1998. Pensions and labor force participation in the UK. *American Economic Review* 88 (2): 173–78.

———. 1999. Pensions and retirement in the UK. In *Social security and retirement around the world,* ed. J. Gruber and D. Wise, 403–35. Chicago: University of Chicago Press.

Blundell, R., C. Meghir, and S. Smith. 2001. Pension incentives and the pattern of retirement in the UK. In *Social security and retirement around the world: Vol. II,* ed. J. Gruber and D. Wise. Chicago: University of Chicago Press.

———. 2002. Pension incentives and the pattern of early retirement. *Economic Journal* 112 (478): C153–C170.

Clark, T., and C. Emmerson. 2003. Privatising provision and attacking poverty?

The direction of UK pension policy under new Labour. *Journal of Pension Economics and Finance* 2 (1): 67–89.

Department for Work and Pensions. 2002. *Simplicity, security and choice: Working and saving for retirement.* Cm. 5677. London: The Stationery Office.

———. 2006. *Security in retirement: Toward a new pensions system.* Cm6841. London: The Stationery Office.

Dilnot, A., R. Disney, P. Johnson, and E. Whitehouse. 1994. *Pensions policy in the UK: An economic analysis.* London: Institute for Fiscal Studies.

Disney, R., C. Emmerson, and S. Tanner. 1999. *Partnership in pensions: An assessment.* London: IFS.

Disney, R., C. Emmerson, and S. Smith. 2003. Pension reform and economic performance in Britain in the 1980s and 1990s. In *Seeking a premier economy: The economic effects of British economic reforms, 1980–2000,* ed. R. Blundell, D. Card, and R. Freeman, 233–72. Chicago: University of Chicago Press.

Disney, R., E. Grundy, and P. Johnson. (eds.). 1997. *The dynamics of retirement: Analyses of the retirement surveys.* Department of Social Security Research Report no. 72. London: Stationery Office.

Disney, R., and D. Hawkes. 2003. Declining employment of older workers: Has Britain turned the corner? In *The labour market under New Labour, the state of working Britain,* ed. R. Dickens, P. Gregg, and J. Wadsworth. Hampshire, England: Palgrave.

Disney, R., C. Meghir, and E. Whitehouse. 1994. Retirement behaviour in Britain. *Fiscal Studies* 15 (1): 24–43.

Disney, R., and S. Smith. 2002. The labour supply effect of the abolition of the earnings rule for older workers in the United Kingdom. *Economic Journal* 112 (478): 136–52.

Disney, R., and G. Stears. 1996. Why is there a decline in defined benefit plan membership? London: Institute for Fiscal Studies Working Paper no. 96/4.

Emmerson, C., and P. Johnson. 2002. Pension provision in the United Kingdom. In *Pension systems and retirement incomes across OECD countries,* ed. R. Disney and P. Johnson. Aldershot, England: Edward Elgar.

Emmerson, C., G. Tetlow, and M. Wakefield. 2006. The Pensions White Paper: Who wins and who loses? *Project Management Institute News,* August.

Emmerson, C., and M. Wakefield. 2003. *Achieving simplicity, security and choice in retirement? An assessment of the government's proposed pension reforms.* Briefing Note no. 36. London: Institute for Fiscal Studies.

Government Actuary's Department. 2003. *Occupational pension schemes 2000: Eleventh survey by the Government Actuary.* London: Government Actuary's Department.

Stock, J., and D. Wise. 1990a. The pension inducement to retire: An option value analysis. In *Issues in the economics of aging,* ed. D. Wise, 205–24. Chicago: University of Chicago Press.

Stock, J., and D. Wise. 1990b. Pensions, the option value of work and retirement. *Econometrica* 58 (5): 1151–80.

Tanner, S. 1998. The dynamics of male retirement behaviour. *Fiscal Studies* 19 (2): 175–96.

12

Fiscal Effects of Social Security Reform in the United States

Courtney Coile and Jonathan Gruber

The Old-Age, Survivors, and Disability Insurance (OASDI) program faces a serious long-term solvency crisis. The 2001 Trustees' Report projects that the OASDI trust funds will be exhausted in 2038 and that an immediate and permanent tax increase of 1.86 percent of taxable payroll will be needed to restore solvency for the next seventy-five years. Over the past several years, many Social Security reforms have been suggested to address the solvency crisis, from further increases in the normal retirement age to partial privatization of the system.

Many of these proposals would improve the fiscal balances of the OASDI program by cutting benefits, raising taxes, or both. However, the fiscal implications of these reforms depend critically not just on the static impacts of the reforms on benefit payments and tax collections, but also on dynamic responses of individuals to changes in program incentives. In particular, there is a large literature over the past two decades that suggests that retirement decisions are responsive to the parameters of the Social Security system. If reform alters retirement patterns, this will in turn impact benefit payments and tax collections, both inside and outside the Social Security system. For example, if raising the early entitlement age for Social Security leads to later retirement, this may significantly improve the government's fiscal position, above and beyond the savings from starting payments later in life.

Courtney Coile is an associate professor of economics at Wellesley College and a faculty research fellow of the National Bureau of Economic Research (NBER). Jonathan Gruber is a professor of economics at the Massachusetts Institute of Technology and a research associate of the National Bureau of Economic Research.

The authors thank David Wise and other members of the International Social Security Working Group for helpful suggestions.

While some previous studies of Social Security and retirement have forecast the effect of various reforms on labor supply, little work in the United States has focused on the impact of reforms on the fiscal position of the federal government. There has been little attempt, to date, to marry dynamic models of retirement responsiveness to estimates of the impact of reform on fiscal balances.

We propose to incorporate labor supply responses into our simulations of the effect of Social Security reforms on older workers' net fiscal contributions to OASDI. Such reforms will have both an automatic effect on fiscal balances by changing contributions and benefits for a given work history (the *mechanical* effect), and an additional effect through labor supply responses to the reform (the *behavioral* effect). We estimate the fiscal implications of both the mechanical and the behavioral effect, using retirement models to predict labor supply responses. The result will be an estimate of the steady-state impact of the reforms on the financial balance sheet of the OASDI program. We also include income and consumption taxes in our analysis in order to examine the effect of the reforms on total government finances.

To be clear, we are not engaging in a full-blown solvency analysis along the lines of that carried out by the Social Security Administration (SSA). We do not consider the impact of reform on both transition and long-run system finances. Rather, for illustrative purposes, we follow one cohort of workers and illustrate the impacts of reforms on the benefits paid to, and the taxes collected from, this cohort. This gives some guide as to the percentage effects of reforms on system balances.

The remainder of the chapter is organized as follows. In section 12.1, we provide some background on the Social Security program and on previous literature on social security and retirement. In section 12.2, we discuss the data and empirical strategy we employ to estimate the effect of reforms on workers' net fiscal contributions to OASDI. In section 12.3, we present our results. In section 12.4, we analyze the distribution effects of the proposed policy changes. In section 12.5, we conclude.

12.1 Background

12.1.1 Institutional Features of Social Security

As this paper focuses on labor supply responses to Social Security reform, a brief overview of the Social Security program is necessary to understand how the program affects retirement; see Diamond and Gruber (1998) for a more detailed review. An individual is entitled to retired worker benefits once he or she has worked forty quarters in covered employment. Benefits are calculated in several steps. Annual earnings are indexed by an average wage index, and the thirty-five highest years of earnings are used to compute the average indexed monthly earnings (AIME).[1] A progressive formula is applied to the AIME to obtain the primary insurance amount (PIA). Finally, the PIA is adjusted to obtain the monthly benefit amount based on when benefits are first received. Individuals claiming at the normal retirement age (NRA, legislated to grow slowly from 65 to 67) receive the PIA. Individuals can receive benefits as early as age 62 (the early retirement age, or ERA), or can delay until age 70. Benefits are reduced by 6.67 percent for each year of receipt prior to the NRA and are increased by a delayed retirement credit of 3 percent to 8 percent for each year receipt is postponed past the NRA, depending on the worker's birth year.[2] Benefit receipt is subject to an earnings test before age 65, whereby earnings above a floor amount reduce current benefits and cause them instead to be paid out (with an actuarial adjustment) upon full retirement. Spouses of beneficiaries also receive a dependent benefit equal to 50 percent of the worker's PIA or a survivor benefit equal to 100 percent of the worker's PIA, although the spouse receives only the larger of this and his or her own retired worker benefit. Benefits are funded with a payroll tax of 12.4 percent, paid half by employers and half by employees.

Additional work affects social security wealth in several ways. First, the additional year of earnings may replace an earlier year of zero or low earnings in the AIME calculation, raising the monthly benefit. Second, work beyond age 62 implies a delay in claiming benefits (if earnings are significantly above the earnings test floor). Benefits are forgone for a year, but future benefits are higher due to the actuarial adjustment. Finally, additional work results in additional payroll taxes. The combination of these three effects determines whether the Social Security system provides a return to additional work that is more or less than actuarially fair.

12.1.2   Previous Related Literature

While there is little work that has incorporated labor supply responses to Social Security reforms into estimates of the effect of reforms on the government's fiscal position, there is a large previous literature that has explored the effect of Social Security on retirement decisions. A brief overview of this literature follows; for a more detailed review, see Diamond and Gruber (1998).

While a few studies have used aggregate information on the labor force behavior of workers at different ages to infer the role played by Social Security, most studies have attempted to specifically model the role that benefits play in determining retirement decisions.[3] Early studies estimated

---

1. Earnings after age 60 are in nominal dollars, increasing the incentive to work at these ages.

2. The delayed retirement credit (DRC) is rising from 3 percent for workers born prior to 1925 to 8 percent for workers born after 1942. For workers with an NRA above 65, benefits are reduced 5 percent per year for receipt more than three years before the NRA.

3. Hurd (1990) and Ruhm (1995) are good examples of studies using aggregate data.

reduced-form models of the retirement decision as a function of social security wealth,[4] however, more recent literature has also incorporated increases in wealth resulting from additional work. Some studies did this by incorporating the accrual of social security wealth resulting from one additional year of work, others by estimating structural models of retirement decisions by workers facing a lifetime budget constraint.[5] Typically, these studies found that Social Security played an important role, albeit one that could only explain a fraction of the decrease in older men's labor supply during the post-WWII era.

Stock and Wise (1990a, b) made the important observation that it is not simply the increment to retirement wealth with one additional year of work that matters, but rather the entire evolution of future wealth with further work. They developed an option value model that posited retirement decisions as a function of the difference between the utility of retirement at the current date and at the date that maximizes one's utility. The critical contribution of this approach is to model retirement decisions in a forward-looking framework that considers the impact of the path of future incentives on retirement. This approach was extended from firm-specific to national data by Samwick (1998), and it shows once again the modest effects of Social Security, but much larger effects of private pensions.

Coile and Gruber (2000) recognized that the vast majority of variation across individuals in option value resulted from wages, and they developed an alternative measure—peak value—that measures the financial gain from delaying retirement to the age at which social security wealth is maximized. They also found that Social Security has a significant but modest effect on retirement decisions.

A final relevant article is Coile and Gruber (2001), which explores whether the Social Security program provides strong incentives or disincentives for work at particular ages. They find that, once payroll taxes are included, the median male worker faces a small tax on work through the Social Security system at ages 55 to 61, a near-zero tax at ages 62 to 64, and a large tax at ages 65 to 69. The actuarial unfairness of the system at some ages suggests that labor supply responses to Social Security reforms may have a beneficial effect on the government's fiscal position if the reforms encourage more years of work at those ages.

---

4. For more recent examples of this literature, see Diamond and Hausman (1984) and Blau (1994).

5. For examples of the former, see Fields and Mitchell (1984) and Hausman and Wise (1985); for examples of the latter, see Burtless (1986), Gustman and Steinmeier (1985, 1986), and Rust and Phelan (1997).

12.2   Data and Empirical Strategy

12.2.1   Data

The data used in the analysis is the Health and Retirement Study (HRS). This is a survey of persons born 1931–1941 and their spouses, with interviews every two years, starting in 1992. The HRS contains extensive information on employment, health, and family structure. For the purposes of this paper, the critical feature is that the HRS is linked to Social Security earnings histories, allowing accurate calculation of the retirement incentives arising from Social Security.[6]

The sample for the analysis is all men and single women in the 1931–1941 birth cohorts who are working at age 55 and have nonmissing Social Security records for themselves and their spouses. Benefits accruing to married women are included in their husband's record (this includes the women's retired worker, dependent, and survivor benefits). We assume that married women retire at the initial ERA, that is, at 62. When we simulate reforms to the system, we continue to assume that women retire at 62 and claim benefits at the first availability. The purpose of maintaining the same retirement age is to avoid building a behavioral response of women into the mechanical effect. The final sample size is 3,060 persons.

For each person in our sample, we have earnings histories that can allow us to compute his or her Social Security benefit entitlement at each retirement age (or age of death). The critical assumption involved in doing so is projecting his or her earnings into future years. In our earlier work, we found that these projections work best if we assume no real earnings growth from the current age forward until retirement. Given these earnings projections, we can also compute the payroll tax obligations of workers at future ages.

A key contribution of our simulations is that we will consider the impact on the entire government fiscal position, not just on Social Security in a vacuum. Doing so requires modeling the impact of additional years of work on income and consumption tax revenue as well, and we subsequently describe our approach for doing so. This approach does not provide a perfect picture of the full fiscal impact of reforms. For example, there will be effects on other, much smaller retirement income support programs when Social Security is reformed, such as the Supplemental Security Income (SSI) program. But these effects are difficult to model, since these other programs may also change through reform. We assume that the

---

6. The HRS also includes information from employers on private pensions. In this analysis, we will ignore pensions, as our focus is on Social Security reform, and it is difficult to forecast how pensions might change in response to a change in Social Security rules.

effects are sufficiently modest that they do not bias our overall assessment of the fiscal implications of reform.

12.2.2 Empirical Strategy

Our goal is to estimate how changes to the Social Security program would affect the net fiscal position of OASDI with respect to a particular cohort of workers, those born between 1931 and 1941, who were working at age 55. Once again, this approach is not designed to provide a full picture of the full implications of reform for program solvency. Rather, it provides a snapshot of the relative magnitude of effects that may be observed when reform impacts a particular slice of birth cohorts.

We calculate social security wealth in the base case for our sample of age-55 workers and their families using the following approach. Each age-55 worker will exit the labor force sometime over the next twenty years, either by retiring or by dying prior to retirement.[7] Thus, there are forty possible exit paths out of the labor force, or forty states of the world, corresponding to retirement or death at each age from 55 to 74. We obtain the weighted average social security wealth by multiplying the probability of each state by the social security wealth received in that state.

The probability of each state is obtained as follows. We calculate the conditional probability of dying at each age from age- and sex-specific U.S. life tables.[8] We calculate the probability of retiring at each age conditional on being in the labor force using models of retirement behavior from Coile and Gruber (2004).[9] The central results from that paper are reproduced in table 12.1. We estimate retirement models as a function of both the level of social security wealth (the expected PDV of net transfers from the Social Security system from your current age forward), and two different dynamic measures of retirement incentives. The first is option value, as pioneered by Stock and Wise (1990a, b). This measure, as previously noted, captures the difference between the utility of retiring today and retiring at the age when utility is maximized, as a function of both future wages and retirement benefit entitlements. Thus, if this is positive, then there are gains to delaying retirement, and these gains rise with the value of the option value term (so that we expect a negative impact of option value on retirement). The second is the peak value, as described in Coile and Gruber (2000). This measure focuses solely on retirement income as opposed to total financial returns to work, in order to distinguish retirement-income effects from wage

---

7. For the purpose of our calculation, we will assume everyone retires by age 74. We do not use workers' observed labor force exit, as many workers will not have exited the labor force by the 2000 HRS. Rather, we use projected labor force exits from the empirical models described herein.

8. Life tables are from the 1995 OASDI Trustees Report, intermediate assumptions case.

9. To be precise, this probability is also conditional on being alive at the beginning of this age and not dying at this age. Thus, 100 percent of workers at each age are accounted for either through exit to death, exit to retirement, or continued labor force participation.

Table 12.1   **Retirement probits**

	Incentive variable			
	Peak value		Option value	
	Age dummies	Linear age	Age dummies	Linear age
Male sample				
SSW	0.1996	0.2926	0.1249	0.2010
	(0.1395)	(0.1344)	(0.1363)	(0.1331)
$10,000 change	(0.0016)	(0.0025)	(0.0010)	(0.0017)
Incentive measure	−0.6618	−0.4983	−0.2106	−0.2368
	(0.2750)	(0.2927)	(0.0522)	(0.0539)
$1,000 change	(−0.0005)	(−0.0004)		
Pseudo R^2	0.1386	0.1386	0.1402	0.1402
Female sample				
SSW	0.2574	0.2881	0.2200	0.2485
	(0.1315)	(0.1320)	(0.1323)	(0.1331)
$10,000 change	(0.0020)	(0.0022)	(0.0017)	(0.0019)
Incentive measure	−0.0307	−0.0878	−0.2441	−0.2723
	(0.3350)	(0.3345)	(0.0753)	(0.0773)
$1,000 change	(−0.00002)	(−0.00007)		
Pseudo R^2	0.1530	0.1530	0.1530	0.1549

Notes: Dependent variable is whether the individual retires this year. Peak value and social security wealth (SSW) are in 100,000s of $1992; option value is in 10,000. Regressions include controls for education, race, experience, marital status, industry, occupation, region, and year, as well as a quartic in earnings, a quartic in lifetime earnings, and the interactions of these quartics (plus same earnings variables for the spouse).

effects (which might be unobservably correlated with tastes for work). So this measure is the difference between the maximum value of the PDV of retirement income and the value if the individual retires today. Once again, as peak value is larger, the returns to delaying retirement rise, so that we expect a negative coefficient in a retirement equation.

Both models also include controls for age, flexible functions of earnings and lifetime earnings, and education, race, region, industry, and occupation dummies. A central issue, which is the focus of our earlier paper, is the correct approach to specifying the impact of age in these retirement models, particularly the use of age dummies versus linear age. If there are strong correlations between wealth or dynamic incentives and particular ages, then including age dummies might absorb some of the impacts of the program on retirement decisions. On the other hand, if there are nonlinear impacts of age on retirement decisions, then including a linear age term may lead to biased estimates of the program's incentive effects. Thus, we estimate the models both ways in table 12.1.

In this work, we have found fairly consistent evidence for significant effects of program incentives on retirement decisions. Table 12.1 shows the key coefficients from these models. In each cell, we show the probit coefficient, the associated standard error, and the impact of a $10,000 increment to SSW, or a $1,000 increment to peak value. For men, peak value and option value each have a negative and significant effect on retirement, while social security wealth has a positive, though not always significant, effect. The results suggest that each $10,000 in social security wealth raises the odds of retirement by 0.1 to 0.25 percentage points, from a rate of 5.7 percentage points. Each $1,000 in peak value, on the other hand, lowers the odds of retirement by 0.04 to 0.05 percentage points. We can't really interpret the option value coefficient as such, since it is in utility terms. Our results are fairly similar for women. The major differences are that the SSW terms are more consistently significant, and the peak value terms are now insignificant.

We apply the coefficients from those models to each individual's characteristics to obtain a predicted probability of retirement at each age for each individual. That is, this model provides us with baseline estimates of retirement by age.

Next, the expected net present discounted value of social security wealth is calculated for each possible labor force exit path (retirement or death at each of the twenty ages 55 to 74). For single workers, social security wealth is simply a sum of future benefits, discounted by time preference and survival probabilities. For married workers it is more complicated, since we must include dependent spouse and survivor benefits and retired worker benefits for the spouse, and account for the joint likelihood of survival of the worker and dependent. We use a real discount rate of 3 percent and survival probabilities from the age- and sex-specific life tables. Finally, we multiply the probability of each state times the social security wealth in that state for each individual, then average over all individuals to obtain the average base case social security wealth for the sample.

This same approach can then be used to compute the fiscal implications of reform, in two steps. First, we measure the impact of reform on both social security wealth and on option/peak value at each age. We can then use these new post-reform values to compute a new odds of retirement at each age, based on our regression coefficients in table 12.1. We assume that mortality is not affected by reform. Second, we multiply these new odds of exit by the new stream of net SSW from either death or retirement at each age. In this way, we obtain the new fiscal position for this cohort from reform.

As this discussion makes clear, however, there are two distinct effects of reform that are of interest: the fiscal effects of reform that arise automatically due to changes in program rules, and those that arise due to labor supply responses. The mechanical effect is the change in social security wealth that arises solely from the change in program rules, holding retirement probabilities constant, while the behavioral effect is the additional change in social security wealth that results from the change in retirement probabilities, holding wealth constant at its postreform level. The fiscal implications of the mechanical and behavioral effects are calculated as follows:

$$\text{Mechanical effect} = \sum_{i=1}^{N}\sum_{s=1}^{48} P_{is}^{B} SSW_{is}^{R} - \sum_{i=1}^{N}\sum_{s=1}^{48} P_{is}^{B} SSW_{is}^{B},$$

$$\text{Behavioral effect} = \sum_{i=1}^{N}\sum_{s=1}^{48} P_{is}^{R} SSW_{is}^{R} - \sum_{i=1}^{N}\sum_{s=1}^{48} P_{is}^{B} SSW_{is}^{R},$$

$$\text{Total effect of return} = \sum_{i=1}^{N}\sum_{s=1}^{48} P_{is}^{R} SSW_{is}^{R} - \sum_{i=1}^{N}\sum_{s=1}^{48} P_{is}^{B} SSW_{is}^{B},$$

where i is individual, s is state (exit to death or retirement at each age), B is base, and R is reform. Thus, the mechanical effect is the impact of letting SSW change from before to after reform, but holding retirement behavior constant; the behavioral effect is the impact of letting exit probabilities change from before to after reform, but holding SSW constant. The sum of the mechanical and behavioral effects is equal to the total effect.

The net present discounted value of income and consumption taxes are computed using the same methodology as social security wealth. Again, there are forty possible exit paths out of the labor force, and each path corresponds to certain expected future income flows. For example, in the case where the worker retires at age 55, there are three possible amounts of household income in each future year, depending on whether the husband, wife, or both are alive in that year. Taxes are computed for each of the three possible income amounts, then the stream of taxes is discounted for time preference and mortality risk. The income taxes paid each year are calculated using a simple tax calculator based on the 2000 U.S. income tax code; households are assumed to take the standard deduction and tax rules regarding the taxation of Social Security benefits are incorporated. Consumption taxes are assumed to be 4.5 percent of income; 4.5 percent is the ratio of state and local sales and excise taxes to personal disposable income for 2000.

12.3   Results

12.3.1   The Reforms

We simulate three different reforms to the U.S. Social Security system. The first reform is a three-year increase in the ERA and NRA, to 65 and 68, respectively (Three-Year Reform). This reform will significantly reduce social security wealth at any age, since benefits receipt begins much later in life. The reform will also reduce incentives for continued work at younger ages, since the peak value of SSW is so much lower; but it will increase incentives for work after age 65, since the actuarial adjustment is now so much larger in that age range.

The second reform is a change in the actuarial adjustment, to 6 percent per year (Actuarial Reform). This is actually only a small change to the current U.S. system, since the actuarial adjustment is equal to 6.67 percent between ages 62 and 65 and is between 5 percent and 7.5 percent above age 65 for workers in these birth cohorts. But this is a much larger change in the other countries in this project, which do not currently have actuarial adjustments. In the U.S. context, this change will lead to a reduction in SSW at younger ages, which will promote retirement, but also a reduction in the dynamic incentive to continue work. At older ages, the effects will vary by birth cohort.

The third reform is a move to a system with a flat 60 percent replacement rate of the AIME at age 65, an early eligibility age of 60, and a 6 percent annual actuarial adjustment between ages 60 and 70 (Common Reform).[10] The third policy is not viewed as being a realistic policy reform for the United States, but is presented to illustrate the effects of moving to a more generous system, more similar to those in European countries. This policy will significantly increase social security wealth, leading to earlier retirement, but will also significantly increase the financial benefits to longer work life, since the dollar benefits from additional work are rising so substantially, while the actuarial adjustment is similar to current law.

One issue that arises in simulating policy reforms is how the reforms will affect individuals' tendency to retire at particular ages, as reflected by the age dummies in the retirement model. For example, two of the three policies change the early retirement age, and it seems quite likely that the spike in the retirement hazard at age 62 might be altered as a result of the change. However, it is difficult to predict exactly how the retirement hazard might change. We propose to deal with this issue by using two alternative assumptions about the age dummies. The first is to leave the age dummies unchanged by the policies, and the second is to shift the age dummies as seems appropriate. For the first policy, we shift the age dummies back by three years, so that the age 62 spike is moved to age 65, the age 65 spike to age 68, and so on. For the second policy, the age dummies are unaffected, while for the third policy, we shift the age 62 dummy to age 60 and make several other small adjustments. We also present results using the linear age model.

12.3.2 Results

The results of the analysis for the typical age-55 household, averaging over married couples and singles, are shown in table 12.2. We present six panels, corresponding to the six specifications we estimate: linear age,

---

10. This system also has a 100 percent survivor benefit, though no dependent spouse benefit.

Table 12.2   Total fiscal impact of reform for average age-55 household

Cost or revenue item	Base	Three-Year Reform	Actuarial Reform	Common Reform	Total change relative to base (%)		
					Three-Year	Actuarial	Common
Peak value, linear age							
Benefits	196,503	160,526	198,763	282,264	-18.3	1.1	43.6
Taxes							
Payroll	58,681	61,362	58,089	57,305	4.6	-1.0	-2.3
Income	86,288	88,000	85,588	90,839	2.0	-0.8	5.3
Consumption	35,221	34,622	35,155	39,895	-1.7	-0.2	13.3
Total	180,191	183,983	178,832	188,038	2.1	-0.8	4.4
Peak value, age dummies (no shift)							
Benefits	193,947	158,400	196,232	282,445	-18.3	1.2	45.6
Taxes							
Payroll	60,419	62,396	59,768	62,054	3.3	-1.1	2.7
Income	87,808	88,595	87,038	96,551	0.9	-0.9	10.0
Consumption	35,504	34,708	35,428	40,981	-2.2	-0.2	15.4
Total	183,731	185,700	182,234	199,585	1.1	-0.8	8.6
Peak value, age dummies (with shift)							
Benefits	193,947	159,678	196,232	279,771	-17.7	1.2	44.3
Taxes							
Payroll	60,419	66,820	59,768	59,939	10.6	-1.1	-0.8
Income	87,808	93,859	87,038	93,800	6.9	-0.9	6.8
Consumption	35,504	35,994	35,428	40,312	1.4	-0.2	13.5
Total	183,731	196,672	182,234	194,051	7.0	-0.8	5.6

(*continued*)

Table 12.2 (continued)

Cost or revenue item	Base	Three-Year Reform	Actuarial Reform	Common Reform	Total change relative to base (%)		
					Three-Year	Actuarial	Common
Option value, linear age							
Benefits	196,839	160,914	199,110	280,870	-18.3	1.2	42.7
Taxes							
Payroll	59,763	62,297	59,393	57,012	4.2	-0.6	-4.6
Income	87,591	89,149	87,181	89,971	1.8	-0.5	2.7
Consumption	35,546	34,938	35,540	39,741	-1.7	0.0	11.8
Total	182,901	186,383	182,114	186,724	1.9	-0.4	2.1
Option value, age dummies (no shift)							
Benefits	194,153	158,791	196,436	279,323	-18.2	1.2	43.9
Taxes							
Payroll	61,229	63,180	60,918	59,638	3.2	-0.5	-2.6
Income	88,766	89,580	88,438	92,940	0.9	-0.4	4.7
Consumption	35,751	34,987	35,766	40,280	-2.1	0.0	12.7
Total	185,746	187,747	185,122	192,857	1.1	-0.3	3.8
Option value, age dummies (with shift)							
Benefits	194,153	160,208	196,436	276,407	-17.5	1.2	42.4
Taxes							
Payroll	61,229	66,541	60,918	57,446	8.7	-0.5	-6.2
Income	88,766	93,697	88,438	89,997	5.6	-0.4	1.4
Consumption	35,751	36,004	35,766	39,579	0.7	0.0	10.7
Total	185,746	196,243	185,122	187,022	5.7	-0.3	0.7

Note: Results are in 2001 euros.

age dummies with no shift in their value from reform, and age dummies with a shift in value from reform, each for the peak and option value models. In each panel, we show rows for: Social Security benefits, payroll taxes, income taxes, consumption taxes, and total tax payments. We show columns for the base case, and then for each of the three reforms. Finally, the last three columns show the percentage effects from each of the three reforms.

Consider the first panel, which shows the peak value model, with linear age controls. In the base case, averaging over the forty possible labor force exit paths, the typical age-55 household has expected future Social Security benefits of €196,503 (2001 euros), expected future Social Security payroll taxes of €58,681, and expected total future taxes of €180,191. It is important to note that the majority of future tax payments come not from payroll taxes but from income taxes. This highlights the value of government-wide simulations, as opposed to simulations that focus on the Social Security system in a vacuum.

The total effect of the Three-Year Reform is to lower benefits, in this case by 18.3 percent to €160,526. Payroll taxes rise, as do income taxes, due to longer working lives. But consumption taxes fall, as the higher labor income does not offset lower Social Security benefits, leading to falling disposable income. In total, tax revenues rise by 2.1 percent, to €183,983.

The effect of the Actuarial Reform is much smaller; benefits rise by only 1.1 percent and taxes fall by 0.8 percent. The effect of the Common Reform is the largest of all, with a rise in benefit payments of 43.6 percent and a total rise in tax payments of 4.4 percent. All six models (peak value versus option value, linear age versus age dummies, with or without shift) generate similar predictions of the effect of the reforms on benefits, though the effect of the reforms on taxes varies more across the models.

Table 12.3 decomposes the total effect of reform into two components, the mechanical effect and the behavioral effect. Once again, we present one panel for each estimated model. Each panel has three sets of columns for the three reforms. In each set of columns, we show the mechanical effect, the behavioral effect, and the total effect of reform.

In the case of Social Security benefits, the mechanical effect is responsible for the vast majority of the total effect. For example, in the peak value model with linear age controls, the Three-Year Reform mechanically cuts benefits by €35,934. Incorporating labor supply responses to the reform has an additional beneficial effect on program solvency, but the effect is very small: benefits drop by a further €44, or less than 0.1 percent of base case benefits. In some of the other models, the behavioral response to this reform actually results in an increase in benefits—for example, in the option value model with age dummy shift, benefits rise by €1,249. However, in all models, the magnitude of the behavioral effect remains very small relative to the magnitude of the mechanical effect.

Table 12.3   Decomposition of the total effect of reform

	Change in present discounted value								
	Three-Year Reform			Actuarial Reform			Common Reform		
	Mechanical	Behavioral	Total	Mechanical	Behavioral	Total	Mechanical	Behavioral	Total
Peak value, linear age									
Benefits	−35,934	−44	−35,978	2,405	−146	2,260	84,312	1,449	85,761
Taxes: Total	−2,706	6,499	3,793	199	−1,558	−1,359	11,119	−3,272	7,848
Net change	−33,228	−6,543	−39,770	2,207	1,412	3,619	73,192	4,721	77,913
Change as % base benefits	−24.0	−4.7	−28.8	1.6	1.0	2.6	53.0	3.4	56.4
Peak value, age dummies (no shift)									
Benefits	−35,146	−401	−35,547	2,314	−30	2,285	83,779	4,718	88,498
Taxes: Total	−2,658	4,627	1,969	196	−1,693	−1,497	11,023	4,831	15,854
Net change	−32,488	−5,028	−37,516	2,118	1,663	3,781	72,756	−113	72,643
Change as % base benefits	−23.8	−3.7	−27.5	1.6	1.2	2.8	53.3	−0.1	53.3
Peak value, age dummies (with shift)									
Benefits	−35,146	876	−34,270	2,314	−30	2,285	83,779	2,044	85,824
Taxes: Total	−2,658	15,599	12,941	196	−1,693	−1,497	11,023	−703	10,320
Net change	−32,488	−14,723	−47,211	2,118	1,663	3,781	72,756	2,748	75,504
Change as % base benefits	−23.8	−10.8	−34.6	1.6	1.2	2.8	53.3	2.0	55.4

					Option value, linear age				
Benefits	−36,031	106	−35,925	2,344	−73	2,270	85,119	−1,088	84,031
Taxes: Total	−2,724	6,206	3,482	196	−983	−787	11,269	−7,446	3,823
Net change	−33,308	−6,100	−39,408	2,147	910	3,058	73,850	6,358	80,208
Change as % base benefits	−24.1	−4.4	−28.5	1.6	0.7	2.2	53.3	4.6	57.9
				Option value, age dummies (no shift)					
Benefits	−35,193	−169	−35,362	2,283	0	2,283	84,398	773	85,171
Taxes: Total	−2,672	4,673	2,000	194	−818	−624	11,139	−4,028	7,111
Net change	−32,521	−4,841	−37,362	2,090	818	2,908	73,259	4,800	78,060
Change as % base benefits	−23.8	−3.5	−27.4	1.5	0.6	2.1	53.6	3.5	57.2
				Option value, age dummies (with shift)					
Benefits	−35,193	1,249	−33,945	2,283	0	2,283	84,398	−2,144	82,254
Taxes: Total	−2,672	13,168	10,496	194	−818	−624	11,139	−9,862	1,276
Net change	−32,521	−11,920	−44,441	2,090	818	2,908	73,259	7,719	80,978
Change as % base benefits	−23.8	−8.7	−32.5	1.5	0.6	2.1	53.6	5.7	59.3

Note: Results are in 2001 euros.

This is the case for the other two reforms as well. For both the Actuarial Reform and the Common Reform, the vast majority of the effect on Social Security payments is through the mechanical effect.

In the case of taxes, the behavioral effect is often larger than the mechanical effect and can vary significantly across models. For example, in the first panel of table 12.3, the mechanical effect of the Three-Year Reform is to reduce taxes by €2,706, while the behavioral effect is to raise taxes by €6,499, so that taxes increase on net. For this reform, the behavioral effect on taxes is particularly pronounced in the models with age dummy shifts in the third and sixth panels. On the other hand, for the Common Reform, the mechanical effects of taxes are much larger in all cases, although the offsetting behavioral effects are of a similar order of magnitude in the option value model with shifting age dummies.

The final rows of each panel in table 12.3 show the net change in the government's fiscal position for this cohort as a result of reform, and that net change as a percentage of baseline benefits. For the Three-Year Reform, we find that there is a total reduction in net government outlays of roughly €40,000 to €47,000, depending on the model. This represents 28 to 35 percent of baseline benefits. The majority of this impact comes from mechanical effects. At most one third, and generally less than one fifth, comes from behavioral effects, and this is exclusively through the tax side.

As noted, the impacts of the Actuarial Reform are much more modest. There is an increase in government outlays of €3,000–€3,800, or 2–2.8 percent of baseline benefit payments. In this case, behavioral effects play a larger role, explaining about one third of the total change in fiscal position.

The Common Reform has the most substantial impact on fiscal positions. Net payments rise by over 50 percent in all simulations. This case also features the smallest relative contribution from behavioral responses; only about 10 percent or less of the effect of reform comes through behavioral responses. This is because most of the fiscal impact of this reform is on the benefits side, not the tax side, so that the small behavioral effect on benefits implies a small behavioral effect overall.

To better understand why the fiscal implications of the behavioral effect on social security wealth are relatively small, it is useful to recall that this is the additional effect of labor supply responses on fiscal balances, holding social security wealth constant at the postreform level. In order for the labor supply responses to have an additional effect on Social Security finances, two conditions must be met: reforms must significantly impact retirement decisions, and the Social Security system (benefits net of payroll taxes) must be *less or more than actuarially fair.* Even if there is no additional beneficial effect on Social Security program finances, reforms may improve overall government finances if they encourage workers to retire later and this results in higher lifetime income and consumption taxes.

Figure 12.1 shows Social Security benefits by age of retirement in the

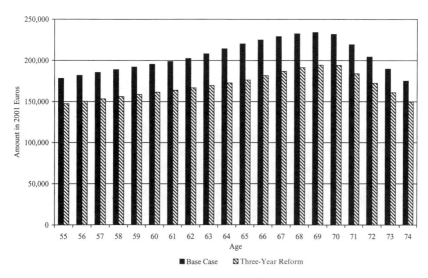

Fig. 12.1   Social Security benefits by age of labor force exit, Three-Year Reform

base case and in the Three-Year Reform case. In the base case, social security wealth rises with age of retirement until peaking at age 69, making it appear that the system provides some return to additional work. However, when payroll taxes are included, the system is close to actuarially fair. For example, social security wealth in the base case rises from about €195,000 at age 60 to about €234,000 at age 69; however, the increase in payroll taxes over the same period (not shown on the graph) is about €44,000, making the net return to additional work a loss of approximately €5,000. Under the Three-Year Reform, benefits are lower but the system (including payroll taxes) remains roughly actuarially fair. Thus, even if this policy change induces people to change their retirement behavior, such changes will have little fiscal impact on the Social Security system, because it is close to actuarially fair.

Figure 12.2 illustrates how the sum of payroll, income, and consumption taxes varies with age of retirement. As discussed previously with respect to payroll taxes, the present discounted value of lifetime taxes rises with age, and this is true for other types of taxes as well. However, while the rise in payroll taxes roughly counteracts the rise in Social Security benefits with later labor force exit, the total rise in taxes greatly exceeds the rise in benefits. As a result, the net fiscal implications of longer work lives is positive: while Social Security is roughly actuarially fair, the increase in income and consumption taxes imply gains to the government from longer work lives.

Figure 12.3 shows the distribution of retirement ages pre- and postreform in the option value model with no shift of the age dummies. The reform is found to reduce the probability of retirement slightly at ages 55 to

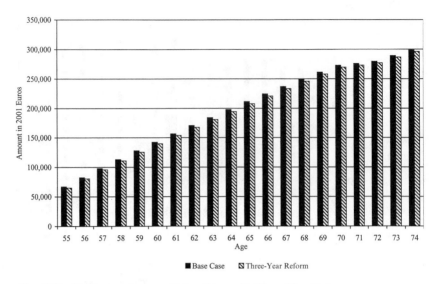

Fig. 12.2 Total taxes by age of labor force exit, Three-Year Reform

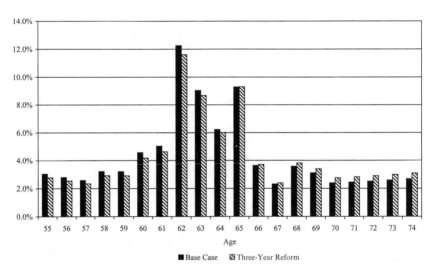

Fig. 12.3 Distribution of retirement ages, Three-Year Reform, option value—age dummies (no shift)

64 and to increase it slightly at ages 66 to 74. But these effects are, in general, fairly small. Thus, it should not be surprising that there is relatively little behavioral effect on fiscal positions from this reform: there is relatively little impact on behavior, and any changes in behavior have modest impacts, because the system is roughly actuarially fair.

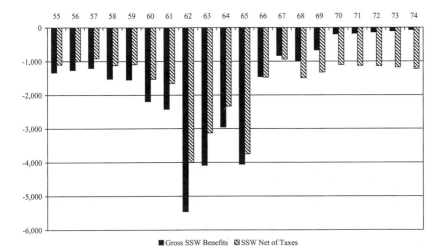

Fig. 12.4   Total effect by age of retirement, Three-Year Reform, option value—age dummies (no shift)

Figure 12.4 puts the information in figures 12.1 to 12.3 together to show the total effect of the reform on social security wealth, both gross and net of all taxes, by age of retirement. The gross and net effects by age are always negative, as this reform is a large benefit cut. The effects are largest at ages 62 to 65, because the retirement probabilities are relatively high at these ages; put simply, most of the fiscal savings from this reform come from people who retire at ages 62 to 65, because there are so many of them.

Figures 12.5 and 12.6 repeat figures 12.3 and 12.4, under the assumption that the age dummies shift by three years as a result of the reform. Here, there are much larger behavioral responses to reform, since we are by construction assuming that there is an enormous change in retirement behavior (by shifting the age dummy coefficients). As one would expect, the retirement probabilities now decline sharply at ages 62 to 64 and rise sharply at ages 65 to 68. As a result, the reform now saves a larger amount of money at ages 62 to 64, since there are so many fewer people retiring then, but costs more money at ages 66 to 68 because of the increase in people retiring at those ages.

Finally, figure 12.7 compares the fiscal implications of reform for one birth cohort as a percentage of GDP for the six models used. In all cases, the mechanical effect leads to a savings of about 0.45 percent of GDP and the behavioral effect leads to an additional savings of about 0.10 percent of GDP, and slightly more in models with age dummy shifts. Thus we conclude that most of the effect of the policy reform on government finances results from the mechanical effect of the change. Labor supply responses to the policy have little additional effect on Social Security program sol-

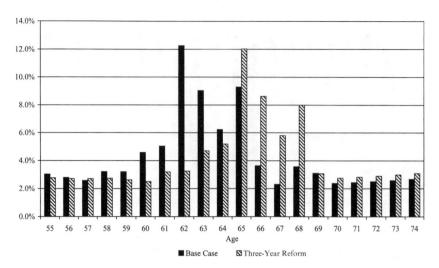

Fig. 12.5   Distribution of retirement ages, Three-Year Reform, option value—age dummies (with shift)

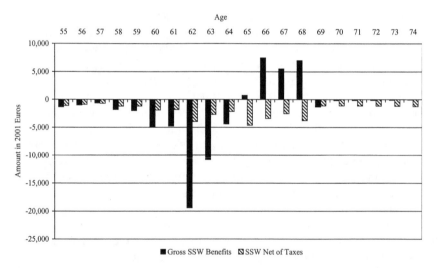

Fig. 12.6   Total effect by age of retirement, Three-Year Reform, option value—age dummies (with shift)

vency because the system is close to actually fair, though they do have a small beneficial effect on total government finances as a result of higher lifetime income and consumption taxes paid.

Next, we examine whether this finding will also apply to the two other reforms, the Actuarial Reform and the Common Reform. Figure 12.8 shows that the system is roughly actuarially fair (once payroll taxes are included)

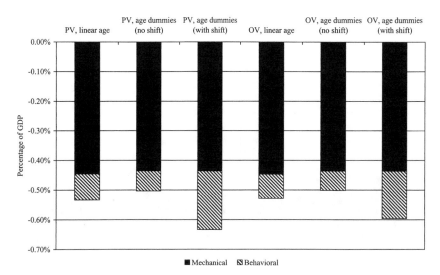

Fig. 12.7   Fiscal implications of reform as a percent of GDP: Three-Year Reform

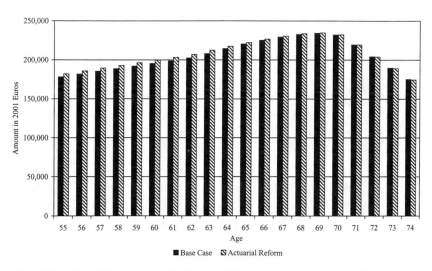

Fig. 12.8   Social Security benefits by age of labor force exit, Actuarial Reform

in both the base case and Actuarial Reform. Figure 12.9 shows that there are only small changes in retirement probabilities resulting from this reform in the option value model with no age dummy shift. Figure 12.10, like figure 12.7, compares the fiscal implications of this reform using all six models. As the reform represents only a small change from the current U.S. system, it is found to cause a mechanical increase in the cost of the program

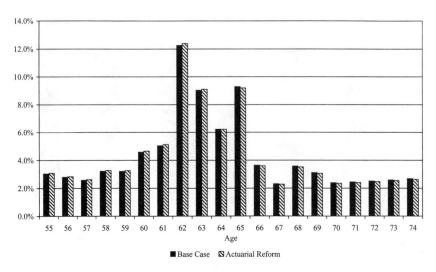

Fig. 12.9   Distribution of retirement ages, Actuarial Reform, option value—age dummies (no shift)

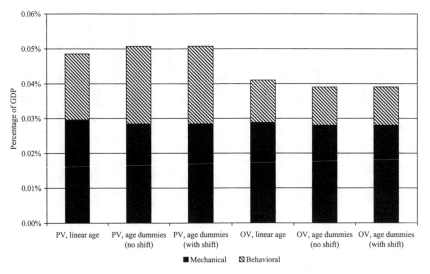

Fig. 12.10   Fiscal implications of reform as a percentage of GDP: Actuarial Reform

of only 0.03 percent of GDP; the behavioral effect raises the cost by an additional 0.01 percent–0.02 percent of GDP.

Figures 12.11 to 12.13 explore the effects of the Common Reform. Under this reform, the system is now more than actuarially fair, as the generous 60 percent replacement rate rewards additional work by more than enough to offset the additional payroll taxes. For example, working from

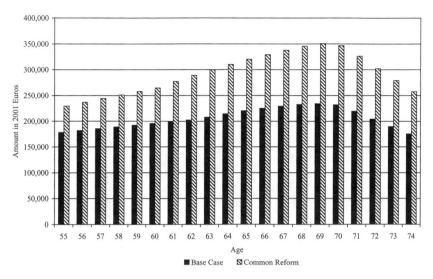

Fig. 12.11   Social Security benefits by age of labor force exit, Common Reform

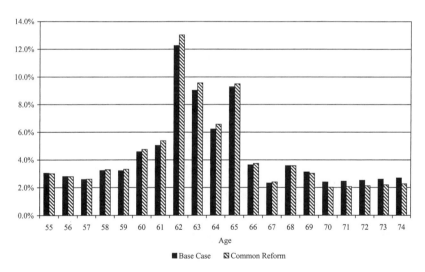

Fig. 12.12   Distribution of retirement ages, Common Reform, option value—age dummies (no shift)

age 60 to age 69 raises social security wealth net of payroll taxes by over €41,000. Due to the wealth effect, this reform induces people to retire earlier, as shown in figure 12.12; as the system is more than fair, earlier retirement will benefit Social Security program finances, though it will hurt overall government finances by lowering lifetime income and consumption taxes. As shown in figure 12.13, the fiscal implications of this reform are a

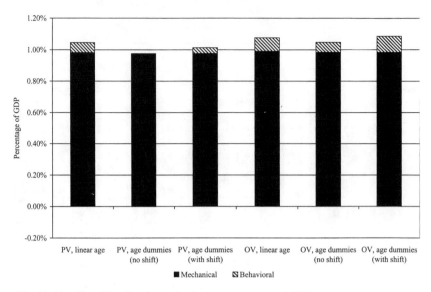

Fig. 12.13   Fiscal implications of reform as a percent of GDP

mechanical increase in program costs of almost 1 percent of GDP and an additional increase in costs of 0.1 percent–0.2 percent of GDP as a result of the behavioral response, as workers retire earlier and pay fewer taxes.

To restate our central conclusion, the fiscal implication of the behavioral effect is quite small relative to the mechanical effect of the reforms, typically on the order of 10–20 percent of the total effect. Reforms may lead to significant changes in retirement behavior, particularly in models including shifts of the age dummies. However, as the Social Security system (including payroll taxes) is roughly actuarially fair, inducing earlier or later retirement has only a second-order effect on program solvency, though it may affect overall government finances by changing the amount of lifetime income and consumption taxes paid.

12.4   Distributional Analysis

Finally, we examine the effect of these reforms on people in different parts of the income distribution. Tables 12.4 and 12.5 show the effect of the three reforms by family AIME quintile using the option value models, first without (table 12.4) and then with (table 12.5) shifts of the age dummies. This comparison implicitly highlights the importance of behavioral effects, since these effects are much larger in the model with age dummy shifts.

In the model without an age dummy shift, the Three-Year Reform is found to affect all quintiles similarly: the change in Social Security benefits net of all taxes is equal to a loss of 19.8 percent of base benefits for the top

Table 12.4   Distribution analysis, optional value—Age dummies (no shift)

	Present discounted value				Change relative to base		
Case	Base	Three-Year Reform	Actuarial Reform	Common Reform	Three-Year Reform	Actuarial Reform	Common Reform
			Quintile 1 (highest)				
Benefits	255,230	207,917	258,921	423,651	−47,313	3,691	168,421
Taxes: Total	340,597	343,794	338,887	351,741	3,198	−1,710	11,144
Net change					−50,511	5,401	157,277
Change as % of base benefits					−19.8	2.1	61.6
			Quintile 2				
Benefits	225,141	184,077	227,998	338,720	−41,064	2,857	113,579
Taxes: Total	220,492	223,587	219,668	230,430	3,096	−823	9,938
Net change					−44,160	3,680	103,641
Change as % of base benefits					−19.6	1.6	46.0
			Quintile 3				
Benefits	204,245	166,976	206,409	290,404	−37,269	2,164	86,159
Taxes: Total	165,641	168,244	165,274	173,308	2,603	−367	7,667
Net change					−39,872	2,531	78,492
Change as % of base benefits					−19.5	1.2	38.4
			Quintile 4				
Benefits	173,991	142,668	175,695	224,095	−31,323	1,704	50,104
Taxes: Total	118,946	120,067	118,760	123,692	1,121	−185	4,746
Net change					−32,444	1,889	45,358
Change as % of base benefits					−18.6	1.1	26.1
			Quintile 5				
Benefits	111,923	92,125	112,919	119,248	−19,788	996	7,325
Taxes: Total	82,635	82,614	82,600	84,680	−21	−35	2,045
Net change					−19,777	1,031	5,280
Change as % of base benefits					−17.7	0.9	4.7

Note: Results are in 2001 euros.

Table 12.5   Distribution analysis, optional value—Age dummies (with shift)

Case	Base	Present discounted value			Change relative to base		
		Three-Year Reform	Actuarial Reform	Common Reform	Three-Year Reform	Actuarial Reform	Common Reform
		Quintile 1 (highest)					
Benefits	255,230	209,460	258,921	419,153	−45,770	3,691	163,923
Taxes: Total	340,597	359,191	338,887	340,770	18,594	−1,710	173
Net change					−64,365	5,401	163,750
Change as % of base benefits					−25.2	2.1	64.2
			Quintile 2				
Benefits	225,141	185,717	227,998	334,951	−39,424	2,857	109,810
Taxes: Total	220,492	234,757	219,668	222,802	14,266	−823	2,311
Net change					−53,690	3,680	107,499
Change as % of base benefits					−23.8	1.6	47.7
			Quintile 3				
Benefits	204,245	168,531	206,409	287,310	−35,713	2,164	83,065
Taxes: Total	165,641	176,672	165,274	167,628	11,030	−367	1,987
Net change					−46,743	2,531	81,079
Change as % of base benefits					−22.9	1.2	39.7
			Quintile 4				
Benefits	173,991	143,909	175,695	222,102	−30,082	1,704	48,112
Taxes: Total	118,946	125,010	118,760	120,400	6,064	−185	1,455
Net change					−36,146	1,889	46,657
Change as % of base benefits					−20.8	1.1	26.8
			Quintile 5				
Benefits	111,923	93,233	112,919	118,026	−18,690	996	6,103
Taxes: Total	82,635	85,135	82,600	83,091	2,500	−35	456
Net change					−21,190	1,031	5,647
Change as % of base benefits					−18.9	0.9	5.0

Note: Results are in 2001 euros.

quintile versus a loss of 17.7 percent of base benefits for the lowest quintile; naturally, the absolute dollar losses are much larger for the top quintile. In the model with an age dummy shift, however, the top quintile experiences a relatively larger loss, 25.2 percent versus 18.9 percent for the lowest quintile. This suggests, therefore, that the behavioral response to the reform is either reducing benefits or increasing tax payments by a larger amount for the highest income quintiles. This effect appears to operate mostly through taxes: given that income taxes are progressive, longer work lives lead to a larger increase in tax payments over the work life for higher-income groups. That is, the longer work life in table 12.5 relative to table 12.4 leads to about €18,000 more in tax payments for the highest income quintile, but only €2,500 more for the lowest income group.

In the Actuarial Reform, gains are small for all quintiles, though they are twice as large as a percent of base benefits (2.1 percent versus 0.9 percent) for the highest quintile relative to the lowest.

In the Common Reform, by contrast, benefits are highly skewed toward the upper quintiles, even in percentage terms. This is because the Common Reform replaces the progressive benefit formula in the current system with a flat 60 percent replacement rate. The top quintile receives an increase in social security wealth net of all taxes equal to 61.6 percent of base benefits, while the bottom quintile receives an increase equal to just 4.7 percent of base benefits; results are similar in the model with shifts of the age dummy.

12.5   Conclusions

Any Social Security reform designed to improve the solvency of the OASDI trust funds will automatically have a beneficial effect on Social Security program finances by cutting benefits or raising taxes (the mechanical effect). But the reform may have an additional beneficial effect on program finances (the behavioral effect) if it encourages workers to retire later and if the Social Security system is less than actuarially fair. Even if there is no effect on program finances, the reform may have a beneficial effect on government finances if it leads workers to retire later and raises the lifetime income and consumption taxes they pay.

We have developed here a microsimulation model to estimate the impact of several reforms to the Social Security system. This model incorporates the behavioral responses of retirement to Social Security entitlements estimated in our earlier work. We have two key findings from this exercise. First, major reforms to the system can have substantial impacts on fiscal balances. Raising the early and normal retirement age by three years improves net fiscal balances by roughly one third of baseline benefits. On the other hand, reducing the early retirement age to 60 and raising the replacement rate to 60 percent would lead to a deterioration of fiscal balances by over one half of baseline benefits.

Second, behavioral responses to system reforms only contribute modestly to fiscal balance effects. This is because the Social Security system as a whole is roughly actuarially neutral. As a result, delaying retirement has little net impact on system finances. However, when other taxes are factored in, delaying retirement does increase net government revenue. Thus, behavioral effects on the system as a whole are not zero, but are dominated by the mechanical effects of reform.

References

Blau, David M. 1994. Labor force dynamics of older men. *Econometrica* 62 (1): 117–56.

Burtless, Gary. 1986. Social Security, unanticipated benefit increases, and the timing of retirement. *Review of Economic Statistics* 53:781–805.

Coile, Courtney, and Jonathan Gruber. 2004. The effect of Social Security on retirement in the United States. In *Social security and retirement around the world: Micro-estimation,* ed. Jonathan Gruber and David A. Wise, 691–729. Chicago: University of Chicago Press.

Coile, Courtney, and Jonathan Gruber. 2000. Social security and retirement. National Bureau of Economic Research Working Paper no. 7830. Cambridge, MA: National Bureau of Economic Research.

———. 2001. Social Security incentives for retirement. In *Themes in the economics of aging,* ed. David Wise, 311–41. Chicago: University of Chicago Press.

Diamond, Peter, and Jonathan Gruber. 1998. Social security and retirement in the United States. In *Social security and retirement around the world,* ed. Jonathan Gruber and David A. Wise, 437–73. Chicago: University of Chicago Press.

Diamond, Peter, and Jerry Hausman. 1984. Retirement and unemployment behavior of older men. In *Retirement and economic behavior,* ed. H. Aaron and G. Burtless, 97–134. Washington, DC: Brookings Institution.

Fields, Gary S., and Olivia S. Mitchell. 1984. Economic determinants of the optimal retirement age: An empirical investigation. *Journal of Human Resources* 19 (2): 245–62.

Gustman, Alan L., and Thomas L. Steinmeier. 1985. The 1983 Social Security reforms and labor supply adjustments of older individuals in the long run. *Journal of Labor Economics* 3 (2): 237–53.

———. 1986. A structural retirement model. *Econometrica* 54 (3): 555–84.

Hausman, Jerry A., and David A. Wise. 1985. Social Security, health status, and retirement. In *Pensions, labor, and individual choice,* ed. David A. Wise, 159–92. Chicago: University of Chicago Press.

Hurd, Michael D. 1990. Research on the elderly: Economic status, retirement, and consumption and saving. *Journal of Economic Literature* 28 (2): 565–637.

Ruhm, Christopher. 1995. Secular changes in the work and retirement patterns of older men. *Journal of Human Resources* 30:362–85.

Rust, John, and Christopher Phelan. 1997. How Social Security and Medicare affect retirement behavior in a world of incomplete markets. *Econometrica* 65 (4): 781–831.

Samwick, Andrew A. 1998. New evidence on pensions, Social Security, and the timing of retirement. *Journal of Public Economics* 70 (2): 207–36.

Stock, James H., and David A. Wise. 1990a. Pensions, the option value of work, and retirement. *Econometrica* 58 (5): 1151–80.

———. 1990b. The pension inducement to retire: An option value analysis. In *The economics of aging,* ed. David Wise, 205–29. Chicago: University of Chicago Press.

Contributors

Michael Baker
Department of Economics
University of Toronto
150 St. George Street
Toronto, Ontario M5S 3G7 Canada

Paul Bingley
Aarhus School of Business
Department of Economics
Prismet, Silkeborgvej 2
DK 8000 Aarhus C Denmark

Richard Blundell
Department of Economics
University College London
Gower Street
London WC1E 6BT, England

Michele Boldrin
Department of Economics
University of Minnesota
Minneapolis, MN 55455

Axel Börsch-Supan
Mannheim Research Institute for the
   Economics of Aging
University of Mannheim
Building L13, 17
D-68131 Mannheim, Germany

Agar Brugiavini
Dipartimento di Scienze Economiche
Università Ca' Foscari di Venezia
S. Giobbe, 873
30121 Venice, Italy

Courtney Coile
Department of Economics
Wellesley College
106 Central Street
Wellesley, MA 02481

Raphael Desmet
Federal Planning Bureau
Avenue des Arts, 47-49, Kunstlaan
1000 Brussels, Belgium

Carl Emmerson
The Institute for Fiscal Studies
7 Ridgmount Street
London WC1E 7AE England

Jonathan Gruber
Department of Economics, E52-355
Massachusetts Institute of Technology
50 Memorial Drive
Cambridge, MA 02142-1347

Nabanita Datta Gupta
The Danish National Institute of
    Social Research
Herluf Trolles Gade 1
DK-1052 Copenhagen, Denmark

Sergi Jiménez-Martín
Department of Economics
Universitat Pompeu Fabra
Ramon Trias Fargas 25-27
08005 Barcelona, Spain

Alain Jousten
Department of Economics
University of Liège
Boulevard du rectorat, 7, Bâtiment B31
4000 Liège, Belgium

Arie Kapteyn
RAND
1776 Main Street
P.O. Box 2138
Santa Monica, CA 90407-2138

Simone Kohnz
Munich Graduate School of
    Economics
Ludwig-Maximilians University
    Munich
Ludwigstr. 28
D-80539 Munich, Germany

Ronan Mahieu
French Ministry of Labor, DARES
39-43, quai André Citroën
75902 Paris Cedex 15 France

Kevin Milligan
Department of Economics
University of British Columbia
#997-1873 East Mall
Vancouver, B.C. Canada V6T 1Z1

Akiko S. Oishi
Faculty of Law and Economics
Chiba University
Yayoi-cho 1-33, Inage-ku
Chiba-city 263-8522 Japan

Takashi Oshio
Graduate School of Economics
Kobe University
2-1, Rokkodai, Nada-Ku
Kobe, Hyogo, 657-8501, Japan

Mårten Palme
Department of Economics
Stockholm University
106 91 Stockholm, Sweden

Peder J. Pedersen
Department of Economics
University of Aarhus
DK-8000 Aarhus C Denmark

Franco Peracchi
Faculty of Economics
Università "Tor Vergata"
Via Columbia, 2
00133 Rome, Italy

Sergio Perelman
CREPP, Department of Economics
University of Liège
Boulevard du Rectorat 7, Bâtiment 31
4000 Liége, Belgium

Pierre Pestieau
University of Liège-Sart Tilman
Boulevard du Rectorat 7, Bâtiment 31
4000 Liège, Belgium

Reinhold Schnabel
Department of Economics
Universität Duisburg-Essen
45117 Essen, Germany

Ingemar Svensson
Swedish Social Insurance Agency
Adolf Fredriks Kyrkogata 8
S-103 51 Stockholm, Sweden

Klaas de Vos
CentERdata
Tilburg University
PO Box 90153
5000 LE Tilburg, The Netherlands

Emmanuelle Walraet
INSEE
105 rue des Français Libres
44274 Nantes Cedex 2 France

David A. Wise
John F. Kennedy School of
    Government
Harvard University
79 John F. Kennedy Street
Cambridge, MA 02138

Author Index

Subject Index